SMILING THROUGH
THE APOCALYPSE

Edited by Harold Hayes

SMILING THROUGH THE APOCALYPSE

ESQUIRE'S HISTORY OF THE SIXTIES

An Esquire Press Book □ *Crown Publishers, Inc., New York for Arnold*

Published by Crown Publishers, Inc., 225 Park Avenue South, New York, New York, 10003 and represented in Canada by the Canadian MANDA Group.

CROWN is a trademark of Crown Publishers, Inc.

Manufactured in the United States of America

Library of Congress Cataloging-in-Publication Data
Smiling through the apocalypse.
"An Esquire Press Book."
1. History, Modern—1945–   I. Esquire, inc.
D840.S54   1987   973.92   87-5349
ISBN 0-517-56557-9

10 9 8 7 6 5 4 3 2 1
First Edition

Contents

PART II: THE GRASS ROOTS OF "NOW"

PART III: EGOS, SUPEREGOS AND IDS

PART IV: SOME FAILURES IN COMMUNICATIONS

Section 1 / The Credibility Gap

Section 2 / The Generation Gap

Section 3 / The Color Gap

PART V: LIVING UP TO OUR COMMITMENT IN VIETNAM

"May you live in the most interesting of times"

—*Traditional Chinese curse*

Introduction to the New Edition

The principal character of this book carried a pen, not a guitar; made notes, not war; and while he wasn't exactly part of the problem *or* the solution, he certainly wasn't a neutral observer.

The protagonist of this book was the nonfiction writer who found himself center-ring at the main event of an era: the Sixties. It was here that he rubbed elbows with heroes and clowns; gaped at death-defying acts all around him; and was bathed and pounded in the red glare of rockets—from America's inner cities to the rice paddies of Vietnam.

He was a liberated army of one. He may recently have been freed of the constraints of daily journalism, or a novelist who'd decided that, in the hurly-burly of the Sixties, fiction wasn't where the action was. Where it was, was out on the street, from Dealey Plaza to the corner of Haight and Ashbury. It was to these war zones that *Esquire* dispatched its foot-soldiers. Many returned with what came to be fashionably known as "new journalism": novelistic, nonfiction writing in which the author often assumed a place.

In the introduction that follows, then-editor Harold Hayes provides the rest of the contemporary context as seen from his vantage point at the close of the decade. On rereading his words and the following pieces, I am struck by an essential fact of this business: that any good magazine that endures to live a rich, long life carries in its bloodstream the strength of its traditions. In the Thirties, when *Esquire* was founded, such writers as Hemingway and Dos Passos also brought the techniques and the temperament of the novelist to the demands of real-world reporting. Under the leadership of founding editor Arnold Gingrich, the magazine dared to combine fiction and fact, and ignited the mixture with a spark of wit.

The same holds true of *Esquire* in the Sixties, when such refugees from newspapers as Talese, Wolfe, and Wicker met up with such literary émigrés as Mailer, Bellow, and Vidal. They and the others in this book—notably newcomers such as Michael Herr and Terry Southern—formed the basis of an extraordinary cast.

As we turn toward the Nineties, we'd do worse than to spend a few precious evenings with this book. For *Esquire* editors, writers, and readers alike, these pages are more than just revealing episodes of past history. The journalism here sets a standard and delivers a challenge: to bring to our times—apocalyptic or not—the hard-won style and substance that grace these pieces. They are our heritage and our inspiration. Month to month, they are the targets we shoot for.

Lee Eisenberg
Editor, *Esquire*
New York City, 1986

Introduction to the First Edition

Decades seldom start on schedule. The Thirties began in '29 with the Depression; the Forties with World War II in '41; the Fifties with the election of Dwight Eisenhower in '52; and the Sixties ten months after the turn of the year when, in his television debate with Jack Kennedy, Richard Nixon's face signaled defeat. But for politicians and journalists, the first day of a decade opens a new epoch, ready or not, and *Esquire* reacted accordingly. In our January 1960 issue, the first paragraph of the lead article (by Arthur Schlesinger Jr.) read:

"At periodic moments in our history, our country has paused on the threshold of a new epoch in our national life, unable for a moment to open the door, but aware that it must advance if it is to preserve its natural vitality and identity. One feels that we are approaching such a moment now—that the mood which had dominated the nations for a decade is beginning to seem thin and irrelevant; that it no longer interprets our desires and needs as a people; that new forms, new energies, new values are straining for expression and release. The Eisenhower epoch—the present period of passivity and acquiescence in our national life—is drawing to a close."

Part prophecy, part wishful thinking. That January issue was published on December 14, having been assembled back in September of 1959. Actually, on Friday, January 1, 1960, no door opened. Khrushchev declared he would disarm Russia unilaterally, the French issued a one-franc coin worth twenty cents and NASA announced plans to cut back space costs. If there were new energies and new values straining for release, most Americans were unaware of them. Rather, life seemed monotonously predictable. The average American was white, prosperous and torpid; a second car and a swimming pool were facts of his life, a new vacation home an immediate possibility. Though there was still plenty to fear from the Russians—perhaps a bomb shelter would prove a wiser investment than a beach house—the mood was benign. Of course the Negro was restless, and many people were distressed by news pictures of police dogs breaking up demonstrations in Alabama. But that was largely a regional problem; elsewhere, America was an ongoing enterprise.

There was no war, the economy was sound (unemployment practically nonexistent) and our democratic institutions, God's church among them, were invulnerable. Arthur Schlesinger was right, however: The Fifties *were* drawing to a close. *Smiling Through the Apocalypse: Esquire's History of the Sixties* is an account of what happened next.

A magazine is a promise, sometimes fulfilled, sometimes not. Responding to events of the day, it seeks to offer a bit more perspective than the shifting realities reported in the daily press, though the permanence of its views is only slightly less subject to change. Between the morning papers and the Cronkite show, there is often very little to add but—and this is the redeeming strength of all magazines today—attitude. The magazine engages its reader and holds him because it shares with him a certain point of view.

To land on the moon is to make news which transcends form: the faster the word gets out, the better. But once established, the fact moves from the simple to the complex, begging interpretation of a thousand varieties. A magazine's promise is the delivery, on a fixed schedule, of its own version of the world, its special attitude toward the reader.

The present-day attitude of *Esquire* was formed out of a reaction to the banality of the Fifties. From the raspberry to the hoax, in words and/or pictures (curiously the pictures always provoked the greatest outrage, especially George Lois's covers) and occasionally with some loss of dignity, the idea was to suggest alternate possibilities to a monolithic view. And how monolithic it was! The passivity of the Fifties was shared by garage mechanics and college presidents.

At *Esquire* our attitude took shape as we went along, stumbling past our traditional boundaries of fashion, leisure, entertainment and literature onto the more forbidding ground of politics, sociology, science and even, occasionally, religion. Any point of view was welcome as long as the writer was sufficiently skillful to carry it off, but we tended to avoid committing ourselves to doctrinaire programs, even though advised on occasion that we might thereby better serve the interests of mankind. None of the programs available would permit us consistently to keep our lines open to the reader, so we stayed loose.

But despite this calloused lack of commitment—or perhaps because of it—we began to form the habit of searching for the right questions. If two superpowers have superbombs, how does one protect itself from the other? Should churches practice segregation? Should Arthur Miller be jailed for refusing to name those of his friends who were Communist? Was reverence due cherished institutions of American life, or irreverence? What evil lurked in the heart of Eisenhower, what virtue in the heart of Alger Hiss?

Raising such questions in the capacity of surrogate readers, we then moved as editors to find the appropriate writers, often the unexpected ones, to answer them. But the attitude, now roughly shaping, would become refined through more complicated means: the precise phrasing of titles—

"JOE," SAID MARILYN MONROE,
JUST BACK FROM KOREA,
"YOU NEVER HEARD SUCH CHEERING."
"YES, I HAVE,"
JOE DiMAGGIO ANSWERED.

—the toning and sharpening "house copy," those introductory copy blocks and captions accompanying visual features; and sometimes—increasingly more often—planning features executed exclusively by the editors to remind readers that we were ever mindful of where their interests lay (the rococo phase of this cycle occurring well into the Sixties with a two-page list entitled "The 100 Best People in the World").

And always, always pounding away on the Idea, ten a week from each staff editor until he either mutinied, buckled or broke through to some dazzlingly fresh concept which gained for the magazine another inch of new ground.

Few magazines have successfully defined their own attitude, and *Esquire* is no exception. For a while we called ours an effort toward a rational view, then satire and then irony. But only humor—of a most complex, often unfunny sort—is sufficiently flexible to cover the larger part of our effort, from black wit to custard-pie burlesque. Against the aridity of the national landscape of the late Fifties we offered to our readers in our better moments the promise of outright laughter; by the end of the Sixties the best we could provide was a bleak grin.

Arriving slightly behind schedule, Jack Kennedy opened the door to an epoch releasing new energies indeed, though it is now clear that many of his constituents missed the point of his coming. What Kennedy wanted was the acceptance of conventional liberal measures to ensure minimum creature comforts, freedom and security; what the country wanted was to be like Jack—young, rich, powerful and attractive. Backing up, like electric currents in a cloudless sky, those new energies collected around him until the terrible spark of his assassination set them loose, traumatizing the country more than any event in recent memory.

"The Rise and Fall of Charisma," Part I of this book, traces through the Sixties the pathetic parabola of the Kennedy spirit, concluding with the Chicago Convention of 1968. But the Kennedy chronicle, like some medieval legend, seems endless. *The Last Kennedy*, a 1968 portrait of Edward by Burton Hersh, was turned in only days before the assassination of Robert and hastily revised to allow for this latest misfortune to strike the president's survivors. In the light of Edward Kennedy's disastrous experience in the Chappaquiddick affair of 1969, Hersh's appraisal appears now slightly out of chronology (and context). But here it stands. Although we are told the House of Kennedy at last has fallen, it will be seen that the theme of this section argues the decline of the Kennedy ideal began even before the president's death. The Hersh piece, like others throughout the book which may seem inconsistent in view of our later knowledge of events, is without further revision because it reflects our impressions of the moment.

"The Grass Roots of 'Now,'" Part II, derives from the section preceding it. As Arthur Schlesinger had predicted, new forms and new values would come along with the new energies, and in *Esquire*'s view the forms tended to define the values. Thus more than a casual interest was expressed by our editors and writers in the diversions of the period—from baton-twirling schools to Las Vegas casinos. No longer was there an archetypal American; standing in his place, self-absorbed and passionate to the point of militancy, was a cluster of groups, some of them harsh and disquieting.

So were some of their new values, six of which underline parts of this book:

Power is an absolute, like truth or justice. (Part I, "The Rise and Fall of Charisma")

Public image is more important than measurable achievement. (Part III, "Egos, Superegos and Ids")

The government lies. (Part IV, Section 1, "The Credibility Gap")

Youth is incorruptible. (Part IV, Section 2, "The Generation Gap")

Minority rights are secured more effectively by intimidation than by legislation or Christian example. (Part IV, Section 3, "The Color Gap")

Patriotism is an irrelevant reason for going to war. (Part V, "Living Up to Our Commitment in Vietnam")

As this is a book about life in the Sixties, it is mostly concerned with the infinite variety of the odd and dissimilar: styles, conspiracies, education, sex, war, cars, establishments,* fads, drugs, Pepsi-Cola contests, murders, sports, riots and fashions. And with people of all kinds: winners, losers, clowns, revolutionaries, fools, mothers, actors, segregationists, topless waitresses, soldiers, villains, fighters, martyrs, hippies, yippies and L.B.J.

But the writer is the only hero.

"If any man have an ear," wrote St. John regarding a terminal point for readers of a wider audience than *Esquire*'s, "let him hear." In the apocalyptic Sixties the message came through clearly, for writers were everywhere, sending back the word. "Creative Agonies," Part VI of this informal history, is concerned with the private lives of our writer kings.

It is doubtful whether even so egocentric an author as Ernest Hemingway saw himself as central to events as have some of the writers through these years, freedom-riding down South, slogging through the Mekong Delta,

---

*More than our share of them, perhaps: establishments on Wall Street, in the art world, the Washington press corps, the literary world, even a baseball establishment. In our pages, conspiracy lovers were fair game—until the Sixties turned around on us. See "The American Establishment" and "An Appreciation of the Nonmilitary Functions of War" in Part IV. The former, published in 1962, spoofs the notion that there is an establishment; the latter, published in 1967, spoofs the notion that there is not.

marching on the Pentagon, backtracking Kansas killers, running from cops in Chicago and so on—keeping witness in the truest sense, and all readers were the richer for it. So were writers, by the way, some of them now millionaires whose celebrity had become international, but troublesome. Because instant communication allowed the possibility of instant success, writers and readers by mid-decade looked expectantly toward the coronation of the Writer of the Year. Saul Bellow, '65, *Herzog*; Truman Capote, '66, *In Cold Blood*; William Styron, '67, *The Confessions of Nat Turner*; Norman Mailer, '68, *The Armies of the Night*; Philip Roth, '69, *Portnoy's Complaint*. But sudden though it was, modern fame could pass quickly. Last year's writer found himself working under an excruciating pressure imposed by the mass reader's perfidy. Despite the unprecedented wealth and glory paid out by the Sixties for higher achievement, the time warp ultimately conspired against him. Talent got him there, but publicity would have to keep him alive. Like everyone else, he too wanted to be young, rich, powerful and attractive. A prominent symptom of his unstrung condition was the emergence of his claims to new literary forms—the "nonfiction novel," "history as literature and literature as history," the "New Journalism." While identifying characteristics of at least two of these forms may be traced back to articles appearing first in *Esquire*, the claim was misleading. Demands of the language remain constant, and varieties in technique are relative matters, drawing from old sources. Separating the spurious from the authentic in most activities through this decade is a task continuing over into the future. But there can be no doubt that ours was a time uniquely blessed with an extraordinary abundance of writing talent, men and women of great originality and style, exquisitely sensitive to the nature of change going on about them.

Most are present in this collection, a number of them having earlier established their reputations independently of *Esquire*. But a few of them first reached a national audience through this magazine and have continued throughout most of the period to identify their principal efforts with ours. These are Gay Talese, Tom Wolfe, Garry Wills,† and, among our by-lined editors, John Berendt and Alice Glaser.

Ironically, many of the better novelists weren't writing much fiction, perhaps because social disintegration forced the writer to view himself as his own protagonist; perhaps, as has been remarked elsewhere, because the times were too stimulating for the interior vision to contain. Although there is no fiction included in this selection, *Esquire* published throughout the Sixties a number of outstanding stories, even serializing through one hectic season the chapters of a Norman Mailer novel turned out to monthly deadline. Possibly

†For the record, William F. Buckley Jr. sent over Garry Wills, who had published, and continues to, in the *National Review*. But as Mr. Buckley would be the first to acknowledge, the editorial intentions of the two periodicals are so dissimilar as to allow the claim, on behalf of *Esquire*'s readers at least, to stand.

the quality of the fiction was superior to that of the nonfiction, the insights more lasting and—as our fiction department insists even to this day—more meaningful a way to view the period. Possibly. But in the Sixties, events seemed to move too swiftly to allow the osmotic process of art to keep abreast, and when we found a good novelist we immediately sought to seduce him with the sweet mysteries of current events.

Even so, for the very best of our writers, no single event yielded a key to the decade. There was too much going on—a fire in the street, a fight at the corner, a burglary in the house next door. The last two articles of our book—the *mano a mano* between William F. Buckley Jr. and Gore Vidal—are as appropriate a conclusion to the Sixties as any other, yielding as they do almost no direct information on the changing times other than by suggesting indirectly—through the bitterness, jealousy, ambition and despair of two of our most eloquent sensibilities—the character of America's collective confusion.

HAROLD HAYES

PART I

THE RISE AND FALL OF CHARISMA

Superman Comes to the Supermarket

by Norman Mailer

In an assignment that was to inspire a different sort of political reporting—more literary and more subjective than before—Norman Mailer covered the 1960 Democratic Convention in Los Angeles, and captured not only the personalities of the candidates, but also the mood of a nation about to chart a new course. Mailer, who was then thirty-seven, was clearly fascinated by the youthful John F. Kennedy and appeared to endorse his candidacy. But, as Mailer stated at the time, the political essay is often a double-edged sword: "Some people may think I'm for Kennedy, but I'm not sure the Kennedy people will think so." This piece was published in November 1960, just before the election.

For once let us try to think about a political convention without losing ourselves in housing projects of fact and issue. Politics has its virtues, all too many of them—it would not rank with baseball as a topic of conversation if it did not satisfy a great many things—but one can suspect that its secret appeal is close to nicotine. Smoking cigarettes insulates one from one's life, one does not feel as much, often happily so, and politics quarantines one from history; most of the people who nourish themselves in the political life are in the game not to make history but to be diverted from the history which is being made.

If that Democratic Convention which has now receded behind the brow of the Summer of 1960 is only half-remembered in the excitements of moving toward the election, it may be exactly the time to consider it again, because the mountain of facts which concealed its features last July has been blown away in the winds of High Television, and the man-in-the-street (that peculiar political term which refers to the quixotic voter who will pull the lever for some reason so salient as: "I had a brown-nose lieutenant once with Nixon's looks," or "that Kennedy must have false teeth"), the not so easily estimated man-in-the-street has forgotten most of

3

what happened and could no more tell you who Kennedy was fighting against than you or I could place a bet on who was leading the American League in batting during the month of June.

So to try to talk about what happened is easier now than in the days of the convention, one does not have to put everything in—an act of writing which calls for a bulldozer rather than a pen—one can try to make one's little point and dress it with a ribbon or two of metaphor. All to the good. Because mysteries are irritated by facts, and the 1960 Democratic Convention began as one mystery and ended as another.

Since mystery is an emotion which is repugnant to a political animal (why else lead a life of bad banquet dinners, cigar smoke, camp chairs, foul breath, and excruciatingly dull jargon if not to avoid the echoes of what is not known), the psychic separation between what was happening on the floor, in the caucus rooms, in the headquarters, and what was happening in parallel to the history of the nation was mystery enough to drown the proceedings in gloom. It was on the one hand a dull convention, one of the less interesting by general agreement, relieved by local bits of color, given two half hours of excitement by two demonstrations for Stevenson, buoyed up by the class of the Kennedy machine, turned by the surprise of Johnson's nomination as vice-president, but, all the same, dull, depressed in its overall tone, the big fiestas subdued, the gossip flat, no real air of excitement, just moments—or as they say in bullfighting— details. Yet it was also, one could argue—and one may argue this yet—it was also one of the most important conventions in America's history, it could prove conceivably to be the most important. The man it nominated was unlike any politican who had ever run for President in the history of the land, and if elected he would come to power in a year when America was in danger of drifting into a profound decline.

A Descriptive of the Delegates: Sons and Daughters of the Republic in a Legitimate Panic; Small-time Practitioners of Small-town Political Judo in the Big Town and the Big Time

Depression obviously has its several roots: it is the doubtful protection which comes from not recognizing failure, it is the psychic burden of exhaustion, and it is also, and very often, that discipline of the will or the ego which enables one to continue working when one's unadmitted emotion is panic. And panic it was I think which sat as the largest single sentiment in the breast of the collective delegates as they came to convene in Los Angeles. Delegates are not the noblest sons and daughters of the Republic; a man of taste, arrived from Mars, would take one look at a convention floor and leave forever, convinced he had seen one of the drearier squats of Hell. If one still smells the faint living echo of a carnival wine, the pepper of a bullfight, the rag, drag, and panoply of a jousting tourney, it is all swallowed and regurgitated by the senses into the fouler cud of a death gas one must rid oneself of—a cigar-smoking, stale-aired, slack-jawed, butt-littered, foul, bleak, hard-working, bureaucratic death gas of language and faces ("Yes those *faces*," says the man from Mars: lawyers, judges, ward heelers, *mafiosos,* Southern goons and grandees, grand old ladies, trade unionists and finks), of pompous words and long pauses which lay like a leaden pain over fever, the fever that one is in, over, or is it that one is just behind history? A legitimate panic for a delegate. America is a nation of experts without roots; we are always creating tacticians who are blind to strategy and strategists who cannot take a step, and when the culture has finished its work the institutions handcuff the infirmity. A delegate is a man who picks a candidate for the largest office in the land, a President who must live with problems whose borders are in ethics, metaphysics, and now ontology; the delegate is prepared for this office of selection by emptying wastebaskets, toting garbage and saying yes at the right time for twenty years in the small political machine of some small or large town; his reward, one of them anyway, is that he arrives at an invitation to the convention. An expert on local catch-as-catch-can, a small-time, often mediocre practitioner of small-town political judo, he comes to the big city with nine-tenths of his mind made up, he will follow the orders of the boss who brought him. Yet of course it is not altogether so mean as that: his opinion is listened to—the boss will consider what he has to say as one interesting factor among five hundred, and what is most important to the delegate, he has the illusion of partial freedom. He can, unless he is severely honest with himself—and if he is, why sweat out the low levels of a political machine?—he can have the illusion that he has helped to choose the candidate, he can even worry most sincerely about his choice, flirt with defection from the boss, work out his own small political gains by the road of loyalty or the way of hard bargain. But even if he is there for no more than the ride, his vote a certainty in the mind of the political boss, able to be thrown here or switched there as the boss decides, still in some peculiar sense he is reality to the boss, the delegate is the great American public, the bar he owns or the law practice, the piece of the union he represents, or the real-estate office, is a part of the political landscape which the boss uses as his own image of how the votes will go, and if the people will like the candidate. And if the boss is depressed by what he sees, if the candidate does not feel right to him, if he has a dull intimation that the candidate is not his sort (as, let us say, Harry Truman was his sort, or Symington might be his sort, or Lyndon Johnson), then vote for him the boss will if he must; he cannot be caught on the wrong side, but he does not feel the pleasure of a personal choice. Which is the center of the panic.

Because if the boss is depressed, the delegate is doubly depressed, and the emotional fact is that Kennedy is not in focus, not in the old political focus, he is not comfortable; in fact it is a mystery to the boss how Kennedy got to where he is, not a mystery in its structures; Kennedy is rolling in money, Kennedy got the votes in primaries, and, most of all, Kennedy has a jewel of a political machine. It is as good as a crack Notre Dame team, all discipline and savvy and go-go-go, sound, drilled, never dull, quick as a knife, full of the salt of hipper-dipper, a beautiful machine; the boss could adore it if only a sensible candidate were driving it, a Truman, even a Stevenson, please God a Northern Lyndon Johnson, but it is run by a man who looks young enough to be coach of the Freshman team, and that is not comfortable at all. The boss knows political machines, he knows issues, farm parity, Forand health bill, Landrum-Griffin, but this is not all so adequate after all to revolutionaries in Cuba who look like beatniks, competitions in missiles, Negroes looting whites in the Congo, intricacies of nuclear fallout, and NAACP men one does well to call Sir. It is all out of hand, everything important is off the center, foreign affairs is now the lick of the heat, and senators are candidates instead of governors, a disaster to the old family style of political measure where a political boss knows his governor and knows who his governor knows. So the boss is depressed, profoundly depressed. He comes to this convention resigned to nominating a man he does not understand, or let us say that, so far as he understands the candidate who is to be nominated, he is not happy about the secrets of his appeal, not so far as he divines these secrets; they seem to have too little to do with politics and all too much to do with the private madnesses of the nation which had thousands—or was it hundreds of thousands—of people demonstrating in the long night before Chessman was killed, and a movie star, the greatest, Marlon the Brando out in the night with them. Yes, this candidate for all his record, his good, sound, conventional liberal record, has a patina of that other life, the second American life, the long electric night with the fires of neon leading down the highway to the murmur of jazz.

An Apparent Digression: A Vivid View of the "City of Lost Angels"; The Democrats Defined; A Pentagon of Traveling Salesmen; Some Pointed Portraits of the Politicians

"I was seeing Pershing Square, Los Angeles, now for the first time . . . the nervous fruithustlers darting in and out of the shadows, fugitives from Times Square, Market Street SF, the French Quarter—

masculine hustlers looking for lonely fruits to score from, anything from the legendary $20 to a pad at night and breakfast in the morning and whatever you can clinch or clip; and the heat in their holy cop uniforms, holy because of the Almighty Stick and the Almightier Vagrancy Law; the scattered junkies, the small-time pushers, the queens, the sad panhandlers, the lonely, exiled nymphs haunting the entrance to the men's head, the fruits with the hungry eyes and the jingling coins; the tough teen-age chicks—'dittybops'—making it with the lost hustlers . . . all amid the incongruous piped music and the flowers—twin fountains gushing rainbow colored: the world of Lonely America squeezed into Pershing Square, of the Cities of Terrible Night, downtown now trapped in the City of lost Angels . . . and the trees hang over it all like some type of apathetic fate."
　　　　　　　　　　　　　　　　　　　—JOHN RECHY: Big Table 3

Seeing Los Angeles after ten years away, one realizes all over again that America is an unhappy contract between the East (that Faustian thrust of a most determined human will which reaches up and out above the eye into the skyscrapers of New York) and those flat lands of compromise and mediocre self-expression, those endless half-pretty repetitive small towns of the Middle and the West whose spirit is forever horizontal and whose marrow comes to rendezvous in the pastel monotonies of Los Angeles architecture.

So far as America has a history, one can see it in the severe heights of New York City, in the glare from the Pittsburgh mills, by the color in the brick of Louisburg Square, along the knotted greedy facades of the small mansions on Chicago's North Side, in Natchez's antebellum homes, the wrought-iron balconies off Bourbon Street, a captain's house in Nantucket, by the curve of Commercial Street in Provincetown. One can make a list; it is probably finite. What culture we have made and what history has collected to it can be found in those few hard examples of an architecture which came to its artistic term, was born, lived and so collected some history about it. Not all the roots of American life are uprooted, but almost all, and the spirit of the supermarket, that homogenous extension of stainless surfaces and psychoanalyzed people, packaged commodities and ranch homes, interchangeable, geographically unrecognizable, that essence of the new postwar SuperAmerica is found nowhere so perfectly as in Los Angeles' ubiquitous acres. One gets the impression that people come to Los Angeles in order to divorce themselves from the past, here to live or try to live in the rootless pleasure world of an adult child. One knows that if the cities of the world were destroyed by a new war, the architecture of the rebuilding would create a landscape which looked, subject to specifications of climate, exactly and entirely like the San Fernando Valley.

It is not that Los Angeles is altogether hideous, it is even by degrees pleasant, but for an Easterner there is never any salt in the wind; it is like

Mexican cooking without chile, or Chinese egg rolls missing their mustard; as one travels through the endless repetitions of that city which is the capital of suburbia with its milky pinks, its washed-out oranges, its tainted lime-yellows of pastel on one pretty little architectural monstrosity after another, the colors not intense enough, the styles never pure, and never sufficiently impure to collide on the eye, one conceives the people who live here—they have come out to express themselves, Los Angeles is the home of self-expression, but the artists are middle-class and middling-minded; no passions will calcify here for years in the gloom to be revealed a decade later as the tesselations of a hard and fertile work, no, it is all open, promiscuous, borrowed, half bought, a city without iron, eschewing wood, a kingdom of stucco, the playground for mass men—one has the feeling it was built by television sets giving orders to men. And in this land of the pretty-pretty, the virility is in the barbarisms, the vulgarities, it is in the huge billboards, the screamers of the neon lighting, the shouting farm-utensil colors of the gas stations and the monster drugstores, it is in the swing of the sports cars, hot rods, convertibles, Los Angeles is a city to drive in, the boulevards are wide, the traffic is nervous and fast, the radio stations play bouncing, blooping, rippling tunes, one digs the pop in a pop tune, no one of character would make love by it but the sound is good for swinging a car, electronic guitars and Hawaiian harps.

So this is the town the Democrats came to, and with their unerring instinct (after being with them a week, one thinks of this party as a crazy, half-rich family, loaded with poor cousins, traveling always in caravans with Cadillacs and Okie Fords, Lincolns and quarterhorse mules, putting up every night in tents to hear the chamber quartet of Great Cousin Eleanor invaded by the Texas-twanging steel-stringing geetarists of Bubber Lyndon, carrying its own mean high-school principal, Doc Symington, chided for its manners by good Uncle Adlai, told the route of march by Navigator Jack, cut off every six months from the rich will of Uncle Jim Farley, never listening to the mechanic of the caravan, Bald Sam Rayburn, who assures them they'll all break down unless Cousin Bubber gets the concession on the garage; it's the Snopes family married to Henry James, with the labor unions thrown in like a Yankee dollar, and yet it's true, in tranquility one recollects them with affection, their instinct is good, crazy family good) and this instinct now led the caravan to pick the Biltmore Hotel in downtown Los Angeles for their family get-together and reunion.

The Biltmore is one of the ugliest hotels in the world. Patterned after the flat roofs of an Italian Renaissance palace, it is eighty-eight times as large, and one-millionth as valuable to the continuation of man, and it would be intolerable if it were not for the presence of Pershing Square, that square block of park with cactus and palm trees, the three-hundred-and-sixty-five-day-a-year convention of every junkie, pot-head, pusher, queen (but you have read that good writing already). For years Pershing Square has been one of the three or four places in America famous to homosexuals, famous not for its posh, the chic is round-heeled here, but because it is one of the avatars of the good old masturbatory sex, dirty with the crusted sugars of smut, dirty rooming houses around the corner where the score is made, dirty book and photograph stores down the street, old-fashioned out-of-the-Thirties burlesque houses, cruising bars, jukeboxes, movie houses; Pershing Square is the town plaza for all those lonely, respectable, small-town homosexuals who lead a family life, make children, and have the Philbrick psychology (How I Joined the Communist Party and Led Three Lives). Yes, it is the open-air convention hall for the small-town inverts who live like spies, and it sits in the center of Los Angeles, facing the Biltmore, that hotel which is a mausoleum, that Pentagon of traveling salesmen the Party chose to house the headquarters of the Convention.

So here came that family, cursed before it began by the thundering absence of Great-Uncle Truman, the delegates dispersed over a run of thirty miles and twenty-seven hotels: the Olympian Motor Hotel, the Ambassador, the Beverly Wilshire, the Santa Ynez Inn (where rumor has it the delegates from Louisiana had some midnight swim), the Mayan, the Commodore, the Mayfair, the Sheraton-West, the Huntington-Sheraton, the Green, the Hayward, the Gates, the Figueroa, the Statler Hilton, the Hollywood Knickerbocker—does one have to be a collector to list such names?—beauties all, with that up-from-the-farm Los Angeles décor, plate-glass windows, patio and terrace, foam-rubber mattress, pastel paints, all of them pretty as an ad in full-page color, all but the Biltmore where everybody gathered every day—the newsmen, the TV, radio, magazine, and foreign newspapermen, the delegates, the politicos, the tourists, the campaign managers, the runners, the flunkies, the cousins and aunts, the wives, the grandfathers, the eight-year-old girls, and the twenty-eight-year-old girls in the Kennedy costumes, red and white and blue, the Symingteeners, the Johnson Ladies, the Stevenson Ladies, everybody —and for three days before the convention and four days into it, everybody collected at the Biltmore, in the lobby, in the grill, in the Biltmore Bowl, in the elevators, along the corridors, three hundred deep always outside the Kennedy suite, milling everywhere, every dark-carpeted grey-brown hall of the hotel, but it was in the Gallery of the Biltmore where one first felt the mood which pervaded all proceedings until the convention was almost over, that heavy, thick, witless depression which was to dominate every move as the delegates wandered and gawked and paraded and set for a spell, there in the Gallery of the Biltmore, that huge depressing alley with its inimitable hotel color, that faded depth of chiaroscuro which unhappily has no depth, that brown which is not a brown, that grey which has no pearl in it, that color which can be described only as hotel-color because the beiges, the tans, the walnuts, the mahoganies, the dull blood rugs, the moaning yellows, the sick greens, the greys and all those dumb browns merge into that lack of color which is an over-large hotel at convention time, with all the small-towners wearing their set, starched faces, that look they get at carnival, all fever and suspicion, and proud to be there, eddying slowly back and forth in that high block-long tunnel of a room with its arched ceiling and square recesses filling every rib of the arch with art work, escutcheons and blazons and other art, pictures I think, I cannot even remember, there was such a hill of cigar smoke the eye had to travel on its way to the ceiling, and at one end there was galvanized-pipe scaffolding and workmen repairing some part of the ceiling, one of them touching up one of the endless squares of painted plaster in the arch, and another worker, passing by, yelled up to the one who was working on the ceiling: "Hey, Michelangelo!"

Later, of course, it began to emerge and there were portraits one could keep, Symington, dogged at a press conference, declaring with no conviction that he knew he had a good chance to win, the disappointment eating at his good looks so that he came off hard-faced, mean, and yet slack—a desperate dullness came off the best of his intentions. There was Johnson who had compromised too many contradictions and now the contradictions were in his face: when he smiled the corners of his mouth squeezed gloom; when he was pious, his eyes twinkled irony; when he spoke in a righteous tone, he looked corrupt; when he jested, the ham in his jowls looked to quiver. He was not convincing. He was a Southern politician, a Texas Democrat, a liberal Eisenhower; he would do no harm, he would do no good, he would react to the machine, good fellow, nice friend—the Russians would understand him better than his own.

Stevenson had the patina. He came into the room and the room was different, not stronger perhaps (which is why ultimately he did not win), but warmer. One knew why some adored him; he did not look like other people, not with press lights on his flesh; he looked like a lover, the simple truth, he had the sweet happiness of an adolescent who has just been given his first major kiss. And so he glowed, and one was reminded of Chaplin, not because they were the least alike in features, but because Charlie Chaplin was luminous when one met him and Stevenson had something of that light.

There was Eleanor Roosevelt, fine, precise, hand-worked like ivory. Her voice was almost attractive as she explained in the firm, sad tones of the first lady in this small town why she could not admit Mr. Kennedy, who was no doubt a gentleman, into her political house. One had the impression of a lady who was finally becoming a woman, which is to say that she was just a little bitchy about it all; nice bitchy, charming, it had a touch of art to it, but it made one wonder if she were not now satisfying the last passion of them all, which was to become physically attractive, for she was better-looking than she had ever been as she spurned the possibilities of a young suitor.

Jim Farley. Huge. Cold as a bishop. The hell he would consign you to was cold as ice.

Bobby Kennedy, that archetype Bobby Kennedy, looked like a West Point cadet, or, better, one of those unreconstructed Irishmen from Kirkland House one always used to have to face in the line in Harvard house football games. "Hello," you would say to the ones who looked like him as you lined up for the scrimmage after the kickoff, and his type would nod and look away, one rock glint of recognition your due for living across the hall from one another all through Freshman year, and then bang, as the ball was passed back, you'd get a bony king-hell knee in the crotch. He was the kind of man never to put on the gloves with if you wanted to do some social boxing, because after two minutes it would be a war, and ego-bastards last long in a war.

Carmine DeSapio and Kenneth Galbraith on the same part of the convention floor. DeSapio is bigger than one expects, keen and florid, great big smoked glasses, a suntan like Man-tan—he is the kind of heavyweight Italian who could get by with a name like Romeo—and Galbraith is tall-tall, as actors say, six foot six it could be, terribly thin, enormously attentive, exquisitely polite, birdlike, he is sensitive to the stirring of reeds in a wind over the next hill. "Our grey eminence," whispered the intelligent observer next to me.

Bob Wagner, the mayor of New York, a little man, plump, groomed, blank. He had the blank, pomaded, slightly worried look of the first barber in a good barbershop, the kind who would go to the track on his day off and wear a green transparent stone in a gold ring,

And then there was Kennedy, the edge of the mystery. But a sketch will no longer suffice.

Perspective from the Biltmore Balcony: The Colorful Arrival of the Hero with the Orange-brown Suntan and Amazingly White Teeth; Revelation of the Two Rivers Political Theory

". . . it can be said with a fair amount of certainty that the essence of his political attractiveness is his extraordinary political intelligence. He has a mind quite unlike that of any other Democrat of this century. It is not literary, metaphysical and moral, as Adlai Stevenson's is. Kennedy is articulate and often witty, but he does not seek verbal polish. No one can doubt the seriousness of his concern with the most serious political matters, but one feels that whereas Mr. Stevenson's political views derive *from a view of life that holds politics to be a mere fraction of existence, Senator Kennedy's primary interest is in politics. The easy way in which he disposes of the question of Church and State—as if he felt that any reasonable man could quite easily resolve any possible conflict of loyalties—suggests that the organization of society is the one thing that really engages his interest."*

—RICHARD ROVERE   *The New Yorker,* July 23, 1960

The afternoon he arrived at the convention from the airport, there was of course a large crowd on the street outside the Biltmore, and the best way to get a view was to get up on an outdoor balcony of the Biltmore, two flights above the street, and look down on the event. One waited thirty minutes, and then a honking of horns as wild as the getaway after an Italian wedding sounded around the corner, and the Kennedy cortege came into sight, circled Pershing Square, the men in the open and leading convertibles sitting backwards to look at their leader, and finally came to a halt in a space cleared for them by the police in the crowd. The television cameras were out, and a Kennedy band was playing some circus music. One saw him immediately. He had the deep orange-brown suntan of a ski instructor, and when he smiled at the crowd his teeth were amazingly white and clearly visible at a distance of fifty yards. For one moment he saluted Pershing Square, and Pershing Square saluted him back, the prince and the beggars of glamour staring at one another across a city street, one of those very special moments in the underground history of the world, and then with a quick move he was out of his car and by choice headed into the crowd instead of the lane cleared for him into the hotel by the police, so that he made his way inside surrounded by a mob, and one expected at any moment to see him lifted to its shoulders like a matador being carried back to the city after a triumph in the plaza. All the while the band kept playing the campaign tunes, sashaying circus music, and one had a moment of clarity, intense as a *déjà vu,* for the scene which had taken place had been glimpsed before in a dozen musical comedies; it was the scene where the hero, the matinee idol, the movie star comes to the palace to claim the princess, or what is the same, and more to our soil, the football hero, the campus king, arrives at the dean's home surrounded by a court of open-singing students to plead with the dean for his daughter's kiss and permission to put on the big musical that night. And suddenly I saw the convention, it came into focus for me, and I understood the mood of depression which had lain over the convention, because finally it was simple: the Democrats were going to nominate a man who, no matter how serious his political dedication might be, was indisputably and willy-nilly going to be seen as a great box-office actor, and the consequences of that were staggering and not at all easy to calculate.

Since the First World War Americans have been leading a double life, and our history has moved on two rivers, one visible, the other under-ground; there has been the history of politics which is concrete, factual, practical and unbelievably dull if not for the consequences of the actions of some of these men; and there is a subterranean river of untapped, ferocious, lonely and romantic desires, that concentration of ecstasy and violence which is the dream life of the nation.

The twentieth century may yet be seen as that era when civilized man and underprivileged man were melted together into mass man, the iron and steel of the nineteenth century giving way to electronic circuits which communicated their messages into men, the unmistakable tendency of the new century seeming to be the creation of men as interchangeable as commodities, their extremes of personality singed out of existence by the psychic fields of force the communicators would impose. This loss of personality was a catastrophe to the future of the imagination, but billions of people might first benefit from it by having enough to eat—one did not know—and there remained citadels of resistance in Europe where the culture was deep and roots were visible in the architecture of the past.

Nowhere, as in America, however, was this fall from individual man to mass man felt so acutely, for America was at once the first and most prolific creator of mass communications, and the most rootless of coun-tries, since almost no American could lay claim to the line of a family which had not once at least severed its roots by migrating here. But, if rootless, it was then the most vulnerable of countries to its own homogeni-zation. Yet America was also the country in which the dynamic myth of the Renaissance—that every man was potentially extraordinary—knew its most passionate persistence. Simply, America was the land where people still believed in heroes: George Washington; Billy the Kid; Lin-coln, Jefferson; Mark Twain, Jack London, Hemingway; Joe Louis, Dempsey, Gentleman Jim; America believed in athletes, rum-runners, aviators; even lovers, by the time Valentino died. It was a country which had grown by the leap of one hero past another—is there a county in all of our ground which does not have its legendary figure? And when the West was filled, the expansion turned inward, became part of an agitated, overexcited, superheated dream life. The film studios threw up their searchlights as the frontier was finally sealed, and the romantic possibili-ties of the old conquest of land turned into a vertical myth, trapped within the skull, of a new kind of heroic life, each choosing his own archetype of a neo-renaissance man, be it Barrymore, Cagney, Flynn, Bogart, Brando or Sinatra, but it was almost as if there were no peace unless one could fight well, kill well (if always with honor), love well and love many, be cool, be daring, be dashing, be wild, be wily, be resourceful, be a brave gun. And this myth, that each of us was born to be free, to wander, to have adventure and to grow on the waves of the violent, the perfumed, and the unexpected, had a force which could not be tamed no matter how the nation's regulators—politicians, medicos, policemen, professors, priests, rabbis, ministers, ideologues, psychoanalysts, builders, executives and endless communicators—would brick-in the modern life with hygiene upon sanity, and middle-brow homily over platitude; the myth would not die. Indeed a quarter of the nation's business must have depended upon its existence. But it stayed alive for more than that—it was as if the message in the labyrinth of the genes would insist that violence was locked with creativity, and adventure was the secret of love.

Once, in the Second World War and in the year or two which followed, the underground river returned to earth, and the life of the nation was intense, of the present, electric; as a lady said, "That was the time when we gave parties which changed people's lives." The Forties was a decade when the speed with which one's own events occurred seemed as rapid as the history of the battlefields, and for the mass of people in America a forced march into a new jungle of emotion was the result. The surprises, the failures, and the dangers of that life must have terrified some nerve of awareness in the power and the mass, for, as if stricken by the orgiastic vistas the myth had carried up from underground, the retreat to a more conservative existence was disorderly, the fear of communism spread like an irrational hail of boils. To anyone who could see, the excessive hysteria of the Red wave was no preparation to face an enemy, but rather a terror of the national self: free-loving, lust-looting, atheistic, implacable—absurdity beyond absurdity to label communism so, for the moral products of Stalinism had been Victorian sex and a ponderous machine of material theology.

Forced underground again, deep beneath all *Reader's Digest* hospital dressings of Mental Health in Your Community, the myth continued to flow, fed by television and the film. The fissure in the national psyche widened to the danger point. The last large appearance of the myth was the vote which tricked the polls and gave Harry Truman his victory in '48. That was the last. Came the Korean War, the shadow of the H-bomb, and we were ready for the General. Uncle Harry gave way to Father, and security, regularity, order, and the life of no imagination were the command of the day. If one had any doubt of this, there was Joe McCarthy with his built-in treason detector, furnished by God, and the damage was done. In the totalitarian wind of those days, anyone who worked in Government formed the habit of being not too original, and many a mind atrophied from disuse and private shame. At the summit there was benevolence without leadership, regularity without vision, security without safety, rhetoric without life. The ship drifted on, that enormous warship of the United States, led by a Secretary of State whose cells were seceding to cancer, and as the world became more fantastic—Africa turning itself upside down, while some new kind of machine man was being made in China—two events occurred which stunned the confidence of America into a new night: the Russians put up their Sputnik, and Civil Rights—that reluctant gift to the American Negro, granted for its effect on foreign affairs—spewed into real life at Little Rock. The national Ego was in shock: the Russians were now in some ways our technological superiors, and we had an internal problem of subject populations equal conceivably in its difficulty to the Soviet and its satellites. The fatherly calm of the General began to seem like the uxorious mellifluences of the undertaker.

Underneath it all was a larger problem. The life of politics and the life of myth had diverged too far, and the energies of the people one knew everywhere had slowed down. Twenty years ago a post-Depression generation had gone to war and formed a lively, grousing, by times inefficient, carousing, pleasure-seeking, not altogether inadequate army. It did part of what it was supposed to do, and many, out of combat, picked up a kind of private life on the fly, and had their good time despite the yaws of the military system. But today in America the generation which respected the code of the myth was Beat, a horde of half-begotten Christs with scraggly beards, heroes none, saints all, weak before the strong, empty conformisms of the authority. The sanction for finding one's growth was no longer one's flag, one's career, one's sex, one's adventure, not even one's booze. Among the best in this newest of the generations, the myth had found its voice in marijuana, and the joke of the underground was that when the Russians came over they could never dare to occupy us for long because America was too Hip. Gallows humor. The poorer truth might be that America was too Beat, the instinct of the nation so separated from its public mind that apathy, schizophrenia, and private beatitudes might be the pride of the welcoming committee any underground could offer.

Yes, the life of politics and the life of the myth had diverged too far. There was nothing to return them to one another, no common danger, no cause, no desire, and, most essentially, no hero. It was a hero America needed, a hero central to his time, a man whose personality might suggest contradictions and mysteries which could reach into the alienated circuits of the underground, because only a hero can capture the secret imagination of a people, and so be good for the vitality of his nation; a hero embodies the fantasy and so allows each private mind the liberty to consider its fantasy and find a way to grow. Each mind can become more conscious of its desire and waste less strength in hiding from itself. Roosevelt was such a hero, and Churchill, Lenin and de Gaulle; even Hitler, to take the most odious example of this thesis, was a hero, the hero-as-monster, embodying what had become the monstrous fantasy of a people, but the horror upon which the radical mind and liberal temperament foundered was that he gave outlet to the energies of the Germans and so presented the twentieth century with an index of how horrible had become the secret heart of its desire. Roosevelt is of course a happier example of the hero; from his paralytic leg to the royal elegance of his geniality he seemed to contain the country within himself; everyone from the meanest starving cripple to an ambitious young man could expand into the optimism of an improving future because the man offered an unspoken promise of a future which would be rich. The sexual and the sex-starved, the poor, the hard-working and the imaginative well-to-do could see themselves in the President, could believe him to be like themselves. So a large part of the country was able to discover its energies because not as much was wasted in feeling that the country was a poisonous nutrient which stifled the day.

Too simple? No doubt. One tries to construct a simple model. The thesis is after all not so mysterious; it would merely nudge the notion that a hero embodies his time and is not so very much better than his time, but he is larger than life and so is capable of giving direction to the time, able to encourage a nation to discover the deepest colors of its character. At bottom the concept of the hero is antagonistic to impersonal social progress, to the belief that social ills can be solved by social legislating, for it sees a country as all-but-trapped in its character until it has a hero who reveals the character of the country to itself. The implication is that without such a hero the nation turns sluggish. Truman for example was not such a hero, he was not sufficiently larger than life, he inspired familiarity without excitement, he was a character but his proportions came from soap opera: Uncle Harry, full of salty common-sense and small-minded certainty, a storekeeping uncle.

Whereas Eisenhower has been the anti-Hero, the regulator. Nations do not necessarily and inevitably seek for heroes. In periods of dull anxiety, one is more likely to look for security than a dramatic confrontation, and Eisenhower could stand as a hero only for that large number of Americans who were most proud of their lack of imagination. In American life, the unspoken war of the century has taken place between the city and the small town the city which is dynamic, orgiastic, unsettling, explosive and accelerating to the psyche; the small town which is rooted, narrow, cautious and planted in the life-logic of the family. The need of the city is to accelerate growth; the pride of the small town is to retard it. But since America has been passing through a period of enormous expansion since the war, the double-four years of Dwight Eisenhower could not retard the expansion, it could only denude it of color, character, and the development of novelty. The small-town mind is rooted—it is rooted in the small town—and when it attempts to direct history the results are disastrously colorless because the instrument of world power which is used by the small-town mind is the committee. Committees do not create, they merely proliferate, and the incredible dullness wreaked upon the American landscape in Eisenhower's eight years has been the triumph of the corporation. A tasteless, sexless, odorless sanctity in architecture, manners, modes, styles has been the result. Eisenhower embodied half the needs of the nation, the needs of the timid, the petrified, the sanctimonious, and the sluggish. What was even worse, he did not divide the nation as a hero might (with a dramatic dialogue as the result); he merely excluded one part of the nation from the other. The result was an alienation of the best minds and bravest impulses from the faltering history which was made. America's need in those years was to take an existential turn, to walk into the nightmare, to face into that terrible logic of history which demanded that the country and its people must become more extraordinary and more adventurous, or else perish, since the only alternative was to offer a false security in the power and the panacea of organized religion, family, and the F.B.I., a totalitarianization of the psyche by the stultifying techniques of the mass media which would seep into everyone's most private associations and so leave the country powerless against the Russians even if the denouement were to take fifty years, for in a competition between totalitarianisms the first maxim of the prizefight manager would doubtless apply: "Hungry fighters win fights."

The Hipster as Presidential Candidate: Thoughts on a Public Man's Eighteenth-Century Wife; Face-to-Face with the Hero; Significance of a Personal Note, or the Meaning of His Having Read an Author's Novel

Some part of these thoughts must have been in one's mind at the moment there was that first glimpse of Kennedy entering the Biltmore Hotel; and in the days which followed, the first mystery—the profound air of depression which hung over the convention—gave way to a second mystery which can be answered only by history. The depression of the delegates was understandable: no one had too much doubt that Kennedy would be nominated, but if elected he would be not only the youngest President ever to be chosen by voters, he would be the most conventionally attractive young man ever to sit in the White House, and his wife—some would claim it—might be the most beautiful first lady in our history. Of necessity the myth would emerge once more, because America's politics would now be also America's favorite movie, America's first soap opera, America's best-seller. One thinks of the talents of writers like Taylor Caldwell or Frank Yerby, or is it rather *The Fountainhead* which would contain such a fleshing of the romantic prescription? Or is it indeed one's own work which is called into question? "Well, there's your first hipster," says a writer one knows at the convention, "Sergius O'Shaugnessy born rich," and the temptation is to nod, for it could be true, a war hero, and the heroism is bona-fide, even exceptional, a man who has lived with death, who, crippled in the back, took on an operation which would kill him or restore him to power, who chose to marry a lady whose face might be too imaginative for the taste of a democracy which likes its first ladies to be executives of home-management, a man who courts political suicide by choosing to go all out for a nomination four, eight, or twelve years before his political elders think he is ready, a man who announces a week prior to the convention that the young are better fitted to direct history than the old. Yes, it captures the attention. This is no routine candidate calling every shot by safety's routine book ("Yes," Nixon said, naturally but terribly tired an hour after his nomination, the TV cameras and lights and microphones bringing out a sweat of fatigue on his face, the words coming very slowly from the tired brain, somber, modest, sober, slow, slow enough so that one could touch emphatically the cautions behind each word, "Yes, I want to say," said Nixon, "that whatever abilities I have, I got from my mother." A tired pause . . . dull moment of warning, ". . . and my father." The connection now made, the rest comes easy, ". . . and my school and my church." Such men are capable of anything.)

One had the opportunity to study Kennedy a bit in the days that followed. His style in the press conferences was interesting. Not terribly popular with the reporters (too much a contemporary, and yet too difficult to understand, he received nothing like the rounds of applause given to Eleanor Roosevelt, Stevenson, Humphrey, or even Johnson), he carried himself nonetheless with a cool grace which seemed indifferent to applause, his manner somehow similar to the poise of a fine boxer, quick with his hands, neat in his timing, and two feet away from his corner when the bell ended the round. There was a good lithe wit to his responses, a dry Harvard wit, a keen sense of proportion in disposing of difficult questions—invariably he gave enough of an answer to be formally satisfactory without ever opening himself to a new question which might go further than the first. Asked by a reporter, "Are you for Adlai as vice-president?" the grin came forth and the voice turned very dry, "No, I cannot say we have considered *Adlai* as a vice-president." Yet there was an elusive detachment to everything he did. One did not have the feeling of a man present in the room with all his weight and all his mind. Johnson gave you all of himself, he was a political animal, he breathed like an animal, sweated like one, you knew his mind was entirely absorbed with the compendium of political fact and maneuver; Kennedy seemed at times like a young professor whose manner was adequate for the classroom, but whose mind was off in some intricacy of the Ph. D. thesis he was writing. Perhaps one can give a sense of the discrepancy by saying that he was like an actor who had been cast as the candidate, a good actor, but not a great one—you were aware all the time that the role was one thing and the man another—they did not coincide, the actor seemed a touch too aloof (as, let us say, Gregory Peck is usually too aloof) to become the part. Yet one had little sense of whether to value this elusiveness, or to beware of it. One could be witnessing the fortitude of a superior sensitivity or the detachment of a man who was not quite real to himself. And his voice gave no clue. When Johnson spoke, one could separate what was fraudulent from what was felt, he would have been satisfying as an actor the way Broderick Crawford or Paul Douglas are satisfying; one saw into his emotions, or at least had the illusion that one did. Kennedy's voice, however, was only a fair voice, too reedy, near to strident, it had the metallic snap of a cricket in it somewhere, it was more impersonal than the man, and so became the least-impressive quality in a face, a body, a selection of language, and a style of movement which made up a better-than-decent presentation, better than one had expected.

With all of that, it would not do to pass over the quality in Kennedy which is most difficult to describe. And in fact some touches should be added to this hint of a portrait, for later (after the convention), one had a short session alone with him, and the next day, another. As one had suspected in advance, the interviews were not altogether satisfactory, they hardly could have been. A man running for President is altogether different from a man elected President: the hazards of the campaign make it impossible for a candidate to be as interesting as he might like to be (assuming he has such a desire). One kept advancing the argument that this campaign would be a contest of personalities, and Kennedy kept returning the discussion to politics. After a while one recognized this was an inevitable caution for him. So there would be not too much point to reconstructing the dialogue since Kennedy is hardly inarticulate about his political attitudes and there will be a library vault of text devoted to it in the newspapers. What struck me most about the interview was a passing remark whose importance was invisible on the scale of politics, but was altogether meaningful to my particular competence. As we sat down for the first time, Kennedy smiled nicely and said that he had read my books. One muttered one's pleasure. "Yes," he said, "I've read . . ." and then there was a short pause which did not last long enough to be embarrassing in which it was yet obvious no title came instantly to his mind, an omission one was not ready to mind altogether since a man in such a position must be obliged to carry a hundred thousand facts and names in his head, but the hesitation lasted no longer than three seconds or four, and then he said, "I've read *The Deer Park* and . . . the others," which startled me for it was the first time in a hundred similar situations, talking to someone whose knowledge of my work was casual, that the sentence did not come out, "I've read *The Naked and the Dead* . . . and the others." If one is to take the worst and assume that Kennedy was briefed for this interview (which is most doubtful), it still speaks well for the striking instincts of his advisers.

What was retained later is an impression of Kennedy's manners which were excellent, even artful, better than the formal good manners of Choate and Harvard, almost as if what was creative in the man had been given to the manners. In a room with one or two people, his voice improved, became low-pitched, even pleasant—it seemed obvious that in all these years he had never become a natural public speaker and so his voice was constricted in public, the symptom of all orators who are ambitious, throttled, and determined.

His personal quality had a subtle, not quite describable intensity, a suggestion of dry pent heat perhaps, his eyes large, the pupils grey, the whites prominent, almost shocking, his most forceful feature: he had the eyes of a mountaineer. His appearance changed with his mood, strikingly so, and this made him always more interesting than what he was saying. He would seem at one moment older than his age, forty-eight or fifty, a tall, slim, sunburned professor with a pleasant weathered face, not even particularly handsome; five minutes later, talking to a press conference on his lawn, three microphones before him, a television camera turning, his appearance would have gone through a metamorphosis, he would look again like a movie star, his coloring vivid, his manner rich, his gestures strong and quick, alive with that concentration of vitality a successful actor always seems to radiate. Kennedy had a dozen faces. Although they were not at all similar as people, the quality was reminiscent of some one like Brando whose expression rarely changes, but whose appearance seems to shift from one person into another as the minutes go by, and one bothers with this comparison because, like Brando, Kennedy's most characteristic quality is the remote and private air of a man who has traversed some lonely terrain of experience, of loss and gain, of nearness to death, which leaves him isolated from the mass of others.

"The next day while they waited in vain for rescuers, the wrecked half of the boat turned over in the water and they saw that it would soon sink. The group decided to swim to a small island three miles away. There were other islands bigger and nearer, but the Navy officers knew that they were occupied by the Japanese. On one island, only one mile to the south, they could see a Japanese camp. McMahon, the engineer whose legs were disabled by burns, was unable to swim. Despite his own painfully crippled back, Kennedy swam the three miles with a breast stroke, towing behind him by a life-belt strap that he held between his teeth the helpless McMahon . . . it took Kennedy and the suffering engineer five hours to reach the island."

The quotation is from a book which has for its dedicated unilateral title, *The Remarkable Kennedys,* but the prose is by one of the best of the war reporters, the former *Yank* editor, Joe McCarthy, and so presumably may be trusted in such details as this. Physical bravery does not of course guarantee a man's abilities in the White House—all too often men with physical courage are disappointing in their moral imagination—but the heroism here is remarkable for its tenacity. The above is merely one episode in a continuing saga which went on for five days in and out of the water, and left Kennedy at one point "miraculously saved from drowning (in a storm) by a group of Solomon Island natives who suddenly came up beside him in a large dugout canoe." Afterward, his back still injured (that precise back injury which was to put him on crutches eleven years later, and have him search for "spinal-fusion surgery" despite a warning that his chances of living through the operation were "extremely limited") afterward, he asked to go back on duty and became so bold in the attacks he made with his PT boat "that the crew didn't like to go out with him because he took so many chances."

It is the wisdom of a man who senses death within him and gambles that he can cure it by risking his life. It is the therapy of the instinct, and who is so wise as to call it irrational? Before he went into the Navy, Kennedy had been ailing. Washed out of Freshman year at Princeton by a prolonged trough of yellow jaundice, sick for a year at Harvard, weak already in the back from an injury at football, his trials suggest the self-hatred of a man whose resentment and ambition are too large for his body. Not everyone can discharge their furies on an analyst's couch, for some angers can be relaxed only by winning power, some rages are sufficiently monumental to demand that one try to become a hero or else fall back into that death which is already within the cells. But if one succeeds, the energy aroused can be exceptional. Talking to a man who had been with Kennedy in Hyannis Port the week before the convention, I heard that he was in a state of deep fatigue.

"Well, he didn't look tired at the convention," one commented.

"Oh, he had three days of rest. Three days of rest for him is like six months for us."

One thinks of that three-mile swim with the belt in his mouth and McMahon holding it behind him. There are pestilences which sit in the mouth and rot the teeth—in those five hours how much of the psyche must have been remade, for to give vent to the bite in one's jaws and yet use that rage to save a life: it is not so very many men who have the apocalyptic sense that heroism is the First Doctor.

If one had a profound criticism of Kennedy it was that his public mind was too conventional, but that seemed to matter less than the fact of such a man in office because the law of political life had become so dreary that only a conventional mind could win an election. Indeed there could be no politics which gave warmth to one's body until the country had recovered its imagination, its pioneer lust for the unexpected and incalculable. It was the changes that might come afterward on which one could put one's hope. With such a man in office the myth of the nation would again be engaged, and the fact that he was Catholic would shiver a first existential vibration of consciousness into the mind of the White Protestant. For the first time in our history, the Protestant would have the pain and creative luxury of feeling himself in some tiny degree part of a minority, and that was an experience which might be incommensurable in its value to the best of them.

A Vignette of Adlai Stevenson; The Speeches: What Happened When the Teleprompter Jammed: How U.S. Senator Eugene McCarthy Played the Matador. An Observation on the Name Fitzgerald

As yet we have said hardly a word about Stevenson. And his actions must remain a puzzle unless one dares a speculation about his motive, or was it his need?

So far as the people at the convention had affection for anyone, it was Stevenson, so far as they were able to generate any spontaneous enthusiasm, their cheers were again for Stevenson. Yet it was obvious he never had much chance because so soon as a chance would present itself he seemed quick to dissipate the opportunity. The day before the nominations, he entered the Sports Arena to take his seat as a delegate—the demonstration was spontaneous, noisy and prolonged; it was quieted only by Governor Collins' invitation for Stevenson to speak to the delegates. In obedience perhaps to the scruple that a candidate must not appear before the convention until nominations are done, Stevenson said no more than: "I am grateful for this tumultuous and moving welcome. After getting in and out of the Biltmore Hotel and this hall, I have decided I know whom you are going to nominate. It will be the last survivor." This dry reminder of the ruthlessness of politics broke the roar of excitement for his presence. The applause as he left the platform was like the dying fall-and-moan of a baseball crowd when a home run curves foul. The next day, a New York columnist talking about it said bitterly, "If he'd only gone through the motions, if he had just said that now he wanted to run, that he would work hard, and he hoped the delegates would vote for him. Instead he made that lame joke." One wonders. It seems almost as if he did not wish to win unless victory came despite himself, and then was overwhelming. There are men who are not heroes because they are too good for their time, and it is natural that defeats leave them bitter, tired, and doubtful of their right to make new history. If Stevenson had campaigned for a year before the convention, it is possible that he could have stopped Kennedy. At the least, the convention would have been enormously more exciting, and the nominations might have gone through half-a-dozen ballots before a winner was hammered into shape. But then Stevenson might also have shortened his life. One had the impression of a tired man who (for a politician) was sickened unduly by compromise. A year of maneuvering, broken promises, and detestable partners might have gutted him for the election campaign. If elected, it might have ruined him as a President. There is the possibility that he sensed his situation exactly this way, and knew that if he were to run for President, win and make a good one, he would first have to be restored, as one can indeed be restored, by an exceptional demonstration of love—love, in this case, meaning that the Party had a profound desire to keep him as their leader. The emotional truth of a last-minute victory for Stevenson over the Kennedy machine might have given him new energy; it would certainly have given him new faith in a country and a party whose good motives he was possibly beginning to doubt. Perhaps the fault he saw with his candidacy was that he attracted only the nicest people to himself and there were not enough of them. (One of the private amusements of the convention was to divine some of the qualities of the candidates by the style of the young women who put on hats and clothing and politicked in the colors of one presiden-tial gent or another. Of course, half of them must have been hired models, but someone did the hiring and so it was fair to look for a common denominator. The Johnson girls tended to be plump, pie-faced, dumb sexy Southern; the Symingteeners seemed a touch mulish, stubborn, good-looking pluggers; the Kennedy ladies were the handsomest; healthy, attractive, tough, a little spoiled—they looked like the kind of girls who had gotten all the dances in high school and/or worked for a year as an airline hostess before marrying well. But the Stevenson girls looked to be doing it for no money; they were good sorts, slightly horsy-faced, one had the impression they played field hockey in college.) It was indeed the pure, the saintly, the clean-living, the pacifistic, the vegetarian who seemed most for Stevenson, and the less humorous in the Kennedy camp were heard to remark bitterly that Stevenson had nothing going for him but a bunch of Goddamn Beatniks. This might even have had its sour truth. The demon-strations outside the Sports Arena for Stevenson seemed to have more than a fair proportion of tall, emaciated young men with thin, wry beards and three-string guitars accompanied (again in undue proportion) by a contingent of ascetic, face-washed young Beat ladies in sweaters and dungarees. Not to mention all the Holden Caulfields one could see from here to the horizon. But of course it is unfair to limit it so, for the Democratic gentry were also committed half en masse for Stevenson, as well as a considerable number of movie stars, Shelley Winters for one: after the convention she remarked sweetly, "Tell me something nice about Kennedy so I can get excited about him."

What was properly astonishing was the way this horde of political half-breeds and amateurs came within distance of turning the convention from its preconceived purpose, and managed at the least to bring the only hour of thoroughgoing excitement the convention could offer.

But then nominating day was the best day of the week and enough happened to suggest that a convention out of control would be a spectacle as extraordinary in the American scale of spectator values as a close seventh game in the World Series or a tied fourth quarter in a professional-football championship. A political convention is after all not a meeting of a corporation's board of directors; it is a fiesta, a carnival, a pig-rooting, horse-snorting, band-playing, voice-screaming medieval get-together of greed, practical lust, compromised idealism, career-advancement, meeting, feud, vendetta, conciliation, of rabble-rousers, fist fights (as it used to be), embraces, drunks (again as it used to be) and collective rivers of animal sweat. It is a reminder that no matter how the country might pretend it has grown up and become tidy in its manners, bodiless in its legislative language, hygienic in its separation of high politics from private life, that the roots still come grubby from the soil, and that politics in America is still different from politics anywhere else because the politics has arisen out of the immediate needs, ambitions, and cupidities of the people, that our politics still smell of the bedroom and the kitchen, rather than having descended to us from the chill punctilio of aristocratic negotiation.

So. The Sports Arena was new, too pretty of course, tasteless in its design—it was somehow pleasing that the acoustics were so bad for one did not wish the architects well; there had been so little imagination in their design, and this arena would have none of the harsh grandeur of Madison Square Garden when it was aged by spectators' phlegm and feet over the next twenty years. Still it had some atmosphere; seen from the streets, with the spectators moving to the ticket gates, the bands playing, the green hot-shot special editions of the Los Angeles newspapers being hawked by the newsboys, there was a touch of the air of promise that precedes a bullfight, not something so good as the approach to the Plaza Mexico, but good, let us say, like the entrance into El Toreo of Mexico City, another architectural monstrosity, also with seats painted, as I remember, in rose-pink, and dark, milky sky-blue.

Inside, it was also different this nominating day. On Monday and Tuesday the air had been desultory, no one listened to the speakers, and everybody milled from one easy chatting conversation to another—it had been like a tepid Kaffeeklatsch for fifteen thousand people. But today there was a whip of anticipation in the air, the seats on the floor were filled, the press section was working, and in the gallery people were sitting in the aisles.

Sam Rayburn had just finished nominating Johnson as one came in, and the rebel yells went up, delegates started filing out of their seats and climbing over seats, and a pullulating dance of bodies and bands began to snake through the aisles, the posters jogging and whirling in time to the music. The dun color of the floor (faces, suits, seats and floor boards), so monotonous the first two days, now lit up with life as if an iridescent caterpillar had emerged from a fold of wet leaves. It was more vivid than one had expected, it was right, it felt finally like a convention, and from up close when one got down to the floor (where your presence was illegal and so consummated by sneaking in one time as demonstrators were going out, and again by slipping a five-dollar bill to a guard) the nearness to the demonstrators took on high color, that electric vividness one feels on the side lines of a football game when it is necessary to duck back as the ballcarrier goes by, his face tortured in the concentration of the moment, the thwomp of his tackle as acute as if one had been hit oneself.

That was the way the demonstrators looked on the floor. Nearly all had the rapt, private look of a passion or a tension which would finally be worked off by one's limbs, three hundred football players, everything from seedy delegates with jowl-sweating shivers to livid models, paid for their work that day, but stomping out their beat on the floor with the hypnotic adulatory grimaces of ladies who had lived for Lyndon these last ten years.

Then from the funereal rostrum, whose color was not so rich as mahogany nor so dead as a cigar, came the last of the requests for the delegates to take their seats. The seconding speeches began, one minute each; they ran for three and four, the minor-league speakers running on the longest as if the electric antennae of television was the lure of the Sirens, leading them out. Bored cheers applauded their concluding Götterdämmerungen and the nominations were open again. A favorite son, a modest demonstration, five seconding speeches, tedium.

Next was Kennedy's occasion. Governor Freeman of Minnesota made the speech. On the second or third sentence his television prompter jammed, an accident. Few could be aware of it at the moment; the speech seemed merely flat and surprisingly void of bravura. He was obviously no giant of extempore. Then the demonstration. Well-run, bigger than Johnson's, jazzier, the caliber of the costumes and decorations better chosen the placards were broad enough, "Let's Back Jack," the floats were garish, particularly a papier-mâché or plastic balloon of Kennedy's head, six feet in diameter, which had nonetheless the slightly shrunken, over-red, rubbery look of a toy for practical jokers in one of those sleazy off-Times Square magic-and-gimmick stores; the band was suitably corny; and yet one had the impression this demonstration had been designed by some hands-to-hip interior decorator who said, "Oh, joy, let's have fun, let's make this *true* beer hall."

Besides, the personnel had something of the Kennedy *élan,* those paper hats designed to look like straw boaters with Kennedy's face on the crown, and small photographs of him on the ribbon, those hats which had come to symbolize the crack speed of the Kennedy team, that Madison Avenue cachet which one finds in bars like P. J. Clarke's, the elegance always giving its subtle echo of the Twenties so that the raccoon coats seem more numerous than their real count, and the colored waistcoats are measured by the charm they would have drawn from Scott Fitzgerald's eye. But there, it occurred to one for the first time that Kennedy's middle name was just that, Fitzgerald, and the tone of his crack lieutenants, the unstated style, was true to Scott. The legend of Fitzgerald had an army at last, formed around the self-image in the mind of every superior Madison Avenue opportunist that he was hard, he was young, he was In, his conversation was lean as wit, and if the work was not always scrupulous, well the style could aspire. If there came a good day . . . he could meet the occasion.

The Kennedy snake dance ran its thirty lively minutes, cheered its seconding speeches, and sat back. They were so sure of winning, there had been so many victories before this one, and this one had been scouted and managed so well, that hysteria could hardly be the mood. Besides, everyone was waiting for the Stevenson barrage which should be at least diverting. But now came a long tedium. Favorite sons were nominated, fat mayors shook their hips, seconders told the word to constituents back in Ponderwaygot County, treacly demonstrations tried to hold the floor, and the afternoon went by; Symington's hour came and went, a good demonstration, good as Johnson's (for good cause—they had pooled their demonstrators). More favorite sons, Governor Docking of Kansas declared "a genius" by one of his lady speakers in a tense go-back-to-religion voice. The hours went by, two, three, four hours, it seemed forever before they would get to Stevenson. It was evening when Senator Eugene McCarthy of Minnesota got up to nominate him.

The gallery was ready, the floor was responsive, the demonstrators were milling like bulls in their pen waiting for the *toril* to fly open——it would have been hard not to wake the crowd up, not to make a good speech. McCarthy made a great one. Great it was by the measure of convention oratory, and he held the crowd like a matador timing their *oles!*, building them up, easing them back, correcting any sag in attention, gathering their emotion, discharging it, creating new emotion on the wave of the last, driving his passes tighter and tighter as he readied for the kill. "Do not reject this man who made us all proud to be called Democrats, do not leave this prophet without honor in his own party." One had not heard a speech like this since 1948 when Vito Marcantonio's voice, his harsh, shrill, bitter, street urchin's voice screeched through the loud-speakers at Yankee Stadium and lashed seventy thousand people into an uproar.

"There was only one man who said let's talk sense to the American people," McCarthy went on, his muleta furled for the *naturales*. "There was only one man who said let's talk sense to the American people," he repeated. "He said the promise of America is the promise of greatness.

This was his call to greatness. . . . Do not forget this man. . . . Ladies and Gentlemen, I present to you not the favorite son of one state, but the favorite son of the fifty states, the favorite son of every country he has visited, the favorite son of every country which has not seen him but is secretly thrilled by his name." Bedlam. The kill. "Ladies and Gentlemen, I present to you Adlai Stevenson of Illinois." Ears and tail. Hooves and bull. A roar went up like the roar one heard the day Bobby Thomson hit his home run at the Polo Grounds and the Giants won the pennant from the Dodgers in the third playoff game of the 1951 season. The demonstration cascaded onto the floor, the gallery came to its feet, the Sports Arena sounded like the inside of a marching drum. A tidal pulse of hysteria, exaltation, defiance, exhilaration, anger and roaring desire flooded over the floor. The cry which had gone up on McCarthy's last sentence had not paused for breath in five minutes, and troop after troop of demonstrators jammed the floor (the Stevenson people to be scolded the next day for having collected floor passes and sent them out to bring in new demonstrators) and still the sound mounted. One felt the convention coming apart. There was a Kennedy girl in the seat in front of me, the Kennedy hat on her head, a dimpled healthy brunette; she had sat silently through McCarthy's speech, but now, like a woman paying her respects to the power of natural thrust, she took off her hat and began to clap herself. I saw a writer I knew in the next aisle; he had spent a year studying the Kennedy machine in order to write a book on how a nomination is won. If Stevenson stampeded the convention, his work was lost. Like a reporter at a mine cave-in I inquired the present view of the widow. "Who can think," was the answer, half frantic, half elated, "just watch it, that's all." I found a cool one, a New York reporter, who smiled in rueful respect. "It's the biggest demonstration I've seen since Wendell Willkie's in 1940," he said, and added, "God, if Stevenson takes it, I can wire my wife and move the family on to Hawaii."

"I don't get it."

"Well, every story I wrote said it was locked up for Kennedy."

Still it went on, twenty minutes, thirty minutes, the chairman could hardly be heard, the demonstrators refused to leave. The lights were turned out, giving a sudden theatrical shift to the sense of a crowded church at midnight, and a new roar went up, louder, more passionate than anything heard before. It was the voice, it was the passion, if one insisted to call it that, of everything in America which was defeated, idealistic, innocent, alienated, outside the Beat, it was the potential voice of a new third of the nation whose psyche was ill from cultural malnutrition, it was powerful, it was extraordinary, it was larger than the decent, humorous, finicky, half-noble man who had called it forth, it was a cry from the Thirties when Time was simple, it was a resentment of the slick technique, the oiled gears, and the superior generals of Fitzgerald's Army; but it was also—and for this reason one could not admire it altogether, except with one's excitement—it was also the plea of the bewildered who hunger for simplicity again, it was the adolescent counterpart of the boss's depression before the unpredictable dynamic of Kennedy as President, it was the return to the sentimental dream of Roosevelt rather than the approaching nightmare of history's oncoming night, and it was inspired by a terror of the future as much as a revulsion of the present.

Fitz's Army held; after the demonstration was finally down, the convention languished for ninety minutes while Meyner and others were nominated, a fatal lapse of time because Stevenson had perhaps a chance to stop Kennedy if the voting had begun on the echo of the last cry for him, but in an hour and a half depression crept in again and emotions spent, the delegates who had wavered were rounded into line. When the vote was taken, Stevenson had made no gains. The brunette who had taken off her hat was wearing it again, and she clapped and squealed when Wyoming delivered the duke and Kennedy was in. The air was sheepish, like the mood of a suburban couple who forgive each other for cutting in and out of somebody else's automobile while the country club dance is on. Again, tonight, no miracle would occur. In the morning the papers would be moderate in their description of Stevenson's last charge.

A Sketch of the Republicans Gathered in Convention: The Choice Between the Venturesome and the Safe; What May Happen at Three o'Clock in the Morning on a Long Dark Night

One did not go to the other convention. It was seen on television, and so too much cannot be said of that. It did however confirm one's earlier bias that the Republican Party was still a party of church ushers, undertakers, choirboys, prison wardens, bank presidents, small-town police chiefs, state troopers, psychiatrists, beauty-parlor operators, corporation executives, Boy-Scout leaders, fraternity presidents, tax-board assessors, community leaders, surgeons, Pullman porters, head nurses and the fat sons of rich fathers. Its candidate would be given the manufactured image of an ordinary man, and his campaign, so far as it was a psychological campaign (and this would be far indeed), would present him as a simple, honest, dependable, hard-working, ready-to-learn, modest, humble, decent, sober young man whose greatest qualification for President was his profound abasement before the glories of the Republic, the stability of the mediocre, and his own unworthiness. The apocalyptic hour of Uriah Heep.

It would then be a campaign unlike the ones which had preceded it. Counting by the full spectrum of complete Right to absolute Left, the political differences would be minor, but what would be not at all minor was the power of each man to radiate his appeal into some fundamental depths of the American character. One would have an inkling at last if the desire of America was for drama or stability, for adventure or monotony. And this, this appeal to the psychic direction America would now choose for itself was the element most promising about this election, for it gave the possibility that the country might be able finally to rise above the deadening verbiage of its issues, its politics, its jargon, and live again by an image of itself. For in some part of themselves the people might know (since these candidates were not old enough to be revered) that they had chosen one young man for his mystery, for his promise that the country would grow or disintegrate by the unwilling charge he gave to the intensity of the myth, or had chosen another young man for his unstated oath that he would do all in his power to keep the myth buried and so convert the remains of Renaissance man as rapidly as possible into mass man. One might expect them to choose the enigma in preference to the deadening certainty. Yet one must doubt America's bravery. This lurching, unhappy, pompous and most corrupt nation—could it have the courage finally to take on a new image for itself, was it brave enough to put into office not only one of its ablest men, its most efficient, its most conquistadorial (for Kennedy's capture of the Democratic Party deserves the word), but also one of its more mysterious men (the national psyche must shiver in its sleep at the image of Mickey Mantle-cum-Lindbergh in office, and a First Lady with an eighteenth-century face). Yes, America was at last engaging the fate of its myth, its consciousness about to be accelerated or cruelly depressed in its choice between two young men in their forties who, no matter how close, dull, or indifferent their stated politics might be, were radical poles apart, for one was sober, the apotheosis of opportunistic lead, all radium spent, the other handsome as a prince in the unstated aristocracy of the American dream. So, finally, would come a choice which history had never presented to a nation before—one could vote for glamour or for ugliness, a staggering and most stunning choice—would the nation be brave enough to enlist the romantic dream of itself, would it vote for the image in the mirror of its unconscious, were the people indeed brave enough to hope for an acceleration of Time, for that new life of drama which would come from choosing a son to lead them who was heir apparent to the psychic loins? One could pause: it might be more difficult to be a President than it ever had before. Nothing less than greatness would do.

Yet if the nation voted to improve its face, what an impetus might come to the arts, to the practices, to the lives and to the imagination of the American. If the nation so voted. But one knew the unadmitted specter in the minds of the Democratic delegates: that America would go to sleep on election eve with the polls promising Kennedy a victory on the day to come, yet in its sleep some millions of Democrats and Independents would suffer a nightmare before the mystery of uncharted possibilities their man would suggest, and in a terror of all the creativities (and some violences) that mass man might now have to dare again, the undetermined would go out in the morning to vote for the psychic security of Nixon the way a middle-aged man past adventure holds to the stale bread of his marriage. Yes, this election might be fearful enough to betray the polls and no one in America could plan the new direction until the last vote was counted by the last heeler in the last ambivalent ward, no one indeed could know until then what had happened the night before, what had happened at three o'clock in the morning on that long dark night of America's search for a security cheaper than her soul.

[November, 1960]

Kennedy Without Tears

by Tom Wicker

On November 22, 1963, the brief Kennedy era came to a sickening end with the death of the president. John F. Kennedy was gone, but the memory lived on, becoming in the minds of some a myth called Camelot. Tom Wicker's brilliant coverage of the assassination for the New York Times *moved* Esquire *to ask him to write an essay that would separate the facts from the image, and give an unsentimental assessment of Kennedy's achievements as president. The story ran in the June 1964 issue. At the* Times, *Wicker went on to become chief of the Washington bureau and later an associate editor and regular columnist.*

Shortly after President Kennedy was shot, the following inscription appeared on a plaque in one of the private bedrooms of the White House:

In this room Abraham Lincoln slept during his occupancy of the White House as President of the United States, March 4, 1861-April 13, 1865.

In this room lived John Fitzgerald Kennedy with his wife Jacqueline Kennedy during the two years, ten months and two days he was President of the United States, January 20, 1961-November 22, 1963.

Before many years pass, that deliberate linkage of two Presidents, that notice chiseled upon history by Jacqueline Kennedy, may seem as inevitable as the Washington Monument. Already, airports and spaceports and river bridges and a cultural center have been named for her husband. Books about him, even phonograph records, are at flood tide and *Profiles in Courage* has returned to the top of The New York *Times* best-seller list. It is almost as if he had never called businessmen sons of bitches, sent the troops to Ole Miss, the refugees to the Bay of Pigs, or kicked the budget sky-high.

Six months after his death, John F. Kennedy is certain to take his place in American lore as one of those sure-sell heroes out of whose face or words or monuments a souvenir dealer can turn a steady buck. There he soon will stand, perhaps in our lifetime—cold stone or heartless bronze, immortal as Jefferson, revered as Lincoln, bloodless as Washington. One can imagine the graven words on his pedestal:

"Ask not what your country can do for you. Ask what you can do for your country."

What his country inevitably will do for John Kennedy seems a curious fate for the vitality and intensity, the wry and derisive style of the man who was the Thirty-fifth President of the United States. His wit surely would have seared the notion of John F. Kennedy International Airport, much less Cape Kennedy—for this was the man who once told the great-great-grandson of John Adams, "It is a pleasure to live in your family's old house, and we hope that you will come by and see us."

One suspects the Eternal Flame might have embarrassed him as much as the Navy did that brilliant Pacific day last June when the strutting admirals put him literally on a flag-draped pedestal aboard an aircraft carrier while the band played *Hail to the Chief* and the jets screamed overhead on taxpayers' money; one of his favorite quips, after all, was that he had gone from Lieutenant J.G. to Commander-in-Chief without any qualifications at all.

I can almost hear that amused Boston voice inquiring, as he once did after reading a favorable Gallup Poll, where all those people who admired him so much were when Congress turned down his school bill in 1961. Staring from Valhalla at himself cast in stone in the middle of some downtown Washington traffic circle, he might well whisper to earthly passersby what he once told 12,000 Democrats in Harrisburg, Pennsylvania:

"I will introduce myself. I am Teddy Kennedy's brother."

And when children rise reverently in some future Fourth of July pageant to recite the chiastic prose of the Kennedy Inaugural Address—the stirring words that raced so many pulses among that "new generation of Americans" to which he appealed—some may recall instead the same rhythm, the same rhetoric, but different words and a more subtle imagination at work:

"We observe tonight not a celebration of freedom but a victory of party, for we have sworn to pay off the same party debt our forebears ran up nearly a year and three months ago. Our deficit will not be paid off in the next hundred days, nor will it be paid off in the first one thousand days, nor in the life of this Administration. Nor, perhaps, even in our lifetime on this planet. But let us begin—remembering that generosity is not a sign of weakness and that ambassadors are always subject to Senate confirmation. For if the Democratic party cannot be helped by the many who are poor, it cannot be saved by the few who are rich. So let us begin."

Now a politician who could laugh at a parody of his noblest speech—let alone make it himself, as Kennedy did the foregoing—obviously was something more intricate in life than the mere sum of the virtues symbolized by the Eternal Flame: purity, steadfastness, warmth, light. A President delighted by the political caricature of Everett McKinley Dirksen, but impatient with the solemn earnestness of Chester Bowles, obviously had a wide streak of Honey Fitz down his spine; yet that same President, confronted with an adulatory mob of hundreds of thousands of cheering Europeans, could not bring himself to respond with more than a halfhearted jab of the arm from the chest—something like a halfback straight-arming a tackler, apologetically. And lest it be imagined that he was merely unemotional, remember that it was the crowd's transmitted frenzy that led Kennedy to make the inspiring but not very wise cry: *Ich bin ein Berliner!*

In the early days of Kennedy's New Frontier (there was bound to be something roguish about a man who could bring the Ivy Leaguers—and himself—to Washington with a slogan that evoked echoes of the Wild West, which appalled most of them), I thought Richard Nixon was perhaps a more interesting *man* than Kennedy. I thought Nixon was, as Conrad wrote of Lord Jim, "one of us." But Kennedy, I thought then, for all his charm and fire and eloquence, was a straightforward political man, who listened to his own rhetoric, contrived his "image" in the comforting faith that a statesman had to get elected before he could do anyone any good, and believed sincerely that his causes were not only right but actually offered solutions to human problems. I thought Kennedy had what Senator Eugene McCarthy called the perfect political mentality— that of a football coach, combining the will to win with the belief that the game is important.

Now, I think that what Kennedy really had of that mentality was a rather peculiar form of the will to win. He wanted power, all right, but something more; "This ability," he once said, "to do things well, and to do them with precision and with modesty, attracts us all." It was a theme to which he often returned—the pursuit of excellence. And as the probability of his political canonization turns toward certainty, and the sad calcification of his humanity into stone and bronze continues, there is not much football coach in the man Kennedy who recalls himself to me most strongly.

If that human Kennedy still seems to me to have been altogether too detached and too controlled to have been, as were Nixon and Lord Jim, "one of us," with all those fascinating hesitancies and inadequacies and torments out of which literature is made, nevertheless he *was* a man "of few days and full of trouble," and for all I know he may even have played "such fantastic tricks before high heaven as to make the angels weep." But the statues will tell us nothing of that.

Not many of them, for instance, will bear inscriptions drawn from his wit—that derisive, barbed, spontaneous wit, just short of mordant, that played so steadily through his speeches and recurred in such stable patterns of wording and attitude that it strikes me in retrospect as the true expression of a point of view, of a way of thinking not subject to time or circumstance or conditions.

It is astonishing, in retrospect, how constantly and boldly this Irish Catholic President, this young man so publicly committed to things like patriotism and public affairs, lampooned politicians, politics, notions, men, systems, myths, himself, even his church. When *The Wall Street Journal* criticized Nixon, Kennedy said, it was like "*L'Osservatore Romano* criticizing the Pope." And Speaker John McCormack denies that Kennedy called him "Archbishop"; "He called me 'Cardinal,' " McCormack recalls.

When the Vatican implied some criticism of Kennedy's campaign efforts to prove himself free of papal influence, Kennedy said ruefully to a pair of reporters: "Now I understand why Henry the Eighth set up his own church."

He and McKinley were the only Presidents ever to address the National Association of Manufacturers, Kennedy told that august body, so "I suppose that President McKinley and I are the only two that are regarded as fiscally sound enough to be qualified." And to the $100-a-plate guests at a glittering political occasion, he confessed: "I could say I am deeply touched, but not as deeply touched as you have been in coming to this luncheon."

Not even the Kennedy family was spared its scion's irreverence. To a dinner of the Alfred E. Smith Foundation during the 1960 campaign, he remarked:

"I had announced earlier this year that if successful I would not consider campaign contributions as a substitute for experience in appointing ambassadors. Ever since I made that statement I have not received one single cent from my father."

Everyone remembers his remark, upon appointing Bob Kennedy Attorney General, that his brother might as well get a little experience before having to practice law; not so many heard him late one night at a Boston dinner last fall when he paid similar respects to the youthful Edward M. Kennedy:

"My last campaign may be coming up very shortly," he said, "but Teddy is around and, therefore, these dinners can go on indefinitely."

The Kennedy wit was so pronounced and so identifiable that it could be reproduced with near exactitude by Ted Sorensen, his speech writer. A deadly serious man, Sorensen's few recorded public jokes included one perfect specimen of Kennedy-style wit.

"There will be a meeting this afternoon of representatives from Baltimore, Atlantic City, San Francisco, Philadelphia, Chicago and other cities interested in holding the 1964 national convention," he said in a mock announcement to a Democratic party gathering. "The meeting will be held in Mayor Daley's room."

In order to laugh—as the Democrats did—one had to know of course that Richard Daley was mayor of Chicago and one of the most powerful figures in the Democratic party—and that the competition for the convention was cutthroat. But Sorensen, as Kennedy always did, had tuned his derision precisely to his audience and the circumstances. The target was the situation—Daley's power, the party's foibles, the audience's pretensions. But whatever the situation, the *point of view* remained constant in Kennedy-style wit; it was the point of view that marked the man.

That point of view, as these few examples show, was a blending of amiable irreverence into a faintly resigned tolerance. It was a point of view that did not expect too much of human beings, even of its possessor; even less did it count heavily upon the wisdom or majesty of politicians; and often enough the political process itself was seen with frank disrespect. Perhaps a British M.P., but no American politician in memory except John Kennedy, would have been capable of the devastating "endorsement" of Senator George Smathers that the President delivered at a fund-raising dinner in Miami Beach:

"I actually came down here tonight to pay a debt of obligation to an old friend and faithful adviser. He and I came to the Eightieth Congress together and have been associated for many years, and I regard him as one of my most valuable counselors in moments of great personal and public difficulty.

"In 1952, when I was thinking about running for the United States Senate, I went to the then Senator Smathers and said, 'George, what do you think?'

"He said, 'Don't do it. Can't win. Bad year.'

"In 1956, I was at the Democratic convention, and I said—I didn't know whether I would run for Vice President or not, so I said, 'George, what do you think?'

" 'This is it. They need a young man. It's your chance.' So I ran—and lost.

"And in 1960, I was wondering whether I ought to run in the West Virginia primary. 'Don't do it. That state you can't possibly carry.'

"And actually, the only time I really got nervous about the whole matter at the Democratic Convention of 1960 was just before the balloting and George came up and he said, 'I think it looks pretty good for you.' "

The audience was already in stitches, but Kennedy had saved the real barb of his wit to the last, for an astonishing punch line in which Smathers appears not only as a target but as part of an apparatus—the Presidency and its problems—that was in itself somewhat ridiculous in its pretensions:

"It will encourage you to know [Kennedy said] that every Tuesday morning . . . we have breakfast together and he advises with me—Cuba, anything else, Laos, Berlin, anything—George comes right out there and gives his views and I listen very carefully."

Nor did he stop with such small targets as Smathers. Composing a birthday telegram to his touchy Vice President, Lyndon Johnson, he once told a reporter, was like "drafting a state document."

When Prime Minister Lester B. Pearson of Canada arrived at Hyannis Port in the Spring of 1963, his reputation as a baseball expert had preceded him. The resident White House baseball nut was Dave Powers, an Irishman of jovial mien who could sing *Bill Bailey Won't You Please Come Home* with marvelous vigah at the drop of a Scotch and soda. After a chilly Cape Cod dinner, Pearson followed Kennedy into seclusion, only to find it shattered by a summons to Powers.

"Dave," the President said, "test him out."

Whereupon Powers put the Prime Minister through an exhaustive baseball catechism, while the President rocked silently in his rocking chair, puffing on a cigar inscrutably, either measuring his man or enjoying the incongruous match—or both. Back and forth flowed the batting averages, managers' names, World Series statistics, and other diamond esoterica, until finally it was Dave Powers, not Mike Pearson, who tripped on some southpaw's 1926 earned run average.

"He'll do," Kennedy said then, with some satisfaction. After which he and Pearson hit it off famously and jointly equipped Canada with nuclear warheads.

Probably the finest piece of work Kennedy did in his eight generally lackluster years in the Senate was his leadership of the fight against reform of the electoral college in 1956. He argued brilliantly for the system as it was and still is. His side prevailed for a number of sound reasons, but not least because Kennedy succeeded in convincing enough Senators that, as he put it, "Falkland's definition of conservatism is quite appropriate—'When it is not necessary to change, it is necessary not to change.'"

That might almost have been Lord Melbourne speaking: *If it was not absolutely necessary, it was the foolishest thing ever done,* Melbourne said of a Parliamentary act. Indeed, Melbourne may have been in Kennedy's mind; for in the course of that brutal exposure of all his habits and persuasions to which Americans subject their President, it was to become known that his favorite book was David Cecil's *Melbourne.*

Probably no monument of the future will record that fact; yet it ought to give biographers pause. If the Kennedy campaign of 1960 meant anything, in terms of the man who waged it, it ought to have meant that Kennedy was a man who aimed to set the country right, who saw no reason it couldn't be done, who intended to let nothing stand in the way of doing it. The President who took office that cold day in January, 1961, saying, "let us begin," seemed to promise that the nation's problems could be solved if only enough brains and vigor and determination and money were applied to them.

Why would such a man enjoy reading of Melbourne, who believed government, in fact most human effort, was futile; who counseled, *When in doubt do nothing*; who said of a proposal to reform the English municipal councils, *We have got on tolerably well with the councils for five hundred years; we may contrive to go on with them for another few years or so*; and who thought the most damaging part of reform was that it aroused extravagant hopes that government and society—even men— might actually be improved.

But perhaps Kennedy was never quite the man the 1960 campaign suggested—just as Melbourne was not quite the fogy a few random quotations might suggest. Melbourne, in fact, as his biographer pictures him, was a man of immense charm and wit, great learning, considerable understanding of human nature, and remarkable courage in going his way—attributes that might be aspired to by any man. Certainly Kennedy possessed some of them and there is evidence to suggest that he shared to some extent Melbourne's skepticism about political and other human efforts at improving the condition of man.

The Kennedy wit certainly implies that he did. So did his remarks on a famous television interview in December of 1962, when he reviewed his first two years in office.

"There is a limitation upon the ability of the United States to solve these problems," he said. " . . . there is a limitation, in other words, upon the power of the United States to bring about solutions. . . . The responsibilities placed on the United States are greater than I imagined them to be and there are greater limitations upon our ability to bring about a favorable result than I had imagined them to be. . . . It is much easier to make the speeches than it is finally to make the judgments. . . ."

And it might have been Melbourne speaking again when he said of his efforts to roll back steel prices: "There is no sense in raising hell and then not being successful. There is no sense in putting the office of the Presidency on the line on an issue and then being defeated."

A few months later, I asked Kennedy at a news conference if he would comment on what I said was a feeling in the country that his Administration seemed "to have lost its momentum and to be slowing down and to be moving on the defensive."

"There is a rhythm to a personal and national and international life and

it flows and ebbs," Kennedy replied. He even conceded—sounding not unlike Melbourne on the Reform Laws—that "Some of our difficulties in Europe have come because the military threat in Europe is less than it has been in the past. In other words, whatever successes we may have had in reducing that military threat to Europe brought with it in its wake other problems. . . ."

Later, Ted Sorensen was to publish a book that in its essence was a discussion of the limitations upon a President—the reasons why, as Kennedy wrote in a foreword, "Every President must endure a gap between *what he would like and what is possible*" (the italics are mine). Once again Sorensen had caught the spirit of his chief and reproduced it; politics was not after all simply a matter of brains and vigor and determination, or even money. Its events, life itself, flowed also from the contrary nature of men, the blind turns of chance, the inertia of custom. And in that same foreword Kennedy quoted Franklin Roosevelt as saying

"Lincoln was a sad man because he couldn't get it all at once. And nobody can."

On a more personal level, some who knew Kennedy well sensed something deeper than skepticism in him, though he was a private man who did not much reveal himself even to men who worked with him for years. He was absolutely fearless about airplanes, for instance, flying anywhere, at any time, in any weather in which he could get aloft, sleeping through anything, scarcely seeming aware that he was off the ground. Yet four persons in his family—his brother, his sister, Ethel Kennedy's parents—had died in aircraft accidents.

Kennedy sometimes discussed the possibility that he would be assassinated with members of his staff. They would be anxious to explain the details of security precautions to him, to show him that it was unlikely it could happen. "If someone is going to kill me," he would say, "they're going to kill me."

And one of those who was close to him believes that Kennedy bothered little about what he was going to do with all those years that presumably would be on his hands when he emerged from the White House at age fifty-one (assuming he won two terms).

"It didn't really concern him," the aide recalls. "He never thought he was going to live to be an old man anyway."

Yet he had his imperatives. A man owed something to the public service. He had to be a patriot. He ought to be physically fit and courageous. (Good war records received special consideration on the New Frontier, and Dave Powers remembers that Kennedy once learned by heart the citation for a medal that had been awarded to General Douglas MacArthur.) A man's job was to act, not talk—to begin, to take the first step in a journey of a thousand miles.

Kennedy has been compared to Franklin Roosevelt and he liked to pose in front of an F.D.R. portrait. In fact, some of his qualities more nearly recall Theodore Roosevelt, the apostle of the big stick, the strenuous life and the bully pulpit. Like T.R., for instance, Kennedy fancied himself in the role of national taste maker—Roosevelt picked up Edward Arlington Robinson and Kennedy adopted Robert Frost. Roosevelt let his rather rigid literary ideas get about and the Kennedys thought they ought to provide White House examples—Casals, Shakespeare and opera in the East Room—for the cultural uplift of the nation. Yet, after an American opera group had sung a scene from *The Magic Flute* in English, after a dinner for the President of India, Kennedy could confess to a group of guests: "I think they ought to sing it in the original language. It doesn't sound right any other way."

There is not much doubt that Kennedy's publicized delight in Ian Fleming's spoof-spy novels doubled Fleming's sales, although there has been no big run on Cecil's *Melbourne*. He kept green, graceful Lafayette Square in Washington from disappearing into the capital's Great Stone Face. One of his last interests was in a plan to redeem Pennsylvania Avenue from army-surplus stores, cheap steak houses and bumbling federal architects. But it was as if art and culture were in the National Interest, like the test-ban treaty and Project Mercury; and if Kennedy was an avid reader of history, he did not seem to suffer from a great personal involvement in drama, music, art. The movies shown in the White House screening room were often the commonplace of Hollywood, and, except in the East Room, Kennedy's favorite music was more nearly Sinatra than Schönberg. As President, his first venture to Broadway took him to the slick musical, *How to Succeed in Business Without Really Trying*. Once, when he had a group of newspapermen in his house at Palm Beach, I stole a look at a stack of recordings; the one on top was a Chubby Checker twist collection.

But the imperatives of taking part, of public service, seemed, like those that moved Teddy Roosevelt, to be genuine and even profound. To the Touchdown Club of New York, he quoted with obvious approval the rather fervent view of T.R. on the matter

"The credit belongs to the man who is actually in the arena—whose face is marred by dust and sweat and blood . . . a leader who knows the great enthusiasms, the great devotions—and spends himself in a worthy cause—who at best if he wins knows the thrills of high achievement—and if he fails at least fails while daring greatly—so that his place shall never be with those cold and timid souls who know neither victory nor defeat."

Many times, he voiced a similar sentiment in his own words. Oddly, the man of detachment, of cool wit and ironic view, preached the "long twilight struggle" in which the most certain thing was that there would be "neither victory nor defeat." Yet, the man of commitment, of action, rejected with robustious Teddy the "cold and timid souls" who had no blood and dust upon their faces. And another quotation he liked to throw at university audiences was the rhetorical question of George William Curtis of Massachusetts:

"Would you have counted him a friend of ancient Greece who quietly discussed the theory of patriotism on that hot summer day through whose hopeless and immortal hours Leonidas and the three hundred stood at Thermopylae for liberty? Was John Milton to conjugate Greek verbs in his library when the liberty of Englishmen was imperiled?"

To the students of George Washington University, Kennedy gave his own answer: "No, quite obviously, the duty of the educated man or woman, the duty of the scholar, is to give his objective sense, his sense of liberty to the maintenance of our society at the critical time."

But in the next breath he was telling the story of someone who went to Harvard years ago and "asked for President Lowell. They said, 'He's in Washington, seeing Mr. Taft.' I know that some other day, when they are asking for the President of your university, they will say that he is over at the White House seeing Mr. Kennedy. They understood at Harvard, and you understand here, the relative importance of a university president and a President of the United States."

If that was a joke, it did not come from one who often gave up "his objective sense, and his sense of liberty." Honey Fitz would sing *Sweet Adeline* until his tonsils gave out, but his grandson was never known to wear a funny hat in public. It may seem a small point, but John Kennedy maintained it literally to his dying day. On November 22, in Fort Worth, he went through the Texas ritual of being presented a cowboy hat—but steadfastly resisted the pleas of two thousand Texans that he put it on.

"Come to Washington Monday and I'll put it on for you in the White House," he joked. But even in that comparative privacy, had he reached it, he would not have worn that hat. The man of detachment had yielded himself enough; he would make his little pushing gesture at the crowds, but he would not wave his arms exuberantly above his head like Eisenhower, or thump his chest like Theodore Roosevelt.

So, despite their similarities, he was radically different from the ebullient T.R. Restraint was his style, not arm-waving. There was nothing detached, nothing ironic, about Roosevelt, who could say and believe it that in the White House "my teaching has been plain morality." Kennedy would never claim more than that he hoped he was a "responsible President"; he would not often speak on television because he believed people would tire of him and stop listening.

Sometimes, it seemed, he even thought of politics, the Presidency itself, as a sporting proposition. Kennedy never tired of exhorting college students to prepare themselves for the public service, but he was seldom stuffy about it. He did not propose, he told the University of North

Carolina student body, to adopt "from the Belgian constitution a provision giving three votes instead of one to college graduates—at least not until more Democrats go to college."

As the campaign of 1960 wore on, the atmosphere around the candidate sometimes seemed almost like one of those parlor games the Kennedys played so often. "Tell me a delegate and I'll tell you who he's for," Kennedy would say to members of his staff, in his best Twenty Questions manner. "Give me a state and I'll give you the delegate breakdown."

The election was so close it inhibited Kennedy; he would point out how closely divided was the country at every opportunity. Yet, he could compare his own disputed election to the plight of a Notre Dame football team that had won a game by means some thought illegal. "And we're not going to give it back," he told the National Football Foundation.

Kennedy disliked the solemn ideologues and myopic Babbitts who crowd American political life—Senator Karl Mundt of South Dakota, for instance—but he delighted in the skillful shenanigans of some who took the game of politics less seriously—even, in some cases, when the voters and taxpayers were taken too. With obvious relish, he once described the operations of the raffish but highly effective Senator Warren Magnuson of Washington as follows:

"He speaks in the Senate so quietly that few can hear him. He looks down at his desk—he comes into the Senate late in the afternoon—he is very hesitant about interrupting other members of the Senate—when he rises to speak, most members of the Senate have left—he sends his messages up to the Senate and everyone says, 'What is it?' And Senator Magnuson says, 'It's nothing important.' And Grand Coulee Dam is built."

The night before he died, Kennedy spoke in tribute to Representative Albert Thomas in Houston, Texas. Not the least of Thomas' achievements over the years had been the enrichment of Houston with federal investments; his most recent coup had been the somewhat controversial establishment there of the Manned Spacecraft Center. Kennedy recounted a bit floridly how Thomas had helped put the United States in a position to fire into space the largest booster rocket bearing the largest "payroll" in history. As the audience laughed, Kennedy hastily corrected the word to "payload."

That slip might have embarrassed most politicians, but it obviously struck Kennedy as funny. "It will be the largest payroll, too," he added, grinning, "and who should know that better than Houston. We put a little of it right in here." Wasn't that what made the wheels go round?

Kennedy laughed out loud when he heard that Everett Dirksen had said that one of his early economic measures would have "all the impact of a snowflake on the bosom of the Potomac." He once carried a letter from de Gaulle around the White House, pointing out its elegances to his staff. It mattered not who won or lost, but how they played the game.

Even the selection of winners of the Medal of Freedom, a sort of royal honors list Mrs. Kennedy and the President invented, was not free in Kennedy's mind from the sporting balance of politics—you scratch mine and I'll scratch yours. When the painter Andrew Wyeth was selected, Kennedy—who had put up an early argument for Ben Shahn—decreed: "Next year, we'll have to go abstract."

One night on his plane, returning to Washington from a speech in Trenton, he talked about his love of boating with a group of us, and confided: "I'd really like to have that yacht Eisenhower laid up in Phila- delphia [the old *Williamsburg*]. But he said he did it for economy reasons and if I took it out of mothballs now they'd never let me hear the end of it." That was how the game was played; all you could do was grin and bear it, and play the game yourself.

Thus, John Kennedy in his pursuit of excellence, his commitment to active service, spent a great deal of his short life playing and thinking politics—running and angling for office, first; pushing political solutions to social and economic problems, second. But that is not necessarily the same thing as being profoundly involved in politics; it is not the same thing as a belief in solutions or the efficacy of politics. Kennedy seemed sometimes to think of himself as taking the first steps he so often urged upon the country and the world; he would use politics, he would propose a program, not with much hope for either, but to raise a question, to start someone thinking, to bring a matter into whatever light there was.

One Saturday morning in 1963 in Los Angeles he appeared at the Hollywood Palladium to address a Democratic women's breakfast; it was the only time I ever heard *Hail to the Chief* played with a twist beat. He was supposed to make "brief remarks"; instead, he plunged in his familiar machine-gun delivery into a half hour of Democratic party evangelism so impassioned and so portentous of phrase that some of my colleagues wrote that he had "kicked off his 1964 campaign." I was so stirred by the speech that I phoned The New York *Times* to hold space for the full text of it. It was a "major address," I assured my editors.

When the transcript came spinning from the White House mimeograph an hour later, I thumbed through it in search of those memorable phrases, those ringing pledges, those grand calls to battle, that had rung through the Palladium. I have that transcript before me now and it confirms my disillusionment; there was nothing there, nothing but rhetoric and deliv- ery. We had seen a performance in which J.F.K. had been playing the game unusually well.

In 1962, Kennedy proposed a Cabinet-level Department of Urban Affairs. Robert C. Weaver, the Administration's housing chief, was to be its Secretary—the first Negro to sit in any President's Cabinet. The proposal was hailed as a political master-stroke. Who could vote, in effect, against Weaver except the Southerners? And who cared about them?

In any event, a great many members of Congress voted against the proposal and it became one of Kennedy's most embarrassing defeats. Not long afterward, I asked him how it had happened.

He took a cigar out of his mouth and answered bluntly: "I played it too cute. It was so obvious it made them mad." In short, he had played the game poorly. I think he often did.

He could go before a captive audience of Democratic old people in Madison Square Garden and shed crocodile tears in behalf of his medical-care plan—and look as political and as uncomfortable as he was. Before an audience in Miami Beach from which he had little further to gain, the A.F.L.-C.I.O., he was so palpably bored, his speech was so blatantly routine and uninspired, that men of more objective political judgment might have booed him from the platform. He went into General Eisenhower's home county during the 1962 campaign and delivered a speech so demagogic and so extravagant in its claims for Democratic virtue and Republican sloth that even the General was enraged and promptly proceeded to emerge from retirement to campaign against him—a development that might have been politically important had not the Cuban crisis changed the whole picture in October. On his Western trip in the Fall of 1963—his last extended tour in the country—Kennedy looked and felt so out of place talking about conservation and nature and wildlife that the reporters following him gave him the nickname "Smokey the Bear"; it was reported by Pierre Salinger at Jackson Lake Lodge that the President actually had seen a moose from the window of his room.

Shortly after Kennedy's death, Carroll Kilpatrick and I visited J. Frank Dobie at the University of Texas and asked him what was the difference between Kennedy and Lyndon Johnson. Mr. Dobie knew Johnson well; he knew Kennedy only as most Americans knew him—as a voice on the radio, a face on the screen, a presence in the land. "Johnson is concerned with means," Mr. Dobie said at once, as if the contrast was obvious. "Kennedy was interested in ends."

A generality, perhaps, but near enough to truth to *ring* true. Kennedy played the game as a political man had to, sometimes brilliantly, often with boredom and ineptitude. But it was not then that he stirred us. Even his memorable campaign of 1960, the finest exercise of his strictly political life, was not politics-as-usual; it was outside the ordinary rules, for Kennedy was a Roman Catholic, an inexperienced younger man, something of an intellectual, who put little trust in traditional politicians, and relied instead upon his own men, his own techniques, his own personality.

Perhaps he had to move beyond the rules, get out of the game, before he really involved himself—and therefore involved other men. His trip to

Europe in 1963 exhilarated him, for instance; he knew he had broken through the traditional wall of diplomatic niceties, spoken above the heads of politicians and governments, and he believed a new generation of Europeans had responded. At his death, his tax bill was mired in Congress, but its mere presentation may yet be the longest step toward lifting American economic policy out of twin ruts of ignorance and cliché. His civil-rights bill was fumbled and botched, but he was the first American President to recognize in the outpouring of events a "moral crisis" in race relations. The long shadow of de Gaulle darkened his European policy, but he had proclaimed on both sides of the Atlantic a commitment to the interdependence of two continents. Nobody could say there would be no nuclear war, but he had taken the "first step" of the test-ban treaty.

That is what haunts me about Kennedy—not just that he was a man of certain admirable visions, but that he had the kind of mind that could entertain vision, the kind of outlook that could put in perspective the gambits and maneuvers of the moment, see truly the futility of most means, the uncertain glory of most ends. Surely he was one of those men "educated in the liberal traditions, willing to take the long look, undisturbed by prejudices and slogans of the moment, who attempt to make an honest judgment on difficult events"; surely he tried to be one of those, to borrow his words again, who could "distinguish the real from the illusory, the long-range from the temporary, the significant from the petty. . . ."

And that is the real irony of John F. Kennedy's coming immortality. For when James Reston asked him in the Summer of 1961, during a long afternoon's talk at Hyannis Port, what kind of a world it was he had in mind, what vision he had of the future, John Kennedy—President of the United States for half a year, perpetrator of the Bay of Pigs, not long home from his "somber" meeting with Khrushchev in Vienna—could reply: "I haven't had time to think about that yet."

It is the classic story of the liberal man in politics. *I claim not to have controlled events,* Lincoln said, *but confess plainly that events have controlled me.* And perhaps it is symbolized in a compelling picture of Kennedy that comes to us from one of Washington's most imposing men.

It is a glimpse from the Cuban missile crisis of October, 1962, a period of great tension at the White House as throughout the world. The personage and the President were alone in Kennedy's oval office discussing what in New Frontier jargon were known as "the options"; that month, the options were pretty grim.

Kennedy rose from his rocking chair, leaving his visitor seated on a sofa. The President went across his office to the French doors that opened on the terrace of the West Executive Wing. Beyond the terrace lay the famous Rose Garden, redesigned like almost everything else about the White House by the elegant stylists who had come to live there. But at its end still towered the famous magnolia planted by Andrew Jackson.

Kennedy stood for a long time, silent, gazing at the garden and the magnolia, his hands behind his back, the burden of decision almost visible on his shoulders. "Well," he said at last, "I guess this is the week I earn my salary."

The detached thinker had been brought to bay by the necessities of the moment. That questing mind with its sensitivity to the complexity of things, to the illusory nature of answers and solutions, had come to the moment of black vs. white. That derisive and worldly wit was stilled in the sheer responsibility of choice. Action and events had overtaken contemplation and vision, and Kennedy shared the plight of Melbourne: *I am afraid the question of the Irish Church can neither be avoided or postponed. It must therefore be attempted to be solved.* And for Kennedy, that fall, humanity itself was the question.

So with his football coach's will to win, with his passion for "the ability to do things well," Kennedy had had his dreams and realized them. But I believe he stood on the sidelines, too, even while the game was going on, measuring his performance, wryly remarking upon it, not much impressed, not much deluded. Perhaps he knew all along that events would control, action overwhelm, means fail to reach ends. "There stands the decision," he wrote, "and there stands the President." Sooner or later, they would be as one.

The decisions he made, the slogans he spoke—let them be carved on the monuments. But for me his epitaph is inscribed on Dave Powers' silver beer mug, that John Kennedy gave him for his birthday last year. It reads:

> There are three things which
> are real:
> God, human folly and laughter.
> The first two are beyond our
> comprehension
> So we must do what we can
> with the third.

No one at the White House knew the source of those lines. I can find the words in no book of quotations. The Library of Congress has not been able to discover who wrote them. But I think I know.

[June, 1964]

Robert's Character

by Patrick Anderson

As attorney general and as the president's brother, Robert Kennedy was the second most powerful man in America. He used this power to shore up the platform of the New Frontier, to run the Democratic party machine, and to protect the Kennedy family's interests. He pursued these ends with dogged single-mindedness, achieving a reputation as a cold, ruthless prosecutor. Pat Anderson worked in the attorney general's office and glimpsed Kennedy in many private and public moments. His article was published in April 1965.

From the moment I joined the Kennedy Administration I was determined to cling to my objectivity—to work long and hard, but deep within me to remain a neutral on the New Frontier.

The reasons for my reserve were perverse and personal. I grew up, a poor and rather puny lad, in a Texas city that applauded wealth and athletic ability in its young. As a result, although I have no religious or racial prejudice, I instinctively distrust the rich and athletic.

Add to this the usual suspicion of the Southwesterner for the Easterner and it is clear that although I was ready to work for Robert Kennedy, that most rich and athletic of Easterners, I was not likely to gaze upon him in unquestioning awe.

Kennedy, as Attorney General, was chairman of the President's Committee on Juvenile Delinquency, and one of his oldest and closest friends, David Hackett, was its executive director. On the recommendation of another Kennedy aide, Hackett hired me, in December of 1961, as information officer for this Committee. I was then a twenty-five-year-old newspaper reporter.

For the next three years my job kept me in and out of the Attorney

General's cavernous, fifth-floor office at the Justice Department, Hackett's office next door, and the press office across the hall. Yet despite this physical proximity, it must be clear that I am not attempting to picture myself as having been a close associate of Robert Kennedy. To the contrary, the point is that I was on the fringes, close enough to Kennedy to see his faults, but not close enough to see his virtues.

Kennedy was surrounded by a group of trusted aides—such as Hackett, Ed Guthman, his press officer, John Nolan, his administrative assistant, and Angie Novello, his personal secretary—and my business was carried on with them. My occasional conversations with Kennedy usually went something like:

"General, would you stand a little closer to the Governor for this next picture?"

"Okay."

In short, I was close enough to Kennedy to ghostwrite for him, but not close enough to rate more than a nod in the hall; close enough to issue invitations in his name, but not close enough to be sure he remembered my name; close enough to see the bickering in his office, but not close enough to see the grand designs in his mind.

It was from this vantage point—a frustrating one for a disciple, perhaps, but not a bad one for a determined neutral—that for two years I observed the second most powerful man in the United States. And in those days to know Robert Kennedy was to know the New Frontier.

Kennedy ran the Justice Department, and ran it well, but that was only the first of his many roles during his brother's Administration. The New Frontier operated on the assumption that there were many great jobs to be done and very few men who could do them correctly. One of the most important men in the Administration once said to me: "There aren't ten men in this country whose judgment I trust." Thus the trusted few worked to exhaustion (and loved it; the real sacrifices of the New Frontier were made by their wives and children), while hundreds of untrusted civil servants and political appointees sat idle.

To say that Kennedy performed many jobs is, of course, to say that he stepped on many toes. Although he was its youngest member, he in effect served as a straw boss over the Cabinet, and if a Cabinet member resented this, there was not a great deal he could do about it. It is true that Kennedy's authority stemmed in part from his own demonstrated abilities, as well as from the fact that he was the President's brother. (Teddy, after all, was not made Secretary of State.) But this factor should not be exaggerated, for Washington understands power much better than it understands talent. It was not Robert Kennedy's talent that caused J. Edgar Hoover to follow his orders after years of dealing directly with the White House, nor was it any loss of ability on Kennedy's part that led Hoover to revert to his old habits after the assassination.

Much of the Attorney General's moonlighting was political. The Kennedys believed that the Democratic National Committee, supposedly their party's political headquarters, could attract top men only during election years. Thus during 1961-63 Robert Kennedy was for all practical purposes the head of the Democratic political machine. While John Kennedy worried about Khrushchev and de Gaulle, Robert Kennedy handled the equally delicate negotiations with Chicago's Mayor Daley, Harlem's Congressman Adam Clayton Powell, Jr., and an endless stream of lesser politicos who had some claim to press the Kennedy flesh and bend the Kennedy ear. It is somewhere recorded that John Kennedy bathed and put on fresh clothing several times each day; one suspects that Robert Kennedy washed his hands many times each day.

It has been said that Kennedy successfully fused the two great traditions of American Attorneys General, the political and the legalistic. Nonetheless, he maintained clear lines between the two. Political matters were negotiable; matters of principle were not. Unsavory political deals were necessary from time to time. Harold Cox of Mississippi, the first Federal judge appointed by President Kennedy, who later referred from the bench to civil-rights workers as "a bunch of chimpanzees" and "a bunch of niggers," was the close friend of Senator James Eastland, chairman of the Senate Judiciary Committee; Judge Cox was the price the Administration had to pay for the confirmation of Judge Thurgood Marshall and other commendable appointments. But there were no negotiations when Democratic politicians were accused of breaking the law: during Kennedy's term, the Justice Department prosecuted two Democratic Congressmen, three State Supreme Court justices, five mayors, two chiefs of police, and three sheriffs.

Many high Administration officials had not had previous political experience and found the bread and butter of everyday politics mildly distasteful. A Democratic sheriff who was the protégé of an important Democratic Senator once sought a letter from Robert Kennedy praising the sheriff's "junior-deputies" program for teen-agers. I drafted a letter and took it for clearance to Byron ("Whizzer") White, the Deputy Attorney General, who later was elevated to the Supreme Court. White asked me if I thought we should endorse the program.

I recited the political background of the request, but White interrupted: "But is the man's program any good?" I was forced to admit that, although I was convinced the "junior-deputies" program was not subversive, I had not considered its merits a major factor. The letter was sent, but not until White had deleted several adjectives.

Another of Kennedy's part-time jobs was at the Defense Department. Although he admired the way Robert McNamara ran his shop, there were periodic crises when the military became involved in political matters and it was necessary for the Attorney General to take over as acting commander in chief. These emergencies included the occupation of Ole Miss, the "schoolhouse-door" confrontation with Governor Wallace at the University of Alabama, and the concealment at various military bases of that outspoken son of Cosa Nostra, Joe Valachi.

Because the underworld had reportedly offered $100,000 for Valachi's life, extreme measures were taken to keep his whereabouts secret prior to his Congressional testimony. But a reporter, acting on a tip, called the commanding general of the Army base where Valachi was concealed and asked the general if Valachi was there. "Sure, we've got him," the general reportedly replied, a bit of candor for which several high Administration officials urged that he be busted to private.

During these crises, I was assisting in the Attorney General's press office and my chief fringe benefit was having Pentagon colonels call me, an enlisted man in the National Guard, for clearance on various routine press announcements. I always suspected that Robert Kennedy, a deck-swabbing seaman during World War II, shared my pleasure in exercising civilian control over the military. Indeed, one of Seaman Kennedy's finest moments, I thought, came when he visited Korea early in 1964 and, according to wire-service reports, was told by a high-ranking general that it would be very difficult to grant his request for a trip to the front lines. "Why would it be difficult, General?" he asked, and got what he wanted. The general learned that there are few experiences in this world quite like having Robert Kennedy push his unsmiling face toward yours and ask, "Why?"

Kennedy also played a major role in Administration programs to help the young and the underprivileged, so much so that Anthony Celebrezze, a man who made the incredible blunder of resigning as Mayor of Cleveland to become Secretary of Health, Education and Welfare, once protested:

"If Bob Kennedy wants to run my Department, let him come take my job."

This was wishful thinking, of course, since Robert Kennedy, like any sensible man, would have jumped off the Capitol dome before he would have taken the H.E.W. job. It sufficed to have trusted Kennedy lieutenants placed in key positions throughout the government. All this was done, of course, in the name of "coordination." This is a popular word in government, but whenever it appears, it is wise to inquire: Who is coordinating whom? During his brother's Administration, Robert Kennedy was coordinating most of the government, either personally or through trusted aides.

One of Kennedy's most trusted aides was Dave Hackett, his close friend since they were schoolboys together at Milton Academy in the early war years. Justice Department legend has it that Hackett was once asked by a reporter if he had gone to school with the Attorney General and replied:

"In those days the Attorney General went to school with *me*."

The statement would have been true, for Hackett was a legendary athlete when Bob Kennedy was still scrambling to make the team. Another school friend, John Knowles, modeled the young athlete-hero of his prizewinning novel, *A Separate Peace,* on Hackett, who went on to be twice named to the U.S. Olympic hockey team.

When Kennedy moved into the Justice Department, Hackett moved into the office next to his. At a time when many young New Frontiersmen were sparing no effort to be popularly identified as such, Hackett was content to operate quietly out of an unmarked office, devoting himself entirely to Kennedy's interests. It was this tough, charming, handsome, calculating man who was given responsibility for the national juvenile-delinquency program, who was charged with launching the Kennedys' "domestic Peace Corps," and who represented Robert Kennedy's interests in the hard bargaining that led to the poverty legislation. It was because I worked for Hackett that I was able to see a great deal of the government, and more than a little of Robert Kennedy.

Kennedy was a strange, complex man, easier to respect than to like, easier to like than to understand; in all, a man to be taken seriously. His love for humanity, however real, seemed greater in the abstract than in individual cases. He was no intellectual, but he was more receptive to other men's ideas than most intellectuals. But even as you made excuses for his weaknesses, there was the fear that you were doing more than he would do for you.

He has been called a simple man; it would be more accurate to say he is many simple men.

There is the simple man who pursued Jimmy Hoffa with such relentlessness that he accomplished the truly stupendous feat of making many people feel sorry for Hoffa. There is the simple man who, introduced to a shy, embarrassed secretary, made an elaborate, boyish curtsy that both put the girl at ease and gave her something to remember for the rest of her life. There is the simple man who, after his brother's death, could tell a reporter in complete honesty that he was thinking about becoming a schoolteacher, while in another corner of his mind little engines were already pondering the complicated Johnson-Wagner-Powell-Buckley gambit that led to his Senate bid.

I once briefed a reporter on the many youth programs Kennedy took part in, and she asked why I thought he spent so much time with children. I suggested that they provided an antidote to the Hoffas and Governor Wallaces he was obliged to deal with so much of the time. During her interview the reporter asked Kennedy if this was true, and he replied with some annoyance: "I just like children; that's all."

Methinks he doth protest too much, that such determined simplicity springs necessarily from a basic complexity. Fitzgerald wrote of Dick and Nicole Diver: ". . . the simplicity of behavior also, the nursery-like peace and goodwill, the emphasis on the simpler virtues, was part of a desperate bargain with the gods and had been attained through struggles she could not have guessed at."

But I do not mean to romanticize Robert Kennedy. There is too much about him to dislike.

Kennedy's most obvious fault is rudeness. His face, when it lacks that boyish, photogenic grin, is not a pleasant sight. It has a certain bony harshness and those ice-blue eyes are not the smiling ones that Irishmen sing songs about. At best, he recalls Fitzgerald's description of Gatsby: "an elegant young roughneck."

It is with this stern visage that Kennedy confronts most of the world. The easy smile, the cheerful greeting—these are rare. He is too preoccupied with the salvation of humanity to be polite to individuals. His friends call this shyness, but the historians of the 1960 campaign do not record that he was ever shy in the pursuit of a stray delegate.

A more perceptive comment came from boxer Cassius Clay who told a writer during the 1964 campaign: "I see Robert Kennedy walking through the streets meeting everybody, shaking everybody's hands, and when he gets into office you gonna need a necktie to go and see him." Clay may have remembered the fate of another heavyweight champion, Floyd Patterson, whose autographed picture adorned Kennedy's office—until he lost the championship.

One summer afternoon in 1963 I saw him, within the space of ten minutes, at his very best and very worst. I went with him to a Washington school where, through his intervention, the swimming pool was being opened to neighborhood children for summer use for the first time. As he inspected the pool, a blustering bureaucrat from the recreation department approached him, hoping for commendation. Instead, he was met with a machine-gun burst of questions:

Q. How deep is the shallow end of the pool?
A. Three feet.
Q. What about children under three feet tall?
A. They can't use the pool.
Q. Why not use a wooden platform to raise the shallow end?
A. It would rot.
Q. Why wasn't the pool to be open on Sundays?
A. None of the pools was ever open on Sundays. . . .

By then the poor man, suddenly become an enemy of tiny tots and Sunday swimming, was almost incoherent. Kennedy turned and walked away without a word.

Grant that the man was a bumbler. A Southern politician would have thrown his arm around his shoulders, listened to his problems—and in five minutes had his promise to build the platform and open on Sundays. But Kennedy had no time for this.

Minutes later, as he left the pool, hundreds of Negro children ran after him, shouting his name and reaching out to touch him. Kennedy moved among them slowly, smiling, rubbing their heads, squeezing their hands, reaching out to the smaller ones who could not get near him. This was not done for show—there were no reporters or photographers along—but because he loved those slum children, loved them as much as he disdained the fool of a bureaucrat who could not give him the answers he wanted.

But I must cling to my viewpoint. It is well and good to love children. But it is a finer thing to be passably pleasant to all of the people all of the time than to play Santa Claus to the poor when the fancy strikes you.

Robert Kennedy's concern for Negro advancement, which won him such hate in the South, was less evident inside the Justice Department. There were plenty of Negroes to be seen—the waiters in his private dining room, the messengers who went out for coffee and sandwiches—but you'd have to look hard for one Negro lawyer in a job of importance.

One day a civil-rights group picketed the Justice Department in protest of its hiring practices and Kennedy went out to speak to them.

"We hire people for their ability, not their race," said Kennedy, who served in a Cabinet filled with men picked solely for their ability, such as Celebrezze and Gronouski.

But what I have called rudeness may more fairly be termed an unconscious assumption of superiority. The Kennedy crowd was above all else an ingroup. Jack was President. Bob made him President and could do sixty push-ups to boot. Jackie was Jackie. Ted was Senator. Sarge ran the Peace Corps like magic. Dave Hackett had been on the Olympic hockey team, twice. Art Schlesinger had a Pulitzer Prize. Pierre hadn't won a Pulitzer, but he had been a child prodigy on the piano. Dean Markham had been the meanest lineman in Harvard football history. Byron White had been a Rhodes Scholar *and* an all-American halfback.

And so it went. Our team can whip your team. (How fleeting, power; in 1961 I attended a party with Ken O'Donnell and Lyndon Johnson; people were debating which was more important.)

Although I never attended a party at Hickory Hill, Kennedy's home, I sometimes shared his guests' thrill vicariously as I helped Dave Hackett write the poems and paint the posters that played such a vital part in the Kennedy merrymaking. I remember one night helping Hackett rewrite a long poem which celebrated a yachting trip he had taken with Bob and Ted.

The gist of the poem was simply that Robert Kennedy was a hell of a fellow. All the other party props—the posters and the funny games—had the same moral. I could not understand a man who would let his closest friends pay homage to him, or friends who would do such a thing, or people who needed props and poems to have a party. Perhaps it is pertinent to remember that Fitzgerald is usually misquoted. He did not say the "rich" are different from you and me; he said the "very rich." I have friends who are rich, but the Kennedys are very rich and perhaps that is the difference. I know no better explanation.

An entire attitude toward life lies behind the simple act of pushing someone into a swimming pool. A man who sprang from modest beginnings, no matter how high he may have risen, will find his hand stayed by visions of the time when there was only one Sunday suit, bought at Easter time and handed down from brother to brother, patched, polished, pressed—preserved with desperate loving care and God forbid that it should ever be pushed into a swimming pool. I once knew a young Texas farmer who made a fortune in oil. In an effort to impress his dates he would rent the ballroom of a San Antonio hotel, hire a band, fly in exotic foods from around the world and after dinner have a cockfight staged on the ballroom floor. Yet I'm positive he could never have pushed anyone into a swimming pool; he knew the value of a good suit of clothing.

I was sometimes a ghost-writer for Robert Kennedy, a man whose intellectual level was forever fixed for me by a report that he listens to recordings of Shakespeare in the shower.

It was standard practice to end his speeches and articles with an erudite quotation. One Sunday, working at home on a piece for the *Saturday Review* on the proposed domestic Peace Corps, I found myself without Bartlett's *Familiar Quotations* and had to rely on memory. I used Donne's "no man is an island," only to be criticized by my wife for triteness. I argued that if Kennedy did in fact know any literary quotations (do you retain what you hear in the shower?) they probably would include "no man is an island." And I will further argue that if a man is going to know only a half-dozen quotations, they *should* include "no man is an island" and "give me liberty or give me death" and others equally trite. One of Kennedy's virtues, perhaps his greatest, is that he understands that truth is often quite simple.

For Kennedy is ruled by heart, not intellect. As one of his most perceptive admirers, Joseph Kraft, said of him: ". . . his view of the world is intensely personal. The Attorney General has almost no interest in abstract ideas." Like Barry Goldwater, he operates almost entirely by instinct. The difference is that Kennedy's instincts ("We must provide genuine opportunities for these people," "My brother cannot launch another Pearl Harbor") are good.

Kennedy's humor deserves more credit than it has received. It ranges from merciless joshing of his friends (as when they collapse halfway through a fifty-mile hike) to extremely caustic comment. One day not long after the Bay of Pigs a group of us watched a Presidential press conference on television in Ed Guthman's office. A reporter asked the President if he planned to unleash Chiang onto the Chinese mainland.

"That'll take their minds off Cuba," Robert Kennedy muttered.

To me, one of his most disturbing traits was his passion for statistics.

Statistics were always referred to as "facts," and his speeches, except for a six-month period in 1963 when novelist Richard Yates wrote them, were rarely more than collections of these statistical "facts," inspiring anecdotes, and erudite quotations. I was often called upon to supply these figures, a job made less tasteful by my utter disbelief in government statistics. But even leaving accuracy aside, I mistrust any man who thinks the best speech is the one with the most statistics.

As far as a speaker and his audience are concerned, it doesn't make the slightest difference whether 800,000 teen-agers are unemployed or a million. What does matter is whether he, or they, can understand what it is for just one child to live in a slum. And this understanding is not a fact that can be held in the fingertips, but a sorrow that must be carried in the heart.

My first doubts about John Kennedy came when I saw, firsthand, that he shared his brother's passion for facts. In October of 1963 I hurriedly wrote a statement on urban problems for the President to use in a Rose Garden ceremony announcing a grant to New Haven. My statement contained around a thousand words which aspired to Sorensenian eloquence, but prudently included several statistics on unemployment and population growth.

Minutes before the ceremony, the President skimmed my statement and then, using it as background, spoke off the cuff. This was standard procedure; both Kennedys could talk better than any of their writers could write.

But, I noted with a sinking heart, the President had used one item from my text verbatim—a statistic on the number of unemployed youth projected for 1970.

"So what?" it might be asked. But I cared about John Kennedy, this stranger to whom I was devoting several irredeemable years, and I found that the only firsthand knowledge I had of him was that he shared his younger brother's mania for "facts."

Skepticism is an occupational hazard of the image-making business. You know that the speeches are ghost-written, the spontaneous demonstrations are intricately planned, the press conferences are rigged so that a friendly reporter will ask the right question. You soon decide that you can learn more about a man from one unguarded handshake than from a dozen State of the Union Messages.

My doubts about Robert Kennedy were based on personal observation, and for all I knew Jack was just Bobby with an extra coat of polish or a better manager. I remembered that proud old Joe Kennedy once said, "Bobby is the one most like me," and I wondered if by Kennedy family standards Robert, not John, might be the ideal Kennedy. Perhaps Jack Kennedy, because of his childhood illnesses and because he was the second son, had merely been tolerated by his family as he read history books and grew soft on intellectuals. I was struck by the fear that perhaps Jack wanted to be like Bob more than Bob wanted to be like Jack.

Doubts such as these were in my mind one evening when, over my protests, one of the secretaries led me into the Attorney General's office to a party the staff was giving for his thirty-eighth birthday.

All office parties are bad, but this one was miserable. About forty employees, from Nick Katzenbach and Burke Marshall to the newest secretary, filed in and formed a circle about Kennedy, who stood alone beside his desk. No one came nearer than six feet to him, except when an aide handed him his "gifts." These included a plastic "hot-line" telephone to Paul Corbin, his political aide at the Democratic National Committee; a used putter (his own, brought from home, which he didn't recognize); and a laboriously designed "Anti-Monopoly" set. After slowly examining each gift he would say in his flat voice, "That's funny," and you suspected he meant funny like a crutch.

He stood in that circle for half an hour. Now and then Guthman or Jim McShane, the Chief U.S. Marshall and one of the funniest men alive, would toss a joke across the void and the girls would titter nervously. The only motion came when people in the circle jockeyed to get in line with the camera that was recording this awesome event.

After the gifts were opened, beer was served and perhaps the party livened up. I never knew because I left, embarrassed for all of us, the gawking guests and the lonely guest of honor.

That was the evening of November 20, 1963.

Two nights later, I read myself to sleep with a poem:

"What songs shall I sing for him that I love?"

I had learned that there is no neutrality. A man must choose and now, too late, I chose that sweet, star-crossed man who had passed beyond my love or sorrow to what we must believe to be a better world.

I did not see Kennedy again until four weeks later at his annual Christmas party for poor children. Several of his aides had been planning the party for months and his guests, seven hundred children from Washington's poorest families, were met with one treat after another from the moment they arrived at the Justice Department.

It was a clear, crisp December day. The children arrived at an inner courtyard where four burly Washington Redskins lifted them into horse-drawn sleighs for a fast ride around the courtyard over tons of artificial ice.

Next they went up the elevator to the Attorney General's office where a three-man clown band was playing and Santa stood beside a Christmas tree with a present for every child. Some of the presents had been sent from around the world to Caroline and John Kennedy, Jr. in the month preceding.

After receiving their presents, the children went down the elevator to the auditorium, where Carol Channing was to entertain after they had all assembled. I was among the staff people who were seeing that everyone got an ice-cream cone and found the bathroom. As the auditorium began to fill, someone suggested that I bring the clown band down to entertain the waiting children.

I went up the the Attorney General's office and was negotiating with the chief clown ("Hell, man, they just sent us up here!") when Robert Kennedy approached us. I explained that the auditorium was filling with children and we thought the clowns would do more good there. He nodded and walked away.

This was during the period when, according to the newspaper columnists, Kennedy was living in a trance. I don't know whether this was true, but I know I was living in a trance and so was everyone I knew who was worth a damn.

A moment later, as the chief clown protested to me that he and his boys weren't going anywhere until they'd had a smoke, Kennedy returned and spoke to me:

"The clowns should be where the children are."

Our eyes met for a long moment and it seemed, incredibly, as if he wanted my agreement.

"Yes, sir," I said, "they should be," and I herded the reluctant clowns downstairs.

[April, 1965]

The Holy Family

by Gore Vidal

The Kennedy legend burned bright, a durable flame fueled by the countless memoirs of loyal courtiers. In Esquire*'s April 1967 issue, Gore Vidal reviewed the books that mythologized JFK and the family's rise to power. An astute political observer—and sometime participant—Vidal had written a play in 1960 based on Kennedy's life, called* The Best Man. *His books of the 1960s include* Washington, D.C. *and* Myra Breckenridge.

From the beginning of the Republic, Americans have enjoyed accusing the first magistrate of kingly ambition. Sometimes seriously but more often derisively the President is denounced as a would-be king, subverting the Constitution for personal ends. From General Washington to the present incumbent, the wielder of power has usually been regarded with suspicion, a disagreeable but not unhealthy state of affairs for both governor and governed. Few Presidents, however, have been accused of wanting to establish family dynasties, if only because most Presidents have found it impossible to select a successor of any sort, much less promote a relative. Each of the Adamses and the Harrisons reigned at an interval of not less than a political generation from the other, while the two Roosevelts were close neither in blood nor in politics. But now something new is happening in the Republic, and, as the Chinese say, we are living "in interesting times."

In 1960, with the election of the thirty-fifth President, the famous ambition of Joseph P. Kennedy seemed at last fulfilled. He himself had come a long way from obscurity to great wealth and prominence; now his eldest surviving son, according to primogeniture, had gone the full distance and become President. It was a triumph for the patriarch. It was also a splendid moment for at least half the nation. What doubts one may have had about the Kennedys were obscured by the charm and intelligence of John F. Kennedy. He appeared to be beautifully onto himself; he was also onto us; there is even evidence that he was onto the family, too. As a result, there were few intellectuals in 1960 who were not beguiled by the spectacle of a President who seemed always to be standing at a certain remove from himself, watching with amusement his own performance. He was an ironist in a profession where the prize usually goes to the cornball. With such a man as chief of state, all things were possible. He would "get America moving again." But then mysteriously the thing went wrong. Despite fine rhetoric and wise commentary, despite the glamour of his presence, we did not move, and if historians are correct when they tell us that Presidents are "made" in their first eighteen months in office, then one can assume that the Kennedy administration would never have fulfilled our hopes, much less his own. Kennedy was of course ill-fated from the beginning. The Bay of Pigs used up much of his credit in the bank of public opinion, while his attempts at social legislation were resolutely blocked by a more than usually obstructive Congress. In foreign affairs he was overwhelmed by the masterful Khrushchev and not until the Cuban missile crisis did he achieve tactical parity with that sly gambler. His administration's one achievement was the test-ban treaty, an encouraging footnote to the Cold War.

Yet today Kennedy dead has infinitely more force than Kennedy living. Though his administration was not a success, he himself has become a world touchstone of political excellence. Part of this phenomenon is attributable to the race's need for heroes, even in deflationary times. But mostly the legend is the deliberate creation of the Kennedy family and its clients. Wanting to regain power, it is now necessary to show that once upon a time there was indeed a Camelot beside the Potomac, a golden age forever lost unless a second Kennedy should become the President. And so, to insure the restoration of that lovely time, the past must be transformed, dull facts transcended, and the dead hero extolled in films, through memorials, and in the pages of books.

Most notorious of the books has been William Manchester's *The Death of a President*. Hoping to stop Mr. Jim Bishop from writing one of his ghoulish *The Day They Shot* sagas, the Kennedys decided to "hire" Mr. Manchester to write their version of what happened at Dallas. Unfortunately, they have never understood that treason is the natural business of clerks. Mr. Manchester's use of Mrs. Kennedy's taped recollections did not please the family. The famous comedy of errors that ensued not only insured the book's success, but also made current certain intimate details which the family preferred for the electorate not to know, like the President's selection of Mrs. Kennedy's dress on that last day in order, as he put it, "to show up those cheap Texas broads," a remark not calculated to give pleasure to the clients of Neiman-Marcus. Also, the family's irrational dislike of President Johnson came through all too plainly, creating an unexpected amount of sympathy for that least sympathetic of magistrates. Aware of what was at stake, Mrs. Kennedy tried to alter a book which neither she nor her brothers-in-law had read. Not since Mary Todd Lincoln has a President's widow been so fiercely engaged with legend if not history. But then legend-making is necessary to the Kennedy future. As a result, most of the recent books about the late President are not so much political in approach as religious. There is the ritual beginning of the book which is the end: the death at Dallas. Then the witness goes back in time to the moment when he first met the Kennedys. He finds them strenuous but fun. Along with riotous good times, there is the constant question: How are we to elect Jack President? This sort of talk was in the open after 1956, but as long ago as 1943, Paul B. Fay, Jr.[1] made a bet that one day Jack would be J.F.K.

From the beginning the godhead shone for those who had the eyes to see. The witness then gives us his synoptic version of the making of the President. Once again we visit cold Wisconsin and dangerous West Virginia (can a young Catholic war hero defeat a Protestant accused of being a draft dodger in a poor mining state where primary votes are bought and sold?). From triumph to triumph the hero proceeds to the convention at Los Angeles where the god is recognized. The only shadow upon that perfect day is cast, significantly, by Lyndon B. Johnson. Like Lucifer he challenged the god at the convention; and was struck down only to be raised again as son of morning. The deal to make Johnson Vice-President still causes violent argument among the new theologians. Pierre Salinger[2] quotes J.F.K. as observing glumly, "The whole story will never be known, and it's just as well that it won't be." Then the campaign itself. The great television debates (Quemoy and Matsu) in which Nixon's obvious lack of class, as classy Jack duly noted, did him in—barely. The narrowness of the electoral victory was swiftly erased by the splendor of the inaugural ("It all began in the cold": Arthur Schlesinger, Jr.[3]). From this point on the thousand days unfold in familiar sequence and, though details differ from gospel to gospel, the story already possesses the quality of a passion play: disaster at Cuba One, triumph at Cuba Two; the eloquent speeches; the fine pageantry; and always the crowds and the glory, ending at Dallas.

With Lucifer now rampant upon the heights, the surviving Kennedys are again at work to regain the lost paradise, which means that books must be written not only about the new incarnation of the Kennedy godhead but

1. *The Pleasure of his Company,* by Paul B. Fay, Jr.
2. *With Kennedy,* by Pierre Salinger.
3. *A Thousand Days,* by Arthur Schlesinger, Jr.

the old. For it is the dead hero's magic that makes legitimate the family's pretensions. As an Osiris-Adonis-Christ figure, J.F.K. is already the subject of a cult that may persist, through the machinery of publicity, long after all memory of his administration has been absorbed by the golden myth now being created in a thousand books to the single end of maintaining in power our extraordinary holy family.

The most recent batch of books about J.F.K., though hagiographies, cannot help but at times illuminate the three themes which dominate any telling of the sacred story: money, image making, family. That is the trinity without which nothing. Mr. Salinger, the late President's press secretary, is necessarily concerned with the second theme, though he touches on the other two. Paul B. Fay, Jr. (a wartime buddy of J.F.K. and Under-Secretary of the Navy) is interesting on every count and since he seems not to know what he is saying, his book is the least calculated and the most lifelike of the ones so far published. Other books at hand are Richard J. Whalen's *The Founding Father* (particularly good on money and family) and Evelyn Lincoln's *My Twelve Years with John F. Kennedy* which, in its simple way, tells us a good deal about those who are drawn to the Kennedys.

While on the clerical staff of a Georgia congressman, Mrs. Lincoln decided in 1952 that she wanted to work for "someone in Congress who seemed to have what it takes to be President"; after a careful canvass, she picked the Representative from the Massachusetts 11th District. Like the other witnesses under review, she never says *why* she wants to work for a future President; it is taken for granted that anyone would, an interesting commentary on all the witnesses from Arthur Schlesinger (whose *A Thousand Days* is the best political novel since *Coningsby*) to Sorensen's more dour *Kennedy*. Needless to say, in all the books there is not only love and awe for the fallen hero who was, in most cases, the witness's only claim to public attention, but there are also a remarkable number of tributes to the holy family. From Jacqueline (Isis-Aphrodite-Madonna) to Bobby (Ares and perhaps Christ-to-be) the Kennedys appear at the very least as demigods, larger than life. Bobby's hardworking staff seldom complained, as Mr. Salinger put it, "because we all knew that Bob was working just a little harder than we were." For the same reason "we could accept without complaint [J.F.K.'s] bristling temper, his cold sarcasm, and his demands for always higher standards of excellence because we knew he was driving himself harder than he was driving us—despite great and persistent physical pain and personal tragedy." Mrs. Lincoln surprisingly finds the late President "humble"—doubtless since the popular wisdom requires all great men to be humble. She refers often to his "deep low voice" (sic), "his proud head held high, his eyes fixed firmly on the goals—sometimes seemingly impossible goals—he set for himself and all those around him." Mr. Schlesinger's lovely threnody at the close of *his* gospel makes it plain that we will not see J.F.K.'s like again, at least not until the administration of Kennedy II.

Of the lot so far, only Mr. Fay seems not to be writing a book with an eye to holding office in the next Kennedy administration. He is garrulous and indiscreet (the Kennedys are still displeased with his memoirs even though a few thousand words were cut from the manuscript on the narrow theological ground that, since certain things he witnessed do not enhance the image, they must be apocrypha). On the subject of the Kennedys and money, Mr. Fay tells a most revealing story. In December, 1959, at Palm Beach the family was assembled; someone mentioned money, "causing Mr. Kennedy to plunge in, fire blazing from his eyes. 'I don't know what is going to happen to this family when I die,' Mr. Kennedy said. 'There is no one in the entire family, except Joan and Teddy, who is living within their means. No one appears to have the slightest concern for how much they spend.' " The tirade ended with a Kennedy sister running from the room in tears, her extravagance condemned in open family session. Characteristically, Jack deflected the progenitor's wrath with the comment that the only "solution is to have Dad work harder." A story which contradicts, incidentally, Mr. Salinger's pious "despite his great wealth and his generosity in contributing all of his salaries as Congressman, Senator and President to charities, the President was not a man to waste pennies."

But for all the founding father's grumbling, the children's attitude toward money—like so much else—is pretty much what he wanted it to be. It is now a familiar part of the sacred story of how Zeus made each of the nine Olympians individually wealthy, creating trust funds which now total some ten million dollars per god or goddess. Also at the disposal of the celestials is the great fortune itself, estimated at one hundred two hundred three hundred or whatever hundred millions of dollars, administered from an office on Park Avenue, to which the Kennedys send their bills, for "the childhood habit of dependence persisted in adult life. As grown men and women the younger Kennedys still look to their father's staff of accountants to keep track of their expenditures and see to their personal finances."[4] There are, of course, obvious limitations to not understanding the role of money in the lives of the majority. The late President was aware of this limitation and he was forever asking his working friends how much money they made; on occasion, he was at a disadvantage because he did not understand the trader's mentality. He missed the point to Khrushchev at Vienna and took offense at what, after all, was simply the boorishness of the marketplace. His father, an old hand in Hollywood, would have understood better the mogul's bluffing.

It will probably never be known how much money Joe Kennedy has spent for the political promotion of his sons. At the moment, an estimated million dollars a year is being spent on Bobby's behalf, and this sum can

4. *The Founding Father,* by Richard J. Whalen.

be matched year after year until 1972, and longer. Needless to say, the sons are sensitive to the charge that their elections are bought. As J.F.K. said of his 1952 election to the Senate, "People say 'Kennedy bought the election. Kennedy could never have been elected if his father hadn't been a millionaire.'. Well, it wasn't the Kennedy name and the Kennedy money that won that election. I beat Lodge because I hustled for three years," etc.[4] But of course without the Kennedy name and the Kennedy money, he would not even have been a contender. Not only was a vast amount of money spent for his election in the usual ways, but a great deal was spent in not so usual ways. For instance, right after the pro-Lodge Boston *Post* unexpectedly endorsed Jack Kennedy for the Senate, Joe Kennedy loaned the paper's publisher $500,000.[4]

But the most expensive legitimate item in today's politics is the making of the image. Highly paid technicians are able to determine with alarming accuracy just what sort of characteristics the public desires at any given moment in a national figure and with adroit handling a personable candidate can be made to seem whatever the Zeitgeist demands. The Kennedys are not of course responsible for applying to politics the techniques of advertising (the two have always gone hand in hand), but of contemporary politicians (the Rockefellers excepted) the Kennedys alone possess the money to maintain one of the most remarkable self-publicizing machines in the history of advertising, a machine which for a time had the resources of the federal government at its disposal.

It is in describing the activities of a chief press officer at the White House that Mr. Salinger is most interesting. A talented image maker, he was responsible, among other things, for the televised press conferences in which the President was seen at his best responding to simple questions with careful and often charming answers. That these press conferences were not very informative was hardly the fault of Mr. Salinger or the President. If it is true that the medium is the message and television is the coolest of all media and to be cool is desirable, then the televised thirty-fifth President was positively glacial in his effectiveness. He was a natural for this time and place, largely because of his obsession with the appearance of things. In fact, much of his political timidity was the result of a quite uncanny ability to sense how others would respond to what he said or did, and if he foresaw a negative response, he was apt to avoid action altogether. There were times, however, when his superb sense of occasion led him astray. In the course of a speech to the Cuban refugees in Miami, he was so overwhelmed by the drama of the situation that he practically launched on the spot a second invasion of that beleaguered island. Yet generally he was cool. He enjoyed the game of pleasing others, which is the actor's art. He was also aware that vanity is perhaps the strongest of human emotions, particularly the closer one comes to the top of the slippery pole. Mrs. Kennedy once told a friend that the last thing Mrs.

Eisenhower had done before leaving the White House was to hang a portrait of herself in the entrance hall. The first thing Mrs. Kennedy had done on moving in was to put the portrait in the basement, on aesthetic, not political grounds. Overhearing this, the President told an usher to restore the painting to its original place. "The Eisenhowers are coming to lunch tomorrow," he explained patiently to his wife, "and that's the first thing she'll look for." Mrs. Lincoln records that before the new Cabinet met, the President and Bobby were about to enter the Cabinet room when the President "said to his brother, 'Why don't you go through the other door?' The President waited until the Attorney General entered the Cabinet room from the hall door, and then he walked into the room from my office."

In its relaxed way Mr. Fay's book illuminates the actual man much better than the other books if only because he was a friend to the President, and not just an employee. He is particularly interesting on the early days when Jack could discuss openly the uses to which he was being put by his father's ambition. Early in 1945 the future President told Mr. Fay how much he envied Fay his postwar life in sunny California while "I'll be back here with Dad trying to parlay a lost P.T. boat and a bad back into a political advantage. I tell you, Dad is ready right now and can't understand why Johnny boy isn't 'all engines full ahead.' " Yet the exploitation of son by father had begun long before the war. In 1940 a thesis written by Jack at Harvard was published under the title *Why England Slept,* with a foreword by longtime, balding, family friend Henry Luce. The book became a best seller and as Joe wrote at the time in a letter to his son,[4] "You would be surprised how a book that really makes the grade with high-class people stands you in good stead for years to come."

Joe was right of course and bookmaking is now an important part of the holy family's home industry. As Mrs. Lincoln observed when J.F.K.'s collection of political sketches "won the Pulitzer prize for biography in 1957, the Senator's prominence as a scholar and statesman grew. As his book continued to be a best seller, he climbed higher upon public-opinion polls and moved into a leading position among Presidential possibilities for 1960."[5] Later Bobby would "write" a book about how he almost nailed Jimmy Hoffa; and so great was the impact of this work that many people had the impression that Bobby had indeed put an end to the career of that turbulent figure.

Most interesting of all the mythmaking was the creation of Jack the war hero. John Hersey first described for *The New Yorker* how Jack's Navy boat was wrecked after colliding with a Japanese ship; in the course of a long swim, the young skipper saved the life of a crewman, an admirable thing to do. Later they were all rescued. Since the officer who survived was Ambassador Kennedy's son, the story was deliberately told and retold as

5. *My Twelve Years with John F. Kennedy,* by Evelyn Lincoln.

an example of heroism unequaled in war's history. Through constant repetition the simple facts of the story merged into a blurred impression that somehow at some point a unique act of heroism had been committed by Jack Kennedy. The last telling of the story was a film starring Cliff Robertson as J.F.K. (the President had wanted Warren Beatty for the part, but the producer thought Beatty's image was "too mixed up").

So the image was created early: the high-class book that made the grade; the much publicized heroism at war; the election to the House of Representatives in 1946. From that point on, the publicity was constant and though the Congressman's record of service was unimpressive, he himself was photogenic and appealing. Then came the Senate, the marriage, the illnesses, the second high-class book, and the rest is history. But though it was Joe Kennedy who paid the bills and to a certain extent managed the politics, the recipient of all this attention was meanwhile developing into a shrewd psychologist. Mr. Fay quotes a letter written him by the new Senator in 1953. The tone is jocular (part of the charm of Fay's book is that it captures as no one else has the preppish side to J.F.K.'s character; he was droll, particularly about himself, in a splendid sort of W. C. Fields way): "I gave everything a good deal of thought. I am getting married this fall. This means the end of a promising political career, as it has been based up to now almost completely on the old sex appeal." After a few more sentences in this vein the groom-to-be comes straight to the point. "Let me know the general reaction to this in the Bay area." He did indeed want to know, like a romantic film star, what effect marriage would have on his career. But then most of his life was governed, as Mrs. Lincoln wrote of the year 1959, "by the public-opinion polls. We were not unlike the people who check their horoscope each day before venturing out." And when they did venture out, it was always to create an illusion. As Mrs. Lincoln remarks in her guileless way: after Senator Kennedy returned to Washington from a four-week tour of Europe, "it was obvious that his stature as a Senator had grown, for he came back as an authority on the current situation in Poland."

It is not to denigrate the late President or the writers of his gospel that neither he nor they ever seemed at all concerned by the bland phoniness of so much of what he did and said, or of what they now say and do. After all, politicians have been pretty much the same since the beginning of history. Part of the game is creating illusion. In fact, the late President himself shortly after Cuba summed up what might very well have been not only his political philosophy but that of the age in which we live. When asked whether or not the Soviet's placement of missiles in Cuba would have actually shifted the balance of world power, he indicated that he thought not, "But it would have politically changed the balance of power. It would have appeared to, and appearances contribute to reality."

From the beginning the holy family has tried to make itself appear to be what it thinks people want rather than what the realities of any situation might require. Since Bobby is thought by some to be ruthless, he must therefore be photographed as often as possible with children, smiling and happy and athletic, in every way a boy's ideal man. Politically, he must *seem* to be at odds with the present administration without ever actually taking any important position that President Johnson does not already hold. Bobby's Vietnamese war dance was particulary illustrative of the technique. A step to the left (let's talk to the Vietcong), followed by two steps to the right, simultaneously giving "the beards"—as he calls them—the sense that he is for peace in Vietnam while maintaining his brother's war policy. Characteristically, the world at large believes that if J.F.K. were alive there would be no war in Vietnam. The mythmakers have obscured the fact that it was J.F.K. who began our active participation in the war when, in 1961, he added to the six hundred American observers the first of a gradual buildup of American troops, which reached twenty thousand at the time of his assassination. And there is no evidence that he would not have persisted in that war for, as he said to a friend shortly before he died, "I have to go all the way with this one." He could not suffer a second Cuba and hope to maintain the appearance of Defender of the Free World at the ballot box in 1964.

The authors of the latest Kennedy books are usually at their most interesting when they write about themselves. They are cautious, of course (except for the jaunty Mr. Fay), and most are thinking ahead to Kennedy II. Yet despite a hope of future preferment, Mr. Salinger's self-portrait is a most curious one. He veers between a coarse unawareness of what it was all about (he never, for instance, expresses an opinion of the war in Vietnam), and a solemn bogusness that is most putting off. Like an after-dinner speaker, he characterizes everyone ("Clark Clifford, the brilliant Washington lawyer"); he pays heavy tribute to his office staff; he praises Rusk and the State Department, remarking that "J.F.K. had more effective liaison with the State Department than any President in history." This would have come as news to the late President, not to mention quite a few of his thirty-four predecessors. Firmly Mr. Salinger puts Arthur Schlesinger in his place, saying that he himself never heard the President express a lack of confidence in Rusk. Mr. Salinger also remarks that though Schlesinger was "a strong friend" of the President (something Mr. Salinger, incidentally, was not), "J.F.K. occasionally was impatient with their [Schlesinger's memoranda] length and frequency." Mrs. Lincoln also weighs in on the subject of the historian-in-residence. Apparently J.F.K.'s "relationship with Schlesinger was never that close. He admired Schlesinger's brilliant mind, his enormous store of information . . . but Schlesinger was never more than an ally and assistant." It is a tribute to Kennedy's gift for compartmentalizing the people in his life that none knew to what extent he saw the others. Mr. Fay was an after-hours buddy.

Mrs. Lincoln was the girl in the office. Mr. Salinger was a technician and not a part of the President's social or private or even, as Mr. Salinger himself admits, political life. Contrasting his role with that of James Hagerty, he writes, "My only policy duties were in the information field. While Jim had a voice in deciding what the administration would do, I was responsible only for presenting that decision to the public in a way and at a time that would generate the best possible reception." His book is valuable only when he discusses the relations between press and government. And of course when he writes about himself. His 1964 campaign for the Senate is nicely told and it is good to know that he lost because he came out firmly for fair housing on the ground that "morally I had no choice—not after sweating out Birmingham and Oxford with John F. Kennedy." This is splendid but it might have made his present book more interesting had he told us something about that crucial period of sweating out. Although he devotes a chapter to telling how he did not take a fifty-mile hike, he never discusses Birmingham, Oxford or the Negro revolution. All in all, his book is pretty much what one might expect of a P.R. man. He papers over personalities with the reflexive and usually inaccurate phrase (Eisenhower and Kennedy "had deep respect for each other"; Mrs. Kennedy has "a keen understanding of the problems which beset mankind"). Yet for all his gift at creating images for others, Mr. Salinger seems not to have found his own. Uneasily he plays at being U.S. Senator, fat boy at court, thoughtful emissary to Khrushchev. Lately there has been a report in the press that he is contemplating writing a novel. If he does, Mr. Harold Robbins may be in the sort of danger that Mr. George Murphy never was. The evidence at hand shows that he has the gift. Describing his divorce from "Nancy, my wife of eight years," Mr. Salinger manages in a few lines to say everything. "An extremely artistic woman, she was determined to live a quieter life in which she could pursue her skills as a ceramicist. And we both knew that I could not be happy unless I was on the move. It was this difference in philosophies, not a lack of respect, that led to our decision to obtain a divorce. But a vacation in Palm Springs, as Frank Sinatra's guest, did much to revive my spirits."

Mr. Fay emerges as very much his own man and it is apparent that he amused the President at a level which was more that of a playmate escorting the actress Angie Dickinson to the Inaugural than as serious companion to the prince. Unlike the other witnesses, Mr. Fay has no pretensions about himself. He tells how "the President then began showing us the new paintings on the wall. 'Those two are Renoirs and that's a Cézanne,' he told us. Knowing next to nothing about painters or paintings, I asked, 'Who are they?' The President's response was predictable. 'My God, if you ask a question like that, do it in a whisper or wait till we get outside. We're trying to give this administration a semblance of class.' " The President saw the joke; he also saw the image which must at all times be projected. Parenthetically, a majority of the recorded anecdotes about Kennedy involve keeping up appearances; he was compulsively given to emphasizing, often with great charm, the division between how things must be made to seem, as opposed to the way they are. This division is noticeable, even in the censored version of Mr. Manchester's *The Death of a President*. The author records that when Kennedy spoke at Houston's coliseum, Jack Valenti, crouched below the lectern, was able to observe the extraordinary tremor of the President's hands, and the artful way in which he managed to conceal them from the audience. This tension between the serene appearance and that taut reality add to the poignancy of the true legend, so unlike the Parson Weems's version Mrs. Kennedy would like the world to accept.

Money, image, family: the three are extraordinarily intertwined. The origin of the Kennedy sense of family is the holy land of Ireland, priest-ridden, superstitious, clannish. While most of the West in the nineteenth century was industrialized and urbanized, Ireland remained a famine-ridden agrarian country, in thrall to politicians, homegrown and British, priest and lay. In 1848, the first Kennedy set up shop in Boston, where the Irish were exploited and patronized by the Wasps; not unnaturally, the Irish grew bitter and vengeful and finally asserted themselves at the ballot box. But the old resentment remained as late as Joe Kennedy's generation; with it flourished a powerful sense that the family is the only unit that could withstand the enemy, as long as each member remained loyal to the others, "regarding life as a joint venture between one generation and the next."[4] To Joe Kennedy, in Bobby's words, "the most important thing . . . was the advancement of his children . . . except for his influence and encouragement, my brother Jack might not have run for the Senate in 1952."[6] (So much for J.F.K.'s comment that it was his own "hustling" that got him Lodge's seat.)

The father is of course a far more interesting figure than any of his sons if only because his will to impose himself upon a society which he felt had snubbed him has been in the most extraordinary way fulfilled. He drove his sons to "win, win, win." But never at any point did he pause to ask himself or them just what it was they were supposed to win. He taught them to regard life as a game of Monopoly (a family favorite): you put up as many hotels as you can on Ventnor Avenue and win. Consequently, some of the failure of his son's administration can be ascribed to the family philosophy. All his life Jack Kennedy was driven by his father and then by himself to be first in politics, which meant to be the President. But once that goal had been achieved, he had no future, no place else to go. This absence of any sense of the whole emerged in the famous exchange between him and James Reston who naïvely (in the context) asked the newly elected President what his philosophy was, what vision did he have

6. *The Fruitful Bough*, privately printed.

of the good life. Mr. Reston got a blank stare for answer. Kennedy apologists are quick to use this exchange as proof of their man's essentially pragmatic nature (pragmatic was a favorite word of the era, even though its political meaning is opportunist). As they saw it: give the President a specific problem and he will solve it through intelligence and expertise. A "philosophy" was simply of no use to a man of action. For a time actual philosophers were charmed by the thought of an intelligent young empiricist fashioning a New Frontier.

Not until the second year of his administration did it become plain that Kennedy was not about to do much of anything. Since his concern was so much with the appearance of things, he was at his worst when confronted with those issues where a moral commitment might have informed not only with passion but with shrewdness his political response. On such bills as Medicare and Civil Rights, had he challenged the Congress in the Truman manner, he might at least have inspired the country, if not the Congress, to follow his lead. But he was reluctant to rock the boat and it is significant that he often quoted Hotspur on summoning spirits from the deep: any man can summon but will the spirits come? J.F.K. never found out; he would not take the chance. His excuse in private for his lack of force, particularly in dealing with the Congress, was the narrow electoral victory of 1960. The second term, he declared, would be the one in which all things might be accomplished. With a solid majority behind him, he could work wonders. But knowing his character, it is doubtful that the second term would have been much more useful than the first. After all, he would have been constitutionally a lame-duck President, perhaps interested in holding the franchise for his brother. The family, finally, was his only commitment and it colored all his deeds and judgment.

In 1960, after listening to him denounce Eleanor Roosevelt at some length, I asked him why he thought she was so much opposed to his candidacy. The answer was quick: "She hated my father and she can't stand it that his children turned out so much better than hers." I was startled at how little he understood Mrs. Roosevelt who, to be fair, did not at all understand him, though at the end she was won by his personal charm. Yet it was significant that he could not take seriously any of her political objections to him (e.g., his attitude to McCarthyism); he merely assumed that she, like himself, was essentially concerned with family, and, envying the father, would want to thwart the son. He was, finally, very much his father's son even though, as all the witnesses are at pains to remind us, he did not share that magnate's political philosophy—which goes without saying since anyone who did could not be elected to anything except possibly the Chamber of Commerce. But the father's confidence in his own wisdom ("I know more about Europe than anybody else in this country," he said in 1940, "because I've been closer to it longer"[4]) and the assumption that he alone knew the absolute inside story about everything is a trait inherited by the sons, particularly Bobby, whose principal objection to the "talking liberals" is that they never know what's really going on, as he in his privileged place does but will not tell. The Kennedy children have always observed our world from the heights.

The distinguished jurist Francis Morrissey tells a most revealing story of life upon Olympus. "During the Lodge campaign, the Ambassador told [Jack and me] clearly that the campaign . . . would be the toughest fight he could think of, but there was no question that Lodge would be beaten, and if that should come to pass Jack would be nominated and elected President. . . . In that clear and commanding voice of his he said to Jack, 'I will work out the plans to elect you President. It will not be any more difficult for you to be elected President than it will be to win the Lodge fight . . . you will need to get about twenty key men in the country to get the nomination for it is these men who will control the convention. . . .' "6

One of the most fascinating aspects of politician-watching is trying to determine to what extent any politician believes what he says. Most of course never do, regarding public statements as necessary noises to soothe the electorate or deflect the wrath of the passionate who are forever mucking things up for the man who wants decently and normally to rise. Yet there are cases of politicians who have swayed themselves by their own speeches. Take a man of conservative disposition and force him to give liberal speeches for a few years in order to be elected and he will, often as not, come to believe himself. There is evidence that J.F.K. often spellbound himself. Bobby is something else again. Andrew Kopkind in *The New Republic* once described Bobby's career as a series of "happenings." The McCarthy friend and fellow traveler of one year emerges as an intense New York liberal in another, and between these two happenings there is no thread at all to give a clue as to what the man actually thinks or who he really is. That consistency which liberals so furiously demanded of the hapless Nixon need not apply to any Kennedy. After all, as the recent gospels point out, J.F.K. himself was slow to become a liberal, to the extent he ever was (in our society no working politician can be radical). As J.F.K. said to James MacGregor Burns, "Some people have their liberalism 'made' by the time they reach their late twenties. I didn't. I was caught in crosscurrents and eddies. It was only later that I got into the stream of things." His comment made liberalism sound rather like something run up by a tailor, a necessary garment which he regrets that he never had time in his youth to be fitted for. Elsewhere he explains those "currents and eddies." Of his somewhat reactionary career in the House of Representatives he said, "I'd just come out of my father's house at the time, and these were the things I knew."7 It is of course a truism that character is formed in one's father's house. Ideas may change but the

7. *Portrait of a President,* by William Manchester.

attitude toward others does not. A father who teaches his sons that the only thing that matters is to be "first, not second, not third"[4] is obviously (should his example be followed) going to be rewarded with energetic sons. Yet it is hardly surprising that to date one cannot determine where the Junior Senator from New York stands on such a straightforward issue (morally if not politically) as the American adventure in Vietnam. Differing with the President as to which cities ought to be bombed in the North does not constitute an alternative policy. His sophisticated liberal admirers, however, do not seem in the least distressed by his lack of a position; instead they delight in the *uses* to which he has put the war in Vietnam in order to embarrass the usurper in the White House.

The cold-blooded jauntiness of the Kennedys in politics has a remarkable appeal for those who also want to rise and find annoying—to the extent they are aware of it at all—the moral sense. Also, the success of the three Kennedy brothers nicely makes hash of the old American belief that by working hard and being good one will deserve (and if fortunate, receive) promotion. A mediocre Representative, an absentee Senator, through wealth and family connections, becomes the President while his youngest brother inherits the Senate seat. Now Bobby is about to become R.F.K. because he is Bobby. It is as if the United States had suddenly reverted to the eighteenth century when the politics of many states were family affairs. In those days, if one wanted a political career in New York one had best be born a Livingston, a Clinton, or a Schuyler; failing that one must marry into the family like Alexander Hamilton, or go to work for them. In a way, the whole Kennedy episode is a fascinating throwback to an earlier phase of civilization. Because the Irish maintained the ancient village sense of the family longer than most places in the West and to the extent that the sons of Joe Kennedy reflect those values and prejudices, they are an anachronism in an urbanized non-family-minded society. Yet the fact that they are so plainly not of this time makes them fascinating; their family story is a glamorous continuing soap opera whose appeal few can resist, including the liberals who, though they may suspect that the Kennedys are not with them at heart, believe that the two boys are educable. At this very moment beside the Charles River a thousand Aristotles dream of their young Alexanders, and the coming heady conquest of the earth.

Meanwhile, the source of the holy family's power is the legend of the dead brother, who did not much resemble the hero of the books under review. Yet the myth that J.F.K. was a philosopher-king will continue as long as the Kennedys remain in politics. And much of the power they exert over the national imagination is a direct result of the ghastliness of what happened at Dallas. But though the world's grief and shock were genuine, it was not entirely for J.F.K. himself. The death of a young leader necessarily strikes an atavistic chord. For thousands of years the man-god was sacrificed to insure with blood the harvest, and there is always an element of ecstasy as well as awe in our collective grief. Also, Jack Kennedy was a television star, more seen by most people than their friends or relatives. His death in public was all the more stunning because he was not an abstraction called The President, but a man the people thought they knew. At the risk of *lèse-divinité,* however, the assassination of President Nixon at, let us say, Cambridge by what at first was thought to be a member of the A.D.A. but later turned out to be a dotty Bircher would have occasioned quite as much national horror, mourning and even hagiography. But in time the terrible deed would have been forgotten for there are no Nixon heirs.

Beyond what one thinks of the Kennedys themselves, there remains the large question: what sort of men ought we to be governed by in the coming years? With the high cost of politics and image making, it is plain that only the very wealthy or those allied with the very wealthy can afford the top prizes. And among the rich, only those who are able to please the people on television are Presidential. With the decline of the religions, the moral sense has become confused, to say the least, and intellectual or political commitments that go beyond the merely expedient are regarded with cheerful contempt not only by the great operators themselves, but also by their admirers and, perhaps, by the electorate itself. Also, to be fair, politicians working within a system like ours can never be much more than what the system will allow. Hypocrisy and self-deception are the traditional characteristics of the middle class in any place and time, and the United States today is the paradigmatic middle-class society. Therefore we can hardly blame our political gamesmen for being, literally, representative. Any public man has every right to try and trick us, not only for his own good but, if he is honorable, for ours as well. However, if he himself is not aware of what he is doing or to what end he is playing the game, then to entrust him with the first magistracy of what may be the last empire on earth is to endanger us all. One does not necessarily demand of our leaders passion (Hitler supplied the age with quite enough for this century) or reforming zeal (Mao Tse-tung is incomparable), but one does insist that they possess a sense of community larger than simply personal power for its own sake, being first because it's fun. Finally, in an age of super-communications, one must have a clear sense of the way things are, as opposed to the way they have been made to seem.

Since the politics of the Kennedys are so often the work of publicists, it is necessary to keep trying to find out just who they are and what they really mean. If only because should *they* be confused as to the realities of Cuba, say, or Vietnam, then the world's end is at hand.

At one time in the United States the popular wisdom maintained that there was no better work for a man to do than to set in motion some idea whose time had not yet arrived, even at the risk of becoming as unpopular as those politicians J.F.K. so much admired in his book and so little emulated in his career. It may well be that it is now impossible for such men to rise to the top in our present system. If so, this is a tragedy. Meanwhile, in their unimaginative fierce way, the Kennedys continue to play successfully the game as they found it. They create illusions and call them facts, and between what they are said to be and what they are falls the shadow of all the useful words not spoken, of all the actual deeds not done. But if it is true that in a rough way nations deserve the leadership they get, then a frivolous and apathetic electorate combined with a vain and greedy intellectual establishment will most certainly restore to power the illusion-making Kennedys. Holy family and bedazzled nation, in their faults at least, are well-matched. In any case, the age of the commune in which we have lived since the time of Jackson is drawing to a close and if historical analogies are of any use at all, the rise of the *signori* is about to begin, and we may soon find ourselves enjoying a strange new era in which all our lives and dreams are presided over by smiling, interchangeable, initial gods.

[April, 1967]

The Last Kennedy

by Burton Hersh

In five short years, the world saw the Kennedy dynasty destroyed—JFK and Robert Kennedy were dead, killed by assassins. In this profile of the youngest Kennedy brother, published in September 1968, Burton Hersh appraised the political strength of Edward Moore Kennedy. The following year, tragedy struck again. The car that Ted Kennedy was driving careened off a bridge in Chappaquiddick. Kennedy survived, but his female companion drowned, and the ensuing controversy clouded his political future.

If the continuing story of the Family Kennedy ever finds literary format, it will probably be as a series of convulsive epilogues recounting all the foreshortened lifetimes, wiped away abruptly each in lunatic turn by yet another tide of fate. This the Kennedys were Irish enough to start out knowing. Edward Moore Kennedy, whose instincts are the most subtle among his generation of brothers, senses fate especially. Even after Eugene McCarthy's upset in New Hampshire forced on Robert Kennedy the expediency of running in the primaries, Ted was reportedly opposed. Once the decision was made, however, he slipped into the familiar harnesses and even worked up enough enthusiasm while in West Virginia to infer, with unaccustomed clumsiness, that he might be back in eight years to campaign for himself. "Bobby's therapy is going to cost the family $8,000,000," Victor Navasky reports Ted as having remarked gloomily once the primary battles started. His foreboding was more than financial.

When the worst was fulfilled, when he appeared at the center of the television screen, clearly in charge of the nation's latest trauma, always referred to as "Senator Edward," it was difficult to remember that only six years ago he had been lumbering, helpless Ted. Back then, well-informed

73

opinion of every imaginable description—the right, the intellectual left, old college classmates, onlookers in general—decided in advance that Ted Kennedy was never going to be anything much more useful to society than a Winthrop House jock whose wind had gotten lousy.

One September evening in 1962, having just proposed to open his political career as the Junior Senator from Massachusetts, Kennedy glanced up from his prepared remarks to hear the issue of his candidacy itself being laid open savagely by his upset opponent. "What are your qualifications for the United States Senate?" Edward J. McCormack Jr. was intoning across a South Boston auditorium platform. "You graduated from law school three years ago. You never worked for a living. You have never run for or held elective office. You are running on a slogan—You can do more for Massachusetts. . . . This is the most insulting slogan I have seen in Massachusetts because it means vote for this man because he has influence, he has connections, he has relations. This is a slogan that insults the President of the United States. . . ."

McCormack's attack, despite the passion with which he was delivering it, had meticulously calculated. Having already been elbowed out of this youngest Kennedy's way for the Democratic Party's formal endorsement, the ambitious thirty-eight-year-old Attorney General of Massachusetts was risking his chances in the primary on a personal assault uninhibited by even the canons of Boston-Irish character assassination.

"I listened to my opponent the other night," McCormack continued, "and he said, 'I want to serve because I care.' You didn't care very much, Ted, when you could have voted between 1953 and 1960 on sixteen occasions and you only voted three times. . . . Do you really care about civil rights? While I was fighting to eliminate the 'black belts' and the ghettos, you were attending a school that is almost totally segregated, the University of Virginia—"

There was a simple wooden rostrum in front of Kennedy; he seemed to hang onto it for balance, the knuckles of his heavy fingers whitening, the muscles of his ox pelvis of a jaw squirming each time he reset it. Kennedy's hewn, somewhat lipless and inexpressive face looked particularly drained for one so congenitally affable; sweat had begun its beading just below his widow's peak.

Late the previous spring, on the recommendation of tactical advisers who wanted to give the open secret of his misdemeanor a chance to ventilate itself, Kennedy had admitted to a Boston *Globe* reporter that he left Harvard after his freshman year because somebody else took a Spanish exam for him. Whatever the scandal-value of the incident, it had pretty much depleted itself over the months of the summer, but the impression lingered: weak. Weak.

By autumn the Massachusetts political air was overhung and threatening with rumors. One insisted that Joe, the Founding Father, and old Joe alone among the Kennedys had much of an appetite for Edward's candidacy. The seat in the Senate his brother the President had occupied—warmed reliably since 1960 by Benjamin Smith II, Jack's room-mate in college—Teddy wanted now. Political appointments out of Washington were reportedly delayed. There was recurrent talk that, win or lose, Ted Kennedy was going to oversee all patronage in Massachusetts after September of 1962.

The paranoia normal to workers for the good of the party grew and provided the Kennedy campaign a special leverage of its own. For McCormack, alliances of a political lifetime had now begun to dissolve. "I'm going after the anti-chutzpah vote," the angry young Attorney General had sworn to friends as he needled the inexperienced Kennedy into open confrontation.

"The thing that fascinates me is Teddy's constant reference to his trips," McCormack went on that embattled evening. "He made two European trips, visited eleven countries in twenty-four days. In South America he visited nine countries in twenty-seven days."

Much of the informed American community shared McCormack's indignation. "It was sporting of Teddy to wait until he was thirty instead of asking for an Act of Congress or a Constitutional Amendment to lower the qualifying age," Inez Robb had written. The Washington *Post,* praising this arriving Kennedy for his modesty, pointedly noted that he had "much to be modest about." The New York *Times* admitted that Kennedy was just old enough for the Senate, but had "few other qualifications," and suggested that "relatives of prominent officials" should "present some solid evidence of talent before they make the sacrifice of starting at the top." "Nepotism!" Scotty Reston exclaimed. Mark De Wolfe Howe of the Harvard Law School circulated a letter throughout the academic world calling Edward Kennedy's candidacy that of a "bumptious newcomer . . . both preposterous and insulting." McCormack himself let it be known that one of his cardinal motives in running was to ward off the most self-evident among Kennedy's domestic blunders: his brother's elevation to the Senate.

McCormack was leaving his audience no doubt at all that evening that he intended to spare his President chagrin. "I worked my way up the political ladder," McCormack, who is himself the nephew of the Speaker of the United States House of Representatives, reminded his audience. "I'm not starting at the top."

For what already seemed like hours Ted Kennedy had been reaching at, clutching at, anything that might somehow drive the exchange back to substantive political issues. Despite Kennedy's carefully rehearsed gestures, his dragged-out nasalized inflections, his decisive down-blading hand motions—in spite of everything, McCormack was somehow keeping real discussion pushed maddeningly away. McCormack lashed out; whatever Ted managed in return went awry, somehow. "We should not have any talk about personalities or families!" Kennedy attempted, finally.

McCormack cracked right down. "And so I ask, since the question of names and families has been injected, if his name was Edward Moore—with his qualifications, with your qualifications, Teddy—if it was Edward Moore your candidacy would be a joke. Nobody's laughing, because his name is not Edward Moore—it is Edward Moore Kennedy."

The debate was one of those exceptional public events helpful to everybody involved in it. Certainly Edward McCormack had gotten a beautiful opportunity to relieve his spleen in front of the television cameras. (Although, when he was later beaten in the primary, he went out of his way to berate the condition of Massachusetts politics generally, and sulked straight through until a chance at another important Democratic office came along a couple of years afterward.) Kennedy himself, as things worked out, profited immediately and measurably from an enormous sympathy backlash. He sensed the effect a couple of days afterward when, as he was campaigning at the door of a factory at quitting time, a seasoned old laborer asked suddenly: "Is it true, like I heard, that you never worked a day in your life, Kennedy?"

The candidate mumbled something to the effect that he hadn't worked much with his hands, really. . . .

"Well, let me tell ya somethin', kid," the seasoned old laborer said, "ya sure ain't missed a hell of a lot."

From that instant, Kennedy realized, he had his seat in the Senate.

This latest, last, most resented, least-seriously-taken of two generations of Kennedys to come to Washington now arrived to begin his career-at-the-top. Insiders around Washington, like academics around Boston, ignored any genuinely accurate picture of Edward Kennedy and devoted themselves to scrutinizing the negative: he was *not* a humorous, charming, detached, intellectualizing man, like Jack; he did not have the clarity, push, hard-edged aggressiveness that made Bobby so effective. The profile of whatever he had done that far in life looked utterly Kennedy-derivative: he went through prep school and, when they let him in again, Harvard; he played end on the football team; his grades were bad enough to keep him out of Harvard Law School but good enough for the University of Virginia, like Bobby's. He spent a season, like both his brothers, reporting for the International News Service. There had been two years as a private first class stationed near Paris in the U.S. Army. He managed Jack Kennedy's campaign for President in the Far West, and carpers at the time liked to blame him for losing California. What most people remembered best was his willingness to go off a major ski jump on somebody's challenge in Wisconsin: to casual knockers this meant he was crazy or irresponsible. After the 1960 election he worked for the office of the Attorney General of Massachusetts, rounded thirty, and ran for Senator.

For anybody interested in picking out more detail, certain other aspects of Kennedy's personality now began to recommend themselves. Once he was out of the Army, he had volunteered and worked in a settlement house in Boston's Negro South End. At Law School he was elected head of the Student Forum and, with John Tunney, now a California Congressman, won the Moot Case contest, a round-robin debate that, like the Ames at Harvard, suggests potential courtroom agility. People who knew him at all began to report that he was an excellent listener, that he remembered and combined ideas well, and that in the end his decisions were largely his own except—even then, except—when influenced directly and strenuously by Bobby. He worked very hard, it was said. He could demand a great deal of anybody who worked for him, but his ambiance, the state of tension he kept around himself, was livable with.

Ted's way with people was variously taken; some who ran into him found him empty, really: bland. "In my opinion he's just a pasteboard mask," somebody remarked to me.

"I don't know what makes Teddy tick, but I'm sure that the fact that he's the youngest son in a family of real abrasive people makes him want to make good. And he's making good," another more caustic and more knowledgeable Kennedy-watcher tipped me early.

Milton Gwirtzman, a young Washington lawyer who has worked one way or the other with most of the Kennedys, and who served as Kennedy's legislative assistant, had much the same viewpoint. Milton is a little oracular—the word in Kennedy circles was that you had to believe in Milton in order to be able to see him clearly—but I think his meaning is plain enough. "While he's growing up," Milton said, innocuous behind his dense Army-pink eyeglasses, "the youngest son doesn't have the physical or mental abilities of the others, so the way he gets along is to be good, nice, easy to get along with. When Ted got to Washington in 1963 he faced substantially the same situation in the Senate, where many envious Senators had *sons* older than he was then. . . . But he made a point of calling them all Senator, and he learned how to have a drink of bourbon with Jim Eastland and address him as Mister Chairman, and they saw that he did his homework, that he was ready to take on the dirty work, like presiding over the Senate, that nobody really likes, and after a while he was—people started to take to him here. His younger-brother characteristics stood him in good stead."

These younger-brother characteristics are well-documented in Kennedy family archives. In 1938, for example, when Joe was settling in as Ambassador to the Court of Saint James's, Edward brought an urgent request home. Might he be permitted to punch a classmate, who had been working him over daily? "You tell me I can't get into fights because Dad is the Ambassador," the six-year-old told Rose earnestly. Permission came; Kennedy already showed an unusual sense of the fitness of whatever he did.

Or even farther back: when Ted was born a full four years after Jean, and thus really the afterthought, the belated end of that generation's model run, Joe traded in the family sailboat *Tenovus* for something larger, *Onemore*. By the time Edward came along Joe's frenetic notorious years as the lone-wolf speculator of Wall Street were pretty much over; having found, at best, marginal acceptance among the Best People of either Boston or New York Society, the Kennedys had removed, spiritually at least, to their own privately mythologized duchy at Hyannis Port, from where they proceeded to establish diplomatic relations with the remainder of America. Joe, who backed Franklin D. Roosevelt early and reminded him of it often, received a series of appointments (Chairman of the Securities and Exchange Commission, head of the Maritime Commission, ultimately that choicest of Ambassadorships). Accordingly, during his impressionable earliest years, little Ted enjoyed very regular exposure to the men who (in a favorite phrase of his own, these days) "move affairs." Until Joe Kennedy's iron-willed America Firstism forced Roosevelt to allow him to resign, F.D.R. took a perverse delight in the machinations of this colicky redheaded Irish-American speculator he himself set loose among the university theorists and tea-table career people of the very early New Deal; the umbilical connection between The Family and the American Government, however slack it went just after World War II, was now unbrokenly established.

One of Joe's penchants had been for pedagogy. "Dad was always very very interested in what went on in school, in sports," Edward Kennedy said when I asked him about his earliest years. "He also took a very great interest in your conduct. For example, I remember he didn't feel I ought to have a bicycle unless others among my classmates did. He tended to keep this kind of discipline up until it became self-generating." Edward developed into the best sailor, tennis player, mountaineer, skier in the family. An exceptional listener always, he sensed beneath the unfettered dinner-table arguments about politics and international affairs the undertow of very large family second-generation governmental ambitions. Big, friendly, low-strung, and, in his father's phrase, affable as an Irish cop, Ted took on the anchor-man responsibilities for the family when his father started failing. He edited a private book, *The Fruitful Bough*, of vignettes about Joe, and put in a lot of weekend duty at Hyannis Port after his father's stroke. *Jack and Bob will run the show, while Ted's in charge of hiding Joe* went a pernicious little couplet just before the election in 1960; whoever wrote that had a maliciously delicate nose for character. "You can see the emotion in his eyes, the interest, but that's all," Ted Kennedy says currently of his father. "These days his concerns are pretty well limited to the activities of his grandchildren. . . ."

Instructions—requests, really—that I got some months ago from Edward Kennedy's very, very able and otherwise rather unbuttoned staff when I was first in Washington suggest the sensitivities that this has engendered. "Don't overplay the role of the staff," I was cautioned, "and don't refer to the Senator either to his face or—more particularly—in print as *Teddy*. This irks him and we hear him muttering about the Teddy treatment sometimes."

Early one otherwise unexceptional June evening in 1964 something happened to Edward Kennedy which may very well have amounted to the most important event in his life up to that time. The rented private aircraft in which he was doing some rather informal campaigning around back Massachusetts went into a spin somehow and crashed nose-first into an apple orchard not far outside Springfield. The pilot and Kennedy's administrative assistant, Edward Moss, were killed; Kennedy, who had been half-standing just behind them almost in the middle of the plane, was dragged out of the wreck in desperate condition. Surgeons at the nearest accessible hospital, after cleaning him up and putting him through a series of probes too sensitive to allow the use of pain-killers, found out little by little that three vertebrae in his lower back had been smashed together, two ribs were cracked, and internal hemorrhaging around his spleen and left kidney was so extensive that until some of it had dissipated there would be no way to discover how much, if any, permanent damage had been done his inner organs. The position of the third lumbar vertebra was especially precarious; it had been driven out sideways so far that one more inch would have snapped his spinal cord and left him a paralytic.

Radio and television reports went out immediately, of course; within hours a party of Kennedys had arrived. The student nurse on duty refused to leave her post or make clear to the group, which included Robert, Governor Peabody, and Ted's wife Joan, which room the Senator was in. The increasingly anxious visitors finally found the young Senator beneath an oxygen tent, "tubes up his nose, things dangling from both his arms," as his wife remembers.

"There are more of us than there is trouble," Bobby told an overtaking newsman shortly. "The Kennedys intend to stay in public life. Good luck is something you make, and bad luck is something you endure."

The near-corpse inside the translucent tent apron, recognizing, perhaps, his wife's characteristic pink dress, showed signs of saying something. "Hi, Joansie," he managed, with difficulty. Then, typically, "Don't worry!"

Kennedy spent the next six months in a series of hookups, most notably a rotating Stryker frame. His mind and his secretary Angelique Voutselas' stenographic pad were increasingly busy. One suspects that such a prolonged brush with death went deep into Edward Kennedy's thinking and feelings. There was a suggestive similarity between his own injury—which, he was told shortly, would leave him physically limited, half-crippled permanently, dependent on a back brace—and that of his assassinated brother Jack. This produced a strange result. People who had gone mountain climbing with Ted, for example, had always commented on his low-keyed calm and stamina and courage; now in times of danger or physical stress he began to show a peculiar detachment. "I could very well understand people's opposition to my original Senatorial candidacy," he told me once when he and I were discussing the subject. "The reservations of others. And I bore no ill feeling toward those people"—he talks like this, very often: those stilted political phrases, those long, cold, dragged-out vowels of Kennedyese—"Today, since then, a number of those people have been helpful. . . ." Then, thinking it over: "Perhaps, had I been somebody else, and had I been asked, I'd have opposed my nomination myself."

This detachment pervades. David Burke, Kennedy's serious, able executive assistant, admits to a palm-clamming tenseness the moment he climbs into any aircraft smaller than a DC-8; Kennedy, for his own macabre reasons, will fly almost anywhere in almost anything, and, since Burke accompanies him often, so must Dave. Kennedy has long since found this out about Burke and, having acquired a pilot's license early in his own life, Edward amuses himself quietly sometimes by unobtrusive little palms-up/palms-down gestures calculated to hint to Burke the way he himself would handle the stick. Circling into Topeka once in a privately owned jet, Kennedy speculated aloud about whether *he* could get the aircraft down, insisting that he could figure out the purpose of all the controls except one mysterious but presumably unimportant little red light. . . . Another time, during a very rugged passage indeed, Kennedy pulled together the deck of cards he was riffling idly and suggested that the ashen Burke pick one at random. Burke complied, fingers shaking. "Isn't it too bad nobody is going to know that is the last thing you ever did," his employer commented stonily.

"Liberalism," among the Kennedys originally, was the kind of term Old Joe liked to lay up in quotes whenever he needed to use it: the liberal in politics was somebody with a heart bleeding all over the carpet, and applesauce for brains. Edward, once his Senate seat was warmed properly, began to show symptoms of an instinctive gut liberalism of approach, a deeply effective, very detailed sense of whom the commonest of people were, and what they really needed. Recently turning over the pages of his photograph album he showed me a picture somebody had taken of him, early in that first campaign, shaking hands all around a machine shop. "If you look closely," he remarked, "you can see that half the people there are without at least *part* of one of their fingers." He turned the binder page over: the next picture showed him soliciting across some kind of conveyor belt tended by a gnomic flour-dusty old man. "That man was kneading the blueberries out as they came through that endless pie-making machine," Kennedy said. "He told me, 'If you want my vote, Kennedy, you'll have to shake my hand.' " The candidate was photographed dripping blueberries halfway to the elbow.

More and more, the legislation Kennedy began to be associated with concerned the plight of the scratch-dirt poor, people suffocating in the impacted slums, the dispossessed and homeless, the old, the immigrants, draftees. He began to spend a lot of his Massachusetts time talking with out-of-work fishermen, with workers in the cranberry bogs. Kennedy became the most knowledgeable man in the Senate about voting-rights problems, about refugee affairs. His concern was unmistakably deep. His sense of the corruptions and dislocations within postwar America became increasingly specific. He began working harder and harder. His day might last from an early tactical discussion in his McLean, Virginia, home at seven in the morning until a post-dinner-party stint with his willing but fading staff people that started at ten p.m. and went on into the morning following. An avid brain picker anyhow, the half-crippled young Senator, trying to formulate a piece of legislation, was likely to import an expert from Harvard or take a jet halfway around the world to find out for himself precisely the relevant facts; these facts had a way of coming back in debate on the floor of the Senate like machine-gun bullets. The legislation he proposed gained a name for being exceptionally well-backgrounded, clear in its intention, and limited in its intention. Typical was his recent amendment to the Administration's O.E.O. (Poverty) Act, which provided in complete detail for the establishment, staffing, and maintenance of forty "neighborhood health center" clinics throughout the worst American city slums. "His proposals are laid in with a rifle, accurately, not with a shotgun," a ranking Republican told me; this made them easier for his conservative opponents to vote for and justify at home. The Democratic leadership on The Hill began to prefer Kennedy's work to the often very abrupt, badly timed, frequently blanketing legislation being brought forward by the Junior Senator from New York.

While Kennedy's intensity at work now approached total preoccupation, his way with whichever people he cared about became more relaxed, simpler, more whimsical. His secretaries tried to stay out of giggling range when, as is most frequently true, he realized he wasn't going to make it home in time to put his three young kids to bed and so was forced to deliver, via telephone, the afternoon's installment of an ongoing animal saga in which he himself plays all the voices. Never ostentatious anyhow (he drives his own Chrysler around, frugally trading it every couple of years), he now made every effort to keep everything as unencumbered as possible for himself.

His reputation—his justification for being there at all—pretty much established in the Senate by 1964, he got himself reelected for a full term from his hospital bed and returned early in 1965 to receive his colleagues' heartfelt welcoming. Then, in September of 1965, came the Morrissey incident.

Francis Xavier Morrissey, Frank Morrissey, had been a municipal judge in the Boston city court system for a good many years before the trip he took to Washington, D.C. which was to make him momentarily famous. Morrissey, essentially an old-line Kennedy-family coat holder, aspired to the dignity of a place on the Federal Bench to cap his career. In fact, the Kennedys owed him. Frank Morrissey had done a great many services for Joe, and when first Jack, and finally Ted, decided to establish their political bases in Massachusetts, Morrissey guided both boys adeptly and with an unmistakable devotion. There had even been talk of a judgeship for Morrissey early in the Kennedy Administration; snooping at the time by the ever-vigilant Boston *Globe* seems to have scared the Administration off. When, much later on and largely as a personal courtesy, one suspects, Edward Kennedy sent along to Lyndon Johnson his recommendation of Morrissey for the judgeship, the political expectation overall was that the President would appoint one of his own among the Massachusetts devoted.

The expectation proved incorrect. In a special conference at the L.B.J. ranch, the President announced that he was going to forward to the Senate for its ratification the long-dormant Morrissey nomination. *Why* is disputed. Some claim that Johnson agreed to the Morrissey idea to hang a man of Morrissey's limited qualifications on the record of the Kennedys. Others regard it as a favor granted Edward in gratitude for the way he had floor-managed the Administration's regional development bill shortly before, and explained that the President had craftily waited until Autumn of 1965 to forward the nomination because The New York *Times* was struck; Johnson's intention here, supposedly, was to give the Kennedys at least a partial news blackout during which to drag hapless Frank Morrissey through.

Unfortunately for Morrissey The Boston *Globe* was not struck. The *Globe,* in an exhaustively researched series of exposés and editorials, exhumed Frank Morrissey's past, his graduation from a Georgia diploma mill, his struggle to pass the Massachusetts bar, his desultory achievements since. Local defenders of the honor of the Bench, like Judge Wyzanski and the Boston chapter of the American Bar Association, disapproved of Morrissey publicly and sternly.

The Washington *Post* picked the story up and attacked from the opposite flank. By the time Frank Morrissey got down to his Senate hearings, conservatives on the Judiciary Committee, scenting vulnerable game, were very nearly drooling. "Certain questions have arisen," Everett Dirksen began—too gently. Then—Morrissey showing up all loquaciousness, his inflections one moment affected and mincing, the next the low, whining South-Boston bleat, pure borderline Irish—Dirksen took him, a little more archly, further: "*Grave* questions have arisen." Finally, "Serious accusations have been leveled—" Morrissey talked some more; liberals all over the chamber were coming up hesitant. Edward Kennedy now spoke on Morrissey's behalf: under unmistakable personal pressure, the Cro-Magnon jaw trembling, very obviously near tears, Kennedy launched a diatribe, recalled the shoeless Irish boy Morrissey was in childhood, his battle for respectability, the regard he earned as a Justice within the Boston Courts. . . . Warming to his subject, Kennedy reprimanded the American Bar Association as an organization narrow-minded enough to have tried to stop the ratification of Louis Brandeis for the Supreme Court. . . .

Dirksen, in too deep to backpedal, called Washington's puzzled press corps together before the committee could vote: he had a "bombshell," which he intended to explode if Morrissey's nomination went further.

Everett Dirksen's "bombshell," when unearthed finally, was a particularly puny little operatic ladyfinger. In 1961 Frank Morrissey and Edward Kennedy, traveling together in Italy where Kennedy had received an award from the American Committee on Italian Migration, vacationed for a day or two on Capri. There they shared a meal with a fellow American who bragged around about it later. The fellow American turned out to be a deported Mafia gangster; apparently Dirksen, somehow digging up the item from an Italian newspaper four years afterward, had some intention of linking publicly the names of Edward Moore Kennedy, Frank Morrissey, and the American criminal underworld.

Appraised of what Dirksen's bombshell was, Kennedy painfully and reluctantly sent the nomination back to the Judiciary Committee to die: *I would want any nominee of mine to be confirmed on a record clear and complete enough. . . .*"I think Teddy learned then," Doyle of The Boston *Globe* told me years afterward, "that you can't buy the whole thing."

More vital than the Dirksen "bombshell" was the realization that no matter what happened, the Morrissey nomination was tarred with notoriety; any Senator who voted for Morrissey—and Kennedy could have compelled the vote, that is commonly agreed—would come away tarred to his constituents too. Every Senator around felt the strain of patronage obligations himself; all understood Kennedy's position; all appreciated the public humiliation—and the private judgment—that killing the nomination involved.

Conservative knives had probably been sharpening for Kennedy since his whirlwind unexpected decision, not months after he hobbled back into the Senate chambers on his silver-headed cane, to buck both the Conservative establishment and the Liberal leadership and try to stick an amendment outlawing local and state poll taxes onto the Administration's 1965 Voting Rights Bill. The oligarchs of Committee Power in the Senate hated the idea of another incursion by Northerners into the sanctified inequities of their vespertine political world; the Liberal wing feared that the Kennedy amendment would cost them votes enough to endanger the bill.

From the vantage point of his Senatorial career, that shaky spring was probably the worst time Kennedy could have chosen to displease elders of both persuasions. He himself had just been selected, with crotchety old Eastland's suffrage, as floor manager of the Administration's expanded Immigration Bill.

To Judiciary Committee Chairman Eastland, a gnarled old moss-bedecked cypress of seniority and Dixieland privilege, young Kennedy had already become one of the trials of advancing age. "Wha' you wan' now, Kennedy," he is reputed to inquire wearily whenever the youngster appears. Sometimes the compromises they work out prove touchy to live with. For example, at the time Kennedy was shepherding his Immigration Bill through, Kennedy finagled, through Eastland, a kind of informal agreement with the Southern bloc that none of them would speak on the subject for the record. Then, on the Senate floor itself, Senator Holland of Florida suddenly got up to ask how many Spanish-speaking "nigras" this liberalization would involve: the Deep South delegation scuttled for the cloakroom *en mêlée*.

Determined whatever the upshots, Kennedy went recruiting for his anti-poll-tax army. Persuasion, old political debts, appeals to democratic principle, implicit logrolling threats, implicit logrolling promises—he employed whichever, in each case, seemed indicated. Mark De Wolfe Howe of Harvard, that very same Mark De Wolfe Howe who had once circulated the academic letter labeling Kennedy's candidacy "both preposterous and insulting," came down to help. "Ted is a real expert at diffusing the opposition," one old Washington hand explains. "He knows just where to look for the opposition's weakness. He might start in working on X, for instance. He knows he'll never get X's vote, but he will have prevented X from dragging Y's vote away from him too." Kennedy opened the debate by delivering a major speech that treated the poll tax in historical terms as a *liberalizing* step in the development of universal suffrage, a means of permitting non-property-holders to vote. It played on the egalitarian impulses of even the most conservative.

Dave Burke had started working for Kennedy just before that. Burke himself was not fully aware, from the Senator's typically circular lines of early inquiry, exactly what his new employer was about; he was startled one afternoon when Kennedy looked up during a Committee meeting and asked for "my poll-tax amendment." Panic-stricken, no lawyer himself, Burke rushed back to the offices for a few lines of legalese to get Kennedy through the Committee session.

Katzenbach, the Attorney General, and Mansfield, the Majority Leader, and the reactionaries assembled marshaled their forces quickly and—almost—too late; the floor vote on the Kennedy Amendment that defeated it went 49-44; three out of five Senatorial Democrats voted *against* their own Administration on this matter. To placate them a provision went into the voting-rights bill requiring that if local or state poll taxes were collected, the much hated Federal registrars must collect them. Katzenbach had hinted broadly that two pending Supreme Court cases dealing with the Virginia poll tax might decide the matter without embarrassing the legislators. Obligated, the Justice Department pushed its suits harder, and on March 25, 1966, the Court reversed itself and found *all* local poll taxes in violation of the Fourteenth Amendment. To Senatorial insiders, operators, Kennedy's parliamentary skill and leadership had left people holding their breaths. "Ted is not as *forceful* in the Senate, yet, as Jack was," says the Republican moderate Thruston Morton, who knew both of them well. "But Teddy is personally more popular. He's much quieter, less in evidence, lower keyed. As a parliamentarian and what, for lack of a better word, I'd call a floor strategist, he's better than Jack. He's patient in debate with those who take an opposite viewpoint. Jack Kennedy, and Bobby after him, could sometimes answer quite shortly, indicate quite clearly his feeling of intellectual superiority to his colleagues. The Senate is a deliberative body; Ted intuitively understands this. He handles the whole thing with a lot more suavity."

The poll-tax fight set a kind of pattern: Edward showed himself almost invariably willing to trade a victory of form—i.e., a vote victory—for one of substance, as when he managed, as part of his Federal gun-control-legislation campaign, to force the Army to stop sponsoring the National Rifle Matches by permitting it to sponsor them one last time. The reapportionment broil, a very stubborn, bitter struggle Kennedy fought over many months in 1967 and ultimately won, is illustrative again of the kind of parliamentary generalship at which he has become so effective. The issue itself arose out of a series of Supreme Court decisions, the so-called one-man-one-vote cases. These required the states to reapportion voting districts according to population shifts since 1904. Once the effort to prevent such a return to democracy through Constitutional Amendment had failed, conservatives like Everett Dirksen, fearful for the erosion of their own pocket boroughs, fell back on legislation that would delay significant redistricting until at least 1972. Kennedy very shortly got upwind of all this, and recruited young Republican Senator Baker of Tennessee (Dirksen's son-in-law, of all men), and beat the obstructive legislation to pieces every time it, or some form of it, came from the House of Representatives. In the course of his inquiry he pinpointed the abuses resulting from later-day gerrymandering and suggested a "compactness and equality" criterion for voting districts that the Supreme Court has now taken under advisement. All these are, certainly, sophisticated issues, the infighting is complicated, but to the convinced libertarian they are in fact the heart and kidneys of a surviving democracy.

Two somewhat more dramatic campaigns had begun to bring Kennedy to the attention of newspaper readers even before Robert's assassination: his early skirmishing with—preparatory, obviously, to a frontal attack on—Congressional defenders of the draft policies, and his investigations into the refugee problems of Vietnam. Kennedy's Vietnamese concern came as an unintended consequence of a look he was forced to take, as Chairman of the Special Subcommittee on Refugees and Escapees, at the human marginalia piling up along the edges of our involvement there. He began to mull over the war's moral purposes, its human and political cost-effectiveness, the way, in detail, it was actually being waged. Overall indictments and geopolitical recommendations are very far from Kennedy's method—his characteristic working principles, his staff people admit, are "Let's preserve our options," or "It's a long road ahead"—but he is obviously deeply troubled. His way of dealing with this is, as usual, to return again and again to the facts. He picks the brains of experts, he empties and re-empties his famously overstuffed attaché case, "the Bag," on trips like his twice-yearly visits to the International Conference on Refugee Affairs at Geneva or his investigations, like the one last January, into the corruption inside Vietnam itself. His speeches detailing the unutterable misery of that nation's two to three million refugees have already worked a powerful effect among his senate colleagues. Further than that he cannot seem to make himself go. As late as the middle of March of 1968, Edward was reported unconvinced of the wisdom of Bobby's challenge. "Now when my brother Bobby recently decided to give an anti-Vietnam-policy speech and showed it to me and asked me what to do," he said a short time before his brother was assassinated, as he opened an Americans for Democratic Action dinner meeting, "I said he should put the speech in a plain brown envelope and send it along to *Ramparts* magazine. Then I took him over to the Senate, and I showed him where his seat was, and I told him a few things I thought would help him get along. . . ."

The war in Vietnam was spitting up the bones of politicians all across the pre-primary landscape the bleak mid-December day I spent in cavalcade across northeast Massachusetts with Kennedy on one of those odd frantic junkets of campaigning-for-its-own-sake he squeezed in whenever he could between stretches in Washington.

He was unconcealably preoccupied with his own incompletely formulated feelings of personal responsibility about the war, and the speech he
made a few minutes later, to students in The Community College in
Haverhill, showed how involved he felt. "It's nice to see so many bright
eyes after that junior prom," he began; then his anchor dropped locally, "I
think this is the biggest group of young people I've seen all in one place
since I had lunch lahst Sunday at my brother Bobby's." His response to the
laugh he got, not much, but enough to warm him up, provoked out of him
genuinely that Kennedy grin of big, long, expensively-cared-for teeth. The
Kennedy Reaction was setting in already, I saw: the co-eds were moving
around inside the scoops of their auditorium folding chairs, crossing
thighs, wriggling, rotating sneaker tips. If this one were not a Kennedy, I
wondered, but just one more very-early-middle-aging politician in his
invariable *suit*, needing a haircut but not upsetting at all, noticeably
jug-eared, his lined neck beginning to fatten—if this one were just anybody at all, wouldn't these enthralled kids see him as unexciting, if not
positively square, in a way?

"Young people are *ahs*king," Kennedy was now opening up, taking on
timbre like an elocution prizewinner, "what have been ow-uh policies that
have sent ow-uh young people to war three times in twenty-five years,
they're ahsking significant questions which *should* be ahsked, they're
forming their *own* idears, for while our elders are concentrating on their
own wealth, their own comfort, this generation says, this is not enough—"

There is much recrossing of mini-skirted legs; Kennedy perorates:
"Oliver Wendell Holmes said, 'Through our great good fortune, in our
youth, our hearts were touched with fire.' " Applause begins prematurely.
'I believe it is important that that fire, in the hearts of our youth, be used
to light a better world. Thank you." He has stepped away already;
half-limping, the outline of the brace visible through the cloth of his suit
jacket, to escape the convergence of the mobs and through the stage door
rear.

In the open country outside Haverhill there was a positively Pentagon-
sized General Electric assembly plant; we pulled up there for fifteen
minutes of nonstop handshaking. The interlude had a kind of Orpheus in
the contemporary lumpen-proletariat Underworld character that dizzies
me now whenever I think about it: the gigantic cinder-block shell of the
place, scorched-smelling throughout with that special space-age hyper-
dryness, like the inside of somebody's television set, where Kennedy,
trailed always by his schedule-panicky handlers, shuffles briskly along
acre after acre of aisles of workbenches, stops periodically for picture-
taking, invades the cafeteria. He weaves in and out of table groupings,
somehow warm and methodical at once, pressing hand after hand after
hand—pressing *thousands* of hands, touching collarbones, pinching
elbows, brushing beneath the cauliflower-like vaccination scars of

worked-out old women with understanding fingertips. Wherever he passes excitement is audible: "Who's eatin'?" one girl employee says, shrugging, to another. "Everybody's runnin' after *him*. Gee, he should come every day."

"He's so much like John Kennedy it's—it's—" The woman is speechless. "He looks like a kid, honestly. Oooh, is he *cute!*"

"I wonder would he like some pea soup," I overhear one dour little soul say to nobody especially; I think she would halfway expect, should she press on Kennedy the paper cup she is holding, that he could in some obscure way bless it for her. By now Kennedy is out behind the heavy glass counters handshaking among the cooks.

At Lawrence, addressing a post-prandial Chamber of Commerce meeting, he tries one of those carefully breath-catching pan-Kennedy jokes: "I am aware that there is a man running for President of the United States, from Minnesota, who has held very high public office. I want to take this occasion to tell all of you here that under no circumstances could I ever support that man from Minnesota—" Applause erupts, too early. "Harold Stassen." The punch line goes all but unattended. Something in this reflex of business-community hatred for McCarthy-as-liberal offends Kennedy's deeply seated impulses; suddenly he has fallen into a delivery strenuous to the point of ranting: ". . . we know that the draft law today is just as unfair, as inequitable, as it was a year ago. Our young people, the ones here coming out of The Community College and the vocational high school, *aren't* going to be deferred, we realize that. . . ." His speech swings straightaway into the Vietnam war itself, its senselessness, the shortsightedness of its human provisions. "What have been the policies that have brought these about? I find it difficult to answer. Are we tied to the shibboleths of the past? Are we astigmatic to this extent?" He introduced the poverty program: "And I think it is well, my friends, to see how we're going to bring industry into the poverty program. This is a challenge you must help us with—"

"Boy, I couldn't have made it any shorter," Kennedy tells Dave Burke, almost apologetically, once he is safely back in the Oldsmobile and en route to Lowell. "That's an important group of people." He turns up a printed card somebody has slipped into his hand while he was folding himself gingerly into the car: "TO HELL WITH THE CONSTITUTION" is lettered crudely across the back. "SUPPORT JOHNSON." The awareness that he has missed his audience is unmistakably depressing. "I should have led them through what the considerations, the implications are if the government increases or doesn't increase taxes," he decides after a while.

At the high school in Lowell, exactly from the moment the car door opens, everything is all right again. A kind of honor guard of very nubile little girls in Prussian-blue uniforms with chevrons reviews Kennedy's approach: he now proceeds beyond them and up the aisle through nymphet pandemonium; pressing to get within benediction reach they scream deliriously, giggle, try to touch, shriek *eeeee*. One overstimulated chestnut-haired bud in an apache T-shirt is obviously out: both eyes glitter blindly in her adolescent ecstasy, she springs on reflex the moment he brushes her hand. "I don't believe it!" she gasps, utterly from the throat; Kennedy has shambled out of her range now and mounts the dais one step at a time, augustly.

The uproar quiets, finally; the mayor of Lowell introduces Kennedy, with point, as the man who *has* done more for Massachusetts. Upon the speaker's lips, quickly wiped away, a strange little fugitive smile is momentarily discernible. "Now let me say, Mister Mayor," the speaker of the day begins, "that this is—" the tumult pitches up again— "that this is the biggest group of young people—that I have seen—since I had lunch with my brother Bobby's family last Sunday. . . ." The laugh he gets is mostly of appreciation; the Senator smiles out benevolently. Kennedy at that moment was fully, visibly, comfortable again; easy; tilling the future.

In June, 1968, he was in San Francisco, closing up the primary shop there after his brother's final victory, when word of the assassination attempt reached him. By the time he got to Los Angeles, Bobby's condition was critical, already deteriorating. As ever, he was the one to give the news to his invalided father. For Edward Kennedy himself the moment was excruciating and fateful: the spiritual inheritance of this star-crossed near-mythological American family—whatever the duties, whatever the wealth and the organization and the charisma, whatever the fugitive piercing glories—the burden of all it had come to mean was his.

It would be hard to ascertain whether Ted had slept at all in the days that followed. He sat up half Tuesday night, and through the morning of surgery in the intensive-care wing of the Good Samaritan Hospital in Los Angeles; by nine o'clock on Thursday he had landed in New York with the body of his brother and was on hand to help drag the coffin off the forklift and slide it onto the bed of a hearse. There was a short receiving ceremony at St. Patrick's Cathedral; after that everybody left but Ted, who prayed into the earliest morning. He came back later that day to watch another night beside the purple-draped catafalque, beneath six flickering candles. People who wandered by noted that he had slumped little by little into the corner of a pew; workmen began to arrive to hammer together the scaffolding for television cameras; Edward Kennedy didn't notice. The people came to file by, forming a line a mile long. A woman said: "I watched on TV and the Kennedys don't cry. I thought I should come down and do some crying for them."

Sometime in the daylight intervals between his vigils he decided to deliver a personal eulogy at the funeral. He stepped up behind the rostrum of the cathedral to speak—his full face a little puffy by then and his mood strained by fatigue. At that moment and for the first time for many Americans, he came sharply into public focus.

"We loved him as a brother," Edward opened, "and as a father and as a son. From his parents and from his older brothers and sister, Joe and Kathleen and Jack, he received an inspiration—" Here Kennedy very nearly faltered, paused, went on. He suggested what Robert had meant to his family, his sense of the inequities of our societies, his hopes for the political and moral redemption to be sought through the upcoming young. He concluded with words he himself had written a few hours before. "There is pride in that, even arrogance, but there is also experience and truth, and in any event it is the only way we can live. That is the way he lived. That is what he leaves us."

When the ceremony was over there was to be the delayed tragedy-broken train ride beneath another afternoon and evening of rains, more hands to shake on the train and at the graveside, more people to thank, to reassure, to wave to, to comfort. Public life, which is undertaken so lightly sometimes, leaves very little private life once the realization of calling is complete. To this family of awkward outsiders which had determined to scramble so for national attention, for wealth, for political power, everything had arrived suddenly, and was as suddenly devastated. Two of Edward's brothers had schemed unsuccessfully for the Vice-Presidential nomination in their seasons; for Edward in 1968, it was obviously and simply a question of accepting it or not, and now that didn't seem to matter much. By now there were only the issues and the facts and the political process and the problems of a people, and the surviving possibility that he himself could still do something about that.

[September, 1968]

Chicago, The Year of Our Lord, 1968

Chicago mayor Richard Daley's police force attacked hundreds of demonstrators in Grant Park during the 1968 Democratic Convention. Eric Sevareid called it "the most disgraceful spectacle in the history of American politics." Esquire had enlisted a varied literary crew—playwright Jean Genet, journalist John Sack, and William Burroughs, author of Naked Lunch—to cover events outside Convention Hall. The images they brought back are among the decade's most graphic and unforgettable.

The Members of the Assembly

by Jean Genet

Chicago reminds me of an animal which curiously is trying to climb on top of itself. Part of the city is transformed by the life—or the parade, in both senses of the term—of the hippies.

Saturday night, about ten o'clock, the young people in Lincoln Park have lighted a kind of bonfire. Close by, scarcely visible in the darkness, a good-sized crowd has formed beneath the trees to listen to a black band—flutes and bongo drums. An American Indian, carrying a furled green flag, explains to us that it will be taken tomorrow to the airport when Senator McCarthy is scheduled to arrive and speak. Unfurled, the flag bears upon its green background the painted image of a seventeen-year-old boy—some say he was Indian, others black—killed two days before by the Chicago police.

The cops arrive, in brief but still unangry waves, to put out the fire and disperse the demonstrators. One word about them: the demonstrators are young people of a gentleness almost too gentle, at least this evening. If couples are stretched out on the grass in the park, it seems to me it is for the purpose of angelic exchanges. Everything strikes me as being very chaste. The darkness of the park is not solely responsible for the fact that all I can see are shadows folded in each other's arms.

A group of demonstrators, which had at first dispersed, has re-formed and is singing a kind of two-syllable chant, not unlike a Gregorian chant, a funeral dirge to the memory of the dead boy. I can scarcely speak of the beauty of this plaintive wail, of the anger and the singing.

Around the park, which is almost totally dark, what I first see is a proliferation of American cars, heavy with chrome, and beyond them the gigantic buildings of the city, each of whose floors is lighted, why I don't know.

Are these four democratic days going to begin with a funeral vigil in memory of a young Indian—or black—murdered by the Chicago police?

If man is, or is searching to be, omnipotent, I am willing to accept Chicago's gigantism; but I should like the opposite to be accepted as well: a city which would fit in the hollow of one's hand.

Sunday, Midway Airport, Chicago. McCarthy's arrival. Almost no police, and the few who do check our press credentials are extremely casual. Across from the press platform itself, actually the empty back of a parked trailer truck, are three similar platforms: one is occupied by a brass-dominated orchestra whose members are men in their thirties and forties, another by a rock group in its twenties. Between them is the platform reserved for McCarthy and his staff. McCarthy's plane is a few minutes late; the crowd massed behind the press platform consists of men and women whose faces reflect that peculiar image which only profound honesty and hope can give.

McCarthy finally arrives; and the crowd comes dramatically to life: every man, woman, and child, shouting "We Want Gene," brandishes signs devoid of the customary slogans but generously bedecked with flowers drawn or painted each according to the bearer's whim, and it is this flower-crowd that McCarthy is going to address. He is extremely relaxed; he smiles; he is about to speak, but the battery of microphones is dead. Sabotage? Smiling, he walks over and tries the mikes of the musical group in its thirties and forties: dead. Still smiling, he tries the mikes of the rock group in its twenties: dead! Finally, he makes his way back to his platform and tries his own microphones, which in the interim have been repaired, at least to some degree. He smiles. He is also serious, and he declares that he will speak only if the men and women the farthest away from the speaker's platform can hear him. Finally, he does speak, and you have all heard what he said on television.

As he leaves the speaker's platform, it seems that no one is protecting him, save for the sea of flowers painted by the hope-filled men and women.

A few hours later, at McCarthy's headquarters in the Hilton Hotel, there again appears to be almost no police security, or if there is any it is subtle, invisible. We are received with great courtesy.

This leads me to what, in my opinion, is one of the basic questions I ask myself: after eight months of campaigning, in order for this little-known Senator—or known all too well through a name steeped in shame—in order for McCarthy to arouse such enthusiasm, what concessions has he made? In what ways has his moral rectitude been weakened?

And yet the fact remains that all his speeches, all his statements, reveal intelligence and generosity. Is it a trick?

For a city with as large a black population as Chicago has, I note that there were very few blacks out to greet and acclaim him.

The First Day: The Day of the Thighs

The thighs are very beautiful beneath the blue cloth, thick and muscular. It all must be hard. This policeman is also a boxer, a wrestler. His legs are long, and perhaps, as you approach his member, you would find a furry nest of long, tight, curly hair. That is all I can see—and I must say it fascinates me—that and his boots, but I can guess that these superb thighs extend on up into an imposing member and a muscled torso, made even firmer every day by his police training in the cops' gymnasium. Higher up, into his arms and hands which must know how to put a black man or a thief out of action.

In the compass of his well-built thighs, I can see . . . but the thighs have moved, and I can see that they are splendid: America has a magnificent, divine, athletic police force, often photographed and seen in dirty books . . . but the thighs have parted slightly, ever so slightly, and through the crack which extends from the knees to the too-heavy member, I can see . . . why, it's the whole panorama of the Democratic Convention with its star-spangled banners, its star-spangled undress, its star-spangled songs, its star-spangled fields, its star-spangled candidates, in short the whole ostentatious parade, but the color has too many facets, as you have seen on your television sets.

What your television fails to bring you is the odor. No: the Odor, which may have a certain connection with order? The reason is that the Democratic Convention is being held right next to the stockyards, and I keep asking myself whether the air is being befouled by the decomposition of Eisenhower or by the decomposition of all America.

A few hours later, about midnight, I join Allen Ginsberg to take part in a demonstration of hippies and students in Lincoln Park: their determination to sleep in the park is their very gentle, as yet too gentle, but certainly poetic, response to the nauseating spectacle of the Convention. Suddenly the police begin their charge, with their grimacing masks intended to terrify: and, in fact, everyone turns and runs. But I am well aware that these brutes have other methods, and far more terrifying masks, when they go hunting for blacks in the ghettos, as they have done for the past hundred and fifty years. It is a good, healthy, and ultimately moral thing for these fair-haired, gentle hippies to be charged at by these louts decked out in this amazing snout that protects them from the effects of the gas they have emitted.

And I should like to end the first day with this: the person who opens her door to receive us as we try to escape from these brutes in blue is a young and very beautiful black woman. Later, when the streets have finally grown calm again, she offers to let us slip out through a back door, which opens onto another street: without the police suspecting it, we have been conjured away and concealed by a trick house. Nonetheless, these enormous thighs of policemen stuffed with LSD, rage, and patriotism were fascinating to see.

Tomorrow: another sleep-in in Lincoln Park, for this Law which is no law must be resisted.

The Second Day: The Day of the Visor

The truth of the matter is that we are bathed in a Mallarméan blue. This second day imposes the azure helmets of the Chicago police. A policeman's black leather visor intrudes between me and the world: a gleaming visor in whose tidy reflections I may be able to read the world, wittingly kept in top condition by numerous, and doubtless daily, polishings. Supporting this visor is the blue cap—Chicago wants us to think that the whole police force, and this policeman standing in front of me, have descended from heaven—made of a top-grade sky-blue cloth. But who is this blue cop in front of me? I look into his eyes, and I can see nothing else there except the blue of the cap. What does his gaze say? Nothing. The Chicago police are, and are not. I shall not pass. The visor and the gaze are there. The visor so gleaming that I can see myself and lose myself in it. I've got to see the continuation of the allegedly Democratic Convention, but the cop in the black visor with the blue eyes is there. Beyond him, I can nonetheless catch a glimpse of a lighted sign above the convention floor: there is an eye and "CBS News," the structure of which, in French as in English, reminds me of "obscene." But who is this policeman in the blue cap and black visor? He is so handsome I could fall into his arms. I look again at his look: at long last I recognize it; it is the look of a beautiful young girl, voluptuous and tender, which is hiding beneath a black visor and blue cap. She loves this celestial color: the Chicago police are feminine and brutal. It does not want its ladies to meekly obey their husbands whose hair is sky blue, dressed in robes of many colors. . . .

And what of the convention? It is democratic, it babbles on, and you have seen it on your screens: it is there for the purpose of concealing from you a game both simple and complex, which you prefer to ignore.

About ten o'clock this evening, part of America has detached itself from the American fatherland and remains suspended between earth and sky. The hippies have gathered in an enormous hall, as starkly bare as the Convention Hall is gaudy. Here all is joy, and in the enthusiasm several hippies burn their draft cards, holding them high for everyone to see: they will not be soldiers, but they may well be prisoners for five years. The hippies ask me to come up onto the stage and say a few words: this youth is beautiful and very gentle. It is celebrating the Un-Birthday of a certain Johnson who, it seems to me, hasn't yet been born. Allen Ginsberg is voiceless: he has chanted too loud and too long in Lincoln Park the night before.

Order, real order, is here: I recognize it. It is the freedom offered to everyone to discover and create himself.

About midnight, again in Lincoln Park, the clergy—also between earth and sky in order to escape from America—is conducting a religious service. I am subjected to another, but also very beautiful, kind of poetry. And what of the trees in the park? At night they bear strange fruit, clusters of young people suspended in their branches. I am as yet unfamiliar with this nocturnal variety: but that's the way it is in Chicago. The clergymen invite us to be seated: they are singing hymns in front of an enormous wooden cross. They joke too, and use slang. "Sit or split," says one of the bantering and slangy priests. "Sit or split." The cross, borne by several clergymen, moves away into the night, and this imitation of the Passion is very mov— I don't have time to finish the word: enormous projectors are turned on directly in front of us, and the police, throwing canisters of tear gas, rush at us. We have to run. Once again it is this police, azure but inexorable, who are pursuing us and pursuing the cross. Spellman-the-cop would have had a good laugh.

We take refuge in Ginsberg's hotel, across the street from the Park: my eyes are burning from the gas: a medic pours water into them, and the water spills over me down to my feet. In short, in their blundering clumsiness, the Americans have tried to burn me and a few minutes later to drown me.

We pause to collect ourselves in Allen Ginsberg's hotel room. And what of the convention? And democracy? The newspapers have kept you posted about them.

We leave the hotel: another azure policeman—or the beautiful girl in drag—holding his billy club in his hand the way, exactly the way, I hold a black American's member—escorts us to our car and opens the door for us: there can be no mistake about it: we are White.

The Third Day: The Day of the Belly

Chicago has fed these policemen's bellies, which are so fat that one must presume that they live on the slaughterhouses required by a city which resembles three hundred Hamburgs piled one on top of the other, and daily consumes three million hamburgers. A policeman's beautiful belly has to be seen in profile: the one barring my route is a medium-sized belly (de Gaulle could qualify as a cop in Chicago). It is medium-sized, but it is well on its way to perfection. Its owner wheedles it, fondles it with both his beautiful but heavy hands. Where did they all come from? Suddenly we are surrounded by a sea of policemen's bellies barring our entrance into the Democratic Convention. When I am finally allowed in, I will understand more clearly the harmony which exists between these bellies and the bosoms of the lady-patriots at the Convention—there is harmony but also rivalry: the arms of the ladies of the gentlemen who rule America have the girth of the policemen's thighs. Walls of bellies. And walls of policemen who encircle us, astonished by our appearance at the Democratic Convention, furious at the unconventional way we're dressed: they are thinking that we are thinking what they know, that is that the Democratic Convention is the Holy of Holies. The mouths of these bellies huddle in hasty conference. Walkie-talkies are barking. All of us in possession of the electronic passes required to enter the Amphitheater. The Chief of Police—wearing civilian clothes and his belly—arrives. He checks our passes, our identification, but obviously a man of taste and discretion, does not ask to see mine. He offers me his hand. I shake it. The bastard. We enter the corridors of the Convention Hall, but only to be allowed into the press section. New police bellies are there, blocking our route again. Can we go in and sit down? Bellies even heavier and more robust tell us there is no room for us inside: within the hallowed halls of the convention segregation is being practiced against four or five white males, who have had the effrontery to come without ties, a mixed band of long-haired and hairless, with a few beards thrown in. After long discussions, we are allowed to go in and sit down. I gather, from the fatigue which has just overwhelmed me, that what I am witnessing is a resounding lie, voluptuous for those who make their living from it. I hear the numbers being announced: they are counting the votes cast by New Jersey and adding them to those cast by Minnesota: never very good at arithmetic, I am amazed that this science is used to choose a President. Finally triumph and pandemonium—their triumph—Humphrey is nominated. The bellies have chosen a representative. This unmad madness, screaming mauve songs, gaudy but grey, this inordinate lie of talking bellies, you have seen and heard its pale reflections on your television screens.

I have an urge to go outside and touch a tree, graze in the grass, screw a goat, in short do what I'm used to doing.

A few hours before going to the convention, where our free and easy manner has petrified the police and made them suspicious, we have taken part in the Peace March organized by David Dellinger in Grant Park. Thousands of young people were there, peacefully listening to Phil Ochs sing and to others talk; we were covered with flowers. A symbolic march set off in the direction of the slaughterhouse. A first row of blacks, then behind them, in rows of eight abreast, anyone who cared to join the demonstration. No one got very far: more bellies charged, firing tear gas at the young people. Trucks filled with armed soldiers drove endlessly back and forth through the streets of Chicago.

To the Hippies

Hippies, young people of the demonstration, you no longer belong to America, which has moreover repudiated you. Hippies with long hair, you are making America's hair curl. But you, between earth and sky, are the beginning of a new continent, an Earth of Fire rising strangely above, or hollowed out below, what once was this sick country—an earth of fire first and, if you like, an earth of flowers. But you must begin, here and now, another continent.

Fourth Day: The Day of the Revolver

Is it necessary to write that everything is over? With Humphrey nominated, will Nixon be master of the world?

The Democratic Convention is closing its doors. The police, here as elsewhere, will be less brutal, if it can. And is the revolver, in turn, going to speak?

The Democratic Convention has made its choice, but where, in what drunken bar, did a handful of democrats make their decision?

Across from the Hotel Hilton, again in Grant Park, a sumptuous happening. The youth have scaled a bronze horse on which is seated a bronze rider. On the horse's mane—whose head is bowed as if in sleep—young blacks and whites are brandishing black flags and red flags. A burning youth, which I hope will burn all its bridges; it is listening, attentive and serious, to a Presidential candidate who was not invited to the convention: Dick Gregory. Gregory is inviting his friends—there are four or five thousand of them in the park—to come home with him. They won't let us march to the Amphitheater, he declares, but there's no law that says you can't come on down to my house for a party. But first, he says, the four or five policemen who have stupidly allowed themselves to be hemmed in by the crowd of demonstrators must be freed. With great wit and humor, Gregory explains how the demonstrators are to walk, no more than two or three abreast, keeping on the sidewalk and obeying all traffic lights. He says that the march may be long and difficult, for he lives in a house in the black ghetto of South Chicago. He invites the two or three beaten delegates (that is, McCarthy delegates) to head the march, for the police whose job it will be to stop the march may be less brutal with them.

We walk along a hedge of armed soldiers.

At long last America is moving, because the hippies have shaken their shoulders.

The Democratic Convention is closing its doors.

A few random thoughts, as usual:

America is a heavy island, too heavy: it would be good, for America, and for the world, for it to be demolished, for it to be reduced to powder.

The danger for America is not Mao's *Thoughts:* it is the proliferation of cameras.

So far as I know, there were no scientists among the demonstrators: is intelligence stupid, or science too easy?

The policemen are made of rubber: their muscles are of hard rubber; the convention itself was pure rubber: Chicago is made of rubber that chews chewing gum; the policemen's thoughts are made out of soft rubber, Mayor Daley of wet rubber. . . .

As we are leaving the Democratic Convention, a young policeman looks at me. Our gazes are already a settling of scores: he has understood that I am the enemy, but not one of the policemen is aware of the natural but invisible road, like that of drugs, which has led me, underground or via the route of heaven, into the United States, although the State Department refused me a visa to enter the country.

Too many star-spangled flags: here, as in Switzerland, a flag in front of every house. America is Switzerland flattened out by a steamroller. Lots of young blacks: will the delegates' hot dogs or the revolver bullet murder the democrats before it is too late?

Fabulous happening. Hippies! Glorious hippies, I address my final appeal to you: children, flower children in every country, in order to fuck all the old bastards who are giving you a hard time, unite, go underground if necessary in order to join the burned children of Vietnam.

—*Translated by Richard Seaver*   [November, 1968]

The Coming of the Purple Better One

by William Burroughs

Saturday August 24, 1968: Arrive O'Hare Airport, Chicago. First visit in 26 years. Last in Chicago during the war where I exercised the trade of exterminator.

"Exterminator. Got any bugs lady?"

"The tools of your trade," said the customs officer touching my cassette recorder.

Driving in from the airport note empty streets newspapers in the wind a ghost town. Taxi strike bus strike doesn't account for the feeling of nobody here. Arrive Sheraton Hotel where I meet Jean Genet. He is dressed in an old pair of corduroy pants no jacket no tie. He conveys a remarkable impact of directness confronting completely whoever he talks to.

Sunday August 25: Out to the airport for the arrival of McCarthy. An estimated fifteen thousand supporters there to welcome him mostly young people. Surprisingly few police. Whole scene touching and ineffectual particularly in retrospect of subsequent events.

Monday August 26: We spend Monday morning in Lincoln Park talking to the Yippies. Jean Genet expresses himself succinctly on the subject of America and Chicago.

"I can't wait for this city to rot. I can't wait to see weeds growing through empty streets."

May not have to wait long. Police in blue helmets many of them wearing one-way dark glasses stand around heavy and sullen. One of them sidles up to me while I am recording and says: "You're wasting film."

Of course the sound track does bring the image track on set so there is not all that much difference between a recorder and a camera.

Another sidles up right in my ear. "They're talking about brutality. They haven't seen anything yet."

The cops know they are the heavies in this show and they are going to play it to the Hilton.

Monday night to the Convention Hall. Cobblestone streets smell of coal gas and stockyards. No place to park. Some citizen rushes out screaming. "You can't park here! I'll call the police! I'll have your car towed away!"

Through line after line of police showing our credentials and finally click ourselves in. Tinny atmosphere of carnivals and penny arcades without the attractions. The barkers are there but no freaks no sideshows no scenic railways.

Up to Lincoln Park where the cops are impartially clubbing Yippies newsmen and bystanders. After all there are no innocent bystanders. What are they doing here in the first place? The worst sin of man is to be born.

Tuesday August 27: The Yippies are stealing the show. I've had about enough of the convention farce without humor barbed wire and cops around a lot of nothing.

Jean Genet says: "It is time for writers to support the rebellion of youth not only with their words but with their presence as well."

It is time for every writer to stand by his words.

Lincoln Park Tuesday night: The Yippies have assembled at the epicenter of Lincoln Park. Bonfires, a cross, the demonstrators singing *The Battle Hymn of the Republic.*

He hath loosed the fateful lightning of his terrible swift sword.

"Wet a handkerchief and put it in front of your face. . . . Don't rub your eyes."

He is trampling out the vintage where the grapes of wrath are stored.

"Keep your cool and stay seated."

He has sounded forth the trumpet that shall never call retreat.

"Sit or split."

At this point I look up to see what looks like a battalion of World War I tanks converging on the youthful demonstrators and I say, "What's with you Martin you wig already?"

He just looks at me and says: "Fill your hand stranger." And hauls out an old rusty police force from 1910 and I take off across Lincoln Park tear-gas canisters raining all around me. From a safe distance I turn around to observe the scene and see it is a 1917 gas attack from the archives. I make the lobby of the Lincoln Hotel where the medics are treating gas victims. The Life-Time photographer is laid out on a bench medics washing his eyes out. Soon he recovers and begins taking pictures of everything in sight. Outside the cops prowl about like aroused tomcats.

Wednesday August 28: Rally in Grant Park to organize a march to the Amphitheatre. I am impressed by the organization that has been built here. Many of the marshals wear crash helmets and blue uniforms. It is difficult to distinguish them from the police. Clearly the emergent Yippie uniform is crash helmet, shoulder pads, and aluminum jockstrap. I find myself in the second row of the nonviolent march feeling rather out of place since nonviolence is not exactly my program. We shuffle slowly forward the marshals giving orders over the loudspeaker.

"Link arms. . . . Keep five feet between rows. . . . You back there watch what you're smoking. . . . Keep your cool. . . . This is a nonviolent march. . . . You can obtain tear-gas rags from the medics. . . ."

We come to a solid line of cops and there is a confab between the cops and the marshals. For one horrible moment I think they will let us march five bloody miles and me with blisters already from walking around in the taxi strike. No. They won't let us march. And being a nonviolent march and five beefy cops for every marcher and not being equipped with bulldozers it is an impasse. I walk around the park recording and playing back, a beauteous evening calm and clear vapor trails over the lake youths washing tear gas out of their eyes in the fountain. Spot of bother at the bridge where the pigs and national guardians have stationed themselves like Horatio but in far greater numbers.

So out to the Convention Hall where they don't like the look of us despite our electronic credentials being in order and call a Secret Service man for clearance. We get in finally and I play back the Grant Park recordings and boo Humphrey to while away the time as they count votes to the all too stupid and obvious conclusion.

What happened Wednesday night when the guard dogs broke loose again is history.

I have described the Chicago police as left over from 1910 and in a sense this is true. Daley and his nightstick authority date back to turn-of-the-century ward politics. They are anachronisms and they know it. This I think accounts for the shocking ferocity of their behavior. Jean Genet, who has considerable police experience, says he never saw such expressions before on allegedly human faces. And what is the phantom fuzz screaming from Chicago to Berlin, from Mexico City to Paris? "We are REAL REAL REAL!!! REAL as this NIGHTSTICK!" As they feel, in their dim animal way, that reality is slipping away from them. Where are all the old cop sets, Clancy? Eating your apple twirling your club the sky goes out against your back. Where are the men you sent up who came around to thank you when they got out? Where is the gold watch the chief gave you when you cracked the Norton case? And where are your pigeons, Clancy? You used to be quite a pigeon fancier remember the feeling you got sucking arrests from your pigeons soft and evil like the face of your whiskey priest brother? Time to turn in your cop suit to the little Jew who will check it off in his book. Won't be needing you after Friday.

The youth rebellion is a worldwide phenomenon that has not been seen before in history. I don't believe they will calm down and be ad execs at thirty as the establishment would like to believe. Millions of young people all over the world are fed up with shallow unworthy authority running on a platform of bullshit. There are five questions that any platform in America must answer not with hot air but with change on a basic level.

1. Vietnam: As I recollect the French were in there quite some years and finally pulled out to repeat the same mistake in Algeria. History tells us this is a war that cannot be won. Perhaps it is not intended to be won but merely as provocation and pretext to start a war with Red China. Looks like some folks figure the only answer to this mess is blow the set up and start over. May have happened several times before what we call history going back about 10,000 years and the human actor being about 500,000 years on set, give a little take a little, so what was he doing for the 480,000 years unaccounted for? If we have come from stone axes to nuclear weapons in ten thousand years this may well have happened before. Brion Gysin has put forward the theory that a nuclear disaster in what is now the Gobi Desert destroyed the civilization that had made such a disaster possible and incidentally gave rise to what he terms "Albino freaks," namely the white race. Any case if we don't want to see the set go America should get out of Vietnam and reach an immediate agreement with Red China.

2. *Alienated youth:* The only establishment that is supported by its young people is Red China. And that is why the State Department does not want Americans to go there. They do not want Americans to realize that any establishment offering young people anything at all will get their support. Because the western establishments are not offering anything. They have nothing to declare but their bad intentions. Let them come all the way out in the open with their bad intentions, declare a Secret Service overwhelming majority, and elect a purple-assed baboon to the Presidency. At this dark hour in the history of the penny arcade, Wednesday troubling all our hearts, the aggressive Southern ape suh fought for you in the perilous Kon-Tiki Room of the Sheraton.

3. *Black Power:* Find out what they want and give it to them. All the signs that mean anything indicate that the blacks were the original inhabitants of this planet. So who has a better right to it?

4. *Our police and judicial system:* What would happen if all the cotton-picking, stupid-assed, bible-belt laws passed by bourbon-soaked state legislators were actually enforced together with all federal and city laws? If every businessman who chiseled on his income tax by one dollar was caught and jailed? If every drug offender was caught and jailed? If every violator of all the laws penalizing sex acts between consenting adults in private was caught and jailed? How many people would be in jail? I think 30,000,000 is a very conservative estimate. And how many cops would it take to detect and arrest these criminals? And how many guards to keep them confined? And how many judges parole officers and court personnel to process them? And how much money would this cost?

Fix yourself on 30,000,000 violators in vast internee camps all united to scream with the inflexible authority of one big mouth. "We want gymnasiums! Libraries! Swimming pools! We want golf courses! Country clubs! Theatres!"

And with every concession they scream for MORE! MORE! MORE!

"The internee delegation in a meeting with the President today demanded as a prerequisite for any talks the 'immediate and unconditional removal of the so-called guards.' "

Senator Bradly rose in the Senate to question the wisdom of setting up what he termed "a separate state of dubious loyalty at the very core of our nation."

"We want tanks! Planes! Submarines!"

"An ominous atmosphere smogged the capital today as peace talks with the internee delegation bogged down."

"We want a space program! We want an atom bomb!"

"The number of internees is swelling ominously . . . forty million . . . fifty million . . . sixty million . . . 'America is a thin shell around a pulsing core of sullen violators.' "

"Today the internees exploded their first atom bomb described as 'a low yield nuclear device.' "

"It may be low yield but it's right on our back porch," said Senator Bradly plaintively.

"Today the internees signed a mutual assistance pact with Red China." As regards our judicial system there are three alternatives:

A. Total enforcement. Is either of our distinguished candidates for the Presidency prepared to support the computerized police terror that such enforcement would entail?

B. An admission that the judicial system is a farce and the laws not really intended to be enforced except in a haphazard sporadic fashion. Is either candidate prepared to make such an admission?

C. Get some bulldozers in here and clean out all this garbage and let no state saloon reel to his drunken feet and start braying about state rights. Is either candidate prepared to advocate the only sensible alternative?

5. *The disappearing dollar:* 1959 Minutes To Go: "I'm absolutely weak I can only just totter home the dollar has collapsed." Figuring ten years time lag the dollar should collapse in 1969. There is something wrong with the whole concept of money. It takes always more and more to buy less and less. Money is like junk. A dose that fixes on Monday won't fix on Friday. We are being swept with vertiginous speed into a worldwide inflation comparable to what happened in Germany after World War I. The rich are desperately stockpiling gold, diamonds, antiques, paintings, medicines, food, liquor, tools and weapons. Any platform that does not propose the basic changes necessary to correct these glaring failures is a farce. What is happening in America today is something that has never happened before in recorded history: *Total confrontation.* The lies are obvious. The machinery is laid bare. All Americans are being shoved by the deadweight of a broken control machine right in front of each other's faces. Like it or not they cannot choose but see and hear each other. How many Americans will survive a total confront?

In Last Resort the Truth

The scene is Grant Park Chicago 1968. A full-scale model of *The Mayflower* with American flags for sails has been set up. A. J. in his Uncle Sam suit steps to a mike on the deck.

"Ladies and gentlemen it is my coveted privilege and deep honor to introduce to you the distinguished Senator and former Justice of the Supreme Court Homer Mandrill known to his many friends as the Purple Better One. No doubt most of you are familiar with a book called *African Genesis* written by Robert Ardrey a native son of Chicago and I may add a true son of America. I quote from Mr. Ardrey's penetrating work: 'When I was a boy in Chicago I attended the Sunday School of a neighborhood Presbyterian church. I recall our Wednesday-night meetings with the simplest nostalgia. We would meet in the basement. There would be a short prayer and a shorter benediction. And we would turn out all the lights and in total darkness hit each other with chairs.'

"Mr. Ardrey's early training tempered his character to face and make known the truth about the origins and nature of mankind. 'Not in innocence and not in Asia was mankind born. The home of our fathers was the African highland on a sky-swept savannah glowing with menace. The most significant of all our gifts was the legacy bequeathed us by our immediate forebears a race of terrestrial, flesh-eating, killer apes. . . . Raymond A. Dart of the University of Johannesburg was the strident voice from South Africa that would prove the southern ape to be the human ancestor. Dart put forward the simple thesis that Man emerged from the anthropoid background for one reason only: because he was a killer. A rock, a stick, a heavy bone was to our ancestral killer ape the margin of survival. . . . And he said that since we had tried everything else we might in last resort try the truth. . . . Man's original nature imposes itself on any human solution.'

"The aggressive southern ape suh, glowing with menace, fought your battles on the perilous veldts of Africa 500,000 years ago. Had he not done so you would not be living here in this great city in this great land of America raising your happy families in peace and prosperity. Who more fitted to represent our glorious Simian heritage than Homer Mandrill himself a descendant of that illustrious line? Who else can restore to this nation the spirit of true conservatism that imposes itself on any human solution? What candidate is better fitted for the highest office in the land at a time when this great republic is threatened by enemies foreign and domestic? Actually there can be only one candidate: the Purple Better One your future President."

To *The Battle Hymn of the Republic* an American flag is drawn aside revealing a purple-assed mandrill (thunderous applause). Led to the mike by Secret Service men in dark suits that bulge suggestively here and there the Purple Better One blinks in bewilderment.

The Technician mixes a bicarbonate of soda and belches into his hand. He is sitting in front of three instrument panels, one labeled P.A. for Purple Ass, one labeled A. for Audience, a third P. for Police. (Crude experiments with rhesus monkeys have demonstrated that small currents of electricity passed through electrodes into the appropriate brain areas can elicit any emotional or visceral response: rage, fear, sexuality, vomiting, sleep, defecation. No doubt with further experimentation these techniques will be perfected and electro-magnetic fields will supersede the use of actual electrodes imbedded in the brain.) He adjusts dials as Homer's mouth moves to a dubbed speech from directional mikes. The features of other candidates are projected onto Homer's face from a laser installation across the park so that he seems to embody and absorb them all.

"At this dark hour in the history of the republic there are grave questions troubling all our hearts. I pledge myself to answer these questions. One question is the war in Vietnam which is not only a war but a holy crusade against the godless forces of international communism. And I say to you if these forces are not contained they will engulf us all." (Thunderous applause.) "And I flatly accuse the administration of criminal diffidence in the use of atomic weapons. Are we going to turn a red white and blue ass to the enemy?" (No! No! No!) "Are we going to fight through to victory at any cost?" (Yes! Yes! Yes!) "I say to you we will win if it takes ten years. We will win if we have to police every blade of grass and every gook in Vietnam." (Thunderous applause.) "And after that we are going to wade in and take care of Chairman Mao and his gang of cutthroat slave drivers." (Thunderous applause.) "And if any country shall open its mouth to carp at the great American task well a single back-handed blow from our mighty Seventh Fleet will silence that impotent puppet of Moscow and Peking.

"Another question is so-called Black Power. I want to go on record as saying I am a true friend to all good Darkies everywhere." (To wild applause a picture of the world-famous statue in Natchitoches Louisiana flashes on screen. As you all know this statue shows a good old Darkie with his hat in his hand and is dedicated to All Good Darkies Everywhere.) Homer's voice chokes with emotion and tears drip off his purple nose. "Why when I was fourteen years old our old yard Nigrah Rover Jones got runned over by a laundry truck and I cried my decent American heart out. And I have a deep conviction that the overwhelming majority of Nigrahs in this country is good Darkies like Rover Jones. However we know that there is in this country today another kind of Nigrah and as long as there is a gas pump handy we all know the answer to that." (Thunderous applause.) "And I would like to say this to followers of the Jewish religion. Always remember we like nice Jews with Jew jokes. As for Nigger-loving communistic agitating Sheenies well just watch yourself Jew boy or we'll cut the rest of it off." (That's telling em Homer.) What about the legalization of marijuana? "Marijuana! Marijuana! Why that's deadlier than cocaine. And what are we going to do about the vile America-hating hoodlums who call themselves hippies, Yippies, and chippies? We are going to put this scum behind bars like the animals they are." (Thunderous applause.) "And I'll tell you something else. A bunch of queers, dope freaks, and degenerated dirty writers is living in foreign lands under the protection of American passports from the vantage point of which they do not hesitate to spit their filth on Old Glory. Well we're going to pull the passports off those dope freaks." (The Technician pushes a sex button and the Simian begins to masturbate.) "Bring them back here and teach them to act like decent Americans." (The Simian emisses, hitting the lens of a Life-Time photographer.) "And I denounce as Communist-inspired the rumors that the dollar collapsed in 1959. I pledge myself to turn the clock back to 1899 when a silver dollar bought a steak dinner and a good piece of ass." (Thunderous applause as a plane writes September 17, 1899, across the sky in smoke.) "I have heard it said that this is a lawless nation that if all the laws in this land were truly enforced we would have thirty percent of the population in jail and the remaining seventy percent on the cops. I say to you if there is infection in this great land it must be cut out by the roots. We will not fall into slack-assed permissive anarchism. I pledge myself to uphold the laws of America and to enforce these hollowed statutes on all violators regardless of race, color, creed or position." (Thunderous applause.) "We will overcome all our enemies foreign and domestic and stay armed to the teeth for years, decades, centuries."

A phalanx of blue-helmeted cops shoulder through the crowd. They stop in front of the deck. The lead cop looks up at A. J. and demands: "Let's see your permits for that purple-assed son of a bitch."

"Permits? We don't have any permits. We don't have to show you any stinking permits. You are talking suh to the future President of America."

The lead cop takes a slip of paper from his shirt pocket and reads MUNICIPAL CODE OF CHICAGO . . . Chapter 98, Section 14: "No person shall permit any dangerous animal to run at large, nor lead any such animal with a chain, rope, or other appliance, whether such animal be muzzled or unmuzzled, in any public way or public place." He folds the paper and shoves it back into his shirt pocket. He points at the Purple Better One. "It's dangerous and we got orders to remove it."

A cop steps forward with a net. The Technician shoves the rage dial all the way up. Screaming, farting, snarling, the Simian leaps off the deck onto the startled officer who staggers back and goes down thrashing wildly on the ground while his fellow pigs stand helpless and baffled not daring to risk a shot for fear of killing their comrade. Finally the cop heaves himself to his feet and throws off the Simian. Panting, bleeding, he stands there his eyes wild. With a scream of rage the Purple Better One throws himself at another patrolman who fires two panicky shots which miss the Simian and crash through a window of the Hilton in the campaign headquarters of a conservative Southern candidate. A photographer from The London *Times* is riddled with bullets by Secret Service men under the misconception he has fired from a gun concealed in his camera. The cop throws his left arm in front of his face. The Simian sinks his canines into the cop's arm. The cop presses his gun against the Simian's chest and pumps in four bullets. Homer Mandrill thuds to the bloody grass, ejaculates, excretes and dies. A. J. points a finger at the cop.

"Arrest that pig!" he screams. "Seize the assassin!"

A. J. was held in $100,000 bail which he posted in cash out of his pocket. Further disturbances erupted at the funeral when a band of vigilantes who call themselves the White Hunters attempted to desecrate the flag-draped body as it was carried in solemn procession through Lincoln Park on the way to its final resting place in Grant Park. The hoodlums were beaten off by A. J.'s guard of Korean Karate experts. The Daughters of the American Revolution who had gathered in front of the Sheraton to protest the legalization of marijuana were charged by police screaming, "Chippies! Chippies! Chippies!" And savagely clubbed to the sidewalk in a litter of diamonds, teeth, blood, mink stoles and handbags.

As the Simian was laid to rest under a silver replica of *The Mayflower* a statue of the Purple Better One in solid gold at the helm, A. J. called for five minutes of silent prayer in memory of our beloved candidate, "Cut down in Grant Park by the bullets of an assassin. . . . A Communistic Jew Nigger inflamed to madness by injections of marijuana. . . . The fact that the assassin had, with diabolical cunning, disguised himself as a police officer indicates the workings of a far-flung communistic plot the tentacles of which may reach into the White House itself. This foul crime shrieks to high heaven. We will not rest until the higher-ups are brought to justice whoever and wherever they may be. I pledge myself to name a suitable and worthy successor. We will overcome. We will realize the aspirations and dreams that every American cherishes in his heart. The American dream can be must be and will be realized. I say to you that Grant Park will be a shrine for all future Americans. In the words of the all-American poet James Whitcomb Riley

'Freedom shall a while repair
'To dwell a weeping hermit there.' "

[November, 1968]

In a Pig's Eye

by John Sack

Be a Chicago pig policeman! Carry a pistol and sleep until noon! Zzz . . . Zzz. . . . On the other hand, he had arrived home at four in the morning, a little mote of CS tear gas still chewing at his throat like cayenne pepper or like sunburn on his shoulders, his Irish eyes still smarting, tired: the wounds of another night of shoving the scroungers from Lincoln Park. "Yippies again" or "Hippies again," he had muttered to Mama, slipping beneath the sheets with the yellow rose of Texas pattern, the $16.92 blanket, the Cross, and hearing his wife answer, *"Ish,"* the random syllable over and above which she had nothing to say of Chicago's disgraceful new visitors. A minute later, and Chicago policeman number 14020 was sleeping—*zzz.*

Now it was twelve noon and "Mama" was in the kitchen to cook scrambled eggs and venison, the kids having had Cheerios already and Winnie a biscuit-bone—*How about Lady! Lassie! Brownie!* the kids all had yelled at him when the puppy arrived, but 14020 had answered, "Those names are so *ordinary.*" A row of the children's photographs, tinted, like *Désirée,* the movie, in purples and pinks, hung in his living room, once a year the Graphic man coming to hang up a bedsheet and wheedle, "Now, let's have a smile!" Behind glass in his dining room, like a Delft set in a whatnot, was 14020's family library, where what he loved best was *The Best-Loved Poems of the American People.* In the event of subversion one could probably break the glass with an ice hammer to listen to America singing. *Listen my children and you shall hear*—a cobblestone bridge and a chiaoscuro horse and rider had risen in 14020's mind's eye on reading this. *In fourteen hundred ninety-two*— *If a task is once begun*— *Lord, let me live like a regular man*— *Oh, say, can you see, by the dawn's early light*—a dewy distillate of the atmosphere that any American boy breathes from birth. Once in school the future patrolman had gotten a D in English from his nattily dressed teacher, rhapsodic quoter of Shelley, toucher of boys' hairless elbows, suspected fairy ("If you stay after school," his friends had advised him merrily, "you'll get an A")—had gotten a D for electing to memorize poetry from *The Best-Loved Poems.* The girls in class had cunningly chosen things from Shelley, but *Hail to thee, blithe birdie* wasn't his coffee-cup and 14020 had sung instead of the land where the venison grows. "*Oh,*" he had begun—"*Oh the north countree is a hard countree,*" old Momo at the front of the room pricking up his delicate ears—"*Oh, tough as a steak was Yukon Jake, Hard-boiled as a picnic egg! He washed his shirt in the Klondike dirt, And drank his rum by the keg,*" a weak electrical impulse going down the Teach's elegant fingers and translating into a "D" at his manicured nails. What the hell—14020 wouldn't be going to Oxford anyway, but to police academy.

Reader, if you would know the psychology of Chicago's normative fuzz, get a copy of *The Best-Loved Poems of the American People* (Garden City, 1936). Get everything else whose tattered and torn bindings bear the same Dewey decimal number and shred 'em, pestle 'em into a powder, wet 'em into a paste, water 'em into a pulp, and warm 'em inside a stove set at 98.6 degrees. And—*voilà,* you've done it, there you've got a pot of Chicago copkopf, homemade psyche, the grey stuff of the second city's blue, a Cream of Wheat of American attitudes that is 192 years old. So thick yet so easily permeable is this oatmeal that no Irish or Polish farmer's heart is actually needed to pump blood to its farthermost cells. Seventy to eighty times a minute a new infusion of oxygen brings life to the most cachectic of America's tried and truisms—*Clean behind your ears*— *Mabel, Mabel, if you're able*— *Do not write "fuck" on your forehead*— *Spare the rod and spoil the child*— *What if your sister marries one*— *Cross at the green not in between*— *Eat your spinach*— *Bathe*— the neat antimacassar rules of the lower middle class: a class, remember, which, with its social inferiors, is a full ninety percent of America's people. Flower children, wearers of wampum, you in omega symbols and ankh crosses, whatever: alas, the different drummer you march to plays in a small chamber orchestra, the hundreds of millions hum the same respectable Oms as Chicago's police. And if these police, at times, tend to forget which are society's laws and which are society's manners—well, would you blame them?

"John! Breakfast is ready, John!" Mama was calling upstairs and 14020 arose, shaved, slipped into his blue police trousers with the Roosevelt era width, buckled on his pistol, nightstick, handcuffs, and Mace, breakfasted on venison, left. "Be careful, John," his wife called after him, as always, and 14020 became another of the visored thousands that the young people knew as "Pigs."

One day during the Convention, a squad of Chicago policemen sat around one of those outdoor tables, X's of redwood beneath it, bolts as big as I-beam rivets, that was a stone's throw—no, a bit farther—from the pasture where the young people, or Yippies, the papers called them, lay in Lincoln Park. Comers and goers to this party of finger cymbalists, *Rat*-readers, rappers, tambourine players, and catnappers went by these ten policemen often, and even their spinster aunts in Kansas would not have cluck-clucked so severely at the passing scene as did these 180-to-220-pound patrolmen. "Hmf! I don't think she should be in a miniskirt," a squad member said as a girl walked by. "Take it to the farm and cultivate it," another snickered, at a Yippie with a pumpkin-colored helmet where all decent people wore a fedora. "*That woman*—" another gasped as a girl in a sweater passed them. "*She doesn't have a brassiere on!*" "Patrio— what do they call it? Patriotism," another of the tittle-tattles said, as boys and girls with a blood-spattered flag of Chicago walked by. "Love of your country. Hmf!"

Lying on the grass (for there were no wastebaskets now in the park, the young people had built up council fires in several and Chicago had removed them all)—littering the area around the picnic table were the *Seed, Militant,* Yippie and other periodicals that the squad had been reading not so much to understand the visitors in Lincoln Park as to have chapters and verses by which to censure them. Typical of these throwaways was a Yippie thing some of whose eighteen demands were so blandly sensible that the Democratic platform itself may have adopted them, *9. A conservation program* [*for*] *preserving our natural resources. 13. A program* [*for*] *cable television.* Other demands had a pedigree in philosophy's history as old as Diogenes, *15. We believe that people should fuck all the time, anytime,* or a partisan in America of the 1960's as respectable as Erich Fromm, *7. The Abolition of pay housing, pay media, pay transportation, pay food, pay education, pay clothing, pay medical help, and pay toilets.* But the joyous forms in which the Yippies put these ideas had acted as rubber stoppers in the policemen's decorous ears, denying all ingress of content. "Yeah, I saw that thing," a Jewish patrolman at the picnic table was telling another. "It said everybody should eff. *You* know," he said, turning to a woman in plain clothes with a LOVE charm between her great bosoms, a policewoman who lowered her eyes demurely to indicate to the squad: she knew. "It isn't so bad if you think those words. But to print them!"

"Any time. Any place. Anyone you want," an Irish patrolman said in dismay.

"What amazes me," the Jewish one went on, "they don't want to work! They want everything handed to them! Shazam! A dinner. Shazam! A car. Shazam! A trip to Miami. But what do they do to earn these?"

"Like they say," the Irishman again. "Some people got to plant food and some people got to dig ditches." For after all, doesn't it say in *The Best-Loved Poems of the American People,*

> *If you want to fill a place*
> *And be useful to the race,*
> *Just get up and take a brace—*
> *Do it now!*

In late afternoon, a Yippie girl on a bicycle came by this redwood table to cry at Chicago's constabulary, "*Pigs!*" And crouching over the handlebars she then whizzed away in Tour de France posture in case the police escalated by hurling a .38 pistol at her pretty brunette head, or firing it. At other times the breeze brought to the squad's ears the insulting cries of "*Soo . . . ie* " and "*Oink oink oink!*" At these, the squad of police chuckled and kept playing hearts. It has been alleged that the suid metaphors got, at last, under the policemen's skins, provoking them to vengeance on Wednesday—absurd. *For sticks and stones may break my bones but names will tra-la la-la*—a worthy old American axiom, that, and if Longfellow's authorship can be shown it might run under the "Inspiration" category in the next, or forty-seventh, printing, of *The B.L.P. of the A.P.* Accordingly, it had a lifetime tenure in every cop's seat of reason, and anyhow: all in the squad could see where in Lincoln Park the pigs really groveled, for whose toes hadn't been washed in one half week? "They sleep on the grass and they call *us* the pigs," an officer at the picnic table said, not at all angry but only amazed at man's great capacity to deceive himself.

Nor did sticks and stones themselves, plastic bags of water, bottles, any of these rile the policemen beyond all endurance as they arched across the stars at eleven that night, the Lincoln Park closing time. "Careful. Here comes a big one," a man in the squad would say, as innocent of indignation as a little kid in Michigan's surf: for he sensibly jests at Budweiser cans who has felt switchblade knives and 22-caliber lead. At midnight when it moved out in a skirmish line, its CS tear gas ahead, its German shepherds on leashes, its CS-infested park as eerie as Spotsylvania in the floodlights of fire trucks, the squad of Chicago police was as casual as G.I.'s on a pick-up-the-cigarettes call, shuffling, chewing their gum, making little jokes like "Push me on into battle, Sergeant." Of anger, the police had as little as the "angry ocean" has whenever it beats on a seawall or shipwrecks a sailor. Spit on the flag, holler "Up yours" to his sister, rape a mother superior, these were the deeds to make an American angry: but a misdemeanor in Lincoln Park was just another day, another dollar. Be wary of the pathetic fallacy: the throw of the tear gas or the heavy fall of the nightstick is not necessarily a passionate act. At one in the morning as the last weeping trespasser fled to the streets of Old Town, the squad was asking serenely, "What do you say? Now? Thank you, Sergeant! Light 'em up!" And out of its blue pockets came the L&Ms and the Panatellas.

Insouciant the police could be, for they recognized that the challenge to their values arose from a too tiny minority of America to pay much attention to. Conversely, the challengers in Lincoln Park had to rage against the "*Facist*" and "*SS* " bullyboys or else resign themselves to the terrible truth that Chicago's police did represent the will of Chicago's people. To realize this, the young people only had to listen in Lincoln Park to the noisy tribunes of the millions of Americans who surrounded them, as millions of white corpuscles surround a germ. Men in their undershirts, women in Shalimar perfume, soldiers in Vietnam insignia:

"All your brothers and sisters are being killed there and you're talking against them!"

"If one American dies by *any* cause, *any* cause, you ought to support him!"

"You people got no right to wave a Communist flag in the United States of America! Because they got a right to cut you down, just like in *Doctor Zhivago!*"

"I'm proud of this country, boy! This is the greatest country in the world!"

"Get out of this country!"

Indeed, the young people just had to look at their subconscious selves to see, even there, the whalebone ethics of America, much as their manifestos damned it. One afternoon, the most awful apprehensions of the cardplayers at the redwood table had really been set to materialize: as a Yippie boy whispered to another, "We got forty chicks who say they'll groove!" For forty girls had vowed to divest themselves of Levis and society's trammels to participate today in a Yippie "ball-in," appropriately in the ball field of Lincoln Park—forty suntanned couples had pledged themselves to roll in the outfield as bare and as gloriously brown as the other team's discarded mitts. Revolution! And equity as well as philosophy was on Yippie's side: society would be monstrous if pretty girls can be tear-gassed and billy-sticked in a public park but cannot be equally and oppositely loved in commiseration. At one o'clock the organizers of this baseball diamond ball—one, a Yippie boy with glasses both of whose hinges had been supplanted by thick wads of adhesive tape, the other with a chain of pop-tops as a brim to a Rip Van Winkle hat—were passing among the Yippie girls to announce: it was starting time, the hour to put their pelvises where all their mouths were. "You people start moving to the ball park," the organizers said. Titters of "You go ahead. We'll watch," were all they heard until, with a heavy heart, the Yippie boys realized that the ball-in had dwindled to a game of one-o-cat and Rip Van Winkle would have to go it alone with his girl friend under a black oak. "We're going to start it here," he told her. "You're the unlucky victim."

"Thanks a lo . . . t."

Rip sat beside her to whisper in her earringed ear.

"*Oh,*" the girl answered him. "Blush blush!"

Rip kissed her prettily on her milky cheek.

"Oh, where is my mo . . . ther?"

Rip looked hurt as a boy from the Aardvark theatre went by and gave her a promotional piece.

"*Bob Dylan. Don't Look Back,*" she started to read cheerfully to Rip Van Winkle. "*So memorable that it rings in the mind for a long time afterwards! The picture is a must for Dylan fans! A fascinating picture! You know, we should go see it. . . .*" A virgin, the unlucky victim had fooled her mother and father that her reputation would be safe today at a girl friend's home in Chicago. Her father worked at Chicago's waterworks, where the rioters' fires in April had lowered the water pressure to where citizens couldn't bathe and raised her father's blood pressure to where he was voting for Wallace. Whenever the victim argued with him he merely said, "Eat your food."

"Screw it," the Yippie boy with adhesive tape on his glasses said. "I'm going to split and go back to New York City. This is bombing out."

And out beyond the outfield fence the same virtuous squad of cops waited, alerted, ready to use their handcuffs to practice what the American people preached, what the Yippies themselves didn't dare to say they secretly believed.

Another afternoon, the young people swept from Lincoln Park to walk south to confront the enemy at his very castle, his GHQ downtown, his pigsty central. Had they chrysanthemums, the colorful boys and girls would have seemed to be en route to a football game as they yelled things like *"Two! Four! Six! Eight! We don't want a po-lice-state!"* At hotel doors the Democratic delegates sat in their wheelchairs, the Ringer's solution dripping from bottles into their arms, their pulse rates ten to twenty times a minute. "What do you think, John?" an Idaho lady asked her delegate husband as the young people passed.

"I think dammit! Look at him there—he hasn't washed his hair in a month!"

"Up against the wall," the young people shouted as they continued down State Street, some wearing beards, some doing Hopi dances, some saying oms. Outstanding among them in NBC and CBS's eyes was a Berkeley girl who sat pickaback on one sturdy boy after another, radiantly smiling, holding aloft a red flag of revolution—a girl in a khaki uniform, a full canteen on her pistol belt. Few of the young in Chicago would work as hard as this living incarnation of socialist realism to win to Revolution's banners the hearts and minds of the city's bourgeois police. *"Look me in the eye, officer,"* she would say bravely as they stood in ranks, confronting them as a sergeant might. "I'm sorry you work over-time today—*but I want to free the people! You know what I mean, don't you?"* Once, one of these patrolmen had really whispered back, "I'm with you, sister," the girl in khaki smiling angelically and stroking his Negro face. But there had been just one.

Already at pigsty central the police were in elbow-to-elbow ranks to safeguard its $50 windows and window displays of Cyclops' or the Statue of Liberty's fingerprints. Therefore it may seem strange that the pied piper whom the glassy eyes of NBC and CBS discovered at the very vanguard of that parade was plainly a Chicago cop, Patrolman Ray Walsh. True, it was excellent tactics to lead these potential troublemakers down a full three-and-a-half miles of State Street till their tired feet conspired with their fallacious sense of having accomplished things to add up into inertia. And to solace the scared pedestrians was an errand that Walsh could be proud of: even the deputy commander with his major's leaves, his electric megaphone, his eyes darting up and about like a Christian in the lion arena, even he had stopped to sympathize with a lady shopper who wanted to flee before the light was green, "Lady, what can I tell you?" And there was a need for Walsh to keep the revolution on its allotted half of the sidewalk. But even so, Walsh was ashamed to have to keep cadence with an army whose very guidons announced its arrant un-Americanism. *"This in my own city,"* he would say to other patrolmen. At night all week he would sit at home in blue police trousers and loden après-ski boots to watch on a color television screen as large as a Delacroix as young people fought his fellow officers in Chicago's streets and chanted at Walter Cronkite, *"The whole—world's—watching!"*

"Uh," his Irish wife had commented as she turned from the shameful

things on the television to Pall Malls and Schlitz on the sofa table. "And today I saw *nuns* there! I see the nuns doing that," she continued, "instead of going home and saying their rosary, my respect for them isn't so great!"

"It makes you kind of sick inside," Walsh had agreed, drinking some Schlitz. Before the week had ended he was to write to Daley about it:

Dear Mayor Daley!

After all your meticulous and wonderful plans to cater to the Democratic convention here, you have to have it spoiled by a handful of men, tyrannical, Communists, leading young men and women into fights and riots with my fellow brothers in Blue.

Mr. Mayor, I'm an ex-serviceman, I have seen action in Korea and it took a lot of will power to control myself from pulling down the Communist flag and everything it stood for. . . .

"It's enough to make you want to quit," he was saying now to Patrolman Steve Stukel. All of Walsh's squad was marching along with the Communists today.

"Twenty-five months over there," Vietnam, "and then I got to see this," Stukel replied. *I'm tired,* he was thinking, *I'm hot, if these people get violent, I'm going to get violent also!*

"I figure, ninety percent of these kids are on dope, one kind or another," said Patrolman George Wertz. He wondered aloud what the puissant chemical was that had fixed that radiant smile on the girl in khaki for lo! already two miles.

"Probably not LSD," Walsh said. "But something like Dexedrine, one of those barbiturates."

"Stimulants," Wertz corrected him.

"Stimulants," Walsh agreed.

"*Revolution! Now!*" the young people screamed as they walked the last mile and a half to the pigsty central. If it weren't for these malcontents it would be Wertz's weekend: a sunny day, a lovely day at Adventureland, no doubt, the cotton candy, the yellow taffy, the children all on the rolly—he called it—coaster saying "*Ooh*" and "*Ah*" ("Daddy," they had asked him once, "can we go on the big one?" "No," Wertz had answered, and they had never asked again). Or else because of the children—and Wertz couldn't blame them, really—today he could dedicate to the toilet seat, to moving it out of harm's way of the bathroom door. It was *crack* all morning and afternoon as the children went to "wash their hands" and *crack* in the other direction as the children went out again. Would you believe it? white, rose, green, beige, toilet seats he had bought at Sears, a dozen at least, $6 apiece, and *crack—crack—crack*—in two or three months apiece they had busted off their hinges, "Good morning, I want to buy another toilet seat." Putting on a spring to lift the seat automatically when the children forgot to—dangerous, one fast *crack* and there would go the water tank. Taking down the bathroom door—now *really,* and even making the door narrower was impractical, how then could he bring in his brand-new bathtub on some other weekend? Right now Wertz's expedient was to stand the toilet seat on the bathroom's mosaic floor for children to put on, take off, as required, like a Chicago telephone book at dinner. It was an indecent situation, though, one that a weekend with a blowtorch and some plumber's lead could rectify if these people were not marching on headquarters under a red banner and crying out, "*Revolution! Now!*"

"Is that a VC flag?" Walsh was saying now to Stukel.

"They got variations," Stukel answered sullenly.

In a way, it was saintly restraint above and beyond the call of their captains for Walsh, the Korean veteran, Stukel, the Vietnam veteran, and Wertz to walk so amenably under the flag of their enemy all afternoon, but duty required them to insure that the orderly flow on Chicago's sidewalks not be impeded by the march. "Now you people are going to be arrested—" even the deputy commander kept shouting it through his megaphone—"arrested, if you take up more than half of the sidewalk," his voice at times obsequious, at other times edgy, in its passion that not a moment be lost in any pedestrian's progress up State Street to Marshall Field's, to Walgreen's, to Ess & Abe Distinctive Ladies Apparel, to Pickard Heim Beauty School, to Loft's, to *Rosemary's Baby,* or to Frank-burger to buy a Choc-o-Shake. This above all, that the relish jar be delivered, that the dress advertising copy be ready by five, and that the $7.50 necktie be bought before the party tonight! One might argue it was these pedestrians that the young people had to revolt against if they're to get a sane society: with a husky cry of "Up against the wall, mothers and fathers," disobeying the deputy commander, snapping out in Zengakuren snakelines, using the flagpole like a Samurai sword and laying about, the boys and girls should have driven all those pedestrians into the lake to be eaten alive by alewives. But so few yards had they crawled from the taffeta bassinets of America that in these, the most meaningful of their encounters in August, instinctively the young people sided one hundred percent with Chicago's police. "Now remember," a boy with a red shirt repeated into his microphone, mistakenly. "We're not against the people who use this street! So walk on the inside of the sidewalk," repeating it, repeating it, until by the squeal of his amplified voice he had half hypnotized himself. "The *in*-side of the *side*-walk, the *in*-side of the *side*-walk," his words became the singsong of a Hadacol salesman as Chicago, unobstructed, hurried on to its sales counters, and to its blotter-covered desks.

"*Your mother sucks . . .*"

It was that false allegation, to Stukel, the Vietnam veteran, that in one split second shattered the unanimity of the young people, the pedestrians, and Chicago's police. *You little*—and Stukel now charged at that offender with his fist clenched, his pistol, his nightstick, his Mace undeployed.

Lewd literature, dirt under fingernails, hair under armpits, sandals where all nice people had gartered socks, even the flag of those odious insurgents who once had shot his helicopter down—all of this he had endured, even the cries of *"Pig"* had passed out of Stukel's other ear. *But nobody says that about my Mother,* not in America he doesn't! Grand old Mother who cooked him spaghetti, the Mother whom he had given on Mother's day a white rose and a dozen red—Mother! Mother who told him stories like, "Why are there just two pallbearers at a Polish funeral? *Because,"* Mother had blurted, too eager to get to the punch line to listen to Stukel's guesses—"because there are just two handles on a garbage can!" *How many buttons are missing today? Nobody knows but Mother. How many playthings are strewn in her way? Nobody knows but Mother.* Mother who is spelled mother, Mother who married dear old—*Take that! And that! And that! And that!*

But before Stukel could strike out to incite a melee on State Street, a sergeant took his shoulder and ordered him, "Forget it." Stukel tried to forget it. The great parade continued on past pigsty central's $50 windows with no nasty incidents—today, half of the sidewalk scrupulously open.

It was Wednesday that the city shook. No thumb in a lovable old Irish sergeant's eye or knee in his groin precipitated it: rather, it began when a boy abused a quite inanimate object. "In the later nineteenth century," Wells says in *The Outline of History* in a chapter on England and France and Germany, "it would have aroused far less hostility to have jeered at God than to have jeered at one of those strange beings, England or France or Germany." And at Wednesday afternoon's rally in Chicago when a speaker suddenly asked, *"What is going on over there,"* and fifteen thousand people looked to their left to see a boy lower a sheet of Nylanin fabric from a wooden pole, the irrepressible strains of *"Say, does that star-spangled banner still wave"* did surge through the Cream of Wheat subconscious of a squad of Chicago policemen, who instinctively charged. Lumber, pieces of asphalt, Rheingold, even a smoke bomb in a vegetable can drove the American patriots back, but it was an item wrapped in Saran material that was really to teach the Department to Know Their Enemy. Sailing ever so lightly toward the squad, splashing apart on the grass, emitting an indisputable odor, the Saran bag brought a mortally horrified shout to the lips of one patrolman. "It's a bag of shit! They're shitting in bags and throwing it!"

Word of this utmost atrocity spread in the ranks of Chicago's police as speedily as the slices did of Johnson's birthday cake at the other side of the city. "It is shit!"

"It is what?"

"It is shit! In the plastic bags!"

"It is shit? *Be careful, there is shit in the plastic bags!*"

"They are animals. . . ."

Two minutes later, the first of the afternoon and evening's one hundred casualties lay on Chicago's grass, a river of blood on his face as though it had cracked like an oyster shell. America's unseen audience who needed no ABC that night for its home entertainment was, perhaps, not aware: to most of Chicago's policemen the targets of their heavy clubs were not Americans but desecrators of America's red white and blue, not human beings but African shit-kicking chimpanzees. It was for America's most cherished beliefs—not for Nazi piggery, sadism, vengeance, relief—that the blows descended. For a young boy to resist, to argue, even to offer excuses—to Chicago's policemen this was intolerable, that a kid should persist in recalcitrance even as the very incarnations of Americanism arrayed themselves before him in a column of blue. Let those who would now demur that the vast majority of *"they"* whose blood was to splatter on Michigan Avenue were innocent citizens—let them carry that argument to where it is still needed: to Asia, where not an American rifle company or air wing couldn't use that caveat. But those who would now find fault with Chicago's police for their extremism in defense of Americanism shall have to vote for Cleaver this month to vote for a Presidential candidate who concurs. As for other Americans, the polls are that 78.7 percent of our neighbors do not consider that Chicago used excessive force. Understandably: it is for these citizens' gods the police did battle, beating the heads that the more hidden persuaders of American society had evidently not reached.

Yet even in most young people the values of the middle classes had trickled. All secondhand was their revolution, rags and textbook tags out of other people's risings in 1848, 1917, the 1930's: cries of "Scab" in support of strikers who only wanted in on the gravy, barricades of Volkswagens that the police could walk by, wallpaper newspapers with no Chicago walls to plaster them on, and automobile honks of "Hell no—We won't go" which were a simple inversion of "Algérie—Française." All of these and Pamplona's bravado of being as close to the bulls as possible even as you're running away. But most of these summer vacationers, of Cheerios had their bones been built: and even the smiling girl in khaki, radiant waver of red, revolutionary extraordinary, could be seen in Chicago as Humphrey began his "I proudly accept . . ." speech and as a thousand voters of the future fled up the avenue from CS clouds—be seen setting against the sneezing, wheezing, weeping tide of humanity to get to a truck with the words, Good Humor. The smiling girl asked there, "Do you have a chocolate fudge cake?"

"No. We only have Popsicles."

"I wanted a chocolate fudge cake."

"Popsicles is all we have."

"No kind of ice cream, then?"

"Nothing but Popsicles."

"*Would you believe it,*" a boy going by remarked. "We're running from tear gas and she's buying Popsicles. The essence of capitalism!"

Reportedly they are now radicalized. Ten, fifteen, twenty years, the theory is, and these boys and girls will be out carrying rifles in America's own Sierra Maestras. Maybe. Let us hope so, anyhow. But the Chicago that has radicalized many has reactionalized twice as many, and these people are mighty not only in numbers but in nightsticks, pistols, CS, armored vehicles, atomic bombs, and, as Chicago teaches, in their readiness to use them—and these people in November vote. Humphrey was nominated and undermined in Chicago, and Nixon will be elected if Super-Nixon allows it: and will become the fifth President to win immortality on Rushmore, in granite with the great ones. Washington at Valley Forge, Jefferson the egalitarian, Lincoln born in a Western cabin, Roosevelt with his stick—all embodied in their physical flesh the very essence of America of their generation. And now Nixon the organization man, Rotary luncheon speaker, adapter, knower of Yukon poetry, owner of dogs, Nixon whom no President since 1920 has equalled in inability to see past the slipcover sensibilities of the middle class. Nixon who even relaxes with the very heart of America thumping outside his hotel room in red neon letters: CARS. Nixon by whose signature the virtues of Chicago's policemen and of their one or two hundred million wards will be ironly implemented in the 1970's— *Law and order— Do not be naughty— Spare the rod and spoil the child— Obey— Eat your spinach— Fit in— Support your local police.*

[November, 1968]

PART II
THE GRASS ROOTS OF "NOW"

Come Alive, America

by Charles and Bonnie Remsberg

Advertising in America reached a creative apex in the Sixties. One of the most outrageous publicity stunts was organized by Pepsi-Cola's advertising team. Based on the principle that the best way to the heart is through the stomach, a sweepstakes contest was held, allowing the winning family to keep, free of charge, all the groceries they could carry out of the store in thirty minutes. In this article, which ran in the February 1965 issue, Charles and Bonnie Remsberg capture the chaos and lunacy of the event.

In the World Headquarters of the Pepsi-Cola Company, an eleven-story glass-and-aluminum structure known to New Yorkers as the Joan Crawford Building, a group of executives met not long ago to discuss a new idea for product promotion. Their goal was to sell more Pepsi-Cola and also to gain for the soft drink a larger place in the hearts and minds of the American people.

What they proposed was a contest. They planned a national sweepstakes of the just-fill-in-the-blank-nothing-to-buy-no-jingle-to-write variety. The grand prize of the contest was to be the *ne plus ultra* for enterprises of this sort, and a discussion of it consumed much of the creative energies of the sales-promotion staff. The gift of a South Sea island was ruled out ("too unreal for general public identification"). So was an around-the-world cruise for two (too few promotable opportunities).

A Pepsi-Cola spokesman said, "We're going to hit people where they live. And what hits them hard, *really* hard? Groceries!"

The winner of the contest and his entire family, wearing roller skates if they so desired, would be turned loose in a supermarket and permitted to keep all the foodstuffs they could take from the shelves and deposit on the check-out counters in the space of thirty minutes. Pepsi executives would pick up the tab on the spot, handing the store manager a negotiable check and a "photogenic" five-foot-long nonnegotiable blowup that he could "keep forever."

According to the press release announcing this event, there would be children and adults "scurrying helter-skelter through the empty aisles of a store, racing against the clock . . . the blur of sprinting slacks and maybe even shorts . . . perhaps a relay system, using basketball tosses to get food from the shelves to the check-out counter . . . the facial expressions on the family's faces as they try to make split-second decisions on the most dollar-rewarding food choices to make . . . the looks on their faces as the check-out tape records higher and higher totals. . . ."

The press release was delivered to newspaper offices wrapped around a six-pound sirloin steak.

The papers printed stories of the promised event. There were television commercials that showed gasping families furiously grasping for packaged foods while crowds of spectators cheered. The word began to spread.

Very little was required of the people who entered the sweepstakes. They had to print their names and addresses (and the name and address of their "favorite retail outlet that sells Pepsi-Cola") on an entry blank and drop the blank into collection hoppers in supermarkets. Within two months, Pepsi-Cola had received 61,000,000 entries, thereby reportedly quadrupling the biggest response from any previous sweepstakes. From the entries, local Pepsi bottlers drew various low-echelon winners. They were guided in this by a Publicity Exploitation Kit which had been sent them by the home office. Many of the bottlers tumbled their group of entries in a cement mixer.

Most of the prizes at this stage consisted of gift certificates. But several entrants in each of the 525 Pepsi franchise areas were permitted "individual shopping sprees" in which they were allowed five, ten, or fifteen minutes to grab as many edibles and potables as possible.

After this prelude, the local bottlers shipped all the entries to the offices of D. L. Blair Corporation, an impartial contest-management company in New York. There, anonymous judges drew the names of fifty state grand-prize winners, each of whom reaped a year's supply of groceries, automotive service and accessories, and Pepsi, 2,496 full bottles of it, or, as one Pepsi official put it in an unguarded moment, "whatever the bladder can take."

Then finally, last July, when the nation's appetite had been properly whetted, Blair officials went back to the pile of entries and plucked out the name of the "top national winner."

It was Opal Miller, forty-seven, a seamstress who lives with her husband, Sharol, a paper-mill roustabout, and three of their nine children in

Taylorville, Illinois, population 8,801. Before the selection was announced to the public, a private investigator reported to Pepsi headquarters that Mrs. Miller was a brown-haired, bespectacled woman of "medium build," white, neat, clean, a "friendly neighbor" in an "average" neighborhood.

Mrs. Miller was called upon to make a statement. She took a pill to help curb her excitement and said, "I just can't believe I'm top. It musta been God's hand leading the hand that picked my entry. It's that miraculous."

Taylorville lies amid the cornfields and soybean patches of central Illinois. On the day before the Millers were to claim their winnings, the town was adorned as if for a holiday. Banners were hung in the courthouse square. They said: Congratulations Opal Miller and Welcome to the Pepsi-Cola Capital of the World. Bunting draped the light poles. The bank displayed a sign calling Mrs. Miller its "Luckiest Customer." The clothing store where she works set forth in red letters this message: Look! We're Bustin' with Pride for Opal Miller!

At the intersection of Pepsi Boulevard and Miller Drive (the two major thoroughfares had been renamed for the occasion), visitors could inspect the modest supermarket where the event was to take place. There, drinking a Pepsi-Cola and surveying the new street markers from under an awning, was a greying, crew-cut man who resembled W. C. Fields. He was the mayor of Taylorville. He said that Taylorville was in the midst of "a volcano, a goodwill volcano.

"Nobody gets anything bad out of something like this, that's what's important. People here are thrilled. They realize this is the only time in their lives and the lifetime of Taylorville that they'll see something like this shopping spree come to pass. Some of the little towns around here are pretty jealous. We even had Miss America."

Miss America, whose four sponsors include the Pepsi-Cola Company, had consented to come to Taylorville as part of the preliminary celebrations. She received a gilded Key to the City and a serenade by a high-school band, which, as it turned out, had not learned how to play *Here She Comes, Miss America.*

"Those kids will probably never have an honor as great as welcoming Miss America," the mayor said.

Miss America had passed out autographed photographs of herself during a luncheon for local businessmen and neighboring mayors. One of the mayors confessed he needed a tranquilizer. After estimating that the Millers' grocery bill would hit $10,000, Miss America praised them as "the kind of people who preserve our American democracy."

The mayor said, "I think her visit, this whole shebang, will make Taylorville the Pepsi-Cola Capital of the World. Of course, we're already the Soybean Capital."

A short, ruddy man with a broad grin and a large tie clasp shaped like a paper clip emerged from the store. In a Brooklyn accent, he announced that he was Bob Windt, Director of Publicity for Pepsi.

"I just got back from a promotion thing in the Far East. The boss told me I wouldn't like this next assignment, Taylorville. But he was wrong. This is more fun than the time I took a horse into the Conrad Hilton Hotel in Chicago or when I had a guy box a kangaroo in 'Frisco. This is really my country down here." He looked down Pepsi Boulevard and smiled. "These are my people." The mayor smiled back.

"Inside the supermarket," Windt said, "there's a real human-interest drama." In honor of Mrs. Miller's winning and the attendant publicity, the store manager was financing a telephone call to the Millers' married daughter who was quartered on an Army base in Germany. The daughter was having a particularly difficult third pregnancy, and Mrs. Miller had hoped that Miss America might ease things by saying hello. But Miss A's chaperone had pointed out that the Queen's contract expressly forbade her to enter grocery stores. Windt explained: "Grocery stores downgrade the Miss America image." So Mr. and Mrs. Miller were placing the call sans celebrity, while a cameraman from nearby Springfield recorded the scene.

Windt had hoped for something more than a cameraman from Springfield. When he had walked away from the mayor, he said: "Frankly, the negative thing about all this is having it in central Illinois. If the winner had only been from Henderson, Nevada [twenty miles from Las Vegas], we'd have planned a three-day weekend and you'd have had to beat the news guys off with a club. Well, maybe the adrenalin will start flowing yet."

The store manager was having trouble completing the Millers' call; neither the daughter nor her spouse seemed to be at home. Mrs. Miller and her husband, who looked like the man in Grant Wood's "American Gothic," were busy in the manager's office figuring the transatlantic time difference and wondering where their daughter could be at so late an hour. (It was nine p.m. in Germany.) Finally Windt suggested they fake the call to accommodate the cameraman, and adjusted the receiver between them.

"Now, *action!*" he ordered. "Mrs. Miller, say something." Mrs. Miller stared blankly at the camera. "Anything . . . 'Hello, how are you?'"

"Hellohowareya," Mrs. Miller said.

"Mr. Miller, say something."

"Hellohowareya," Mr. Miller said.

"No biz like show biz," Windt muttered.

When the camera stopped whirring, Windt left to track down "a police whistle that blows with authority" to signal the start of the race the next morning, and the Millers followed the store manager back to the meat counter. A staff of butchers was stacking up nearly two tons of choice meats and double-checking a list of the Millers' preferences: 125 sirloins, seventy hams, seventy-five roasts, 250 porterhouses, twenty turkeys, etc.

The manager predicted that more than $5,000 worth of meat would be brimming over the top when the Millers raced down the aisles. Mr. Miller whistled appreciatively.

"Don't waste time trying to compare cuts," the manager told them. "Just grab whatever you see. Remember, seconds are dollars."

Mrs. Miller nodded. "Can we keep whatever we got in our hands when the final bell rings, or do we hafta drop it?"

"Keep it," the manager said. The Millers smiled at each other. "Now if you happen to drop or break anything when you're running, just leave it on the floor and grab more. We'll have boys stationed in the aisles to sweep up."

Much of the merchandise, the manager pointed out, was stocked on the shelves and stacked in aisles in shipping cartons, the tops of which had been cut off diagonally. "Take the whole thing. Don't waste time picking out individual items. We've got salmon, canned chickens, vegetables, everything stacked like that. If you're in doubt, just grab. Whatever you do, don't stop."

"Oh, we won't!" Mrs. Miller promised. "This is gonna be *mar*velous! But wouldn't it be wonderful if all nine kids was still at home and could be in on this?"

Even with only three offspring eligible to run, if Miss America's $10,000 estimate proved accurate, their grocery haul, plus the value of the 1964 Mercury station wagon which they were being given, would nearly double their combined yearly income, thereby raising them to a much higher tax bracket. The Millers were asked how they felt about that aspect of their windfall.

"We got the tax bite licked," Mr. Miller said.

"We're borrowin' money," Mrs. Miller added. "The Pepsi people have been just wonderful. They told us this was the smart thing to do rather than give up a once-in-a-lifetime opportunity for something like taxes."

Mr. Miller had spent several evenings with a diagram of the store, mapping out an elaborate battle attack. He and two of the three eligible sons—nineteen-year-old Jackie, a motorcycle buff, and thirteen-year-old Ronnie, a Little League catcher—would run relays to clean out the meat counter, while Mrs. Miller and nine-year-old David went for frozen foods, coffee and other light items. David, however, would need a mother's guiding hand. "A boy that young don't understand and might take just anything. Something nice but cheap, like candy or potato chips.

"Of course, we're going to take some Pepsi," Mr. Miller added. "Pepsi first and last." Mrs. Miller gave a thoughtful nod.

Both remarked that they were delighted with the store's compactness. Normally they shopped at a rangier supermarket, but lately had been boycotting it because it was being struck and they were opposed to crossing union picket lines. Now they were seeing the importance of a social conscience firsthand. "The meat counter over at that place is lots farther from the check-out stands," Mrs. Miller said. "We wouldn't be able to get near as much."

The store manager said he, too, was glad things worked out as they did. "This will bring in new customers, even from out of town. It'll be a status symbol to shop where Mrs. Miller shopped."

On Pepsi Boulevard, outside the store, the mayor was staring apprehensively at storm clouds overhead. He suggested a tour of the special displays in the downtown store windows. "Our businessmen used their inventive genius to honor the Millers and Pepsi. Miss America herself judged the windows."

Around the courthouse square, Taylorville's inventive genius was everywhere apparent. Most of the displays had been designed with promotional material supplied by the local Pepsi bottler. They featured mannequins (some wearing only bras and girdles) capped with paper Pepsi hats, alternating rows of Diet and Regular Pepsi cartons, corrugated paper Pepsi signs, glossy prints of Miss America holding a Pepsi, and hand-lettered posters congratulating Opal Miller—all before backdrops of gigantic red-white-and-blue Pepsi bottle caps. Reportedly, it had been extremely difficult for Miss America to narrow the field to *the* most outstanding display from among so many competitors. Down the street, a deliveryman, with furtive caution, toted a case of Coca-Cola into a drugstore just as the heavens opened up. A downpour.

Bob Windt was slouched in a chair in the hotel lobby, toying with a foot-long red-and-yellow plastic whistle and staring at the rain. A Pepsi photographer from New York was trying to cheer him: "I saw a woman drinking a Coke downtown, so I smashed her in the face." Windt said nothing.

He looked at the latest copy of the Taylorville *Breeze-Courier* which had kept on top of the story ever since Mrs. Miller's entry was drawn. Now, on the eve of the running, its twelve pages were filled with fifty-four display ads, praising the Millers and Pepsi-Cola under such headlines as: ANOTHER MILESTONE IN TAYLORVILLE'S HISTORY; TAYLORVILLE'S BOWLED 'EM OVER AGAIN; CONGRATULATIONS FOR MAKING SUCH AN UNFORGETTABLE EXPERIENCE POSSIBLE! The advertisers included the county sheriff and a local pest-control firm. The copy revealed that the shopping event was touching off a number of related contests. One tavern, for instance, was offering a "free thirty-minute eating-and-drinking spree for the customer who comes closest to guessing the dollar value of the Millers' total take."

Windt was still brooding. "This contest was too honest, so we came up with Taylorville. Hell, in Henderson we'd have even had Telstar."

Mr. Miller was partly to blame for the lack of journalistic enthusiasm, Windt decided, because he had not taken more days off from his job to join in preliminary promotional activities. "He could have asked for his vacation now," Windt said. "But he just sat there with his nose out of joint and didn't say anything."

The phone rang. ABC-TV was on the line from Chicago. Windt's face brightened. "That old adrenalin. Before this is over, *Time* and *Life* will be begging for stills!"

The rain was over by evening. Pepsi Boulevard had been blocked off in front of the store, and a dozen city laborers were there, noisily throwing together sets of wooden bleachers from the high-school football field. The choice center seats were to be roped off for the Miller kin and other dignitaries. The other seats were to be on a first-come first-served basis. "People will be here early," a worker said. "They know the TV cameras will sweep across the crowd." To assure *some* visibility for all, glaziers were removing the supermarket's large plate-glass front windows.

Inside, electricians were checking the efficiency of the wiring. Extra lines had been added. An independent moviemaker, hired by Pepsi, crammed a camera and a cameraman into a shopping cart and careened it up and down the aisles, rehearsing camera angles. The ABC crew, freshly arrived from Chicago, scanned the scene and declared that things weren't commercial enough. They suggested that prominent Pepsi signs be pasted atop cash registers directly in front of the TV camera platform. Stock boys, some of whom would work all night, were corraling one hundred extra shopping carts, three thousand paper bags and mountains of S&H Green Stamps, while other employees dismantled display cases of cigarettes, phonograph records, kitchen utensils and other non-foodstuffs which the Millers would not be permitted to grab during the race. "We decided to get these thing out of the way rather than have Mrs. Miller get excited and grab something she can't have," the manager explained.

Near the check-out counter, Bob Windt was in a rage over the cans of Jewel Mixed Nuts and the boxes of Chef Boy-Ar-Dee Pizza mix flanking a Pepsi display. "Terrible, terrible!" he bellowed to Tony Becker, a hulking Pepsi troubleshooter from Chicago who would be master of ceremonies for the running. "Our stake in this is to promote Pepsi. I don't give a damn about mixed nuts. Get 'em outa here or cover 'em up with Pepsi!"

Becker tried to explain that nuts and pizza could be considered "related food items" and that Pepsi "often ties in with related food items promotion-wise," but a fresh crisis was already pushing Windt's blood pressure to new heights. The wall clock Becker had chosen as "official timer" was imprinted only with the name of the supermarket. "When the cameras flash to the clock for the time, we want PEPSI to come out on the screen. I've had a hard enough time getting some of these news guys down here without blowing it like this," Windt said. In a hasty conference, he and Becker decided that a Pepsi clock would be designated "official," but to avoid hard feelings from the store staff, the first clock would be kept in reserve "in case of emergency."

Two aisles over, another important conference was underway. Two Pepsi promotion experts from New York had cornered the store manager and were informing him that the Millers would not be permitted to carry food in the pasteboard shipping cartons, despite the fact that their briefings and battle plans had been built around this stratagem. "We're mostly interested in something exciting, something *visual*," one of them explained in a confidential tone. "We might have a prism lens, say, that'll make Mrs. Miller suddenly be eight Mrs. Millers to the camera's eye. Basically, it will be better if they just carry what they can in their arms."

"Besides," said the other man, "we don't want to take a bath on this."

"Without the cartons," the first expert added, "the unexpected is more likely to happen. Why, we may be dragging those people up off the floor by the time thirty minutes is over."

All evening a steady stream of townsfolk filed down to the store to watch the preparations—mothers with babes in arms, grizzled old men, housewives in slacks and hair curlers, kids with baseball gloves and bubble gum, young farmers with sun-leathered faces, businessmen with cigars. Some sat on the bleachers for hours, staring at the activity inside the store or plotting their own imaginary assault on the shelves or ruminating over the tragic fact that six of the Miller brood had already flown the nest and thus they were ineligible for the spree.

The editor of the *Breeze-Courier* had just returned from a country-club banquet honoring the Millers for all they'd done for Taylorville.

"You know, Pepsi has hit on a real fine idea. We're a gluttonous race, I guess, but the idea of the supermarket, the grocery-store phenomenon and all, really thrills people. It's like the hunt. You get to sack the game yourself."

A husband and wife walked past, carrying youngsters in pajamas. "At least there's five of 'em," the man was saying. "They'll be able to get something. If some guy had won who was taking care of a seventy-five-year-old mother or something, hell, she wouldn't be able to grab nothing."

Miller Day (so designated by mayoral proclamation) dawned. On an early morning radio interview, a Pepsi executive said: "Out of all forty-eight states, the national spotlight is focused today on Taylorville." The bleachers were already filling (some local shops had given employees time off to attend) and inside the manager was assuring a group of nervous pink-smocked checkers that each of them would have a chance to handle the Millers' groceries and that there would be extra checkers standing by in case anyone got overly excited and had to quit. Two empty semi-trailers had been jockeyed into the parking lot; whatever couldn't be crammed into the station wagon the semi-trailers would carry to storage lockers the Millers had rented in the next town, and a uniformed cop was on hand to direct shopping-cart traffic. The festival crowd swigged free cups of Pepsi, tapped time to the Sousa marches blaring from a loudspeaker, and waved eagerly at TV cameramen and press photographers. Then, when a woman in black slacks and sneakers entered the store, followed by three sneakered boys and a man, someone shouted: "Is that *her?*"

It was. Taylorville's queen for a day walked directly to the manager's office and opened her purse.

"I'm going to take off my rings and my watch and anything that might hamper me in any way," Mrs. Miller announced. Her hair had been set gratuitously by a local beauty operator. Her sneakers were donated by J. C. Penney. She joined the rest of her family for a final reconnaissance of the battlefield. Women in the crowd looked on with unveiled envy as Mrs. Miller experimentally wrapped her arms around a tall stack of canned chickens. The store manager said, "Don't worry about being neat at the check-out counters, just dump the stuff and *go!*"

Finally, just before the zero hour of nine-thirty, Tony Becker got on top of a sturdy safe at the front of the store, grabbed a microphone, and said: "It's almost spree time! Millers, get on your marks!" As one, the five Millers dropped to a crouch at the check-out counters, their eyes on the twentieth-century cornucopia arrayed before them. "Awright, folks, let's count 'em down like a Sa-turn rocket. *Ten . . . nine . . . eight. . . .*"

Four thousand voices thundered in unison. In a second-story window across the street, an American Legion volunteer pressed the official bugle to his lips. At the base of the safe, Bob Windt put the police whistle to his lips. Alongside the Millers, the store manager raised a pearl-handled starter's pistol.

"*. . . three . . . two . . . one . . . GO!*"

Bugle blast, whistle shrill, revolver crack. The crowd shrieked as the Millers sprinted down the aisles, followed closely by the movie man in the shopping cart. In a blur of flying legs and snatching hands, they swarmed over the shelves like locusts through a cornfield. "Go! Go! Go!" the crowd chanted. Becker turned the march music double volume, and the bugler blared a cavalry charge.

Cash registers began to ring as Jackie dumped two dozen steaks on the counter. His mother staggered up with three huge frozen turkeys, and someone yelled: "Atta boy, Mrs. Miller!" Little David, momentarily bewildered, finally got his bearings and began heaving boxes of chocolate milk flavoring into the check-out aisles, where adult store employees scrambled frantically to pick them up. At the brimming meat counter, Mr. Miller loaded Ronnie to the chin with rib roasts. A sympathetic butcher, seeing sweat pouring down the boy's face, held a cup of water to his lips. "Not too much now," his father said. Alarmed Pepsi officials, noting that only the youngest of the Millers had remembered the "Pepsi first" pledge, rushed to a Pepsi display and grabbed a dozen cartons for them. The first shopping cart was loaded now, but in the frenzy the sacker rammed it through a glass door en route to the parking lot, then kicked the broken glass aside and raced on. Becker called on the crowd to give him the old Taylorville yell.

Bob Windt surveyed the scene with rapture. "This is great. We're in the greatest business in the world—*philanthropy*!"

For thirty minutes, the scream of the crowd, the blare of the music, the clang of the cash registers, the steady avalanche of steaks, bananas, sugar, shortening, coffee, cake mixes, frozen shrimp, fish, tea, honey-glazed hams in champagne sauce never slackened. Then suddenly, moments after the meat counter was stripped bare and Mrs. Miller dumped an armload of Metrecal on the counter, Becker bellowed: "We're coming down to the wire now! Pandemonium—*let it break loose!*" The crowd went out of control. People jumped up and down on the bleachers. They threw their paper Pepsi cups into the air. And as the sound of their voices reached the pitch of hysteria, there was a general movement, a surge toward the ravaged store. The final gun sounded.

Each panting Miller was handed a Pepsi. Flashbulbs popped. Jubilantly, the store manager announced the grand-total food value: $6,274.64, plus Green Stamps.

The Millers stopped smiling. "That's not as much as we'd planned on," Mrs. Miller said. She looked around to see what they had missed.

"Well, we don't wanna be big hogs. Just little ones," said her husband.

Then the crowd closed in and well-wishers smothered the winners with hugs and kisses.

Out in the parking lot people were inspecting the seventy-five loaded carts stretched under the boiling sun, and those fortunate enough to be neighbors or friends of the Millers were letting everyone else know about it. Someone shouted that the grocery grabbers had gotten twenty-eight twenty-five-pound bags of sugar. Someone else counted sixty one-pound cans of coffee. Another spotted a dozen bags of charcoal briquettes.

"Charcoal briquettes!" a woman said. "That's not foodstuffs! I thought they were only supposed to get foodstuffs!"

Windt was pushing through the crowd now, trying to get the truck loading started. He was asked what his next promotional idea might be.

"Well, I'll just sit back, study the elements and see what develops. Something will come up. I've been foolin' 'em since I was twelve, so what the hell?"

A man wearing a Pepsi-Cola shirt came past, and he was holding a radio shaped like a Pepsi dispenser. The volume was turned up to the limit, and a commercial that had made its debut that day came booming out:

"Come alive,

Come alive,

You're in the Pepsi generation."

[February, 1965]

Las Vegas (What?). Las Vegas (Can't Hear You! Too Noisy). *Las Vegas!!!*

by Tom Wolfe

If a house in the suburbs represented the American dream of domesticity, a trip to Las Vegas was the ultimate hedonistic getaway. In this classic example of the "new journalism," Tom Wolfe makes vivid the surreal quality of a totally wired city promising untold riches in the middle of the desert. Wolfe was a staff member of the New York Herald Tribune *when this piece was published in February 1964.*

"Hernia, hernia, hernia, hernia, hernia, hernia, hernia, hernia, hernia, hernia, hernia, hernia, hernia, HERNia; hernia, HERNia, hernia, hernia, hernia, hernia, HERNia, HERNia, HERNia; hernia, hernia, hernia, hernia, hernia, hernia, hernia, eight is the point, the point is eight; hernia, hernia, HERNia; hernia, hernia, hernia, hernia, all right, hernia, hernia, hernia, hernia, hard eight, hernia, hernia, hernia, HERNia, hernia, hernia, hernia, HERNia, hernia, hernia, hernia, HERNia, hernia, hernia, hernia, hernia. . . ."

"What is all this *hernia hernia* stuff?"

This was Raymond talking to the wavy-haired fellow with the stick, the dealer, at the craps table about 3:45 Sunday morning. The stickman had no idea what this big wiseacre was talking about, but he resented the tone. He gave Raymond that patient arch of the eyebrows known as a Red Hook brush-off, which is supposed to convey some such thought as, I am a very tough but cool guy, as you can tell by the way I carry my eyeballs low in the pouches, and if this wasn't such a high-class joint we would take wiseacres like you out back and beat you into jellied madrilene.

At this point, however, Raymond was immune to subtle looks.

The stickman tried to get the game going again, but every time he would start up his singsong, by easing the words out through the nose, which seems to be the style among craps dealers in Las Vegas—"All right, a new shooter . . . eight is the point, the point is eight" and so on—Raymond would start droning along with him in exactly the same tone of voice, "Hernia, hernia, hernia; hernia, HERNia, HERNia, hernia; hernia, hernia, hernia."

Everybody at the craps table was staring in consternation to think that anybody would try to needle a tough, hip, elite *soldat* like a Las Vegas craps dealer. The gold-lamé odalisques of Los Angeles were staring. The Western sports, fifty-eight-year-old men who wear Texas string ties, were staring. The old babes at the slot machines, holding Dixie Cups full of nickels, were staring at the craps tables, but cranking away the whole time.

Raymond, who is thirty-four years old and works as an engineer in Phoenix, is big but not terrifying. He has the sort of thatchwork hair that grows so low all along the forehead there is no logical place to part it, but he tries anyway. He has a huge, prognathous jaw, but it is as smooth, soft and round as a melon, so that Raymond's total effect is that of an Episcopal divinity student.

The guards were wonderful. They were dressed in cowboy uniforms like Bruce Cabot in *Sundown* and Robert Taylor in many another Western and they wore sheriff's stars.

"Mister, is there something we can do for you?"

"The expression is 'Sir,' " said Raymond. "You said 'Mister.' The expression is 'Sir.' How's your old Cosa Nostra?"

Amazingly, the casino guards were easing Raymond out peaceably, without putting a hand on him. I had never seen the fellow before, but possibly because I had been following his progress for the last five minutes, he turned to me and said, "Hey, do you have a car? This wild stuff is starting again."

The gist of it was that he had left his car somewhere and he wanted to ride up the Strip to the Stardust, one of the big hotel-casinos. I am describing this big goof Raymond not because he is a typical Las Vegas tourist, although he has some typical symptoms, but because he is a good example of the marvelous impact Las Vegas has on the senses. Raymond's senses were at a high pitch of excitation, the only trouble being that he was going off his nut. He had been up since Thursday afternoon, and it was now about 3:45 a.m. Sunday. He had an envelope full of pep pills—amphetamine—in his left coat pocket and an envelope full of Equanils—meprobamate—in his right pocket, or were the Equanils in the left and the pep pills in the right? He could tell by looking, but he wasn't going to look anymore. He didn't care to see how many were left.

He had been rolling up and down the incredible electric-sign gauntlet of Las Vegas' Strip, U.S. Route 91, where the neon and the par lamps—

bubbling, spiraling, rocketing, and exploding in sunbursts ten stories high out in the middle of the desert—celebrate one-story casinos. He had been gambling and drinking and eating now and again at the buffet tables the casinos keep heaped with food day and night, but mostly hopping himself up with good old amphetamine, cooling himself down with meprobamate, then hooking down more alcohol, until now, after sixty hours, he was slipping into the symptoms of toxic schizophrenia.

He was also enjoying what the prophets of hallucinogen call "consciousness expansion." The man was psychedelic. He was beginning to isolate the components of Las Vegas' unique bombardment of the senses. He was quite right about "this *hernia hernia* stuff." Every casino in Las Vegas is, among the other things, a room full of craps tables with dealers who keep up a running singsong that sounds as though they are saying "hernia, hernia, hernia, hernia, hernia" and so on. There they are day and night, easing a running commentary through their nostrils. What they have to say contains next to no useful instruction. Its underlying message is, We are the initiates, riding the crest of chance. That the accumulated sound comes out "hernia" is merely an unfortunate phonetic coincidence. Actually, it is part of something rare and rather grand: a combination of baroque stimuli that brings to mind the bronze gongs, no larger than a blue plate, that Louis XIV, his ruff collars larded with the lint of the foul Old City of Byzantium, personally hunted out in the bazaars of Asia Minor to provide exotic acoustics for his new palace outside Paris.

The sounds of the craps dealer will be in, let's say, the middle register. In the lower register will be the sound of the old babes at the slot machines. Men play the slots too, of course, but one of the indelible images of Las Vegas is that of the old babes at the row upon row of slot machines. There they are at six o'clock Sunday morning no less than at three o'clock Tuesday afternoon. Some of them pack their old hummocky shanks into Capri pants, but many of them just put on the old print dress, the same one day after day, and the old hob-heeled shoes, looking like they might be going out to buy eggs in Tupelo, Mississippi. They have a Dixie Cup full of nickels or dimes in the left hand and an Iron-Boy work glove on the right hand to keep the calluses from getting sore. Every time they pull the handle, the machine makes a sound much like the sound a cash register makes before the bell rings, then the slot pictures start clattering up from left to right, the oranges, lemons, plums, cherries, bells, bars, buckaroos—the figure of a cowboy riding a bucking bronco. The whole sound keeps churning up over and over again in eccentric series all over the place, like one of those random-sound radio symphonies by John Cage. You can hear it at any hour of the day or night all over Las Vegas. You can walk down Fremont Street at dawn and hear it without even walking in a door, that and the spins of the wheels of fortune, a boring and not very popular sort of simplified roulette, as the tabs flap to a stop. As an overtone, or at times simply as a loud sound, comes the babble of the casino crowds, with an occasional shriek from the craps tables, or, anywhere from four p.m. to six a.m., the sound of brass instruments or electrified string instruments from the cocktail-lounge shows.

The crowd and band sounds are not very extraordinary, of course. But Las Vegas' Muzak is. Muzak pervades Las Vegas from the time you walk into the airport upon landing to the last time you leave the casinos. It is piped out to the swimming pool. It is in the drugstores. It is as if there were a communal fear that someone, somewhere in Las Vegas, was going to be left with a totally vacant minute on his hands.

Las Vegas has succeeded in wiring an entire city with this electronic stimulation, day and night, out in the middle of the desert. In the automobile I rented, the radio could not be turned off, no matter which dial you went after. I drove for days in a happy burble of Action Checkpoint News, *Monkey No. 9, Donna, Donna, the Prima Donna,* and picking-and-singing jingles for the Frontier Bank and the Fremont Hotel.

One can see the magnitude of the achievement. Las Vegas takes what in other American towns is but a quixotic inflammation of the senses for some poor salary mule in the brief interval between the flagstone rambler and the automatic elevator downtown and magnifies it, foliates it, embellishes it into an institution.

For example, Las Vegas is the only town in the world whose skyline is made up neither of buildings, like New York, nor of trees, like Wilbraham, Massachusetts, but signs. One can look at Las Vegas from a mile away on Route 91 and see no buildings, no trees, only signs. But such signs! They tower. They revolve, they oscillate, they soar in shapes before which the existing vocabulary of art history is helpless. I can only attempt to supply names—Boomerang Modern, Palette Curvilinear, Flash Gordon Ming-Alert Spiral, McDonald's Hamburger Parabola, Mint Casino Elliptical, Miami Beach Kidney. Las Vegas' sign makers work so far out beyond the frontiers of conventional studio art that they have no names themselves for the forms they create. Vaughan Cannon, one of those tall, blond Westerners, the builders of places like Las Vegas and Los Angeles, whose eyes seem to have been bleached by the sun, is in the back shop of the Young Electric Sign Company out on East Charleston Boulevard with Herman Boernge, one of his designers, looking at the model they have prepared for the Lucky Strike Casino sign, and Cannon points to where the sign's two great curving faces meet to form a narrow vertical face and says:

"Well, here we are again—what do we call that?"

"I don't know," says Boernge. "It's sort of a nose effect. Call it a nose."

Okay, a nose, but it rises sixteen stories high above a two-story building. In Las Vegas no farseeing entrepreneur buys a sign to fit a building he owns. He rebuilds the building to support the biggest sign he can get up the money for and, if necessary, changes the name. The Lucky Strike Casino today is the Lucky Casino, which fits better when recorded in sixteen stories of flaming peach and incandescent yellow in the middle of the Mojave Desert. In the Young Electric Sign Co. era signs have become the architecture of Las Vegas, and the most whimsical, Yale-seminar-frenzied devices of the two late geniuses of Baroque Modern, Frank Lloyd Wright and Eero Saarinen, seem rather stuffy business, like a jest at a faculty meeting, compared to it. Men like Boernge, Kermit Wayne, Ben Mitchem and Jack Larsen, formerly an artist for Walt Disney, are the designer-sculptor geniuses of Las Vegas, but their motifs have been carried faithfully throughout the town by lesser men, for gasoline stations, motels, funeral parlors, churches, public buildings, flop-houses and sauna baths. A San Francisco artist and jewelry designer, who lived for three years in Plainfield, New Jersey, near unspeakable Route 22, is in Las Vegas for the first time, driving down the Strip. "Wonderful," she says. "New Jersey has spread across the Continental Divide at last."

Then there is a stimulus that is both visual and sexual—the Las Vegas buttocks décolletage. This is a form of sexually provocative dress seen more and more in the United States, but avoided like Broadway message-embroidered ("Kiss Me, I'm Cold") underwear in the fashion pages, so that the euphemisms have not been established and I have no choice but clinical terms. To achieve buttocks décolletage a woman wears bikini-style shorts that cut across the round fatty masses of the buttocks rather than cupping them from below, so that the outer-lower edges of these fatty masses, or "cheeks," are exposed. I am in the cocktail lounge of the Hacienda Hotel, talking to managing director Dick Taylor about the great success his place has had in attracting family and tour groups, and all around me the waitresses are bobbing on their high heels, bare legs and décolletage-bare backsides, set off by pelvis-length lingerie of an uncertain denomination. I stare, but I am new here. At the White Cross Rexall drugstore on the Strip a pregnant brunette walks in off the street wearing black shorts with buttocks décolletage aft and illusion-of-cloth nylon lingerie hanging fore, and not even the old mom's-pie pensioners up near the door are staring. They just crank away at the slot machines. On the streets of Las Vegas, not only the show girls, of which the town has about two hundred fifty, bona fide, in residence, but girls of every sort, including, especially, Las Vegas' little high-school buds, who adorn what locals seeking roots in the sand call "our city of churches and schools," have taken up the chic of wearing buttocks décolletage step-ins under flesh-tight slacks, with the outline of the undergarment showing through fashionably. Others go them one better. They achieve the effect of having been dipped once, briefly, in Helenca stretch nylon. More and more they look like those wonderful old girls out of Flash Gordon who were wrapped just once over in Baghdad pantaloons of clear polyethylene with only

Flash Gordon between them and the insane red-eyed assaults of the minions of Ming. It is as if all the hip young suburban gals of America named Lana, Deborah and Sandra, who gather wherever the arc lights shine and the studs steady their coiffures in the plate-glass reflection, have convened in Las Vegas with their bouffant hair above and anatomically stretch-pant-swathed little bottoms below, here on the new American frontier. But exactly!

None of it would have been possible, however, without one of those historic combinations of nature and art that creates an epoch. In this case, the Mojave Desert plus the father of Las Vegas, the late Benjamin "Bugsy" Siegel.

Bugsy was an inspired man. Back in 1944 the city fathers of Las Vegas, their Protestant rectitude alloyed only by the giddy prospect of gambling revenues, were considering the sort of ordinance that would have preserved the town with a kind of Colonial Williamsburg dinkiness in the motif of the Wild West. All new buildings would have to have at least the facade of the sort of place where piano players used to wear garters on their sleeves in Virginia City around 1880. In Las Vegas in 1944, it should be noted, there was nothing more stimulating in the entire town than a Fremont Street bar where the composer of *Deep in the Heart of Texas* held forth and the regulars downed fifteen-cent beer.

Bugsy pulled into Las Vegas in 1945 with several million dollars that, after his assassination, was traced back in the general direction of gangster-financiers. Siegel put up a hotel-casino such as Las Vegas had never seen and called it the Flamingo—all Miami Modern, and the hell with piano players with garters and whatever that was all about. Everybody drove out Route 91 just to gape. Such shapes! Boomerang Modern supports, Palette Curvilinear bars, Hot Shoppe Cantilever roofs and a scalloped swimming pool. Such colors! All the new electrochemical pastels of the Florida littoral: tangerine, broiling magenta, livid pink, incarnadine, fuchsia demure, Congo ruby, methyl green, viridine, aquamarine, phenosafranine, incandescent orange, scarlet-fever purple, cyanic blue, tessellated bronze, hospital-fruit-basket orange. And such signs! Two cylinders rose at either end of the Flamingo—eight stories high and covered from top to bottom with neon rings in the shape of bubbles that fizzed all eight stories up into the desert sky all night long like an illuminated whisky-soda tumbler filled to the brim with pink champagne.

The business history of the Flamingo, on the other hand, was not such a smashing success. For one thing, the gambling operation was losing money at a rate that rather gloriously refuted all the recorded odds of the gaming science. Siegel's backers apparently suspected that he was playing both ends against the middle in collusion with professional gamblers who hung out at the Flamingo as though they had liens on it. What with one thing and another, someone decided by the night of June 20, 1947, that Benny Siegel, lord of the Flamingo, had had it. He was shot to death in Los Angeles.

Yet Siegel's aesthetic, psychological and cultural insights, like Cézanne's, Freud's and Max Weber's, could not die. The Siegel vision and the Siegel aesthetic were already sweeping Las Vegas like gold fever. And there were builders of the West equal to the opportunity. All over Las Vegas the incredible electric pastels were repeated. Overnight the Baroque Modern forms made Las Vegas one of the few architecturally unified cities of the world—the style was Late American Rich—and without the bother and bad humor of a City Council ordinance. No enterprise was too small, too pedestrian or too solemn for The Look. The Supersonic Carwash, the Mercury Jetaway, Gas Vegas Village and Terrible Herbst gasoline stations, the Par-a-Dice Motel, the Palm Mortuary, the Orbit Inn, the Desert Moon, the Blue Onion Drive-In—on it went, like Wildwood, New Jersey, entering Heaven.

The atmosphere of the six-mile-long Strip of hotel-casinos grips even those segments of the population who rarely go near it. Barely twenty-five-hundred feet off the Strip, over by the Convention Center, stands Landmark Towers, a shaft thirty stories high, full of apartments, supporting a huge circular structure shaped like a space observation platform, which was to have contained the restaurant and casino. Somewhere along the way Landmark Towers went bankrupt, probably at that point in the last of the many crises when the construction workers *still* insisted on spending half the day flat on their bellies with their heads, tongues and eyeballs hanging over the edge of the tower, looking down into the swimming pool of the Playboy Apartments below, which has a "nudes only" section for show girls whose work calls for a tan all over.

Elsewhere, Las Vegas' beautiful little high-school buds in their buttocks-décolletage stretch pants are back on the foam-rubber upholstery of luxury broughams peeling off the entire chick ensemble long enough to establish the highest venereal-disease rate among high-school students anywhere north of the yaws-rotting shanty jungles of the Eighth Parallel. The Negroes who have done much of the construction work in Las Vegas' sixteen-year boom are off in their ghetto on the west side of town, and some of them are smoking marijuana, eating peyote buttons and taking horse (heroin), which they get from Tijuana, I mean it's simple, baby, right through the mails, and old Raymond, the Phoenix engineer, does not have the high life to himself.

I am on the third floor of the Clark County Courthouse talking to Sheriff Captain Ray Gubser, another of these strong, pale-eyed Western-builder types, who is obligingly explaining to me law enforcement on the Strip, where the problem is not so much the drunks, crooks or roughhousers, but these nuts on pills who don't want to ever go to bed, and they have hallucinations and try to bring down the casinos like Samson. The county has two padded cells for them. They cool down after three or four days and they turn out to be somebody's earnest breadwinner back in Denver or Minneapolis, loaded with the right credentials and pouring soul and apologiae all over the county cops before finally pulling out of never-never land for good by plane. Captain Gubser is telling me about life and eccentric times in Las Vegas, but I am distracted. The captain's office has windows out on the corridor. Coming down the corridor is a covey of girls, skipping and screaming, giggling along, their heads exploding in platinum-and-neon-yellow bouffants or beehives or raspberry-silk scarves, their eyes appliquéd in black like mail-order decals, their breasts aimed up under their jerseys at the angle of antiaircraft automatic weapons, and, as they swing around the corner toward the elevator, their glutei maximi are bobbing up and down with their pumps in the inevitable buttocks décolletage pressed out against black, beige and incarnadine stretch pants. This is part of the latest shipment of show girls to Las Vegas, seventy in all, for the "Lido de Paris" revue at the Stardust, to be entitled *Bravo!*, replacing the old show, entitled *Voilà*. The girls are in the County Courthouse getting their working papers, and fifteen days from now these little glutei maximi and ack-ack breasts with stars pasted on the tips will be swinging out over the slack jaws and cocked-up noses of patrons sitting at stageside at the Stardust. I am still listening to Gubser, but somehow it is a courthouse where mere words are beaten back like old atonal Arturo Toscanini trying to sing along with the NBC Symphony. There he would be, flapping his little toy arms like Tony Galento shadowboxing with fate, bawling away in the face of union musicians who drowned him without a bubble. I sat in on three trials in the courthouse, and it was wonderful, because the courtrooms are all blond-wood modern and look like sets for TV panel discussions on marriage and the teen-ager. What the judge has to say is no less formal and no more fatuous than what judges say everywhere, but inside of forty seconds it is all meaningless because the atmosphere is precisely like a news broadcast over Las Vegas' finest radio station, KORK. The newscast, as it is called, begins with a series of electronic wheeps out on that far edge of sound where only quadrupeds can hear. A voice then announces that this is Action Checkpoint News. "The news—all the news—flows first through Action Checkpoint!—then reaches You! at the speed of Sound!" More electronic wheeps, beeps and lulus, and then an item: "Cuban Premier Fidel Castro nearly drowned yesterday." Urp! Wheep! Lulu! No news a KORK announcer has ever brought to Las Vegas at the speed of sound, or could possible bring, short of word of the annihilation of Los Angeles, could conceivably compete within the brain with the giddiness of this electronic jollification.

The wheeps, beeps, freeps, electronic lulus, Boomerang Modern and Flash Gordon sunbursts soar on through the night over the billowing hernia—hernia sounds and the old babes at the slots—until it is 7:30 a.m. and I am watching five men at a green-topped card table playing poker. They are sliding their Bee-brand cards into their hands and squinting at the pips with a set to the lips like Conrad Veidt in a tunic collar studying a code message from S.S. headquarters. Big Sid Wyman, the old Big-Time gambler from St. Louis, is there, with his eyes looking like two poached eggs engraved with a road map of West Virginia, after all night at the poker table. Sixty-year-old Chicago Tommy Hargan is there with his topknot of white hair pulled back over his little pink skull and a mountain of chips in front of his old caved-in sternum. Sixty-two-year-old Dallas Maxie Welch is there, fat and phlegmatic as an Indian Ocean potentate. Two Los Angeles biggies are there exhaling smoke from candela-green cigars into the gloom. It looks like the perfect vignette of every Big Time back room, "athletic club," snooker house and floating poker game in the history of the guys-and-dolls lumpen-bourgeoisie. But what is all this? Off to the side, at a rostrum, sits a flawless little creature with bouffant hair and Stridex-pure skin who looks like she is polished each morning with a rotary buffer. Before her on the rostrum is a globe of coffee on a hot coil. Her sole job is to keep the poker players warmed up with coffee. Meantime, numberless uniformed lackeys are cocked and aimed about the edges to bring the five Big Timers whatever else they might desire, cigarettes, drinks, napkins, eyeglass-cleaning tissues, plug-in telephones. All around the poker table, at a respectful distance of ten feet, is a fence with the most delicate golden pickets. Upon it, even at this narcoleptic hour, lean men and women in their best clothes watching the combat of the titans. The scene is the charmed circle of the casino of the Dunes Hotel. As everyone there knows, or believes, these fabulous men are playing for table stakes of fifteen or twenty thousand dollars. One hundred dollars rides on a chip. Mandibles gape at the progress of the battle. And now Sid Wyman, who is also a vice-president of the Dunes, is at a small escritoire just inside the golden fence signing a stack of vouchers for such sums as $4500, all printed in the heavy Mondrianesque digits of a Burroughs business check-making machine. It was as if America's guys-and-dolls gamblers had somehow been tapped upon the shoulders, knighted, initiated into a new aristocracy.

Las Vegas has become, just as Bugsy Siegel dreamed, the American Monte Carlo—without any of the inevitable upper-class baggage of the Riviera casinos. At Monte Carlo there is still the plush mustiness of the nineteenth-century noble lions—of Baron Bleichroden, a big winner at roulette who always said, "My dear friends, it is so easy on Black." Of Lord Jersey, who won seventeen maximum bets in a row—on black, as a matter of fact—nodded to the croupier, and said, "Much obliged, old sport, old sport," took his winnings to England, retired to the country and never gambled again in his life. Or of the old Duc de Dinc who said he could win only in the high-toned Club Privé, and who won very heavily one night, saw two Englishmen gaping at his good fortune, threw them every mille note he had in his hands and said, "Here. Englishmen without money are altogether odious." Thousands of Europeans from the lower orders now have the money to go to the Riviera, but they remain under the century-old status pall of the aristocracy. At Monte Carlo there are still Wrong Forks, Deficient Accents, Poor Tailoring, Gauche Displays, Nouveau Richness, Cultural Aridity—concepts unknown in Las Vegas. For the grand debut of Monte Carlo as a resort in 1879 the architect Charles Garnier designed an opera house for the Place du Casino; and Sarah Bernhardt read a symbolic poem. For the debut of Las Vegas as a revue in 1946 Bugsy Siegel hired Abbott and Costello, and there, in a way, you have it all.

           I am in the office of Major A. Riddle—Major is his name—the president of the Dunes Hotel. He combs his hair straight back and wears a heavy gold band on his little finger with a diamond sunk into it. As everywhere else in Las Vegas, someone has turned on the air conditioning to the point where it will be remembered, all right, as Las Vegas-style air conditioning. Riddle has an appointment to see a doctor at 4:30 about a crimp in his neck. His secretary, Maude McBride, has her head down and is rubbing the back of her neck. Lee Fisher, the P.R. man, and I are turning ours from time to time to keep the pivots from freezing up. Riddle is telling me about "the French war" and moving his neck gingerly. The Stardust bought and imported a version of the Lido de Paris spectacular, and the sight of all those sequined giblets pooning around on flamingo legs inflamed the tourists. The Tropicana fought back with the Folies Bergère, the New Frontier installed "Paree Ooh La La," the Hacienda reached for the puppets "Les Poupées de Paris," and the Silver Slipper called in Lili St. Cyr, the stripper, which was going French after a fashion. So the Dunes has bought up the third and last of the great Paris girlie shows, the Casino de Paris. Lee Fisher says, "And we're going to do things they *can't* top. In this town you've got to move ahead in quantum jumps."

           Quantum? But exactly! The beauty of the Dunes' Casino de Paris show is that it will be beyond art, beyond dance, beyond spectacle, even beyond the titillations of the winking crotch. The Casino de Paris will be a behemoth piece of American calculus, like Project Mercury.

           "This show alone will cost us two and a half million a year to operate and one and a half million to produce," Major A. Riddle is saying. "The costumes alone will be fantastic. There'll be more than five hundred costumes and—well, they'll be fantastic.

           "And this machine—by the time we get through expanding the stage, this machine will cost us $250,000."

           "Machine?"

"Yes. Sean Kenny is doing the staging. The whole set moves electronically right in front of your eyes. He used to work with this fellow Lloyd Wright?"

"Frank Lloyd Wright?"

"Yes. Kenny did the staging for *Blitz*. Did you see it? Fantastic. Well, it's all done electronically. They built this machine for us in Glasgow, Scotland, and it's being shipped here right now. It moves all over the place and creates smoke and special effects. We'll have everything. You can stage a bombardment with it. You'll think the whole theatre is blowing up.

"You'll have to program it. They had to use the same mechanism that's in the Skybolt Missile to build it. It's called a 'Celson' or something like that. That's how complicated this thing is. They have to have the same thing as the Skybolt Missile."

As Riddle speaks, one gets a wonderful picture of sex riding the crest of the future. Whole tableaux of bare-bottomed Cosmonaughties will be hurtling around the Casino de Paris Room of the Dunes Hotel at fantastic speed in elliptical orbits, a flash of the sequined giblets here, a blur of the black-rimmed decal eyes there, a wink of the crotch here and there, until, with one vast Project Climax for our times, Sean Kenny, who used to work with this fellow Frank Lloyd Wright, presses the red button and the whole yahooing harem, shrieking ooh-la-la amid the din, exits in a mushroom cloud.

The allure is most irresistible not to the young but the old. No one in Las Vegas will admit it—it is not the modern, glamorous notion—but Las Vegas is a resort for old people. In those last years, before the tissue deteriorates and the wires of the cerebral cortex hang in the skull like a clump of dried seaweed, they are seeking liberation.

At eight o'clock Sunday morning it is another almost boringly sunny day in the desert, and Clara and Abby, both about sixty, and their husbands, Earl, sixty-three, and Ernest, sixty-four, come squinting out of the Mint Casino onto Fremont Street.

"I don't know what's wrong with me," Abby says. "Those last three drinks, I couldn't even feel them. It was just like drinking fizz. You know what I mean?"

"Hey," says Ernest, "how about that place back 'ere? We ain't been back 'ere. Come on."

The others are standing there on the corner, squinting and looking doubtful. Abby and Clara have both entered old babehood. They have that fleshy, humped-over shape across the back of the shoulders. Their torsos are hunched up into fat little loaves supported by bony, atrophied leg stems sticking up into their hummocky hips. Their hair has been fried and dyed into improbable designs.

"You know what I mean? After a while it just gives me gas," says Abby. "I don't even feel it."

"Did you see me over there?" says Earl. "I was just going along, nice and easy, not too much, just riding along real nice. You know? And then, boy, I don't know what happened to me. First thing I know I'm laying down fifty dollars. . . . "

Abby lets out a great belch. Clara giggles.

"Gives me gas," Abby says mechanically.

"Hey, how about that place back 'ere?" says Ernest.

". . . Just nice and easy as you please. . . . "

". . . get me all fizzed up. . . . "

"Aw, come on. . . . "

And there at eight o'clock Sunday morning stand four old parties from Albuquerque, New Mexico, up all night, squinting at the sun, belching from a surfeit of tall drinks at eight o'clock Sunday morning, and—marvelous!—there is no one around to snigger at what an old babe with decaying haunches looks like in Capri pants with her heels jacked up on decorated wedgies.

"Where do we *come* from?" Clara said to me, speaking for the first time since I approached them on Fremont Street. "He wants to know where we come from. I think it's past your bedtime, sweets."

"Climb the stairs and go to bed," said Abby.

Laughter all around.

"Climb the stairs" was Abby's finest line. At present there are almost no stairs to climb in Las Vegas. Avalon homes are soon to go up, advertising "Two-Story Homes!" as though an incredibly lavish and exotic concept. As I talked to Clara, Abby, Earl and Ernest, it came out that "climb the stairs" was a phrase they brought along to Albuquerque with them from Marshalltown, Iowa, those many years ago, along with a lot of other baggage, such as the entire cupboard of Protestant taboos against drinking, lusting, gambling, staying out late, getting up late, loafing, idling, lollygagging around the streets and wearing Capri pants—all designed to deny a person short-term pleasures so he will center his energies on bigger, long-term goals.

"We was in 'ere"—the Mint—"a couple of hours ago, and that old boy was playing the guitar, you know, 'Walk right in, set right down,' and I kept hearing an old song I haven't heard for twenty years. It has this little boy and his folks keep telling him it's late and he has to go to bed. He keeps saying, 'Don't make me go to bed and I'll be good.' Am I *good*, Earl? Am I *good*?"

The liberated cortex in all its glory is none other than the old babes at the slot machines. Some of them are tourists whose husbands said, *Here is fifty bucks, go play the slot machines,* while they themselves went off to more complex pleasures. But most of these old babes are part of the permanent landscape of Las Vegas. In they go to the Golden Nugget or the Mint, with their Social Security check or their pension check from the Ohio telephone company, cash it at the casino cashier's, pull out the Dixie Cup and the Iron-Boy work glove, disappear down a row of slots and get on with it. I remember particularly talking to another Abby—a widow, sixty-two years old, built short and up from the bottom like a fire hydrant. After living alone for twelve years in Canton, Ohio, she had moved out to Las Vegas to live with her daughter and her husband, who worked for the Army.

"They were wonderful about it," she said. "Perfect hypocrites. She kept saying, you know, 'Mother, we'd be delighted to have you, only we don't think you'll *like* it. It's practically a fron*tier* town,' she says. 'It's so *gar*ish,' she says. So I said, I told her, 'Well, if you'd rather I didn't come. . . .' 'Oh, no!' she says. I wish I could have heard what her husband was saying. He calls me 'Mother.' '*Moth*er,' he says. Well, once I was here, they figured, well, I *might* make a good baby-sitter and dishwasher and duster and mopper. The children are nasty little things. So one day I was in town for something or other and I just played a slot machine. It's fun—I can't describe it to you. I suppose I lose. I lose a little. And *they* have fits about it. 'For God's sake, Grandmother,' and so forth. They always say '*Grand*-mother' when I am supposed to 'act my age' or crawl through a crack in the floor. Well, I'll tell you, the slot machines are a *whole lot* better than sitting in that little house all day. They kind of get you; I can't explain it."

The childlike megalomania of gambling is, of course, from the same cloth as the megalomania of the town. And, as the children of the liberated cortex, the old guys and babes are running up and down the Strip around the clock like everybody else. It is not by chance that much of the entertainment in Las Vegas, especially the second-stringers who perform in the cocktail lounges, will recall for an aging man what was glamorous twenty-five years ago when he had neither the money nor the freedom of spirit to indulge himself in it. In the big theatre-dining room at the Desert Inn, The Painted Desert Room, Eddie Fisher's act is on and he is saying cozily to a florid guy at a table right next to the stage, "Manny, you know you shouldn'a sat this close—you know you're in for it now, Manny, baby," while Manny beams with fright. But in the cocktail lounge, where the idea is chiefly just to keep the razzle-dazzle going, there is Hugh Farr, one of the stars of another era in the West, composer of two of the five Western songs the Library of Congress has taped for posterity, *Cool Water* and *Tumbling Tumbleweed,* when he played the violin for the Sons of the Pioneers. And now around the eyes he looks like an aging Chinese savant, but he is wearing a white tuxedo and powder-blue leather boots and playing his sad old Western violin with an electric cord plugged in it for a group called The Country Gentlemen. And there is Ben Blue, looking like a waxwork exhibit of vaudeville, doffing his straw skimmer to reveal the sculptural qualities of his skull. And down at the Flamingo cocktail lounge—Ella Fitzgerald is in the main room—there is Harry

James, looking old and pudgy in one of those toy Italian-style show-biz suits. And the Ink Spots are at the New Frontier and Louis Prima is at the Sahara, and the old parties are seeing it all, roaring through the dawn into the next day, until the sun seems like a par lamp fading in and out. The casinos, the bars, the liquor stores are open every minute of every day, like a sempiternal wading pool for the childhood ego. ". . . Don't make me go to bed. . . ."

Finally the casualties start piling up. I am in the manager's office of a hotel on the Strip. A man and his wife, each about sixty, are in there, raging. Someone got into their room and stole seventy dollars from her purse, and they want the hotel to make it up to them. The man pops up and down from a chair and ricochets back and forth across the room, flailing his great pig's-knuckle elbows about.

"What kind of security you call that? Walk right in the god-dern room and just help themselves. And where do you think I found your security man? Back around the corner reading a god-dern detective magazine!"

He had scored a point there, but he was wearing a striped polo shirt with a hip Hollywood solid-color collar, and she had on Capri pants, and hooked across their wrinkly old faces they both had rimless, wraparound French sunglasses of the sort young-punk heroes in *nouvelle vague* movies wear, and it was impossible to give any earnest contemplation to a word they said. They seemed to have the great shiny popeyes of a praying mantis.

"Listen, Mister," she is saying, "I don't care about the seventy bucks. I'd lose seventy bucks at your craps table and I wouldn't think nothing of it. I'd play seventy bucks just like that, and it wouldn't mean nothing. I wouldn't regret it. But when they can just walk in—and you don't give a damn—for Christ's sake!"

They are both zeroing in on the manager with their great insect corneas. The manager is a cool number in a white-on-white shirt and silver tie.

"This happened three days ago. Why didn't you tell us about it then?"

"Well, I was gonna be a nice guy about it. Seventy dollars," he said, as if it would be difficult for the brain to grasp a sum much smaller. "But then I found your man back there reading a god-dern detective magazine. *True Detectives* it was. Had a picture on the front of some floozie with one leg up on a chair and her garter showing. Looked like a god-derned athlete's-foot ad. Boy, I went into a slow burn. But when I am burned up, I am *burned up!* You get me, Mister? There he was, reading the god-derned *True Detectives.*"

"Any decent hotel would have insurance," she says.

The manager says, "I don't know a hotel in the world that offers insurance against theft."

"Hold on, Mister," he says, "are you calling my wife a liar? You just get smart, and I'm gonna pop you one! I'll pop you one right now if you call my wife a liar."

At this point the manager lowers his head to one side and looks up at the old guy from under his eyebrows with a version of the Red Hook brush-off, and the old guy begins to cool off.

But others are beyond cooling off. Hornette Reilly, a buttery hipped baggage from New York City, is lying in bed with a bald-headed guy from some place who has skin like oatmeal. He is asleep or passed or something. Hornette is relating all this to the doctor over the Princess telephone by the bed.

"Look," she says, "I'm breaking up. I can't tell you how much I've drunk. About a bottle of brandy since four o'clock, I'm not kidding. I'm in bed with a guy. Right this minute. I'm talking on the telephone to you and this slob is lying here like an animal. He's all fat and his skin looks like oatmeal—what's happening to me? I'm going to take some more pills. I'm not kidding, I'm breaking up. I'm going to kill myself. You've got to put me in Rose de Lima. I'm breaking up, and I don't even know what's happening to me."

"So naturally you want to go to Rose de Lima."

"Well, yeah."

"You can come by the office, but I'm not sending you to Rose de Lima."

"Doctor, I'm not kidding."

"I don't doubt that you're sick, old girl, but I'm not sending you to Rose de Lima to sober up."

The girls do not want to go to the County Hospital. They want to go to Rose de Lima, where the psychiatric cases receive milieu therapy. The patients dress in street clothes, socialize and play games with the staff, eat well and relax in the sun, all paid for by the State. One of the folk heroines of the Las Vegas floozies, apparently, is the call girl who last year was spending Monday through Friday at Rose de Lima and "turning out," as they call it, Saturdays and Sundays on the Strip, to the tune of $200 to $300 a weekend. She looks upon herself not as a whore, or even a call girl, but as a lady of assignation. When some guy comes to the Strip and unveils the little art-nouveau curves in his psyche and calls for two girls to perform arts upon one another, this one consents to be the passive member of the team only. A Rose de Lima girl, she draws the line.

At the County Hospital the psychiatric ward is latched, bolted, wired up and jammed with patients who are edging along the walls in the inner hall, the only place they have to take a walk other than the courtyard.

A big brunette with the remnants of a beehive hairdo and decal eyes and an obvious pregnancy is the liveliest of the lot. She is making eyes at everyone who walks in. She also nods gaily toward vacant places along the wall.

"Mrs.————is refusing medication," a nurse tells one of the psychiatrists. "She won't even open her mouth."

Presently the woman, in a white hospital tunic, is led up the hall. She looks about fifty, but she has extraordinary lines on her face.

"Welcome home," says Dr.————.

"This is not my home," she says.

"Well, as I told you before, it has to be for the time being."

"Listen, you didn't analyze me."

"Oh, yes. Two psychiatrists examined you—all over again."

"You mean that time in jail."

"Exactly."

"You can't tell anything from that. I was excited. I had been out on the Strip, and then all that stupid—"

Three-fourths of the 640 patients who clustered into the ward last year were casualties of the Strip or the Strip milieu of Las Vegas, the psychiatrist tells me. He is a bright and energetic man in a shawl-collared black silk suit with brass buttons.

"I'm not even her doctor," he says. "I don't know her case. There's nothing I can do for her."

Here, securely out of sight in this little warren, are all those who have taken the loop-the-loop and could not stand the centripety. Some, like Raymond, who has been rocketing for days on pills and liquor, who has gone without sleep to the point of anoxia, might pull out of the toxic reaction in two or three days, or eight or ten. Others have conflicts to add to the chemical wackiness. A man who has thrown all his cash to the flabby homunculus who sits at every craps table stuffing the take down an almost hidden chute so it won't pile up in front of the customers' eyes; a man who has sold the family car for next to nothing at a car lot advertising "Cash for your car—*right now*" and then thrown that to the homunculus, too, but also still has the family waiting guiltlessly, guilelessly back home; well, he has troubles.

" . . . After I came here and began doing personal studies," the doctor is saying, "I recognized extreme aggressiveness continually. It's not merely what Las Vegas can do to a person, it's the type of person it attracts. Gambling is a very aggressive pastime, and Las Vegas attracts aggressive people. They have an amazing capacity to louse up a normal situation."

The girl, probably a looker in more favorable moments, is pressed face into the wall, cutting glances at the doctor. The nurse tells her something and she puts her face in her hands, convulsing but not making a sound. She retreats to her room, and then the sounds come shrieking out. The doctor rushes back.

Other patients are sticking their heads out of their rooms along the hall. "The young girl?" a quiet guy says to a nurse. "The young girl," he says to somebody in the room.

But the big brunette just keeps rolling her decal eyes.

Out in the courtyard—all bare sand—the light is a kind of light-bulb twilight. An old babe is rocking herself back and forth on a straight chair and putting one hand out in front from time to time and pulling it in toward her bosom.

It seems clear enough to me. "A slot machine?" I say to the nurse, but she says there is no telling.

" . . . and yet the same aggressive types are necessary to build a frontier town, and Las Vegas is a frontier town, certainly by any psychological standard," Dr.——is saying. "They'll undertake anything and they'll accomplish it. The building here has been incredible. They don't seem to care what they're up against, so they do it."

I go out to the parking lot in back of the County Hospital and it doesn't take a second; as soon as I turn on the motor I'm swinging again with Action Checkpoint News, *Monkey No. 9, Donna, Donna, the Prima Donna* and friendly picking and swinging for the Fremont Hotel and Frontier Federal. Me and my big white car are sailing down the Strip and the Boomerang Modern, Palette Curvilinear, Flash Gordon Ming-Alert Spiral, McDonald's Hamburger Parabola, Mint Casino Elliptical and Miami Beach Kidney sunbursts are exploding in the Young Electric Sign Company's Grand Gallery for all the sun kings. At the airport there was that bad interval between the rental-car stall and the terminal entrance, but once through the automatic door the Muzak came bubbling up with *Song of India.* On the upper level around the ramps the slots were cranking away. They are placed like "traps," a word Las Vegas picked up from golf. And an old guy is walking up the ramp, just off the plane from Denver, with a huge plastic bag of clothes slung over the left shoulder and a two-suiter suitcase in his right hand. He has to put the suitcase down on the floor and jostle the plastic bag all up around his neck to keep it from falling, but he manages to dig into his pocket for a couple of coins and get going on the slot machines. All seems right, but walking out to my plane I sense that something is missing. Then I recall sitting in the cocktail lounge of the Dunes at three p.m. with Jack Heskett, district manager of the Federal Sign and Signal Corporation, and Marty Steinman, the sales manager, and Ted Blaney, a designer. They are telling me about the sign they are building for the Dunes to put up at the airport. It will be five thousand square feet of free-standing sign, done in flaming-lake red on burning-desert gold. The d—the D—alone in the word Dunes, written in Cyrillic modern, will be practically two stories high. An inset plexiglas display, the largest revolving, trivision plexiglas sign in the world, will turn and show first the Dunes, with its twenty-two-story addition, then the seahorse swimming pool, then the new golf course. The scimitar curves of the sign will soar to a huge roaring diamond at the very top. "You'll be able to see it from an airplane fifteen miles away," says Jack Heskett. "Fifty miles," says Lee Fisher. And it will be sixty-five feet up in the air—because the thing was, somebody was out at the airport and they noticed there was only one display to be topped. That was that shaft about sixty feet high with the lit-up globe and the beacon lights, which is to say, the control tower. Hell, you can only see that forty miles away. But exactly!

[February, 1964]

Twirling at Ole Miss

by Terry Southern

Even with the many upheavals of the era, certain scenes remained to be played as they had been for years, untouched by the shock waves of war, riots, and drugs. Such were the classes of the Dixie National Baton Twirling Institute held on the University of Mississippi campus. In this piece, published in February 1963, Terry Southern takes a guided tour of one of the last holdouts of Southern Americana—a summer school for teenybopper baton twirlers.

In an age gone stale through the complex of bureaucratic inter-dependencies, with its tedious labyrinth of technical specialization, each contingent upon the next, and all aimed to converge into a single totality of meaning, it is a refreshing moment indeed when one comes across an area of human endeavor absolutely sufficient unto itself, pure and free, no strings attached—the cherished and almost forgotten *l'art pour l'art*. Such is the work being carried forward now at the Dixie National Baton Twirling Institute, down at the campus of Ole Miss—a visit to which is well worthwhile these days, if one can keep one's wits about.

In my case, it was the first trip South in many years, and I was duly apprehensive. For one thing, the Institute is located just outside Oxford, Mississippi—and, by grotesque coincidence, Faulkner's funeral had been held only the day before my arrival, lending a grimly surreal aura to the nature of my assignment . . . namely, to get the story on the Baton Twirling Institute. Would reverting to the Texas twang and callousness of my youth suffice to see me through?

Arriving in Oxford then, on a hot midday in July, after the three-hour bus ride from Memphis, I stepped off in front of the Old Colonial Hotel

149

and meandered across the sleepy square toward the only sign of life at hand—the proverbial row of shirt-sleeved men sitting on benches in front of the county courthouse, a sort of permanent jury.

"Howdy," I say, striking an easy stance, smiling friendly-like, "Whar the school?"

The nearest regard me in narrow surmise: they are quick to spot the stranger here, but a bit slow to cotton. One turns to another.

"What's that he say, Ed?"

Big Ed shifts his wad, sluices a long spurt of juice into the dust, gazes at it reflectively before fixing me again with gun-blue-cold eyes.

"Reckon you mean, 'Whar the school *at*?', don't you, stranger?"

Next to the benches, and about three feet apart, are two public drinking fountains, and I notice that the one boldly marked "For Colored" is sitting squarely in the shadow cast by the justice symbol on the courthouse façade—to be entered later, of course, in my writer's notebook, under "Imagery, sociochiaroscurian, hack."

After getting directions (rather circuitous, I thought—being farther put off by what I understood, though perhaps in error, as a fleeting reference to "the Till case") I decided to take a cab, having just seen one park on the opposite side of the square.

"Which is nearer," I asked the driver, "Faulkner's house or his grave?"

"Wal," he said without looking around, "now that would take a little studyin', if you were gonna hold a man to it, but offhand I'd say they were pretty damn near the same—about ten minutes from where we're sittin' and fifty cents each. They're in opposite directions."

I sensed the somehow questionable irony of going from either to the Baton Twirling Institute, and so decided to get over to the Institute first and get on with the coverage.

"By the way," I asked after we'd started, "where can a man get a drink of whiskey around here?" It had just occurred to me that Mississippi is a dry state.

"Place over on the county line," said the driver, "about eighteen miles; cost you four dollars for the trip, eight for the bottle."

"I see."

He half turned, giving me a curious look.

"Unless, of course, you'd like to try some 'nigger-pot.' "

"Nigger-pot? Great God yes, man," I said in wild misunderstanding, "let's go!"

It soon developed, of course, that what he was talking about was the unaged and uncolored corn whiskey privately made in the region, and also known as "white lightning." I started to demur, but as we were already in the middle of the colored section, thought best to go through with it. Why not begin the sojourn with a genuine Dixieland experience—the traditional jug of corn?

As it happened the distiller and his wife were in the fields when we reached the house, or hut as it were, where we were tended by a Negro boy of about nine.

"This here's a mighty fine batch," he said, digging around in a box of kindling wood and fetching out unlabeled pints of it.

The taxi driver, who had come inside with me, cocked his head to one side and gave a short laugh, as to show we were not so easily put upon.

"Why, boy," he said, "I wouldn't have thought you was a drinkin' man."

"Nosuh, I ain't no drinkin' man, but I sure know how it suppose to taste—that's 'cause times nobody here I have to *watch* it and I have to *taste* it too, see it workin' right. We liable lose the whole batch I don't know how it suppose to taste. You all taste it," he added, holding out one of the bottles and shaking it in my happy face. "You see if that ain't a fine batch!"

Well, it had a pretty good taste all right—a bit edgy perhaps, but plenty of warmth and body. And I did have to admire the pride the young fellow took in his craft. You don't see much of that these days—especially among nine-year-olds. So I bought a couple of bottles, and the driver bought one, and we were off at last for the Institute.

The Dixie National Baton Twirling Institute holds its classes in a huge, sloping, fairyland grove on the campus of Ole Miss, and it resembles something from another age. The classes had already begun when I stepped out of the cab, and the sylvan scene which stretched before me, of some seven-hundred girls, nymphs and nymphets all, cavorting with their staffs in scanty attire beneath the broadleaf elms, was a sight to spin the senses and quicken the blood. Could I but have donned satyr's garb and rushed savagely among them! But no, there was this job o'work to get on with—dry, factual reportage—mere donkey work, in fact. I decided the correct procedure was to first get some background material, and to this end I sought out Don Sartell, "Mister Baton" himself, Director of the Institute. Mr. Sartell is a handsome and personable young man from north of the Mason-Dixon line, highly intelligent, acutely attuned to the needs of the young, and, needless to say, extremely dexterous *avec les doigts*. (By way of demonstrating the latter he once mastered a year's typing course in a quick six hours—or it may have been six days, though I do recall that it was an impressive and well-documented achievement.)

"Baton twirling," he tells me straight off, "is the second largest girl's youth movement in America—the first, of course, being the Girl Scouts." (Veteran legman, I check this out later. Correct.) "The popularity of baton twirling," he explains, "has a threefold justification: (1) it is a sport which can be practiced alone; (2) it does not, unlike other solo sports (sailing, skiing, shooting, etc.), require expensive equipment; and (3) it does not, again like the aforementioned, require travel, but, on the contrary, may be practiced in one's own living room or backyard."

"Right," I say. "So far, so good, Mister Baton—but what about the intrinsics? I mean, just what is the point of it all?"

"The point, aside from the simple satisfaction of mastering a complex and highly evolved skill, is the development of self-confidence, poise, ambidexterity, disciplined coordination, et cetera."

I asked if he would like a drink of nigger-pot. He declined graciously: he does not drink or smoke. My place, I decided, is in the grove, with the groovy girls—so, limbering up my 600-page, eight-dollar copy of *Who's Who in Baton Twirling,* I take my leave of the excellent fellow and steal toward the sylvan scene below, ready for anything.

                     The development of American baton twirling closely parallels the history of emancipation of our women. A larger version of this same baton (metal with a knob on the end) was first used, of course, to direct military marching bands, or, prior to that, drum corps—the baton being manipulated in a fairly straight-forward, dum-de-dum, up-and-down manner. The idea of *twirling* it—and finally even *flinging* it—is, obviously, a delightfully girlish notion.

Among those most keenly interested in mastering the skill today are drum majorettes from the high schools and colleges of the South and Midwest, all of which have these big swinging bands and corps of major-ettes competing during the half at football games. In the South, on the higher-educational level, almost as much expense and training goes into these groups as into the football team itself, and, to persons of promise and accomplishment in the field, similar scholarships are available. Girls who aspire to become majorettes—and it is generally considered the smartest status a girl can achieve on the Southern campus—come to the Institute for preschool training. Or, if she is already a majorette, she comes to sharpen her technique. Many schools send a girl, or a small contingent of them, to the Institute to pick up the latest routines so that they can come back and teach the rest of the corps what they have learned. Still others are training to be professionals and teachers of baton twirling. Most of these girls come every year—I talked to one from Honey Pass, Arkansas, a real cutie pie, who had been there for eight consecutive years, from the time she was nine. When I asked if she would like a drink of pot, she replied pertly: "*N . . . o . . . .* spells 'No'!" Such girls are usually championship material, shooting for the Nationals.

Competitions to determine one's degree of excellence are held regularly under the auspices of the National Baton Twirling Association, and are of the following myriad categories: *Advanced Solo; Intermediate Solo; Beginners Solo; Strutting Routine; Beginners Strutting Routine; Military*

Marching; Flag; Two-Baton; Fire Baton; Duet; Trio; Team; Corps; Boys; Out-of-State; and others. Each division is further divided into age groups: 0-6, 7-8, 9-10, 11-12, 13-14, 15-16, 17 and over. The winner in each category receives a trophy, and the first five runners-up receive medals. This makes for quite a bit of hardware riding on one session, so that a person in the baton-twirling game does not go too long without at least token recognition—and the general run of *Who's Who* entries ("eight trophies, seventy-three medals") would make someone like Audie Murphy appear rudely neglected.

The rules of competition, however, are fairly exacting. Each contestant appears singly before a Judge and Scorekeeper, and while the Judge observes and relays the grading to the Scorekeeper, the girl goes through her routine for a closely specified time. In Advanced Solo, for example, the routine must have a duration of not less than two minutes and twenty seconds, and not more than two and thirty. She is scored on general qualities relating to her degree of accomplishment—including *showmanship, speed,* and *drops,* the latter, of course, counting against her, though not so much as one might suppose. Entrance fees average about two dollars for each contestant. Some girls use their allowance to pay it.

In the Institute's grove—not unlike the fabled Arcadia—the groups are ranged among the trees in various states of learning. The largest, most central and liveliest of these groups is the one devoted to the mastery of Strutting. Practice and instruction in Strutting are executed to records played over a public-address system at an unusually loud volume—a sort of upbeat rock and roll with boogie-woogie overtones. *Dixie, The Stripper,* and *Potato Peel* were the three records in greatest use for this class—played first at half speed, to learn the motions, then blasted at full tempo. Strutting is, of course, one of the most fantastic body-movement phenomena one is likely to see anywhere. The deliberate narcissistic intensity it requires must exceed even that of the Spanish flamenco dancer. High-style (or "all-out") Strutting is to be seen mainly in the South, and what it resembles more than anything else is a very contemporary burlesque-house number—with the grinds in and the bumps out. It is the sort of dance one associates with jaded and sequin-covered washed-out blondes in their very late thirties—but Ole Miss, as is perhaps well known, is in "the heartland of beautiful girls," having produced two Miss Americas and any number of runners-up, and to watch a hundred of their nymphets practice the Strut, in bathing suits, short shorts, and other such skimp, is a visual treat which cuts anything the Twist may offer the viewer. It is said, incidentally, that the best Strutting is done at the colored schools of the South, and that of these the greatest of all is to be seen at Alabama State Teachers College. That jazz trends have decisively influenced the style of Strutting in recent years is readily acknowledged, and is highly apparent indeed.

At the Institute, the instructor of the Strut stands on a slightly raised platform facing her class, flanked by her two assistants. She wears dark glasses, tight rolled shorts, and looks to be about 34-22-34. She's a swinger from Pensacola, Florida, a former National Senior Champion and Miss Majorette of America, now turned pro. When not at the Dixie Institute at the University of Mississippi, or a similar establishment, she gives private lessons at her own studio, for four to six dollars an hour, and drives a Cadillac convertible.

As for other, more academic, aspects of baton twirling, an exhibition was given the first evening by members of the cadre—all champions, and highly skilled indeed. It is really quite amazing what can be done with a baton, and no one could have been more surprised than your correspondent. The members of the cadre can literally walk those sticks over every inch of the body, almost it seems without touching them. This is especially effective at night when they use a thing called the "fire baton," with a torch flaming at each end.

Instruction in speed and manipulation of this sort is a long and nerve-racking process. There is something almost insane about the amount of sheer effort and perseverance which seems to go into achieving even a nominal degree of real excellence—and practice of four hours a day is not uncommon. And yet the genuine and really impressive skill which is occasionally displayed makes it difficult to consider the art as so totally ridiculous as one would have previously believed—though, of course, another might argue that such achieved excellence only makes it more ridiculous—or perhaps not so much ridiculous as absurd. In fact, in the existentialist sense, it might well be considered as the final epitome of the absurd—I mean, people starving in India and that sort of thing, and then others spending four hours a day skillfully flinging a metal stick about. *Ça alors!* In any case it has evolved now into a highly developed art and a tightly organized movement—though by no means one which has reached full flower. For one thing, a nomenclature—that hallmark of an art's maturity—has not yet been wholly formalized. Theoretically, at least, there should be a limit to the number of possible manipulations, each of which could legitimately be held as distinct from all others—that is to say, a repertory which would remain standard and unchanged for a period of time. The art of baton twirling has not yet reached that stage, however, and innovations arise with such frequency that there does not exist at present any single manual, or similarly doctrinaire work, on the subject. Doubtless this is due in large part to the comparative newness of the art as a large and intensely active pastime—the Dixie National Baton Twirling Institute, for example, having been founded as recently as 1951. The continuing evolution of the art as a whole is reflected in the names of the various manipulations. Alongside the commonplace (or classic) designations, such as *arabesque, tour-jeté, cradles,* etc., are those of more exotic or contemporary flavor: *bat, walk-over, pretzel,* and the like . . . and all, old or new, requiring countless hours of practice.

During the twirling exhibition I fell into conversation with a couple of graduate law students, and afterward went along with them to the campus coffee shop, "Rebel Devil" or whatever it is called—nearly all shops there have the word "Rebel" in them—and we had an interesting talk. Ole Miss prides itself, among other things, on having the only law school in the state which is accredited by the American Bar Association—so that these two graduate law students were not without some claim to representing a certain level of relative advancement in the community of scholars. They were clean-cut young men in their mid-twenties, dressed in summer suits of tasteful cut. In answer to a question of mine, we talked about Constitutional Law for ten minutes before I realized they were talking about *State* Constitutional Law. When it became apparent what I was driving at, however, they were quick to face the issue squarely.

"*We* nevuh had no Negra problem heah," said one of them, shaking his head sadly. He was a serious young man wearing glasses and the mien of a Harvard divinity student. "Theah just *weren't* no problem—wasn't till these *agi-ta-tors* came down heah started all this problem business."

They were particularly disturbed about the possible "trouble, an' I mean *real* trouble" which would be occasioned by the attempted registration of a Negro student [James Meredith] which was threatening to take place quite soon, during that very summer session, in fact. As it happened, the authorities managed to delay it; I did, however, get a preview of things to come.

"Why they'll find *dope* in his room the first night he's heah," the other student said, "dope, a gun, something—*anything,* just plant it in theah an' *find* it! And out he'll go!"

They assured me that they themselves were well above this sort of thing, and were, in fact, speaking as mature and nonviolent persons.

"But now these heah young *unduh* graduates, they're hot-headed. Why, do you know how *they* feel? What *they* say?"

Then to the tune of *John Brown's Body,* the two graduate law students begin to sing, almost simultaneously: "*Oh we'll bury all the niggers in the Mississippi mud . . .*", singing it rather loudly it seemed to me—I mean if they were just documenting a point in a private conversation—or perhaps they were momentarily carried away, so to speak. In any event, and despite a terrific effort at steely Zen detachment, the incident left me somewhat depressed, so I retired early, to my comfortable room in the Alumni House, where I sipped the white corn and watched television. But I was not destined to escape so easily, for suddenly who should appear on the screen but old Governor Faubus himself—in a gubernatorial campaign rant—with about six cross-purpose facial tics going strong, and in general looking as mad as a hatter. At first I actually mistook it for a rather tasteless and heavy-handed parody of the governor. It could not, I thought, really be Faubus, because why would the network carry an Arkansas primary campaign speech in Mississippi? Surely not just for laughs. Later I learned that while there is such a thing in television as a *nation*wide hookup for covering events of national importance, there is also such a thing as a *South*wide hookup.

The Institute's mimeographed schedule, of which I had received a copy, read for the next day as follows:

7:30	Up and at 'em
8-9	Breakfast—University Cafeteria
9-9:30	Assembly, Limber up, Review—Grove
9:30-10:45	Class No. 4
10:45-11:30	Relax—Make Notes
11:30-12:45	Class No. 5
1-2:30	Lunch—University Cafeteria
2:30-4	Class No. 6
4-5:30	Swim Hour
6:30-7:30	Supper—University Cafeteria
7:30	Dance—Tennis Court
11	Room Check
11:30	Lights Out (No EXCEPTIONS)

The "*Up and at 'em*" seemed spirited enough, as did the "No EXCEPTIONS" being in heavy capitals; but the rest somehow offered little promise, so, after a morning cup of coffee, I walked over to the library, just to see if they really had any books there—other than books on Constitutional Law, that is. Indeed they did, and quite a modern and comfortable structure it was, too, air-conditioned (as was, incidentally, my room at the Alumni House) and well-lighted throughout. After looking around for a bit, I carefully opened a mint first-edition copy of *Light in August,* and found "nigger-lover" scrawled across the title page. I decided I must be having a run of bad luck as, a few minutes later, I suffered still another minor trauma on the steps of the library. It was one of those incredible bits of irony which sometimes do occur in life, but are never suitable for fiction—for I had completely put the title-page incident out of my mind and was sitting on the steps of the library, having a smoke, when this very amiable gentleman of middle age paused in passing to remark on the weather (102°) and to inquire in an oblique and courteous way as to the nature of my visit. An immaculate, pink-faced man, with pince-nez spectacles attached by a silver loop to his lapel, nails buffed to a gleam, he carried a smart leather briefcase and a couple of English-literature textbooks which he rested momentarily on the balustrade as he continued to smile down on me with what seemed to be extraordinary happiness.

"My, but it's a mighty warm day, an' that's no lie," he said, withdrawing a dazzling white-linen handkerchief and touching it carefully to his brow, ". . . an' I expect you all from up Nawth," he added with a twinkle, "find it especially so!" Then he quite abruptly began to talk of the "natural tolerance" of the people of Mississippi, speaking in joyfully objective tones, as though it were, even to him, an unfailing source of mystery and delight.

"Don't mind nobody's business but yoah own!" he said, beaming and nodding his head—and it occurred to me this might be some kind of really weirdly obscured threat, the way he was smiling; but no, evidently he was just remarkably good-natured. " 'Live an' let live!' That's how the people of Mississippi feel—always have! Why, look at William Faulkner, with all his notions, an' him livin' right ovah heah in Oxford all the time an' nobody botherin' him—just let him go his own way—why we even let him teach heah at the University one yeah! That's right! I know it! Live an' let live— you can't beat it! I'll see you now, you heah?" And his face still a glittering mask of joviality, he half raised his hand in good-by and hurried on. Who was this strange, happy educator? Was it he who had defaced the title page? His idea of tolerance and his general hilarity gave one pause. I headed back to the grove, hoping to recover some equilibrium. There, things seemed to be proceeding pretty much as ever.

"Do you find that your costume is an advantage in your work?" I asked the first seventeen-year-old Georgia Peach I came across, she wearing something like a handkerchief-size Confederate flag.

"Yessuh, I *do*," she agreed, with friendly emphasis, tucking her little blouse in a bit more snugly all around, and continuing to speak in that oddly rising inflection peculiar to girls of the South, making parts of a reply sound like a question: "Why, back home near Macon . . . Macon, Georgia? At Robert E. Lee High? . . . we've got these outfits with *tassels!* And a little red-and-gold skirt? . . . that, you know, sort of *flares out?* Well, now they're awful pretty, and of course they're *short* and everything, but I declare those tassels and that little skirt get in my way!"

The rest of the day passed without untoward incident, with my observing the Strut platform for a while, then withdrawing to rest up for the Dance, and perhaps catch the Faub on video again.

                    The Dance was held on a boarded-over outdoor tennis court, and was a swinging affair. The popular style of dancing in the white South is always in advance of that in the rest of white America; and, at any given moment, it most nearly resembles that which is occurring at the same time in Harlem, which is invariably the forerunner of whatever is to become the national style. I mused on this, standing there near the court foul line, and (in view of the day's events) pursued it to an interesting generalization: perhaps *all* the remaining virtues, or let us say, positive traits, of the white Southerner—folk song, poetic speech, and the occasional warmth and simplicity of human relationships—would seem rather obviously to derive from the colored culture there. Due to my magazine assignment, I could not reveal my findings over the public-address system at the dance—and, in fact, thought best to put them from my mind entirely, and get on with the coverage—and, to that end, had a few dances and further questioned the girls. Their view of the world was quite extraordinary. For most, New York was like another country—queer, remote, and of small import in the scheme of things. Several girls spoke spiritedly of wanting to "get into television," but it always developed that they were talking about programs produced in Memphis. Memphis, in fact, was definitely the mecca, yardstick and *summum bonum*. As the evening wore on, I found it increasingly difficult, despite the abundance of cutie pieness at hand, to string along with these values, and so finally decided to wrap it up. It should be noted too, that girls at the Dixie National are under extremely close surveillance both in the grove and out.

The following day I made one last tour, this time noting in particular the instruction methods for advanced twirling techniques: *1-, 2-, 3-finger rolls, wrist rolls, waist roll, neck roll,* etc. A pretty girl of about twelve was tossing a baton sixty feet straight up, a silver whir in the Mississippi sunlight, and she beneath it spinning like an ice skater, and catching it behind her back, not having moved an inch. She said she had practiced it an hour a day for six years. Her hope was to become "the best there is at the high toss and spin"—and she was now up to seven complete turns before making the catch. Was there a limit to the height and number of spins one could attain? No, she guessed not.

After lunch I packed, bid adieu to the Dixie National and boarded the bus for Memphis. As we crossed the Oxford square and passed the courthouse, I saw the fountain was still shaded, although it was now a couple of hours later than the time before. Perhaps it is always shaded—cool and inviting, it could make a person thirsty just to see it.

[February, 1963]

The Naked Luncheon

by Gina Berriault

In June 1964, topless swimsuits in Europe were front-page news in America. It wasn't long before a bar called the Condor in North Beach, California, went topless, with scores of bars following. Gina Berriault, who has lived on the West Coast most of her life, wrote about the reaction to burgers served up with cheesecake. The article was published in February 1966. Berriault contributed both articles and short stories to Esquire *during the Sixties, and her short fiction has been collected in a number of books, the most recent being* The Infinite Passion of Expectation: Twenty-five Stories.

She descends from the ceiling, down through a round hole that is draped with red velvet around its edges and with gold fibrillar loops of braid. The gilded piano that, during the preliminary performances of two orange-and-black fringed dancers shuffling and shaking, has appeared to float from the ceiling, now descends slowly on its tracks and cables; it is her support, her special piano with its insides removed. Visible first are the high-heeled beige pumps, then the ankles, the calves, the knees, the thighs of the turning legs, while the tension bounds upward, struck continual blows, like a strength-measuring machine at Funland, by the amplified fanfare from the four musicians on the stage. She is wearing nylon nude-colored tights, a French-cut bikini bottom of pink cloth that surprisingly reaches almost to the navel, a white wig of a starlet, page-boy cut, pearly-white lipstick, black awnings of eyelashes, and bare breasts rather large for her small body and a trifle more pendulous than globular. She is in constant motion, after the blasting introduction when the piano rests at last on the floor, and the dancing figure is made to appear twelve times faster by the spotlight that goes on and almost off constantly, reminiscent of the unnerving light on the top of a police car. The music blares, the

words are unseparated. It is sound beyond sound so that only the impact of
the waves is felt; one is caught in the din like a mouse in the amplified
guitar. She moves the pearly mouth like Monroe; it opens but no word is
heard in the din. There is something silent and pantomimic about the
frantic figure within the blasting music as if it danced in the unreal center
of a hurricane. After a kind of climax involving both music and body, the
figure calms, the piano begins to rise. Up goes the white wig through the
ceiling, up go the breasts, up go the legs. Carol Doda disappears, and once
again the piano stands against the ceiling on air while the crowds along the
sidewalk are ushered in by flashlight and half the audience rises and moves
out from the darkness, illuminated on its way by a light from somewhere
that turns the white shirts of the men a luminescent violet as if a globe
burned within each chest.

                    He puts into my hands a jigsaw puzzle. After it
is assembled it will be a giant color photograph of Carol Doda, the same as
on the cover of the box, facing front in a purple, topless swimsuit, one arm
up and one arm down, pale hair straight to her shoulders, and on the
crown of her head a red-and-purple spray of feathers. The man who gives
me this gift is the biggest press agent I've ever seen in the smallest office
I've ever seen, once a broom closet, perhaps, or a toilet when The Condor
was a bar called the Black Condor. Expanded now into a nightclub, The
Condor has a red-brick facade, arched windows with red glass, and
fringed shades, and this triangular office in which I am wedged forms part
of the jut at the corner of Broadway and Columbus. The desk is miniature
and so is the typewriter; once, for a time, a three-foot midget served as
master of ceremonies and this may have been his sanctum, but times have
changed. In one corner are shelves piled with newspapers and magazines,
and when the big man stands on a cane chair to bring down a newspaper
from the top shelf it is almost unbelievable.

"On June 17, 1964," he begins, as if it were a world-shaking date. He
was at the house of his boss, Gino, watching television. It was the time
when the topless swimsuits were being introduced by the newspapers, and
on the front page of the *Chronicle* that day was a photo of a four-year-old
girl wearing one. "You want to know how to pack the place?" he asked his
boss. "No four-year-olds," said Gino. At that time Carol Doda was a
waitress at The Condor who did some dancing on a piano that stayed on
the floor. Unfortunately, President Johnson was about to campaign in the
city the first time she danced topless. "We couldn't get coverage," the
press agent recalls. But notoriety came by way of a disc jockey who,
through the glass of his booth, saw the topless suit held up by Gino, and
the second night the place, as predicted, was packed. Within forty-eight
hours Big Al's and The Off Broadway went topless, and not long after that
a host of other clubs in North Beach—among them the El Cid, the

Galaxie, Pierre's, Tipsy's, and several jigger-size bars around the periphery, where the only entertainment before had been the sour humor of the habitués.

"Some people are saying that her breasts are silicone," I begin, hesitantly.

It was he who gave out the secret, he admits. He gave it out, three months after injections were begun, to a columnist whose observations are as essential to a great many in the San Francisco area as their Librium or their Dexedrine, and now, passing by the even longer lines before The Condor, one hears the word silicone in questions and in answers. "She was mad at me at first," he admits, this admission as eager as the other, "but now she's glad to talk about it. Let's face it, when you go from a 34 to a 44 you can't keep it a secret. When a woman grows like that it's like getting pregnant. They call her Miss Silicone of 1965." I fail to ask who *they* stands for. "It sounds cruel," he admits, "but she doesn't care because this is what the public wants and this is what it's getting. This is the sex symbol that Hollywood didn't build."

She is also, I am told, the Pinup Girl of the Year for the men aboard the aircraft carrier U.S.S. *Kittyhawk,* who have requested a photograph of her to accompany them, as their letter puts it, on their "cruise to Vietnam." He will oblige with five thousand photographs. "Isn't that quite a number?" I ask. "They can give out the extra ones when they get to Vietnam," he replies.

Just as a matter of curiosity, because he is not yet thirty and has to his credit, already, this burgeoning of the entire North Beach, I ask him about his past. As the spirit behind Personalities of California, an enterprise quiescent now because of his involvement at The Condor and other topless clubs, he put professional athletes—wrestlers, baseball and football players—into supermarkets for autographing appearances. The women, he claims, loved it, they flocked in. "This old woman brought her Bible for Pepper Gomez to sign." As I leave the broom closet I see Tony, one of the three owners of The Condor, sitting, with a beatific smile, under a Gay Nineties chandelier.

Whether you are man or woman, there is an initial shock on finding yourself surrounded by nude women, or women who appear in the dim and nude-color light to be nude. At The Off Broadway, as your eyes grow accustomed to the half-dark and to the bareness, you are then able to perceive pointed gold pasties over nipples, nylon flesh-colored tights, bras on some and rayon or nylon panties such as can be picked up on a Macy's bargain table, stretch girdles and two-piece swimsuits, and to perceive, within bras or behind the spangled pasties, small breasts and medium-sized breasts along with the larger ones, and even a hollow chest from improper posture, and, within a girdle, a protruding belly as after a childbirth. They are, at second and third glance, very human and as if in a dormitory, running around to find their clothes. These are the performing non-performers, some at ease, one sweetly pigeon-toed and awkward, with a touch of humiliation where the clothes used to be, standing to take an order with a kind of protective slumping-in of pelvis and breasts, and these are the ones who are being ridiculed in print by another columnist, this one minor, who demands bodily perfection of the girls who serve him his breaded veal cutlets while his own imperfections are concealed beneath his tailor-hung suit.

Voss Boreta, The Off Broadway owner, with the smooth, dark face of the nightclub owner in any movie, talks with happy accommodation about the trials as we sit across from each other at a table that affords a view of the large and low-ceilinged room filled with the usual well-dressed couples and small groups of men and lone men, served by waitresses everywhere bare and bumping and easing by, and engaged by five convulsive girls on as many platforms all around the room, in net trousers and no more except shoes, and by the Beatle-like group on the stage and a long, lean blonde vocalist in a trance and yellow pajamas who dances incessantly as she sings. For several days in the Spring of 1965 the trials were given the front pages, the TV newscasts, and the gossip columns, and those persons who, before, were not aware of the preponderant importance of the topless dancers over other figures of the world scene were now made aware. And when the judges and the jury, upon his advice, ruled that the topless conduct was not outraging of public decency and the girls removed their covering again, there were even larger crowds on the sidewalks waiting for the ones inside to come out.

Before the nighttime topless fashion shows, The Off Broadway booked top or near-top entertainers, and then had topless fashion shows at lunchtime, parading the girls only around the tables. When the arrests began, Boreta at once staged a fashion show at night. In all, he was arrested three times. "We paid Trini Lopez $7500 a week," he tells me. "It's like—fill up a bag and give it to Trini. The total payroll, for him and everybody else, was about $13,000 a week. Now we're even more packed and the payroll is $7000, total." The dancers, still in a frenzy up there on their platforms, after what seems to be close to half an hour, not varying their routine but at least changing platforms, are paid $25 to $30 a night. The waitresses get $12.50 and their tips. There are thirty-eight girls employed on two shifts, and if Boreta runs short his brother supplies him. "My brother's got The Cellar. Before topless, if he got twenty people a night he was lucky. Now he can't handle them all. Chris Boreta—running for Board of Supervisors."

The stage is now clear for the fashion show, and there appears a tall and slender model with champagne-color hair, a gliding walk, and eyes that appear to glow on and off. The yellow-pajamas vocalist, now in the hatcheck booth with a microphone in her hand, parodies the commentary of a *haute-couture* show as the model glides across the stage in a green dress with a neckline so plunging it bares the breasts and the navel. She is a dancer from Las Vegas and so is the model who follows her, very tall, very slender, in a silver-grey dress that appears to be conventional. It is, however, a trick dress, for once on the stage she gives it a graceful tug and down comes the top. On the white-painted brick walls are life-size photos of a bare Yvonne D'Angers. Now she herself appears from out the door that leads to the kitchen and to the dressing room downstairs, an incomparable and somewhat confounding fusion of eighteenth-century French courtesan and girlie-magazine model. The wig is high and as white as Christmas-tree snow, the lips pearly-white, the eyelids weighted with olack canopies, the walk slow with a gliding jog in the hips, the breasts globular, glowing faintly, perhaps with lotion, under the transparent lavender chiffon. Off in a corner of the room there is a glass stall where once a girl showered in what was called champagne. It is now a dressing room where Yvonne strips down to nothing behind white translucent curtains as the light inside dims down. In a red baby doll she emerges, rubs her back against the pillar at the edge of the stage, and, with utmost grace, lowers the top. Finding something amusing in the uplifted faces of the men below her, she laughs to herself, her breasts shaking with perfect timing. Now she lies down on the chaise longue that is covered with white fur, her legs up along the pillar, her breasts down almost under the chins of the nearest patrons, while the microphone voice, which strangely now appears to be Yvonne's mind in interior monologue, cautions *Don't touch. Just look.* She shifts position, she chooses one close patron and beckons slowly with the forefinger, and now the voice begins to make moaning, panting, husky sighs. *Hi, there, tiger. How are you? Get up, are you resisting? I'm sure you've bragged about it for years. Now stand up and do something.* The patron, a large man in a rather iridescent grey summer suit, won't stand up. *Oh, you really do have problems,* says the voice, and it is this terrorizing joke that brings him to his feet to bend his head over the face that, once again, is upside down on the edge of the chaise longue. Yvonne purses her lips upward as the patron bends his head downward; then, almost upon contact, the microphone voice, belonging again to the girl in the hatcheck booth, saying, "And that, ladies and gentlemen, was Yvonne D'Angers," sends her bounding up, running across the stage to her glass shower case, her mass of snowy hair shaking.

Down past the kitchen, down the stairs to the basement, and past a red-jacketed busboy playing solitaire standing up at the napery shelves, I come to the dressing room and find Yvonne settled nude in a chair before her dressing table, brushing a fake nail on the forefinger of the blonde Las Vegas girl. The fingernail, held up for my inspection, appears afflicted with a humpy cornification. "Then you file it down," explains the Las

Vegas girl, "and put on the polish. Oh, yes, they last . . ." and each girl displays her long, gold-tipped fingers.

There are racks of garments, transparent and opaque, of many colors, a small couch, and on the dressing tables, among the jars and bottles, some Listerine mouthwash and a bottle of witch hazel. Around the large mirror before Yvonne are perhaps twenty photographs of herself. She tells me that her father sells Citroëns to the Persians, that when she was a school-girl in Paris she walked by the Moulin Rouge and saw a photograph of a nude couple in a fishnet and heard that suggestive things were done in the dance. "Oh, how I wanted to see that act," she tells me. It is her smiling, obliging history. The brunette model, who has been dancing on the stage upstairs, in a sequined crotch piece and high heels, a shuffle-footed, on-a-dime dance with graceful wavings of her arms, now runs in. She throws a transparent, yellow, ruffled capelet around her shoulders and sits on the sofa to combine her observations on Las Vegas with those of the champagne blonde, who is her room-mate. They were given, they tell me, a chance to tour with a troupe in Europe, but turned it down because of the dog quarantine in England. Their three sheepdogs would have been detained six months, and none of them could have borne so long a separation. Someone outside reminds the girls the show begins again in three minutes.

The atmosphere, the next day at noon, is slightly different at The Off Broadway. There are fewer women, no musicians, and in among the waitresses with their pasties and their girdles and their bras, as before, is one with a green-striped cotton dress and low heels. Had she come in late and found no time to remove her clothes? It was at her table I was given a chair by the hostess and I ask her why she wears a dress. "It's just that when I'm out among strangers I prefer to wear clothes." It has an anachronistic sound here, like a medieval superstition. She is unmarried, a girl with a guileless face, who hastens to tell me that she is not the only one, that another girl, who also worked there before the place went topless and who is now on vacation, also wears a dress. A plump girl with lingerie bra and girdle is standing nearby. "Why aren't you topless?" I ask her. "I don't believe in it," she answers. "I believe in illusion." Of an amiable girl with pasties and panties I ask how the pasties are made to stay on. "With surgical glue," she replies. And how do you remove them? "With an ouch." One of the girls is now gliding across the stage in an orange transparent gown. "She's got a beautiful face," says an elderly man to his male companions around a small table. "I'm interested in those things. I used to be a mortician." The amiable waitress appears to be in a state of discomfort; there is a hint in her arms of a need to hug herself. "I'm cold," she confides. I ask if there is a device for extending the nipples while one sleeps, as I have noticed the extraordinary length of those on the model now passing among the tables. "They're the oddest nipples I've ever seen," the waitress agrees. "There may be a device, but I don't know of any." She has been a waitress for six years and has worked as a topless one for six months. "Are you molested by the men?" I ask. "No such luck," she replies and goes off to attend to her tables.

I turn my attention to the seven men at my table. They are all with a carbide company, the one across the table informs me, and one of the seven is telling the others about the salesman in the silicone division in San Francisco who sends out pictures of Carol Doda, before and after. Laughter follows this and jokes: "If I ever see silicone again, I'll recognize it," and, "You know what you'll hear now—Do you love me for my silicone or for myself?" The man across from me wears heavy glasses that appear to have behind them meditative eyes. No, it's not a convention, he tells me. Just a few people with the company from around the country. He himself is from New York. "Are they silicone?" he asks me as Yvonne passes by, and I tell him I am uninformed.

"In a sense," he comments, "it's like creating a freak in a circus. Nature did a grand job, better with some than with others. But one time people thought bleaching hair was gross, so maybe I'm behind the times. I'm a leg man, myself." He laughs. The others have left the table. He stands up, pats my shoulder. "It's just a joint with a gimmick," he says. What other products does his company manufacture? I ask. "Plastics, batteries, antifreeze, sapphires. . . ."

The plastic surgeon I call on informs me that the injections of liquid silicone by means of a needle into multiple areas of the breast is regarded as unethical by the California Society of Plastic Surgeons, for whom he speaks. Since the use of the medical-grade silicone is not approved by the Federal Drug Administration, manufacturers cannot release it and those persons injecting silicone are using either an industrial grade or are obtaining some other similar type of silicone compound. Because the silicone is promising, however, the F.D.A. has approved the release of the medical grade to several university medical centers for use only in small areas of the body, with injections into the breast specifically excluded. The reason for this exclusion, he explains, is that the ultimate fate of the material in the body is still uncertain. For one thing, it may disguise the presence of a breast tumor, and, for another, experiments have shown that sometimes a portion of the material injected locally disappears and may be carried to other areas of the body. "Where it goes we don't know."

Some silicone, I learn from a chemical engineer-salesman, resembles a thick motor oil. Sand is the starting material and silicone is an organic, modified polymer of sand. It is called dimethylpolysiloxane. He himself has not sold silicone to doctors, he assures me, but he knows that doctors purchase it anonymously. "It's as easy to buy as milk," I am told. "Any large-volume item is impossible to keep track of. So the medical profession, if they dictate their ethics, will have to do the policing, not the industry." His company has no medical-grade silicone, but the industrial grade, he is sure, is as pure. Its other uses? I ask. "Silicone rubber, used by the aerospace industry and by the missile industry for seals and gaskets. And by the urethane industry in foam for furniture, automobiles, insulation. . . ."

Dave Rosenberg, the press agent, is waiting at Enrico's, inside, past the customers sitting in the open around the small, marble-top tables, each with its single rose in a vase. Surprised to find him there because I had thought the interview was to be between Carol Doda and myself, I realize, as we sit down to wait for her, that his presence should have been expected; he is an integral and anxious part of her image. He wears a sky-blue sweater and orders a double Coke. "You heard of George and Teddy and The Condors?" he asks me. "We got a new record, a 45, *Ain't That Loving You, Baby?* We're going to put them up in a helicopter—George and Teddy—and drop 10,000 ping-pong balls on San Francisco. I get home at three in the morning and sit up thinking, thinking, always thinking up new ideas."

She comes in smiling, swinging a black bag, wearing a black-and-red poor-boy sweater, dark-green bell-bottom trousers, and high-heeled black pumps. Dave has told me that she is a frustrated person. I bring up the subject and he answers first. "She gets all kinds of publicity. She gets more publicity than almost anybody except maybe Mamie Van Doren or Jayne Mansfield. She wants to go places. Let's face it, I want to go places, too."

"I think about it day and night," says Carol. "I don't want to be topless forever. I like productional shows—Las Vegas, New York, Europe. I've been in *Der Spiegel* magazine in Germany, the London *Times,* and *Spectator*—they know me in Europe. Anybody else would be touring, but I'm still at The Condor. They helped me get this far, but now they're holding me back. Something's got to explode."

I bring up the possibility that in a year from now every major city in the country will have topless dancers and the fact of her being the original one might have no bearing in the presence of hundreds or thousands of other topless dancers. Since she has no manager, I suggest that she find one. She agrees. "I have to go on to greater heights . . ." and, turning to Dave, she suggests that he phone to New York.

"You could phone Gypsy Rose Lee," he proposes. "You could ask her about a manager." Carol was on Gypsy's TV program, he informs me, and answered questions about the silicone. "At the end of the show Gypsy says to the women, *The bus for the silicone doctor loads out front right after the show*. It was banned in L.A." He tells me that he gets around three calls a week from women who want to know where they can get the treatments.

"Why do women do it . . ." I begin.

"Do they do it for men or for themselves?" asks Dave of Carol, interpreting my question with fewer complications than I had intended for it.

"Not for men," says Carol. "I do it for myself. Men are animals. They don't care how a woman looks."

"We care, we care," protests Dave, shifting his weight in the small chair. "Some beautiful women, they look gorgeous with makeup. You see them in the morning and you want to give them a broom and send them on their way."

"Is there," I ask her, "any resentment? How does it affect you erotically?"

"What's that mean?" she asks.

"It means love," explains Dave.

"No," she replies, musing on resentment. "Because it's part of me. It's me. It becomes a part of yourself. When I see my old pictures I tear them up."

The three of us leave Enrico's, passing two men at one of the tables on the edge of the sidewalk, who lean out to watch her after she has gone by. Carol and I, walking behind Dave for a few yards, are both obscured from oncoming pedestrians. It isn't until they get past him that they see she is there.

There is a place called Mother's. On its windows are painted, in luminous red and black, nude women standing life-size, reminiscent of stained-glass figures. One enters into a chamber of uterine-red walls, rippled and folded in bas-relief as if frozen in the midst of contraction. In the men's room, I am told, there is an *assemblage* of tin soldiers and comic strips, and in the ladies' room there is one of broken dolls. Maria is introduced as the "labacious" dancer, or perhaps the microphone plays tricks. She is the girl who has been sitting at the bar in a black and silver kimono. "No dogs," warns a patron against the wall, a young man with the face of an aristocratic alcoholic. "No dogs," he repeats. Maria, growing at once agitated by the music, wears a bra that is not a bra. It acts as a spangled shelf for the bare breasts. She rolls her buttocks and strokes her breasts at the suggestion of the drummer who is singing out his many directions. And here, as in other clubs, the dancer's body seems to be undergoing a kind of frantic confinement in a yell leader's psyche of close-together legs and ebullient school spirit. There are no bumps, no grinds, there is no carnality here or impending carnality, and perhaps that is what is missing most because it is what we are led to expect. There are only the routines, up and down the block, of pistol pantomime with index fingers from the hips, of shotgun loading, of pony riding to music playing that very moment on a dozen radio stations in the area, and there are patrons' Sing Alongs, with clapping above the head, similar to Simon Says. What *is* present is something of Pop Art, the multi-static squares of race-cars, canned soup, pie wedges, motorcycles, and a movie star nude on a hamburger, what *is* present is an obstinate childlike innocence of the same kind that puts a fighting-cock cartoon on the helmets of our bomber pilots and drops toys a day after bombs. Over at the Red Balloon, one swoops down a slide, to the blast of a horn and the pop of rifles from the shooting gallery, into a carnival where patrons can throw balls at a target to knock a topless girl out of bed and, for a moment, into view, and where strip poker is played for a dollar a hand and the only one who strips is the girl. And down at the corner at Benny the Bum's, a small bar, Joyce, the Negro waitress, in black boots and net overblouse, snaps her fingers and shuffles on a little platform, sometimes lifting her blouse in a parody of the other *haute-couture* parody with, "Now I'm gonna show my lil tiddies."

Up in the dressing room at The Condor, in the few minutes before her last appearance for that night, Carol Doda removes the simple black dress she has been wearing while chatting with the patrons at the bar. Underneath, ready for the act, are the flesh-color tights, and tonight there is a grey bit of bikini bottom with what appears to be a silver braid bobbing at the back. She turns before the mirror. "I remind myself of a horse," she says, laughing, flipping up the braid. "A beer-wagon horse or the ones that pulled the fire trucks." She has, I notice, a beautiful back.

Was the silicone her own idea?

"It was suggested to me," she answers me. She was afraid at first, she thought about it a month, but the doctor reassured her. "But I paid for it myself. *I* paid for it." She describes for me how it's done. "Once a week for a year. It's pumped in with a big needle, like a horse needle. At first it feels too firm. It's like breast now, it feels soft."

She tells me about a letter she has received that day from the mother of a teen-age boy. It has upset her. She tore the letter up, but the pieces are still around if I want to read it. Reverends write to her, informing her that she needs help. There is a fragility to her face, the makeup appears to weigh on it, and there is a quick, natural animation in her gestures. What hurts her most, she tells me, are the kids calling her nasty names along the street and the women calling her a witch. She has no friends, her girl friends turned against her. "You know why? They're afraid. They don't want me to be famous. But I must have something that has to *be*. I know why Marilyn killed herself. Everybody steps on you. Judy Garland, who knows all about emotional upsets, was by to see me. And Gypsy Rose Lee, she came by with her little Mexican dog."

The dressing room looks like a McAllister Street second-hand store. There is a couch and a dresser that in 1930 were probably bargain pieces, old grey lockers that might have been salvaged from a ship. Shoes of the other two girls, now dancing below, lie about on the floor; clothes are thrown over chairs. From below rises the fanfare for her descent. We climb into what appears to be a tunnel and run along in it, bent over. It is a passageway four feet high and about that wide. "It's like being in the war," she says. "You know, a foxhole." We come to a hole in the floor. It is the hole through which she descends, a square one made to appear round from below with the use of a hoop from which hang the red velvet folds and the gold loops. Obviously she is standing on something solid, for she doesn't fall through, feet first. She descends, checking on the stability of her eyelashes and the artful dishevelment of her bangs even as her ankles and legs are beginning to appear to the audience below and the music moans and bellows and throws itself against the ceiling. On my knees I peer over the edge. She is almost down, and as I gaze on the crown of her head I am startled to see the fabric of the wig in which are rooted the white tendrils of hair.

There, gazing down through the hole at the dancing figure in the flashing light, I am reminded again, as I have been reminded of it in the presence of the other bewigged and breasty entertainers, of the story *Gogol's Wife,* by the Italian writer, Tommaso Landolfi. The wife is a balloon doll that Gogol pumps up to the proportions that he wishes, more on one day, less on another, with variations of each part. The color of her hair is changeable, on other areas in addition to her head, and even the color of her skin. But after some years of this ideal mating, while he is entertaining a guest, and the wife, plump that night and blonde, is sitting on a pile of cushions, she speaks: "I want to go poo-poo," she says slyly. It is the beginning of the end. She begins to show signs of aging, grows bitter and religious, and bears a child. And so, torn between love and disgust, he is driven at last to destroy her. He pumps her up until she explodes and is no more.

[March, 1966]

PART III
EGOS, SUPEREGOS AND IDS

Literary Notes on Khrushchev

by Saul Bellow

Nikita Khrushchev was a colorful orator, and his audacious rhetorical style was making headlines when this article ran in March 1961. Esquire *asked Saul Bellow to analyze the Russian premier because Bellow's novels had dealt with powerful men affected by the spirit and events of their time. Already the author of* The Adventures of Augie March *and* The Victim, *Bellow interrupted work on* Herzog *to do this piece.*

Khrushchev, the heir of Lenin and Stalin, Malenkov's successor and the evident head of the Russian oligarchy, has stamped his image on the world and compels us to think about him. It is hard of course to believe that this bald, round, gesticulating, loud man may be capable of overcoming, of ruining, perhaps of destroying us.

"It's him, Khrushchev, dat nut," a garage attendant on Third Avenue said to me last September as the fleet of Russian Cadillacs rushed by. This time Khrushchev was a self-invited visitor. He did not arrive with our blessings, and he did not have our love, but that didn't seem to matter greatly to him. He was able, nevertheless, to dominate the headlines, the television screens, the U.N. Assembly and the midtown streets. An American in his position, feeling himself unwanted and, even worse, unloved, would have been self-effacing. Not Khrushchev. He poured it on, holding press conferences in the street and trading insults from his balcony with the crowd, singing snatches of the *International,* giving a pantomime uppercut to an imaginary assassin. He played up to the crowd and luxuriated in its attention, behaving like a comic artist in a show written and directed by himself. And at the U.N., roaring with anger, interrupting

Mr. Macmillan, landing his fists on the desk, waving a shoe in the air, hugging his allies and bugging his opponents, surging up from his seat to pump the hand of the elegant black Nkrumah in his gilt crimson toga or interrupting his own blasts at the West to plug Soviet mineral water, suddenly winsome, Khrushchev the charmer, not once did he give up the center of the stage. And no one seemed able to take it from him.

Balzac once described the statesman as a "monster of self-possession." He referred of course to the bourgeois statesman. Khrushchev is another sort of fish altogether. And since his début on the world scene shortly after Stalin died and Malenkov "retired," Khrushchev—running always a little ahead of Bulganin—has astonished, perplexed, bamboozled and appalled the world. If the traditional statesman is a prodigy of self-possession, Khrushchev seems instead to give himself away. He seems to be a man of candor, just as Russia seems to be a union of socialist republics. Other statesmen are satisfied to represent their countries. Not so Khrushchev. He wishes to personify Russia and the Communist cause.

                                           Timidity will get us nowhere. If we want to understand him we must give the imagination its freedom and let it, in gambler's language, go for broke. Anyway, he compels us to think of him. We have him continually under our eyes. He is in China, he is in Paris and Berlin and San Francisco, and he performs everywhere. In Austria he inspects a piece of abstract sculpture and, with an astonished air, he asks the artist to tell him what the devil it stands for. Listening or pretending to listen, he observes that the sculptor will have to hang around forever to explain his incomprehensible work. He arrives in Finland in time to attend the birthday celebration of its president; he pushes the poor man aside and frolics before the cameras, eats, drinks, fulminates and lets himself be taken home. In America, on his first visit, his progress across the land was nothing less than spectacular. And no fifteenth-century king could have been more *himself,* whether with the press, with Mr. Garst on the farm, with dazzling dolls of Hollywood, or with the trade-union leaders in San Francisco. "You are like a nightingale," he said to Walter Reuther. "It closes its eyes when it sings, and sees nothing and hears nobody but itself." In Hollywood with Spyros Skouras, he matched success stories, each protagonist trying to prove that he rose from greater depths. "I was a poor immigrant." "I began working when I learned to walk—I was a shepherd boy, a factory laborer, I worked in the coal pits, and now I am Prime Minister of the great Soviet State." Neither of them mentioned the cost of his rise to the public-at-large: Skouras said nothing of the effects of Hollywood on the brains of Americans nor did Khrushchev mention deportations and purges. We who had this greatness thrust upon us had no spokesman in the debate. But then people in show business have always enjoyed a peculiar monopoly of patriotism. The mixture of ideology and entertainment on both sides brought about an emotional crisis on the West Coast, and it was here that Khrushchev was provoked into disclosing some of his deeper feelings. "When we were in Hollywood, they danced the cancan for us," he told the meeting of the trade-union leaders in San Francisco. "The girls who dance it have to pull up their skirts and show their backsides. They are good, honest actresses, but have to perform that dance. They are compelled to adapt themselves to the tastes of depraved people. People in your country will go to see it, but Soviet people would scorn such a spectacle. It is pornographic. It is the culture of surfeited and depraved people. Showing that sort of film is called freedom in this country. Such 'freedom' doesn't suit us. You seem to like the 'freedom' of looking at backsides. But we prefer freedom to think, to exercise our mental faculties, the freedom of creative progress." I take these words from a semi-official Russian-sponsored publication. It does not add what some American reports added, namely, that the Premier here raised his coattails and exposed his rear to the entire gathering as he swooped into a parody of the cancan.

This, friends, is art. It is also an entirely new mode of historical interpretation by the world leader of Marxist thought who bodily, by the use of his own person, delivers a critique of Western civilization. It is, moreover, theatre. And we are its enthralled and partly captive audience. Khrushchev's performance is, in the term used by James Joyce, an epiphany, a manifestation which summarizes or expresses a whole universe of meanings. "We will bury you," Khrushchev has told the capitalist world, and though it has since been said over and over that this is merely a Ukrainian figure of speech, meaning, "We will exceed you in production," I think that in watching this dance we might all feel the itching of the nose which, according to superstition, means that someone is walking on our graves. We would not be far out in seeing auguries of death in this cancan. The "culture of surfeited and depraved people" is doomed. That is the meaning of his brutal and angry comedy. It is also what he means when he plays villain and buffoon to the New York public. To him this is the slack, shallow, undisciplined and cultureless mob of a decadent capitalist city. Still, life is very complicated, for if the Hollywood cancan is poor stuff, what can we say of the products of socialist realism with their pure and loyal worker-heroes and their sweet and hokey maidens? Khrushchev himself is far above such junk. It is possible to conclude from this that in a dictatorship the tyrant may suck into himself all the resources of creativity and leave the art of his country impoverished.

It may, in fact, take not only Russia but the entire world to feed the needs of a single individual. For it can't be ideology alone that produces such outbursts; it must be character. "I have often thought," wrote William James, "that the best way to define a man's character would be to seek out the particular mental or moral attitude in which, when it came upon him, he felt himself most intensely active and alive. At such moments there is a voice inside which speaks and says: '*This* is the real me!' " So perhaps Khrushchev feels himself, or attempts to reach himself, in these outbursts. And perhaps it is when the entire world is watching him soar and he is touching the limits of control that he feels most alive. He does not exhibit great range of feelings. When he takes off the rudimentary masks of bureaucratic composure or peasant dignity or affability, he is angry or jeering. But fear is not the best school for expressiveness, and no man could be an important party functionary under Stalin without the ability to live in fear. We cannot therefore expect him to be versatile. He had, however, what it took to finish the course, the nerves, the control, the patience, the piercing ambition, the strength to kill and to endure the threat of death. It would be premature to say that he has survived all that there is to survive in Russia, but it is a safe guess that in the relief of having reached first place he is whooping it up. Instead of having been punished for his crimes he has become a great leader, which persuades him that life is inherently dramatic. And in his joy at having reversed the moral-accounting system of bourgeois civilization he plays his role with ever greater spirit.

Our ablest political commentators have used theatrical metaphors to describe Khrushchev's behavior. Mr. Sulzberger in The New York *Times* speaks of the "fierce illogic of a Brendan Behan play." Others have been reminded of the Leningrad circus, and a British psychologist has suggested that Khrushchev may have made a study of Pavlov's conditioned reflex. After Pavlov had rewarded his dogs for responding to given signals, he scrambled the pattern and the animals suffered an hysterical breakdown. Our leaders, amid flowers and smiles and exchanges of charm, made appointments to meet Khrushchev at the Summit only to find that he had turned into the Great Boyg of the northern snows who deafened them with snarls and stunned them with ice. If Khrushchev had needed instruction in the technique of blowing hot and cold he could have gotten it from Hitler, who made a great deal of noise in the world, rather than from Pavlov, who made very little. From Hitler he might have learned that angry demonstrations unnerve well-conducted people, and that in statesmanship the advantage always lies with the unprincipled, the brutal and the insane. Hitler could at will convulse himself with rage and, when he had gained his ends, be coolly correct to his staff, all in a matter of moments. Khrushchev does not seem to have this combination of derangement and cold political technique which threatens the end of the world in fire and ice. But does he need lessons from Professor Pavlov in psychological techniques? Teach your granny to suck an egg.

No, the dramatic metaphor is the best one, and in trying to place his style, even before I had seen Khrushchev in action during his recent American visit, a short, buoyant, ruddy, compact, gesturing, tough man—it struck me that Marcel Marceau, another mime appearing in *The Overcoat* at a New York theatre, and Khrushchev, at the other side of town, had both been inspired by the Russian comic tradition. The masterpiece of that tradition is Gogol's *Dead Souls*. From Gogol's landlords and peasants, grotesquely thickheaded or just as grotesquely shrewd, provincial autocrats, creeps, misers, officials, gluttons, gamblers and drunkards, Khrushchev seems to have taken many of the elements of his comic style. He is one of Gogol's stout men who "know better than thin men how to manage their affairs. The thin ones are more often employed on special missions, or are merely 'on the staff,' scurrying hither and thither; their existence is somehow too slight, airy and altogether insubstantial. The stout ones are never to be found filling ambiguous posts, but only straightforward ones; if they sit down anywhere, they do so solidly and firmly, so that, though their position may creak and bend beneath them, they never fall off."

When the occasion demands more earnestness he plays the Marxist. Speaking at the U.N. he made me think, when he called for colonial liberation, of Trotsky in the first years of the Russian Revolution and in particular of Trotsky's conduct during the signing of the Treaty of Brest-Litovsk. There, to the amazement of the German generals, he delayed the negotiations in order to make speeches calling on the world proletariat to support and extend the revolution. Those days are gone forever, of course. They were gone even before Lenin died. And there is a great difference between the fresh revolutionary ardor of Trotsky and the stale agitational technique of an old party hack. Still, when it suits him, Khrushchev is a Marxist. Defending the poor working girls of Hollywood, he delivered the judgment of Marxian orthodoxy on their wriggling and kicking (more of the alienating labor imposed by capitalism on humanity).

There are certain similarities between Khrushchev's Marxism and the liberal ideology of Western businessmen. They make use of it at their convenience. Khrushchev, however, enjoys a considerable advantage in that the needs of Russian history and those of his own personality have coincided so that he is able at times to follow his instincts without restraint. He has besides a great contempt for the representatives of the West who are unable to do without the brittle, soiled and compromised conventions of civilized diplomacy. It is the great coma, the deep sleep, and he despises the sleepers and takes advantage of them. The pictures taken at the Summit reveal the extent of his success. General de Gaulle's mouth is drawn very small in a pucker of foreboding and distaste. Mr. Macmillan seems deeply hurt. Former President Eisenhower looks sad, but also opinionated. Things have gone wrong again, but it is certainly no fault of his. Together, the three must have seemed to Khrushchev like Keats's "still unravished brides of quietness." And it is not hard to guess what he, the descendant of serfs, risen to a position of such might, must have experienced. Confronting the leaders of the bourgeois West, so long feared and hated, he saw himself to be tougher, deeper and more intelligent than any of them. And, in expressing his feelings, more free.

It's hard to know whether the Khrushchev we saw banging with his shoe at the U.N. Assembly is the "real" Khrushchev. But one of the privileges of power seems to be the privilege of direct emotional self-expression. It is not a privilege exercised by many people in the West, so far as I can see.

"Men who have arrived can do what they like," declared the *Daily News* recently in one of its snappy ads. "There was a guy who liked spaghetti and beer, but when he became a junior executive, he thought it more fitting to order steak and asparagus. It was only when he became president of his company that he felt assured enough to go back to spaghetti and beer."

Such are the privileges of power, but bafflingly enough, apart from artists and tyrants, few people, even among company presidents, feel strong enough to tell the world how they feel. New York's Police Commissioner Kennedy, a man who has apparently arrived, could not, some time ago, express his honest views as to the religious convictions of the Jewish members of the force. Everyone knows that the commissioner is not anti-Semitic. Yet the New York Rabbinate felt compelled, as did Mayor Wagner, for formal reasons, to ask for a retraction. So it's not easy to speak one's mind. Even the artists have taken cover, disguising themselves as bank clerks and veiling their sayings. That leaves us with the tyrants. (Is it only a coincidence that Emily Post died during Khrushchev's visit?)

Masked in smiles and peasant charm, or in anger, the Russian Premier releases his deepest feelings and if we are not shaken by them it is because we are not in close touch with reality. In the West the connections between opinion, feeling and bodily motion have been broken. We have lost the expressive power. It is in the use of such power, falsely exploiting his Russian and peasant background, that Khrushchev has shown himself to be an adept. He has a passion always ready to exploit and, though he lies, he has the advantage. The principles of Western liberalism seem no longer to lend themselves to effective action. Deprived of the expressive power, we are awed by it, have a hunger for it and are afraid of it. Thus we praise the grey dignity of our soft-spoken leaders, but in our hearts we are suckers for passionate outbursts, even when those passionate outbursts are hypocritical and falsely motivated.

The best lack all conviction
While the worst are full of passionate intensity.

At times Khrushchev goes beyond Gogolian comedy; this is no longer the amiable chiseler who stuffs himself with fish or pancakes dipped in butter. Gogol's Chichikov, to congratulate himself when he has pulled a fast one, dances in the privacy of his room. But Khrushchev goes into his cancan before the world public with a deep and gnomish joy. Here is a man whom all the twisted currents of human purpose have brought within reach of world power. At a time when public figures show only secondary or tertiary personal characteristics, he appears to show only primary ones. He wears his instincts on his sleeve or like Dostoevski's Father Karamazov, that corrupt and deep old man, he feigns simplicity.

When the charm and irony wear thin, he shows himself to be a harsh, arbitrary and complicated man. It was a simple enough matter for him to have joked contemptuously with Spyros Skouras; in debate with well-informed men who press him closely he becomes abusive, showing that the habit of authority has made him inflexible. He seems unable to discuss any matter except on his own terms. Nature, history, Russian Marxism and, perhaps most of all, the fact that he has survived under Stalin make it impossible for him to entertain other views. What amounted in Paris to ex-President Eisenhower's admission of a blunder must have seemed to him incredible. He lives under an iron necessity to be right. What he perhaps remembers best about men who were not right is their funerals. For him the line between the impossible and the possible is drawn with blood, and foreigners who do not see the blood must appear preposterous to him.

[March, 1961]

Frank Sinatra Has a Cold

by Gay Talese

In this profile, published in April 1966, Gay Talese managed to get beyond Sinatra's postnasal drip and personal guard to size up the star just before he turned fifty. Talese began contributing his offbeat and fascinating stories to Esquire *in 1960, when he was only twenty-eight and a writer for the* New York Times. *His books include* The Kingdom and the Power, Honor Thy Father, *and a forthcoming memoir.*

Frank Sinatra, holding a glass of bourbon in one hand and a cigarette in the other, stood in a dark corner of the bar between two attractive but fading blondes who sat waiting for him to say something. But he said nothing; he had been silent during much of the evening, except now in this private club in Beverly Hills he seemed even more distant, staring out through the smoke and semidarkness into a large room beyond the bar where dozens of young couples sat huddled around small tables or twisted in the center of the floor to the clamorous clang of folk-rock music blaring from the stereo. The two blondes knew, as did Sinatra's four male friends who stood nearby, that it was a bad idea to force conversation upon him when he was in this mood of sullen silence, a mood that had hardly been uncommon during this first week of November, a month before his fiftieth birthday.

Sinatra had been working in a film that he now disliked, could not wait to finish; he was tired of all the publicity attached to his dating the twenty-year-old Mia Farrow, who was not in sight tonight; he was angry that a CBS television documentary of his life, to be shown in two weeks, was reportedly prying into his privacy, even speculating on his possible friendship with Mafia leaders; he was worried about his starring role in an hour-long NBC show entitled *Sinatra—A Man And His Music,* which would require that he sing eighteen songs with a voice that at this particular moment, just a few nights before the taping was to begin, was weak and sore and uncertain. Sinatra was ill. He was the victim of an ailment so common that most people would consider it trivial. But when it gets to Sinatra it can plunge him into a state of anguish, deep depression, panic, even rage. Frank Sinatra had a cold.

Sinatra with a cold is Picasso without paint, Ferrari without fuel—only worse. For the common cold robs Sinatra of that uninsurable jewel, his voice, cutting into the core of his confidence, and it affects not only his own psyche but also seems to cause a kind of psychosomatic nasal drip within dozens of people who work for him, drink with him, love him, depend on him for their own welfare and stability. A Sinatra with a cold can, in a small way, send vibrations through the entertainment industry and beyond as surely as a President of the United States, suddenly sick, can shake the national economy.

For Frank Sinatra was now involved with many things involving many people—his own film company, his record company, his private airline, his missile-parts firm, his real-estate holdings across the nation, his personal staff of seventy-five—which are only a portion of the power he is and has come to represent. He seemed now to be also the embodiment of the fully emancipated male, perhaps the only one in America, the man who can do anything he wants, *anything,* can do it because he has the money, the energy, and no apparent guilt. In an age when the very young seem to be taking over, protesting and picketing and demanding change, Frank Sinatra survives as a national phenomenon, one of the few prewar products to withstand the test of time. He is the champ who made the big comeback, the man who had everything, lost it, then got it back, letting nothing stand in his way, doing what few men can do: he uprooted his life, left his family, broke with everything that was familiar, learning in the process that one way to hold a woman is not to hold her. Now he has the affection of Nancy and Ava and Mia, the fine female produce of three generations, and still has the adoration of his children, the freedom of a bachelor, he does not feel old, he makes old men feel young, makes them think that if Frank Sinatra can do it, it can be done; not that *they* could do it, but it is still nice for other men to know, at fifty, that it can be done.

But now, standing at this bar in Beverly Hills, Sinatra had a cold, and he continued to drink quietly and he seemed miles away in his private world, not even reacting when suddenly the stereo in the other room switched to a Sinatra song, *In the Wee Small Hours of the Morning.*

It is a lovely ballad that he first recorded ten years ago, and it now inspired many young couples who had been sitting, tired of twisting, to get up and move slowly around the dance floor, holding one another very close. Sinatra's intonation, precisely clipped, yet full and flowing, gave a deeper meaning to the simple lyrics—"In the wee small hours of the morning / while the whole wide world is fast asleep / you lie awake, and think about the girl . . ."*—it was, like so many of his classics, a song that evoked loneliness and sensuality, and when blended with the dim light and the alcohol and nicotine and late-night needs, it became a kind of airy aphrodisiac. Undoubtedly the words from this song, and others like it, had put millions in the mood, it was music to make love by, and doubtless much love had been made by it all over America at night in cars, while the batteries burned down, in cottages by the lake, on beaches during balmy summer evenings, in secluded parks and exclusive penthouses and furnished rooms, in cabin cruisers and cabs and cabanas—in all places where Sinatra's songs could be heard were these words that warmed women, wooed and won them, snipped the final thread of inhibition and gratified the male egos of ungrateful lovers; two generations of men had been the beneficiaries of such ballads, for which they were eternally in his debt, for which they may eternally hate him. Nevertheless here he was, the man himself, in the early hours of the morning in Beverly Hills, out of range.

The two blondes, who seemed to be in their middle thirties, were preened and polished, their matured bodies softly molded within tight dark suits. They sat, legs crossed, perched on the high bar stools. They listened to the music. Then one of them pulled out a Kent and Sinatra quickly placed his gold lighter under it and she held his hand, looked at his fingers: they were nubby and raw, and the pinkies protruded, being so stiff from arthritis that he could barely bend them. He was, as usual, immaculately dressed. He wore an oxford-grey suit with a vest, a suit conservatively cut on the outside but trimmed with flamboyant silk within; his shoes, British, seemed to be shined even on the bottom of the soles. He also wore, as everybody seemed to know, a remarkably convincing black hairpiece, one of sixty that he owns, most of them under the care of an inconspicuous little grey-haired lady who, holding his hair in a tiny satchel, follows him around whenever he performs. She earns $400 a week. The most distinguishing thing about Sinatra's face are his eyes, clear blue and alert, eyes that within seconds can go cold with anger, or glow with affection, or, as now, reflect a vague detachment that keeps his friends silent and distant.

Leo Durocher, one of Sinatra's closest friends, was now shooting pool in the small room behind the bar. Standing near the door was Jim Mahoney, Sinatra's press agent, a somewhat chunky young man with a square jaw and narrow eyes who would resemble a tough Irish plainclothesman if it were not for the expensive continental suits he wears and his exquisite shoes often adorned with polished buckles. Also nearby was a big, broad-shouldered two-hundred-pound actor named Brad Dexter

*©*Redd Evans Music Corp.*

who seemed always to be thrusting out his chest so that his gut would not show.

Brad Dexter has appeared in several films and television shows, displaying fine talent as a character actor, but in Beverly Hills he is equally known for the role he played in Hawaii two years ago when he swam a few hundred yards and risked his life to save Sinatra from drowning in a riptide. Since then Dexter has been one of Sinatra's constant companions and has been made a producer in Sinatra's film company. He occupies a plush office near Sinatra's executive suite. He is endlessly searching for literary properties that might be converted into new starring roles for Sinatra. Whenever he is among strangers with Sinatra he worries because he knows that Sinatra brings out the best and worst in people—some men will become aggressive, some women will become seductive, others will stand around skeptically appraising him, the scene will be somehow intoxicated by his mere presence, and maybe Sinatra himself, if feeling as badly as he was tonight, might become intolerant or tense, and then: headlines. So Brad Dexter tries to anticipate danger and warn Sinatra in advance. He confesses to feeling very protective of Sinatra, admitting in a recent moment of self-revelation: "I'd kill for him."

While this statement may seem outlandishly dramatic, particularly when taken out of context, it nonetheless expresses a fierce fidelity that is quite common within Sinatra's special circle. It is a characteristic that Sinatra, without admission, seems to prefer: *All the Way; All or Nothing at All.* This is the Sicilian in Sinatra; he permits his friends, if they wish to remain that, none of the easy Anglo-Saxon outs. But if they remain loyal, then there is nothing Sinatra will not do in turn—fabulous gifts, personal kindnesses, encouragement when they're down, adulation when they're up. They are wise to remember, however, one thing. He is Sinatra. The boss. *Il Padrone.*

I had seen something of this Sicilian side of Sinatra last summer at Jilly's saloon in New York, which was the only other time I'd gotten a close view of him prior to this night in this California club. Jilly's, which is on West Fifty-second Street in Manhattan, is where Sinatra drinks whenever he is in New York, and there is a special chair reserved for him in the back room against the wall that nobody else may use. When he is occupying it, seated behind a long table flanked by his closest New York friends—who include the saloonkeeper, Jilly Rizzo, and Jilly's azure-haired wife, Honey, who is known as the "Blue Jew"—a rather strange ritualistic scene develops. That night dozens of people, some of them casual friends of Sinatra's, some mere acquaintances, some neither, appeared outside of Jilly's saloon. They approached it like a shrine. They had come to pay respect. They were from New York, Brooklyn, Atlantic City, Hoboken. They were old actors, young actors, former prizefighters, tired trumpet players, politicians, a boy with a cane. There was a fat lady who said she remembered Sinatra when he used to throw the *Jersey Observer* onto her front porch in 1933. There were middle-aged couples who said they had heard Sinatra sing at the Rustic Cabin in 1938 and "We knew then that he really had it!" Or they had heard him when he was with Harry James's band in 1939, or with Tommy Dorsey in 1941 ("Yeah, that's the song, *I'll Never Smile Again*—he sang it one night in this dump near Newark and we danced . . ."); or they remembered that time at the Paramount with the swooners, and him with those bow ties, The Voice; and one woman remembered that awful boy she knew then—Alexander Dorogokupetz, an eighteen-year-old heckler who had thrown a tomato at Sinatra and the bobby-soxers in the balcony had tried to flail him to death. Whatever became of Alexander Dorogokupetz? The lady did not know.

And they remembered when Sinatra was a failure and sang trash like *Mairzy Doats,* and they remembered his comeback and on this night they were all standing outside Jilly's saloon, dozens of them, but they could not get in. So some of them left. But most of them stayed, hoping that soon they might be able to push or wedge their way into Jilly's between the elbows and backsides of the men drinking three-deep at the bar, and they might be able to peek through and *see* him sitting back there. This is all they really wanted; they wanted to see him. And for a few moments they gazed in silence through the smoke and they stared. Then they turned, fought their way out of the bar, went home.

Some of Sinatra's close friends, all of whom are known to the men guarding Jilly's door, do manage to get an escort into the back room. But once they are there they, too, must fend for themselves. On the particular evening, Frank Gifford, the former football player, got only seven yards in three tries. Others who had somehow been close enough to shake Sinatra's hand did *not* shake it; instead they just touched him on the shoulder or sleeve, or they merely stood close enough for him to see them and, after he'd given them a wink of recognition or a wave or a nod or called out their names (he has a fantastic memory for first names), they would then turn and leave. They had checked in. They had paid their respects. And as I watched this ritualistic scene, I got the impression that Frank Sinatra was dwelling simultaneously in two worlds that were not contemporary.

On the one hand he is the swinger—as he is when talking and joking with Sammy Davis, Jr., Richard Conte, Liza Minelli, Bernice Massi, or any of the other show-business people who get to sit at *the* table; on the other, as when he is nodding or waving to his *paisanos* who are close to him (Al Silvani, a boxing manager who works with Sinatra's film company; Dominic Di Bona, his wardrobe man; Ed Pucci, a 300-pound former football lineman who is his aide-de-camp), Frank Sinatra is *Il Padrone.* Or better still, he is what in traditional Sicily have long been called *uomini rispettati*—men of respect: men who are both majestic and humble, men who are loved by all and are very generous by nature, men whose hands are kissed as they walk from village to village, men who would *personally* go out of their way to redress a wrong.

Frank Sinatra does things *personally*. At Christmas time, he will personally pick dozens of presents for his close friends and family, remembering the type of jewelry they like, their favorite colors, the sizes of their shirts and dresses. When a musician friend's house was destroyed and his wife was killed in a Los Angeles mud slide a little more than a year ago, Sinatra personally came to his aid, finding the musician a new home, paying whatever hospital bills were left unpaid by the insurance, then personally supervising the furnishing of the new home down to the replacing of the silverware, the linen, the purchase of new clothing.

The same Sinatra who did this can, within the same hour, explode in a towering rage of intolerance should a small thing be incorrectly done for him by one of his *paisanos*. For example, when one of his men brought him a frankfurter with catsup on it, which Sinatra apparently abhors, he angrily threw the bottle at the man, splattering catsup all over him. Most of the men who work around Sinatra are big. But this never seems to intimidate Sinatra nor curb his impetuous behavior with them when he is mad. They will never take a swing back at him. He is *Il Padrone*.

At other times, aiming to please, his men will overreact to his desires: when he casually observed that his big orange desert jeep in Palm Springs seemed in need of a new painting, the word was swiftly passed down through channels, becoming ever more urgent as it went, until finally it was a *command* that the jeep be painted *now*, immediately, yesterday. To accomplish this would require the hiring of a special crew of painters to work all night, at overtime rates; which, in turn, meant that the order had to be bucked back up the line for further approval. When it finally got back to Sinatra's desk, he did not know what it was all about; after he had figured it out he confessed, with a tired look on his face, that he did not care when the hell they painted his jeep.

Yet it would have been unwise for anyone to anticipate his reaction, for he is a wholly unpredictable man of many moods and great dimension, a man who responds instantaneously to instinct—suddenly, dramatically, wildly he responds, and nobody can predict what will follow. A young lady named Jane Hoag, a reporter at *Life*'s Los Angeles bureau who had attended the same school as Sinatra's daughter, Nancy, had once been invited to a party at Mrs. Sinatra's California home at which Frank Sinatra, who maintains very cordial relations with his former wife, acted as host. Early in the party Miss Hoag, while leaning against a table, accidentally with her elbow knocked over one of a pair of alabaster birds to the floor, smashing it to pieces. Suddenly, Miss Hoag recalled, Sinatra's daughter cried, "Oh, that was one of mother's favorite . . ."—but before she could complete the sentence, Sinatra glared at her, cutting her off, and while forty other guests in the room all stared in silence, Sinatra walked over, quickly with his finger flicked the *other* alabaster bird off the table, smashing it to pieces, and then put an arm gently around Jane Hoag and said, in a way that put her completely at ease, "That's okay, kid."

               Now Sinatra said a few words to the blondes. Then he turned from the bar and began to walk toward the poolroom. One of Sinatra's other men friends moved in to keep the girls company. Brad Dexter, who had been standing in the corner talking to some other people, now followed Sinatra.

The room cracked with the clack of billiard balls. There were about a dozen spectators in the room, most of them young men who were watching Leo Durocher shoot against two other aspiring hustlers who were not very good. This private drinking club has among its membership many actors, directors, writers, models, nearly all of them a good deal younger than Sinatra or Durocher and much more casual in the way they dress for the evening. Many of the young women, their long hair flowing loosely below their shoulders, wore tight, fanny-fitting Jax pants and very expensive sweaters; and a few of the young men wore blue or green velour shirts with high collars and narrow tight pants, and Italian loafers.

It was obvious from the way Sinatra looked at these people in the poolroom that they were not his style, but he leaned back against a high stool that was against the wall, holding his drink in his right hand, and said nothing, just watched Durocher slam the billiard balls back and forth. The younger men in the room, accustomed to seeing Sinatra at this club, treated him without deference, although they said nothing offensive. They were a cool young group, very California-cool and casual, and one of the coolest seemed to be a little guy, very quick of movement, who had a sharp profile, pale blue eyes, blondish hair, and squared eyeglasses. He wore a pair of brown corduroy slacks, a green shaggy-dog Shetland sweater, a tan suede jacket, and Game Warden boots, for which he had recently paid $60.

Frank Sinatra, leaning against the stool, sniffling a bit from his cold, could not take his eyes off the Game Warden boots. Once, after gazing at them for a few moments, he turned away; but now he was focused on them again. The owner of the boots, who was just standing in them watching the pool game, was named Harlan Ellison, a writer who had just completed work on a screenplay, *The Oscar*.

Finally Sinatra could not contain himself.

"Hey," he yelled in his slightly harsh voice that still had a soft, sharp edge. "Those Italian boots?"

"No," Ellison said.

"Spanish?"

"No."

"Are they *English* boots?"

"Look, I donno, man," Ellison shot back, frowning at Sinatra, then turning away again.

Now the poolroom was suddenly silent. Leo Durocher who had been poised behind his cue stick and was bent low just froze in that position for a second. Nobody moved. Then Sinatra moved away from the stool and walked with that slow, arrogant swagger of his toward Ellison, the hard tap of Sinatra's shoes the only sound in the room. Then, looking down at Ellison with a slightly raised eyebrow and a tricky little smile, Sinatra asked: "You expecting a *storm?*"

Harlan Ellison moved a step to the side. "Look, is there any reason why you're talking to me?"

"I don't like the way you're dressed," Sinatra said.

"Hate to shake you up," Ellison said, "but I dress to suit myself."

Now there was some rumbling in the room, and somebody said, "Com'on, Harlan, let's get out of here," and Leo Durocher made his pool shot and said, "Yeah, com'on."

But Ellison stood his ground.

Sinatra said, "What do you do?"

"I'm a plumber," Ellison said.

"No, no, he's not," another young man quickly yelled from across the table. "He wrote *The Oscar.*"

"Oh, yeah," Sinatra said, "well I've seen it, and it's a piece of crap."

"That's strange," Ellison said, "because they haven't even released it yet."

"Well, I've seen it," Sinatra repeated, "and it's a piece of crap."

Now Brad Dexter, very anxious, very big opposite the small figure of Ellison, said, "Com'on, kid, I don't want you in this room."

"*Hey,*" Sinatra interrupted Dexter, "can't you see I'm talking to this guy?"

Dexter was confused. Then his whole attitude changed, and his voice went soft and he said to Ellison, almost with a plea, "*Why do you persist in tormenting me?*"

The whole scene was becoming ridiculous, and it seemed that Sinatra was only half-serious, perhaps just reacting out of sheer boredom or inner despair; at any rate, after a few more exchanges Harlan Ellison left the room. By this time the word had gotten out to those on the dance floor about the Sinatra-Ellison exchange, and somebody went to look for the manager of the club. But somebody else said that the manager had already heard about it—and had quickly gone out the door, hopped in his car and drove home. So the assistant manager went into the poolroom.

"I don't want anybody in here without coats and ties," Sinatra snapped.

The assistant manager nodded, and walked back to his office.

It was the morning after. It was the beginning of another nervous day for Sinatra's press agent, Jim Mahoney. Mahoney had a headache, and he was worried but not over the Sinatra-Ellison incident of the night before. At the time

Mahoney had been with his wife at a table in the other room, and possibly he had not even been aware of the little drama. The whole thing had lasted only about three minutes. And three minutes after it was over, Frank Sinatra had probably forgotten about it for the rest of his life—as Ellison will probably remember it for the rest of *his* life: he had had, as hundreds of others before him, at an unexpected moment between darkness and dawn, a scene with Sinatra.

It was just as well that Mahoney had not been in the poolroom; he had enough on his mind today. He was worried about Sinatra's cold and worried about the controversial CBS documentary that, despite Sinatra's protests and withdrawal of permission, would be shown on television in less than two weeks. The newspapers this morning were full of hints that Sinatra might sue the network, and Mahoney's phones were ringing without pause, and now he was plugged into New York talking to the *Daily News*'s Kay Gardella, saying: ". . . that's right, Kay . . . they made a gentleman's agreement to not ask certain questions about Frank's private life, and then Cronkite went right ahead: 'Frank, tell me about those associations.' *That* question, Kay—*out!* That question should never have been asked. . . ."

As he spoke, Mahoney leaned back in his leather chair, his head shaking slowly. He is a powerfully built man of thirty-seven; he has a round, ruddy face, a heavy jaw, and narrow pale eyes, and he might appear pugnacious if he did not speak with such clear, soft sincerity and if he were not so meticulous about his clothes. His suits and shoes are superbly tailored, which was one of the first things Sinatra noticed about him, and in his spacious office opposite the bar is a red-muff electrical shoe polisher and a pair of brown wooden shoulders on a stand over which Mahoney can drape his jackets. Near the bar is an autographed photograph of President Kennedy and a few pictures of Frank Sinatra, but there are none of Sinatra in any other rooms in Mahoney's public-relations agency; there once was a large photograph of him hanging in the reception room but this apparently bruised the egos of some of Mahoney's other movie-star clients and, since Sinatra never shows up at the agency anyway, the photograph was removed.

Still, Sinatra seems ever present, and if Mahoney did not have legitimate worries about Sinatra, as he did today, he could invent them—and, as worry aids, he surrounds himself with little mementos of moments in the past when he did worry. In his shaving kit there is a two-year-old box of sleeping tablets dispensed by a Reno druggist—the date on the bottle marks the kidnapping of Frank Sinatra, Jr. There is on a table in Mahoney's office a mounted wood reproduction of Frank Sinatra's ransom note written on the aforementioned occasion. One of Mahoney's mannerisms, when he is sitting at his desk worrying, is to tinker with the tiny toy train he keeps in front of him—the train is a souvenir from the Sinatra film, *Von Ryan's Express;* it is to men who are close to Sinatra what the PT-109 tie clasps are to men who were close to Kennedy—and Mahoney then proceeds to roll the little train back and forth on the six inches of track; back and forth, back and forth, click-*clack* click-*clack*. It is his Queeg-thing.

Now Mahoney quickly put aside the little train. His secretary told him there was a *very* important call on the line. Mahoney picked it up, and his voice was even softer and more sincere than before. "Yes, Frank," he said. "Right . . . right . . . yes, Frank. . . . "

When Mahoney put down the phone, quietly, he announced that Frank Sinatra had left in his private jet to spend the weekend at his home in Palm Springs, which is a sixteen-minute flight from his home in Los Angeles. Mahoney was now worried again. The Lear jet that Sinatra's pilot would be flying was identical, Mahoney said, to the one that had just crashed in another part of California.

On the following Monday, a cloudy and unseasonably cool California day, more than one hundred people gathered inside a white television studio, an enormous room dominated by a white stage, white walls, and with dozens of lights and lamps dangling: it rather resembled a gigantic operating room. In this room, within an hour or so, NBC was scheduled to begin taping a one-hour show that would be televised in color on the night of November 24 and would highlight, as much as it could in the limited time, the twenty-five-year career of Frank Sinatra as a public entertainer. It would not attempt to probe, as the forthcoming CBS *Sinatra* documentary allegedly would, that area of Sinatra's life that he regards as private. The NBC show would be mainly an hour of Sinatra singing some of the hits that carried him from Hoboken to Hollywood, a show that would be interrupted only now and then by a few film clips and commercials for Budweiser beer. Prior to his cold, Sinatra had been very excited about this show; he saw here an opportunity to appeal not only to those nostalgic, but also to communicate his talent to some rock-and-rollers—in a sense, he was battling The Beatles. The press releases being prepared by Mahoney's agency stressed this, reading: "If you happen to be tired of kid singers wearing mops of hair thick enough to hide a crate of melons . . . it should be refreshing to consider the entertainment value of a video special titled *Sinatra—A Man And His Music.* . . . "

But now in this NBC studio in Los Angeles, there was an atmosphere of anticipation and tension because of the uncertainty of the Sinatra voice. The forty-three musicians in Nelson Riddle's orchestra had already arrived and some were up on the white platform warming up. Dwight Hemion, a youthful sandy-haired director who had won praise for his television special on Barbra Streisand, was seated in the glass-enclosed control booth that overlooked the orchestra and stage. The camera crews, technical teams, security guards, Budweiser ad men were also standing between the floor lamps and cameras, waiting, as were a dozen or so ladies who worked as secretaries in other parts of the building but had sneaked away so they could watch this.

A few minutes before eleven o'clock, word spread quickly through the long corridor into the big studio that Sinatra was spotted walking through the parking lot and was on his way, and was looking fine. There seemed great relief among the group that was gathered; but when the lean, sharply dressed figure of the man got closer, and closer, they saw to their dismay that it was not Frank Sinatra. It was his double. Johnny Delgado.

Delgado walks like Sinatra, has Sinatra's build, and from certain facial angles does resemble Sinatra. But he seems a rather shy individual. Fifteen years ago, early in his acting career, Delgado applied for a role in *From Here to Eternity*. He was hired, finding out later that he was to be Sinatra's double. In Sinatra's latest film, *Assault on a Queen,* a story in which Sinatra and some fellow conspirators attempt to hijack the *Queen Mary,* Johnny Delgado doubles for Sinatra in some water scenes; and now, in this NBC studio, his job was to stand under the hot television lights marking Sinatra's spots on the stage for the camera crews.

Five minutes later, the real Frank Sinatra walked in. His face was pale, his blue eyes seemed a bit watery. He had been unable to rid himself of the cold, but he was going to try to sing anyway because the schedule was tight and thousands of dollars were involved at this moment in the assembling of the orchestra and crews and the rental of the studio. But when Sinatra, on his way to his small rehearsal room to warm up his voice, looked into the studio and saw that the stage and orchestra's platform were not close together, as he had specifically requested, his lips tightened and he was obviously very upset. A few moments later, from his rehearsal room, could be heard the pounding of his fist against the top of the piano and the voice of his accompanist, Bill Miller, saying, softly, "Try not to upset yourself, Frank."

Later Jim Mahoney and another man walked in, and there was talk of Dorothy Kilgallen's death in New York earlier that morning. She had been an ardent foe of Sinatra for years, and he became equally uncomplimentary about her in his nightclub act, and now, though she was dead, he did not compromise his feelings. "Dorothy Kilgallen's dead," he repeated, walking out of the room toward the studio. "Well, guess I got to change my whole act."

When he strolled into the studio the musicians all picked up their instruments and stiffened in their seats. Sinatra cleared his throat a few times and then, after rehearsing a few ballads with the orchestra, he sang *Don't Worry About Me* to his satisfaction and, being uncertain of how long his voice could last, suddenly became impatient.

"Why don't we tape this mother?" he called out, looking up toward the glass booth where the director, Dwight Hemion, and his staff were sitting. Their heads seemed to be down, focusing on the control board.

"Why don't we tape this mother?" Sinatra repeated.

The production stage manager, who stands near the camera wearing a headset, repeated Sinatra's words exactly into his line to the control room: "Why don't we tape this mother?"

Hemion did not answer. Possibly his switch was off. It was hard to know because of the obscuring reflections the lights made against the glass booth.

"Why don't we put on a coat and tie," said Sinatra, then wearing a high-necked yellow pullover, "and tape this. . . ."

Suddenly Hemion's voice came over the sound amplifier, very calmly: "Okay, Frank, would you mind going back over. . . ."

"Yes I *would* mind going back," Sinatra snapped.

The silence from Hemion's end, which lasted a second or two, was then again interrupted by Sinatra saying, "When we stop doing things around here the way we did them in 1950, maybe we . . ." and Sinatra continued to tear into Hemion, condemning as well the lack of modern techniques in putting such shows together; then, possibly not wanting to use his voice unnecessarily, he stopped. And Dwight Hemion, very patient, so patient and calm that one would assume he had not heard anything that Sinatra had just said, outlined the opening part of the show. And Sinatra a few minutes later was reading his opening remarks, words that would follow *Without a Song,* off the large idiot-cards being held near the camera. Then, this done, he prepared to do the same thing on camera.

"Frank Sinatra Show, Act I, Page 10, Take 1," called a man with a clapboard, jumping in front of the camera—*clap*—then jumping away again.

"Did you ever stop to think," Sinatra began, "what the world would be like without a song? . . . It would be a pretty dreary place. . . . Gives you something to think about, doesn't it? . . ."

Sinatra stopped.

"Excuse me," he said, adding, *"Boy,* I need a drink."

They tried it again.

"Frank Sinatra Show, Act I, Page 10, Take 2," yelled the jumping guy with the clapboard.

"Did you ever stop to think what the world would be like without a song? . . ." Frank Sinatra read it through this time without stopping. Then he rehearsed a few more songs, once or twice interrupting the orchestra when a certain instrumental sound was not quite what he wanted. It was hard to tell how well his voice was going to hold up, for this was early in the show; up to this point, however, everybody in the room seemed pleased, particularly when he sang an old sentimental favorite written more than twenty years ago by Jimmy Van Heusen and Phil Silvers—*Nancy,* inspired by the first of Sinatra's three children when she was just a few years old.

"If I don't see her each day
I miss her. . . .
Gee what a thrill
Each time I kiss her. . . ."

As Sinatra sang these words, though he has sung them hundreds and hundreds of times in the past, it was suddenly obvious to everybody in the studio that something quite special must be going on inside the man, because something quite special was coming out. He was singing now, cold or no cold, with power and warmth, he was letting himself go, the public arrogance was gone, the private side was in this song about the girl who, it is said, understands him better than anybody else, and is the only person in front of whom he can be unashamedly himself.

Nancy is twenty-five. She lives alone, her marriage to singer Tommy Sands having ended in divorce. Her home is in a Los Angeles suburb and she is now making her third film and is recording for her father's record company. She sees him every day; or, if not, he telephones, no matter if it be from Europe or Asia. When Sinatra's singing first became popular on radio, stimulating the swooners, Nancy would listen at home and cry. When Sinatra's first marriage broke up in 1951 and he left home, Nancy was the only child old enough to remember him as a father. She also saw him with Ava Gardner, Juliet Prowse, Mia Farrow, many others, has gone on double dates with him. . . .

"She takes the winter
And makes it summer. . . .
Summer could take
Some lessons from her. . . ."

Nancy now also sees him visiting at home with his first wife, the former Nancy Barbato, a plasterer's daughter from Jersey City whom he married in 1939 when he was earning $25 a week singing at the Rustic Cabin near Hoboken.

The first Mrs. Sinatra, a striking woman who has never remarried ("When you've been married to Frank Sinatra . . . " she once explained to a friend), lives in a magnificent home in Los Angeles with her younger daughter, Tina, who is seventeen. There is no bitterness, only great respect and affection between Sinatra and his first wife, and he has long been welcome in her home and has even been known to wander in at odd hours, stoke the fire, lie on the sofa and fall asleep. Frank Sinatra can fall asleep anywhere, something he learned when he used to ride bumpy roads with band ·buses; he also learned at that time, when sitting in a tuxedo, how to pinch the trouser creases in the back and tuck the jacket under and out, and fall asleep perfectly pressed. But he does not ride buses anymore, and his daughter Nancy, who in her younger days felt rejected when he slept on the sofa instead of giving attention to her, later realized that the sofa was one of the few places left in the world where Frank Sinatra could get any privacy, where his famous face would neither be stared at nor cause an abnormal reaction in others. She realized, too, that things normal have always eluded her father: his childhood was one of loneliness and a drive toward attention, and since attaining it he has never again been certain of solitude. Upon looking out the window of a home he once owned in Hasbrouck Heights, New Jersey, he would occasionally see the faces of teen-agers peeking in; and in 1944, after moving to California and buying a home behind a ten-foot fence on Lake Toluca, he discovered that the only way to escape the telephone and other intrusions was to board his paddle boat with a few friends, a card table and a case of beer, and stay afloat all afternoon. But he has tried, insofar as it has been possible, to be like everyone else, Nancy says. He wept on her wedding day, he is very sentimental and sensitive. . . .

"What the hell are you doing up there, Dwight?"

Silence from the control booth.

"Got a party or something going on up there, *Dwight?*"

Sinatra stood on the stage, arms folded, glaring up across the cameras toward Hemion. Sinatra had sung *Nancy* with probably all he had in his voice on this day. The next few numbers contained raspy notes, and twice his voice completely cracked. But now Hemion was in the control booth out of communication; then he was down in the studio walking over to where Sinatra stood. A few minutes later they both left the studio and were on the way up to the control booth. The tape was replayed for Sinatra. He watched only about five minutes of it before he started to shake his head. Then he said to Hemion: "Forget it, just forget it. You're wasting your time. What you got there," Sinatra said, nodding to the singing image of himself on the television screen, "is a man with a cold." Then he left the control booth, ordering that the whole day's performance be scrubbed and future taping postponed until he had recovered.

Soon the word spread like an emotional epidemic down through Sinatra's staff, then fanned out through Hollywood, then was heard across the nation in Jilly's saloon, and also on the other side of the Hudson River in the homes of Frank Sinatra's parents and his other relatives and friends in New Jersey.

When Frank Sinatra spoke with his father on the telephone and said he was feeling awful, the elder Sinatra reported that *he* was also feeling awful: that his left arm and fist were so stiff with a circulatory condition he could barely use them, adding that the ailment might be the result of having thrown too many left hooks during his days as a bantamweight almost fifty years ago.

Martin Sinatra, a ruddy and tattooed little blue-eyed Sicilian born in Catania, boxed under the name of "Marty O'Brien." In those days, in those places, with the Irish running the lower reaches of city life, it was not uncommon for Italians to wind up with such names. Most of the Italians and Sicilians who migrated to America just prior to the 1900's were poor and uneducated, were excluded from the building-trades unions dominated by the Irish, and were somewhat intimidated by the Irish police, Irish priests, Irish politicians.

One notable exception was Frank Sinatra's mother, Dolly, a large and very ambitious woman who was brought to this country at two months of age by her mother and father, a lithographer from Genoa. In later years Dolly Sinatra, possessing a round red face and blue eyes, was often mistaken for being Irish, and surprised many at the speed with which she swung her heavy handbag at anyone uttering "Wop."

By playing skillful politics with North Jersey's Democratic machine, Dolly Sinatra was to become, in her heyday, a kind of Catherine de Medici of Hoboken's third ward. She could always be counted upon to deliver six hundred votes at election time from her Italian neighborhood, and this was her base of power. When she told one of the politicians that she wanted her husband to be appointed to the Hoboken Fire Department, and was told, "But, Dolly, we don't have an opening," she snapped, "*Make* an opening."

They did. Years later she requested that her husband be made a captain, and one day she got a call from one of the political bosses that began, "Dolly, congratulations!"

"For what?"

"*Captain* Sinatra."

"Oh, you finally made him one—thank you very much."

Then she called the Hoboken Fire Department.

"Let me speak to *Captain* Sinatra," she said. The fireman called Martin Sinatra to the phone, saying, "Marty, I think your wife has gone nuts." When he got on the line, Dolly greeted him:

"Congratulations, *Captain* Sinatra!"

Dolly's only child, christened Francis Albert Sinatra, was born and nearly died on December 12, 1915. It was a difficult birth, and during his first moment on earth he received marks he will carry till death—the scars on the left side of his neck being the result of a doctor's clumsy forceps, and Sinatra has chosen not to obscure them with surgery.

After he was six months old, he was reared mainly by his grandmother. His mother had a full-time job as a chocolate dipper with a large firm and was so proficient at it that the firm once offered to send her to the Paris office to train others. While some people in Hoboken remember Frank Sinatra as a lonely child, one who spent many hours on the porch gazing into space, Sinatra was never a slum kid, never in jail, always well-dressed. He had so many pants that some people in Hoboken called him "Slacksey O'Brien."

Dolly Sinatra was not the sort of Italian mother who could be appeased merely by a child's obedience and good appetite. She made many demands on her son, was always very strict. She dreamed of his becoming an aviation engineer. When she discovered Bing Crosby pictures hanging on his bedroom walls one evening, and learned that her son wished to become a singer too, she became infuriated and threw a shoe at him. Later, finding she could not talk him out of it—"he takes after me"—she encouraged his singing.

Many Italo-American boys of his generation were then shooting for the same star—they were strong with song, weak with words, not a big novelist among them: no O'Hara, no Bellow, no Cheever, nor Shaw; yet they could communicate *bel canto*. This was more in their tradition, no need for a diploma; they could, with a song, someday see their names in lights . . . *Perry Como* . . . *Frankie Laine* . . . *Tony Bennett* . . . *Vic Damone* . . . but none could see it better than *Frank Sinatra.*

Though he sang through much of the night at the Rustic Cabin, he was up the next day singing without a fee on New York radio to get more attention. Later he got a job singing with Harry James's band, and it was there in August of 1939 that Sinatra had his first recording hit—*All or Nothing at All.* He became very fond of Harry James and the men in the band, but when he received an offer from Tommy Dorsey, who in those days had probably the best band in the country, Sinatra took it; the job paid $125 a week, and Dorsey knew how to feature a vocalist. Yet Sinatra was very depressed at leaving James's band, and the final night with them was so memorable that, twenty years later, Sinatra could recall the details to a friend: ". . . the bus pulled out with the rest of the boys at about half-past midnight. I'd said good-bye to them all, and it was snowing, I remember. There was nobody around and I stood alone with my suitcase in the snow and watched the taillights disappear. Then the tears started and I tried to run after the bus. There was such spirit and enthusiasm in that band, I hated leaving it. . . ."

But he did—as he would leave other warm places, too, in search of something more, never wasting time, trying to do it all in one generation, fighting under his *own* name, defending underdogs, terrorizing top dogs. He threw a punch at a musician who said something anti-Semitic, espoused the Negro cause two decades before it became fashionable. He also threw a tray of glasses at Buddy Rich when he played the drums too loud.

Sinatra gave away $50,000 worth of gold cigarette lighters before he was thirty, was living an immigrant's wildest dream of America. He arrived suddenly on the scene when DiMaggio was silent, when *paisanos* were mournful, were quietly defensive about Hitler in their homeland. Sinatra became, in time, a kind of one-man Anti-Defamation League for Italians in America, the sort of organization that would be unlikely for them because, as the theory goes, they rarely agreed on anything, being extreme individualists: fine as soloists, but not so good in a choir; fine as heroes, but not so good in a parade.

When many Italian names were used in describing gangsters on a television show, *The Untouchables,* Sinatra was loud in his disapproval. Sinatra and many thousands of other Italo-Americans were resentful as well when a small-time hoodlum, Joseph Valachi, was brought by Bobby Kennedy into prominence as a Mafia expert, when indeed, from Valachi's testimony on television, he seemed to know less than most waiters on Mulberry Street. Many Italians in Sinatra's circle also regard Bobby Kennedy as something of an Irish cop, more dignified than those in Dolly's day, but no less intimidating. Together with Peter Lawford, Bobby Kennedy is said to have suddenly gotten "cocky" with Sinatra after John Kennedy's election, forgetting the contribution Sinatra had made in both fund-raising and in influencing many anti-Irish Italian votes. Lawford and Bobby Kennedy are both suspected of having influenced the late President's decision to stay as a house guest with Bing Crosby instead of Sinatra, as originally planned, a social setback Sinatra may never forget. Peter Lawford has since been drummed out of Sinatra's "summit" in Las Vegas.

"Yes, my son is like me," Dolly Sinatra says, proudly. "You cross him, he never forgets." And while she concedes his power, she quickly points out, "He can't make his mother do anything she doesn't want to do," adding, "Even today, he wears the same brand of underwear I used to buy him."

Today Dolly Sinatra is seventy-one years old, a year or two younger than Martin, and all day long people are knocking on the back door of her large home asking her advice, seeking her influence. When she is not seeing people and not cooking in the kitchen, she is looking after her husband, a silent but stubborn man, and telling him to keep his sore left arm resting on the sponge she has placed on the armrest of a soft chair. "Oh, he went to some terrific fires, this guy did," Dolly said to a visitor, nodding with admiration toward her husband in the chair.

Though Dolly Sinatra has eighty-seven godchildren in Hoboken, and still goes to that city during political campaigns, she now lives with her husband in a beautiful sixteen-room house in Fort Lee, New Jersey. This home was a gift from their son on their fiftieth wedding anniversary three years ago. The home is tastefully furnished and is filled with a remarkable juxtaposition of the pious and the worldly—photographs of Pope John and Ava Gardner, of Pope Paul and Dean Martin; several statues of saints and holy water, a chair autographed by Sammy Davis, Jr. and bottles of bourbon. In Mrs. Sinatra's jewelry box is a magnificent strand of pearls she had just received from Ava Gardner, whom she liked tremendously as a daughter-in-law and still keeps in touch with and talks about; and hung on the wall is a letter addressed to Dolly and Martin: "The sands of time have turned to gold, yet love continues to unfold like the petals of a rose, in God's garden of life . . . may God love you thru all eternity. I thank Him, I thank you for the being of one. Your loving son, Francis. . . ."

Mrs. Sinatra talks to her son on the telephone about once a week, and recently he suggested that, when visiting Manhattan, she make use of his apartment on East Seventy-second Street on the East River. This is an expensive neighborhood of New York even though there is a small factory on the block, but this latter fact was seized upon by Dolly Sinatra as a means of getting back at her son for some unflattering descriptions of his childhood in Hoboken.

"What—you want me to stay in *your* apartment, in *that* dump?" she asked. "You think I'm going to spend the night in *that* awful neighborhood?"

Frank Sinatra got the point, and said, "Excuse *me*, Mrs. Fort Lee."

After spending the week in Palm Springs, his cold much better, Frank Sinatra returned to Los Angeles, a lovely city of sun and sex, a Spanish discovery of Mexican misery, a star land of little men and lithe women sliding in and out of convertibles in tense tight pants.

Sinatra returned in time to see the long-awaited CBS documentary with his family. At about nine p.m. he drove to the home of his former wife, Nancy, and had dinner with her and their two daughters. Their son, whom they rarely see these days, was out of town.

Frank, Jr., who is twenty-two, was touring with a band and moving cross country toward a New York engagement at Basin Street East with The Pied Pipers, with whom Frank Sinatra sang when he was with Dorsey's band in the 1940's. Today Frank Sinatra, Jr., whom his father says he named after Franklin D. Roosevelt, lives mostly in hotels, dines each evening in his nightclub dressing room, and sings until two a.m., accepting graciously, because he has no choice, the inevitable comparisons. His voice is smooth and pleasant, and improving with work, and while he is very respectful of his father, he discusses him with objectivity and in an occasional tone of subdued cockiness.

Concurrent with his father's early fame, Frank, Jr. said, was the creation of a "press-release Sinatra" designed to "set him apart from the common man, separate him from the realities: it was suddenly Sinatra, the electric magnate, Sinatra who is supernormal, not super*human*, but super*normal*. And here," Frank, Jr. continued, "is the great fallacy, the great bullshit, for Frank Sinatra *is* normal, *is* the guy whom you'd meet on a street corner. But this other thing, the supernormal guise, has affected Frank Sinatra as much as anybody who watches one of his television shows, or reads a magazine article about him. . . .

"Frank Sinatra's life in the beginning was so normal," he said, "that nobody would have guessed in 1934 that this little Italian kid with the curly hair would become the giant, the monster, the great living legend. . . . He met my mother one summer on the beach. She was Nancy Barbato, daughter of Mike Barbato, a Jersey City plasterer. And she meets the fireman's son, Frank, one summer day on the beach at Long Branch, New Jersey. Both are Italian, both Roman Catholic, both lower-middle-class summer sweethearts—it is like a million bad movies starring Frankie Avalon. . . .

"They have three children. The first child, Nancy, was the most normal of Frank Sinatra's children. Nancy was a cheerleader, went to summer camp, drove a Chevrolet, had the easiest kind of development centered around the home and family. Next is me. My life with the family is very, very normal up until September of 1958 when, in complete contrast to the rearing of both girls, I am put into a college-preparatory school. I am now away from the inner family circle, and my position within has never been remade to this day. . . . The third child, Tina. And to be dead honest, I really couldn't say what her life is like. . . ."

The CBS show, narrated by Walter Cronkite, began at ten p.m. A minute before that, the Sinatra family, having finished dinner, turned their chairs around and faced the camera, united for whatever disaster might follow. Sinatra's men in other parts of town, in other parts of the nation, were doing the same thing. Sinatra's lawyer, Milton A. Rudin, smoking a cigar, was watching with a keen eye, an alert legal mind. Other sets were watched by Brad Dexter, Jim Mahoney, Ed Pucci; Sinatra's makeup man, "Shotgun" Britton; his New York representative, Henri Giné; his haberdasher, Richard Carroll; his insurance broker, John Lillie; his valet, George Jacobs, a handsome Negro who, when entertaining girls in *his* apartment, plays records by Ray Charles.

And like so much of Hollywood's fear, the apprehension about the CBS show all proved to be without foundation. It was a highly flattering hour that did not deeply probe, as rumors suggested it would, into Sinatra's love life, or the Mafia, or other areas of his private province. While the documentary was not authorized, wrote Jack Gould in the next day's New York *Times,* "it could have been."

Immediately after the show, the telephones began to ring throughout the Sinatra system conveying words of joy and relief—and from New York came Jilly's telegram: "WE RULE THE WORLD!"

The next day, standing in the corridor of the NBC building where he was about to resume taping his show, Sinatra was discussing the CBS show with several of his friends, and he said, "Oh, it was a gas."

"Yeah, Frank, a helluva show."

"But I think Jack Gould was right in the *Times* today," Sinatra said. "There should have been more on the *man*, not so much on the music. . . ."

They nodded, nobody mentioning the past hysteria in the Sinatra world when it seemed CBS was zeroing in on the *man*; they just nodded and two of them laughed about Sinatra's apparently having gotten the word "bird" on the show—this being a favorite Sinatra word. He often inquires of his cronies, "How's your bird?"; and when he nearly drowned in Hawaii, he later explained, "Just got a little water on my bird"; and under a large photograph of him holding a whisky bottle, a photo that hangs in the home of an actor friend named Dick Bakalyan, the inscription reads: "Drink, Dickie! It's good for your bird." In the song, *Come Fly With Me,* Sinatra sometimes alters the lyrics—". . . just say the words and we'll take our birds down to Acapulco Bay. . . ."

Ten minutes later Sinatra, following the orchestra, walked into the NBC studio which did not resemble in the slightest the scene here of eight days ago. On this occasion Sinatra was in fine voice, he cracked jokes between numbers, nothing could upset him. Once, while he was singing *How Can I Ignore the Girl Next Door,* standing on the stage next to a tree, a television camera mounted on a vehicle came rolling in too close and plowed against the tree.

"Kee-rist!" yelled one of the technical assistants.

But Sinatra seemed hardly to notice it.

"We've had a slight accident," he said, calmly. Then he began the song all over from the beginning.

When the show was over, Sinatra watched the rerun on the monitor in the control room. He was very pleased, shaking hands with Dwight Hemion and his assistants. Then the whisky bottles were opened in Sinatra's dressing room. Pat Lawford was there, and so were Andy Williams and a dozen others. The telegrams and telephone calls continued to be received from all over the country with praise for the CBS show. There was even a call, Mahoney said, from the CBS producer, Don Hewitt, with whom Sinatra had been so angry a few days before. And Sinatra was *still* angry, feeling that CBS had betrayed him, though the show itself was not objectionable.

"Shall I drop a line to Hewitt?" Mahoney asked.

"Can you send a fist through the mail?" Sinatra asked.

He has everything, he cannot sleep, he gives nice gifts, he is not happy, but he would not trade, even for happiness, what he is. . . .

He is a piece of our past—but only we have aged, he hasn't . . . we are dogged by domesticity, he isn't . . . we have compunctions, he doesn't . . . it is our fault, not his. . . .

He controls the menus of every Italian restaurant in Los Angeles; if you want North Italian cooking, fly to Milan. . . .

Men follow him, imitate him, fight to be near him . . . there is something of the locker room, the barracks about him . . . bird . . . bird. . . .

He believes you must play it big, wide, expansively—the more open you are, the more you take in, your dimensions deepen, you grow, you become more what you are—bigger, richer. . . .

"He is better than anybody else, or at least they think he is, and he has to live up to it."
                                                                        —NANCY SINATRA, JR.

"He is calm on the outside—inwardly a million things are happening to him."
                                                                        —DICK BAKALYAN

"He has an insatiable desire to live every moment to its fullest because, I guess, he feels that right around the corner is extinction."   —BRAD DEXTER

"All I ever got out of any of my marriages was the two years Artie Shaw financed on an analyst's couch."   —AVA GARDNER

"We weren't mother and son—we were buddies."   —DOLLY SINATRA

"I'm for anything that gets you through the night, be it prayer, tranquilizers or a bottle of Jack Daniel."   —FRANK SINATRA

Frank Sinatra was tired of all the talk, the gossip, the theory—tired of reading quotes about himself, of hearing what people were saying about him all over town. It had been a tedious three weeks, he said, and now he just wanted to get away, go to Las Vegas, let off some steam. So he hopped in his jet, soared over the California hills across the Nevada flats, then over miles and miles of desert to The Sands and the Clay-Patterson fight.

On the eve of the fight he stayed up all night and slept through most of the afternoon, though his recorded voice could be heard singing in the lobby of The Sands, in the gambling casino, even in the toilets, being interrupted every few bars however by the paging public address: ". . . Telephone call for Mr. Ron Fish, Mr. Ron Fish . . . *with a ribbon of gold in her hair.* . . . Telephone call for Mr. Herbert Rothstein, Mr. Herbert Rothstein . . . *memories of a time so bright, keep me sleepless through dark endless nights.* . . ."

Standing around in the lobby of The Sands and other hotels up and down the strip on this afternoon before the fight were the usual prefight prophets: the gamblers, the old champs, the little cigar butts from Eighth Avenue, the sportswriters who knock the big fights all year but would never miss one, the novelists who seem always to be identifying with one boxer or another, the local prostitutes assisted by some talent in from Los Angeles, and also a young brunette in a wrinkled black cocktail dress who was at the bell captain's desk crying, "But I want to speak to Mr. Sinatra."

"He's not here," the bell captain said.

"Won't you put me through to his room?"

"There are *no* messages going through, Miss," he said, and then she turned, unsteadily, seeming close to tears, and walked through the lobby into the big noisy casino crowded with men interested only in money.

Shortly before seven p.m., Jack Entratter, a big grey-haired man who operates The Sands, walked into the gambling room to tell some men around the blackjack table that Sinatra was getting dressed. He also said that he'd been unable to get front-row seats for everybody, and so some of the men—including Leo Durocher, who had a date, and Joey Bishop, who was accompanied by his wife—would not be able to fit in Frank Sinatra's row but would have to take seats in the third row. When Entratter walked over to tell this to Joey Bishop, Bishop's face fell. He did not seem angry; he merely looked at Entratter with an empty silence, seeming somewhat stunned.

"Joey, I'm *sorry*," Entratter said when the silence persisted, "but we couldn't get more than six together in the front row."

Bishop still said nothing. But when they all appeared at the fight, Joey Bishop was in the front row, his wife in the third.

The fight, called a holy war between Muslims and Christians, was preceded by the introduction of three balding ex-champions, Rocky Marciano, Joe Louis, Sonny Liston—and then there was *The Star-Spangled Banner* sung by another man from out of the past, Eddie Fisher. It had been more than fourteen years ago, but Sinatra could still remember every detail: Eddie Fisher was then the new king of the baritones, with Billy Eckstine and Guy Mitchell right with him, and Sinatra had been long counted out. One day he remembered walking into a broadcasting studio past dozens of Eddie Fisher fans waiting outside the hall, and when they saw Sinatra they began to jeer, "Frankie, Frankie, I'm *swooning, I'm swooning*." This was also the time when he was selling only about 30,000 records a year, when he was dreadfully miscast as a funny man on his television show, and when he recorded such disasters as *Mama Will Bark,* with Dagmar.

"I growled and barked on the record," Sinatra said, still horrified by the thought. "The only good it did me was with the dogs."

His voice and his artistic judgment were incredibly bad in 1952, but even more responsible for his decline, say his friends, was his pursuit of Ava Gardner. She was the big movie queen then, one of the most beautiful women in the world. Sinatra's daughter Nancy recalls seeing Ava swimming one day in her father's pool, then climbing out of the water with that fabulous body, walking slowly to the fire, leaning over it for a few moments, and then it suddenly seemed that her long dark hair was all dry, miraculously and effortlessly back in place.

With most women Sinatra dates, his friends say, he never knows whether they want him for what he can do for them now—or will do for them later. With Ava Gardner, it was different. He could do nothing for her later. She was on top. If Sinatra learned anything from his experience with her, he possibly learned that when a proud man is down a woman cannot help. Particularly a woman on top.

Nevertheless, despite a tired voice, some deep emotion seeped into his singing during this time. One particular song that is well remembered even now is *I'm A Fool to Want You,* and a friend who was in the studio when Sinatra recorded it recalled: "Frank was really worked up that night. He did the song in one take, then turned around and walked out of the studio and that was that. . . . "

Sinatra's manager at that time, a former song plugger named Hank Sanicola, said, "Ava loved Frank, but not the way he loved her. He needs a great deal of love. He wants it twenty-four hours a day, he must have people around—Frank is that kind of guy." Ava Gardner, Sanicola said, "was very insecure. She feared she could not really hold a man . . . twice he went chasing her to Africa, wasting his own career. . . . "

"Ava didn't want Frank's men hanging around all the time," another friend said, "and this got him mad. With Nancy he used to be able to bring the whole band home with him, and Nancy, the good Italian wife, would never complain—she'd just make everybody a plate of spaghetti."

In 1953, after almost two years of marriage, Sinatra and Ava Gardner were divorced. Sinatra's mother reportedly arranged a reconciliation, but if Ava was willing, Frank Sinatra was not. He was seen with other women. The balance had shifted. Somewhere during this period Sinatra seemed to change from the kid singer, the boy actor in the sailor suit, to a man. Even before he had won the Oscar in 1953 for his role in *From Here to Eternity,* some flashes of his old talent were coming through—in his recording of *The Birth of the Blues,* in his Riviera-nightclub appearance that jazz critics enthusiastically praised; and there was also a trend now toward L.P.'s and away from the quick three-minute deal, and Sinatra's concert style would have capitalized on this with or without an Oscar.

In 1954, totally committed to his talent once more, Frank Sinatra was selected Metronome's "Singer of the Year," and later he won the U.P.I. disc-jockey poll, unseating Eddie Fisher— who now, in Las Vegas, having sung *The Star-Spangled Banner,* climbed out of the ring, and the fight began.

Floyd Patterson chased Clay around the ring in the first round, but was unable to reach him, and from then on he was Clay's toy, the bout ending in a technical knockout in the twelfth round. A half hour later, nearly everybody had forgotten about the fight and was back at the gambling tables or lining up to buy tickets for the Dean Martin-Sinatra-Bishop nightclub routine on the stage of The Sands. This routine, which includes Sammy Davis, Jr. when he is in town, consists of a few songs and much cutting up, all of it very informal, very special, and rather ethnic—Martin, a drink in hand, asking Bishop: "Did you ever see a Jew jitsu?"; and Bishop, playing a Jewish waiter, warning the two Italians to watch out "because I got my own group—the *Matzia*."

Then after the last show at The Sands, the Sinatra crowd, which now numbered about twenty—and included Jilly, who had flown in from New York; Jimmy Cannon, Sinatra's favorite sports columist; Harold Gibbons, a Teamster official expected to take over if Hoffa goes to jail—all got into a line of cars and headed for another club. It was three o'clock. The night was young.

They stopped at The Sahara, taking a long table near the back, and listened to a baldheaded little comedian named Don Rickles, who is probably more caustic than any comic in the country. His humor is so rude, in *such* bad taste, that it offends no one—it is *too* offensive to be offensive. Spotting Eddie Fisher among the audience, Rickles proceeded to ridicule him as a lover, saying it was no wonder that he could not handle Elizabeth Taylor; and when two businessmen in the audience acknowledged that they were Egyptians, Rickles cut into them for their country's policy toward Israel; and he strongly suggested that the woman seated at one table with her husband was actually a hooker.

When the Sinatra crowd walked in, Don Rickles could not be more delighted. Pointing to Jilly, Rickles yelled: "How's it feel to be Frank's tractor? . . . Yeah, Jilly keeps walking in front of Frank clearing the way." Then, nodding to Durocher, Rickles said, "Stand up, Leo, show Frank how you slide." Then he focused on Sinatra, not failing to mention Mia Farrow, nor that he was wearing a toupee, nor to say that Sinatra was washed up as a singer, and when Sinatra laughed, everybody laughed, and Rickles pointed toward Bishop: "Joey Bishop keeps checking with Frank to see what's funny."

Then, after Rickles told some Jewish jokes, Dean Martin stood up and yelled, "Hey, you're always talking about the Jews, never about the Italians," and Rickles cut him off with, "What do we need the Italians for—all they do is keep the flies off our fish."

Sinatra laughed, they all laughed, and Rickles went on this way for nearly an hour until Sinatra, standing up, said, "All right, com'on, get this thing over with. I gotta go."

"Shaddup and sit down!" Rickles snapped. "I've had to listen to you sing. . . ."

"Who do you think you're talking to?" Sinatra yelled back.

"Dick Haymes," Rickles replied, and Sinatra laughed again, and then Dean Martin, pouring a bottle of whisky over his head, entirely drenching his tuxedo, pounded the table.

"Who would ever believe that staggering would make a star?" Rickles said, but Martin called out, "Hey, I wanna make a speech."

"Shaddup."

"No, Don, I wanna tell ya," Dean Martin persisted, "that I think you're a great performer."

"Well, thank you, Dean," Rickles said, seeming pleased.

"But don't go by me," Martin said, plopping down into his seat, "I'm drunk."

"I'll buy that," Rickles said.

By four a.m. Frank Sinatra led the group out of The Sahara, some of them carrying their glasses of whisky with them, sipping it along the sidewalk and in the cars; then, returning to The Sands, they walked into the gambling casino. It was still packed with people, the roulette wheels spinning, the crapshooters screaming in the far corner.

Frank Sinatra, holding a shot glass of bourbon in his left hand, walked through the crowd. He, unlike some of his friends, was perfectly pressed, his tuxedo tie precisely pointed, his shoes unsmudged. He never seems to lose his dignity, never lets his guard completely down no matter how much he has drunk, nor how long he has been up. He never sways when he walks, like Dean Martin, nor does he ever dance in the aisles or jump up on tables, like Sammy Davis.

A part of Sinatra, no matter where he is, is never there. There is always a part of him, though sometimes a small part, that remains *Il Padrone*. Even now, resting his shot glass on the blackjack table, facing the dealer, Sinatra stood a bit back from the table, not leaning against it. He reached under his tuxedo jacket into his trouser pocket and came up with a thick but *clean* wad of bills. Gently he peeled of a one-hundred-dollar bill and placed it on the green-felt table. The dealer dealt him two cards. Sinatra called for a third card, overbid, lost the hundred.

Without a change of expression, Sinatra put down a second hundred-dollar bill. He lost that. Then he put down a third, and lost that. Then he placed two one-hundred-dollar bills on the table and lost those. Finally, putting his sixth hundred-dollar bill on the table, and losing it, Sinatra moved away from the table, nodding to the man, and announcing, "Good dealer."

The crowd that had gathered around him now opened up to let him through. But a woman stepped in front of him, handing him a piece of paper to autograph. He signed it then *he* said, "Thank you."

In the rear of The Sands' large dining room was a long table reserved for Sinatra. The dining room was fairly empty at this hour, with perhaps two dozen other people in the room, including a table of four unescorted young ladies sitting near Sinatra. On the other side of the room, at another long table, sat seven men shoulder-to-shoulder against the wall, two of them wearing dark glasses, all of them eating quietly, speaking hardly a word, just sitting and eating and missing nothing.

The Sinatra party, after getting settled and having a few more drinks, ordered something to eat. The table was about the same size as the one reserved for Sinatra whenever he is at Jilly's in New York; and the people seated around this table in Las Vegas were many of the same people who are often seen with Sinatra at Jilly's or at a restaurant in California, or in Italy, or in New Jersey, or wherever Sinatra happens to be. When Sinatra sits to dine, his trusted friends are close; and no matter where he is, no matter how elegant the place may be, there is something of the neighborhood showing because Sinatra, no matter how far he has come, is still something of the boy from the neighborhood—only now he can take his neighborhood with him.

In some ways, this quasi-family affair at a reserved table in a public place is the closest thing Sinatra now has to home life. Perhaps, having had a home and left it, this approximation is as close as he cares to come; although this does not seem precisely so because he speaks with such warmth about his family, keeps in close touch with his first wife, and insists that she make no decision without first consulting him. He is always eager to place his furniture or other mementos of himself in her home or his daughter Nancy's, and he also is on amiable terms with Ava Gardner. When he was in Italy making *Von Ryan's Express,* they spent some time together, being pursued wherever they went by the *paparazzi.* It was reported then that the *paparazzi* had made Sinatra a collective offer of $16,000 if he would pose with Ava Gardner; Sinatra was said to have made a counter offer of $32,000 if he could break one *paparazzi* arm and leg.

While Sinatra is often delighted that he can be in his home completely without people, enabling him to read and think without interruption, there are occasions when he finds himself alone at night, and *not* by choice. He may have dialed a half-dozen women, and for one reason or another they are all unavailable. So he will call his valet, George Jacobs.

"I'll be coming home for dinner tonight, George."

"How many will there be?"

"Just myself," Sinatra will say. "I want something light, I'm not very hungry."

George Jacobs is a twice-divorced man of thirty-six who resembles Billy Eckstine. He has traveled all over the world with Sinatra and is devoted to him. Jacobs lives in a comfortable bachelor's apartment off

Sunset Boulevard around the corner from Whiskey à Go Go, and he is known around town for the assortment of frisky California girls he has as friends—a few of whom, he concedes, were possibly drawn to him initially because of his closeness to Frank Sinatra.

When Sinatra arrives, Jacobs will serve him dinner in the dining room. Then Sinatra will tell Jacobs that he is free to go home. If Sinatra, on such evenings, should ask Jacobs to stay longer, or to play a few hands of poker, he would be happy to do so. But Sinatra never does.

This was his second night in Las Vegas, and Frank Sinatra sat with friends in The Sands' dining room until nearly eight a.m. He slept through much of the day, then flew back to Los Angeles, and on the following morning he was driving his little golf cart through the Paramount Pictures movie lot. He was scheduled to complete two final scenes with the sultry blonde actress, Virna Lisi, in the film, *Assault on a Queen.* As he maneuvered the little vehicle up the road between the big studio buildings, he spotted Steve Rossi who, with his comedy partner Marty Allen, was making a film in an adjoining studio with Nancy Sinatra.

"Hey, Dag," he yelled to Rossi, "stop kissing Nancy."

"It's part of the film, Frank," Rossi said, turning as he walked.

"In the garage?"

"It's my Dago blood, Frank."

"Well, cool it," Sinatra said, winking, then cutting his golf cart around a corner and parking it outside a big drab building within which the scenes for *Assault* would be filmed.

"Where's the fat director?" Sinatra called out, striding into the studio that was crowded with dozens of technical assistants and actors all gathered around cameras. The director, Jack Donohue, a large man who has worked with Sinatra through twenty-two years on one production or other, has had headaches with this film. The script had been chopped, the actors seemed restless, and Sinatra had become bored. But now there were only two scenes left—a short one to be filmed in the pool, and a longer and passionate one featuring Sinatra and Virna Lisi to be shot on a simulated beach.

The pool scene, which dramatizes a situation where Sinatra and his hijackers fail in their attempt to sack the *Queen Mary,* went quickly and well. After Sinatra had been kept in the water shoulder-high for a few minutes, he said, "Let's move it, fellows—it's cold in this water, and I've just gotten over one cold."

So the camera crews moved in closer, Virna Lisi splashed next to Sinatra in the water, and Jack Donohue yelled to his assistants operating the fans, "Get the waves going," and another man gave the command, *"Agitate!"* and Sinatra broke out in song. "Agitate in rhythm," then quieted down just before the cameras started to roll.

Frank Sinatra was on the beach in the next situation, supposedly gazing up at the stars, and Virna Lisi was to approach him, toss one of her shoes near him to announce her presence, then sit near him and prepare for a passionate session. Just before beginning, Miss Lisi made a practice toss of her shoe toward the prone figure of Sinatra sprawled on the beach. As she tossed her shoe, Sinatra called out, "Hit me in my bird and I'm going home."

Virna Lisi, who understands little English and certainly none of Sinatra's special vocabulary, looked confused, but everybody behind the camera laughed. She threw the shoe toward him. It twirled in the air, landed on his stomach.

"Well, that's about three inches too high," he announced. She again was puzzled by the laughter behind the camera.

Then Jack Donohue had them rehearse their lines, and Sinatra, still very charged from the Las Vegas trip, and anxious to get the cameras rolling, said, "Let's try one." Donohue, not certain that Sinatra and Lisi knew their lines well enough, nevertheless said okay, and an assistant with a clapboard called, "419, Take 1," and Virna Lisi approached with the shoe, tossed it at Frank lying on the beach. It fell short of his thigh, and Sinatra's right eye raised almost imperceptibly, but the crew got the message, smiled.

"What do the stars tell you tonight?" Miss Lisi said, delivering her first line, and sitting next to Sinatra on the beach.

"The stars tell me tonight I'm an idiot," Sinatra said, "a gold-plated idiot to get mixed up in this thing. . . . "

"Cut," Donohue said. There were some microphone shadows on the sand, and Virna Lisi was not sitting in the proper place near Sinatra.

"419, Take 2," the clapboard man called.

Miss Lisi again approached, threw the shoe at him, this time falling short—Sinatra exhaling only slightly—and she said, "What do the stars tell you tonight?"

"The stars tell me I'm an idiot, a gold-plated idiot to get mixed up in this thing. . . . " Then, according to the script, Sinatra was to continue, " . . . do you know what we're getting into? The minute we step on the deck of the *Queen Mary,* we've just tattooed ourselves," but Sinatra, who often improvises on lines, recited them: " . . . do you know what we're getting into? The minute we step on the deck of that mother's-ass ship. . . . "

"*No,* no," Donohue interrupted, shaking his head, "I don't think that's right."

The cameras stopped, some people laughed, and Sinatra looked up from his position in the sand as if he had been unfairly interrupted.

"I don't see why that can't work . . . " he began, but Richard Conte, standing behind the camera, yelled, "It won't play in London."

Donohue pushed his hand through his thinning grey hair and said, but not really in anger, "You know, that scene was pretty good until somebody blew the line. . . ."

"Yeah," agreed the cameraman, Billy Daniels, his head popping out from around the camera, "it was a pretty good piece. . . ."

"Watch your language," Sinatra cut in. Then Sinatra, who has a genius for figuring out ways of not reshooting scenes, suggested a way in which the film could be used and the "mother" line could be rerecorded later. This met with approval. Then the cameras were rolling again, Virna Lisi was leaning toward Sinatra in the sand, and then he pulled her down close to him. The camera now moved in for a close-up of their faces, ticking away for a few long seconds, but Sinatra and Lisi did not stop kissing, they just lay together in the sand wrapped in one another's arms, and then Virna Lisi's left leg just slightly began to rise a bit, and everybody in the studio now watched in silence, not saying anything until Donohue finally called out:

"If you ever get through, let me know. I'm running out of film."

Then Miss Lisi got up, straightened out her white dress, brushed back her blonde hair and touched her lipstick, which was smeared. Sinatra got up, a little smile on his lips, and headed for his dressing room.

Passing an older man who stood near a camera, Sinatra asked, "How's your Bell & Howell?"

The older man smiled.

"It's fine, Frank."

"Good."

In his dressing room Sinatra was met by an automobile designer who had the plans for Sinatra's new custom-built model to replace the $25,000 Ghia he has been driving for the last few years. He also was awaited by his secretary, Tom Conroy, who had a bag full of fan mail, including a letter from New York's Mayor John Lindsay; and by Bill Miller, Sinatra's pianist, who would rehearse some of the songs that would be recorded later in the evening for Sinatra's newest album, *Moonlight Sinatra.*

While Sinatra does not mind hamming it up a bit on a movie set, he is extremely serious about his recording sessions; as he explained to a British writer, Robin Douglas-Home: "Once you're on that record singing, it's you and you alone. If it's bad and gets you criticized, it's you who's to blame—no one else. If it's good, it's also you. With a film it's never like that; there are producers and scriptwriters, and hundreds of men in offices and the thing is taken right out of your hands. With a record, you're it. . . ."

> But now the days are short
> I'm in the autumn of the year
> And now I think of my life
> As vintage wine
> From fine old kegs. . . .

It no longer matters what song he is singing, or who wrote the words—they are all *his* words, *his* sentiments, they are chapters from the lyrical novel of his life.

Life is a beautiful thing
　As long as I hold the string. . . .

When Frank Sinatra drives to the studio, he seems to dance out of the car across the sidewalk into the front door; then, snapping his fingers, he is standing in front of the orchestra in an intimate, airtight room, and soon he is dominating every man, every instrument, every sound wave. Some of the musicians have accompanied him for twenty-five years, have gotten old hearing him sing *You Make Me Feel So Young*.

When his voice is on, as it was tonight, Sinatra is in ecstasy, the room becomes electric, there is an excitement that spreads through the orchestra and is felt in the control booth where a dozen men, Sinatra's friends, wave at him from behind the glass. One of the men is the Dodgers' pitcher, Don Drysdale ("Hey, Big D," Sinatra calls out, "*hey*, baby!"); another is the professional golfer, Bo Wininger; there are also numbers of pretty women standing in the booth behind the engineers, women who smile at Sinatra and softly move their bodies to the mellow mood of his music:

　Life is a beautiful thing
　　As long as I hold the string. . . .
　"*Will this be moon love*
　　Nothing but moon love
　Will you be gone when the dawn
　　Comes stealing through. . . ."

After he is finished, the record is played back on tape, and Nancy Sinatra, who has just walked in, joins her father near the front of the orchestra to hear the playback. They listen silently, all eyes on them, the king, the princess; and when the music ends there is applause from the control booth, Nancy smiles, and her father snaps his fingers and says, kicking a foot, "*Ooba-deeba-boobe-do!*"

Then Sinatra calls to one of his men. "Hey, Sarge, think I can have a half-a-cup of coffee?"

Sarge Weiss, who had been listening to the music, slowly gets up.

"Didn't mean to wake ya, Sarge," Sinatra says, smiling.

Then Weiss brings the coffee, and Sinatra looks at it, smells it, then announces, "I thought he'd be nice to me, but it's *really* coffee. . . ."

There are more smiles, and then the orchestra prepares for the next number. And one hour later, it is over.

The musicians put their instruments into their cases, grab their coats, and begin to file out, saying good-night to Sinatra. He knows them all by name, knows much about them personally, from their bachelor days, through their divorces, through their ups and downs, as they know him. When a French-horn player, a short Italian named Vincent DeRosa, who has played with Sinatra since The Lucky Strike "Hit Parade" days on radio, strolled by, Sinatra reached out to hold him for a second.

"Vicenzo," Sinatra said, "how's your little girl?"

"She's fine, Frank."

"Oh, she's not a *little* girl anymore," Sinatra corrected himself, "she's a big girl now."

"Yes, she goes to college now. U.S.C."

"That's great."

"She's also got a little talent, I think, Frank, as a singer."

Sinatra was silent for a moment, then said, "Yes, but it's very good for her to get her education first, Vicenzo."

Vincent DeRosa nodded.

"Yes, Frank," he said, and then he said, "Well, good-night, Frank."

"Good-night, Vicenzo."

After the musicians had all gone, Sinatra left the recording room and joined his friends in the corridor. He was going to go out and do some drinking with Drysdale, Wininger, and a few other friends, but first he walked to the other end of the corridor to say good-night to Nancy, who was getting her coat and was planning to drive home in her own car.

After Sinatra had kissed her on the cheek, he hurried to join his friends at the door. But before Nancy could leave the studio, one of Sinatra's men, Al Silvani, a former prizefight manager, joined her.

"Are you ready to leave yet, Nancy?"

"Oh, thanks, Al," she said, "but I'll be all right."

"Pope's orders," Silvani said, holding his hands up, palms out.

Only after Nancy had pointed to two of her friends who would escort her home, and only after Silvani recognized them as friends, would he leave.

The rest of the month was bright and balmy. The record session had gone magnificently, the film was finished, the television shows were out of the way, and now Sinatra was in his Ghia driving out to his office to begin coordinating his latest projects. He had an engagement at The Sands, a new spy film called *The Naked Runner* to be shot in England, and a couple more albums to do in the immediate months ahead. And within a week he would be fifty years old. . . .

> *Life is a beautiful thing*
> *As long as I hold the string*
> *I'd be a silly so-and-so*
> *If I should ever let go. . . .*

Frank Sinatra stopped his car. The light was red. Pedestrians passed quickly across his windshield but, as usual, one did not. It was a girl in her twenties. She remained at the curb staring at him. Through the corner of his left eye he could see her, and he knew, because it happens almost every day, that she was thinking, *It looks like him, but is it?*

Just before the light turned green, Sinatra turned toward her, looked directly into her eyes waiting for the reaction he knew would come. It came and he smiled. She smiled and he was gone.

[April, 1966]

Bogie in Excelsis

by Peter Bogdanovich

It was almost ten years after the death of Humphrey Bogart when this article was published in September 1964. All around the world, a cult had grown up that was dedicated to keeping Bogie's legend alive. Writer/director Peter Bogdanovich, whose movie credits include The Last Picture Show *and* Paper Moon, *wrote frequently on Hollywood in the pages of* Esquire.

Usually he wore the trench coat unbuttoned, just tied with the belt, and a slouch hat, rarely tilted. Sometimes it was a captain's cap and a yachting jacket. Almost always his trousers were held up by a cowboy belt. You know the kind: one an Easterner, waiting for a plane out of Phoenix, buys just as a joke and then takes a liking to. Occasionally, he'd hitch up his slacks with it, and he often jabbed his thumbs behind it, his hands ready for a fight or a dame.

Whether it was Sirocco or Casablanca, Martinique or Sahara, he was the only American around (except maybe for the girl) and you didn't ask him how he got there, and he always worked alone—except for the fellow who thought he took care of him, the rummy, the piano player, the one *he* took care of, the one you didn't mess with. There was very little he couldn't do, and in a jam he could do anything: remove a slug from a guy's arm, fix a truck that wouldn't start. He was an excellent driver, knowing precisely how to take those curves or how to lose a guy that was tailing him. He could smell a piece of a broken glass and tell you right away if there'd been poison in it, or he could walk into a room and know just where the button was that opened the secret door. At the wheel of a boat, he was beautiful.

His expression was usually sour and when he smiled only the lower lip moved. There was a scar on his upper lip, maybe that's what gave him the faint lisp. He would tug meditatively at his earlobe when he was trying to figure something out and every so often he had a strange little twitch—a kind of backward jerk of the sides of his mouth coupled with a slight squinting of the eyes. He held his cigarette (a Chesterfield) cupped in his hand. He looked right holding a gun.

Unsentimental was a good word for him. "Leave 'im where he is," he might say to a woman whose husband has just been wounded. "I don't want 'im bleeding all over my cushions." And blunt: "I don't like you. I don't like your friends and I don't like the idea of her bein' married to you." And straight: "When a man's partner is killed he's supposed to do something about it. It doesn't make any difference what you thought of him. He was your partner and you're supposed to do something about it."

He was tough; he could stop you with a look or a line. "Go ahead, slap me," he'd say, or, "That's right, go for it," and there was in the way he said it just the right blend of malice, gleeful anticipation and the promise of certain doom. He didn't like taking orders. Or favors. It was smart not to fool around with him too much.

As far as the ladies were concerned, he didn't have too much trouble with them, except maybe keeping them away. It was the girl who said if he needed anything, all he had to do was whistle; he never said that to the girl. Most of the time he'd call her "angel," and if he liked her he'd tell her she was "good, awful good."

Whatever he was engaged in, whether it was being a reporter, a saloon-keeper, a gangster, a detective, a fishing-boat owner, a D.A., or a lawyer, he was impeccably, if casually, a complete professional. "You take chances," someone would say. "I get paid to," was his answer. But he never took himself too seriously. What was his job, a girl would ask. Conspiratorially, he'd lean in and say with the slightest flicker of a grin, "I'm a private dick on a case." He wasn't going to be taken in by Art either; he'd been to college, but he was a bit suspicious of the intellectuals. If someone mentioned Proust, he'd ask, "Who's he?", even though he knew.

Finally, he was wary of Causes. He liked to get paid for taking chances. He was a man who tried very hard to be Bad because he knew it was easier to get along in the world that way. He always failed because of an innate goodness which surely nauseated him. Almost always he went from belligerent neutrality to reluctant commitment. From: "I stick my neck out for nobody." To: "I'm no good at being noble, but it doesn't take much to see that the problems of three little people don't amount to a hill o' beans in this crazy world." At the start, if the question was, "What are your sympathies?", the answer was invariably, "Minding my own business." But by the end, if asked why he was helping, risking his life, he might say, "Maybe 'cause I like you. Maybe 'cause I don't like them." Of course it was always "maybe" because he wasn't going to be that much of a sap, wasn't making any speeches, wasn't going to be a Good guy. Probably he rationalized it: "I'm just doing my job." But we felt good inside. We knew better.

Several months ago, the New Yorker Theatre in Manhattan ran a cycle of thirty Humphrey Bogart movies. A one-day double bill of *The Big Sleep* and *To Have and Have Not* broke all their attendance records. "I had two hundred people sitting on the floor," said Daniel Talbot, owner of the 830-seat revival house and one of the two producers of *Point of Order.* "It was wild. I had to turn away a couple of hundred people. And that audience! First time Bogie appeared they applauded, and that was just the beginning. Any number of scenes got hands. And the laughs! Bogart is very hot right now," Talbot explained. "It's more than a cult, it's something else too. He's not consciously hip, but hip by default. You get the feeling that he lives up to the Code. Anyone who screws up deserves the fate of being rubbed out by Bogart. He's also very American, and his popularity, I think, is a reaction to this currently chic craze for foreign films and things foreign in general. With Bogart you get a portrait of a patriot, a man interested in the landscape of America. I think he's an authentic American hero—more existential than, say, Cooper, but as much in the American vein, and more able to cope with the present." Talbot paused and grinned. "Frankly, I just like to watch him at work. He hits people beautifully."

The French have a more intellectual, if nonetheless affectionate, approach to Bogart and the legend he has left behind. As Belmondo stares mystically at a photo of Bogart in Godard's *Breathless,* slowly exhaling cigarette smoke and rubbing his lip with his thumb, he murmurs wistfully, "Bogie . . ." and you can almost hear his director's thoughts, echoed, for instance, in the words of the late André Bazin, probably France's finest film critic. "Bogart is the man with a past," he wrote in *Cahiers du Cinéma* in 1957, a month after Bogart died. "When he comes into a film, it is already 'the morning after'; sardonically victorious in his macabre combat with the angel, his face scared by what he has seen, and his step heavy from all he has learned, having ten times triumphed over his death, he will surely survive for us this one more time. . . . The Bogartian man is not defined by his contempt for bourgeois virtues, by his courage or cowardice, but first of all by his existential maturity which little by little transforms life into a tenacious irony at the expense of death." Of course, the French too can have a more basic approach. "Finally in full color," wrote Robert Lachenay in the same magazine, "we see Bogie as he was in real life—as he was to Betty Bacall every night on his pillow. . . . I loved Bogart even better then. . . ."

The Bogart cult has been perpetuated for the last several years in colleges all over the United States. "I met a Harvard fellow recently," said writer Nathaniel Benchley, "who believed in only two things: the superiority of Harvard and the immortality of Humphrey Bogart." During every exam period in Cambridge, it has become customary for the Brattle Theatre to run a Bogart film festival. Sometimes they don't even list the pictures; they just put a large photograph of him outside the theatre. It seems to be enough. Walk into the Club Casablanca (in the same building) and ask one of the undergraduates. "Bogart has a coolness you can't get away from," he might tell you. "It's a wryness, a freedom," he'll say, at the same time denying that there is a real cult and that he's just so refreshing, so pleasantly removed from their academic world. "There's no crap about Bogart," another student may observe. "He's also kind of anti-European and pro-American. Like he dumps on the European, you know what I mean?" By this time his date won't be able to control herself any longer. "He's so masculine!" she'll blurt out. "He's so fantastically tough!" Was he? "He satirized himself a great deal," said writer Betty Comden. Raymond Massey recalled an incident during the shooting of *Action in the North Atlantic* (1943): "The scene called for our doubles to jump from the bridge of a burning tanker into the water below, which was aflame with oil. Bogie turned to me and said, '*My* double is braver than yours.' I said that wasn't so, that *my* double was the braver man. Then Bogie looked at me and he said, 'The fact is I'm braver than you are.' I said that was nonsense. And the next thing I knew we did the doggone stunt ourselves." Massey chuckled. "I burned my pants off and Bogie singed his eyebrows."

To Joseph L. Mankiewicz, who directed him in *The Barefoot Contessa* (1954), Bogart's toughness was a façade. "You'd be having dinner with him," he said, "and someone would come over and you could just see the tough guy coming on." And to Chester Morris: "He had a protective shell of seeming indifference. He wasn't, but he did a lotta acting offstage. He liked to act tough, liked to talk out of the side of his mouth." Writer Nunnally Johnson said Bogart was convinced that people would have been disappointed if he didn't act tough with them. "A fan came over during dinner one time," said Johnson, "and Bogie told him to beat it. When the guy got back to his table I heard his companion say, quite happily, 'See, I told ya he'd insult you.'" Johnson reflected a moment. "But he was a lot tougher than I would be and a lot tougher than most people I know. I remember one time Judy Garland and her husband, Sid Luft, were at his home. Now Luft was a big alley fighter and a good deal broader than Bogart. But Bogie got annoyed about something or other and he walked right over to Luft, who also was a good head taller, and nodded at Judy. 'Would you take that dame out of this house,' he said, 'and never come back.' Luft kind of looked at him a moment and then he took her out." Johnson smiled. "Bogie took big risks."

Adlai Stevenson didn't find him that way. "He wasn't tough, not really," said the Ambassador. "He was, to me, a nonconformist. He had a cynicism without being unhealthy. He had great curiosity and an arch kind of skepticism." And still another opinion: "He was a pushover," said Lauren Bacall.

"I never broke through his barrier," said critic John McLain. "I don't think anyone really got underneath. Bogart didn't unburden himself to men. He loved to be in love and with a woman. I think he came closer to leveling with them than with anybody." Bogart married four women during his fifty-seven years, each of them an actress: Helen Mencken (1926), Mary Phillips (1928), the late Mayo Methot (1938), and in 1945, Lauren Bacall. "I think once a person was out, they were really out," said Truman Capote, discussing the divorces. "He had emotional attachments."

The Bogart-Methot marriage was a stormy one. "Their neighbors were lulled to sleep," Dorothy Parker once said, "by the sounds of breaking china and crashing glass." Johnson recalled that Methot once had Bogart followed. "She was very jealous and positive that he was playing around. But Bogie never had a weakness for dames. The only weakness he ever had was for a drink and a talk." Johnson smiled. "Bogie soon found out a guy was tailing him, and he called up the fellow's agency. 'Hello, this is Humphrey Bogart,' he said. 'You got a man on my tail. Would you check with him and find out where I am.' "

The first time Bogart met Betty Bacall was coming out of director Howard Hawks' office. She had made a test for Hawks, who had discovered her and first teamed the couple in *To Have and Have Not* (1945). "I saw your test," Bogart said to her. "We're gonna have a lotta fun together." It was with Bacall that he had his only children, a boy named Steve, which is what she called Bogart in that first movie, and a girl named Leslie Howard, after the actor who had insisted that Bogart be cast in the film version of *The Petrified Forest* (1936), the movie that really began his picture career. "He missed her when they were apart," Capote said. "He loved her. He used to talk a terrific line, but he was monogamous. Although that isn't entirely true—he fell in love with Bacall while he was still married to Mayo."

Bogart put it this way: "I'm a one-woman man and I always have been. I guess I'm old-fashioned. Maybe that's why I like old-fashioned women, the kind who stay in the house playing *Roamin' in the Gloamin'*. They make a man think he's a man and they're glad of it." The stories go that Bogart was a heavy drinker, but Johnson thinks otherwise. "I don't think Bogie drank as much as he pretended to," he said. "Many's a time I was with him, the doorbell would ring, and he'd pick up his glass just to go answer the door. He couldn't have been as good at his job if he drank as much as he was supposed to have."

But Bogart did drink. "I think the world is three drinks behind," he used to say, "and it's high time it caught up." On one occasion he and a friend bought two enormous stuffed panda bears and took them as their dates to El Morocco. They sat them in chairs at a table for four and when an ambitious young lady came over and touched Bogart's bear, he shoved her away. "I'm a happily married man," he said, "and don't touch my panda." The woman brought assault charges against him, and when asked if he was drunk at four o'clock in the morning, he replied, "Sure, isn't everybody?" (The judge ruled that since the panda was Mr. Bogart's personal property, he could defend it.)

But Bogart didn't have to drink to start trouble. "He was an arrogant bastard," said Johnson, grinning. "It's kinda funny, this cult and everything. When he was alive, as many people hated him as loved him. I always thought of him as somewhat like Scaramouche." Johnson chuckled. "What was it? 'Born with the gift of laughter and the sense that the world was mad. . . .' He'd start a skirmish and then sit back and watch the consequences. Of course, there was nearly always something phony about the guy he was needling. Needle is the wrong word—howitzer would be more like it. The other fellow could use deflating, but it didn't take all that artillery."

The Holmby Hills Rat Pack, which Bogart initiated and which died with him, sprang from this distaste for pretense. "What is a rat?" he once explained. "We have no constitution, charter or bylaws, yet, but we know a rat when we see one. There are very few rats in this town. You might say that rats are for staying up late and drinking lots of booze. We're against squares and being bored and for lots of fun and being real rats, which very few people are, but if you're a real rat, boy! Our slogan is, 'Never rat on a rat.' A first principle is that we don't care who likes us as long as we like each other. We like each other very much."

John McClain tells of the yacht club Bogart belonged to and of the people who rented the large house next door for a summer. They were the Earls and they Dressed for Dinner. The members of the club (who were never invited) used to peer over their fence, watching the lush festivities. McClain had been invited to a Sunday dinner and had asked if he might bring Bogart along as they would be together on his yacht over the weekend. As they docked, McClain reminded Bogart to dress for the occasion and went off to get ready himself. Bogart went into the club for a drink or two. "After a while," McClain recalled, "Bogie announced to everyone in the club, 'My dear friends, the Earls,' he said, 'are having an open house and they want you all to come.' And into the Earl house comes Bogie followed by about thirty people, all wearing shorts and sport shirts and sneakers." McClain laughed. "It was pretty funny, actually, but I was furious at the time."

"He could be very wrong too," said Benchley. "One time at '21' I was standing at the bar with a couple of friends and Bogie got up from his table and came over. 'Are you a homosexual?' he said to one of them, just like that. The fellow looked rather taken aback and said he didn't see that it was any of his business. 'Well are you?' said Bogie. 'Come on, we got a bet going at the table.' The fellow said, 'Since you ask, no.' I think Bogie could feel he'd been wrong and he turned to the other guy with us and asked him if *he* was a homosexual. The guy said no. He asked me and I said no and then he said, 'Well, I am,' and kinda minced away. He knew he'd been wrong."

A few weeks after Bogart's death, Peter Ustinov said, in a speech: "Humphrey Bogart was an exceptional character in a sphere where characters are not usually exceptional. To a visitor hot from the cold shores of England, he would put on an exaggerated Oxford accent and discuss the future of the 'British Empah' as though he wrongheadedly cared for nothing else in the wide world. His aim was to shake the newcomer out of his assumed complacency by insults which were as shrewdly observed as they were malicious. . . . The way into his heart was an immediate counterattack in a broad American accent, during which one assumed a complicity between him and his *bête noire*, Senator McCarthy, in some dark scheme. . . . It was in the character of the man that he smiled with real pleasure only when he had been amply repaid in kind."

Capote would go along with that: "The turning point in our friendship—the beginning really—was during *Beat the Devil* (1954). Bogie and John Huston and some others, they were playing that game—you know the one, what d'ya call it—you take each other's hand across a table and try to push the other's arm down. Well, it just happens that I'm very good at that game. So, anyway, Bogie called over, 'Hey, Caposy.' That's what he called me, 'Caposy.' He said, 'C'mon, Caposy, let's see you try this.' And I went over and I pushed his arm down. Well, he looked at me. . . . He had such a suspicious mind, he was sure that Huston had cut off my head and sewed it onto someone else's body. 'Let's see you do that again,' he said. And again I pushed his arm down. So he said once more, and I said I would only if we bet a hundred dollars, which we did. I won again and he paid me, but then he came over and he started sort of semi-wrestling with me. It was something they did. He was crushing me and I said, 'Cut that *owat*,' and he said, 'Cut that *owat*.' I said, 'Well, do,' and he said, 'Why?' I said, 'Because you're hurting me.' But he kept right on squeezing, so I got my leg around behind him and pushed and over he went. He was flat on his can looking up at me. And from then on we were very good friends."

"Bogie's needling tactics were quite calculated," Johnson explained. "I had lunch with him and Betty at Romanoff's one time and she was giving him hell about some row at a party. He'd provoked it, of course. 'Someday somebody's gonna belt you,' she said, and he said, 'No, that's the art of it—taking things up to that point and then escaping.'"

In 1947, Bogart led a march to Washington to protest the investigations of the Un-American Activities Committee. Some people labeled him a pinko. He didn't like that. "I am an American," he said. Bogart's political freethinking was considered dangerous in Hollywood. In 1952, however, he campaigned most actively for Stevenson for President. "He never seemed to give a damn what people thought or said," Mr. Stevenson recalled. "And it was quite perilous in those days to be a Democrat, especially one partisan to me. He was disdainful about anybody trying to muscle about in a free country."

"He wasn't an extremist in anything," said Miss Bacall, "except telling the truth. You had to admire Bogie. He always said what he thought. 'Goddamnit,' he used to say, 'if you don't want to hear the truth, don't ask me.' "

"That's true," Johnson agreed. "Everything he did was honest. He used to say, 'What's everybody whispering about? I've got cancer!' He'd say, 'For Christ's sake, it's not a venereal disease.' "

Bogart also said that the only point in making money is "so you can tell some big shot to go to hell." And: "I have politeness and manners. I was brought up that way. But in this goldfish-bowl life, it is sometimes hard to use them."

His widow thinks it was more than just good manners Bogart had. Finally, she'll tell you, "He was an old-fashioned man, a great romantic. And very emotional. He would cry when a dog died. You should have seen him at our wedding, tears streaming down his face. He told me that he started thinking about the meaning of the words. He was tough about life and totally uncompromising, but I remember he went to see Steve at nursery school and when he saw him sitting at his little desk, he cried."

Alistair Cooke met the Bogarts on the Stevenson campaign train and he remembered sitting with them one afternoon and saying that, of course, Stevenson wouldn't win. " 'What!' said Bogie, astounded. 'Not a prayer, I'm afraid,' I said. 'Why you son of a bitch,' Betty said, 'that's a fine thing to say.' 'Look,' I said, 'I'm a reporter. You're the lieutenants.' We bet ten dollars on it and when Stevenson lost he paid it to me. But he didn't really think I'd take it. You know what he said? 'It's a hell of a guy who bets against his own principles.' "

Cooke commented on this Bogart trait in an article he wrote for *The Atlantic Monthly* (May, 1957). "A touchy man who found the world more corrupt than he had hoped . . . he invented the Bogart character and imposed it on a world impatient of men more obviously good. And it fitted his deceptive purpose like a glove. . . . From all . . . he was determined to keep his secret: the rather shameful secret, in the realistic world we inhabit, of being a gallant man and an idealist."

Other friends detected a similar quality in Bogart. Mankiewicz called it, "A sadness about the human condition. He had a kind of eighteenth-century, Alexander Pope nature. I think he would have made a superb Gatsby. His life reflected Gatsby's sense of being an outsider." Stevenson found "a wistful note in him, as there often is in thinking people. He was much more profound than one might think." And Capote called him lost. "It was his outstanding single characteristic—that something almost pathetic. Not that he would ever ask for sympathy, far from it. It just always seemed to me as though he were permanently lonely. It gave him a rather poetic quality, don't you think?"

That secret inner world of Humphrey Bogart was reflected in his passion for sailing and his love for the *Santana*, his boat, on which he went off whenever he could, accompanied by a few friends. They used to drink Drambuies and play dominoes or just sail. He had learned early about the sea, having left school (at their request) at seventeen and joined the Navy. It was on the troopship *Leviathan* that he received the injury that permanently scarred his upper lip. "Sailing. That was the part of him no one could get at," Capote said. "It wasn't anything materialistic. It was some kind of inner soul, an almost mystical hideaway."

If the *Motion Picture Herald*'s annual Fame Poll of the Top Ten movie stars can be trusted, it appears that Bogart's peak years of popularity were 1943-1949, during and just after World War II. Cooke explained it this way: "He was . . . a romantic hero inconceivable in any time but ours. . . . When Hitler was acting out scripts more brutal and obscene than anything dreamed of by Chicago's North Side or the Warner Brothers, Bogart was the only possible antagonist likely to outwit him and survive. What was needed was no Ronald Colman, Leslie Howard or other knight of the boudoir, but a conniver as subtle as Goebbels. Bogart was the very tough gent required, and to his glory he was always, in the end, on our side."

He didn't get his Oscar, however, until 1952 (for *The African Queen*), and popped up on the top ten again in 1955, a little more than a year before he died. Betty Comden: "I don't think this cult is anything new. . . . " Adolph Green: "No. . . ." Comden: "Bogart never stopped being popular. . . ." Green: "There are so few originals around. . . ." Comden: "Bogart's style had an innate sophistication. . . ." Green: "He was less an actor . . ." Comden: ". . . than a personality." Bogart agreed. "Sure I am. It took fifteen years to make us personalities. Gable and Cooper can do anything in a picture, and people would say, 'Oh, that's just good old Clark.' "

"His great basic quality," said Ustinov, "was a splendid roughness. Even when perfectly groomed, I felt I could have lit a match on his jaw. . . . He knew his job inside out, and yet it was impossible not to feel that his real soul was elsewhere, a mysterious searching instrument knocking at doors unknown even to himself. . . ."

Perhaps this is what Bogart's admirers sense. "There was something about him that came through in every part he played," said Miss Bacall. "I think he'll always be fascinating—to this generation and every succeeding one. There was something that made him able to be a man of his own and it showed through his work. There was also a purity, which is amazing considering the parts he played. Something solid too. I think as time goes by we all believe less and less. Here was someone who believed in something."

"Like all really great stars," said director George Cukor, "he had a secret. You never really know him altogether. He also had boldness of mind, freedom of thought—a buccaneer. I think these young people haven't seen him," he went on, trying to explain the cult. "They're simply rediscovering him. After all, Bogie had class."

"The average college student would sooner identify with Bogart than, say, Sinatra, don't you think?" said Mankiewicz. "He had that rather intellectual disrespect for authority. Also I don't think anyone ever really believed that Bogart was a gangster—that's what fascinated people. Bogart never frightened them."

"It's angry youth," Chester Morris said. "They're cheering for the heavy today. Everything must be nonconformist. They'd also like to do the kind of things he did. He was a forerunner of James Bond." Benchley: "He's a hero without being a pretty boy."

"Could it be anything as simple as sex appeal?" Capote wondered. "He had an image of sophisticated virility and he projected it remarkably well. And with such humor. At last, he had such style that it doesn't wither, it doesn't age, it doesn't date. Like Billie Holiday."

"I think Robin Hood has always been attractive," said Adlai Stevenson.

Before the adulation, there must be something to adulate. And this must be created. "If a face like Ingrid Bergman's looks at you as though you're adorable," Bogart once said, "everyone does. You don't have to act very much." The late Raymond Chandler thought otherwise: "All Bogart has to do to dominate a scene is to enter it." Evidently it wasn't always that way. In 1922, playing one of his first stage roles, he was reviewed by Alexander Woollcott: "His performance could be mercifully described as inadequate." But two years later, of another performance, Woollcott again: "Mr. Bogart is a young actor whose last appearance was recorded by your correspondent in words so disparaging that it is surprising to find him still acting. Those words are hereby eaten." It would figure that Bogart often used to quote the first review but never the second.

" 'Why, I'm a National Institution,' he used to say," Capote recalled. "He was very proud of his success and fame. But he was most serious about his acting. He thought of it as a profession, one that he was curious about, knew something about. After all, it was almost the sum total of his life. In the end, Bogart really was an artist. And a very selective one. All the gestures and expressions were pruned down and pruned down. One time I watched *The Maltese Falcon* with him and he sat there, muttering in that hoarse way, criticizing himself in the third person. 'Now he's gonna come in,' he'd say. 'Then he's gonna do this and that's where he does the wrong thing.' I gathered during the silences that he liked it. It was braggadocio through silence."

Howard Hawks directed Bogart in his two most archetypal roles, as Harry (Steve) Morgan in *To Have and Have Not* and Philip Marlow in *The Big Sleep* (1946). "He was extremely easy to work with," Hawks said. "Really underrated as an actor. Without his help I couldn't have done what I did with Bacall. Not many actors would sit around and wait while a girl steals a scene. But he fell in love with the girl and the girl with him, and that made it easy."

Bogart used to say that an audience was always a little ahead of the actor. "If a guy points a gun at you," he explained, "the audience knows you're afraid. You don't have to make faces. You just have to believe that you are the person you're playing and that what is happening is happening to you."

Ustinov acted with Bogart once, in a comedy called *We're No Angels* (1955). "Bogart had an enormous presence," he said, "and he carried the light of battle in his eye. He wished to be matched, to be challenged, to be teased. I could see a jocular and quarrelsome eye staring out of the character he was playing into the character I was playing—rather as an experienced bullfighter might stare a hotheaded bull into precipitate action."

"When the heavy, full of crime and bitterness," said Bogart, "grabs his wounds and talks about death and taxes in a husky voice, the audience is his and his alone."

This emotion, elicited so consciously from his movie audiences, ironically became a reality. His death was horribly, heart-breakingly in character. He died on January 14, 1957, of a cancer of the esophagus, and it had taken well over a year to kill him. "These days," he said, "I just sit around and talk to my friends, the people I like." Which is what he did.

"I went to see him toward the end," said Ambassador Stevenson. "He was very ill and very weak, but he made a most gallant effort to keep gay. He had an intolerance for weakness, an impatience with illness."

"I went a few times," Capote said. "Most of his friends went, some almost every day, like Sinatra. Some were very loyal. He seemed to bring out the best in them all. He looked so awful, so terribly thin. His eyes were huge and they looked so frightened. They got bigger and bigger. It was real fear and yet there was always that gay, brave self. He'd have to be brought downstairs on the dumbwaiter and he'd sit and wait and wait for his Martini. He was only allowed one, I think, or two. And that's how we used to find him, smoking and sipping that Martini."

During that time, his wife rarely left the house, though her friends and even Bogart urged her to go out more often. When someone asked why she had only been out six or seven times in ten months, Bogart replied: "She's my wife and my nurse. So she stays home. Maybe that's the way you tell the ladies from the broads in this town."

"He went through the worst and most agonizing pain any human can take," said Dr. Maynard Brandsma. "I knew this and when I'd see him I'd ask, 'How is it?' Bogie would always answer simply, 'Pretty rough.' He never complained and he never whimpered. I knew he was dying and during the last weeks I knew he knew it too."

"I saw him twenty-three days before he died," said Cukor. "He couldn't come downstairs anymore and he was heavily sedated. He kept closing his eyes. Still he'd be telling jokes and asking to hear the gossip. But his voice was the wonder. That marvelous voice. It was absolutely alive. It was the last thing that died."

His death came in the early morning and that day the papers carried the news to the world. Most of the reports were similar. Quite a few of them told it this way: "Usually he kissed his wife Lauren Bacall and said, 'Good night.' But according to Dr. Michael Flynn, this time he put his hand on her arm and murmured in his familiar brusque fashion, 'Good-bye, kid.' "

Whether it really happened that way or not is beside the point. Bogart the man and Bogart the hero had merged until now one couldn't tell the difference between the two, if indeed there ever had been any. He had walked through seventy-five movie nights for his public and it was too late now to change the image, too late to alter a legend that had really just begun.

[September, 1964]

The Loser

by Gay Talese

Floyd Patterson was the first man in the history of boxing to twice capture the world heavyweight championship. He was also the youngest title holder— only twenty-one years old—when he knocked out Archie Moore in 1956 and succeeded retired champion Rocky Marciano. Patterson lost the title to Ingemar Johansson of Sweden in 1959, won it back one year later, then, on September 25, 1962, lost it again when he was knocked out by Sonny Liston in one round. His repeated attempts to win back the title were unsuccessful. This profile by Gay Talese was published in March 1964, one month after a promising newcomer named Cassius Clay triumphed over Liston and became the new champion.

At the foot of a mountain in upstate New York, about sixty miles from Manhattan, there is an abandoned country clubhouse with a dusty dance floor, upturned barstools, and an untuned piano; and the only sounds heard around the place at night come from the big white house behind it—the clanging sounds of garbage cans being toppled by raccoons, skunks, and stray cats making their nocturnal raids down from the mountain.

The white house seems deserted, too; but occasionally, when the animals become too clamorous, a light will flash on, a window will open, and a Coke bottle will come flying through the darkness and smash against the cans. But mostly the animals are undisturbed until daybreak, when the rear door of the white house swings open and a broad-shouldered Negro appears in grey sweat clothes with a white towel around his neck.

He runs down the steps, quickly passes the garbage cans and proceeds at a trot down the dirt road beyond the country club toward the highway. Sometimes he stops along the road and throws a flurry of punches at imaginary foes, each jab punctuated by hard gasps of his breathing—

"*hegh-hegh-hegh*"—and then, reaching the highway, he turns and soon disappears up the mountain.

At this time of morning farm trucks are on the road, and the drivers wave at the runner. And later in the morning other motorists see him, and a few stop suddenly at the curb and ask:

"Say, aren't *you* Floyd Patterson?"

"No," says Floyd Patterson. "I'm his brother, Raymond."

The motorists move on, but recently a man on foot, a disheveled man who seemed to have spent the night outdoors, staggered behind the runner along the road and yelled, "Hey, Floyd Patterson!"

"No, I'm his brother, Raymond."

"Don't tell *me* you're not Floyd Patterson. I know what Floyd Patterson looks like."

"Okay," Patterson said, shrugging, "if you want me to be Floyd Patterson, I'll be Floyd Patterson."

"So let me have your autograph," said the man, handing him a rumpled piece of paper and a pencil.

He signed it—"Raymond Patterson."

One hour later Floyd Patterson was jogging his way back down the dirt path toward the white house, the towel over his head absorbing the sweat from his brow. He lives alone in a two-room apartment in the rear of the house, and has remained there in almost complete seclusion since getting knocked out a second time by Sonny Liston.

In the smaller room is a large bed he makes up himself, several record albums he rarely plays, a telephone that seldom rings. The larger room has a kitchen on one side and, on the other, adjacent to a sofa, is a fireplace from which are hung boxing trunks and T-shirts to dry, and a photograph of him when he was the champion, and also a television set. The set is usually on except when Patterson is sleeping, or when he is sparring across the road inside the clubhouse (the ring is rigged over what was once the dance floor), or when, in a rare moment of painful honesty, he reveals to a visitor what it is like to be the loser.

"Oh, I would give up anything to just be able to work with Liston, to box with him somewhere where nobody would see us, and to see if I could get past three minutes with him," Patterson was saying, wiping his face with the towel, pacing slowly around the room near the sofa. "I *know* I can do better. . . . Oh, I'm not talking about a rematch. Who would pay a nickel for another Patterson-Liston fight? I know *I* wouldn't. . . . But all I want to do is get past the first round."

Then he said, "You have no idea how it is in the first round. You're out there with all those people around you, and those cameras, and the whole world looking in, and all that movement, that excitement, and *The Star-Spangled Banner,* and the whole nation hoping you'll win, including the President. And do you know what all this does? It blinds you, just blinds you. And then the bell rings, and you go at Liston and he's coming at you, and you're not even aware that there's a referee in the ring with you.

". . . Then you can't remember much of the rest, because you don't want to. . . . All you recall is, all of a sudden you're getting up, and the referee is saying, 'You all right?' and you say, 'Of *course* I'm all right,' and he says, 'What's your name?' and you say, 'Patterson.'

"And then, suddenly, with all this screaming around you, you're down again, and you know you have to get up, but you're extremely groggy, and the referee is pushing you back, and your trainer is in there with a towel, and people are all standing up, and your eyes focus directly at no one person—you're sort of floating.

"It is not a *bad* feeling when you're knocked out," he said. "It's a *good* feeling, actually. It's not painful, just a sharp grogginess. You don't see angels or stars; you're on a pleasant cloud. After Liston hit me in Nevada, I felt, for about four or five seconds, that everybody in the arena was actually in the ring with me, circled around me like a family, and you feel warmth toward all the people in the arena after you're knocked out. You feel lovable to all the people. And you want to reach out and kiss everybody—men and women—and after the Liston fight somebody told me I actually blew a kiss to the crowd from the ring. I don't remember that. But I guess it's true because that's the way you feel during the four or five seconds after a knockout. . . .

"But then," Patterson went on, still pacing, "this good feeling leaves you. You realize where you are, and what you're doing there, and what has just happened to you. And what follows is a hurt, a confused hurt—not a physical hurt—it's a hurt combined with anger; it's a what-will-people-think hurt; it's an ashamed-of-my-own-ability hurt . . . and all you want then is a hatch door in the middle of the ring—a hatch door that will open and let you fall through and land in your dressing room instead of having to get out of the ring and face those people. The worst thing about losing is having to walk out of the ring and face those people. . . ."

Then Patterson walked over to the stove and put on the kettle for tea. He remained silent for a few moments. Through the walls could be heard the footsteps and voices of the sparring partners and the trainer who live in the front of the house. Soon they would be in the clubhouse getting things ready should Patterson wish to spar. In two days he was scheduled to fly to Stockholm and fight an Italian named Amonti, Patterson's first appearance in the ring since the last Liston fight.

Next he hoped to get a fight in London against Henry Cooper. Then, if his confidence was restored, his reflexes reacting, Patterson hoped to start back up the ladder in this country, fighting all the leading contenders, fighting often, and not waiting so long between each fight as he had done when he was a champion in the ninety-percent tax bracket.

His wife, whom he finds little time to see, and most of his friends think he should quit. They point out that he does not need the money. Even he admits that, from investments alone on his $8,000,000 gross earnings, he should have an annual income of about $35,000 for the next twenty-five years. But Patterson, who is only twenty-nine years old and barely scratched, cannot believe that he is finished. He cannot help but think that it was something more than Liston that destroyed him—a strange, psychological force was also involved, and unless he can fully understand what it was, and learn to deal with it in the boxing ring, he may never be able to live peacefully anywhere but under this mountain. Nor will he ever be able to discard the false whiskers and moustache that, ever since Johansson beat him in 1959, he has carried with him in a small attaché case into each fight so he can slip out of the stadium unrecognized should he lose.

"I often wonder what other fighters feel, and what goes through their minds when they lose," Patterson said, placing the cups of tea on the table. "I've wanted so much to talk to another fighter about all this, to compare thoughts, to see if he feels some of the same things I've felt. But who can you talk to? Most fighters don't talk much anyway. And I can't even look another fighter in the eye at a weigh-in, for some reason.

"At the Liston weigh-in, the sportswriters noticed this, and said it showed I was afraid. But that's not it. I can never look *any* fighter in the eye because . . . well, because we're going to fight, which isn't a nice thing, and because . . . well, once I actually did look a fighter in the eye. It was a long, long time ago. I must have been in the amateurs then. And when I looked at this fighter, I saw he had such a nice face . . . and then he looked at *me* . . . and *smiled* at me . . . and *I* smiled back! It was strange, very strange. When a guy can look at another guy and smile like that, I don't think they have any business fighting.

"I don't remember what happened in that fight, and I don't remember what the guy's name was. I only remember that, ever since, I have never looked another fighter in the eye."

The telephone rang in the bedroom. Patterson got up to answer it. It was his wife, Sandra. So he excused himself, shutting the bedroom door behind him.

Sandra Patterson and their four children live in a $100,000 home in an upper-middle-class white neighborhood in Scarsdale, New York. Floyd Patterson feels uncomfortable in this home surrounded by a manicured lawn and stuffed with furniture, and, since losing his title to Liston, he has preferred living full time at his camp, which his children have come to know as "daddy's house." The children, the eldest of whom is a daughter named Jeannie now seven years old, do not know exactly what their father does for a living. But Jeannie, who watched the last Liston-Patterson fight on closed-circuit television, accepted the explanation that her father performs in a kind of game where the men take turns pushing one another down; he had his turn pushing them down, and now it is their turn.

The bedroom door opened again, and Floyd Patterson, shaking his head, was very angry and nervous.

"I'm not going to work out today," he said. "I'm going to fly down to Scarsdale. Those boys are picking on Jeannie again. She's the only Negro in this school, and the older kids give her a rough time, and some of the older boys tease her and lift up her dress all the time. Yesterday she went home crying, and so today I'm going down there and plan to wait outside the school for those boys to come out, and. . . ."

"How old are they?" he was asked.

"Teen-agers," he said. "Old enough for a left hook."

Patterson telephoned his pilot friend, Ted Hanson, who stays at the camp and does public-relations work for him, and has helped teach Patterson to fly. Five minutes later Hanson, a lean white man with a crew cut and glasses, was knocking on the door; and ten minutes later both were in the car that Patterson was driving almost recklessly over the narrow, winding country roads toward the airport, about six miles from the camp.

"Sandra is afraid I'll cause trouble; she's worried about what I'll do to those boys; she doesn't want trouble!" Patterson snapped, swerving around a hill and giving his car more gas. "She's just not firm enough! She's afraid . . . she was afraid to tell me about that groceryman who's been making passes at her. It took her a long time before she told me about that dishwasher repairman who comes over and calls her 'baby.' They all know I'm away so much. And that dishwasher repairman's been to my home about four, five times this month already. That machine breaks down every week. I guess he fixes it so it breaks down every week. Last time, I laid a trap. I waited forty-five minutes for him to come, but then he didn't show up. I was going to grab him and say, 'How would you like it if I called *your* wife *baby*? You'd feel like punching me in the nose, wouldn't you? Well, that's what I'm going to do—if you ever call her *baby* again. You call her Mrs. Patterson; or Sandra, if you know her. But you don't know her, so call her Mrs. Patterson.' And then I told Sandra that these men, this type of white man, he just wants to have some fun with colored women. He'll never marry a colored woman, just wants to have some fun. . . ."

Now he was driving into the airport's parking lot. Directly ahead, roped to the grass airstrip, was the single-engine green Cessna that Patterson bought and learned to fly before the second Liston fight. Flying was a thing Patterson had always feared—a fear shared by, maybe inherited from, his manager, Cus D'Amato, who still will not fly.

D'Amato, who took over training Patterson when the fighter was seventeen or eighteen years old and exerted a tremendous influence over his psyche, is a strange but fascinating man of fifty-six who is addicted to Spartanism and self-denial and is possessed by suspicion and fear: he avoids subways because he fears someone might push him onto the tracks; never has married; never reveals his home address.

"I must keep my enemies confused," D'Amato once explained. "When they are confused, then I can do a job for my fighters. What I do not want in life, however, is a sense of security; the moment a person knows security, his senses are dulled—and he begins to die. I also do not want many pleasures in life; I believe the more pleasures you get out of living, the more fear you have of dying."

Until a few years ago, D'Amato did most of Patterson's talking, and ran things like an Italian *padrone*. But later Patterson, the maturing son, rebelled against the Father Image. After losing to Sonny Liston the first time—a fight D'Amato had urged Patterson to resist—Patterson took flying lessons. And before the second Liston fight, Patterson had conquered his fear of height, was master at the controls, was filled with renewed confidence—and knew, too, that even if he lost, he at least possessed a vehicle that could get him out of town, fast.

But it didn't. After the fight, the little Cessna, weighed down by too much luggage, became overheated ninety miles outside of Las Vegas. Patterson and his pilot companion, having no choice but to turn back, radioed the airfield and arranged for the rental of a larger plane. When they landed, the Vegas air terminal was filled with people leaving town after the fight. Patterson hid in the shadows behind a hangar. His beard was packed in the trunk. But nobody saw him.

Later the pilot flew Patterson's Cessna back to New York alone. And Patterson flew in the larger, rented plane. He was accompanied on this flight by Hanson, a friendly, forty-two-year-old, thrice-divorced Nevadan who once was a crop duster, a bartender, and a cabaret hoofer; later he became a pilot instructor in Las Vegas, and it was there that he met Patterson. The two became good friends. And when Patterson asked Hanson to help fly the rented plane back to New York, Hanson did not hesitate, even though he had a slight hangover that night—partly due to being depressed by Liston's victory, partly due to being slugged in a bar by a drunk after objecting to some unflattering things the drunk had said about the fight.

Once in the airplane, however, Ted Hanson became very alert. He had to, because, after the plane had cruised a while at 10,000 feet, Floyd Patterson's mind seemed to wander back to the ring, and the plane would drift off course, and Hanson would say, "Floyd, Floyd, how's about getting back on course?", and then Patterson's head would snap up and his eyes would flash toward the dials. And everything would be all right for a while. But then he was back in the arena, reliving the fight, hardly believing that it had really happened. . . .

"*. . . And I kept thinking, as I flew out of Vegas that night, of all those months of training before the fight, all the roadwork, all the sparring, all the months away from Sandra . . . thinking of the time in camp when I wanted to stay up until eleven-fifteen p.m. to watch a certain movie on* The Late Show. *But I didn't because I had roadwork the next morning. . . .*

"*. . . And I was thinking about how good I'd felt before the fight, as I lay on the table in the dressing room. I remember thinking, 'You're in excellent physical condition, you're in good mental condition—but are you vicious?' But you tell yourself, 'Viciousness is not important now, don't think about it now; a championship fight's at stake, and that's important enough and, who knows?, maybe you'll get vicious once the bell rings.'*

"*. . . And so you lay there trying to get a little sleep . . . but you're only in a twilight zone, half asleep, and you're interrupted every once in a while by voices out in the hall, some guy's yelling 'Hey, Jack,' or 'Hey, Al,' or, 'Hey, get those four-rounders into the ring.' And when you hear that, you think, 'They're not ready for you yet.' So you lay there . . . and wonder, 'Where will I be tomorrow? Where will I be three hours from now?' Oh, you think all kinds of thoughts, some thoughts completely unrelated to the fight . . . you wonder whether you ever paid your mother-in-law back for all those stamps she bought a year ago . . . and you remember that time at two a.m. when Sandra tripped on the steps while bringing a bottle up to the baby . . . and then you get mad and ask: 'What am I thinking about these things for?' . . . and you try to sleep . . . but then the door opens and somebody says to somebody else, 'Hey, is somebody gonna go to Liston's dressing room to watch 'em bandage up?'*

"*. . . And so then you know it's about time to get ready. . . . You open your eyes. You get off the table. You glove up, you loosen up. Then Liston's trainer walks in. He looks at you, he smiles. He feels the bandages and later he says, 'Good luck, Floyd,' and you think, 'He didn't have to say that; he must be a nice guy.'*

"*. . . And then you go out, and it's the long walk, always a long walk, and you think, 'What am I gonna be when I come back this way?' Then you climb into the ring. You notice Billy Eckstine at ringside leaning over to talk to somebody, and you see the reporters—some you like, some you don't like—and then it's* The Star-Spangled Banner, *and the cameras are rolling, and the bell rings. . . .*

"*. . . How could the same thing happen twice? How? That's all I kept thinking after the knockout. . . . Was I fooling these people all these*

*years? . . . Was I ever the champion? . . . And then they lead you out
of the ring . . . and up the aisle you go, past those people, and all you
want is to get to your dressing room, fast . . . but the trouble was in Las
Vegas they made a wrong turn along the aisle, and when we got to the end,
there was no dressing room there . . . and we had to walk all the way
back down the aisle, past the same people, and they must have been
thinking, 'Patterson's not only knocked out, but he can't even find his
dressing room. . . .'*

"*. . . In the dressing room I had a headache. Liston didn't hurt me
physically—a few days later I only felt a twitching nerve in my teeth—it
was nothing like some fights I've had: like that Dick Wagner fight in '53
when he beat my body so bad I was urinating blood for days. After the
Liston fight, I just went into the bathroom, shut the door behind me, and
looked at myself in the mirror. I just looked at myself and asked, 'What
happened?', and then they started pounding on the door, and saying,
'Com'on out, Floyd, com'on out; the press is here, Cus is here, com'on out,
Floyd. . . .'*

"*. . . And so I went out, and they asked questions, but what can you
say? What you're thinking about is all those months of training, all the
conditioning, all the depriving; and you think, 'I didn't have to run that
extra mile, didn't have to spar that day, I could have stayed up that night
in camp and watched* The Late Show. . . . *I could have fought this fight
tonight in no condition. . . .'*"

"Floyd, Floyd," Hanson had said, "let's get back on course. . . ."

Again Patterson would snap out of his reverie, and refocus on the
omniscope, and get his flying under control. After landing in New Mexico,
and then in Ohio, Floyd Patterson and Ted Hanson brought the little
plane into the New York airstrip near the fight camp. The green Cessna
that had been flown back by the other pilot was already there, roped to the
grass at precisely the same spot it was on this day five months later when
Floyd Patterson was planning to fly it toward perhaps another fight—this
time a fight with some schoolboys in Scarsdale who had been lifting up his
little daughter's dress.

Patterson and Ted Hanson untied the plane, and Patterson got a rag
and wiped from the windshield the splotches of insects. Then he walked
around behind the plane, inspected the tail, checked under the fuselage,
then peered down between the wing and the flaps to make sure all the
screws were tight. He seemed suspicious of something. D'Amato would
have been pleased.

"If a guy wants to get rid of you," Patterson explained, "all he has to do
is remove these little screws here. Then, when you try to come in for a
landing, the flaps fall off, and you crash."

Then Patterson got into the cockpit and started the engine. A few moments later, with Hanson beside him, Patterson was racing the little plane over the grassy field, then soaring over the weeds, then flying high above the gentle hills and trees. It was a nice takeoff.

Since it was only a forty-minute flight to the Westchester airport, where Sandra Patterson would be waiting with a car, Floyd Patterson did all the flying. The trip was uneventful until, suddenly behind a cloud, he flew into heavy smoke that hovered above a forest fire. His visibility gone, he was forced to the instruments. And at this precise moment, a fly that had been buzzing in the back of the cockpit flew up front and landed on the instrument panel in front of Patterson. He glared at the fly, watched it crawl slowly up the windshield, then shot a quick smash with his palm against the glass. He missed. The fly buzzed safely past Patterson's ear, bounced off the back of the cockpit, circled around.

"This smoke won't keep up," Hanson assured. "You can level off."

Patterson leveled off.

He flew easily for a few moments. Then the fly buzzed to the front again, zigzagging before Patterson's face, landed on the panel and proceeded to crawl across it. Patterson watched it, squinted. Then he slammed down at it with a quick right hand. Missed.

Ten minutes later, his nerves still on edge, Patterson began the descent. He picked up the radio microphone—"Westchester tower . . . Cessna 2729 uniform . . . three miles northwest . . . land in one-six on final . . ."—and then, after an easy landing, he climbed quickly out of the cockpit and strode toward his wife's station wagon outside the terminal.

But along the way a small man smoking a cigar turned toward Patterson, waved at him, and said, "Say, excuse me, but aren't you . . . aren't you . . . Sonny Liston?"

Patterson stopped. He glared at the man, bewildered. He wasn't sure whether it was a joke or an insult, and he really did not know what to do.

"Aren't you Sonny Liston?" the man repeated, quite serious.

"No," Patterson said, quickly passing by the man, "I'm his brother."

When he reached Mrs. Patterson's car he asked, "How much time till school lets out?"

"About fifteen minutes," she said, starting up the engine. Then she said, "Oh, Floyd, I just should have told Sister, I shouldn't have. . . ."

"*You* tell Sister; *I'll* tell the boys. . . ."

Mrs. Patterson drove as quickly as she could into Scarsdale, with Patterson shaking his head and telling Ted Hanson in the back, "Really can't understand these school kids. This is a religious school, and they want $20,000 for a glass window—and yet, some of them carry these racial prejudices, and it's mostly the Jews who are shoulder-to-shoulder with us, and. . . ."

"Oh, Floyd," cried his wife, "Floyd, *I* have to get along here . . . you're not here, *you* don't live here, *I*. . . ."

She arrived at the school just as the bell began to ring. It was a modern building at the top of a hill, and on the lawn was the statue of a saint and, behind it, a large white cross. "There's Jeannie," said Mrs. Patterson.

"Hurry, call her over here," Patterson said.

"Jeannie! Come over here, honey."

The little girl, wearing a blue school uniform and cap, and clasping books in front of her, came running down the path toward the station wagon.

"Jeannie," Floyd Patterson said, rolling down his window, "point out the boys who lifted your dress."

Jeannie turned and watched as several students came down the path; then she pointed to a tall, thin curly-haired boy walking with four other boys, all about twelve to fourteen years of age.

"Hey," Patterson called to him, "can I see you for a minute?"

All five boys came to the side of the car. They looked Patterson directly in the eye. They seemed not at all intimidated by him.

"You the one that's been lifting up my daughter's dress?" Patterson asked the boy who had been singled out.

"Nope," the boy said, casually.

"Nope?" Patterson said, caught off guard by the reply.

"Wasn't him, Mister," said another boy. "Probably was his little brother."

Patterson looked at Jeannie. But she was speechless, uncertain. The five boys remained there, waiting for Patterson to do something.

"Well, er, where's your little brother?" Patterson asked.

"Hey, kid!" one of the boys yelled. "Come over here."

A boy walked toward them. He resembled his older brother; he had freckles on his small, upturned nose, had blue eyes, dark curly hair and, as he approached the station wagon, he seemed equally unintimidated by Patterson.

"You been lifting up my daughter's dress?"

"Nope," the boy said.

"*Nope!*" Patterson repeated, frustrated.

"Nope, I wasn't lifting it. I was just touching it a little. . . ."

The other boys stood around the car looking down at Patterson, and other students crowded behind them, and nearby Patterson saw several white parents standing next to their parked cars; he became self-conscious, began to tap nervously with his fingers against the dashboard. He could not raise his voice without creating an unpleasant scene, yet could not retreat gracefully; so his voice went soft, and he said, finally:

"Look, boy, I want you to stop it. I won't tell your mother—that might get you in trouble—but don't do it again, okay?"

"Okay."

The boys calmly turned and walked, in a group, up the street.

Sandra Patterson said nothing. Jeannie opened the door, sat in the front seat next to her father, and took out a small blue piece of paper that a nun had given her and handed it across to Mrs. Patterson. But Floyd Patterson snatched it. He read it. Then he paused, put the paper down, and quietly announced, dragging out the words, "*She didn't do her religion.* . . ."

Patterson now wanted to get out of Scarsdale. He wanted to return to camp. After stopping at the Patterson home in Scarsdale and picking up Floyd Patterson, Jr., who is three, Mrs. Patterson drove them all back to the airport. Jeannie and Floyd, Jr., were seated in the back of the plane, and then Mrs. Patterson drove the station wagon alone up to camp, planning to return to Scarsdale that evening with the children.

It was four p.m. when Floyd Patterson got back to the camp, and the shadows were falling on the clubhouse, and on the tennis court routed by weeds, and on the big white house in front of which not a single automobile was parked. All was deserted and quiet; it was a loser's camp.

The children ran to play inside the clubhouse; Patterson walked slowly toward his apartment to dress for the workout.

"What could I do with those school boys?" he asked. "What can you do to kids of that age?"

It still seemed to bother him—the effrontery of the boys, the realization that he had somehow failed, the probability that, had those same boys heckled someone in Liston's family, the school yard would have been littered with limbs.

While Patterson and Liston both are products of the slum, and while both began as thieves, Patterson had been tamed in a special school with help from a gentle Negro spinster; later he became a Catholic convert, and learned not to hate. Still later he bought a dictionary, adding to his vocabulary such words as "vicissitude" and "enigma." And when he regained his championship from Johansson, he became the Great Black Hope of the Urban League.

He proved that it is not only possible to rise out of a Negro slum and succeed as a sportsman, but also to develop into an intelligent, sensitive, law-abiding citizen. In proving this, however, and in taking pride in it, Patterson seemed to lose part of himself. He lost part of his hunger, his anger—and as he walked up the steps into his apartment, he was saying, "I became the good guy. . . . After Liston won the title, I kept hoping that he would change into a good guy, too. That would have relieved me of the responsibility, and maybe I could have been more of the bad guy. But he didn't. . . . It's okay to be the good guy when you're winning. But when you're losing, it is no good being the good guy."

Patterson took off his shirt and trousers and, moving some books on the bureau to one side, put down his watch, his cuff links and a clip of bills.

"Do you do much reading?" he was asked.

"No," he said. "In fact, you know I've never finished reading a book in my whole life? I don't know why. I just feel that no writer today has anything for me; I mean, none of them has felt any more deeply than I have, and I have nothing to learn from them. Although Baldwin to me seems different from the rest. What's Baldwin doing these days?"

"He's writing a play. Anthony Quinn is supposed to have a part in it."

"Quinn?" Patterson asked.

"Yes."

"Quinn doesn't like me."

"Why?"

"I read or heard it somewhere; Quinn had been quoted as saying that my fight was disgraceful against Liston, and Quinn said something to the effect that he could have done better. People often say that—*they* could have done better! Well I think that if *they* had to fight, *they* couldn't even go through the experience of waiting for the fight to begin. They'd be up the whole night before, and would be drinking, or taking drugs. They'd probably get a heart attack. I'm sure that, if I was in the ring with Anthony Quinn, I could wear him out without even touching him. I would do nothing but pressure him, I'd stalk him, I'd stand close to him. I wouldn't touch him, but I'd wear him out and he'd collapse. But Anthony Quinn's an old man, isn't he?"

"In his forties."

"Well, anyway," Patterson said, "getting back to Baldwin, he seems like a wonderful guy. I've seen him on television and, before the Liston fight in Chicago, he came by my camp. You meet Baldwin on the street and you say, 'Who's this poor slob?'—he seems just like another guy; and this is the same impression *I* give people when they don't know me. But I think Baldwin and me, we have much in common, and someday I'd just like to sit somewhere for a long time and talk to him. . . ."

Patterson, his trunks and sweat pants on, bent over to tie his shoelaces, and then, from a bureau drawer, took out a T-shirt across which was printed *Deauville*. He has several T-shirts bearing the same name. He takes good care of them. They are souvenirs from the high point of his life. They are from the Deauville Hotel in Miami Beach, which is where he trained for the third Ingemar Johansson match in March of 1961.

Never was Floyd Patterson more popular, more admired than during that winter. He had visited President Kennedy; he had been given a $35,000 jeweled crown by his manager; his greatness was conceded by sportswriters—and nobody had any idea that Patterson, secretly, was in possession of a false moustache and dark glasses that he intended to wear out of Miami Beach should he lose the third fight to Johansson.

It was after being knocked out by Johansson in their first fight that Patterson, deep in depression, hiding in humiliation for months in a remote Connecticut lodge, decided he could not face the public again if he lost. So he bought false whiskers and a moustache, and planned to wear them out of his dressing room after a defeat. He had also planned, in leaving his dressing room, to linger momentarily within the crowd and perhaps complain out loud about the fight. Then he would slip undiscovered through the night and into a waiting automobile.

Although there proved to be no need for bringing disguise into the second or third Johansson fights, or into a subsequent bout in Toronto against an obscure heavyweight named Tom McNeeley, Patterson brought it anyway; and, after the first Liston fight, he not only wore it during his thirty-hour automobile ride from Chicago to New York, but he also wore it while in an airliner bound for Spain.

"As I got onto this plane, you'd never have recognized me," he said. "I had on this beard, moustache, glasses and hat—and I also limped, to make myself look older. I was alone. I didn't care what plane I boarded; I just looked up and saw this sign at the terminal reading 'Madrid,' and so I got on that flight after buying a ticket.

"When I got to Madrid I registered at a hotel under the name 'Aaron Watson.' I stayed in Madrid about four or five days. In the daytime I wandered around to the poorer sections of the city, limping, looking at the people, and the people stared back at me and must have thought I was crazy because I was moving so slow and looked the way I did. I ate food in my hotel room. Although once I went to a restaurant and ordered soup. I hate soup. But I thought it was what old people would order. So I ate it. And after a week of this, I began to actually think I was somebody else. I began to believe it. And it is nice, every once in a while, being somebody else."

Patterson would not elaborate on how he managed to register under a name that did not correspond to his passport; he merely explained, "With money, you can do anything."

Now, walking slowly around the room, his black silk robe over his sweat clothes, Patterson said, "You must wonder what makes a man do things like this. Well, I wonder too. And the answer is, I don't know . . . but I think that within me, within every human being, there is a certain weakness. It is a weakness that exposes itself more when you're alone. And I have figured out that part of the reason I do the things I do, and cannot seem to conquer that one word—*myself*—is because . . . is because . . . I am a coward. . . ."

He stopped. He stood very still in the middle of the room, thinking about what he had just said, probably wondering whether he should have said it.

"I am a coward," he then repeated, softly. "My fighting has little to do with that fact, though. I mean you can be a fighter—and a *winning* fighter—and still be a coward. I was probably a coward on the night I won the championship back from Ingemar. And I remember another night, long ago, back when I was in the amateurs, fighting this big, tremendous man named Julius Griffin. I was only a hundred fifty-three pounds. I was petrified. It was all I could do to cross the ring. And then he came at me, and moved close to me . . . and from then on I don't know anything. I have no idea what happened. Only thing I know is, I saw him on the floor. And later somebody said, 'Man, I never saw anything like it. You just jumped up in the air, and threw thirty different punches. . . .' "

"When did you first think you were a coward?" he was asked.

"It was after the first Ingemar fight."

"How does one see this cowardice you speak of?"

"You see it when a fighter loses. Ingemar, for instance, is not a coward. When he lost the third fight in Miami, he was at a party later at the Fontainebleau. Had I lost, I couldn't have gone to that party. And I don't see how he did. . . ."

"Could Liston be a coward?"

"That remains to be seen," Patterson said. "We'll find out what he's like after somebody beats him, how he takes it. It's easy to do anything in victory. It's in defeat that a man reveals himself. In defeat I can't face people. I haven't the strength to say to people, 'I did my best, I'm sorry, and what not.' "

"Have you no hate left?"

"I have hated only one fighter," Patterson said. "And that was Ingemar in the second fight. I had been hating him for a whole year before that—not because he beat me in the first fight, but because of what he did after. It was all that boasting in public, and his showing off his right-hand punch on television, his thundering right, his 'toonder and lightning.' And I'd be home watching him on television, and *hating* him. It is a miserable feeling, hate. When a man hates, he can't have any peace of mind. And for one solid year I hated him because, after he took everything away from me, deprived me of everything I was, he *rubbed it in*. On the night of the second fight, in the dressing room, I couldn't wait until I got into the ring. When he was a little late getting into the ring, I thought, 'He's holding me up; he's trying to unsettle me—well, I'll get him!' "

"Why couldn't you hate Liston in the second match?"

Patterson thought for a moment, then said, "Look, if Sonny Liston walked into this room now and slapped me in the face, then you'd see a fight. You'd see the fight of your life because, then, a principle would be involved. I'd forget he was a human being. I'd forget I was a human being. And I'd fight accordingly."

"Could it be, Floyd, that you made a mistake in becoming a prize-fighter?"

"What do you mean?"

"Well, you say you're a coward; you say you have little capacity for hate; and you seemed to lose your nerve against those schoolboys in Scarsdale this afternoon. Don't you think you might have been better suited for some other kind of work? Perhaps a social worker, or. . . ."

"Are you asking why I continue to fight?"

"Yes."

"Well," he said, not irritated by the question, "first of all, I love boxing. Boxing has been good to me. And I might just as well ask you the question: 'Why do you write?' Or, 'Do you retire from writing every time you write a bad story?' And as to whether I should have become a fighter in the first place, well, let's see how I can explain it. . . . Look, let's say you're a man who has been in an empty room for days and days without food . . . and then they take you out of that room and put you into another room where there's food hanging all over the place . . . and the first thing you reach for, you eat. When you're hungry, you're not choosy, and so I chose the thing that was closest to me. That was boxing. One day I just wandered into a gymnasium and boxed a boy. And I beat him. Then I boxed another boy. I beat him, too. Then I kept boxing. And winning. And I said, 'Here, finally, is something I can do!'

"Now I wasn't a sadist," he quickly added. "But I liked beating people because it was the only thing I could do. And whether boxing was a sport or not, I wanted to make it a sport because it was a thing I could succeed at. And what were the requirements? Sacrifice. That's all. To anybody who comes from the Bedford-Stuyvesant section of Brooklyn, sacrifice comes easy. And so I kept fighting, and one day I became heavyweight champion, and I got to know people like you. And you wonder how I can sacrifice, how I can deprive myself so much. You just don't realize where I've come from. You don't understand where I was when it began for me.

"In those days, when I was about eight years old, everything I got—I stole. I stole to survive, and I did survive, but I seemed to hate myself. My mother told me I used to point to a photograph of myself hanging in the bedroom and say, 'I don't like that boy!' One day my mother found three large X's scratched with a nail or something over that photograph of me. I don't remember doing it. But I do remember feeling like a parasite at home. I remember how awful I used to feel at night when my father, a longshoreman, would come home so tired that, as my mother fixed food before him, he would fall asleep at the table because he was that tired. I would always take his shoes off and clean his feet. That was my job. And I felt so bad because here I was, not going to school, doing nothing, just watching my father come home; and on Friday nights it was even worse. He would come home with his pay, and he'd put every nickel of it on the table so my mother could buy food for all the children. I never wanted to be around to see that. I'd run and hide. And then I decided to leave home and start stealing—and I did. And I would never come home unless I brought something that I had stolen. Once I remember I broke into a dress store and stole a whole mound of dresses, at two a.m., and here I was, this little kid, carrying all those dresses over the wall, thinking they were all the same size, my mother's size, and thinking the cops would never notice me walking down the street with all those dresses piled over my head. They did, of course. . . . I went to the Youth House. . . ."

Floyd Patterson's children, who had been playing outside all this time around the country club, now became restless and began to call him, and Jeannie started to pound on his door. So Patterson picked up his leather bag, which contained his gloves, his mouthpiece and adhesive tape, and walked with the children across the path toward the clubhouse.

He flicked on the light switches behind the stage near the piano. Beams of amber streaked through the dimly lit room and flashed onto the ring. Then he walked to one side of the room, outside the ring. He took off his robe, shuffled his feet in the rosin, skipped rope, and then began to shadowbox in front of the spit-stained mirror, throwing out quick combinations of lefts, rights, lefts, rights, each jab followed by a "*hegh-hegh-hegh-hegh*." Then, his gloves on, he moved to the punching bag in the far corner, and soon the room reverberated to his rhythmic beat against the bobbling bag—rat-tat-tat-*tetteta*, rat-tat-tat-*tetteta*, rat-tat-tat-*tetteta, rat-tat-tat-*tetteta!*

The children, sitting on pink leather chairs moved from the bar to the fringe of the ring, watched him in awe, sometimes flinching at the force of his pounding against the leather bag.

And this is how they would probably remember him years from now: a dark, solitary, glistening figure punching in the corner of a forlorn spot at the bottom of a mountain where people once came to have fun—until the clubhouse became unfashionable, the paint began to peel, and Negroes were allowed in.

As Floyd Patterson continued to bang away with lefts and rights, his gloves a brown blur against the bag, his daughter slipped quietly off her chair and wandered past the ring into the other room. There, on the other side of the bar and beyond a dozen round tables, was the stage. She climbed onto the stage and stood behind a microphone, long dead, and cried out, imitating a ring announcer, "Ladieeees and gentlemen . . . tonight we present. . . ."

She looked around, puzzled. Then, seeing that her little brother had followed her, she waved him up to the stage and began again: "Ladiees and gentlemen . . . tonight we present . . . *Floydie Patterson. . . .*"

Suddenly, the pounding against the bag in the other room stopped. There was silence for a moment. Then Jeannie, still behind the microphone and looking down at her brother, said, "Floydie, come up here!"

"No," he said.

"Oh, come up here!"

"*No*," he cried.

Then Floyd Patterson's voice, from the other room, called: "Cut it out. . . . I'll take you both for a walk in a minute."

He resumed punching—rat-tat-tat-*tetteta*—and they returned to his side. But Jeannie interrupted, asking, "Daddy, how come you sweating?"

"Water fell on me," he said, still pounding.

"Daddy," asked Floyd, Jr., "how come you spit water on the floor before?"

"To get it out of my mouth."

He was about to move over to the heavier punching bag when the sound of Mrs. Patterson's station wagon could be heard moving up the road.

Soon she was in Patterson's apartment cleaning up a bit, patting the pillows, washing the teacups that had been left in the sink. One hour later the family was having dinner together. They were together for two more hours; then, at ten p.m., Mrs. Patterson washed and dried all of the dishes, and put the garbage out in the can—where it would remain until the raccoons and skunks got to it.

And then, after helping the children with their coats and walking out to the station wagon and kissing her husband good-bye, Mrs. Patterson began the drive down the dirt road toward the highway. Patterson waved once, and stood for a moment watching the taillights go, and then he turned and walked slowly back toward the house.

[March, 1964]

PART IV

SOME FAILURES IN COMMUNICATIONS

SECTION 1

THE
CREDIBILITY
GAP

The American Establishment

by Richard H. Rovere

Is there an American Establishment, a tightly knit group that wields undue power and influence? In this landmark piece published in May 1962, Richard Rovere slyly "proved" its existence and poked fun at the era's various definitions of the term. The article was later used to introduce his book The American Establishment, *which contained other reports, opinions, and speculations. Rovere, who is best known for his work as* The New Yorker's *Washington correspondent, was a frequent contributor to* Esquire.

"To understand the United States today, it is necessary to know something about the Establishment. Most citizens don't realize it exists. Yet the Establishment makes its influence felt from the President's Cabinet to the professional life of a young college teacher who wants to obtain a foundation grant for research. It affects the nation's policies in almost every area." —The News and Courier *of Charleston, S.C., October 18, 1961*

It is now, of course, conceded by most fair-minded and objective authorities that there is an Establishment in America—a more or less closed and self-sustaining institution that holds a preponderance of power

Note: Some of this material originally appeared in the *American Scholar* ("Notes on the Establishment in America," Vol. 30, No. 4, Autumn, 1961, pp. 489-495). Many readers professed to be puzzled by my approach. Some even asked if I intended my work to be taken seriously. I found their questions disheartening and, I might as well add, more than a bit offensive. They cast doubt not only on my own integrity but on that of the distinguished journal which had the courage to publish my findings. The *American Scholar* is, after all, an official publication of the United Chapters of Phi Beta Kappa. Its editors, of whom I am one, would certainly not be parties to a hoax. I might add, however, that the present work entirely exhausts my knowledge of the subject. Readers wishing further information are advised to get in touch with their in our more or less open society. Naturally, Establishment leaders pooh-pooh the whole idea; they deny the existence of the Establishment, and disclaim any connection of their own with it, and insist that they are merely citizens exercising citizens' rights and responsibilities. They often maintain that the real power is held by some other real or imagined force—the voters, the Congress, the comsymps, Madison Avenue, the rich, the poor, and so forth. This is an ancient strategy; men of power have always known how to use it. "Wouldst thou enjoy first rank?" St. John Chrysostom wrote. "Then cede it to another."[1] *The News and Courier* is absolutely right.

Conceptions of the Establishment, to be sure, differ widely, just as do conceptions of the Church, the State, and other important institutions. Hilary Masters, a leading member of the Dutchess County school of sociologists, defined it in a recent lecture[2] as "the legitimate Mafia."[3] To William F. Buckley, Jr. and his collaborators on the *National Review* it is almost interchangeable with the "Liberal Machine," which turns out the "Liberal Line." Their Establishment includes just about everyone in the

---

friendly F.B.I. agent or the House Committee on Un-American Activities. They may also buy The New York *Times* and read between the lines.

1. *Homilies,* 388.
2. Before the Edgewater Institute, Barrytown, N.Y., July 4, 1961. Vide *Proceedings,* 1961, pp. 37-51. Also see Masters' first-rate monograph *Establishment Watering Places,* Shekomeko Press, 1957.
3. It was the figure of speech, not the actual analogy, that seemed so striking and appropriate. Actually, the analogy was not actual—and doubtless was not intended to be regarded as such. The Establishment exists; the Mafia does not exist. Modern scholarship has pretty well destroyed the myth of the Mafia. (Vide, "The Myth of the Mafia," in *The End of Ideology,* by Daniel Bell, The Free Press, Glencoe, Illinois, 1960.) Bell cites a report by Serrell Hillman, a journalist who went all over the country to find out if there really was a Mafia at work in this country. He checked in at the Federal Bureau of Investigation and asked the top men there if they believed in the Mafia. They said they did not. Chicago Crime Commission—same story. [Hillman could not check with Central Intelligence Agency because it is forbidden by statute to intervene in domestic affairs.] But he did talk with innumerable police officials, criminal lawyers, criminals, private detectives, and the like—none of whom could put him on the trail of the Mafia. He was eventually forced to the conclusion that the only people who believed in it were (1) Senator Estes Kefauver, of Tennessee; (2) Hearst crime reporters; and (3) The Treasury Department's Bureau of Narcotics. Senator Kefauver once described the Mafia in concrete terms. "The Mafia," he said, "is the cement that helps to bind the Costello-Adonis-Lansky syndicate of New York and the Accardo-Guzik-Fischetti syndicate of Chicago." This sounds good but isn't. Note that tricky word "helps." Besides, it is unproved that there is any cement. If I may interject a purely personal note here, I may say that I have done a bit of work on my own. One day, in the Summer of 1960, I was on an airplane (United Air Lines, Flight 420) and learned that the Honorable Frank S. Hogan, District Attorney of New York County, was a fellow passenger. The air was turbulent, and seat belts had to be fastened, so I could not approach the famous prosecutor myself. I asked a stewardess if she would deliver a note to Mr. Hogan. She said she would be delighted. My note read: "Dear Mr. District Attorney: Is there a Mafia?" His reply was prompt and categorical.

country except themselves,[4] and the great hidden, enlightened majority of voters who would, if only they were given the chance, put a non-Establishment man in the White House and have John Kenneth Galbraith recalled from India, or left there and relieved of his passport. Galbraith, himself a pioneer in the field of Establishment studies, sees the Establishment as a rather small group of highly placed and influential men who embody the best of the Conventional Wisdom and can be trusted with substantial grants of power by any responsible group in the country. The perfect Establishment type, in his view, would be the Republican called to service in a Democratic administration (e.g., the present Secretary of the Treasury, Douglas Dillon) or the vice versa. "They are the *pivotal* people," he observed in one of his earlier studies. (The italics are his.) That was before his appointment as the Establishment's man in New Delhi. (He is not a member of his own Establishment, however, for he could not hope to be held over in a Republican administration.)

The fact that experts disagree on exactly what the Establishment is and how it works does not mean that they are talking about different things or about something that does not exist. Experts disagree about the Kingdom of God. This is not an argument against its existence; plainly the Kingdom of God is many things. Differences of opinion over the meaning of "justice" have given rise to one of the most honored professions in the world. One dogmatic Marxist may quarrel with another over the proper "role of the proletariat" and even about who should and who should not be counted as belonging to the "bourgeoisie." This does not make a fiction or a meaningless abstraction of either the proletariat or the bourgeoisie. The Establishment can be thought of in many different ways, all of them empirically valid in one or another frame of reference. Masters, Buckley, Galbraith, and Corradini[5] look upon the Establishment from quite different points of

"No, Virginia, there is not," he wrote. Still and all, I think that Masters' phrase caught the spirit of the thing admirably. Dante's *Inferno* was a product of the imagination, but it has helped many men to approach the reality of beauty and even the beauty of reality. The Establishment really is the cement that binds the Rockefeller-Gill-Sulzberger syndicate in New York to the Stevenson-Field-Sandburg syndicate in Chicago.

4. It is characteristic of most thinkers and writers on the subject to define the Establishment in such a way as to keep themselves outside it and even victimized by it. Werner von Fromm has suggested that they all tend toward a mild paranoia, and what little clinical evidence there is tends to support him. The one exception known to me is François Grund, a French economist of conservative leanings, who has applied to the Establishment Burke's phrases for the nobility—"an ornament of the civil order . . . the Corinthian capital of . . . society." Both von Fromm's and Grund's observations are to be found in the 1961 Edgewater *Proceedings*.

5. H. D. Corradini, author of *Patterns of Authority in American Society* (Gainesville Press, 1958). Corradini, an anthropologist, draws a striking parallel between the American Establishment and the Ydenneks, an intertribal council that still functions in Canada.

view—which grow in the main out of their differing disciplines—but they
would have no difficulty in agreeing that Douglas Dillon is true-blue or
that, say, Senator Thomas J. Dodd of Connecticut is on the outside
looking in—disapprovingly, in his case. Despite their differences of
emphasis and approach, none of them would have many reservations
about the *News and Courier*'s definition:

"The Establishment is a general term for those people in finance,
business, and the professions, largely from the Northeast, who hold the
principal measure of power and influence in this country irrespective of
what administration occupies the White House. . . . [It is] a working
alliance of the near-socialist professor and the internationalist Eastern
banker calling for a bland bipartisan approach to national politics."[6]

For my own part, I think the definition is a pretty good one. I would cavil
a bit at the notion that "the Establishment is a general term," etc. It is a
good deal more than a collective noun, as I shall make clear. Moreover,
there is a slight ambiguity in the phrase "principal measure of power." Too
many journalists, awed by their observations of the Establishment at work,
leap to the conclusion that its power is not only great but invariably decisive.
This is by no means the case. There are powerful anti-Establishment forces
at work, and frequently they prevail. It seems to me perfectly clear, for example, that the Establishment has never found a way of controlling Congress.[7] Indeed, there are times when Congress appears to be nothing more
or less than a conspiracy to louse up the plans of the Establishment. Whatever the Establishment wants, it often seems, Congress mulishly opposes.

Nor has the Establishment ever made much headway in such fields as
advertising, television or motion pictures. The basic orientation of the
leaders in all these fields is anti-Establishment, and what Establishment
strength exists is concentrated mainly on the lower levels—in advertising,
the copywriters; in television, certain of the news departments (most
notably at Columbia Broadcasting); and in the motion pictures, a few
writers and actors. Still, Establishment strength in these areas is generally
unimpressive. In Hollywood, to take a simple example, ICMPAFPWJ,
the Independent Committee of the Motion Picture Arts for Freedom and

6. The newspaper's anti-Establishment bias is plain enough, as is the editorialist's
   sense of exclusion. "Southerners have no place in the Establishment," he writes
   "except for a domesticated handful who have turned their backs on regional
   beliefs." For "regional beliefs" read Senator Strom Thurmond and Governor Orval
   Faubus.
7. From time to time, it has managed to hold a balance of power in the Senate, but it
   has never done even this much in the House. *The Congressional Monthly* for
   January, 1962, surveying the entire performance of the first session of the Eighty-
   seventh Congress, found that only nineteen members of the House had Establishment voting records of better than eighty percent. Of the nineteen, who accounted
   for less than five percent of the total membership, twelve were Democrats, seven
   were Republicans. Fourteen were from the eastern seaboard, two from California,
   and one each from Oregon, Louisiana, and Minnesota.

Peace With Justice, an Establishment front, held a fund-raising meeting in the Beverly Wilshire Hotel on November 20, 1961. Only twenty-eight persons attended, and the take for the evening, after eloquent pleas for support from Paul Newman and Joanne Woodward, was $3,067.50. (Of this amount, $2,900 was in the form of pledges, only about fifteen percent of which, in all likelihood, were actually redeemable.) On the very same evening, at the Beverly Hilton, the National Foundation for Amoebic Dysentery raised more than five times as much, all in cash or checks of that date, from three times as many people.

The Establishment does not control everything, but its influence is pervasive, and it succeeds far more often than its antagonists in fixing the major goals of American society. Though it does not, as I have noted, come anywhere close to controlling Congress, Congress is everlastingly *reacting* to it. Within the next couple of years, for example, Congress will spend a good part of its time fighting the Establishment program for a great revision of American trade practices and for eventual American association with the European Common Market. This whole scheme was cooked up at a three-day meeting of the Executive Committee at the Sheraton-Park in Washington immediately after President Kennedy's inauguration on January 20, 1961.[8] The odds are heavily against the Establishment winning this battle in 1962 or even in 1963. The important thing, though, is that the Establishment has taken the initiative and put its great antagonist on the defensive. Practically everyone is agreed that in time the victory, even in this difficult matter, will go to the Establishment.

The Establishment is not, of course, at any level a membership organization in the sense that it collects dues, issues cards, or holds meetings openly under its own auspices. It is a coalition of forces, the leaders of which form the top directorate, or Executive Committee—referred to sometimes as "Central." At the lower levels, organization is quite loose, almost primitive in some cases, and this is one of the facts that explains the differences in definition among experts. In the upper reaches, though, certain divisions have achieved a high degree of organization. For instance, the directors of the Council on Foreign Relations make up a sort of Presidium for that part of the Establishment that guides our destiny as a

8. The meeting had been called not for this purpose alone, but to review the state of the world generally at the start of the new President's term. The question of American intervention in Cuba, for example, was discussed at length and, eventually, tabled because the Committee members were so divided among themselves. A resolution was passed urging President Kennedy to meet with Nikita Khrushchev "at an early date with a view to determining whether any basis for negotiations to reduce tensions presently exists." The Common Market matter came up when Roscoe Gist reported that George Ball, Undersecretary of State for Economic Affairs, wished to pressure the United Kingdom into joining the Common Market and looked to a day when we, too, might belong. By a vote of 23-5, with two abstentions, he was authorized to go ahead.

nation.[9] (The unimpeachable source, a dissident Executive Committee member who leaked the story about the Common Market decision, said that the Gist Subcommittee appointed to work on the Common Market matter had only two members not drawn from the Council.) The presidents and senior professors of the great Eastern universities frequently constitute themselves as *ad hoc* Establishment committees. Now and then, the Executive Committee regroups as an Establishment front for some particular end. In the Summer of 1961, as a case in point, when anti-Establishment forces in Congress and elsewhere threatened the President's foreign-aid program, the Establishment, at the request of the White House, hastily formed the Citizens' Committee for International Development and managed to bull through a good deal of what the President wanted. The Establishment has always favored foreign aid. It is, in fact, a matter on which Establishment discipline may be invoked.

Summing up the situation at the present moment, it can, I think, be said that the Establishment maintains effective control over the Executive and Judicial branches of government; that it dominates most of American education and intellectual life; that it has very nearly unchallenged power in deciding what is and what is not respectable opinion in this country. Its authority is enormous in organized religion (Roman Catholics[10] and fundamentalist Protestants to one side), in science, and, indeed, in all the learned professions except medicine. It is absolutely unrivaled in the great new world created by the philanthropic foundations—a fact which goes most of the way toward explaining why so little is known about the Establishment and its workings. Not one thin dime of Rockefeller, Carnegie, or Ford money has been spent to further Establishment studies.[11]

If it were not for the occasional formation of public committees such as the Citizens' Committee for International Development, Establishment schol-

9. The President, of course, has Constitutional responsibility for foreign affairs, and I am not suggesting that any recent President has abdicated to the CFR. But policy and strategy are worked out in the Council and reach the President by way of the State Department, which, of course, is largely staffed and always directed by Council members.

10. It should be noted, though, that it is becoming influential in Catholic journalism. A content survey of twelve leading Catholic periodicals showed thirty-eight percent of the text to be Establishment inspired.

11. The situation approaches scandal at times. The foundations and universities have subsidized a number of first-rate Establishment scholars. Daniel Bell, H. E. Corradini, Alfred Kazin, and Mary McCarthy have received Guggenheim Fellowships or other such benefactions, but always for something other than Establishment studies. A few universities—Florida, Southern Methodist, Ramona, Virginia Military Institute, and Michigan State—have done what little they could to help out, and so have a few of the less-well-heeled foundations. But there is a general lockout in the richer and better-known institutions. Some have even gone so far as to encourage what might be called "red-herring scholarship"—efforts to prove that

ars would have a difficult time learning who the key figures are. Committee rosters serve Establishmentologists in the same way that May Day photographs of the reviewing stand above Lenin's tomb serve the Kremlinologists. By close analysis of them, by checking one list of names against another, it is possible to keep tabs quite accurately on the Executive Committee. A working principle generally agreed upon by Establishment scholars is this: If in the course of a year a man's name turns up fourteen times in paid advertisements in, or collective letters to, The New York *Times,* the official Establishment daily, it is about fourteen to one that he is a member of the Executive Committee. (I refer, naturally, to advertisements and letters pleading Establishment causes.) There are, to be sure, exceptions. Sometimes a popular athlete or movie actor will, innocently or otherwise, allow himself and his name to be exploited by the Establishment. He might turn up twenty times a year and still have no real status in the institution. But that is an exception. The rule is as stated above.

One important difference between the American Establishment and the party hierarchy in Russia is that the Establishment chairman is definitely *not* the man in the center of the picture or the one whose name is out of alphabetical order in the listings. The secret is astonishingly well kept. Some people, to be sure, have argued that when, as happens most of the time, the Establishment has a man of its own in the White House, he automatically becomes chairman just as he automatically becomes commander-in-chief of the Armed Forces. I am quite certain that this is not the case. For one thing, the Establishment rarely puts one of its tried and trusted leaders in the White House. Dwight Eisenhower and John F. Kennedy have both served the Establishment and been served by it, but neither is or ever was a member of the innermost circle. Both, indeed, were admitted with some reluctance on the part of senior members, and Eisenhower's standing has at times been most insecure.

I am not sure who the chairman of the Establishment is today, although I would not be altogether surprised to learn that he is Dean Rusk. By a thrust of sheer intuition, though, I did get the name of the 1958 chairman and was rather proud of myself for doing so. In that year, I discovered that J. K. Galbraith had for some time been surreptitiously at work in Establishment studies, and he told me that he had found out who was running the thing. He tested me by challenging me to guess the man's name. I thought hard for a while and was on the point of naming Arthur Hays Sulzberger, of The New York *Times,* when suddenly the right name

---

something other than the Establishment dominates the country. A notorious example is C. Wright Mills' *The Power Elite* (Oxford University Press, 1956). It was subsidized by the Huntington Hartford Foundation, Columbia University's Social Science Research Council, and Brandeis University. Even the parent body, the British Establishment, got into the act through the Oxford University Press, which, Mills admits, went "beyond the ordinary office of publisher in helping me get on with this."

sprang to my lips. "John J. McCloy," I exclaimed. "Chairman of the Board of the Chase Manhattan Bank, once with Cadwalader, Wickersham & Taft, and a partner in Cravath, de Gersdorff, Swaine & Wood, as well as, of course, Milbank, Tweed, Hope, Hadley & McCloy; former United States High Commissioner in Germany; former President of the World Bank; liberal Republican; chairman of the Ford Foundation and chairman—my God, how could I have hesitated!—of the Council on Foreign Relations, Inc.; Episcopalian." "That's the one," Galbraith said. He congratulated me for having guessed what it had taken him so much patient research to discover.

The Establishment is not monolithic in structure or inflexible in doctrine. There is an Establishment "line," but adherence is compulsory only on certain central issues, such as foreign aid. On economic affairs, for example, several views are tolerated. The accepted range is from about as far left as, say, Walter Reuther to about as far right as, say, Dwight Eisenhower. A man cannot be for *less* welfareism than Eisenhower, and to be farther left than Reuther is considered bad taste.[12] Racial equality is another matter on which the Establishment forbids dissent. Opposition to integration is a cause for expulsion, or at least suspension for not less than a year, unless it is mere "token" opposition. The only *white* Southern members of the Establishment in anything like good standing are reconstructed Southerners or Southerners the Establishment has reason to believe would be reconstructed if political circumstances would allow it. Take Senator William Fulbright of Arkansas. He is a pillar of the Establishment even though he votes with the unenlightened on racial matters. The Council on Foreign Relations gave him an "A-1" rating when he was up for chairman of the Senate Foreign Relations Committee.[13] The Executive Committee accepts him because it assumes his heart is in the right place. He is, after all, a former Rhodes scholar and a former university president. Moreover, the Fulbright scholarships have provided an enormous subsidy for Establishment intellectuals.

12. Setting the limitations on the left is not much of a problem nowadays, for the left has been inching toward the center at the rate of about seven inches per year; the only extreme positions in this epoch are on the right, and these are inadmissible. It is interesting to consider the change that has come over the Establishment in the last twenty years. In their views on government intervention and related questions, Wendell Willkie in the early Forties and Dwight Eisenhower in the early Sixties seemed peas from the same pod. But Willkie in his time was regarded as an economic liberal, whereas Eisenhower in ours is clearly a conservative. It has been estimated that by 1968, views such as Eisenhower's will be considered excessively rightist—as Barry Goldwater's are today—and will not be tolerated.
13. It exercised the veto power, though, when he was proposed as Secretary of State. It wanted Dean Rusk to get the job, and used Fulbright's record on racial questions as an argument against Fulbright's candidacy.

The Establishment has lately been having a most difficult time with those of its members—clergy, scientists, and academicians, in the main—who have joined the Committee for a Sane Nuclear Policy. The Executive Committee—in particular that powerful "hard-line" faction led by Dean Acheson and Roscoe Gist—has no use at all for this organization and would deal very sharply with its supporters if they did not include so many people who incorporate most of the Establishment virtues. Exactly what stand it will take remains to be seen.

In nonpolitical affairs, great doctrinal latitude is not only tolerated but encouraged. In religion, the Establishment is rigorously disestablishmentarian. Separatism is another matter on which discipline may be invoked.[14] Like a citywide ticket in New York, the Executive Committee is carefully balanced religiously as well as racially. (The only important difference is that several places are kept for nonbelievers.) The only proscribed views are the noisier ones. Though he now and then gets an audience in the White House, Billy Graham is *persona non grata* in Establishment circles. Monsignor Fulton J. Sheen is regarded as a Catholic Billy Graham and is similarly a pariah.

Reinhold Niebuhr is the official Establishment theologian, and Bishop Angus Dun is the chaplain.

In matters of public policy, it may be said that those principles and policies that have the editorial support of The New York *Times* are at the core of Establishment doctrine. And those irregularities and eccentricities that receive sympathetic *consideration* in The *Times* (not only on the editorial page but in the Sunday Magazine and the Book Review) are within the range of Establishment doctrinal tolerance.

It is essential to an understanding of the Establishment to recognize its essentially *national* characteristics. *The whole of its power is greater than the sum of its parts.* Its leading figures have national and international reputations, but very often are persons of only slight influence or standing in the cities and states from which they come. Former Chairman McCloy, for example, cuts a lot of ice in Washington, Geneva, Paris, London, Rio de Janeiro, Bonn, Moscow, and Tokyo, but practically none in Manhattan. In Albany, he is almost unknown. The relative weakness of the Establishment in the states undoubtedly helps to explain the shellackings it repeatedly gets in Congress. Statewide—or one might say, statewise—it is often torn by a kind of factionalism that seldom afflicts its national and

14. "The Establishment," the Reverend F. Q. Shafer said, in the first of his 1961 Geist Lectures at Brownlee Seminary, "takes the view that religion is a matter of conscience and has no place in politics or in education. It evidently sees no contradiction between this and its endlessly repeated dictum that politics and education must always be informed by conscience."

international operations. In New York, for example, Averell Harriman and Nelson Rockefeller have often found themselves locked in combat like Grant and Lee; in Washington, they are Alphonse and Gaston. And so it goes.

A state-by-state canvass of Establishment strengths and weaknesses was conducted by Perry Associates, a St. Louis firm, in 1959. Some of the highlights follow:

In three states—Texas, Oklahoma, and North Dakota—the Establishment is virtually outlawed. There are no restrictive or repressive measures on the statute books, but there is persistent harassment by police and other officials. The American Civil Liberties Union had expressed some interest in arranging a test case, but no suitable one was found. Despite constant police surveillance, there is considerable underground Establishment activity in the Dallas area and in San Antonio.

The Indiana authorities are openly hostile to the Establishment, and there has been continuing agitation for a law requiring Establishment agents to register with the Attorney General and be fingerprinted. It is hard to see what would be accomplished by this, for the Perry people could find no trace of Establishment activity anywhere in Indiana, except at Indiana University, in Bloomington. The faculty people there are state employees anyway and can quite easily be dealt with. In neither Nebraska nor Idaho could *any* Establishment influence be found. There were only the faintest traces in Wyoming, New Hampshire, Utah, and Florida.

Florida was the one Southern state in which Establishment forces seemed exceedingly weak. Elsewhere, it was learned, nearly all those who described themselves as "moderates" were actually connected with the Establishment.

The big centers are, as one might expect, the states with large cities and large electoral votes: New York, California, Illinois, Pennsylvania, Ohio, and Massachusetts. A rather surprising case, though, was Kansas, which ranked ahead of New Jersey and Maryland.

For some reason, Establishment studies have attracted few historians. Most of the work thus far has been undertaken by journalists, economists, sociologists, and psychologists. In consequence, very little has been done to uncover the origins of the Establishment. One British historian, Keith E. D. Smith-Kyle, maintains, in *America in the Round* (Polter & Polter, Ltd., London, 1956), that "the American pretense to equality was, to speak bluntly, given the lie by the formation in the early days of the Republic of the sort of 'command' group similar in most respects to what Britons nowadays speak of as 'The Establishment.' By 1847, when the Century Association was founded in New York, power had been consolidated in a handful of hands. From then on, whenever there was a 'laying on of hands,' the blood in those extremities was the very blood that had coursed through those that had molded the clay of life in the so-called Federal period."

It is plain that Smith-Kyle is trying to say, in a roundabout British way, that a hereditary aristocracy runs the show here. He is as wrong-headed in this matter as he is in most others.[15] American students, though they number few trained historians[16] among them and none of a celebrity that compares with Smith-Kyle's, subscribe almost unanimously to the proposition that the Establishment came into being at a far later date—to be exact, as well as neat, at the turn of the century. They see the institution forming during the administration of Theodore Roosevelt, who by common consent was the first Establishment President—and in a way the last.[17] The Founding Fathers of today's group zeroed in on T. R. as if they had caught him in a perfect bombsight. Consider them all, a few of them still alive, all of them within living memory: Henry L. Stimson, William Allen White, Nicholas Murray Butler, Robert Frost, Albert Beveridge, Abraham Hummel, Joseph Choate, William Travers Jerome, Jacob Riis, Charles Evans Hughes, Felix Frankfurter, Ida M. Tarbell, Joseph Pulitzer, Martin Provensen, Lincoln Steffens, Benson Frost, Learned Hand, W. Adolphe Roberts, Jane Addams, Nelson W. Aldrich, Eleanor Alice Burgess, John Hay, John Ray, John Jay Chapman, Van Wyck Brooks, Carl Schurz, Hamlin Garland, Oscar Straus, Winthrop Chanler, James R. Bourne, Whitelaw Reid, and Gifford Pinchot.[18]

There, plainly, was the first Executive Committee!

Some uninformed publicists confuse the Establishment with the Organization. The two could not be more different. The Establishment Man and the Organization Man could not be more different, or more at odds. The Establishment uses the Organization from time to time, as a ruling group must in an industrial and commercial society. But it devoutly hopes that in time the Organization will wither away. The Organization would like to overthrow the Establishment. It had a near success when it ran its 1960 chairman, Richard M. Nixon, for President of the United States.

15. Vide, his revolting apology for Munich, *The Noble Experiment* (Heineken, London), and his blatantly Stalinist *The Bear and the Jug* (Bafer & Bafer, 1949).

16. Arthur Schlesinger, Jr., has done some fairly decent work in the past, vide *The General and the President* (with Richard H. Rovere), but his judgments are suspect because of his own connections with the Establishment.

17. This is a rather fine point. Since Roosevelt's time, every President except Harding and Truman has taken office with full Establishment approval. So far as can be determined though, no one has ever gone directly from the Executive Committee to the office of Chief Executive. Woodrow Wilson is sometimes cited as an exception, but it is dubious in the extreme that he was one. Charles Evans Hughes, his 1916 opponent, was an Executive Committee man.

18. I am indebted for this list to F. W. Dupee's illuminating study *The Suckleys of Wildercliff and the Origins of the Establishment,* No. IV in the *Occasional Papers* published by the Mid-Hudson Historical Society. Mr. Dupee is professor of English at Columbia University and perhaps the country's leading authority on Henry James.

The New York *Times* has no close rival as an Establishment daily. Technological advance is making it possible for The *Times* to become a national newspaper. This development should add immeasurably to the growth of the institution's powers.

Most Establishment personnel get at least one newspaper besides The *Times*, in order to keep up with Walter Lippmann. Papers that carry both Lippmann and Joseph Alsop are in good standing with the Establishment and get a lot of advertising that way.

There are some specialized magazines but none of general circulation that can be described as official or semi-official organs. I have pondered long over the case of *Time* magazine and have concluded that it has no real place in the Establishment. It goes too far in attacking Establishment positions and it has treated many Establishment members with extreme discourtesy and at times with vulgarity. The Establishment fears *Time*, of course, and it now and then shows cravenness in its attempts to appease it by putting Henry Luce on some commission or other (on freedom of the press, national goals, and so forth), or by giving his wife some political job. But the Luce publications generally must be considered as outside the Establishment.

Now that control of *Newsweek* has passed to Philip L. Graham, publisher of The Washington *Post*, it may be that the Establishment will adopt it as an official weekly.

U. S. News and World Report is widely read, but held in low regard.

Foreign Affairs has, within its field, the authority of *Pravda* and *Izvestia*.

Harper's, The Atlantic, and *The New Yorker* all have Establishment clienteles, but none can be regarded as official. The *Saturday Review* was once heavily patronized but no longer is. *The New Republic* is coming up. *The Nation* has long since gone down. A few of the younger Establishment intellectuals read *Partisan Review*, but the more sophisticated ones regard it as stuffy and prefer *The Noble Savage*, edited by Saul Bellow and issued in April and November by the World Publishing Company.

As Thomas R. Waring, the noted Southern journalist, has pointed out, "The significance of the Establishment can be discovered by finding out who is *not* a member." No one has yet compiled a complete list of nonmembers, but the following names may help significance seekers to get their bearings. These people are known to be nonmembers:

The Honorable Lyndon B. Johnson, Vice-President of the United States.

The Honorable Richard M. Nixon, former Vice-President of the United States.

The Honorable John Nance Garner, former Vice-President of the United States.

Cus D'Amato, prominent New York sportsman and manager of Floyd Patterson, the heavyweight champion of the world.

J. Edgar Hoover, Director, Federal Bureau of Investigation.

General of the Army Douglas MacArthur.

Allen Ginsberg, poet.

The Honorable James A. Farley, former Chairman, Democratic National Committee.

Fowler Harbison, President, Ramona College.

James Hoffa, President, International Brotherhood of Teamsters.

Hetherington Wells, Chairman of the Board, Consolidated Hydraulics, Inc.

Spruille Braden, diplomatist. (Here is a curious case indeed. Former Ambassador Braden has held many leading positions in the Establishment and is even now a member of the Council on Foreign Relations. But he is also a member of the national council of the John Birch Society. He was read out of the Establishment on April 14, 1960, before his John Birch connections were known.)

Sherman Adams, formerly the assistant to the President of the United States.

Drew Pearson, syndicated columnist.

Edgar Queeny, Chairman of the Board, Monsanto Chemical Corporation.

Charles Goren, bridge expert.

Charles A. Lindbergh, aviator.

The Honorable John MacCormack, Speaker, House of Representatives.

The Reverend Norman Vincent Peale, pastor, Marble Collegiate Church of New York (Dutch Reformed) and author of *The Power of Positive Thinking*.

Cyrus S. Eaton, industrialist and philanthropist.

The Honorable Everett McKinley Dirksen, United States Senator from Illinois and the minority leader of the Senate.

Dr. Edward Teller, nuclear physicist, often known as "Father of the Hydrogen Bomb."

Conrad Hilton, hotel executive.

The Honorable Richard J. Hughes, Governor of New Jersey.

Michael J. Quill, President, Transport Workers Union.

Morris Fishbein, M.D., editor and official, American Medical Association.

George Sokolsky, syndicated columnist.

Duke Snider, Los Angeles Dodgers.

John L. Lewis, President, United Mine Workers of America.

Carleton Putnam, writer, former Chairman of the Board, Delta Air Lines.

The Establishment has in its top councils some people who appear to the unsophisticated to be oppositionists. For example, Norman Thomas, the Socialist leader; Norman Mailer, the self-styled "hipster" novelist; and Norman Podhoretz, the firebrand editor of *Commentary,* all enjoy close relations with leading figures on the Executive Committee. The Reverend Martin Luther King has been proposed for membership on the Executive Committee. On March 3, 1962, a planning committee that met for three days at the Royalton Hotel in New York reported that "we need informed, constructive criticism fully as much as we need support" and urged the recruitment of "people who will take a long, cold look at our policies and procedures and candidly advise us of any weaknesses they see. We recommend that in the cases of people playing this indispensable role of 'devil's advocate,' all discipline be suspended."

It is interesting to observe the workings of the Establishment in Presidential politics. As I have pointed out, it rarely fails to get one of its members, or at least one of its allies, into the White House. In fact, it generally is able to see to it that both nominees are men acceptable to it. It is never quite powerful enough, though, to control a nominating convention or actually to dictate nominations. National conventions represent regional interests much as Congress does, and there is always a good deal of unarticulated but nonetheless powerful anti-Establishment sentiment at the quadrennial gatherings of both Republicans and Democrats. Nevertheless, the great unwashed who man the delegations understand—almost intuitively, it seems—that they cannot win without the Establishment, and the more responsible among them have the foresight to realize that even if they did win they couldn't run the country without assistance from the Executive Committee. Over the years, a deal has been worked out that is almost an operating rule of American politics. The rule has been formulated by the novelist Margaret Creal in this way:

When an Establishment man is nominated for the Presidency by either party, the Vice-Presidential candidate must be drawn from outside the Establishment. When, as has occasionally happened, the Establishment is denied the Presidential nomination, it must be given the Vice-Presidential nomination.

The system has worked almost perfectly for the last thirty years. In that time, the only non-Establishment man in the White House has been Harry Truman, and he had been Franklin Roosevelt's non-Establishment Vice-President. Putting Henry Wallace aside as a pretty far-out case and not counting Alben Barkley (a Vice-President's Vice-President), the Vice-Presidents have all been non-Establishment: John Nance Garner, Harry Truman, Richard Nixon, and Lyndon Johnson.

Now observe what happens when the Establishment has to yield first place, as it had to do at the Republican convention in 1960. Richard Nixon, a non-Establishment Vice-President, simply could not be denied the Presidential nomination. So the Establishment Republicans demanded and of course obtained Henry Cabot Lodge. There was a similar case in 1936, when the Republicans went outside the Establishment to nominate Alf Landon for first place. The Vice-Presidential candidate was Colonel Frank Knox, the publisher of the Chicago *Daily News,* and later Roosevelt's Secretary of the Navy. Four years later, the Establishment nominated Wendell Willkie on the Republican ticket and agreed to Charles McNary, distinctly non-Establishment. In 1944, it was Dewey (Establishment) and Bricker (Non). The Establishment was particularly powerful in 1948 and not only got Dewey again but Earl Warren. In 1952, the usual deal was made in both parties: Eisenhower versus Stevenson (Establishment) and Nixon and Sparkman (Non). Same thing in 1956, with Estes Kefauver in for Sparkman.

The Russians have caught on to the existence of the Establishment and understand some of its workings quite well. Nikita Khrushchev showed himself to be no slouch when he told Walter Lippmann, last spring, that President Kennedy was controlled by Nelson Rockefeller. Many people regarded this as depressing evidence of the grip of old-school Marxism on Khrushchev's mind. They thought he was mistaking a faded symbol of industrial and mercantile power for the real wielder of authority under People's Capitalism. He was doing nothing of the sort. He was facing the facts of Establishment life. Not as a Standard Oil heir but as an Establishment agent, Nelson Rockefeller had forced the Republicans to rewrite their platform so that it conformed very closely to Chester Bowles's Democratic platform and provided for a vigorous anti-Communist defense program. Where did the central ideas of both platforms originate? In—where else?—the studies made by the Rockefeller Panel for the Rockefeller Brothers Fund and published as *Prospect for America.* Who was on the Rockefeller Panel? Here are just a few of the names, left and right:

Dean Rusk	Lucius D. Clay
Chester Bowles	Arthur F. Burns
Jacob Potofsky	Henry Luce[19]
Anna Rosenberg	Oveta Culp Hobby
Henry Kissinger	David Sarnoff
(Director of the project)	

And when Kennedy became President, from what foundation did he get his Secretary of State? The Rockefeller Foundation, of course.

19. The outsider inside. I once asked an authority on the parent body, the British Establishment, how he accounted for the sudden eminence of Barbara Ward. He explained that every Establishment agency (the B.B.C. directors, for example) had to have at least one woman and one Roman Catholic. Miss Ward was a neat package deal.

[May, 1962]

How I Signed Up at $250 a Month for the Big Parade Through Havana Bla-Bla-Bla and Wound Up in Guatemala with the CIA

by Terry Southern

America under the leadership of Kennedy had its share of embarrassments, among them the abortive invasion of Cuba known as "The Bay of Pigs." Planned by the C.I.A. under Eisenhower, the mission was approved by the newly inaugurated Kennedy administration and proceeded on April 17, 1961. Esquire later learned that before the supposedly clandestine invasion, active recruiting had been going on in broad daylight on the streets of Miami. The following interview with one of the volunteers was published in June 1963.

One night not long ago I was sitting around the White Horse Tavern, in New York City's colorful Greenwich Village, having a quick game of chess with a self-styled internationally famous blitz-chess champ. Six snappy ones and I pretty well had the game sewed up, when the champ suddenly said: "Say, see that guy at the bar—he was in the Cuban fiasco."

"Cut the diversionary crap, Champ," I countered, not bothering to look around, tapping the board of play instead, "and face up to the power." I had slapped the old de Sade double cul-de-sac on his Lady—and, as Bill Seward says, that's a rumble nobody can cool.

"No, man," insisted the champ in petulance, "I'm not kidding—just ask him and see."

Well, to make a short preface even terse (the champ, by the way, interfered with the pieces when I did look around, and so eked out another shoddy win), I investigated further to find that it was, in fact, true: this man *had* participated in the Cuban fiasco, of April 17, 1961, right up to the eleventh-hour moment of the fiasco proper, "Bad Day at the Pig Bay." His story was so interesting that my immediate hope was to share it with whatever sort of sensitive readership I could muster, and to that end I invited him over to my place for some drinks and a couple of hours tape-recording of his curious tale. Here then is the story of Boris Grgurevich, thirty-three, born and raised in New York City; it is a verbatim transcript of the recorded interview:

Well, now let me ask you this, how did you get involved in this Cuban fiasco?

It was *cold,* man . . . you know, like January. You remember that big snowstorm? When they pulled all the cars off the street? Yeah, well that was it. . . . *Cold.* And this friend of mine, Ramón, comes by. I know him ten, fifteen years, but you know, haven't seen him for a while, so there's a big bla-bla hello scene . . . and he was running from something, I mean that was pretty obvious, but he was always very high-strung, moving around a lot—Miami, L.A., Mexico—and right away he says, "Man, let's go to *Miami,* where it's *WARM.*" And he had this *car,* and well, I mean it wasn't difficult him talking me into going, because of the weather and all. So that was the first thing—we went down to Miami.

Had he mentioned anything about Cuba before you left for Miami?

No, man, he didn't say anything about *Cuba*—or maybe he *did* mention it, you know, fleetingly . . . like "bla-bla-bla the Cuban situation," or some crap like that, but we were just going to *Miami.* I mean he probably *did* mention it, because he was *born* in Cuba, you dig, and speaks Spanish and so on—but Castro was all right with me . . . I mean he had that *beard,* you know, and he seemed pretty interesting. No, we didn't talk about that, we get down to Miami, and we have three great days at the track, and then we have four terrible ones—we were reduced to moving in with Jimmy Drew, a guy I know there. And so Ramón's taking me around—I mean, he knows Miami, see, and there's a *liquor* store in the neighborhood and he introduces me to this guy owns the liquor store—nice guy to know, owns a liquor store, and we get very friendly, you know, and he's giving us bottles of *rum.* Well, he's *Cuban,* dig, and he and Ramón start yakking it up about *Cuba* and "bla-bla Castro" and so on, and now he's talking about the *"invasion"* and how he's going to get back what they *took* from him and all that jive. And naturally I'm *agreeing* with him—well I mean he keeps laying this *rum* on us, about three bottles a day . . . but he's, well he was obviously full of crap, a kind of middle-aged hustler businessman . . . and all these cats hanging around the liquor store all looked like *hoods,* but sort of *failing,* you know? Anyway, we were meeting all these hood-faces hanging around this liquor store, mostly Cubans, or born in Cuba, and one of them took us to this . . . well, they had this recruiting station, you know, where they're all signing up for the *invasion,* and Ramón, well he's getting more and more excited about this—he's a *salesman* actually, I mean that's what he does, you know, in

real life, sell things, and so he's selling himself on this idea, invading
Cuba . . . and of course he was selling me on it too.

Well, now this recruiting—this station—was this being done quite
openly?

Openly? Well, man, it was open twenty-four hours a day. You know,
like in the middle of town.

This was about the time Cuba raised this question in the U.N. and the
U.S. delegation so emphatically denied it. If recruitment was being done
as openly as you suggest, how could they deny it?

Well, use your bean, man—what are they supposed to do, *admit* it?

All right, now let me ask you this, what was Ramón's idea exactly—I
mean, if the invasion was successful, did he think he would get something
out of it?

Well, Ramón's what you might call an *essentialist*—and he just more or
less figures that the man with the gun is, you know, *the man with the gun.*

And how did you feel about it?

The money was the thing that interested me—I mean we'd had these
four very bad days at the track, and I had no *money.* Well, they were
offering two-fifty a month and, you know, room and board, and . . . let's
see, what else . . . yeah, *a trip to Guatemala.* But I guess the main thing
was these cats at the recruiting station, giving this big spiel about "bla-
bla-bla the American Government, the C.I.A., the U.S. Army," and so on.
I mean the picture *they* were painting had *battleships* in it, Dad—you
know, rockets against pitchforks. Well man, I mean how could we lose?
Cuba versus America—are you kidding?

So it was pretty obvious even then that it was an American project?

Well *of course,* man—that was the whole pitch. You don't think they
could have got these guys in there any other way, do you? I mean most of
these guys were just sort of tired, middle-aged businessmen, or young
hustlers . . . *they* weren't going to do anything, anybody could see that.
It was like they were recruiting for the *parade,* you know, to march
through Havana—and these guys were joining up to be *in* the parade,
that's all. I mean there was a *slight* pretense at a front—the *Juan Paula
Company,* that's the way the checks were paid, from the *Juan Paula
Company*—and then there were some of these C.I.A. faces running
around, trying to make a cloak-and-dagger scene out of it, but that was
just sort of a *game* with them. I mean everybody in Miami knew about the
recruiting.

Did you meet other Americans who wanted to go?

Well, they didn't want Americans, you see, they wanted *Cubans*—for
the big parade, dig? So you had to be Cuban, or if you were American, like
Ramón, you had to be born in Cuba. But yeah, there were some other
Americans down there, trying to get in—guys from the South mostly,
these real . . . you know, anything-is-better-than-home types. Most of

them had been in the Army or something like that. But they didn't want them—they wanted Cubans.

So how did you get in?

Well, man, I mean they didn't make an *issue* of it or anything like that, not as far as *I* was concerned, because we had gotten sort of friendly with them, these C.I.A. cats . . . and they weren't bad guys really—I mean they thought *they* were doing the right thing and they thought *we* were doing the right thing, so we had a pretty good relationship with them. They were nice guys actually—just sort of goofy.

Where did you see the first C.I.A. person? At the recruiting station?

That's right, they would fool around this recruiting station . . . but they were sort of flunky types. The first, what you might call "higher-echelon" C.I.A. face, was this guy directing the loading, you know, when we left for the airport. Young, dapper, sort of prematurely grey, crew-cut, very square, would-be-hip-looking cat. I guess he was a faggot really.

How did you get to the airport?

Well, one night about a week after we signed up and had finished taking these physicals they said, "Okay, this is it"—you know, very dramatic—and they picked us up, there were about ninety of us altogether, in these trucks . . . sort of like moving vans, and, well, went to the airport.

Was this the Miami International Airport?

No man, it was some kind of abandoned *military* airport. Took us about an hour to get there—then we were inside this huge hangar, and that's where they issued the uniforms. Khaki uniforms, shoes, and all that jazz. Then we get on the plane . . . C-47 . . . with the windows taped up, you know, no light, very cloak-and-dagger. And the trip . . . well, we took off that night and landed the next morning. Guatemala. And it was *hot,* man . . . wow, was it *hot.* Cats falling out all over the place—I mean, *these* guys were in no shape to start with, and then this *heat.* Well, there were these trucks there to pick us up—sort of red, commercial-type trucks, like farm trucks, you know, big open trucks. And they took us from the airstrip to the camp—that was outside Retalhuleu, the airstrip—and it takes about an hour and a half to get to Trax, the camp, the last half hour very *steep,* like straight up a mountain. First we pass a Guatemalan outpost, then a Cuban one. And it's all *lava*—the campsite was all lava . . . cut right out of the side of this mountain about 8,000 feet up. It was laid out in three levels, you dig, like huge terraces. The first level had the firing range, parade ground, the second had the barracks, mess hall, and so on, and then at the top was where the C.I.A. lived—separate, with their own mess hall, movie, and all that. Anyway it's all lava . . . like crushed coral, you know, crunch, crunch, crunch, everywhere you step. And it was supposed to be a secret camp, but of course everyone knew about it—I mean they were fifteen hundred guys up there eventually, blasting away all day—rifles, machine guns, mortars. And it was written up in all the newspapers and magazines—including *Bohemia Libre.* Know that one? It's the big anti-Communist magazine there.

Was this formerly a Guatemalan army camp?

No, man, this was formerly *nothing.* They were still working on it when I got there—I mean the camp was built for this, you know, this particular project, and they were still working on it.

Well, had you gotten to know any of the other men yet? What were they like?

You mean the guys on the plane? Well, let's see, there was this guy, Martinez . . . he was about fifty-two or -three, had been in the Batista army, a clerk—beautiful handwriting . . . well, you know the type, man, a *clerk.* And he was there because that was all he knew—the army and how to write. I mean that was the whole story with him. And then you get someone else, like this kid Raúl—young country boy, thinks his old man has been beat for a couple of *cows* or something. Very sincere cat. Well, you know, man, there were all kinds, like any army. Mostly pretty simple cats though—well, you know, like any army.

Can you describe the camp more fully?

It was the usual scene, man—a *camp.* A military *camp.* The barracks . . . well, a couple of them were quonset huts, but most of them were just ordinary wooden barracks—hold about seventy guys, something like that. Mess hall, orderly room, quartermaster, motor pool, and so on . . . like an ordinary American Army camp . . . a little shabbier maybe, you know, more makeshift.

How was the food?

Well, that was a pretty funny scene all right—that whole mess-hall scene. They had these three American cooks, you dig, and lot of Guatemalans to do KP—with a couple of translators, you know, so the cooks could tell the Guatemalans what to do—and the food was okay, sort of typical American fare, but the Cubans didn't particularly dig it. I mean they like different things, you know—black beans, rice, pork, they eat a lot of pork. Anyway a lot of times they wouldn't eat in the mess hall—they would cop a *pig* somewhere, you know, off a farmer, somebody like that . . . trade him a gun for it, anything—I mean, there were, you know, quite a few little black-market operations going on. So they would have this pig . . . a live, squealing *pig,* man, and they'd butcher it right outside the barracks and build a big fire and cook it. They have a ball—a kind of little *fiesta,* you know, singing and dancing, lushing it up, cooking this pig. It was a crazy scene.

Did you start your training right away?

Yeah, you started off as a group. . . . They would keep all the guys who arrived together as a group, right through Basic Training—you know, marching, calisthenics, rifle range, and so on. And then they would train you for some specialty—like mortar, machine gun, or something.

But we didn't get started until the next day. I mean there was a little confusion when we arrived, because there had just been a take-over the night before—a Batista coup—and the San Román boys had taken over. These were two brothers, Pepe and Roberto San Román—they were very tight with the Americans. See, the Americans never knew what was happening—I mean, they lived apart, ate apart, none of them spoke Spanish, and they never had any idea what was going on in camp—so if some guy came to them and said "bla-bla-bla Communist plot" or some crap like that, why they had to *believe* him—they really had no choice, they always had to take the word of the guy who was telling them. So they'd say: "Okay, *you* take over—get those Commies outta there!"

Had there actually been a plot?

No, man, this was just *politicking*. There was a lot of maneuvering going on, you dig—I mean, these guys were sort of divvying up the spoils, you know, even before they got there. That's how sure of themselves they were. And so the San Román brothers finally came out on top. Short-lived though it proved to be.

Anyway they had these three cats in the can—not the regular stockade, but a tin-roof shack built just to hold these guys. They were the ones who had taken all the weight in the coup—you know, supposed to be Communist spies. It was like that shack in *The Bridge on the River Kwai,* and those cats were in there for *three months,* man. Nobody was allowed near them except whoever was guarding the shack—and the C.I.A. guy who brought their chow . . . and, that's right, there were a couple of G-2 faces would question them sometimes. But they never cracked—I saw them the day they came out—they were strong cats, man.

Do you suppose they were Communist spies?

Well, I think they were just strong, dangerous cats, man—who, you know, disagreed with the Batista clique. So when they pulled off this coup, these guys caught all the heat.

So the San Román brothers became . . . what, the commandants of the camp?

Well, Frank Bender, the C.I.A. guy, was in charge of the operation—I mean he was in charge of the *whole* thing, you dig, but Pepe San Román was *nominally* the camp commander, from the, you know, Cuban point of view—and Roberto, he was in charge of the heavy-weapons company, the four-point-two mortars . . . that was the most important company in the outfit.

What were the American instructors like?

Well, they were all specialists—you know, *instructors,* mostly from the Army: World War II, Korean War, or young cats from, I don't know, *Ohio* or some weird place like that. There were about thirty-five or forty of them. And it was just a gig for them. They were getting seven-fifty, and they were usually pretty conscientious about whatever it was they were teaching—they didn't have any particular interest in the political side of it. They were sort of typical Army faces—but *specialists*, you know, pretty humorless cats, except for the guy training the paratroopers, and he was about half off his nut. And some of them, being from the South and all, were very color conscious—they didn't really *like* the Cubans, you know, because they were different. And of course they were very down on any kind of *mixture,* and the Cubans . . . well, my company commander, for example, was a mulatto—big six-foot-two cat, very temperamental, would shout himself hoarse, that kind of guy, you know? A very uneven cat—one day he would be great, outgoing, very friendly, and the next a mean mother. Anyway the fact that these guys didn't really dig the Cubans, and were down on color, and couldn't speak Spanish—it gave, well, a kind of comic-opera quality to the thing in front.

Would you talk to them about what was going on?

Well, you know, they don't crack—I mean you ask them a direct question and they fade you right out. But, of course, in most cases they didn't know what was going on themselves. Like we used to buzz these instructors—you know, "When are we leaving bla-bla-bla?" but they just "Man, we don't know, we're waiting for orders," that kind of thing.

I don't understand why they couldn't get C.I.A. people who spoke Spanish.

Well, man, I'm inclined to believe that they'd rather *not* have guys who speak the language—I really think their fear is that deep . . . you know? I mean they figure that if these cats get to *talking* to these people they might be in some way *corrupted* by them, you dig. Like they don't trust their own boys, that's what it amounts to. And you can see their point in a way—because there was really nothing holding these cats together . . . they were all there for different reasons, mostly *personal* reasons—and of course because they thought they were going to *win,* that was the main thing. But there was no single idea behind it—you know, the sort of sense of purpose you need to pull off something like that. There were too many guys just looking out for number one—you know, *collectors* . . . they collected things. When it came time to ship out for the invasion, some of those guys had so much *stuff,* man—stuff they had copped . . . transistor radios, binoculars, anything they could cop. They would be carrying an extra pack full of this crap—I'm surprised they could even get off the landing craft with all that weight. They thought they were going on a picnic. Not all of them naturally—I mean there were some sensitive faces there too—sort of fatalistic cats, like this kid Juan on the mortars . . . he used to say: "Land on Monday, get captured on Tuesday, and shot on Wednesday." Very sensitive, sort of morbid type. So it was like that, all fragmented. A lot of different factions and ideas. But the real nucleus of the outfit, the heavy-weapons company, was very strong—they knew their jobs, and they were ready to fight. Well, they were just *wasted,* guys like that. And then there was a huge bunch of goof-offs—cats who had never done *anything,* and weren't going to start now. A lot of them stayed in the guardhouse, you know, like *permanently*—and they had it pretty good . . . they would let them out for chow, they'd get to go to the head of the line, that sort of thing. Some of them were very popular with the men, like clowns. They let all of them out just before the invasion, and a lot of them were made sergeants and so on.

What were the weapons you trained with?

Well, we started with the carbine and the M-1, then the M-3—that's the one that replaced the Thompson, you know, looks like a grease gun? And the Army .45, of course. And then the bazooka, machine gun, and mortar—finally the heavy mortars. That was the largest thing they had . . . these four-point-two mortars. And the Cubans dug that part of it—you know, the shooting. Especially the mortars—they were really *good* with the mortars. Primitive cats, you know, very good with their hands . . . and they'd do great things with the mortars, like dead reckoning, very unorthodox, and it would wig these C.I.A. faces, because they were all specialists—you know, they had learned by the numbers, and that's how they were trying to teach it—and one of these cats, like a young farm boy, would step up and just estimate the distance and drop it right in the top of a barrel about seventy-five yards away . . . and it would flip the instructor. "Tell him that's not the right way to do it," he'd say to the interpreter.

Were all the weapons American?

Everything was American, man. Blankets . . . well, you know *everything.*

What else do you recall about the training?

The training was a big drag, except on the firing range, that was pretty interesting. Very corny lectures and training films . . . well, there were a couple of paratrooper films that weren't bad. And we had this group, you know, which was *training* to be paratroops, and they were a gas . . . about a hundred and twenty guys, they were being trained by this guy from California, very funny cat, like something out of a movie, about forty years old, very *tough*—you know the type, fires a 30-caliber machine gun from the hip. And this was the toughest training on the base. But it was a big joke—I mean *this* cat and his paratroopers, it was like Ali Baba and his hundred and twenty thieves. They would go through the most outlandish things you can imagine in order to cop a pig or something off another company—like one guy pretending he's hanging himself, you know, to attract attention, while the other cats cop the pig. They were a wild bunch of studs, man—the paratroopers.

Did you have any tanks there?

No, the tanks never came to the camp—they were put directly on the ship. The tank crews arrived along toward the end, but they had already been trained—in New Orleans I believe.

What did you train for after you finished Basic?

Well, Ramón and I decided that *telegraphy* might be a good thing—I mean they wanted some guys to train for it, so five of us went into that. But it wasn't as easy as it sounded—you know, da-da-dit all day long in a box about the size of a phone booth. Very hot, man, and *coffee flies* . . . terrible, you have to hit them mop-mop-mop and nothing happens. Extremely difficult to kill. The telegraphy hut was right next to the *church,* you dig—it was just a shack, but there were these *priests* . . . not Cuban, *Spanish* . . . Spanish priests, man—they had imported these cats, and *they* were *something.* Very pretentious, very contemptuous of the Cubans—spoke Spanish with a lisp, you know? And one of these cats was too much—weird face, had a weird turn of mind . . . he had been there when they were building the camp, and a guy had been killed . . . fell from a cliff where they were working. And this priest . . . well, we'd step outside the hut, for a smoke, and he would engage us in conversation, like "Why don't you come to church and bla-bla-bla?"—so we'd talk to him and he'd tell about this guy falling over the cliff, but in extreme detail, man . . . how they found the body, how there were traces of where he had clutched at the grass trying to keep from going over the edge, and so on.

When did you learn that you weren't going to take part in the invasion itself?

Not until the very last minute, We had *no idea* we weren't going, and it was a big drag, man—I mean we'd been there *three months,* dig, and we wanted to *go.* We bugged the hell out of the Americans, Ramón and I, trying to get on that ship—but they wouldn't crack. "There's nothing we can do, your names weren't on the list," was all they would say. There were fourteen of us who didn't go—Ramón, myself, Molinet, who was the quartermaster, the guy in charge of the motor pool, one of the priests, two guys who were clerks, and about seven guys who were on weapons. We were all sore as hell about it—because of course we were sure we were going to win . . . but it wasn't just that—I mean we'd been through a lot together during those three months, and we wanted to go with them.

What do you suppose the reason was?

Well, it wasn't *coincidence,* I'm pretty sure of that. One story was that we were supposed to become cadre—you know, and help train the next group. Like replacing part of the C.I.A. you dig. I don't believe it was because Ramón and I were American, because there was one other American there, a translator for the cooks, and he went.

And when did you learn the outcome of the invasion?

Well we set up this shortwave radio, with a huge antenna, and listened—tuned in directly to Cuba. And at first it sounded like it was a success . . . so there was a big celebration got started—then after a while Castro came on, announcing how he wiped us out. And that brought everyone down, you know, very hard.

I simply can't understand how they could make such a mess of it.

Well, man, it was one of those things. They *wanted* to do it, but they wanted to do it without really *doing* it—you know, like a broad. So that was that . . . and the camp became a terrible drag after that, and of course everyone wanted to *leave*—you know, back to civilization. But these recruits kept arriving from Miami, about two hundred of them during the next couple of weeks—and this brought on the weirdest scenes of the whole time there . . . because these cats were *bugged,* man. I mean it was obviously a dead issue, and these guys wanted to go back to Miami. But the Americans were still trying to keep up some kind of training routine—you know, "Keep 'em busy, good for morale," the old Army crap. But these guys' attitude was "Okay, we lost, so let's get the hell out of here." And they didn't want to do anything. They had a meeting and sent a delegation up to see the Americans and told them they didn't want to drill or anything, they wanted to go back to the States. Well, that wigged the Americans—they thought it was "Communist agitation." See, they were still waiting for orders from Washington about what the hell they were supposed to do next. Anyway, the same day one of the toughest of these cats draws guard duty, and when the guy wakes him, he says, "If you wake me up again I'll blow your head off"—you know, *that* kind of reaction. Well, this guy goes back to the orderly room and tells Martinez Arbona, the guy who was acting camp commander, and Martinez Arbona comes down to the barracks and says, "This is insubordination, bla-bla-bla," and the other guy starts to beat him up. So Martinez cuts out, up the hill, tells the Americans—and this *really* flips them. Now it's a "Communist mutiny," you dig, and they're scared out of their wits. "We've gotta get those guns away from them!" But they had no idea how to go about it, so they were wigging completely. Well, *we* all knew they weren't Communists—I mean they just wanted to get the hell *out* of there. We told the C.I.A. cats, "Man, all you have to do is tell them to *turn in the guns and they can go home.*" But they kept trying to figure out some tricky muscle way of doing it—and God knows what would have happened if we hadn't gone down and told them if they would turn in the guns they could go home. And of course that's what they did. But the Americans never did really believe it—they were very suspicious of them . . . kept them completely separated from the rest of us. And when we got to the airstrip, they sent them right out . . . you know, like thank God they're gone!

So everybody went back to Miami?

Yeah, we get back to Miami, go to the recruiting station—that's where they'd been sending our checks, dig—pick those up, and go our separate ways. Very sad scene at the recruiting place because they've got the lists of guys that got wiped or captured, and relatives and so on are falling by to look at the lists. And we talked to a couple of guys who got away—swam out and got picked up by boats.

What did they have to say about the invasion?

What did they say? "We got wiped, man. . . *wiped*."

[June, 1963]

The Dark Side of L.B.J.

by James Deakin

In the 1964 presidential election Lyndon Baines Johnson ran against Conservative Barry Goldwater, whose campaign slogan was "In your heart, you know he's right." When all the votes were in, Johnson had won by a popular margin greater than any other candidate before him. But, as James Deakin shows in this profile published in August 1967, Johnson's crudeness and deception were to cast a shadow over his political prowess.

The place: The Texas ranch of Senate Majority Leader Lyndon B. Johnson.

The time: Several years ago.

A young man arrives at the ranch to run a routine political errand. While he is waiting in the living room, Johnson strides in, picks up the telephone and calls his press secretary, George Reedy, who is staying in the guesthouse down the road. He gives Reedy a monumental chewing out.

"He was using language that I had never heard one human being use to another," recalls the political worker, now an official of the University of Texas. "He called him every filthy name in the book and some that aren't. I don't think I'll ever forget it."

Finally, Johnson hangs up the phone. He turns to the young man and says, "Now, let's give George his Christmas present." He leads the way outside to an expensive new station wagon, drives it down to the guest-house and toots merrily on the horn. When Reedy comes out, Johnson gives him the station wagon. To the astonished witness, the Senator observes: "You never want to give a man a present when he's feeling good. You want to do it when he's down."

271

In the chronicles of the American Presidency, it is not uncommon to find striking differences between public and private conduct. Beneath the outward rectitude are the usual weaknesses of spirit and failings of flesh: arrogance, pride and vanity (Woodrow Wilson, Franklin Roosevelt); sadism (Calvin Coolidge); liquor (U. S. Grant); neurotic evasion (James Buchanan); persecution complex (John Adams) and sexual insecurity (Warren Harding). At least one President, Harding, broke under this often-cruel duality. Others, like Grover Cleveland with his bastard child, surmounted the inherent hypocrisy of politics. Most Presidents have felt the need to conceal their personal imperfections, although only a few have made a fetish of it. The majority have been reasonably confident the people would forgive or forget and that history's verdict would be based on their official actions, not their private shortcomings.

In the case of the thirty-sixth Chief Executive, Lyndon Baines Johnson, the gap between the public pose and the private reality has proved to be as wide and awesome as any in the history of the republic. There may not be, literally, two Lyndon Johnsons. But he often appears to be the Yang and Yin, the light and dark force, of American politics.

Confronted with a double-identity problem, Johnson has reacted characteristically. He has not been content to live, more or less comfortably, with his shortcomings and trust the voters to do the same. He has sought to cast himself in heroic dimensions. He has appeared in a bewildering variety of shining roles—the wise savior of democracy, the parliamentary master, the cautious guardian of the nuclear trigger, the conqueror of poverty, disease and illiteracy at home and in the four corners of the earth, the Horatio Alger of his generation, the devoted son of a model mother, and most of all, the humble servant of a great people. He has identified himself with Lincoln, F.D.R. and a host of other eminent Americans. He is clean, brave, reverent, a veritable pantheon of Boy Scout virtues. He is the Paul Bunyan of Presidents and the glowing embodiment of the American Dream, played center stage under a spotlight that rarely dims, to applause that never stops, if he can help it.

His most familiar public pose is humility. His head bowed meekly, speaking in a smarmy mumble, he delivers a modest little sermon about the flag ("I have seen the sunrise on Mont Blanc, but the most beautiful vision these eyes ever beheld was the flag of my country in a foreign land") or the scourge of poverty ("As I looked into this African mother's eyes, I saw the same look . . . that I saw in my own mother's eyes when she was determined that her children would have food, clothes and an education") or the right of dissent from his Vietnam policy. This last homily takes an invariable form. Everybody has a right to disagree. It is part of our God-given freedom. Go ahead, criticize me. It's okay. I can bear it. (A brave little smile.) That's what your President is paid for. (And remember, I'm the only President you've got.)

But the dark side of Lyndon Johnson insistently intrudes upon the performance. Just as the courageous youth is saving the fair maiden, he is revealed as the one who foreclosed the mortgage in the first place. White House reporters groan inwardly when they see one of Johnson's humility bits coming, for they have glimpsed the hard man beneath the mush: Johnson slicing up a reporter for asking a "chicken-shit" question; Johnson impugning another newsman's patriotism for daring to inquire critically about the Dominican intervention, Johnson bludgeoning Senator Frank Church for his reservations about the Vietnam war ("Okay, Frank, next time you need a dam in Idaho, ask Walter Lippmann for one"); Johnson excoriating another Vietnam critic as "that (obscenity) Hartke"; Johnson neutralizing a diplomat's career with a stroke of his pen across a promotion list because the man once disagreed with him; Johnson cutting a team of magazine reporters ("Someone ought to do an article on *you* and your damn profession, your First Amendment"); Johnson warning the Republicans via the grapevine that if they press him too hard on Bobby Baker, some G.O.P. tax returns will be audited; Johnson in a bloody undercover war to the death with Bobby Kennedy, no holds barred, no quarter asked or given.

The disparity between Lyndon Johnson's public character and private nature is so profound that one can only be astonished at the task the man has set himself—to create a fictional human being for public consumption. He has, as Stewart Alsop has said, a "constant itch to try to be what he isn't." The measure of his failure is the endless gossip about the dark side of his nature—now a source of worldwide concern.

Beyond doubt, this Texan is one of the most complicated men ever to occupy the White House, perhaps the most complicated. His mind is fathomless; the subtlety of his mental processes rivals that of Lincoln. His grasp of the machinery of government is unparalleled; to hear him hold forth on fiscal policy is a breathtaking experience, considering how little most Presidents knew about this subject. His mastery of the intricate legislative arts is unexcelled. His ability at Congressional persuasion, although a little impaired these days, was once the eighth wonder of the world, and his political memory approaches the genius level.

But in the best Victorian tradition, Lyndon Johnson has a secret life. Within it lives a man subject to wide fluctuations from exhilaration to irritability to rage to withdrawal. White House reporters have grown accustomed to these dramatic changes in Johnson's mood. On the crest one day, ebullient, full of zest and verve, talking incessantly, dashing hither and yon, he may sink into a deep gloom twenty-four hours later. Then he retreats, goes perfunctorily through his schedule of public appearances, races through his speeches and hastens back to the privacy of his office. During one of his upswings, he often goes on a marathon talking jag that leaves reporters limp and their editors inundated with reams of copy. The White House "regulars"—reporters assigned full time to cover the President—have learned to steel themselves against what they describe as "the whirling-dervish effect." A typical example was March 12, 1966, a Saturday.

On that day, a group of state governors had come to the White House for what was scheduled as a routine discussion of federal-state relations. Johnson, however, turned the meeting into a full-scale, action-packed, razzle-dazzle briefing on the Vietnam situation. In the lead role, of course, was the President himself. As supporting players, he called in Vice-President Hubert Humphrey; Secretary of State Dean Rusk; Secretary of Defense Robert S. McNamara; General Earle G. Wheeler, Chairman of the Joint Chiefs of Staff; General Maxwell D. Taylor, special Presidential adviser on Vietnam; General Ellis Williamson, who had just returned from the war zone; Courtenay Valenti, the curly-haired daughter of then-Presidential aide Jack Valenti, and four dogs.

On the same day, Johnson met with the executive committee of the National Governors' Conference, held a press conference to report on the meeting, met with the governors of the Appalachian states, held another press conference to report on *that* meeting, presided at a three-hour briefing at which Rusk, McNamara and the generals reported to the governors on the Vietnam situation, held a third press conference to report on that meeting, announced the appointment of former Governor Farris Bryant of Florida as Director of the Office of Emergency Planning, and then played with Courtenay Valenti and his four dogs for a half hour while photographers snapped pictures. Two meetings, three press conferences, a three-hour briefing and a romp, and all in time for the Sunday papers. It had been a good, upbeat day for Lyndon Johnson.

But when he goes into one of his winters of despair—often produced by a critical news story or column—it is another matter. The President makes himself very scarce, as the record of his press conferences shows. With complete justification, Johnson asserts that he has held as many or more meetings with reporters as any of his predecessors, but the key indicator of his moods is the way the press conferences are grouped. He may hold three, four or five in the space of a few weeks and then go for many weeks without holding any at all. In the three weeks between February 27 and March 21 of this year, for instance, he held four news conferences. After that, six weeks elapsed before he met again with reporters, on May 3.

In the incestuous Washington community of politicians, bureaucrats, lawyers, diplomats and newspapermen, stories about Johnson's vanity sweep the circuit. When he became President, White House photographers soon learned that the right side of his face was off limits, since Johnson considers his left profile more photogenic. For a long time, photographers were herded over to the left side of the room when he held a press conference, but in recent months some infiltration to the right has been permitted. Similarly, there was a long period during which Johnson wore contact lenses when speaking from a text in public, rather than use his glasses. He is back to wearing them openly now, but during the time he was not, a hapless Signal Corps enlisted man ran afoul of the Johnson temper. A few minutes before a White House ceremony, the Signal Corpsman placed the lectern in the correct position for reading, then left the room. At this point, Jack Valenti wandered in, judged the lectern to be a little close and moved it back a few inches. Johnson had to strain to see the text but got through the ceremony. Then, in a towering rage, he summoned the Corpsman to his office and demanded of the bewildered soldier: "Son, are you trying to - - - - me?"

Although he has relaxed somewhat in these respects, the Johnson vanity is a well-established phenomenon. Shortly after becoming President, he assigned government photographer Yoichi Okamoto to the White House as his personal photographer. Okamoto is the President's shadow; quiet and unobtrusive, he goes wherever Johnson goes and is present at virtually every Presidential meeting, noiselessly clicking away. Several times a week, Johnson goes over the big batch of prints turned in by "Okie." Those he likes most, he keeps. Others he sends to those who appear in the pictures with him. If a reporter shows up in a picture, he is likely to get a note from the President's personal secretary, Juanita Roberts, saying: "The President was looking through some of his pictures today and thought you might like to have the enclosed." The pictures usually are large color shots, eminently suitable for a prominent place on the wall.

Johnson also has a predilection for plaques, but of a more enduring kind. If Texans want to put up monuments to him even though he is still alive, well why not? There is, for instance, his restored birthplace near Stonewell, his restored boyhood home in Johnson City, the soon-to-be-restored log cabin of his grandfather, Sam Ealy Johnson, Sr., a state park, a Lyndon B. Johnson lake, a projected Lyndon B. Johnson library at the University of Texas, and a plaque on the wall of the Pedernales Electric Cooperative proclaiming it to be "a product of the faith, ability and foresight of Lyndon Baines Johnson, President of the United States of America, while Congressman for the Tenth District, 1938."

The President's unwearying revisitations to his birthplace and his boyhood home have provided an endurance test for reporters and, once rested, interesting exercises in psychological speculation. Weekend after weekend, they speed down the narrow roads and lurch across the fields trying to keep up with the President as he pokes around in the faded memorabilia of his childhood, sifting out impressions of his past that begin to explain his complexity.

First, there is the picture of a small boy in an oversize cowboy hat, staring unwinkingly into an old-fashioned camera from a dusty front porch. Like the kids in Katherine Anne Porter's *Noon Wine*, digging in the ragweed, already squinting under the relentless sun, a little grubby, a little unwilling to go to school, restlessly energetic, suspicious of strangers. (In *Noon Wine*, when Olaf Helton came to work on Mr. Thompson's Texas farm, one of the Thompson boys called him "Big Swede" and ridiculed him; Lyndon Johnson was to say in later life that the trouble with foreigners was that "they're not like folks you were reared with.")

Then a restless red-neck youth, vaguely and inarticulately discontented, a drifter until he tires of working with his hands for pocket money and decides to go to college. Then a young Congressman from the sticks, clawing his way up in a town casually dominated by Eastern Brahmins (in *The Johnson Eclipse,* Leonard Baker notes that "the 'American Establishment' . . . excluded Lyndon Johnson for years"). Then a Senator and Senate Majority Leader, coming into his own as a professional among professionals in the one branch of government where Southern non-Establishment types have the best chance of rising to the top of the pecking order. Then a three-year eclipse as Vice-President, pouring out his frustrated vanity in transatlantic telephone calls to Walter Jenkins during trips to Europe. Johnson would ask Jenkins anxiously whether the New York and Washington papers played his trip "outside" (on page one) that day; when they did not, reporters recall, he would sink into despondency. Then a cosmic accident, and Lyndon Johnson is President. His ego blooms again like a giant tropical flower.

It is often said that alcohol is the fuel on which Washington runs. It is not. Ego and ambition, in equal parts, are the fuels. At the top, ambition drives a national government. It drives Johnson, who is hell-bent on being as great a President as Franklin Roosevelt. Despite Vietnam, despite the polls, despite Walter Lippmann and The New York *Times*, he wants to rank with F.D.R., and he is going at it as hard as he can, the only way he knows how. A veteran White House correspondent has commented that the thing to remember about Johnson is that, unlike some other men who reached the top, the mere fact of achieving the Presidency did not satisfy his ambition. It remains as an elemental and unfulfilled force even at the pinnacle. A great deal of what Johnson does can best be understood in the context of that ambition—and the insecurity of a man who is not sure he is going to make it, who has never been sure he was going to make it.

His sister, Mrs. Birge Alexander, recalls that as a boy he was the "bossy" one in the family. Not long after he was elected to the House, a group of elderly Senators journeying South to the funeral of one of their colleagues were astounded when a gangling young man bounced into the railroad car and began pumping their hands vigorously while proclaiming, "Ah'm Lyndon Johnson, glad to meet you," and "Proud to make your acquaintance." At the following Christmastime, according to Rowland

Evans and Robert Novak in *Lyndon B. Johnson: The Exercise of Power*, government officials who scarcely knew the young Congressman "were amazed when fat holiday turkeys arrived from Lyndon and Lady Bird Johnson."

When he reached the Senate via the famous 87-vote "landslide" of 1948, he began honing to perfection a set of classic techniques, some of them honorable, with which to further his ambitions. He worked hard, boasting that he could cram two days' work into one by taking an afternoon nap in between. (It was not an idle boast; he is still, today, an immensely hard worker, expecting all those around him to be the same.) He did favors, he logrolled, and he and Lady Bird entertained the power-houses of the Senate at small dinner parties at their house on Thirtieth Place. "These informal dinners," Evans and Novak point out, "gave Johnson a singular insight into the Senate's inner problems. Senators and their idiosyncrasies were analyzed there as they could never be on the floor and seldom in the cloakroom. At these parties, the men spoke frankly and unguardedly . . . and Johnson stored up in a few years a penetrating understanding of the world of the Senate." Later, as Majority Leader, Johnson built up a big batch of political I.O.U.'s by breaking with tradition to give several freshman Democratic Senators, including John F. Kennedy, a seat on a major committee.

On the darker side, Johnson poked into all the Senatorial closets he could find and rattled the bones of the skeletons. A liberal Senator has said that the Texan, as Majority Leader, ran "a little F.B.I." on Capitol Hill, using his big staff, wide acquaintanceship and his own sensitive antennae to accumulate a vast store of political secrets and gossip.

During the 1964 Presidential campaign, a four-man pool of reporters usually rode with Johnson on his Air Force jet (the pools have since been discontinued), and the President relaxed between campaign stops by recounting intimate stories about the great and near-great figures of contemporary American politics. To his small audience, he seemed to have a salacious anecdote about every prominent political personality of the last thirty years, rattling off descriptions of their sexual behavior and eccentricities until even the hard-bitten correspondents blanched. On one occasion, Johnson told of an incident involving a well-known American diplomat of the New Deal era whose tastes were unorthodox. While on a train trip, Johnson said, the diplomat encountered a porter in the washroom, and "he had that porter's britches down before he knew what hit him." He ridiculed the lofty moral tone taken by one of his political rivals, saying: "Why, when he was in Spain on that military trip, he laid every woman he could get his hands on." On one of his trips abroad as Vice-President, Johnson was asked by reporters how he had got along with an internationally famous statesman.

"I had my hand halfway up his leg before he knew what was happening," he replied.

In this phase of Johnson's secret life, he becomes that familiar figure, the American Yahoo—the big-talker whose specialty is the off-color joke. Robert Sherill, in *The Accidental President*, has written that "the President sometimes gets a little drunk at parties and . . . tells smutty stories until [Lady Bird's] face freezes and cracks." It is important, however, to keep this side of Johnson's personality in perspective. He does indeed know a great many dirty jokes—and so did Abraham Lincoln. He does use profanity in his private conversations—and so did Harry S. Truman and John F. Kennedy. The Presidents of the United States are men under pressure, and most of them, in these days at least, do not relax by reading the Bible. By itself, Johnson's blue language means nothing. It has little relevance to his official actions. Unlike his browbeating of subordinates, which makes it difficult for him to attract able men to government service, his smutty jokes have little effect on the course of government. What is significant, in his case, is that Johnson himself has succeeded in drawing attention to his private profanity by endeavoring to present himself publicly as a sort of Mary Poppins in the White House.

Johnson's jokes and similes are heavily animalistic and scatological. They emphasize bathroom functions. On one occasion, when he learned that a national magazine was preparing a story on his personal finances, he called in the editors and spent hours wheedling and cajoling them and uttering veiled warnings about higher postal rates, in an unsuccessful effort to squelch the article. The President insisted that the editors should come to him if they wanted accurate information. Then he gave a graphic men's-room example of the kind of personal information he would not expect them to print unless they had checked the statistics firsthand.

With the Easterners who froze him out for so many years, Johnson's scatology takes on strong overtones of the bravado that covers up insecurity. He seems to be saying to them: If I was too crude for you then, I'll be even cruder now. One of the most dignified of Kennedy's cabinet officers, a man of impeccable Establishment credentials, was rocked to the depths of his Ivy League soul when he was summoned into conference with the new President and found himself in the bathroom while Johnson bestrode the executive commode. An editor of a Midwestern newspaper attended one of the bathroom conferences when he was called to the Johnson ranch to discuss possible posts in the new Administration. Another Kennedy holdover asserts that he was summoned to the ranch early one morning and directed into the bathroom, where he sat on the side of the tub and received his instructions for the day while Johnson obtained relief. The Kennedy man says he mentioned the incident later to a woman who had been a member of Johnson's staff for years. "What's so unusual about that?" she replied. "He's been doing that with me for years."

Shortly after persuading a prominent Establishment educator to take a top Administration job, Johnson introduced him to the mule-skinner side of his new responsibilities. As the President posed for pictures with the new official, a photographer complimented Johnson on his civil-rights presentation to Congress. The Chief Executive let loose a flow of pleased profanity. The educator's face froze as Johnson declared that before he was through, every blankety-blank, so-and-so, unprintable mother's son in the United States would be able to go freely to the polling place and vote. Later, a reporter commented on the incident to the new official, who smiled weakly and said he had been in the Army, after all, and had heard some strong language in his time.

Some of Johnson's stories reveal the coarsening, almost brutalizing effect of his years in the slaughterhouse politics of the Lone Star State. One of his favorite jokes concerns a popular Texas sheriff who was running for reelection. The sheriff's opponents had been trying unsuccessfully to think of a good campaign issue to use against him. Finally, one man suggested that "we spread a rumor that he - - - -s pigs." Another protested that "you know he doesn't do that." "I know," said the first man, "but let's make the sonofabitch deny it."

It is interesting to note how closely Johnson's patterns of private conduct conform to an American stereotype: the adult drugstore cowboy. One of his biographers, Philip Geyelin, in *Lyndon B. Johnson and the World*, writes that Johnson "cannot remember having read six books all the way through since college." Veteran White House correspondents can recall only one book on international problems that he has ever mentioned reading—Barbara Ward's *The Rich Nations and the Poor Nations*. He is eternally restless, seldom able to sit through a movie, but instead turning constantly to talk to others in the audience. He is not a stamp collector, a piano player, a golfer or a sailor (although he occasionally tears around Lyndon B. Johnson Lake in a big motorboat). He cares nothing for art or the theatre, both of which he leaves to Lady Bird. When he is not working, there are only two things he really likes to do. He likes to get in his car at the ranch and cruise around, like a teen-ager on Saturday night, except that he is visually caressing his land rather than a teeny-bopper in a mini-skirt. And he likes to sit around the living room in the evening with some cronies, drinking Scotch (at his instruction, the White House insists he drinks bourbon, an American product) and rehashing the day's legislative triumph.

The first aspect of Johnson's secret life to gain currency was his tendency to bully, and this has severely handicapped his efforts to attract outstanding men to his Administration. Despite the valiant efforts of several generations of his staff (in the White House under Johnson, a generation is six months to a year) to portray him as the ideal boss, reports spread rapidly about his bullyragging, temper outbursts and cruel sarcasm. Finally, confronted with a matter of common knowledge, staff members took a new tack. Acknowledging that the chief occasionally dressed down a subordinate, they described it as a sort of initiation rite. Not until a new man had been dressed down by L.B.J., said his aides, could he consider himself admitted fully to the President's trust and confidence. A noble try, but it hardly accounted for the fact that the hazing never stopped.

At least it can be said of Johnson's bullying that he is a virtuoso, not a one-note man. Chewing out the immediate members of his staff, he uses a frontal assault. To an aide who had kept the Vice-President cooling his heels outside the oval office for a few minutes, Johnson raged, "If you ever keep Hubert waiting again, I'll kick your ass down that hall." When he saw reporters in casual conversation with this same assistant at an airport, Johnson hurried over and informed the newsmen bluntly that they were wasting their time, that *he*—jerking his thumb at the staffer—was just a flunky who didn't know anything and that if they wanted information they should come to the President.

With high-ranking Administration officials not on the immediate White House staff, Johnson switches from threats to sarcasm. One of his key advisers, an immensely hardworking man who customarily puts in a twelve-hour day, waited in his office one evening until eight or nine o'clock in case the President wanted him. When no call came, the official departed to join his wife at a theatre. Shortly after he left, Johnson called. Bright and early the next morning, the official's home telephone rang. The voice on the other end was venomous. "Hello, playboy," said Johnson. One aspect of Johnson's temper is that it is not always genuine; evidence attests that he can turn his wrath on and off for its effect on some hapless aide. Stewart Alsop has told of one visitor who found the President in a pleasant mood. He "chatted amiably for a few minutes, then glanced at a paper on his desk, excused himself, picked up a telephone and gave some nameless subordinate . . . a brutal dressing down, then pleasantly resumed the interrupted conversation."

During one stay at the ranch, Johnson let it be known that next to Lady Bird, the person most important to him was George Reedy. Recalling the station-wagon episode, reporters received this information dubiously. A kind and scholarly man whose travail seemed akin, both in intensity and duration, to that of the Israelites in Egypt, Reedy set some sort of record for service with Johnson. But at length even he moved on, like so many others who endured the *Sturm und Drang* for shorter periods. The staff turnover under Johnson has been phenomenal, the resignations continual—Horace Busby, McGeorge Bundy, Jack Valenti, Reedy, Henry Hall Wilson, Jr., Lee White, Bill Moyers, Hayes Redmond. And this list does not include several Kennedy holdovers who left early in the game. The high rate of turnover in the White House staff under Johnson has created a chronic shortage of top-level Presidential assistants, the men who, next to the President himself, probably have the most to say about the daily operation of the government. By law, the chief executive can have fourteen special assistants paid up to $30,000 a year. Johnson now has ten.

Those who have worked for Lyndon Johnson once are usually reluctant to return to the indignities and the sarcasm. For the past several months, the President has been trying without success to lure a onetime associate, now a top business executive, back into government as a member of his cabinet. And others shy away from government service after hearing the stories—Johnson routing a cabinet officer out of bed after midnight to come over to the White House and listen to him talk about inconsequentials, Johnson transparently staging a meeting of the entire cabinet for the benefit of reporters, then walking out and leaving a staff subord'.1ate to preside while captive heads of great departments recite like schoolboys.

As a result, important government posts—the Attorney General, the Secretary of Commerce, the Urban Affairs Secretary, the chairmanship of key regulatory agencies—have gone vacant for long periods of time. To fill them, Johnson often has had to appoint career men from within the government, some able, some cautious bureaucratic time servers. Lacking rejuvenation and the cross-pollination of ideas from the outside, his Administration has been notable for its shortage of imagination, especially in foreign affairs. It is not too much to say that the intellectual mediocrity of the Johnson Administration has stemmed in large measure from the sad spectacle of a man who doesn't know how to handle subordinates wisely. "They're all afraid of him," a former aide has said. "You can't get good work and good advice from men when they are afraid of you."

With reporters, Johnson operates as he does with his staff. He probes for their weaknesses, and if he finds a feeble defense he bores in. If he encounters resistance, however, he is likely to back off. A press conference exchange illustrated both facets:

Reporter: Mr. President, in connection with the appointment to the Housing and Urban Affairs Department, there have been reports of a task force headed by Dr. Wood, which recommended—

Johnson: *What* reports? I want to know who reports what.

Reporter: There have been published reports in the newspapers.

Johnson: Whose?

Reporter: There have been published reports in newspapers.

Johnson: Well, who published it? That's what I want to know.

Reporter: I saw something in The Washington *Post*, for one.

Johnson: Go ahead. The Washington *Post*. What did The Washington *Post* say?

Reporter: That a task force headed by Professor Wood had recommended the transfer of the community-action program and the Office of Economic Opportunity to the new [Urban Affairs] department, and there have been subsequent reports that you have decided against this. Can you make any comment on that?

Johnson: I would say that, insofar as a report that I have made a decision on the matter, it is more propaganda than accurate. I have made no decision. We will, in the days ahead, consider a good many reorganization proposals, but the best authority for a Presidential decision is the President or the press secretary, and you can always get guidance on that if you have the time or disposition to obtain it.

So far, so good. It had been a nice, routine job of bullyragging, with the President interrupting the newsman before he could finish his question, and then browbeating him for good measure. But at this point something unusual occurred. Disgusted with the whole performance, the reporter added a comment in a bitter tone, as well-trained seals are definitely not supposed to do.

Reporter: That's why I asked you.

Johnson had turned to answer another question. His head jerked around in obvious surprise, and he flared back. You got it. That's why I told you.

The episode took an interesting turn. For several weeks thereafter, the reporter found Presidential courtesy lavished upon him. When he asked questions at subsequent press conferences, Johnson addressed him as "Mister Jones." He interrupted his answers to other questions to amplify his responses to Jones's queries. He made other reporters wait—"I think Mr. Jones had a question over there." He had his staff track down additional information for Mr. Jones. Another White House newsman has commented that Johnson is never nicer to him than just after he has written a critical column about the President.

The other side of Lyndon Johnson's ambition is his insecurity. On one occasion he was escorting a group of young men through the White House living quarters. When they got to his bedroom, he went over to a table and picked up a sheaf of papers. Here is one marked "top secret," he said, waving the documents. Here is one for "my eyes only." He told them that he could not let them see the documents, "but they're very important." The young men gaped as the leader of the world's most powerful nation brandished the tangible proof of his own importance. Like the residents of Columbus, Ohio, in Thurber's time, he seems always to be looking over his shoulder in anticipation that someone is going to tell him that he didn't win after all. More than a year after taking office, and after winning a smashing election victory of his own, he had the word passed to reporters that he had been responsible for forty percent of Kennedy's New Frontier program, a claim that did not square with his legislative inactivity as Vice-President. In private conversations, he has minimized Kennedy's accomplishments, often in scathing accents, while publicily eulogizing the fallen leader. He was, as Evans and Novak point out, "*both* men: the detractor of Kennedy and the keeper of Kennedy's memory."

Ever since he began his ascent to power, Johnson's dealings with the Washington press corps have been touchy. For his part, Johnson wants the news reported as he chooses and when he chooses. For their part, reporters have been hard pressed, more so than with most Presidents, to separate their personal reactions to Johnson from their professional responsibility to report and analyze his official actions. The conflict antedates his Presidency. Throughout his career, Johnson has blandly deceived reporters and through them the public, and the deception has extended from small personal matters to large policy issues. When Johnson was Majority Leader, a veteran Congressional reporter for a major news service finally decided to stop interviewing him. The late House Speaker Sam Rayburn remonstrated with the reporter. Rayburn pointed out that the Senate leader was an important news source and that the newsman could not afford to bypass him. The reporter replied that he could not afford to file misleading stories, either.

On a trip to Texas in his Senate days, Johnson escorted a group of reporters around his ranch. They stopped in front of a ramshackle shanty bearing the unmistakable marks of a hard life. In reverent tones, the Senator identified this almost-log cabin as the place in which he was reared to manhood. His mother, who happened to be along, listened to the Abe Lincoln spiel for a while and then spoke up. "Why, Lyndon," she said, "you *know* we had a nice house over on the other side of the farm."

When Johnson exaggerates the humbleness of his origins or the valor of his ancestors, it's a relatively harmless matter, although it doesn't do his image any good. But when he injects the same hyperbole into foreign relations, it can do lasting damage to the reputation of the United States government—as in the case of the crisis in the Dominican Republic. At a press conference on June 17, 1965, in what one observer called "a truly alarming stream of Presidential consciousness," he elaborated on his reasons for sending the Marines into Santo Domingo. Said Johnson: "Some 1,500 innocent people were murdered and shot, and their heads cut off, and . . . as we talked to our Ambassador to confirm the horror and tragedy and the unbelievable fact that they were firing on Americans and the American Embassy, he was talking to us from under a desk while bullets were going through his windows, and he had a thousand American men, women and children assembled in the hotel who were pleading with their President for help to preserve their lives. We didn't start that. We didn't intervene. We didn't kill anyone."

It was a graphic picture, but unfortunately it wasn't true. The U.S.

Ambassador in Santo Domingo, William Tapley Bennett, said later that he did not remember any bullets coming into his office, and he did not take cover under his desk. No one was beheaded by the Dominican insurgents. No American citizens were harmed—although two newsmen were shot by U.S. Marines. It should be borne in mind, too, that when Johnson made his press conference statement on June 17, almost three weeks had elapsed since the first Marine contingents were sent in—plenty of time in which to check the facts.

Although reporters didn't realize it at the time, the credibility problem arose at Johnson's first press conference as President, on December 7, 1963. When he was asked about the size of the federal budget then being prepared, Johnson pointed out that Kennedy's last budget had been $98,800,000,000. Then he noted that about $3,500,000,000 would have to be added to this figure to cover "built-in" increases and new programs. Reporters came away with the impression that the new budget would be between $102,000,000,000 and $103,000,000,000.

A few days later, the spending total changed again. At the President's Texas vacation headquarters, officials spread the word that the new budget would be about $100,000,000,000. At other times, Johnson let it be known that the range would be 98 to 102 billion. But when the budget was submitted to Congress, it was none of these figures—not 98, 99, 100, 102 or 103 billion. It was 97.9 billion, and this was later reduced to 97.3 billion. Johnson had his victory. He had kept spending under the Kennedy level. And the reporters and the public had their first lesson in what to expect from the new President: calculated confusion.

In terms of Johnson's credibility, however, it was a Pyrrhic victory. When budget-making time rolled around again the following year, a White House aide, obviously acting under instructions, told reporters that the new figure probably would be between 104 and 106 billion. He was greeted with stony silence. This time, no one filed a story, except for one lady correspondent who had not been in Texas the previous year. When this budget was submitted, it was not 104 or 106 billion. It was 99.7 billion. It might be argued that the varying figures merely meant that a final decision hadn't been reached. But in that case, since the federal budget affects business planning across the country, why say anything at all before the final total was reached?

Since those early days, case after case has come to light in which the President or officials speaking for him have treated the truth with utmost casualness. There has been deception on both the military and diplomatic aspects of the Vietnam war, on the budget, on the Great Society program, on taxes, on pay increases for federal employees, on the aluminum price increase, on the President's health, on the appointment of Abe Fortas to the Supreme Court, and on a long list of other official and personal matters.

When The Washington *Post* reported that Johnson would ask for a four-billion-dollar cut in excise taxes, the President spread the word that this was false. A few months later, he asked Congress to cut excise taxes by 3.9 billion. When The Washington *Star* reported that Johnson would recommend a three percent average pay increase for federal employees, he complained that the story was erroneous. A short time later, he proposed a three percent average pay increase for federal employees. When the aluminum companies announced they were raising prices, the government countered with an announcement that it would sell 200,000 tons of stockpiled aluminum on the open market, which would have the effect of driving prices down. The White House said there was "no connection whatsoever" between the two actions, but later Johnson boasted privately about his role in forcing the aluminum companies to back down and said he had personally talked to a vice-president of Alcoa.

In October, 1965, Johnson announced that he would undergo surgery for removal of his gallbladder. He told reporters that "a thorough examination showed this to be the only trouble." After the operation, it was announced that the surgeons had removed a kidney stone as well. And under questioning by newsmen, the President's personal physician disclosed that Johnson had still another stone in his left kidney and that this had been known "for some years."

One sunny day in July, 1965, the President presided at a ceremony in the rose garden. Afterward, he invited reporters into his office for an impromptu news conference. One newsman asked him whether he could say anything about his plans for filling the vacancy on the Supreme Court that had been created by the appointment of Justice Arthur Goldberg as Ambassador to the United Nations. Johnson replied flatly that he had not even begun to consider the matter, and the reporters filed stories to that effect. The President did not use any of the many phrases available to a President when he does not want to answer a question but does not want to mislead the public either. The next day, he announced the appointment of Abe Fortas to succeed Goldberg on the court.

Johnson does not seem able to let well enough alone. There is no constitutional or legal requirement that a President answer reporters' questions. There are many times when he is well advised not to. But Johnson, it seems, has to see whether his hand is still quicker than the public eye.

Secrecy is a passion for Johnson: It may stem from his upbringing in the Byzantine political world of Texas. But in the White House, this secrecy has caused him nothing but trouble. Bill Moyers has said that "fundamental to [Johnson's] operations . . . is surprise, which keeps his foes off balance. He wants to retain the advantage of calling his own signals and deciding on his own timing." This is obviously good strategy, but there is a strong risk that it will first confuse, then antagonize and finally alienate the public.

As a grey deceiver, President Johnson has virtuoso range, from the minutiae of family history to the number of American troops in Vietnam and their mission. At Camp Stanley in South Korea, on his Asian tour last year, he told American servicemen proudly that "my great-great grand-father died at the Alamo." A search by a Texas historical society, alas, failed to unearth any evidence to support this patriotic allusion.

A preoccupation with secrecy for its own sake can lead up some ludicrous paths. Some time ago, Philip Potter of the Baltimore *Sun,* who is a friend of the President, wrote a detailed story about Johnson's plans for a new Food for Peace program. The story appeared a few days before Johnson was ready to announce the new program. After reading the story, the President canceled the announcement and ordered his staff to burn the mimeographed news releases dealing with the new program. Months later, the new Food for Peace plan was put into effect, but in a piecemeal fashion, one step at a time, to conceal the fact that Potter's story had been correct. Moreover, the White House conducted an inquiry to determine who had leaked the story to Potter. A cabinet-level official was picked as the culprit, although he was innocent. The official later said he was given "unshirted hell" for his alleged transgression. The President did not speak to Potter for months afterward.

In these and dozens of other instances, Johnson has drawn too deeply on the credibility bank. He has cried wolf too often, to the point where many reporters view with suspicion almost everything that he or his spokesmen say. This goes beyond a mere spat; it has sunk deep into the fabric. The relationship between the President and the Washington press corps has settled into a pattern of weary cynicism.

When Johnson's deputy press secretary, Robert Fleming, told newsmen recently that there was no indication an announcement on the supersonic transport plane would be made in the near future, the reporters immediately began boning up on background information about the project so they would be ready to write their stories. Sure enough, the announcement came just one day later.

By overdrawing his credibility account, Johnson has given up, volun-tarily, one of the chief weapons of leadership. The good faith of the prince, Machiavelli wrote, is his greatest asset. To be followed loyally, the chieftain must be trusted. This dark side of Lyndon Johnson, emerging despite his efforts at concealment, has eroded trust and, if you agree with Machiavelli, has impeded his quest for greatness.

The world, Anthony Trollope observed, is a place of hard words and harsh judgments. Lyndon Johnson has operated in this world as he found it, and as he thought it was. A hard, harsh man, he has bulled and battered his way through it to the top. But once there, it became his obligation to offer moral leadership, for this, as his mentor, Franklin Roosevelt, commented, is what is expected and required of the American President. Johnson has tried hard, but he is not an inspirational figure. His crude behavior intrudes as a shadow between the thought and the action. He has lived too long with Trollope's despairing summary.

Once Lyndon Johnson was complaining to a senior statesman that he wasn't liked, and he incautiously inquired why.

"Let's face it, Mr. President," replied the elder. "You just aren't a likable man."

[August, 1967]

An Appreciation of the Nonmilitary Functions of War

This piece first appeared in a longer form in the December 1967 issue of Esquire *introduced as follows: "This report is 28,000 words in length and so depressing that you may not be able to take it. But if you persist, Merry Christmas to you anyway, and on earth war, ill-will toward men." The version printed here—considerably shorter, but no less depressing—was published in the original edition of* Smiling Through the Apocalypse *with the note below by way of explanation.*

The military, or ostensible, function of the war system requires no elaboration. It is often necessary for a national military establishment to create a need for its unique powers—to maintain the franchise, so to speak. And a healthy military apparatus requires regular "exercise," by whatever rationale seems expedient, to prevent its atrophy.

The nonmilitary functions of the war system are more basic. They exist not merely to justify themselves but to serve broader social purposes. If and when war is eliminated, the military functions it has served will end

From a "leaked" government document entitled, in Esquire, "On the Possibility and Desirability of Peace," and later, in book form, "Report from Iron Mountain." The document purported to be the result of a three-year study by 15 of the country's most distinguished intellectuals, concluding that the economic, political and social institutions of modern man would fail without the existence of war to sustain them. The article was believed to be a deliberate hoax, devised out of the fertile imagination of Leonard Lewin (who claimed in the article only to be the conduit for a member of the committee who felt the public had a right to know the committee's recommendations to the government) to satirize, among other things, the nation's dependence on professional "expertise." A measure of its success in this paranoic decade was a bulletin from the State Department to all American embassies disclaiming knowledge of the report.

with it. But its nonmilitary functions will not. It is essential, therefore, that we understand their significance before we can reasonably expect to evaluate whatever institutions may be proposed to replace them.

Economic

The production of weapons of mass destruction has always been associated with economic "waste." The term is pejorative, since it implies a failure of function. But no human activity can properly be considered wasteful if it achieves its contextual objective. ". . . The attacks that, since the time of Samuel's criticism of King Saul, have been leveled against military expenditures as waste may well have concealed or misunderstood the point that some kinds of waste may have a larger social utility."[1]

In the case of military "waste," there is indeed a larger social utility. It derives from the fact that the "wastefulness" of war production is exercised entirely outside the framework of the economy of supply and demand. As such, it provides the only critically large segment of the total economy that is subject to complete and arbitrary central control. If modern industrial societies can be defined as those which have developed the capacity to produce more than is required for their economic survival (regardless of the equities of distribution of goods within them), military spending can be said to furnish the only balance wheel with sufficient inertia to stabilize the advance of their economies.

This function is often viewed, oversimply, as a device for the control of surpluses. One writer on the subject puts it this way: "Why is war so wonderful? Because it creates artificial demand . . . the only kind of artificial demand, moreover, that does not raise any political issues: *war, and only war, solves the problem of inventory*."[2] The reference here is to shooting war, but it applies equally to the general war economy as well. "It is generally agreed," concludes, more cautiously, the report of a panel set up by the U.S. Arms Control and Disarmament Agency, "that the greatly enlarged public sector since World War II, resulting from heavy defense expenditures, has provided additional protection against depressions, since this sector is not responsive to contraction in the private sector and provides a sort of buffer or balance wheel in the economy."[3]

But even in the context of the general civilian economy war cannot be

1. Arthur I. Waskow, *Toward the Unarmed Forces of the United States* (Washington: Institute for Policy Studies, 1966), p. 9. (This is the unabridged edition of the text of a report and proposal prepared for a seminar of strategists and Congressmen in 1965; it was later given limited distribution among other persons engaged in related projects.)
2. David T. Bazelon, "The Politics of the Paper Economy," *Commentary* (November 1962), p. 409.
3. *Economic Impacts of Disarmament* (Washington: U.S.G.P.O., January 1962).

considered wholly "wasteful." Without a long-established war economy, and without its frequent eruption into large-scale shooting war, most of the major industrial advances known to history, beginning with the development of iron, could never have taken place. Weapons technology structures the economy. According to the writer cited above, "Nothing is more ironic or revealing about our society than the fact that hugely destructive war is a very progressive force in it. . . . War production is progressive because it is production that would not otherwise have taken place. (It is not so widely appreciated, for example, that the civilian standard of living *rose* during World War II.)"[4] This is not "ironic or revealing," but essentially a simple statement of fact.

War spending, considered pragmatically, has been a consistently positive factor in the rise of gross national product and of individual productivity. A former Secretary of the Army has carefully phrased it for public consumption thus: "If there is, as I suspect there is, a direct relation between the stimulus of large defense spending and a substantially increased rate of growth of gross national product, it quite simply follows that defense spending *per se* might be countenanced *on economic grounds alone* [emphasis added] as a stimulator of the national metabolism."[5] Actually, the fundamental nonmilitary utility of war in the economy is far more widely acknowledged than the scarcity of such affirmations as that quoted above would suggest.

But *negatively* phrased public recognitions of the importance of war to the general economy abound. The most familiar example is the effect of "peace threats" on the stock market; e.g., "Wall Street was shaken yesterday by news of an apparent peace feeler from North Vietnam, but swiftly recovered its composure after about an hour of sometimes indiscriminate selling,"[6] Other incidental examples are to be found in the pressures brought to bear on the Department of Defense when it announces plans to close down an obsolete facility (as a "wasteful" form of "waste"), and in the usual coordination of stepped-up military activities (as in Vietnam in 1965) with dangerously rising unemployment rates.

Although we do not imply that a substitute for war in the economy cannot be devised, no combination of techniques for controlling employment, production, and consumption has yet been tested that can remotely compare to it in effectiveness.

Political

The political functions of war are essentially organizational. First of all,

4. David T. Bazelon, "The Scarcity Makers," *Commentary* (October 1962), p. 298.
5. Frank Pace, Jr., in an address before the American Bankers' Association, September 1957.
6. A random example, taken in this case from a story by David Deitch in the New York *Herald Tribune* (9 February 1966).

the existence of a society as a political "nation" requires as part of its definition an attitude of relationship toward other "nations." This is what we usually call a foreign policy. But a nation's foreign policy can have no substance if it lacks the means of enforcing its attitude toward other nations—which is to say that it is organized to some degree for war. War, then, as we have defined it to include all national activities that recognize the possibility of armed conflict, is itself the defining element of any nation's existence vis-à-vis any other nation. Since it is historically axiomatic that the existence of any form of weaponry insures its use, we have used the word "peace" as virtually synonymous with disarmament. By the same token, "war" is virtually synonymous with nationhood. The elimination of war implies the inevitable elimination of national sovereignty and the traditional nation-state.

The war system not only has been essential to the existence of nations as independent political entities, but has been equally indispensable to their stable internal political structure. Without it, no government has ever been able to obtain acquiescence in its "legitimacy," or right to rule its society. The possibility of war provides the sense of external necessity without which no government can long remain in power. The historical record reveals instance after instance where the failure of a regime to maintain the credibility of a war threat led to its dissolution, by the forces of private interest, of reactions to social injustice, or of other disintegrative elements.

The basic authority of a modern state over its people resides in its war powers. (There is, in fact, good reason to believe that codified law had its origins in the rules of conduct established by military victors for dealing with the defeated enemy, which were later adapted to apply to all subject populations.[7] On a day-to-day basis, it is represented by the institution of police, armed organizations charged expressly with dealing with "internal enemies" in a military manner. Like the conventional "external" military, the police are also substantially exempt from many civilian legal restraints on their social behavior. In some countries, the artificial distinction between police and other military forces does not exist. On the long-term basis, a government's emergency war powers—inherent in the structure of even the most libertarian of nations—define the most significant aspect of the relation between state and citizen.

In advanced modern democratic societies, the war system has provided political leaders with another political-economic function of increasing importance: it has served as the last great safeguard against the elimination of necessary social classes. As economic productivity increases to a level further and further above that of minimum subsistence, it becomes more and more difficult for a society to maintain distribution patterns insuring the existence of "hewers of wood and drawers of water." The

7. *Vide* L. Gumplowicz, in *Geschichte der Staatstheorien* (Innsbruck: Wagner, 1905) and earlier writings.

further progress of automation can be expected to differentiate still more sharply between "superior" workers and what Ricardo called "menials," while simultaneously aggravating the problem of maintaining an unskilled labor supply.

The arbitrary nature of war expenditures and of other military activities make them ideally suited to control these essential class relationships. Obviously, if the war system were to be discarded, new political machinery would be needed at once to serve this vital subfunction. Until it is developed, the continuance of the war system must be assured, if for no other reason, among others, than to preserve whatever quality and degree of poverty a society requires as an incentive, as well as to maintain the stability of its internal organization of power.

Sociological

Under this heading, we will examine a nexus of functions, the most obvious of which is the time-honored use of military institutions to provide antisocial elements with an acceptable role in the social structure. The disintegrative, unstable social movements loosely described as "fascist" have traditionally taken root in societies that have lacked adequate military or paramilitary outlets to meet the needs of these elements. The current euphemistic clichés—"juvenile delinquency" and "alienation"—have had their counterparts in every age. In earlier days these conditions were dealt with directly by the military without the complications of due process, usually through press gangs or outright enslavement. But it is not hard to visualize, for example, the degree of social disruption that might have taken place in the United States during the last two decades if the problem of the socially disaffected of the post-World War II period had not been foreseen and effectively met. The younger, and more dangerous, of these hostile social groupings have been kept under control by the Selective Service System.

This system and its analogues elsewhere furnish remarkably clear examples of disguised military utility. Informed persons in this country have never accepted the official rationale for a peacetime draft—military necessity, preparedness, etc.—as worthy of serious consideration. But what has gained credence among thoughtful men is the rarely voiced, less easily refuted, proposition that the institution of military service has a "patriotic" priority in our society that must be maintained for its own sake. Ironically, the simplistic official justification for Selective Service comes closer to the mark, once the nonmilitary functions of military institutions are understood. As a control device over the hostile, nihilistic, and potentially unsettling elements of a society in transition, the draft can again be defended, and defended quite convincingly, as a "military" necessity.

It must be noted also that the Armed Forces in every civilization have provided the principal state-supported haven for what we now call the "unemployable." The typical European standing army (of fifty years ago) consisted of ". . . troops unfit for employment in commerce, industry, or agriculture, led by officers unfit to practice any legitimate profession or to conduct a business enterprise."[8] This is still largely true, if less apparent. In a sense, this function of the military as the custodian of the economically or culturally deprived was the forerunner of most contemporary civilian social-welfare programs, from the W.P.A. to various forms of "socialized" medicine and Social Security. It is interesting that liberal sociologists currently proposing to use the Selective Service System as a medium of cultural upgrading of the poor consider this a *novel* application of military practice.

Although it cannot be said absolutely that such critical measures of social control as the draft require a military rationale, no modern society has yet been willing to risk experimentation with any other kind. Even during such periods of comparatively simple social crises as the so-called Great Depression of the 1930's, it was deemed prudent by the government to invest minor make-work projects, like the "Civilian" Conservation Corps, with a military character, and to place the more ambitious National Recovery Administration under the direction of a professional army officer at its inception. Today, at least one small Northern European country, plagued with uncontrollable unrest among its "alienated youth," is considering the expansion of its armed forces, despite the problem of making credible the expansion of a nonexistent external threat.

In general, the war system provides the basic motivation for primary social organization. In so doing, it reflects on the societal level the incentives of individual human behavior. The most important of these, for social purposes, is the individual psychological rationale for allegiance to a society and its values. Allegiance requires a cause; a cause requires an enemy. This much is obvious; the critical point is that the enemy that defines the cause must seem genuinely formidable. Roughly speaking, the presumed power of the "enemy" sufficient to warrant an individual sense of allegiance to the society must be proportionate to the size and complexity of the society. Today, of course, that power must be one of unprecedented magnitude and frightfulness.

It follows, from the patterns of human behavior, that the credibility of a social "enemy" demands similarly a readiness of response in proportion to its menace. In a broad social context, "an eye for an eye" still characterizes the only acceptable attitude toward a presumed threat of aggression, despite contrary religious and moral precepts governing personal conduct. The remoteness of personal decision from social consequence in a modern society makes it easy for its members to maintain this attitude without

8. K. Fischer, *Das Militar* (Zurich: Steinmetz Verlag, 1932), pp. 42-43.

being aware of it. A recent example is the war in Vietnam; a less recent one was the bombing of Hiroshima and Nagasaki. In each case, the extent and gratuitousness of the slaughter were abstracted into political formulae by most Americans, once the proposition that the victims were "enemies" was established. The war system makes such an abstracted response possible in nonmilitary contexts as well. A conventional example of this mechanism is the inability of most people to connect, let us say, the starvation of millions in India with their own past conscious political decision-making. Yet the sequential logic linking a decision to restrict grain production in America with an eventual famine in Asia is obvious, unambiguous, and unconcealed.

What gives the war system its preeminent role in social organization, as elsewhere, is its unmatched authority over life and death. It must be emphasized again that the war system is not a mere social extension of the presumed need for individual human violence, but itself in turn serves to rationalize most nonmilitary killing.

A brief look at some defunct premodern societies is instructive. One of the most noteworthy features common to the larger, more complex, and more successful of ancient civilizations was their widespread use of the blood sacrifice. If one were to limit consideration to those cultures whose regional hegemony was so complete that the prospect of "war" had become virtually inconceivable—as was the case with several of the great pre-Columbian societies of the Western Hemisphere—it would be found that some form of ritual killing occupied a position of paramount social importance in each. Invariably, the ritual was invested with mythic or religious significance; as with all religious and totemic practice, however, the ritual masked a broader and more important social function.

In these societies, the blood sacrifice served the purpose of maintaining a vestigial "earnest" of the society's capability and willingness to make war—i.e., kill and be killed—in the event that some mystical—i.e., unforeseen—circumstance were to give rise to the possibility. It was primarily, if not exclusively, a symbolic reminder that war had once been the central organizing force of the society, and that this condition might recur.

It does not follow that a transition to total peace in modern societies would require the use of this model, even in less "barbaric" guise. But the historical analogy serves as a reminder that a viable substitute for war as a social system cannot be a mere symbolic charade. It must involve real risk of real personal destruction, and on a scale consistent with the size and complexity of modern social systems.

Ecological

Man, like all other animals, is subject to the continuing process of adapting to the limitations of his environment. But the principal mechanism he has utilized for this purpose is unique among living creatures. To forestall the inevitable historical cycles of inadequate food supply, post-Neolithic man destroys surplus members of his own species by organized warfare.

Ethologists[9] have often observed that the organized slaughter of members of their own species is virtually unknown among other animals. Man's special propensity to kill his own kind (shared to a limited degree with rats) may be attributed to his inability to adapt anachronistic patterns of survival (like primitive hunting) to his development of "civilizations" in which these patterns cannot be effectively sublimated. It may be attributed to other causes that have been suggested, such as a maladapted "territorial instinct," etc. Nevertheless, it exists and its social expression in war constitutes a biological control of his relationship to his natural environment that is peculiar to man alone.

War has served to help assure the *survival* of the human species. But as an evolutionary device to *improve* it, war is almost unbelievably inefficient. With few exceptions, the selective processes of other living creatures promote both specific survival *and* genetic improvement. When a conventionally adaptive animal faces one of its periodic crises of insufficiency, it is the "inferior" members of the species that normally disappear. In human societies, those who fight and die in wars for survival are in general its biologically stronger members. This is natural selection in reverse.

The regressive genetic effect of war has been often noted and equally often deplored, even when it confuses biological and cultural factors[10] The disproportionate loss of the *biologically* stronger remains inherent in traditional warfare. It serves to underscore the fact that survival of the species, rather than its improvement, is the fundamental purpose of natural selection, if it can be said to have a purpose, just as it is the basic premise of this study.

But as the polemologist Gaston Bouthoul[11] has pointed out, other institutions that were developed to serve this ecological function have proved even less satisfactory. (They include such established forms as these: infanticide, practiced chiefly in ancient and primitive societies; sexual mutilation; monasticism; forced emigration; extensive capital punishment, as in old China and eighteenth-century England; and other similar, usually localized, practices.)

9. *Vide* most recently K. Lorenz, in *Das Sogenannte Böse: zur Naturgeschichte der Aggression* (Vienna: G. Borotha-Schoeler Verlag, 1964).
10. As in recent draft-law controversy, in which the issue of selective deferment of the culturally privileged is often carelessly equated with the preservation of the biologically "fittest."
11. G. Bouthoul, in *La Guerre* (Paris: Presses universitaires de France, 1953) and many other more detailed studies. The useful concept of "polemology," for the study of war as an independent discipline, is his, as is the notion of "demographic relaxation," the sudden temporary decline in the rate of population increase after major wars.

Man's ability to increase his productivity of the essentials of physical life suggests that the need for protection against cyclical famine may be nearly obsolete.[12] It has thus tended to reduce the apparent importance of the basic ecological function of war, which is generally disregarded by peace theorists. Two aspects of it remain especially relevant, however. The first is obvious: current rates of population growth, compounded by environmental threat of chemical and other contaminants, may well bring about a new crisis of insufficiency. If so, it is likely to be one of unprecedented global magnitude, not merely regional or temporary.

The second relevant factor is the efficiency of modern methods of mass destruction. They offer, perhaps paradoxically, the first opportunity in the history of man to halt the regressive genetic effects of natural selection by war. Nuclear weapons are indiscriminate. Their application would bring to an end the disproportionate destruction of the physically stronger members of the species (the "warriors") in periods of war. Whether this prospect of genetic gain would offset the unfavorable mutations anticipated from post-nuclear radioactivity we have not yet determined.

Another secondary ecological trend bearing on projected population growth is the regressive effect of certain medical advances. Pestilence, for example, is no longer an important factor in population control. The problem of increased life expectancy has been aggravated. These advances also pose a potentially more sinister problem, in that undesirable genetic traits that were formerly self-liquidating are now medically maintained. Many diseases that were once fatal at preprocreational ages are now cured; the effect of this development is to perpetuate undesirable susceptibilities and mutations. It seems clear that a new quasi-eugenic function of war is now in process of formation that will have to be taken into account in any transition plan. For the time being, the Department of Defense appears to have recognized such factors, as has been demonstrated by the planning under way by the Rand Corporation to cope with the breakdown in the ecological balance anticipated after a thermonuclear war. The Department has also begun to stockpile birds, for example, against the expected proliferation of radiation-resistant insects, etc.

Cultural and Scientific

The declared order of values in modern societies gives a high place to the so-called "creative" activities, and an even higher one to those associated with the advance of scientific knowledge. Widely held social values can be translated into political equivalents, which in turn may bear on the nature of a transition to peace. The dependence, therefore, of cultural and

12. This seemingly premature statement is supported by one of our own test studies. But it hypothecates both the stabilizing of world population growth and the institution of fully adequate environmental controls. Under these two conditions, the probability of the permanent elimination of involuntary global famine is 68 percent by 1976 and 95 percent by 1981.

scientific achievement on the war system would be an important consideration in a transition plan even if such achievement had no inherently necessary social function.

Of all the countless dichotomies invented by scholars to account for the major differences in art styles and cycles, only one has been consistently unambiguous in its application to a variety of forms and cultures. However it may be verbalized, the basic distinction is this: Is the work war-oriented or is it not? Among primitive peoples, the war dance is the most important art form. Elsewhere, literature, music, painting, sculpture, and architecture that has won lasting acceptance has invariably dealt with a theme of war, expressly or implicitly, and has expressed the centricity of war to society. The war in question may be national conflict, as in Shakespeare's plays, Beethoven's music, or Goya's paintings, or it may be reflected in the form of religious, social, or moral struggle, as in the work of Dante, Rembrandt, and Bach. Aesthetic and moral standards have a common anthropological origin, in the exaltation of bravery, the willingness to kill and risk death in tribal warfare.

It is also instructive to note that the character of a society's culture has borne a close relationship to its war-making potential, in the context of its times. It is no accident that the current "cultural explosion" in the United States is taking place during an era marked by an unusually rapid advance in weaponry. This relationship is more generally recognized than the literature on the subject would suggest. For example, many artists and writers are now beginning to express concern over the limited creative options they envisage in the warless world they think, or hope, may be soon upon us. They are currently preparing for this possibility by unprecedented experimentation with meaningless forms; their interest in recent years has been increasingly engaged by the abstract pattern, the gratuitous emotion, the random happening, and the unrelated sequence.

The relationship of war to scientific research and discovery is more explicit. War is the principal motivational force for the development of science at every level, from the abstractly conceptual to the narrowly technological. Modern society places a high value on "pure" science, but it is historically inescapable that all the significant discoveries that have been made about the natural world have been inspired by the real or imaginary military necessities of their epochs.

Beginning with the development of iron and steel, and proceeding through the discoveries of the laws of motion and thermodynamics to the age of the atomic particle, the synthetic polymer, and the space capsule, no important scientific advance has not been at least indirectly initiated by an implicit requirement of weaponry. More prosaic examples include the transistor radio (an outgrowth of military communications requirements), the assembly line (from Civil War firearms needs), the canal lock, and so on. A typical adaptation can be seen in a device as modest as the common lawn mower; it developed from the revolving scythe devised by Leonardo da Vinci to precede a horse-powered vehicle into enemy ranks.

The most direct relationship can be found in medical technology. For example, a giant "walking machine," an amplifier of body motions invented for military use in difficult terrain, is now making it possible for many previously confined to wheelchairs to walk. The Vietnam war alone has led to spectacular improvements in amputation procedures, blood-handling techniques, and surgical logistics. It has stimulated new large-scale research on malaria and other tropical parasite diseases; it is hard to estimate how long this work would otherwise have been delayed, despite its enormous nonmilitary importance to nearly half the world's population.

[December, 1967]

SECTION 2

THE GENERATION GAP

My Generation

by Frank Conroy

The Fifties was a time of progress for ordinary Americans: the population rose by 28 million and Americans were better fed and better housed than ever before. Yet the decade also saw an unprecedented arms race, and fear of the Bomb disturbed the normalcy symbolized by Ike's ear-to-ear grin. The startling contrast between daily life and Armageddon left the young with little to say, but one of their number, Frank Conroy, spoke up for the Silent Generation in the October 1968 issue.

I remember asking, as a very young child, what was in the newspapers when there wasn't a war going on. That was the Second World War, the war to eradicate evil from the face of the earth, the war in which all Americans believed. Victory gardens, V-Mail, Gold Star Mothers, ration books and air-raid drills were the order of the day. People talked lustfully of three-inch-thick steaks, automobile tires and real butter. My father carried in his vest pocket his own personal sugar dispenser for coffee and my mother could be reduced to tears by a run in her stockings. The rationing of food, the enemy without, common hardship, common purpose and the almost godlike presence of Franklin Delano Roosevelt served to unify the country as it had perhaps never been unified before. If the First World War, however bloody, had been a bit of a lark, the Second was quite clearly a war of survival. Americans did not expect to lose, yet they knew they'd have to fight like hell to win. The discovery of the death camps of Central Europe resolved all questions as to what the war had been about. The forces of light against the forces of darkness, that was what we believed, and no American thirty-two years old can be un-touched by that memory.

301

We hated the evil Germans and the treacherous Japs, scorned the weak Italians, loved the stalwart Russians, the plucky English and the wise Chinese. The double-fuselage P-38 was the fastest plane we knew about, the B-25 our image of power. It was, to use Fitzgerald's phrase, "bracing to be an American." Then came the atomic bomb and it was no longer quite so bracing.

It goes without saying that the effects of the bomb on the American mind were profound. We who were children at the time, with our childlike sensitivity to mystery, magic, and the unknown, with our social antennae fully extended to pull in all sorts of information, regardless of its usefulness (the ravenous hunger of children's minds, storing everything away undigested, stockpiling the recognizable, the unrecognizable and the ephemeral against a future time), were perhaps most deeply affected. We felt exhilaration at the indisputable proof that America was the strongest power on earth, apprehension because the power was mysterious, and most significantly we felt guilt, secret guilt that verged on the traitorous, guilt we could not possibly talk about. Our political apathy later, as college students in the Eisenhower years, seems to me to trace directly to our inability to reorganize those simple, propagandistic concepts of democracy and political morality which had been our wartime heritage, and which the bomb had rendered untenable.

The war ended, the United Nations was born at Dumbarton Oaks, and America moved into a new phase. We grew toward adolescence during the postwar boom, a period of expansion and prosperity unparalleled in the history of man, a time of busy optimism during which America seemed to concern herself entirely with adult matters. The kids, and there were not many of us in those days, were more or less left out of things. We inhabited a shadow area within the culture—nothing was important about us except the fact that eventually we'd grow up. We were embarrassed at our minority and most of us kept quiet, attempting not to call attention to ourselves.

We were the last generation to grow up without television. The radio was our thing—*The Lone Ranger, The Green Hornet, Mr. and Mrs. North,* etc. When television arrived we greeted it in a state of tremendous excitement. Movies at home! Free! It was too good to be true. And of course it was. It disappointed, was oddly dull after the initial novelty had worn off, unsettlingly hypnogenetic, vaguely inducive of claustrophobia. TV was technically crude in those days, inferior in every way to the marvelously cathartic medium of films, so we kept on paying quarters to get into the children's sections of our neighborhood theatres. And we got a lot for our money. The programs changed every three or four days, with newsreel, cartoon, short, trailers and a double feature. I used to go to Loew's Orpheum, see the show, and then sneak into the balcony to wait for vaudeville at eight o'clock. Movies were a way of life.

We became teen-agers when to be a teen-ager was nothing, the lowest of the low. Our heroes were not of our own age group. For the most part they were athletes—Jackie Robinson, Joe DiMaggio, Sugar Ray Robinson. Our music was Dixieland jazz (a revival was going on at the time), pop music, and, for some of us, bebop. (When I met my wife's aged grandmother years later she turned to me, fixed me with her steel-blue New England eyes and said: "Ah, Mr. Conroy, I understand you are interested in music. Please tell me about bobeep.") At the age of fifteen I saw Charlie Parker on the stage of Carnegie Hall. Our clothing, manners and life-styles were unoriginal—scaled-down versions of what we saw in the adults. We had no sense of group identity, perhaps not much less than the teen-age generations that had preceded us, but unquestionably less than the generation that was to follow ten years later. We were mysteriously disenfranchised—the best-looking girls at high school would ignore the boys of their own age and prefer to go out with older men.

In college we were named. The Silent Generation. The Apathetic Generation. There was no doubt about it. The sleepy Eisenhower years. America in a trance, drifting leisurely through a long golf game while the clouds gathered. Among students it was hard to find a rebel, virtually impossible to find a Marxist, a mystic, a reformer, or indeed, anyone who felt very strongly about anything. When my roommate and I discovered secret fraternities in our college, a college which advertised itself probably to be fraternity-free, and exposed them in the newspaper, there was a bit of talk but not much more. Most students thought it was a ploy from the psychology department. One can imagine what would happen now.

We believed in civil rights but did nothing active about it. Picketing was unheard of, protest vaguely uncool. It was enough to send a few bucks to the N.A.A.C.P., an organization we believed to be utterly safe, no more and perhaps even less militant than the Parent-Teachers Association. We were not afraid of Negroes and so made no attempt, as the students do today, to identify ourselves with their power.

Our sexual mores were conservative in the extreme. It was the time of going steady. Fiercely monogamous, we frowned on playing the field and lived as if we were already married. Virginity in girls was not expected, but faithfulness most certainly was. Promiscuity, which we interpreted as going out with more than one person at a time, was a grievous sin. Our key words were discretion, privacy and propriety. Needless to say, we lived and breathed hypocrisy.

No one knew anything about drugs in those days. Marijuana, which was to sweep through all levels of American society during the next decade, was smoked, as far as I know, by only two students in my college of five hundred. Heroin and cocaine were thought to be extremely dangerous (as they doubtless are) and no one would have dreamed of experimenting with them. LSD, Methedrine, and amyl nitrite were unknown. Mind-expansion was not a meaningless term, however. We read Blake, Zen, science fiction, the Christian mystics, and various studies on E.S.P. and psychic phenomena. We blew our minds without drugs. I remember lying, at the age of nineteen, in the enclosed garden of the Bryn Mawr library, under the cherry tree, watching the stars for hour after hour, aware that light from unimaginable distances was collecting in my eye, getting high on the universe. College was a straight scene for us. We didn't come across pot until many years later.

Our literary heroes were more likely to be figures from the past than from our own time. Most of us felt closer to the sixteenth, eighteenth, and nineteenth centuries than to the seventeenth or the twentieth. James Joyce, whom rightly or wrongly we thought of as a nineteenth-century writer, the penultimate romantic, was a god. We took apart his difficult prose without the least sense of resentment, dissecting clues as eagerly as Talmudic scholars. *Portrait of the Artist* and *Ulysses* were books we knew well. The difficulties of *Finnegans Wake* were thought by us to be the inevitable result of the depth of Joyce's art rather than any failure of Joyce's mind. It would have been sacrilegious to suggest psychosis, and we scorned Stanislaus for having done so. Beckett was respected as much for having been Joyce's secretary as for his writings.

Closer to our own time, we admired Faulkner, Hemingway, Fitzgerald, early Steinbeck, and hated Wolfe, Dos Passos, Sinclair Lewis and James T. Farrell. Among young writers we liked Mailer, Capote, Styron and Salinger (who turned out not to live up to our expectations). There was a flurry about Francoise Sagan, mainly because she was nineteen, but on the whole we recognized her as a creation of the advertising age. The Beats were just beginning, Kerouac, et al., and we greeted them with a certain amount of suspicion, convinced that art was not that easy. Our standards were rather high, I think. The New Critics had filled us with an almost religious awe of language. We read Leavis, Edmund Wilson and Eliot as well, taking it all very seriously, worrying over every little point as if Truth and Beauty hung in the balance. The conservatism that colored so much of our experience did not evaporate when we dealt with literature. We defended literary art as if it were a castle under seige, in imminent danger of being destroyed by the vulgarians. In every college or university I knew anything about the most hated course was Social Science, as much a result of the incredibly rotten prose of the texts as it was of our disinterest in things social. We winced at bad prose, all of us, even the mathematicians and physicists who were presumably more interested in symbols than in language. We were neat, very neat, and sloppiness of any kind irritated us.

Fitzgerald calls a generation that reaction against the fathers which seems to occur about three times a century. There is the possibility that time has collapsed since he wrote those words, that life has accelerated to the point where changeovers occur much more rapidly, but nevertheless it is clear that those of us now in our early thirties were not a generation in any self-conscious sense. We had no leaders, no program, no sense of our own power, and no culture exclusively our own. Rather than saying, "Don't trust anyone over thirty," we would have been much more likely to say, "Don't trust anyone *under* thirty," or perhaps just, "Don't trust anyone." It is hard to believe that little more than ten years has gone by. Imagining, for the moment, American society as a huge mind, the students today can be thought of as representing the unconscious—they are pure emotion, they act first and figure it out later, they are the route through which revolutionary power is expressed—but most importantly they feel themselves to be a part of the social organism, they are the unconscious sensing the dimensions of the whole mind and their role within it. We felt nothing remotely like that. We were much more suspicious of society, without faith in its ability to respond to our minority voice. We were filled with precocious cynicism. We were stoics in our youth.

Now, as we come into power, we are aware of the paucity of our history. We have generation envy. How colorless were our times! Fitzgerald's people believed in their world—it really mattered who won the Princeton-Harvard game, it really meant something to appear at the theatre or the opera—and because they believed in their world they owned it. Until the Depression destroyed them they must have had a marvelous time. Styron's people had the war, a real war, a long, elaborate educational event plunging them directly into life. They had to learn to swim after they were in the water and, however sad their time, it was not dull. Brackman's people have faith. In a nonreligious age they have rediscovered faith. They are experimenters, revolutionaries and freethinkers, possessed by their own creative force. They have their own particular kinds of sillinesses, of course, but they believe they can change the world, and recent evidence suggests they are correct in that assumption. It is no accident that they follow us, they are most immediately in revolt against the banality of those who immediately preceded them. We have already learned a great deal from them, and will learn more. We will never be like them, nor do we want to be, but we perhaps stand to gain more from their example than anyone else. We are still young, after all, relatively late bloomers, but still young. Our strength lies in our fluency in all languages now spoken in America, the old and the new. In tremendously exciting times, we stand at the exact center of American culture, ready for anything.

[October, 1968]

There Goes (Varoom! Varoom!) That Kandy-Kolored (Thphhhhhh!) Tangerine-Flake Streamline Baby (Rahghhh!) Around the Bend (Brummmmmmmmmmmmmmmm.....

by Tom Wolfe

The affluence of the Sixties made it possible for more and more teenagers to own cars of their own. In addition to being a symbol of freedom, mobility, and independence, the automobile became a form of self-expression, and in customized-car design we see the first emergence of teen folk art. At age thirty-two, still somewhat new to journalism, Tom Wolfe signed this piece, published in November 1963 and his first for Esquire, Thomas K. Wolfe, *to "clear up, a generation from now, any possible confusion as to which Wolfe wrote* Look Homeward, Angel.*"*

"This is the decade when the postwar babies come of age. In the automobile business, coming of age means the age at which they enter the automobile market. It adds up to twelve and a half million more young people in these age groups by 1970—an increase of more than one million per year!"
—L. A. Iacocca, Vice-President of
Ford Motor Company, and Ford Division General Manager

The first good look I had at customized cars was at an event called a "Teen Fair," held in Burbank, a suburb of Los Angeles beyond Hollywood. This was a wild place to be taking a look at art objects—eventually, I should say, you have to reach the conclusion that these customized cars *are* art objects, at least if you use the standards applied in a civilized society. But I will get to that in a moment. Anyway, about noon you drive up to a place that looks like an outdoor amusement park, and there are three serious-looking kids, like the cafeteria committee in high school, taking tickets, but the scene inside is quite mad. Inside, two things hit you. The first is a huge platform a good seven feet off the ground with a hully-gully band—everything is electrified, the bass, the guitars, the saxo-

306

phones—and (two) behind the band, on the platform, about two hundred kids are doing frantic dances called the hully-gully, the bird, and the shampoo. As I said, it's noontime. The dances the kids are doing are very jerky. The boys and girls don't touch, not even with their hands. They just ricochet around. Then you notice that all the girls are dressed exactly alike. They have bouffant hairdos—all of them—and slacks that are, well, skintight does not get the idea across; it's more the conformation than how tight the slacks are. It's as if some lecherous old tailor with a gluteus-maximus fixation designed them, striation by striation. About the time you've managed to focus on this, you notice that out in the middle of the park is a huge, perfectly round swimming pool; really rather enormous. And there is a Chris-Craft cabin cruiser in the pool, going around and around, sending up big waves, with more of these bouffant babies bunched in the back of it. In the water, suspended like plankton, are kids in Scuba-diving outfits; others are tooling around underwater, breathing through a snorkel. And all over the place are booths, put up by shoe companies and guitar companies and God knows who else, and there are kids dancing in all of them—dancing the bird, the hully-gully, and the shampoo—with the music of the hully-gully band piped all over the park through loudspeakers.

All this time, Tex Smith, from *Hot Rod Magazine*, who brought me over to the place, is trying to lead me to the customized-car exhibit—"Tom, I want you to see this car that Bill Cushenberry built, The Silhouette"—which is to say, here are two hundred kids ricocheting over a platform at high noon, and a speedy little boat barreling around and around and around in a round swimming pool, and I seem to be the only person who is distracted. The customized-car exhibit turns out to be the Ford Custom Car Caravan, which Ford is sending all over the country. At first, with the noise and peripheral motion and the inchoate leching you are liable to be doing, what with bouffant nymphets rocketing all over the place, these customized cars do not strike you as anything very special. Obviously they *are* very special, but the first thing you think of is the usual—you know, that the kids who own these cars are probably skinny little hoods who wear T-shirts and carry their cigarette packs by winding them around in the T-shirt up near the shoulder.

But after a while, I was glad I had seen the cars in this natural setting, which was, after all, a kind of Plato's Republic for teen-agers. Because if you watched anything at this fair very long, you kept noticing the same thing. These kids are absolutely maniacal about form. They are practically religious about it. For example, the dancers: none of them ever smiled. They stared at each other's legs and feet, concentrating. The dances had no grace about them at all, they were more in the nature of a hoedown, but everybody was concentrating to do them exactly *right*. And the bouffant kids all had form, wild form, but form with rigid standards, one gathers.

Even the boys. Their dress was prosaic—Levis, Slim Jims, sport shirts, T-shirts, polo shirts—but the form was consistent: a stovepipe silhouette. And they all had the same hairstyle: some wore it long, some short, but none of them had a part; all that hair was brushed back straight from the hairline. I went by one of the guitar booths, and there was a little kid in there, about thirteen, playing the hell out of an electric guitar. The kid was named Cranston something or other. He looked like he ought to be named Kermit or Herschel; all his genes were kind of horribly Okie. Cranston was playing away and a big crowd was watching. But Cranston was slouched back with his spine bent like a sapling up against a table, looking gloriously bored. At thirteen, this kid was being fanatically cool. They all were. They were all wonderful slaves to form. They have created their own style of life, and they are much more authoritarian about enforcing it than are adults. Not only that, but today these kids—especially in California—have *money*, which, needless to say, is why all these shoe merchants and guitar sellers and the Ford Motor Company were at a Teen Fair in the first place. I don't mind observing that it is this same combination—money plus slavish devotion to form—that accounts for Versailles or St. Mark's Square. Naturally, most of the artifacts that these kids' money-plus-form produce are of a pretty ghastly order. But so was most of the paraphernalia that developed in England during the Regency. I mean, most of it was on the order of starched cravats. A man could walk into Beau Brummel's house at 11 a.m., and here would come the butler with a tray of wilted linen. "These were some of our failures," he confides. But then Brummel comes downstairs wearing one perfect starched cravat. Like one perfect iris, the flower of Mayfair civilization. But the Regency period did see some tremendous formal architecture. And the kids' formal society has also brought at least one substantial thing to a formal development of a high order—the customized cars. I don't have to dwell on the point that cars mean more to these kids than architecture did in Europe's great formal century, say, 1750 to 1850. They are freedom, style, sex, power, motion, color—everything is right there.

Things have been going on in the development of the kids' formal attitude toward cars since 1945, things of great sophistication that adults have not been even remotely aware of, mainly because the kids are so inarticulate about it, especially the ones most hipped on the subject. They are not from the levels of society that produce children who write sensitive analytical prose at age seventeen, or if they do, they soon fall into the hands of English instructors who put them onto Hemingway or a lot of goddamn-and-hungry-breast writers. If they ever write about a highway again, it's a rain-slicked highway and the sound of the automobiles passing over it is like the sound of tearing silk (not that one household in ten thousand has heard the sound of tearing silk since 1945).

Anyway, we are back at the Teen Fair and I am talking to Tex Smith and to Don Beebe, a portly young guy with a white sport shirt and Cuban sunglasses. As they tell me about the Ford Custom Car Caravan, I can see that Ford has begun to comprehend this teen-age style of life and its potential. The way Ford appears to figure it is this: Thousands of kids are getting hold of cars and either hopping them up for speed or customizing them to some extent, usually a little of both. Before they get married they pour *all* their money into this. If Ford can get them hooked on Fords now, after the kids are married they'll buy new Fords. Even the kids who aren't full-time car nuts themselves will be influenced by which car is considered "boss." They use that word a lot, "boss." The kids used to consider Ford the hot car, but then, from 1955 to 1962, Chevrolet became the favorite. They had big engines and were easy to hop up, the styling was simple, and the kids could customize them easily. In 1959, and more so in 1960, Plymouth became a hot car, too. In 1961 and 1962, it was all Chevrolet and Plymouth. Now Ford is making a big push. A lot of the professional hot-rod and custom-car people, adults, will tell you that now Ford is the hot car, but you have to discount some of it, because Ford is laying money on everybody right and left, in one form or another. In the Custom Car Caravan, all the cars have been fashioned out of Ford bodies except the ones that are completely handmade, like the aforementioned Silhouette.

Anyway, Don Beebe is saying, over a loudspeaker, "I hate to break up that dancing, but let's have a little drag racing." He has a phonograph hooked up to the loudspeaker, and he puts on a record, produced by Riverside Records, of drag-strip sounds, mainly dragsters blasting off and squealing from the starting line. Well, he doesn't really break up the dancing, but a hundred kids come over, when they hear the drag-strip sounds, to where Beebe has a slot-racing stand. Slot-racing is a model-train-type game in which two model drag racers, each about five inches long, powered by electricity, run down a model drag strip. Beebe takes a microphone and announces that Dick Dale, the singer, is here, and any-body who will race Dick at the slot-racing stand will get one of his records. Dick Dale is pretty popular among the kids out here because he sings a lot of "surfing" songs. The surfers—surfboard riders—are a cult much admired by all the kids. They have their own argot, with adjectives like "hang ten," meaning the best there is. They also go in for one particular brand of customizing: they take old wood-bodied station wagons, which they call "woodies" and fix them up for riding, sleeping and hauling surfing equipment for their weekends at the beach. The surfers also get a hell of a bang out of slot-racing for some reason, so with Dick Dale slot-racing at the Teen Fair, you have about three areas of the arcane teen world all rolled into one.

Dick Dale, rigged out in Byronic shirt and blue cashmere V-neck sweater and wraparound sunglasses, singer's mufti U.S.A., has one cord with a starter button, while a bouffant nymphet from Newport named

Sherma, Sherma of the Capri pants, has the other one. Don Beebe flashes a starting light and Sherma lets out a cry, not a thrilled cry, just nerves, and a model 1963 Ford and a model dragster go running down the slot board, which is about chest high. The slot board is said to be one-twenty-fifth the actual size of a drag strip, which somehow reminds you of those incredible stamp-size pictures in the dictionary with the notation that this is one-hundredth the size of a real elephant. A hundred kids were packed in around the slot racers and did not find it incredible. That is, they were interested in who would win, Dick Dale or Sherma. I'm sure they had no trouble magnifying the slot racers twenty-five times to the size of the full-blown, esoteric world of hot rods and custom cars.

I met George Barris, one of the celebrities of the custom-car world, at the Teen Fair. Barris is the biggest name in customizing. He is a good example of a kid who grew up completely absorbed in this teen-age world of cars, who pursued the pure flame and its forms with such devotion that he emerged an artist. It was like Tiepolo emerging from the studios of Venice, where the rounded Grecian haunches of the murals on the Palladian domes hung in the atmosphere like clouds. Except that Barris emerged from the auto-body shops of Los Angeles.

Barris invited me out to his studio—only he would never think of calling it that, he calls it Kustom City—at 10811 Riverside Drive in North Hollywood. If there is a river within a thousand miles of Riverside Drive, I saw no sign of it. It's like every place else out there: endless scorched boulevards lined with one-story stores, shops, bowling alleys, skating rinks, tacos drive-ins, all of them shaped not like rectangles but like trapezoids, from the way the roofs slant up from the back and the plate-glass fronts slant out as if they're going to pitch forward on the sidewalk and throw up. The signs are great, too. They all stand free on poles outside. They have horribly slick doglegged shapes that I call boomerang modern. As for Kustom City—Barris grew up at the time when it was considered sharp to change all the C's to K's. He also sells Kandy Lac to paint cars Kandy Kolors with, and I know that sibilant C in City must have bothered the hell out of him at some point. It's interesting, I think, that he still calls the place Kustom City, and still sells Kandy Kolors, because he is an intelligent person. What it means is, he is absolutely untouched by the big amoeba god of Anglo-European sophistication that gets you in the East. You know how it is in the East. One day you notice that the boss's button-down shirt has this sweet percale roll to it, while your own was obviously slapped together by some mass-production graph keepers who are saving an eighth of inch of cloth per shirt, twelve inches per bolt or the like, and this starts eating at you.

Barris, whose family is Greek, is a solid little guy, five feet seven, thirty-seven years old, and he looks just like Picasso. When he's working, which is most of the time, he wears a heavy white T-style shirt, faded off-white pants cut full with pleats in the manner of Picasso walking along a Mediterranean bluff in the wind at Rapallo, and crepe-sole slipper-style shoes, also off-white. Picasso, I should add, means nothing to Barris, although he knows who he is. It's just that to Barris and the customizers there is no one great universe of form and design called Art. Yet that's the universe he's in. He's not building cars, he's creating forms.

Barris starts taking me through Kustom City, and the place looks like any other body shop at first, but pretty soon you realize you're in a *gallery*. This place is full of cars such as you have never seen before. Half of them will never touch the road. They're put on trucks and trailers and carted all over the country to be exhibited at hot-rod and custom-car shows. They'll run, if it comes to that—they're full of big, powerful, hopped-up chrome-plated motors, because all that speed and power, and all that lovely apparatus, has tremendous emotional meaning to everybody in customizing. But it's like one of these Picasso or Miro rugs. You don't walk on the damn things. You hang them on the wall. It's the same thing with Barris' cars. In effect, they're sculpture.

For example, there is an incredible object he built called the XPAK-400 air car. The customizers love all that X jazz. It runs on a cushion of air, which is beside the point, because it's a pure piece of curvilinear abstract sculpture. If Brancusi is any good, then this thing belongs on a pedestal, too. There is not a straight line in it, and only one true circle, and those countless planes, and tremendous baroque fins, and yet all in all it's a rigid little piece of solid geometrical harmony. As a matter of fact, Brancusi and Barris both developed out of a design concept that we can call Streamlined Modern or Thirties Curvilinear—via utterly different roads, of course—and Barris and most other custom artists are carrying this idea of the abstract curve, which is very tough to handle, on and on and on at a time when your conventional designers—from architects to the guys who lay out magazines—are all Mondrian. Even the young Detroit car stylists are all Mondrian. Only the aircraft designers have done anything more with the Streamline, and they have only because they're forced to by physics, and so on. I want to return to that subject in a minute, but first I want to tell you about another car Barris was showing me.

This was stuck back in a storeroom. Barris wasn't interested in it any more since he did it nine years ago. But this car—this old car, as far as Barris was concerned—was like a dream prefiguration of a very hot sports car, the Quantum, that Saab has come out with this year after a couple of years of consultation with all sorts of aerodynamic experts and advance-guard designers. They're beautiful cars—Saab's and Barris'. They're the same body, practically—with this lovely topology rolling down over the tunneled headlights, with the whole hood curving down very low to the ground in front. I told Barris about the similarity, but he just shrugged; he is quite used to some manufacturer coming up with one of his cars five or six years later.

Anyway, Barris and I were walking around the side of Kustom City, through the parking lot, when I saw an Avanti, the new Studebaker sports model, very expensive. This one had paper mock-ups added to the front and the rear, and so I asked Barris about it. That wasn't much, he said; starting with the paper mock-ups, it brought the hood out a foot with a chic slope to it. He was doing the same sort of thing in the back to eliminate that kind of loaf-of-bread look. It really makes the car. Barris doesn't regard this as a very major project. It may end up in something like a kit you can buy, similar to the old Continental kits, to rig up front and back.

If Barris and the customizers hadn't been buried in the alien and suspect underworld of California youth, I don't think they would seem at all unusual by now. But they've had access to almost nothing but the hot-rod press. They're like Easter Islanders. Suddenly you come upon the astonishing objects, and then you have to figure out how they got there and why they're there.

If you study the work of Barris or Cushenberry (the aforementioned Silhouette) or Ed Roth or Darryl Starbird (can you beat that name?), I think you come up with a fragment of art history. Somewhere back in the Thirties, designers, automobile designers among them, came up with the idea of the streamline. It sounded "functional," and on an airplane it is functional, but on a car it's not, unless you're making a Bonneville speed run. Actually, it's baroque. The streamline is baroque abstract or baroque modern or whatever you want to call it. Well, about the time the stream-line got going—in the Thirties, you may recall, we had curved buildings (like the showpieces later, at the World's Fair)—in came the Bauhaus movement, which was blown-up Mondrian, really. Before you knew it, everything was Mondrian—the Kleenex box: Mondrian; the format of the cover of *Life* Magazine: Mondrian; those bled-to-the-edge photograph layouts in *Paris-Match*: Mondrian. Even automobiles: Mondrian. They call Detroit automobiles streamlined, but they're not. If you don't believe it, look down from an airplane at all the cars parked on a shopping-center apron, and except that all the colors are pastel instead of primary, what have you got? A Mondrian painting. The Mondrian principle, those straight edges, is very tight, very Apollonian. The streamline principle, which really has no function, which curves around and swoops and flows just for the thrill of it, is very free Dionysian. For reasons I don't have to labor over, the kids preferred the Dionysian. And since Detroit blew the thing, the Dionysian principle in cars was left to people in the teen-age netherworld, like George Barris.

Barris was living in Sacramento when he started customizing cars in 1940. As the plot develops, you have the old story of the creative child, the break from the mold of the parents, the garret struggle, the bohemian life, the first success, the accolade of the esoteric following, and finally the money starts pouring in. With this difference: We're out on old Easter Island, in the buried netherworld of teen-age Californians, and those objects, those cars, they have to do with the gods and the spirit and a lot of mystic stuff in the community.

Barris told me his folks were Greeks who owned a restaurant, and "they wanted me to be a restaurant man, like very other typical Greek, I guess," he said. But Barris, even at ten, was wild about cars, carving streamlined cars out of balsam wood. After a few years, he got a car of his own, a 1925 Buick, then a 1932 Ford. Barris established many of the formal conventions of customizing himself. Early in the game he had clients, other kids who paid him to customize their cars. In 1943 he moved to Los Angeles and landed in the middle of the tremendous teen-age culture that developed there during the war. Family life was dislocated, as the phrase goes, but the money was pouring in, and the kids began to work up their own style of life—as they've been doing ever since—and to establish those fanatic forms and conventions I was talking about earlier. Right in the heart of it, of course, was the automobile. Cars were hard to come by, what with the war, so the kids were raiding junkyards for parts, which led to custom-built cars, mostly roadsters by the very nature of it, and also to a lot of radical, hopped-up engines. All teen-age car nuts had elements of both in their work—customizing and hot-rodding, form and power—but tended to concentrate on one or the other. Barris—and Ed Roth later told me it was the same with him—naturally gravitated toward customizing. In high school, and later for a brief time at Sacramento College and the Los Angeles Art Center, he was taking what he described to me as mechanical drawing, shop, and free art.

I liked this term "free art." In Barris' world at the time, and now for that matter, there was no such thing as great big old fructuous Art. There was mechanical drawing and then there was free art, which did not mean that it was liberating in any way, but rather that it was footloose and free and not going anywhere in particular. The kind of art that appealed to Barris, and meant something to the people he hung around with, was the automobile.

Barris gets a wonderful reflective grin on his face when he starts talking about the old days—1944 to 1948. He was a hot-rodder when hot-rodders were hot-rodders, that's the kind of look he gets. They all do. The professional hot-rodders—such as the Petersen magazine syndicate (*Hot Rod Magazine* and many others) and the National Hot Rod Association—have gone to great lengths to obliterate the memory of the gamey hot-rod days, and they try to give everybody in the field transfusions of Halazone so that the public will look at the hot-rodders as nice boys with short-sleeved sport shirts just back from the laundry, and a chemistry set, such an interesting hobby.

In point of fact, Barris told me, it was a lurid time. Everybody would meet in drive-ins, the most famous of them being the Piccadilly out near Sepulveda Boulevard. It was a hell of a show, all the weird-looking roadsters and custom cars, with very loud varoom-varoom motors. By this time Barris had a '36 Ford roadster with many exotic features.

"I had just come from Sacramento, and I wasn't supposed to know anything. I was a tourist, but my car was wilder than anything around. I remember one night this kid comes up with a roadster with no door handles. It looked real sharp, but he had to kick the door from the inside to open it. You should have seen the look on his face when he saw mine—I had the same thing, only with electric buttons."

The real action, though, was the drag racing, which was quite, but quite, illegal.

"We'd all be at the Piccadilly or some place, and guys would start challenging each other. You know, a guy goes up to another guy's car and looks it up and down like it has gangrene or something, and he says: 'You wanna *go*?' Or, if it was a real grudge match for some reason, he'd say, 'You wanna go for pink slips?' The registrations on the cars were pink; in other words, the winner got the other guy's car.

"Well, as soon as a few guys had challenged each other, everybody would ride out onto this stretch of Sepulveda Boulevard or the old divided highway, in Compton, and the guys would start dragging, one car on one side of the center line, the other car on the other. Go a quarter of a mile. It was wild. Some nights there'd be a thousand kids lining the road to watch, boys and girls, all sitting on the sides of their cars with the lights shining across the highway."

But George, what happened if some ordinary motorist happened to be coming down the highway at this point?

"Oh, we'd block off the highway at each end, and if some guy wanted to get through anyway, we'd tell him, 'Well, Mister, there are going to be two cars coming down both sides of the road pretty fast in a minute, and you can go through if you want to, but you'll just have to take your best shot.'

"They always turned around, of course, and after a while the cops would come. Then you *really* saw something. Everybody jumped in their cars and took off, in every direction. Some guys would head right across a field. Of course, all our cars were so hopped up, the cops could never catch anybody.

"Then one night we got raided at the Piccadilly. It was one Friday night. The cops came in and just started loading everybody in the wagons. I was sitting in a car with a cop who was off duty—he was a hot-rodder himself—or they would have picked me up, too. Saturday night everybody came back to the Piccadilly to talk about what happened the night before, and the cops came back again and picked up three hundred fifty that night. That pretty well ended the Piccadilly."

From the very moment he was on his own in Los Angeles, when he was about eighteen, Barris never did anything but customize cars. He never took any other kind of job. At first he worked in a body shop that took him on because so many kids were coming by wanting this and that done to their cars, and the boss really didn't know how to do it, because it was all esoteric teen-age stuff. Barris was making next to nothing at first, but he never remembers feeling hard up, nor does any kid out there today I talked to. They have a magic economy or something. Anyway, in 1945 Barris opened his own shop on Compton Avenue, in Los Angeles, doing nothing but customizing. There was that much demand for it. It was no sweat, he said; pretty soon he was making better than $100 a week.

Most of the work he was doing then was modifying Detroit cars— chopping and channeling. Chopping is lowering the top of the car, bringing it nearer to the hood line. Channeling is lowering the body itself down between the wheels. Also, they'd usually strip off all the chrome and the door handles and cover up the wheel openings in the back. At that time, the look the kids liked was to have the body lowered in the back and slightly jacked up in the front, although today it's just the opposite. The front windshield in those days was divided by a post, and so chopping the top gave the car a very sinister appearance. The front windshield always looked like a couple of narrow, slitty little eyes. And I think this, more than anything else, diverted everybody from what Barris and the others were really doing. Hot-rodders had a terrible reputation at that time, and no line was ever drawn between hot-rodders and custom-car owners, because, in truth, they were speed maniacs, too.

This was Barris' chopped-and-channeled Mercury period. Mercuries were his favorite. All the kids knew the Barris styling and he was getting a lot of business. What he was really doing, in a formal sense, was trying to achieve the kind of streamlining that Detroit, for all intents and purposes, had abandoned. When modified, some of the old Mercuries were more streamlined than any standard model that Detroit has put out to this day. Many of the coupes he modified had a very sleek slope to the back window that has been picked up just this year in the "fastback" look of the Rivieras, Sting Rays, and a few other cars.

At this point Barris and the other customizers didn't really have enough capital to do many completely original cars, but they were getting more and more radical in modifying Detroit cars. They were doing things Detroit didn't do until years later—tailfins, bubble tops, twin headlights, concealed headlights, "Frenched" headlights, the low-slung body itself. They lifted some twenty designs from him alone. One, for example, is the way cars now have the exhaust pipes exit through the rear bumper or fender. Another is the bullet-shaped, or breast-shaped if you'd rather, front bumpers on the Cadillac.

Barris says "lifted," because some are exact down to the most minute details. Three years ago when he was in Detroit, Barris met a lot of car designers and, "I was amazed," he told me. "They could tell me about cars I built in 1945. They knew all about the four-door '48 Studebaker I restyled. I chopped the top and dropped the hood and it ended up a pretty good-looking car. And the bubbletop I built in 1954—they knew all about it. And all this time we thought they frowned on us."

Even today—dealing with movie stars and auto manufacturers and all sorts of people on the outside—I think Barris, and certainly the others, still feel psychologically a part of the alien teen-age netherworld in which they grew up. All that while they were carrying the torch for the Dionysian Streamline. They were America's modern baroque designers—and, oddly enough, "serious" designers, Anglo-European-steeped designers, are just coming around to it. Take Saarinen, especially in something like his T.W.A. terminal at Idlewild. The man in his last years came around to baroque modern.

It's interesting that the customizers, like sports-car fans, have always wanted cars minus most of the chrome—but for different ideals. The sports-car owner thinks chrome trim interferes with the "classic" look of his car. In other words, he wants to simplify the thing. The customizer thinks chrome interferes with something else—the luxurious baroque Streamline. The sports-car people snigger at tailfins. The customizers love them and, looked at from a baroque standard of beauty, they are really not so trashy at all. They are an inspiration, if you will, a wonderful fantasy extension of the curved line, and since the car in America is half fantasy anyway, a kind of baroque extension of the ego, you can build up a good argument for them.

Getting back to Easter Island, here were Barris and the others with their blowtorches and hard-rubber mallets, creating their baroque sculpture, cut off from the rest of the world and publicized almost solely via the teen-age grapevine. Barris was making a fairly good living, but others were starving at this thing. The pattern was always the same: a guy would open a body shop and take on enough hack collision work to pay the rent so that he could slam the door shut at 2 p.m. and get in there and do his custom jobs, and pretty soon the guy got so he couldn't even face *any* collision work. Dealing with all those crusty old arteriosclerotic bastards takes up all your *time*, man, and so they're trying to make a living doing nothing but custom work, and they are starving.

The situation is a lot like that today, except that customizing is beginning to be rationalized, in the sense Max Weber used that word. This rationalization, or efficient exploitation, began in the late Forties when an $80-a-week movie writer named Robert Petersen noticed all the kids pouring money into cars in a little world they had created for themselves, and he decided to exploit it by starting *Hot Rod Magazine*, which clicked right away and led to a whole chain of hot-rod and custom-car magazines. Petersen, by the way, now has a pot of money and drives Maseratis and other high-status-level sports cars of the Apollonian sort, not the Dionysian custom kind. Which is kind of a shame, because he has the money to commission something really incredible.

Up to that time the only custom-car show in the country was a wild event Barris used to put on bereft of any sort of midwifery by forty-two-year-old promoters with Windsor-knot ties who usually run low-cost productions. This car show was utterly within the teen-age netherworld, with no advertising or coverage of any sort. It took place each spring—during the high-school Easter vacations—when all the kids, as they still do, would converge on the beach at Balboa for their beer-drinking-Faschung rites, or whatever the Germans call it. Barris would rent the parking lot of a service station on a corner for a week, and kids from all over California would come with their customized cars. First there would be a parade; the cars, about a hundred fifty of them, would drive all through the streets of Balboa, and the kids would line the sidewalks to watch them; then they'd drive back to the lot and park and be on exhibit for the week.

Barris still goes off to Balboa and places like that. He likes that scene. Last year at Pacific Ocean Park he noticed all these bouffant babies and got the idea of spraying all those great puffed-up dandelion heads with fluorescent water colors, the same Kandy Kolors he uses on the cars. Barris took out an air gun, the girls all lined up and gave him fifty cents per, and he sprayed them with these weird, brilliant color combinations all afternoon until he ran out of colors. Each girl would go skipping and screaming away out onto the sidewalks and the beaches. Barris told me, "It was great that night to take one of the rides, like the Bubble Ride, and look down and see all those fluorescent colors. The kids were bopping [dancing] and running around."

The Bubble is a ride that swings out over the ocean. It is supposed to be like a satellite in orbit.

"But the fellows sky-diving got the best look as they came down by parachute."

In 1948 Petersen put on the first custom-car show in the Los Angeles armory, and this brought customizing out into the open a little. A wild-looking Buick Barris had remodeled was one of the hits of the show, and he was on his way, too.

At some point in the Fifties a lot of Hollywood people discovered Barris and the customizers. It was somewhat as if the literary set had discovered the puppeteer, Tony Sarg, during the Thirties and deified him in a very arty, in-groupy way, only I think in the case of Hollywood and

Barris there was something a lot more in-the-grain about it. The people who end up in Hollywood are mostly Dionysian sorts and they feel alien and resentful when confronted with the Anglo-European ethos. They're a little slow to note the difference between topsides and sneakers, but they appreciate Cuban sunglasses.

In his showroom at Kustom City, down past the XPAK-400 air car, Barris has a corner practically papered with photographs of cars he has customized or handmade for Hollywood people: Harry Karl, Jayne Mansfield, Elvis Presley, Liberace, and even celebrities from the outside like Barry Goldwater (a Jaguar with a lot of airplane-style dials on the dashboard) and quite a few others. In fact, he built most of the wild cars that show-business people come up with for publicity purposes. He did the "diamond-dust" paint job on the Bobby Darin Dream Car, which was designed and built by Andy DiDia of Detroit. That car is an example, par excellence, of baroque streamlining, by the way. It was badly panned when pictures of it were first published, mainly because it looked like Darin was again forcing his ego on the world. But as baroque modern sculpture—again, given the fantasy quotient in cars to begin with—it is pretty good stuff.

As the hot-rod and custom-car-show idea began catching on, and there are really quite a few big ones now, including one at the Coliseum up at Columbus Circle last year, it became like the culture boom in the other arts. The big names, particularly Barris and Roth but also Starbird, began to make a lot of money in the same thing Picasso has made a lot of money in: reproductions. Barris' creations are reproduced by AMT Models as model cars. Roth's are reproduced by Revel. The way people have taken to these models makes it clearer still that what we have here is no longer a car but a design object, an *objet*, as they say.

Of course, it's not an unencumbered art form like oil painting or most conventional modern sculpture. It carries a lot of mental baggage with it, plain old mechanical craftsmanship, the connotations of speed and power and the aforementioned mystique that the teen-age netherworld brings to cars. What you have is something more like sculpture in the era of Benvenuto Cellini, when sculpture was always more tied up with religion and architecture. In a lot of other ways it's like the Renaissance, too. Young customizers have come to Barris' shop, for example, like apprentices coming to the feet of the master. Barris said there were eleven young guys in Los Angeles right now who had worked for him and then gone out on their own, and he doesn't seem to begrudge them that.

"But they take on too much work," he told me. "They want a name, fast, and they take on a lot of work, which they do for practically nothing, just to get a name. They're usually undercapitalized to begin with, and they take on too much work, and then they can't deliver and they go bankrupt."

There's another side to this, too. You have the kid from the small town in the Midwest who's like the kid from Keokuk who wants to go to New York and live in the Village and be an artist and the like, he means, you know, things around home are but *hopelessly*, totally square, home and all that goes with it. Only the kid from the Midwest who wants to be a custom-car artist goes to Los Angeles to do it. He does pretty much the same thing. He lives a kind of suburban bohemian life and takes odd jobs and spends the rest of his time at the feet of somebody like Barris, working on cars.

I ran into a kid like that at Barris'. We were going through his place, back into his interiors—car interiors—department, and we came upon Ronny Camp. Ronny is twenty-two, but he looks about eighteen because he has teen-age posture. Ronny is, in fact, a bright and sensitive kid with an artistic eye, but at first glance he seems always to have his feet propped up on a table or something so you can't walk past, and you have to kind of bat them down, and he then screws up his mouth and withdraws his eyeballs to the optic chiasma and glares at you with his red sulk. That was the misleading first impression.

Ronny was crazy over automobiles and nobody in his hometown, Lafayette, Indiana, knew anything about customizing. So one day Ronny packs up and tells the folks, This is it, I'm striking out for hip territory, Los Angeles, where a customizing artist is an artist. He had no idea where he was going, you understand, all he knew was that he was going to Barris' shop and make it from there. So off he goes in his 1960 Chevrolet.

Ronny got a job at a service station and poured every spare cent into getting the car customized at Barris'. His car was right there while we were talking, a fact I was very aware of, because he never looked at me. He never took his eyes off that car. It's what is called semi-custom. Nothing has been done to it to give it a really sculptural quality, but a lot of streamlining details have been added. The main thing you notice is the color—tangerine flake. This paint—one of Barris' Kandy Kolor concoctions—makes the car look like it has been encrusted with chips of some kind of semi-precious ossified tangerine, all coated with a half-inch of clear lacquer. There used to be very scholarly and abstruse studies of color and color symbolism around the turn of the century, and theorists concluded that preferences for certain colors were closely associated with rebelliousness, and these are the very same colors many of the kids go for—purple, creosote yellow, various violets and lavenders and fuchsias and many of these Kandy Kolors.

After he got his car fixed up, Ronny made a triumphal progress back home. He won the trophy in his class at the national hot-rod and custom-car show in Indianapolis, and he came tooling into Lafayette, Indiana, and down the main street in his tangerine-flake 1960 Chevrolet. It was like Ezra Pound going back to Hamilton, New York, with his Bollingen plaque and saying, Here I am, Hamilton, New York. The way Ronny and Barris tell it, the homecoming was a big success—all the kids thought Ronny was all right, after all, and he made a big hit at home. I can't believe the part about home. I mean, I can't really believe Ronny made a hit with a tangerine-flake Chevrolet. But I like to conjecture about his parents. I don't know anything about them, really. All I know is, *I* would have had a hell of a lump in my throat if I had seen Ronny coming up to the front door in his tangerine-flake car, bursting so flush and vertical with triumph that no one would ever think of him as a child of the red sulk—Ronny, all the way back from California with his grail.

Along about 1957, Barris started hearing from the Detroit auto manufacturers.

"One day," he said, "I was working in the shop—we were over in Lynwood then—and Chuck Jordan from Cadillac walked in. He just walked in and said he was from Cadillac. I thought he meant the local agency. We had done this Cadillac for Liberace, the interior had his songs, all the notes, done in black and white Moroccan leather, and I thought he wanted to see something about that. But he said he was from the Cadillac styling center in Detroit and they were interested in our colors. Chuck'—he's up there pretty good at Cadillac now, I think—said he had read some articles about our colors, so I mixed up some samples for him. I had developed a translucent paint, using six different ingredients, and it had a lot of brilliance and depth. That was what interested them. In this paint you look through a clear surface into the color, which is very brilliant. Anyway, this was the first time we had any idea they even knew who we were."

Since then Barris has made a lot of trips to Detroit. The auto companies, mainly GM and Ford, pump him for ideas about what the kids are going for. He tells them what's wrong with their cars, mainly that they aren't streamlined and sexy enough.

"But, as they told me, they have to design a car they can sell to the farmer in Kansas as well as the hot dog in Hollywood."

For that reason—the inevitable compromise—the customizers do not dream of working as stylists for the Detroit companies, although they deal with them more and more. It would be like René Magritte or somebody going on the payroll of Continental Can to do great ideas of Western man. This is an old story in art, of course, genius vs. the organization. But the customizers don't think of corporate bureaucracy quite the way your conventional artist does, whether he be William Gropper or Larry Rivers, namely, as a lot of small-minded Babbitts, venal enemies of culture, etc. They just think of the big companies as part of that vast mass of *adult* America, sclerotic from years of just being too old, whose rules and ideas weigh down upon Youth like a vast, bloated sac. Both Barris and Roth have met Detroit's Young Stylists, and seem to look upon them as monks from another country. The Young Stylists are designers Detroit recruits from the art schools and sets up in a room with clay and styluses and tells to go to it—start carving models, dream cars, new ideas. Roth especially cannot conceive of anyone having any valid concepts about cars who hasn't come out of the teen-age netherworld. And maybe he's right. While the Young Stylists sit in a north-lit studio smoothing out little Mondrian solids, Barris and Roth carry on in the Dionysian loop-the-loop of streamlined baroque modern.

I've mentioned Ed Roth several times in the course of this without really telling you about him. And I want to, because he, more than any other of the customizers, has kept alive the spirit of alienation and rebellion that is so important to the teen-age ethos that customizing grew up in. He's also the most colorful, and the most intellectual, and the most capricious. Also the most cynical. He's the Salvador Dali of the movement—a surrealist in his designs, a showman by temperament, a prankster. Roth is really too bright to stay within the ethos, but he stays in it with a spirit of luxurious obstinacy. Any style of life is going to produce its celebrities if it sticks to its rigid standards, but in the East a talented guy would most likely be drawn into the Establishment in one way or another. That's not so inevitable in California.

I had been told that Roth was a surly guy who never bathed and was hard to get along with, but from the moment I first talked to him on the telephone he was an easy guy and very articulate. His studio—and he calls it a studio, by the way—is out in Maywood, on the other side of the city from North Hollywood, in what looked to me like a much older and more run-down section. When I walked up, Roth was out on the apron of his place doing complicated drawings and lettering on somebody's ice-cream truck with an airbrush. I knew right away it was Roth from pictures I had seen of him; he has a beatnik-style beard. "Ed Roth?" I said. He said yeah and we started talking and so forth. A little while later we were sitting in a diner having a couple of sandwiches and Roth, who was wearing a short-sleeved T-shirt, pointed to this huge tattoo on his left arm that says "Roth" in the lettering style with big serifs that he uses as his signature. "I had that done a couple of years ago because guys keep coming up to me saying, 'Are you Ed Roth?' "

Roth is a big, powerful guy, about six feet four, two hundred seventy pounds, thirty-one years old. He has a constant sort of court attendant named Dirty Doug, a skinny little guy who blew in from out of nowhere, sort of like Ronny Camp over at Barris'. Dirty Doug has a job sweeping up in a steel mill, but what he obviously lives for is the work he does around Roth's. Roth seems to have a lot of sympathy for the Ronny Camp-Dirty Doug syndrome and keeps him around as a permanent fixture. At Roth's behest, apparently, Dirty Doug has dropped his last name, Kinney, altogether, and refers to himself as Dirty Doug—not

Doug. The relationship between Roth and Dirty Doug—which is sort of Quixote and Sancho Panza, Holmes and Watson, Lone Ranger and Tonto, Raffles and his sidekick—is part of the folklore of the hot-rod and custom-car kids. It even crops up in the hot-rod comic books, which are an interesting phenomenon in themselves. Dirty Doug, in this folklore, is every rejected outcast little kid in the alien netherworld, and Roth is the understanding, if rather overly pranksterish, protective giant or Robin Hood—you know, a good-bad giant, not part of the Establishment.

Dirty Doug drove up in one of his two Cadillacs one Saturday afternoon while I was at Roth's, and he had just gone through another experience of rejection. He has two Cadillacs, he said, because one is always in the shop. Dirty Doug's cars, like most customizers', are always in the process of becoming. The streaks of "primer" paint on the Cadillac he was driving at the time had led to his rejection in Newport. He had driven to Newport for the weekend. "All the cops have to do is see paint like that and already you're 'one of those hot-rodders,' " he said. "They practically followed me down the street and gave me a ticket every twenty-five feet. I was going to stay the whole weekend, but I came on back."

At custom-car shows, kids are always asking Roth, "Where's Dirty Doug?", and if Dirty Doug couldn't make it for some reason, Roth will recruit any kid around who knows the pitch and install him as Dirty Doug, just to keep the fans happy.

Thus Roth protects the image of Dirty Doug even when the guy's not around, and I think it becomes a very important piece of mythology. The thing is, Roth is not buying the act of the National Hot Rod Association, which for its own reasons, not necessarily the kid's reasons, is trying to assimilate the hot-rod ethos into conventional America. It wants to make all the kids look like candidates for the Peace Corps or something.

The heart of the contretemps between the NHRA Establishment and Roth can be illustrated in their slightly different approach to drag racing on the streets. The Establishment tries to eliminate the practice altogether and restricts drag racing to certified drag strips and, furthermore, lets the people know about that. They encourage the hot-rod clubs to help out little old ladies whose cars are stuck in the snow and then hand them a card reading something like, "You have just been assisted by a member of the Blue Bolt Hot Rod Club, an organization of car enthusiasts dedicated to promoting safety on our highways."

Roth's motto is: "Hell, if a guy wants to go, let him *go*."

Roth's designs are utterly baroque. His air car—the Rotar—is not nearly as good a piece of design as Barris', but his beatnik Bandit is one of the great *objets* of customizing. It's a very Rabelaisian *tour de force*—a twenty-first century version of a '32 Ford hot-rod roadster. And Roth's new car, the Mysterion, which he was working on when I was out there, is another *tour de force,* this time in the hottest new concept in customizing, asymmetrical design. Asymmetrical design, I gather, has grown out of the fact that the driver sits on one side of the car, not in the middle, thereby giving a car an eccentric motif to begin with. In Roth's Mysterion—a bubbletop coupe powered by two 406-horsepower Thunderbird motors—a thick metal arm sweeps up to the left from the front bumper level, as from the six to the three on a clock, and at the top of it is an elliptical shape housing a bank of three headlights. No headlights on the right side at all; just a small clearance light to orient the oncoming driver. This big arm, by the way, comes up in a spherical geometrical arc, not a flat plane. Balancing this, as far as the design goes, is an arm that comes up over the back of the bubbletop on the right side, like from the nine to the twelve on a clock, also in a spherical arc, if you can picture all this. Anyway, this car takes the streamline and the abstract curve and baroque curvilinear one step further, and I wouldn't be surprised to see it inspiring Detroit designs in the years to come.

Roth is a brilliant designer, but as I was saying, his conduct and his attitude dilutes the Halazone with which the Establishment is trying to transfuse the whole field. For one thing, Roth, a rather thorough-going bohemian, kept turning up at the car shows in a T-shirt. That was what he wore at the big National Show at the New York Coliseum, for example. Roth also insists on sleeping in a car or station wagon while on the road, even though he is making a lot of money now and could travel first class. Things came to a head early this year when Roth was out in Terre Haute, Indiana, for a show. At night Roth would just drive his car out in a cornfield, lie back on the front seat, stick his feet out the window and go to sleep. One morning some kid came by and saw him and took a picture while Roth was still sleeping and sent it to the model company Roth has a contract with, Revel, with a note saying, "Dear Sirs: Here is a picture of the man you say on your boxes is the King of the Customizers." The way Roth tells it, it must have been an extraordinary good camera, because he says, with considerable pride, "There were a bunch of flies flying around my feet, and this picture showed all of them."

Revel asked Roth if he wouldn't sort of spruce up a little bit for the image and all that, and so Roth entered into a kind of reverse rebellion. He bought a full set of tails, silk hat, boiled shirt, cuff links, studs, the whole apparatus, for $215, also a monocle, and now he comes to all the shows like that. "I bow and kiss all the girls' hands," he told me. "The guys get pretty teed off about that, but what can they do? I'm being a perfect gentleman."

To keep things going at the shows, where he gets $1000 to $2000 per appearance—he's that much of a drawing card—Roth creates and builds one new car a year. This is the Dali pattern, too. Dali usually turns out one huge and (if that's possible any more) shocking painting each year or so and ships it on over to New York, where they install it in Carstairs or hire a hall if the thing is too big, and Dali books in at the St. Regis and appears on television wearing a rhinoceros horn on his forehead. The new car each year also keeps Roth's model-car deal going. But most of Roth's income right now is the heavy business he does in Weirdo and Monster shirts. Roth is very handy with the airbrush—has a very sure hand—and one day at a car show he got the idea of drawing a grotesque cartoon on some guy's sweat shirt with the airbrush, and that started the Weirdo shirts. The typical Weirdo shirt is in a vein of draftsmanship you might call Mad Magazine Bosch, very slickly done for something so grotesque, and will show a guy who looks like Frankenstein, the big square steam-shovel jaw and all, only he has a wacky leer on his face, at the wheel of a hot-rod roadster, and usually he has a round object up in the air in his right hand that looks like it is attached to the dashboard by a cord. This, it turns out, is the gearshift. It doesn't look like a gearshift to me, but every kid knows immediately what it is.

"Kids *love* dragging a car," Roth told me. "I mean they really love it. And what they love the most is when they shift from low to second. They get so they can practically *feel* the r.p.m.'s. They can shift without hardly hitting the clutch at all."

These shirts always have a big caption, and usually something rebellious or at least alienated, something like "MOTHER IS WRONG" or "BORN TO LOSE."

"A teen-ager always has resentment to adult authority," Roth told me. "These shirts are like a tattoo, only it's a tattoo they can take off if they want to."

I gather Roth doesn't look back on his own childhood with any great relish. Apparently his father was pretty strict and never took any abiding interest in Roth's creative flights, which were mostly in the direction of cars, like Barris'.

"You've got to be real careful when you raise a kid," Roth told me several times. "You've got to spend time with him. If he's working on something, building something, you've got to work with him." Roth's early career was almost exactly like Barris', the hot rods, the drive-ins, the drag racing, the college (East Los Angeles Junior College and UCLA), taking mechanical drawing, the chopped and channeled '32 Ford (a big favorite with all the hot-rodders), purple paint, finally the first custom shop, one stall in a ten-stall body shop.

"They threw me out of there," Roth said, "because I painted a can of Lucky Lager beer on the wall with an airbrush. I mean, it was a perfect can of Lucky Lager beer, all the details, the highlights, the seals, the small print, the whole thing. Somehow this can of Lucky Lager beer really bugged the guy who owned the place. Here was this can of Lucky Lager beer on *his* wall."

The Establishment can't take this side of Roth, just as no Establishment could accommodate Dadaists for very long. Beatniks more easily than Dadaists. The trick has always been to absorb them somehow. So far Roth has resisted absorption.

"We were the real gangsters of the hot-rod field," Roth said. "They keep telling us we have a rotten attitude. We have a different attitude, but that doesn't make us rotten."

Several times, though, Roth would chuckle over something, usually some particularly good gesture he had made, like the Lucky Lager, and say, "I am a real rotten guy."

Roth pointed out, with some insight, I think, that the kids have a revealing vocabulary. They use the words "rotten," "bad" and "tough" in a very fey, ironic way. Often a particularly baroque and sleek custom car will be called a "big, bad Merc" (for Mercury) or something like that. In this case "bad" means "good," but it also retains some of the original meaning of "bad." The kids know that to adults, like their own parents, this car is going to look sinister and somehow like an assault on their style of life. Which it is. It's rebellion, which the parents don't go for—"bad," which the kids *do* go for, "bad" meaning "good."

Roth said that Detroit is beginning to understand that there are just a hell of a lot of these bad kids in the United States and that they are growing up. "And they want a better car. They don't want an old man's car."

Roth has had pretty much the same experience as Barris with the motor companies. He has been taken to Detroit and feted and offered a job as a designer and a consultant. But he never took it seriously.

"I met a lot of the young designers," said Roth. "They were nice guys and they know a lot about design, but none of them has actually done a car. They're just up there working away on those clay models."

I think this was more than the craftsman's scorn of the designer who never actually does the work, like some of the conventional sculptors today who have never chiseled a piece of stone or cast anything. I think it was more that the young Detroit stylists came to the automobile strictly from art school and the abstract world of design—rather than via the teen-age mystique of the automobile and the teen-age ethos of rebellion. This status-group feeling is very important to Roth, and to Barris, for that matter, because it was only because of the existence of this status group—and this style of life—that custom-car sculpture developed at all.

With the Custom Car Caravan on the road—it has already reached Freedomland—the manufacturers may be well on the way to routinizing the charisma, as Max Weber used to say, which is to say bringing the whole field into a nice, safe, vinyl-glamorous marketable ball of polyethylene. It's probably already happening. The customizers will end up like those poor bastards in Haiti, the artists, who got too much, too soon, from Selden Rodman and the other folk-doters on the subject of primitive genius, so they're all down there at this moment carving African masks out of mahogany—what I mean is, they never *had* an African mask in Haiti before Selden Rodman got there.

I think Roth has a premonition that something like that is liable to happen, although it will happen to him last, if at all. I couldn't help but get a kick out of what Roth told me about his new house. We had been talking about how much money he was making, and he told me how his taxable income was only about $6200 in 1959, but might hit $15,000 this year, maybe more, and he mentioned he was building a new house for his wife and five kids down at Newport, near the beach. I immediately asked him for details, hoping to hear about an utterly baroque piece of streamlined architecture.

"No, this is going to be my wife's house, the way she wants it, nothing way out; I mean, she has to do the home scene." He has also given her a huge white Cadillac, by the way, unadorned except for his signature—"Roth"—with those big serifs, on the side. I saw the thing, it's huge, and in the back seat were his children, very sweet-looking kids, all drawing away on drawing pads.

But I think Roth was a little embarrassed that he had disappointed me on the house, because he told me his idea of the perfect house—which turned out to be a kind of ironic parable:

"This house would have this big, round living room with a dome over it, you know? Right in the middle of the living room would be a huge television set on a swivel so you could turn it and see it from wherever you are in the room. And you have this huge easy chair for yourself, you know the kind that you can lean back to about ninety-three different positions and it vibrates and massages your back and all that, and this chair is on tracks, like a railroad yard.

"You can take one track into the kitchen, which just shoots off one side of the living room, and you can ride backward if you want to and watch the television all the time, and of course in the meantime you've pressed a lot of buttons so your TV dinner is cooking in the kitchen and all you have to do is go and take it out of the oven.

"Then you can roll right back into the living room, and if somebody rings the doorbell you don't move at all. You just press a button on this big automatic console you have by your chair and the front door opens, and you just yell for the guy to come in, and you can keep watching television.

"At night, if you want to go to bed, you take another track into the bedroom, which shoots off on another side, and you just kind of roll out of the chair into the sack. On the ceiling above your bed you have another TV set, so you can watch all night."

Roth is given, apparently, to spinning out long Jean Shepherd stories like this with a very straight face, and he told me all of this very seriously.

I guess I didn't look like I was taking it very seriously, because he said, "I have a TV set over the bed in my house right now—you can ask my wife."

I met his wife, but I didn't ask her. The funny thing is, I did find myself taking the story seriously. To me it was a sort of parable of the Bad Guys, and the Custom Sculpture. The Bad Guys built themselves a little world and got onto something good and then the Establishment, all sorts of Establishments, began closing in, with a lot of cajolery, thievery and hypnosis, and in the end, thrown into a vinyl Petri dish, the only way left to tell the whole bunch of them where to head in was to draw them a huge asinine picture of themselves, which they were sure to like. After all, Roth's dream house is nothing more than his set of boiled shirt and tails expanded into a whole universe. And he is not really very hopeful about that either.

[November, 1963]

Turning on the World

by Timothy Leary

The Psychedelic Era manifested in the rainbow paintings of Peter Max and in songs like "Lucy in the Sky with Diamonds" was inextricably caught up in the use of drugs. Dr. Timothy Leary, a lecturer at Harvard, became famous when he advocated the widespread use of LSD, a synthetic drug with mind-expanding capabilities, in his crusade for a more peaceful world. Leary wrote widely of the psychedelic experience and included this piece, published in July 1968, in his book High Priest.

By the Fall of 1960 there was in existence an informal international network of scientists and scholars who had taken the psychedelic trip and who foresaw the powerful effect that the new alkaloids would have on human culture. The members of this group differed in age and temperament, and had varying ideas about tactics, but the basic vision was common to all—we believed these wondrous plants and drugs could free man's consciousness and bring about a new conception of man, his psychology and philosophy.

There was Albert Hofmann, who had invented LSD, who dreamed the utopian dream, but who was limited by the cautious politics of Sandoz Pharmaceuticals. What a frustrating web his genius had woven for Sandoz. How could a medical-drug house make a profit on a revelation pill?

Sandoz knew they had patented the most powerful mind-changing substance known to man. They expected to make millions when the psychiatric profession learned how to use LSD, and they were continually disappointed to discover that human society didn't want to have its mind changed, didn't want to touch a love-ecstasy potion.

In 1960 a top executive of Sandoz leaned across the conference table and said jokingly to me, LSD isn't a drug at all. It's a food. Let's bottle it in Coca-Cola and let the world have it. And his legal counsel frowned and said that foods still come under the jurisdiction of the Food and Drug Administration.

By 1966, when LSD was crowding Vietnam for the headlines, officials of Sandoz Pharmaceuticals were groaning, We wish we had never heard of LSD.

I do really wish to destroy it! cried Frodo. Or well, to have it destroyed. I am not made for perilous quests. I wish I had never seen the Ring! Why did it come to me? Why was I chosen?   —The Lord of The Rings

There were the detached philosophers—Aldous Huxley, Father Murray, Gerald Heard, Alan Watts, Harry Murray, Robert Gordon Wasson—who knew that the new drugs were reintroducing the platonic-gnostic vision. These men had read their theological history and understood both the glorious possibility and the angered reaction of the priestly establishment. They were not activists but sage observers.

Then there were the turned-on doctors—psychiatrists who had taken the trip, and came back hoping to fit the new potions into the medical game. Humphrey Osmond, witty, wise, cultured, had invented the name psychedelic and tolerantly wondered how to introduce a harmony-ecstasy drug into an aggressive-puritanical social order. Sidney Cohen, Keith Ditman, Jim Watt, Abram Hoffer and Nick Chewelos hoped to bring about a psychiatric renaissance and a new era of mental health with the new alchemicals.

And there was that strange, intriguing, delightful cosmic magician called Al Meyner, the rum-drinking, swashbuckling, Roman Catholic frontier salesman who promoted uranium ore during the Forties and who took the trip and recognized that LSD was the fissionable material of the mind and who turned on Osmond and Hoffer to the religious mystical meaning of their psychotomimetic drug. Al Meyner set out to turn on the world and flew from country to country with his leather bag full of drugs, claiming to have turned on bishops and obtained *nihil obstat* from Pope John. When the medical society complained that only doctors could give drugs, Meyner bought himself a doctor's degree from a Kentucky diploma mill and swept through northern California turning on scientists and professors and God seekers.

Right from the beginning this dedicated group of ring bearers was rent with a basic disagreement. There were those who said work within the system. Society has assigned the administration of drugs to the medical profession. Any non-doctor who gives or takes drugs is a dope fiend. Play ball with the system. Medicine must be the vanguard of the psychedelic movement. Any nonmedical use of psychedelic drugs would create a new marijuana mess and set back research into the new utopia.

The medical point of view made little sense to religious philosophers. Aldous Huxley called the psychedelic experience a gratuitous grace. His vibrant flame-colored wife, Laura, agreed. So, in gentle tones, did Huston Smith and Alan Watts and Gerald Heard.

And so did Allen Ginsberg, who had discovered the Buddha nature of drugs along with other writers.

I had been visited by most of the psychedelic eminences by this time and was under steady pressure to make the Harvard psychedelic research a kosher-medically-approved project. Everyone was aware of the potency of Harvard's name. Timothy, you are the key figure, said Dr. Al Meyner; I'm just old deputy-dog Al at your service. But the message was clear: Keep it respectable and medical.

And now here was Allen Ginsberg, the secretary-general of the world's poets, beatniks, anarchists, socialists, free-sex/love cultists.

November 26, 1960, the sunny Sunday afternoon that we gave Allen Ginsberg the mushrooms, started slowly. First in the cycle of breakfasts at noon were my son Jack Leary and his friend Bobbie, who had spent the night. Bobbie went off to Mass. When I came down I found Donald, an uninvited raccoon hipster-painter from New York, solemnly squatting at the table gnawing at toast and bacon. Frank Barron, who was visiting, and the poets, Allen Ginsberg and Peter and Lafcadio Orlovsky, remained upstairs and we moved around the kitchen with that Sunday-morning hush, not wanting to wake the sleepers. Lafcadio, Peter's brother, was on leave from a hospital.

About twelve-thirty the quiet exploded into family noise. Bobbie was back from church where he had excitedly told his father about the party we had given the night before for the Harvard football team and how I had given the boys, Bobbie and Jack, a dollar each for being bartenders.

I toted up the political profit and loss from this development. The Harvard football team rang up a sale. But the boys bartending? Bobbie's father is Irish so that's all right. All okay.

Then wham, the door opened and in flooded Susan Leary, my daughter, with three teen-age girls, through the kitchen, upstairs to get clothes, down to make a picnic lunch, up again for records, out, and then back for the ginger ale.

By now the noise had filtered upstairs and we could hear the late sleepers moving around and the bathroom waters running, and down came Frank Barron, half-awake, to fry codfish cakes for his breakfast. And then, Allen Ginsberg and Peter. Allen hopped around the room with nearsighted crow motions cooking eggs, and Peter sat silent, watching.

Afterward the poets fell to reading The *Times* and Frank moved upstairs to Susan's room to watch a pro football game on TV. I told Allen to make himself at home and got beers and went up to join Frank. Donald the painter had been padding softly around the house watching with his big, soft creature eyes and sniffing in corners and at the bookcase and the record cabinets. He had asked to take mushrooms in the evening and was looking for records of Indian peyote drum music.

At dusk, Allen Ginsberg, hunched over a teacup, peering out through his black-rimmed glasses, the left lens bisected by a break, started telling of his experiences with ayahuasco, the fabled visionary vine of the Peruvian jungles. He had followed the quest of Bill Burroughs, sailing south for new realms of consciousness, looking for the elixir of wisdom. Sitting, sweating with heat, lonely in a cheap hotel in Lima, holding a wad of ether-soaked cotton to his nose with his left hand and getting high and making poetry with his right hand, and then traveling by second-class bus with Indians up through the Cordillera de los Andes and then more buses and hitchhiking into the Montaña jungles and shining rivers, wandering through steaming equatorial forests. Then the village Pucallpa, and the negotiations to find the *curandero* [guide], paying him with *aguardiente,* and the ritual itself, swallowing the bitter stuff, and the nausea and the colors and the drums beating and sinking down into thingless void, into the great eye that brings it all together, and the terror of the great snake coming. The old *curandero,* wrinkled face bending over him and Allen telling him, *culebra,* and the *curandero* nodding clinically and blowing a puff of smoke to make the great snake disappear and it did.

The fate of fire depends on wood; as long as there is wood below, the fire burns above. It is the same in human life; there is in man likewise a fate that lends power to his life.   —I Ching

I kept asking Allen questions about the *curandero.* I wanted to learn the rituals, to find out how other cultures (older and wiser than ours) had handled the visionary business. I was fascinated by the ritual thing. Ritual is to the science of consciousness what experiment is to external science. I was convinced that none of our American rituals fit the mushroom experience. Not the cocktail party. Not the psychiatrist. Not the teacher-minister role. I was impressed by what Allen said about his own fear and sickness whenever he took drugs and about the solace and comforting strength of the *curandero,* about how good it was to have someone there who knew, who had been to those far regions of the mind and could tell you by a look, by a touch, by a puff of smoke that it was all right, go ahead, explore the strange world, it's all right, you'll come back, it's all right, I'm here back on familiar old human earth when you need me, to bring you back.

Allen was going to take the mushrooms later that night and he was shaping me up to help him. Allen was weaving a word spell, dark eyes gleaming through the glasses, chain-smoking, moving his hands, intense, chanting trance poetry. Frank Barron was in the study now, and with him Lafcadio Orlovsky.

A car came up the driveway and in a minute the door opened, and Donald, furry and moist, ambled in. He had brought his friend, an anthropology student from Harvard, to be with him when he tripped. Donald asked if his friend could be there during the mushroom session. I liked the idea of having a friend present for the mushrooms, someone to whom you could turn at those moments when you needed support, so I said, Sure, but he couldn't take the pills because he was a university student. Everyone was warning us to keep our research away from Harvard to avoid complications with the university health bureau and to avoid the rumors. He wasn't hungry so I mixed him a drink and then I got the little round bottle and pulled out the cotton topping and gave Donald 30 mg. and Allen Ginsberg 36.

Allen started bustling around getting his cave ready. I brought Susan's record player up to his room and he took some Beethoven and Wagner from the study and he turned out the lights so that there was just a glow in the room. I told him we'd be checking back every fifteen minutes and he should tell me if he wanted anything.

By the time I got downstairs Donald was already high, strolling around the house on dainty raccoon feet with his hands clasped behind his back, thinking and digging deep things. I stayed in the study writing letters, reading The *Times*. I had forgotten about the anthropology student. He was waiting in the kitchen.

After about thirty minutes I found Donald in the hallway. He called me over earnestly and began talking about the artificiality of civilization. He was thinking hard about basic issues and it was obvious what was going on with him—clearing his mind of abstractions, trying to get back behind the words and concepts.

And if he succeeds in assigning the right place to life and to fate, thus bringing the two into harmony, he puts his fate on a firm footing. These words contain hints about the fostering of life as handed on by oral tradition in the secret teachings of Chinese yoga. —I Ching

The anthropology student was standing by, watching curiously, and Donald asked if he minded leaving so that he could talk to me privately. Anthro went back to the kitchen and Donald continued talking about the falseness of houses and machines and deploring the way man cut himself off from the vital stuff with his engines and structures. I was trying to be polite and be a good *curandero* and support him and tell him, great boy, stay with it and work it out.

Susan came back from her friends' about this time and went upstairs to her homework, and I followed her up to check on Allen. He was lying on top of the blanket. His glasses were off and his black eyes, pupils completely dilated, looked up at me. Looking down into them they seemed like two deep, black, wet wells and you could look down them way through the man Ginsberg to something human beyond. The eye is such a defenseless, naïve, trusting thing. PROFESSOR LEARY CAME INTO MY ROOM, LOOKED IN MY EYES, AND SAID I WAS A GREAT MAN. THAT DETERMINED ME TO MAKE AN EFFORT TO LIVE HERE AND NOW.   —Allen Ginsberg

Allen was scared and unhappy and sick. And still he was lying there voluntarily, patiently searching, pushing himself into panics and fears, into nausea, trying to learn something, trying to find meaning. Shamelessly weak and shamelessly human and greatly classic. Peter was lying next to him, eyes closed, sleeping or listening to the record. I GOT NAUSEOUS SOON AFTER—SAT UP IN BED NAKED AND SWALLOWED DOWN THE VOMIT THAT BE-SIEGED FROM MY STOMACH AS IF AN INDEPENDENT BEING DOWN THERE WAS REBELLING AT BEING DRAGGED INTO EXISTENCE.

On the way downstairs I checked Susan's room. She was curled up on the carpet, with her books scattered around her and reading in the shadows. I scolded her about ruining her eyes and flicked on the two wall bulbs. Downstairs Frank was still at the study desk. Anthro was wandering in the living room and told me that Donald had gone outside. The rule we had set up was that no one would leave the house and the idea of Donald padding down Beacon Street in a mystic state chilled me. Out on the front porch I turned on the two rows of spotlights that flooded the long winding stone stairs and started down, shielding my eyes and shouting Donald. Halfway down I heard him answering back and saw him standing under an oak tree on the lower lawn. I asked him how he was, but he didn't talk, just stood there looking wise and deep. He was barefoot and higher than Piccard's balloon. I want to talk to you, but first you must take off your shoes. Okay, why not? I sat down to unlace my shoes and he squatted alongside and told about how the machines complicate our lives and how cold and hot were abstractions and how we didn't really need houses and shoes and clothes because it was just our concepts that made us think we needed these things. I agreed with him and followed what his mind was doing, suspending for a moment the clutch of the abstract but at the same time shivering from the November wind and wanting to get back behind the warm glow of the windows.

The young anthropology student was standing in the hallway. I told him that Donald was doing fine, great mystical stuff, philosophizing without concepts. He looked puzzled. He didn't want a drink or food. I walked upstairs and found the door to Allen's room closed. I waited for a while, not knowing what to do and then knocked softly and said softly, Allen I'm here now and will be back in a few minutes. *Paradise Lost*, A BOOK I'D NEVER UNDERSTOOD BEFORE—WHY MILTON SIDED WITH LUCIFER THE REBEL IN HEAVEN.

I GOT UP OUT OF BED AND WALKED DOWNSTAIRS NAKED, ORLOVSKY FOLLOWING ME, CURIOUS WHAT I WOULD DO AND WILLING TO GO ALONG

IN CASE I DID ANYTHING INTERESTINGLY EXTRAVAGANT. URGING ME ON IN FACT, THANK GOD.

Susan was sitting cross-legged on her bed brushing her hair when there came a patter of bare feet on the hallway carpet. I got to the door just in time to see naked buttocks disappearing down the stairway. It was Peter. I was grinning when I went back to see Susan. Peter is running around without any clothes on. Susan picked up her paraphernalia—curlers, brush, pins, and trotted up to the third floor. I headed downstairs.

When I got to the study Frank was leaning back in his chair behind the desk, grinning quizzically. In front of the desk looking like medieval hermits were Allen and Peter, both stark naked. I WENT IN AMONG THE PSYCHOLOGISTS IN STUDY AND SAW THEY TOO WERE WAITING FOR SOMETHING VAST TO HAPPEN ONLY IT REQUIRED SOMEONE AND THE MOMENT TO MAKE IT HAPPEN—ACTION, REVOLUTION. No, Allen had on his glasses and as I came in he peered out at me and raised his finger in the air. Hey, Allen, what goes on? Allen had a holy gleam in his eye and he waved his finger. I'm the Messiah. I've come down to preach love to the world. We're going to walk through the streets and teach people to stop hating. I DECIDED I MIGHT AS WELL BE THE ONE TO DO SO—PRONOUNCED MY NAKEDNESS AS THE FIRST ACT OF REVOLUTION AGAINST THE DESTROYERS OF THE HUMAN IMAGE.

Well, Allen, that sounds like a pretty good idea. Listen, said Allen, do you believe that I'm the Messiah. THE NAKED BODY BEING THE HIDDEN SIGN. Look, I can prove it. I'm going to cure your hearing. Take off your hearing machine. Your ears are cured. Come on, take it off, you don't need it. AND GRABBED THE TELEPHONE TO COMMUNICATE MY DECISION—WANTED TO HOOK UP KHRUSHCHEV, KEROUAC, BURROUGHS, IKE, KENNEDY, MAO TSE-TUNG, MAILER, ETC.

Frank was still smiling. Peter was standing by, watching seriously. The hearing aid was dumped on the desk. That's right. And now your glasses, I'll heal your vision too. The glasses were laid on the desk too. ALL IN ONE TELEPHONE LINE AND GET THEM ALL TO COME IMMEDIATELY TO HARVARD TO HAVE SPECTRAL CONFERENCE OVER THE FUTURE OF THE UNIVERSE.

Allen was peering around with approval at his healing. But Allen, one thing. What? Your glasses. You're still wearing them. Why don't you cure your own vision. Allen looked surprised. Yes, you're right. I will. He took off his glasses and laid them on the desk.

Now Allen was a blind Messiah squinting around to find his followers. Come on. We're going down to the city streets to tell the people about peace and love. And then we'll get lots of great people onto a big telephone network to settle all this warfare bit.

Fine, said Frank, but why not do the telephone bit first, right here in the house. Frank was heading off the pilgrimage down the avenue naked.

Who we gonna call, said Peter. Well, we'll call Kerouac on Long Island, and Kennedy and Khrushchev and Bill Burroughs in Paris and Norman

Mailer in the psycho ward in Bellevue. We'll get them all hooked up in a big cosmic electronic love talk. War is just a hang-up. We'll get the love-thing flowing on the electric Bell Telephone network. Who we gonna call first, said Peter. Let's start with Khrushchev, said Allen.

Look, why don't we start with Kerouac on Long Island. In the meantime, let's pull the curtains, said Frank. There's enough going on in here so I don't care about looking outside. Allen picked up the white telephone and dialed Operator. The two thin figures leaned forward wrapped up in a holy fervor trying to spread peace. The dear noble innocent helplessness of the naked body. They looked as though they had stepped out of a quattrocento canvas, apostles, martyrs, dear fanatic holy men. Allen said, Hello, operator, this is God, I want to talk to Kerouac. To whom do I want to talk? Kerouac. What's my name? This is God. G-O-D. Okay. We'll try Capitol 7-0563. Where? Northport, Long Island. There was a pause. We were all listening hard. Oh. Yes. That's right. That's the number of the house where I was born. Look, operator, I'll have to go upstairs to get the number. Then I'll call back.

Allen hung up the receiver. What was all that about, Allen? Well, the operator asked me my name and I said I was God and I wanted to speak to Kerouac and she said, I'll try to do my best, sir, but you'll have to give me his number and then I gave her the number of my mother's house. I've got Kerouac's number upstairs in my book. Just a minute and I'll get it.

Back at the phone, Allen was shouting to Jack. He wanted Jack to come up to Cambridge and then he wanted Jack's mother to come too. Jack had a lot to say because Allen held the phone, listening for long spaces. Frank was still sitting behind the desk smiling. Donald and the anthro student were standing in the hallway looking in curiously. I walked over to explain. Allen says he is the Messiah and he's calling Kerouac to start a peace and love movement. Donald wasn't interested. He went on telling me about the foolishness of believing in hot and cold. It occurred to me that Allen and Peter were proving his point. The phone call continued and finally I walked back in and said, Hey, Allen, for the cost of this phone call we could pay his way up here by plane. Allen shot an apologetic look and then I heard him telling Jack, Okay, Jack, I have to go now, but you've got to take the mushrooms and let's settle this quarrel between Kennedy and Khrushchev. BUT NEEDED MY GLASSES—THOUGH HAD YELLED AT LEARY THAT HE DIDN'T NEED HIS EARPIECE TO HEAR THE REAL VIBRATIONS OF THE COSMOS. HE WENT ALONG WITH ME AGREEABLY.

Allen and Peter were sitting on the big couch in the living room and Allen was telling us about his visions, cosmic electronic networks, and how much it meant to him that I told him he was a great man and how this mushroom episode had opened the door to women and heterosexuality and how he could see new womanly body visions and family life ahead. BUT THEN I BEGAN BREATHING AND WANTING TO LIE DOWN AND REST.

Peter's hand was moving back and forth on Allen's shoulder. It was the first time that Allen had stood up to Jack and he was sorry about the phone bill but wasn't it too bad that Khrushchev and Kennedy couldn't have been on the line and, hey, what about Norman Mailer in that psychiatric ward in Bellevue, shouldn't we call him.

I don't think they'd let a call go through to him, Allen. Well, it all depends on how we come on. I don't think coming on as Allen Ginsberg would help in that league. I don't think coming on as the Messiah would either. Well, you could come on as big psychologists and make big demanding noises about the patient. It was finally decided that it was too much trouble.

Still *curandero,* I asked if they wanted anything to eat or drink. Well, how about some hot milk. IF I ATE OR SHIT AGAIN I WOULD TURN BACK TO MERE NON-MESSIAH HUMAN. Allen and Peter went upstairs to put on robes and I put some cold milk in a pan and turned on the stove. Donald was still moving around softly with his hands behind his back. Thinking. Watching. He was too deep and Buddha for us to swing with and I later realized that I hadn't been a very attentive *curandero* for him and that there was a gulf between Allen and him never closed and that the geographic arrangement was too scattered to make a close loving session. Of course, both of them were old drug hands and ready to go off on their own private journeys and both wanted to make something deep and their own.

Anthro's role in all of this was never clear. He stood in the hallway watching curiously but for the most part we ignored him, treated him as an object just there but not involved and that, of course, was a mistake. Any time you treat someone as an object rest assured he'll do the same and that was the way that score was going to be tallied.

We ended up with a great scene in the kitchen. I bustled around pouring the hot milk into cups, and the poets sat around the table looking like Giotto martyrs in checkered robes. Lafcadio came down and we got him some food and he nodded yes when I asked him about ice cream and Allen started to talk about his visions and about the drug scene in New York and, becoming eloquent, wound up preaching with passion about the junkies, helpless, hooked, lost, thin, confused creatures, sick and the police and the informers. I SAW THE BEST MINDS OF MY GENERATION DESTROYED BY MADNESS, STARVING HYSTERICAL NAKED, DRAGGING THEM-SELVES THROUGH THE NEGRO STREETS AT DAWN LOOKING FOR AN ANGRY FIX. And then we started planning the psychedelic revolution. Allen wanted everyone to have the mushrooms. Who has the right to keep them from some-one else? And there should be freedom for all sorts of rituals, too. The doctors could have them and there should be *curanderos,* and all sorts of good new holy rituals that could be developed and ministers have to be involved. Although the church is naturally and automatically opposed to mushroom visions, still the experience is basically religious and some ministers would see it and start using them. But with all these groups and organizations and new rituals, there still had to be room for the single, lone, unattached, non-groupy individual to take the mushrooms and go off and follow his own rituals—brood big cosmic thoughts by the sea or roam through the streets of New York, high and restless, thinking poetry, and writers and poets and artists to work out whatever they were working out.

Allen Ginsberg hunched over the kitchen table, shabby robe hiding his thin white nakedness, cosmic politician. Give them the mystic vision. They'll see it's good and honest and they'll say so publicly and then no one from the police or the narcotics bureau can put them down. And you're the perfect persons to do it. Big serious scientist professors from Harvard. That's right. I can't do it. I'm too easy to put down. Crazy beatnik poet. Let me get my address book. I've got lots of connections in New York and we'll go right down the list and turn them all on.

Now Allen Ginsberg, stooping over the kitchen table peering at his address book. There's Robert Lowell and Muriel Rukeyser, and LeRoi Jones. And Dizzy Gillespie. And the painters. And the publishers. He was chanting out names of the famous and the talented. He was completely serious, dedicated, wound up in the crusade. I'M NEARSIGHTED AND PSY-CHOPATHIC ANYWAY. AMERICA, I'M PUTTING MY QUEER SHOULDER TO THE WHEEL.

And so Allen spun out the cosmic campaign. He was to line up influentials and each weekend I would come down to New York and we'd run mushroom sessions. This fit our Harvard research plans perfectly. Our aim there was to learn how people reacted, to test the limits of the drug, to get creative and thoughtful people to take them and tell us what they saw and what we should do with the mushrooms. Allen's political plan was appealing, too. I had seen enough and read enough in Spanish of the anti-vision crowd, the power-holders with guns, and the bigger and better men we got on our team the stronger our position. And then, too, the big-name bit was intriguing. Meeting and sharing visions with the famous.

It was around midnight. Donald still seemed high and would walk in and out of the room, silently, hands behind his back, Talmudic raccoon, studying the kitchen crowd seriously, and then padding out. The anthropology student had joined us around the table. We had given him something to drink and he was listening to the conversation and saying nothing. He made some comment about schedules back to Cambridge and it was time for him to make the last train, so I drove him down to the station. He asked some questions about the scientific meaning of the mushroom research and it was clear that he didn't understand what had happened and what we were doing. There wasn't time to explain and I felt badly that he had been dragged into a strange situation. We had made the rule that people could bring their friends when they took the mushrooms and this seemed like a good idea for the person taking the mushrooms but it was just beginning to dawn on me that the problem never was with the person taking the drug but rather the people who didn't. Like Brother Toriblo, the Spanish monk, who talked about cruelty and drunkenness caused by the Sacred Mushrooms. It's okay to bring a friend, but he should take the mushrooms with you. And poor Anthro, it turned out, wasn't even a friend of Donald's and as it turned out didn't like him and was clearly bewildered by and critical of what he had seen and heard and the nakedness of the poets. His train was about due and I was too preoccupied by what Allen had been saying to feel like explaining to Anthro. The uneasy feeling persisted and I suggested that he not tell people about the mystic visions and the naked crusaders because this might be misunderstood and he said he wouldn't talk about it and we shook hands and he left.

That was Sunday night. By Monday afternoon the rumors were spreading around Harvard Yard.

Beatniks. Orgies. Naked poets. Junkies. Homosexuality. Drug parties. Tried to lure a decent naïve graduate student into sin. Wild parties masquerading as research. Queers. Beards. Criminal types.

The chairman of my department called me. What the hell is going on, Tim? Two graduate students have come to me indignant—demanding that your work be stopped.

I laughed. I'll send you the reports from the session as soon as they are typed. It was a good session. God would approve. We're learning a lot.

The disapproving gaze of the establishment was on us. You should fear the wary eyes of the servants of Sauron were the words of Elrond. I do not doubt that news . . . has already reached him, and he will be filled with wrath.

—The Lord of The Rings

In the months that followed we began to see ourselves as unwitting agents of a social process that was far too powerful for us to control or more than dimly understand. A historical movement that would inevitably change man at the very center of his nature, his consciousness.

We did sense that we were not alone. The quest for internal freedom, for the elixir of life, for the draught of immortal revelation was not new. We were part of an ancient and honorable fellowship which had pursued this journey since the dawn of recorded history. We began to read the accounts of earlier trippers—Dante, Hesse, René Daumal, Tolkien, Homer, Blake, George Fox, Swedenborg, Bosch, and the explorers from the Orient—tantrics, Sufis, Bauls, Gnostics, hermetics, Sivaites, sadhus.

From this moment on my days as a respectable establishment scientist were numbered. I just couldn't see the new society given birth by medical hands, or psychedelic sacraments as psychiatric tools.

From this evening on my energies were offered to the ancient underground society of alchemists, artists, mystics, alienated visionaries, dropouts and the disenchanted young, the sons arising.   [July, 1968]

The Life and Death of a Hippie

by Anthony Lukas

The hippies met police power with Flower Power. They placed daisies in rifle barrels and preached peace, love, and happiness. And if the world happened not to be sunny all the time, they turned on to its possibilities with regular doses of grass, mescaline, and LSD. In this piece, published in May 1968, Anthony Lukas wrote about the brief, problematic life of a hippie named James Hutchinson, aka Groovy. Lukas, then a reporter for the New York Times, *is the author of several books, including the Pulitzer Prize winner* Common Ground.

On dusky, brown summer mornings, as the big trailer trucks snort toward Woonsocket, the sour-sweet smells of dough baking mix with diesel fumes over Dexter Street. At the open windows of Gorman's Bakery ("Home of Gorman's Fortified Bread"), men with beefy forearms covered in white powder stand sniffing another day in Central Falls, Rhode Island. The steam from the ovens, the choking flour, the heat slowly rising from the macadam roadway, the fumes from the trucks' grinding gears and hissing brakes, all work up a powerful thirst in a man. So one figure raises a ghostly white hand in a window, beckons to a boy sitting across the street on the stoop of a three-story frame house, and asks him to bring three Seven-Ups from the soda fountain at Barry's News Store down the block.

The boy nods and moves off in his peculiar stride, bouncing up and down on the balls of his feet, his body bent sharply forward from the waist, his hands jammed deep in the pockets of his brown leather jacket, his head drawn down between his hunched-up shoulders in the manner of one of the big brown turtles in Scott's Pond. A few minutes later he comes bouncing back, a paper tray with the three Seven-Ups balanced precariously on his head, his silver harmonica flashing in his mouth, playing *Fingertips* to an audience of grinning, flour-white bakers.

This is how one of Gorman's bakers remembered James "Groovy" Hutchinson a few weeks after his nude body was found last October 8 beside that of his friend, Linda Fitzpatrick, in a Greenwich Village basement—their heads bashed in with bricks.

Linda's murder attracted nationwide attention, largely because of her family's social standing. The Fitzpatricks live in a graceful, thirty-room mansion on Doubling Road in Greenwich, Connecticut, a mile from the Greenwich Country Club. Mr. Fitzpatrick, a Princeton graduate, made a small fortune in the spice business and Linda had all the advantages money and position could provide: Greenwich Country Day School, Old-fields School in Baltimore, vacations in Bermuda. But, at least in the last months of her life, there was another side—pot, LSD, crash pads and warlocks—a side her family professed to know nothing about. Because of the gap between her two worlds and the depth of her parents' insulation, Linda quickly became a symbol of the profound alienation of many middle-class youths.

But Groovy was virtually ignored, dismissed by most of the press as a "tattooed drifter." Yet he was an original, a tortured tumbleweed among the flower children, many of whom were products of the manicured lawns and gladiolus beds of New Rochelle and Great Neck.

Most of the hippies dropped quite deliberately from suburbia into the East Village and Haight-Ashbury, seeking the bizarre and the immediate. But Groovy was a true dropout from society, who quite by chance found the hippie scene ready to drop into. Two decades ago he would have dropped out anyway and ended at best a gentle, aimless wanderer through America's shantytowns, at worst a leather-jacketed motorcycle tough. In the East Village he was an all-too-easy luminary, reflecting the gleam in the eyes of a thousand runaways. But to have starred in Central Falls, before an audience of bakers lined up in the windows of a great brick box, among the trucks and the filling stations and the railroad tracks and the junkyards—that may have been one of his finest hours.

Central Falls is the very essence of a New England mill town come on evil days. Wedged onto a sandy slab where the Seekonk and Blackstone Rivers meet just north of Providence, it lies at the southern end of the Blackstone valley, once a center of New England's textile industry. Towns like Saylesville, Valley Falls, Quinnville and Albion all had their big, sooty, brick mills which somehow managed to spin fine white yarn and cloth without a hint of its grimy origin. But after World War II most of the mills moved South, drawn by cheap labor and new power, leaving behind them stagnant pools of unemployment and depression.

With the mills gone, Central Falls has eighty-one manufacturing plants left, employing only 3,812 persons. Corning Glass and Standard Romper Company are the only major plants in town; the rest are mostly small companies lodged in converted mills, producing machines, paper, shoes and food products. There are jobs for the young, but men over forty, who spent their best years in the textile mills, find it hard to get work. Central Falls has a welfare case load of seventeen hundred, the fourth largest in the state, although there are fourteen communities with bigger populations. The city has lost population every census since 1930—when it had 25,898 persons—to 1965—when it had 18,677.

One thing Central Falls has plenty of is liquor licenses—sixty-four, or one for every two hundred ninety-one persons—and there is a bar on nearly every corner, most of them rough workmen's taverns that sell more beer than Scotch and more Scotch than gin. It's a tough city too, sometimes called "Little Chicago," known particularly for its numerous bookies. Other than drinking, playing the horses or, perhaps, bingo there isn't much to do in Central Falls. There's one movie—Holiday Cinema—and one bowling alley—Bill's Bowlaway. Central Falls calls itself, "The friendly city with the forward look," but one teen-ager says, "You can look right through it."

That's the way Central Falls apparently likes it. The city has elected the same mayor—Raymond J. Morissette—five straight times; last November after his latest victory, the mayor's son said, "It's a little like the way it was with the New York Yankees."

There are only four business streets of significance in Central Falls, enclosing most of the city's 1.27 square miles. "If you want to find a guy," explains one teen-ager, "you drive down Broad, left on Hunt, left on Dexter and then left on Clay. If they ain't there, they're out of town." In between are row after row of three-story frame houses where the conglomerate people of Central Falls live—about half of French-Canadian origin, twenty-seven percent Irish and English, ten percent Polish, five percent Syrian and two and a half percent Portuguese.

Jimmy Hutchinson's family is Portuguese on his mother's side, and his mother, Esther, and her large family were the chief influences in his young life. Esther was one of fourteen children born to Mr. and Mrs. Manuel Joseph of Lincoln, Rhode Island, where Mr. Joseph worked in a mill. While she was still young, the family moved to Pawtucket, just across the New Haven Railroad tracks from Central Falls, and it was there at nineteen—in the midst of World War II—that she married Joseph J. Hutchinson, then a sailor stationed at Quonset Point. After the war, the Hutchinsons moved to Pawtucket, where Esther helped support the family by making jewelry.

Esther was a dark-haired, well-built girl with Mediterranean good looks and a Mediterranean temperament to match. After her divorce from Mr. Hutchinson, she married a truck driver named Bob Benoit, but they separated several years ago. Esther had two children by Mr. Hutchinson—George, who was born in 1944 but was adopted while still an infant by the sister of Mr. Hutchinson's sister-in-law, and Jimmy, who was born February 19, 1946, in Pawtucket. She also had two children by Mr. Benoit: Brenda, now ten years old, and Ronald, now three.

The family lived in Pawtucket until Jimmy was about five and then moved to a comfortable old frame house on Tiffany Street in Central Falls. Jimmy went to kindergarten at the Kendall Street School and then on to first grade in 1952. It was that year that Jimmy's "learning problems"—as the school system called them—began to show up. His performance in the first grade was so poor that he had to repeat the grade the next year. The following year, when the family moved back to Pawtucket for a brief stay, Jimmy went on to second grade and then through third grade at the High Street School, but school records show that he was a "low achiever, a borderline student, with difficulty in reading, spelling and comprehension." They also show a "below-average I.Q." A school official said Jimmy evidently "tried hard, did what he could with what he had, but he didn't have much."

So when the family moved back to Central Falls in 1956, the School Department there assigned Jimmy to an "ungraded class" at the Hedley Avenue School. Miss Sara Kerr, who was the principal and school psychologist at Hedley Avenue, explains that the ungraded class was a remedial program to prepare "under-achieving children" to return to the normal grade progression. "As soon as Jimmy's achievement matched his age we would have put him back in a regular grade," Miss Kerr said. But it never did and he remained in the ungraded class for five long years.

Miss Kerr, a bird-like, sharp-featured woman with blue-tinted white hair which stands up sharply from her head, is now retired from the school system, but she spoke warmly about her former student the other day as she perched on an ornate armchair in the Victorian parlor of her home a few blocks from the Hedley Avenue School.

"Jimmy, poor Jimmy, was emotionally disturbed, a badly upset boy—and that came out in a severe reading problem as well as some behavioral problems. He had no motivation, no desire to learn and he was always disturbing the classes. I never found any meanness in him. We had some kids who killed flies and tortured them. Jimmy never did anything like that. He was just clowning. But the teachers couldn't put up with his capers so they'd send him to me.

"I can remember him, oh so well, standing there in the doorway of my office. He was always so well-dressed, beautiful clothes, no little girl could have been more fastidious. He'd just stand there so neat and clean-looking and I'd say, 'Oh, Jimmy, not again!' and he'd start to cry, wiping his eyes on his sleeve. And we'd sit and talk and I'd ask him why he couldn't pay attention and do his work. He'd just nod and sniffle and say, 'Yes, Miss Kerr.' He was a poor, bewildered boy.

"One night I kept him after school. I was determined that he was going to do a single little arithmetic problem, but he couldn't do it, he just couldn't.

"I can assure you for those five years he was never neglected or ignored; he was getting the very best remedial education available. The class was small—fifteen kids—and they had a teacher especially trained for remedial work. We worked and worked with Jimmy to erase his deficits, until I guess we finally came to the conclusion that there were just impediments to academic learning."

But Jimmy posed an increasingly difficult discipline problem. Coupled with this was the fact that he was fifteen by the end of his fifth year and bigger than most of the other kids in the ungraded class. As Miss Kerr recalls it, the superintendent came over one day and said, "Miss Kerr, we've got to try something else with this boy."

The "something else" was Central Falls Trade School, but in between his mother arranged psychiatric outpatient treatment for him at Butler Hospital. He underwent this treatment on and off for the next year.

His teachers agree that Jimmy was emotionally disturbed, that all his clowning was his way of saying, Notice me, pay attention. But by the second year at the Hedley Avenue School he was already getting most of his attention outside school—in a gang of which he was the informal but undisputed leader.

There was Ernie St. Angelo, a hulking boy with a barrel chest and huge hands which could squeeze a Narragansett beer can flat; there was his brother, Steve St. Angelo, a thin, dark-haired youth with a sensitive face; there were the Zenone brothers, Danny and Jimmy; Russell Wilson, Dave Quebec, Eddie Marco, Gary Larosee and sometimes Jimmy's older brother, George Carbary, down from North Attleboro.

But of them all, Ernie St. Angelo was closest to Jimmy, more like a brother than George. "Every day after school," Ernie recalls, "we used to go down to his house on Tiffany Street. Hutchy's Corner, we used to call it, 'cause we called him Hutchy—that's one of the things we called him. And Hippity-hop too, because of the funny way he walked, bouncing up and down like that—oh, yeh, and Bouncy, we called him Bouncy too."

Jimmy collected nicknames like other kids collected rocks or bottle caps. Groovy, the last one, came much later, the casual gift of a casual friend in New Orleans. But in Central Falls there was Jungle Jim, a name he got after he cut another kid with a machete. There was Gander, "because he used to goose guys." There was Steve Ribs, which the gang started calling him one day when he hung on a vine over Scott's Pond making the Tarzan call—"Aaaahhh"—with his puny chest stuck out and ribs showing all over. There was Rock Hutchinson, which he gave himself one night, a night Eddie Marco, another gang member, remembers well: "We useta go drinking on Friday nights. One night we got all dressed up.

He had bought some new clothes, a new trench coat and these new square shades. So we come down the street and he says, 'Dig me. I'm Rock Hutchinson. See, girls. You've got a chance to go out with Rock Hutchinson now!' And everything. Ah, he was too much."

Jimmy, the gang remembers, would do anything and usually carried the rest of them along. "We wouldn't of ever done this stuff unless Hutchy done it first," Ernie St. Angelo recalls. "You wouldn't see him one day. And next day he'd come and tell you what he done. And you'd say, 'No, you didn't,' and he'd say, 'C'mon, I'll show ya.' And he'd do it, too. He'd do anything. I'll tell ya he was a nut. A nut! But he was funny. If somebody was on their deathbed and they don't want to see nobody the one I would advise them to see would have been Hutchinson because I tell you he would have had 'em out of that bed. He was that funny. He was funny not being funny. Even when he got mad the faces he useta make was funny. Serious he was funny.

"I'll tell ya the kind of the things he useta do. When we were real young we useta go down to the dump. There was this bum who useta live down there, Slim the Bum, he was a real dirty old guy living in this shack, a shack made out of doors off old houses they tore down. We was all scared of him because he was kind of crazy, sort of trapped in the head, you know. We useta throw stones at him and watch him skip. But not Hutchy. Hutchy would go up there and shake hands with him, you know? Pat him on the back and say, 'How ya doin', Slim. How's the wife and kids?' It useta really break us up. One day I says, 'Jimmy, why do you go down there and do that stuff with Slim?' and he says, 'Aw, Slim's my buddy.'

"There just wasn't anything he wouldn't do. I remember when we was 'bout thirteen or fourteen, we started going down to the slaughterhouse to ride the wild pigs. The first time I ever went was with my cousin. So I spread the word around Central Falls: 'I know a place we can go and ride pigs.' So when Hutchy heard this, he never rode any pigs before, but he says, 'Come on, let's go.'

"Well see, it was a whole day. You'd hop the freight train in Central Falls. And then you'd go up to Pawtucket where it stopped and you'd hop the big freight coming by and that would take you right out to Providence and you'd get off when it slowed down after the lights and go over to the slaughterhouse. Now they got these pigs all in this big pen waiting to be slaughtered and they'd go nuts because they can sense the smell of death coming from the other pigs being killed. See, you ought to watch out. 'Cause they have the male and the female pigs. Now if you ride the female pigs it's all right, but if you ride a male pig, it's all over. They'll bite you to death.

"Well, Hutchy, he didn't care. He got on this big male, must have been about three hundred pounds. They got some big pigs down there. He rode him all around. And then he got off it, and he started skiing in the muck, you know, the crap. We useta do that. You'd grab their tail and just ride on your feet. And right in the center of the floor was this big hole, a hole about four feet deep where everything drains into it. And Hutchy was skiing by it and he went right into it, right up to his waist. He come home all stinking and everything and his mother says, 'Where were you?' and he says, 'Oh, I was down to the stables, riding the horses.' And she sniffs again and she says, 'They was no horses.' Oh, he was too much!''

"Jimmy was always gettin' himself messed up like that," Eddie Marco chimed in joyously. "One day me and Hutchy and a few other kids, we went down to the pond and there was soft mud down there, you'd run over it and it would start getting all pliable, like jelly. You'd run across it and it would bounce as you ran. And if you stood in a spot for long you'd sink, it was something like hard quicksand.

"And Hutchy was jumping up and down and everybody's telling him, 'Start running.' But he says, 'No, this thing can't suck me up.' So we turn around and a minute later Hutchy's screaming for help. He was up to his knees and was screaming, 'It's eating me up.' So we got boards and pushed 'em out there and pulled him out."

Now the gang was really off, one Hutchy exploit tripping on the heels of another.

"I remember one time he bought a case of Ruppert's," Ernie said. "He used to love Ruppert's beer. So he put it down on the ground and he had a stick, one of those voodoo sticks they used to have, you know, with those shrunken heads. He jammed this stick into the case and he gets down on his knees and everything and he goes, 'Oh, Ruppert's Goddess. Oh, Ruppert's Goddess. You're so good to me.' He went to extremes. Anything you did with him, you'd try and keep up with him, you know, so he wouldn't make you look stupid. But mostly you couldn't. He'd start joking and you'd start joking to keep up with him and before you know it you're running out of jokes and this kid's still going, got a book in his head or something.

"One time we was out in Lincoln Woods at this park they have out there. And there were these four guys singing round the snack bar. They was pretty good you know, maybe semipros, and they had everybody gathered round them listening. So Hutchy, he had these bongo drums, and he went over and sat down across the path on the grass, and he started playing the drums. He wasn't so good, really, but he played real hot, and these people round the singers started coming over one by one. He just took them away. Finally, the singers gave up too and came over. At first they was kinda mad, but then they started laughing and said, 'What are you going to do?'

"Sure, he was a clown. He was half clown, half nut and all hot. Why did he act that way? I don't know. Maybe down deep he might have thought he was really a fool. He probably was hiding something, a bad feeling inside, a feeling that no one really liked him 'cause he was a fool. So he was going to be a bigger fool than even they thought."

Jimmy's problems stemmed, in part, from what could hardly have been a secure, serene home life. His mother stopped working in jewelry factories and collected Aid to Dependent Children. She was still lively and attractive when she left Mr. Benoit.

Friends say she did her best with the cramped five-room apartment on the third floor of the green frame building at 818 Dexter Street, where she moved with her three children from Tiffany Street. Jimmy had his own room leading off the kitchen, decorated with pictures of Elvis Presley and James Brown, his childhood idols, and scattered with records, model cars and airplanes he made and the comic books he pored over but could never quite read.

Jimmy doted on his younger sister, Brenda, and often spent nights baby-sitting with her. His mother says he was "a good son, always doing something for me, for everybody. He never talked the hippie line or nothin' like that. I don't understand how my son could ever have lived that life in all that filth and everything. He was always clean, liked clothes and everything. And he liked to work. And he wasn't unhappy or anything. He never said nothin' about worrying or nothin' like that."

In September, 1962, at the age of sixteen, after a year at the Butler Center, Jimmy entered the machinist's class at Central Falls Trade School, which was in a grey Quonset hut not far from the high school.

The machine shop, at the rear of the hut, is small and jammed with grey steel lathes, grinders, drill presses, spindles and milling machines. On the walls, hammers, awls and wrenches hang on nails, each over its own black outline. Above them is a neatly lettered sign, WE AIM TO KEEP THIS PLACE CLEAN—PLEASE HELP. Grey lockers bear a seemingly endless roster of French-Canadian names: "Plamondon, Trottier, Bernier, Rocheleal."

The teacher also is of French-Canadian descent; he is Louis Sarault Jr., a lean, deliberate, thoughtful man who takes sociology and psychology courses "so I can understand these boys and my own job a little better.

"Sure I had Jimmy in my shop for three years," he recalls. "I remember the day he arrived. Dr. Calcutt, who was superintendent then, marched him over himself. He told me Jimmy came from an ungraded class, that he'd gotten through only the third grade. Normally the trade school accepts only kids who've gone through the eighth grade. But Dr. Calcutt said, 'Let's give him another chance, Louis. See what you can do with him.' Well, that wasn't unusual. Old Sarault usually got all the problem kids. I like the challenge.

"I got to say Jimmy tried here. He wasn't too shifty with a paper and pencil. If he could write more than his name he didn't show me. If I asked him how much is half of fifteen he'd scratch his head and say that's a tough one. You need more than that in a technical shop like this. I couldn't talk trig to him. I had to do his thinking for him.

"But he made himself some nice tools. I remember this diestock he made, welded it himself. It was so good I kept it around as a model, threw it away only last year.

"And in some respects he had a good head. He could reason. He wouldn't take an unnecessary chance if it jeopardized his safety. He was a real con artist, foxy. In fact, in the con sense of the word, you'd have to say he was sharper than most of the other kids. He'd smile at you, but underneath you knew he was saying, 'I'm putting you on, Sarault.' And his friendship—you'd almost have to say alliance—with Ernie St. Angelo was a very shrewd one. Ernie's a big boy and he could take care of Jimmy, but he's not too smart, while Jimmy had it up there in the way you need it on the street.

"He was skinny, real skinny, but if he thought there was an easy mark in the class he'd go after him." One of his classmates said he once took on Ronald Fanion, a little kid with glasses, and that Sarault caught them and said: "If you guys want to fight, then stand up like men, right next to each other, and swap punches in the arm."

(Ernie St. Angelo remembers that fight. "Ya, it was really funny. Hutchy knew Fanion was nearsighted and couldn't see for nothin'. So he said I'll fix 'em. He filled his shirt pocket with nuts and bolts and scraps of metal. Fanion threw a shot at him, took the pocket off and cut his hand bad.")

Sarault remembers that Jimmy went after Ralph Johnson, a kid who also looked like a mark. "But Ralphie punched him out real good, made a cream puff of him. Up till then the shop had been a little wary of Jimmy because he talked tough. But once they saw him in action against Johnson they knew he was nothing.

"Under his toughness, Jimmy was pretty timid. Once or twice when I disciplined him he'd cry. A boy of sixteen! A kid needs to be wanted, he needs to be loved, and I don't know how much of that he had at home. Once when he got in trouble I told him to bring his mother in. She was all agitated and said, 'I'm through with him; I've told him he has to conform, but he won't. I've had enough.'

"He'd been tossed around a lot. He said he didn't remember his father. But he carried his father's picture around in his billfold—a sharp-looking sailor in his Navy whites, his hat cocked back on his head, a little moustache. Jimmy said he wanted to be just like his father and go into the Navy. I think I pleased him once when I said he looked a little like his father. He kept wanting to grow a moustache like his father's, but I wouldn't let him. Every once in a while the fuzz would start sprouting under his nose and I'd say, 'Shave it off, Jimmy.' And he would. A couple of years later I saw him on the street here and sure enough he had a little moustache, just the spitting image of his father's.

"Jimmy got through okay right up to May of his final year and those last ten days the seniors got off to get caps and gowns and all that. Then he went and got in some bad trouble."

This was the machete incident. According to members of the gang who were there, Jimmy had persuaded Gerry Bergevine, a twenty-nine-year-old neighbor, to buy him some beer. Some other kids tried to take it away from him and a "real punch-'em-up" developed. A friend managed to throw Jimmy a machete and in the fight Jimmy cut seventeen-year-old Albie Nickerson on the arms so badly Albie had to be taken to the hospital. After a hearing before Judge Guillaume Myette, Jimmy was held for the Grand Jury in $1,500 bail.

"That really blew up a storm," Sarault recalls. "Dr. Calcutt, who had gone out of his way to help Jimmy, said, 'Louis, I don't see how we can give him a diploma now.' But I knew Jimmy wanted that diploma in the worst kind of way. After all those years in the ungraded class, you can't blame him. He was tired of hearing people say all he did was mush. So, although I don't think he attended graduation, he was given his diploma."

Three weeks after he got his diploma, Jimmy got another break. The Grand Jury declined to indict him, apparently because Nickerson refused to testify.

Perhaps because of his close call, Jimmy seemed to plunge into work that summer. He worked briefly for Tuppet Screw Company in Central Falls and in September switched over to the New England Paper Tube Company in Pawtucket, where he developed a reputation as a hard worker.

At first, as a floor boy, pushing two-wheeled handcarts of paper tubes around the four-story building, he averaged forty-nine hours a week— nine hours on weekdays and four hours on Saturday. Then, in January, 1966, he became a baler, raking wastepaper from a huge chute into compressing machines, then trotting downstairs seven or eight times a day to wire up the bales of packed paper. As a baler he averaged sixty-one and three-quarter hours a week, working all the day shift and part of the night shift in a room filled with the roar of the nearby splitting machines and the hiss of the relentlessly moving mountain of wastepaper.

"He was a real comedian," recalls Frank, his foreman. "He was loud and you could hear him clowning all over, even with all the machines going. But it didn't bother me none. My rule is if it doesn't hurt work it doesn't hurt me, and Jimmy worked good. He was absent only seventy hours in twenty months and he was late only three times—hell, that's a better record than mine."

To the gang, most of whom were working only sporadically, Jimmy's spate of industriousness was just another sign he was nutty ("Hutchy was a working fool," Ernie said). He put most of his money (which got up to about $87 a week before taxes) in a credit union, at first for a car and then for a motorcycle.

But he had no luck with his purchases. He bought Albie Nickerson's '57 white Ford convertible, but Steve St. Angelo ran it into a tree. Then Jimmy bought a motorcycle—a Japanese Yamaha—and within a few days cracked that up.

"Yeh, the Yamaha went into a gas station but Hutchy didn't," Ernie recalls. "He and these other kids were out on this rainy night. It was real slick and at the entrance to the station he jammed on the brake. He did a swan dive over the handlebars and the bike just rolled into the station and cracked up. Hutchy was all banged up, but still clowning. He told me the story all Japanese like, you know, 'Ah, velly honorable bike. So solly, have tell you velly sad tale. Learn number-one lesson—with Japanese bike you do not put front brake on in rain.' "

The motorcycles were part of a new style the gang had adopted even before Jimmy and Ernie left trade school. They began calling themselves the "Mondos" to differentiate them from the "Collegians," another gang across town. The Collegians hung out on Broad Street around Eddie's Ice Cream Parlor and Izzy's Grill. They wore white sneakers, chinos or Levis, white shirts and close-cropped hair. The Mondos hung out on Dexter Street around Sparky's Restaurant and Duchesneau's Drug Store. They wore black pointed boots with high Cuban heels, black leather jackets, black pants with tapered bottoms, their long hair slicked back with grease.

Jimmy was the sharpest dresser of all the Mondos—everything black except the white buttons on his shirt, a white silk tie, a red vest and maybe a little snap-visor corduroy hat. By now his arms—and chest and legs— were heavily tattooed. He had a girl on his left arm, a little baby with boxing gloves marked "Baby Jim," some dice and lucky sevens. ("The first one he got was a torch with a scroll saying 'Mom,' " recalls Ernie. "I can remember when he got it. We went down to Rocky's Tattoo Parlor in Providence and he says, 'Aw, it's nothin', we get a tattoo, it's nothin'. You go first.' I says, 'Why me?' He says, 'Look at ya, ya big gorilla'—he used to call me that—'you're a big gorilla, look at the fat on ya. Look at me. I'm like a pole.' So I got this on here and he says, 'How was it?' and I said, 'It's nothin', Hutch, you'll like it!' So he gets up there trying to show how brave he was and the guy started the machine and started on his arm and you could hear all kinds of grunts. But he was smiling like it wasn't hurting him. He also had these hinges. Usually they'd put on these big hinges, like they have on sea chests, right at the inside of the elbow, but his arm was too skinny so they put one of these door hinges on. Every time he met somebody new he'd show him the hinges on his arms or legs and he'd bend the arm or leg and say, '*Eeeekkk, eeeekkk,*' like one of those creaky doors.")

With his square dark glasses tilted down on his nose, his little corduroy hat cocked back, all his hinges creaking, Jimmy could often be found early in the evenings leaning against the windows of Duchesneau's Drug Store entertaining the rest of the Mondos with his renowned rendition of Little Stevie Wonder's *Fingertips*. First he would play it on the harmonica, doing a jiggly little dance on the sidewalk as he played. Then he would take the harmonica out of his mouth and, spreading his arms wide, would imitate the blind Negro singer's wail: *Say, yeh, yeh, yeh, yeh, yeh, yeh/Just a little bit of soul, oohhwwaa, oohhwwaa, oohhwwaa/Yeh, yeh, yeh/Clap your hands just a little bit louder/Clap your hands just a little bit louder/Yeh, yeh, yeh, yeh.*

Then he would do his other favorite, James Brown, or he would do a Jackie Gleason or Red Skelton routine he had seen on TV, and the Mondos would roar and slap their knees and shout, "Oh, Hutchy, you're some hot ticket."

Sometimes the Mondos would spend the whole evening in front of Duchesneau's or Sparky's, watching the girls, or "snappers," as they called them. "They'd never really do anything, you know," recalls teen-age Karen Conroy. "They'd just cross their arms in front and watch you real close and say, 'Dig her.' " There were some "snappers" who hung out with the Mondos, girls like Connie Oakley, Cathy Malloy, Madeleine Gilbert. Jimmy knew them all, dated Cathy, but like most of the Mondos he never got serious about girls. On Friday nights the Mondos would often wander up to the dances at Holy Trinity but only to watch the girls go in and then make appropriate remarks.

Almost every spring there was a clash between the Mondos and the Collegians on Dexter Street, but most of the time they only growled at each other. They rarely got into serious trouble with the police. Occasionally they would steal empty bottles from construction sites and cash them in, or pull false alarms and watch the fire trucks race up, or drop lighted cigarettes in mailboxes and watch the smoke seep out; and one Halloween a Mondo was arrested for possession of eggs ("Yeh, believe it or not, possession of eggs! 'Course he'd been throwing them at police cars").

The police didn't like the Mondos and they took a particular dislike to Jimmy. "They thought he was a wise guy," Ernie said. "They really used to get on him. 'Course they used to ride all of us. You're out on a corner with another guy, see, and they'd come along, tell you to move. And you ain't doing nothing. There's old men across the street, about ten of them, and they don't kick them off. Hutchy really hated that and I guess he told some of the cops off 'cause they'd really go after him. I seen cops hit him in the legs with clubs hard enough to knock him on the ground and double him up with pain— just for standing on the corner!"

Most of the time, though, Jimmy was shrewd enough to stay out of serious trouble. If he wanted to raise a little hell he'd let others take the risks. "There was this guy who would do anything for Jimmy," says Ernie. "He was always following us Mondos around and we couldn't stand him. He was a hot ticket all right but we couldn't stand him because he had such a big mouth. So most of us just used to tell him to buzz off. But old Hutchy was too shrewd. He'd say to this guy, 'If you want to hang with us you gotta show us you can do something. Why don't you steal a car and come back and pick us up? But for God's sake make it a good one. No old buggies.' We all laughed 'cause we didn't think the guy could steal anything. But a little while later he came around the corner with a red T-bird, for Chrissakes. We all climbed in, laughing and all, and this guy was so small he couldn't hardly reach the pedals, but Jimmy, he held him up by the seat of the pants and told him, 'On, James,' like he was a chauffeur or something."

With the rest of the gang, and particularly with his buddy, Ernie, Jimmy could be more than generous. Ernie remembers once he needed another hundred dollars to get a car he wanted. "Hutchy said, 'I'll give it to ya.' This is while he was working at the paper-tube place and he had plenty of dough. I said, 'Naw, I don't want your money.' But he went to the bank on Friday and drawed out a hundred and he come to my house and says, 'Here, Ernie, here's the money. Go buy the car. And then when you get the car we'll all go along.' That's the kind of guy he was. Listen. He was a well-loved kid, not well-liked, well-loved." The other Mondos agreed. Eddie Marco said emotionally: "There always was and always will be a Hutchinson."

Others found him less appealing. Seventeen-year-old Wayne Robichaud said, "Well, I guess he was okay to the kids who were his friends, but he used to pick on some of us smaller kids. I was a little scared of him." Nineteen-year-old Ken Moore said, "He could be rough. I remember once I walked by a car where he and a girl were in the backseat. I knocked on the window and he came out after me with this knife."

The Collegians remember that Jimmy carried a knife his last few years in Central Falls, "all kinds of knives, big ones, small ones, curved ones, switchblades." The Mondos concede this, but insist it was largely for self-defense. "He was only ninety pounds, for crying out loud. The guy couldn't fight with his hands. He didn't have no defense with his hands."

But it was a knife which ultimately got Jimmy into big trouble. On October 22, 1965, he and Steve St. Angelo went out to celebrate Steve's seventeenth birthday. "We decided to go over to North Attleboro, Massachusetts, and do the town," Steve recalls. "We hit a few of the spots in town and then we drove over to the V.F.W. hall where they was having this teen-aged dance."

Officers Robert Bray and Antonio J. Casale stationed outside the hall later reported that they observed the two boys "staggering" up to the door and "demanding" admission about nine o'clock. "They smelled strongly of alcohol, were unsteady on their feet and their speech was incoherent," the report said. "They became loud and boisterous and began to hit the paneled wall of the lobby when they were refused admission." They were placed under arrest, but Officer Bray noticed Hutchinson had his left hand in the pocket of his leather jacket and ordered him to remove it. Hutchinson did not respond. According to Bray, he then put one hand on Hutchinson's left wrist and began patting the outside of the pocket with his other hand to see if it contained a gun or a knife. "In the process," Bray's report reads, "Hutchinson's left hand came up and forward, still in his left pocket, and a sharp pointed weapon in his left-hand coat pocket penetrated the pocket and came in contact with Bray's right hand, puncturing the palm of his hand, drawing blood."

The sharp pointed weapon, still kept in an envelope in the North Attleboro police station, is a piece of steel about four inches long with two sharp blades protruding at right angles at each end. When the bar, wrapped in cotton and Scotch tape, is held in a man's clenched fist, the two blades jut out just beyond the knuckles.

The boys were taken to the police station where Jimmy was charged with assault and battery with a dangerous weapon, possession of a dangerous weapon, drunkenness and disturbance of the peace. Steve was charged with drunkenness and disturbing the peace.

Ernie St. Angelo, who went up to North Attleboro that night, recalls that even then Jimmy was still clowning. "He had his hands handcuffed behind his back and every time the cops turned their backs he kept stepping through them so his hands would be in front. The cops didn't know how he did it. Then back in the cell he and Stevie unrolled this toilet paper, draped it all over the cell and through the bars and started singing *Happy Birthday*. When the cops came back to tell them to shut up, Jimmy said, 'Jeez, it's my buddy's birthday, aren't you going to even wish him happy birthday?' "

At his arraignment the next morning, Jimmy pleaded not guilty to all four charges and was held in $1,125 bail. When he could not put up the bail he was taken to the New Bedford House of Correction where he was held until the hearing on October 29, when he was bound over for the Grand Jury. On February 11, the Bristol County Grand Jury indicted him.

Within a week after the indictment, Jimmy was talking seriously about leaving Central Falls.

The Mondos say he had always wanted to travel. Eddie Marco remembers: "When we were twelve, a bunch of us took our bikes and went all the way to the Red Bridge in Providence. Hutchy wanted to keep going, but I had a little Mickey Mouse watch and I said I had to be home for five o'clock supper. So I turned around and came back. Gee, I didn't see the rest of them until after eight. They said Hutchy just wouldn't stop, he wanted to go all the way to New York. 'Course, he had an English bike. He could go faster than we could."

Later, he took to riding the freights in and around Providence and he would give his friends a tour of the city from the top of a freight car. Once, Ernie recalls, "He went right up to the front of a freight and asked the engineer, 'Buddy, can I drive your train?' And the guy started screaming at him and Hutchy says, 'No offense, no offense.' "

Still later, he and the other Mondos would drive to New York for weekends, fill up the car with liquor they could buy legally there at eighteen and sell it to minors in Central Falls.

In New York, the Mondos usually went to Greenwich Village, which fascinated Jimmy. "He always wanted to go down there," Ernie says. "We never wanted to, but he kept saying, 'Oh, I want to see them guys with the long hair.' One time we was in this bar down there and the American Beatles were playing. We were sitting at a table, plastered, so Hutchy calls this guy over, when they had a break, and he grabbed the kid's hair. 'Excuse me,' he says real nice. 'Is that your real hair?' Then he started pulling. We was all laughing. Finally the kid says, 'All right, already.' "

Early in April, 1966, Jimmy told his brother, George Carbary, that he was going to leave home. "He didn't know where he was going to go," George recalls. "He said he just wanted to change the scenery. He wanted me to come with him, but I said I couldn't go. Then, before I knew it—boom, he was gone."

Jimmy withdrew all his savings from the credit union and he and Dave Quebec, one of the Mondos, bought a car. He packed a small suitcase with a couple of sports jackets, two pairs of pants, some underwear and socks, telling his mother that he might send for the rest of his clothes as soon as he was settled. He gave his record player and his large record collection to his sister, Brenda.

Jimmy worked his last day at the Paper Tube Company on April 22 and the next day he and Quebec drove to New York. His mother received a postcard dated the twenty-third from New York with a picture of the New York skyline under the printed legend, "Just Arrived in New York." It read: "Having fun. Can't complain as yet. Say hi to Ronnie, Brenda and everyone for me. Okay. Love, Jim H." His friends presume that Quebec wrote this and subsequent postcards for the still almost illiterate Jimmy.

Shortly after they arrived in New York, Jimmy and Quebec apparently joined an itinerant carnival known as Amusements of America, a New Jersey outfit which toured the Eastern Seaboard with a string of Ferris wheels, merry-go-rounds, "thrill rides" and "children's rides." It is not clear just what Jimmy did for the carnival. Once he told his brother that he and Quebec helped put up and tear down the tents. Another time he said he sold tickets in a freak show.

The record of his travels for the next eight months is told largely in a series of laconic postcards he sent his mother. The next was from Hagerstown, Maryland, later in April: "Hi, ma. Heading for Canada. How's the family? Fine I hope. See you soon. Jim." The card from Philadelphia on May 3 said he was "doing all right and don't need anything." In the following weeks the carnival played a series of one-week stands in New Jersey and Pennsylvania. On August 28 came a card from Ottawa, Canada: "Hi, Mom. Had a wonderful time here. Going back to the U. S. now. Will hear from me soon. Doing fine. Being good. Your best son, love, Jimmy."

Soon after he came back to this country, Jimmy left Amusements of America and joined a smaller carnival run by David B. Endy of Miami, Florida, as it headed South. In September, he sent his mother a card from Enfield, North Carolina, saying, "Took in the sights here—moving on to a new town."

Early in January, 1967, a barber known as "Frenchy," who ran "Frenchy's Barbershop" a few doors down from Jimmy's house in Central Falls, was on vacation in Hollywood, Florida, and wandered into a carnival at a shopping center there. He spotted Jimmy standing by a sideshow. "I remember him very well 'cause he was one of the first round here to wear his hair long. He never wanted any off the top. I said, 'How ya doing, Jimmy.' He said 'Oh, okay, I guess.' "

Jimmy apparently stayed on in Hollywood after the carnival left because on February 7 he sent his mother another postcard from there saying, "Having a good time and going up to New Orleans today."

In New Orleans, Jimmy worked at odd jobs, waiting to pick up with another carnival on its northern swing. Then in late February he was staying at a small hotel in the French Quarter when he met another young ex-carnival worker from Kansas City named Ronald Johnson. Johnson, also dubbed "Galahad," remembers the meeting this way:

"There was this Spanish kid I knew down there—he and I'd been going out with the same chick—and one night I didn't have a place to stay so the Spanish kid said come on up to my place. I went up there and Groovy was up there with this other kid named Chris. At first Groovy came on a little uptight, sort of teed off, you know, because those two guys were goofing off all the time while he was working and paying the rent. But the next day Groovy and I got to rappin' and found out the things we had in common. That wasn't only carnivals. There were lots of things. But the main thing was we both liked to goof on people, you know, blow people's minds, doing weird, fantastic things.

"After that Groovy stopped working mostly and we just goofed off together, just horsing around with the longhairs in Jackson Park and all over the French Quarter." (In these weeks Jimmy acquired at least four things—a tattoo of "Bourbon Street" in fancy lettering; a piece of parchment printed like a diploma, "Nobody of the Year Award," and inscribed under it, "James Hutchinson," which Jimmy later hung in his New York pad; the nickname Groovy, which as Galahad recalls came from a guy in a bar one night, an agent in a carnival; and the drug habit. Galahad is a little vague about when Groovy first began taking drugs. The Mondos say he was "a wino"—a drinker—in Central Falls and never did more with drugs than sniff glue. But soon after he met Galahad he was apparently taking LSD regularly.)

"One day," Galahad recalls, "we was sitting in his hotel room, just rappin', rappin' about carnivals, and we just decided to take off, like the carnivals weren't due yet and we could catch them in Philly. So we hitchhiked up to New York, took us about a week. We spent this one wild night just wandering around Memphis but mostly we kept on the road."

Galahad and Groovy arrived in New York on April 1 and as Galahad remembers it they went first to Times Square. "We ran into some kids up there who were tripping on LSD and were on their way to the movies. We asked where we could stay and they suggested the Peace Eye Bookstore down in the Village. So we went down there and ended up staying a couple of weeks."

The Peace Eye, at 383 East Tenth Street in the heart of the East Village, was a hippie bookstore featuring psychedelic literature and the underground press. It was owned by Ed Sanders, the leader of The Fugs. The Jade Companions were staying in the back room and allowed Galahad and Groovy to camp there for about three weeks. They got their food in exchange for a little work around the place, most of it by Groovy.

"One day," Galahad recalls, "Groovy told me he wanted to open a crash pad where homeless kids could stay. I don't know where he got the idea. There weren't any crash pads down in New Orleans. I think he got the idea from some girl he met. Finally we met this other chick who said she'd let us use her pad, really her boyfriend's pad, over on Eleventh Street, as long as we paid the rent—$35 a month."

The pad was Apartment 11 on the third floor of a dingy tenement at 622 East Eleventh Street. On the door was a hand-lettered sign: "Galahad's Pad, protector of all that is righteous and holy." For the next three months, it served as the most renowned of the East Village's crash pads, where the homeless and the friendless could stay as long as they liked. Sometimes Groovy and Galahad would return a runaway child to frantic parents and be rewarded with a television set or money. ("We're in the people business," Groovy once said.) But at most times there were twenty to thirty assorted hippies staying there and, later, a whole host of visitors—newsmen, television cameramen, curiosity seekers and policemen, always policemen.

The police concentration on the pad was later explained in an affidavit filed by Police Commissioner Howard Leary before the United States

District Court. The commissioner said there had been "a number of entries" to the apartment "occasioned by constant requests . . . from other police departments, but most frequently from parents themselves to find minors, runaway teen-agers in the East Village area of New York City. Usually the parents themselves have heard that their children are living at Apartment 11 at 622 East Eleventh Street."

The commissioner's affidavit was filed in response to a suit on behalf of Galahad, Groovy and several other defendants by John Mage, their lawyer, and Paul Chevigny of the New York Civil Liberties Union. The suit charged that the police were conducting a campaign of "harassment, including dragnet arrests, invasions of privacy and searches" against the defendants. The suit, filed in June, 1967, cited eight specific instances prior to May 6 on which the police entered the apartment "without consent, warrant or other lawful cause" and intrusions after that "on an almost daily basis."

Among the instances were:

One on April 27 when, according to Mage, a member of the Narcotics Squad banged on the door and demanded entrance. He arrested Groovy for impairing the morals of a minor—a girl found in the apartment. Groovy spent the night in jail, but the next morning the case was dismissed on arraignment when the girl was found to be over sixteen.

One on May 6 when the police again demanded entrance. Under instructions from Mage, who became their lawyer after Groovy's arrest, Groovy and Galahad demanded a warrant. But according to the suit the police said they did not need a warrant and "forced their way in." About fifteen persons were arrested and taken to the Ninth Precinct but were released the next morning without being charged.

One on May 19 when police again banged on the door, searched the apartment, arrested Groovy and several others on narcotics charges, which were dismissed next morning in Court.

John Mage, a boyish-looking but deeply committed young lawyer, recalls: "After one of the mass arrests I called the Ninth Precinct and complained that this was something out of 1938 Berlin. I guess because I was a lawyer they assumed that I was a married old man with children because the detective said, 'What if your daughter was running around with these hippies?' I said if I had a daughter I'd expect the police to treat her justly, as all people ought to be treated, and the detective shouted, 'These aren't people, they're bedbugs and they should be exterminated.' "

In answering the suit, Commissioner Leary said, "I believe the police officers have acted in good faith to enforce the laws of the State in these situations." But shortly after the suit was filed—and a parallel action against the detectives involved was brought before the Police Review Board—the police entries of the apartment stopped.

Even after that, the pad was threatened by an ever-increasing horde of newsmen seeking the bizarre and the way out. "Neither Galahad nor Groovy knew how to cope with this kind of publicity," recalls Don McNeill of *The Village Voice*. "It just blew Galahad's mind, almost destroyed him. It was just incredible to see how the media's attention contorted the guy."

Groovy was less affected by it because he was more naïve. Eve Cary, who works for the Civil Liberties Union, recalls a wide-eyed Groovy coming up to her at one of the court hearings and saying, "*Time* magazine, the society magazine," wanted to interview him.

"Groovy was just gleefully enjoying everything that happened to him," John Mage said. "Even during the worst of the arrests he just ate up the attention. Newsmen were baffled and amazed to find somebody down there who would talk to them at any time, tell them absolutely anything that came into his head."

Groovy struck others as somehow different, more truly innocent than most of the hippies. June Tauber, a "straight" girl who met him several times last summer, recalls that he made a particular impression on her the night of the Tompkins Square riot. "Most of the hippies, the whole thing, was so dark, dirty, almost Hogarthian. Except for Groovy. He was ebullient, hopping and leaping around, buzzing around Galahad like a butterfly, his little, dark, dancing eyes, his teeny, teeny features, small, delicate, light and bouncy, almost childlike in the midst of that dreary affair."

Another friend remembers Groovy one night as he and other hippies waited for hours amid the forbidding marble columns of the Criminal Court for Galahad to be released on bail: "Groovy would go careening around the hall like a kid on the last day of school, in and out of pillars, leaping, prancing, then skidding sideways to a grinning halt before the largest cluster of psychedelic brethren. For variety he would play softly on his harmonica, breaking into a little jig every few bars."

Steve Golden, who covered the East Village for The New York *Times* last summer, says: "Galahad was the brains of the organization, quick, sharp, though no genius. Groovy wasn't so smart, but he could feel, which Galahad couldn't. Groovy had the vitality, the energy. He was the only one who could put down Galahad without getting him mad. I think of them as Don Quixote and Sancho Panza or maybe Paul Douglas and Judy Holliday in *Born Yesterday*."

One day Galahad and Groovy were sighted on St. Mark's Place in the heart of hippieland. Galahad had on a fireman's hat and was wheeling a shopping cart in which was a big fire extinguisher. Groovy would scurry ahead and light a piece of paper in the gutter and then Galahad would race up and put it out. They would panhandle from the bystanders and then Groovy would race ahead and light another piece of paper. (Galahad liked the act, which Groovy had invented, and told him to hold onto the extinguisher. But when they got together that night Groovy didn't have the extinguisher. "What you do with it?" Galahad demanded. "I don't know," Groovy said. "I think I gave it to somebody.")

Groovy seemed to enjoy giving things away in the Village—part of his newfound "digger" ethos. Sometimes he would stand on the street corner and when he saw someone whose face he liked he would go up and plant a bottle cap in his open palm. "I just want you to have it," he'd tell the bewildered pedestrian.

He also gave away drugs—LSD, speed, pot—or sold them at prices far below those charged by the more professional dealers.

Suddenly in midsummer Groovy took off for Woodstock, New York, about ninety miles up the Hudson, where a hippie scene was developing. He drove up with some friends and they stayed about a month. Galahad recalls that Groovy talked vaguely about starting some sort of rural "commune" there patterned after those that were sprouting in the California hills, but his Woodstock friends say he never did anything about it.

"Mostly we just clowned around the Café Espresso in the middle of town, and Groovy was the chief clown," one friend recalls. "One night he pulled some grass out of the ground, you know, real green cow-type grass, and he rolled it up in a cigarette paper and went up to these proper villagers and said, 'Hey, you want a joint of grass, man?' Ya had to laugh. Oh, another night, you know, the tables of the café were in this little sunken courtyard with their tops just about level with the sidewalk and one night Groovy just stepped off the sidewalk onto one of the tables and asked these tourists for a light. It broke everybody up—except the tourists. They just sat there and looked amazed."

Groovy and his friends had no place to stay in Woodstock. They moved around, sleeping in fields and barns. One week they stayed at a camp in the woods near Bob Dylan's house and visited several times with the folk singer-poet. Later, somebody said, they'd found a vacant barn and on a rainy July 23, Groovy, two other boys and two girls went out there to sleep. About 1 a.m., acting on a complaint by the owner, two Woodstock constables arrested the five for trespassing. The two girls were later released in custody of their parents. But the boys appeared the next day before Justice of the Peace Milton Houst and were sentenced to fifty days in jail or $50 fine.

One of the boys arrested with him recalls that Groovy seemed happy in jail. "In the cell he met this old Negro he'd known on the carnival circuit and rapped with him for hours about the old days. When I got out he asked me not to tell anybody he was there because he wanted to stay in, get some rest and three square meals a day for a while. He was already pretty strung out on drugs by then and I think he just liked the idea of fifty days of peace and quiet. But somebody called Galahad in New York and he came up and paid the fine."

A few weeks after Groovy got out of jail he and Galahad hit the road again. "We were just tired of the scene," Galahad recalls. They rode with some friends from Woodstock up to Montreal (Groovy wanted to see Expo) and then out to Denver. One night they were stopped in a small South Dakota town by a policeman who wanted to see their identification. "Groovy said he didn't have any eye-dentification," Galahad remembers. "But he said he had some tattoos. The cop said he just wanted to see an I.D. card. But Groovy kept showing him his tattoos. It really blew that cop's mind."

In Denver they were picked up by a girl in her Volkswagen bus and they drove with her and six others to Haight-Ashbury in San Francisco, where Galahad and Groovy put up in the Digger Free Store.

One day Steve Golden ran into Groovy at the Haight-Ashbury Free Clinic, which gave hippies free medical care. "He was wearing the only clothes I ever saw him wear anywhere—a dark shirt under a navy-blue pea jacket, scruffy blue jeans and a blue wool Ridgway cap with a button on the top. But he looked a lot worse than he had in New York. He was sitting on an overstuffed couch, his hands folded in his lap and when I said hello he looked up and said, 'Hi.' His eyes were much duller, his skin had turned sallow and he had a four day's growth of beard. I tried to talk with him but I got little response. He said he needed some vitamins, but the clinic didn't have them and he didn't have money to buy them. I offered him $5, but he wouldn't take it. He said he didn't feel well enough to peddle the *Berkeley Barb* like the others were doing, but he'd panhandle some."

Late in August, Groovy and Galahad left for New York because Galahad had a date in Court. Passing through Chicago, Groovy pulled a freak-out which is still Galahad's favorite. "We were busted for loitering and this cop started frisking Groovy. Groovy had this electric razor in one pocket and when the cop touched the razor case Groovy suddenly yelled, 'Careful, it'll explode and blow us all up.' Boy, the cop yanked his hands away like it was a hot stove."

Back in New York the two friends saw less of each other than before. They stayed in different pads, although they would usually get together at least once a day. "We still looked after each other like brothers," Galahad says, "but he was really strung out on speed [Methedrine] by then. Seemed like every time I saw him he was on that stuff, always speedin' all over the place, moving around, circulating, grooving with all the people. I couldn't keep up with him at the end. I didn't have all the energy he did. I wasn't on speed then."

Steve Golden recalls seeing Groovy one day at a be-in. "His little face, which always looked a bit like John Carradine's, was getting down to bones. His chin was sharpened, his cheeks hollowed. His body, which was always thin, still seemed okay, but his face looked like it was starting to die."

Jim Fouratt, a leader of the Jade Companions of the Flowered Dance and other East Village community groups, also saw Groovy several times after he got back from California. "He was getting more and more frantic, still playing the court jester to Galahad's king, a minstrel in the midst of all that ruin. He was frightening to look at, all wasted away from the drugs, he looked like a skeleton dancing and singing."

Sometime around this time Groovy met Linda Fitzpatrick, the girl from Greenwich, Connecticut. Nobody paid much attention to her because Groovy was always with girls in the Village—girls named Fran, Shelly, Vina.

He spent part of his last day in a sleeping bag in front of the Psychedelicatessen next to Linda. At dawn the next morning their bodies were discovered in the boiler room on Avenue B.

Groovy's head was badly mutilated by the brick, but the family insisted on an open casket at the funeral so the undertaker worked a day and a half to fix it up. On October 13, he was buried in Highland Memorial Park in Johnston, Rhode Island. Ernie St. Angelo, Danny Zenone and most of the other Mondos were there. So were Galahad and about thirty other flower children from the Village. Galahad played Groovy's harmonica briefly over the grave. "I know how Groovy would have wanted it," he said. "Like this."

In the reams of press coverage which followed the murder, Groovy was beatified. One feature writer saw him as "his generation's young rebel, a fugitive from the meanness and materialism he saw around him. An urban Huck Finn. The modern runaway from mendacity and phony respectability. A hot-gospeling psychedelic seeker of lost souls."

After reading most of the stories, Ernie St. Angelo said: "Hutchy would have been in his glory if he was alive and could read all this. He would have loved the crazy things they're saying. He always wanted to be the leader of the laughers.

[May, 1968]

My Generation

by Jacob Brackman

The Sixties was a time of rude awakening. The social and political fabric split at the seams. It seemed there were no longer observers, only participants who were part of the problem, part of the solution, and always part of the story. This essay, published in October 1968, documents the radicalization of the nation's Baby Boom generation.

No, no breather yet for reminiscence, no nostalgia, no wistful catalog of names and feats. The biggest crop in national history, War Baby boom; *Hibakusha,* survivors of Hiroshima. Happening now. Our fathers had played out our chances for us. Next time the lamps start going out, no one shall ever see them lit again. Half America under twenty-five, stirring, rumbling: unbuttoned potentiality, exquisite and terrible. First to grow from infancy with Rootie Kazootie and Mr. Wizard, with access to perspective, incredible information about the world; supersaturated with grey emanations. First to grow in the shadow of extinction, first to gamble piously with human chemistry, gripped in a fever for eleventh-hour salvation. The adult secondary, keying on us, cotton-mouthed, their legs near gone, barking signals of our estrangement up to their big forward wall: which way would we cut, or charge, and when? Rushing to their mailboxes, devouring the magazines—something was happening here, the kids were going crazy, black ones burning city blocks, white ones occupying great universities (my God, and holding *hostages*), out to levitate the Pentagon with obscene chants, capping joints instead of kegs at the Delta House, ten thousand self-exiled to Canada, not even *trying* to get through anymore. "Stop us?" Cohn-Bendit laughed. "Slap at water."

The magazine editors fumbling for the angle that won't look ridiculous, eavesdropping in the bar cars, pleading with their adolescent children ("Something's happening here, right? Tell Daddy"). Searching out those few among us who cared, for a time still, to talk, uncertain what they listened for, or could hear. The media men set us questions, subverted in a thousand nuances: How did it feel when (*read*: Kennedy, Schwerner, Rockwell, King, Kennedy) was shot? When did you reject your parents' attitude toward (*read*: sex, religion, the Republican Party)? Did you turn nihilistic when they beat you in a Mississippi jail? Didn't you realize they were sick individuals? Isn't pot, come on now, just running away from reality? Does Gene McCarthy give you hope? You can't believe disruption helps your cause? Do you dig (*read*: maxi-skirts, Che, Nehru jackets)? Well, what other country's better? You think you'd like to live in China? . . . Our disappointment ran so deep we goofed all over them. "Your dog is chewing on my arm." "For a kicks sort of thing, you know what I mean?" "You go on build it up, mother, we gonna burn it down." "Don't think twice, it's all right, Ma (I'm only bleeding)." "I don't know, man, all around me I see cats plugging at their games, and I can't put them down, man; I can't even locate my own head."

Scott, born to the American century, sharing its war-rent Teens and profligate Twenties, winning a First in the Newman field day, pledging Cottage Club at Princeton; too long and too intensely pursuing meager collegiate dreams of wealth and glory, jazzy flapper fun, of heroics on the gridiron, on the battlefield, with the deb of the moment on a sawdusted ballroom floor: *There was an orchestra—Bingo-Bango/Playing for us to dance the tango/And the people all clapped as we arose/For her sweet face and my new clothes.* . . . You called yourselves "lost" and rather fancied the notion; cut the strings to your discredited elders, to their witch hunts and Prohibitions, their Teapot Domes. And after all the football and the classy North Shore parties, the Riviera gilt by association, there glistened a more seductive bauble, bigger than the Ritz—to be a great writer: an American Turgenev. Till in the Thirties, all your barren aspirations cracked, or rather, played themselves out: "Horror and waste— waste and horror—what I might have been and done that is lost, spent, gone, dissipated, unrecapturable." We are setting off where you broke down, Fitzboomski, a sensibility delicate as tears, you took too long to realize how lost you were. We arrived precociously at consciousness, with nothing to live up to.

Perhaps the writer must make plain that his presumptuous "we" isn't shorthand for a clear temper of ideas, statistically accessible, but for a kind of Early-Warning System, which gets its fix from marginal characters, from madmen, yes, and outlaws, reduced to a fraction of their significance by the vast denominator that has remained—will always remain—the same: "In what he called 'the most extensive survey of its kind ever undertaken,' pollster George Gallup found that the political views of voters between the ages of twenty-one and twenty-nine differ hardly at all from the views of those thirty to forty-nine. 'A lot of this talk about this group's being a maverick generation must be considered ridiculous,' Gallup told reporters. 'People should not worry about the future of this country. It's in good hands.' The most recent survey, he said, shows Nixon polling forty-four percent to Kennedy's thirty-seven percent." Who were we then? No torpid cross-section, median deadwood, we had no cutoff age. With vague and wide connections we stretched ten years on campus, fifteen, at least, through rock and dope. Of one hundred million, we were a fringe, but we were making more noise than was our due, attaching converts in their pubescence; and fringes of our own, too woolly, too scary for even us to believe, were burgeoning around us. We did not enjoy the company of all our finest peers by any means, for there were scientists, ponderers, decent liberals who had removed themselves inexorably from us, as if the times were quite like other times and there was still a future for business as usual. Yet, at their remove, they felt a sense of loss. And those who joined us relinquished all prospects for return. We nurtured a daring premise: we were of historical moment, critical, unprecedented, containing within ourselves the fullness of time. Some great wind was brewing as we breathed; not a new generation, but a new notion of generation with new notions of its imperatives. We would not default, succumb to the certainties of age, gulp pills, compromise maturely, lubricate our adulthoods with facile resignations. We would not be normal. For normality was now disease—hacking coughs, quilted stomachs and cold loins, the sniveling bitterness of diminished hopes—and if we were to live propitiously in our era, we would have to define normality anew. We might say no, after long childhoods of indulgence, to the sudden demands of our complicity. We might not, on schedule, relinquish our freedom. We might remain forever infants, joyous beggars, dependent on the system, refusing our contributions yet ready enough to consume. Though distribution was presently askew, or demented, technology has already created wealth enough to sustain us all. We might innovate for Health across the boards: new jokes, sex, politics, learning—a massive reclamation of the cities of our souls. Or so we mused when we were on, and up. When we were off, and down, we could envision ourselves forty-year-old waifs, with pee stains on our underwear, drifting without callings in a society we could neither convert nor make sense of. For in a single day we could waver between something like optimism and a despair so deadly it seemed there was no acre of earth where we would be permitted to gather with those we loved and share a creditable life—a despair that suggested we were the first generation that could imagine declining its bid to inherit the earth.

In 1952, the year I started going to the movies alone, M-G-M released a film called *It's a Big Country,* with, well, real spirit, and an amazing cast—Ethel Barrymore, Keefe Brasselle, Gary Cooper, Van Johnson, Gene Kelly, Janet Leigh, George Murphy—and lots of lines like: "I'm just a guy who loves America. What a country! Greatest in the world and I'm proud to be a part of it. *Sure . . .* we got our problems. But we'll lick 'em." The other night I caught it again on TV and short-circuited back to a past I scarcely recalled. Between vignettes, the camera swept past bustling cities and waving fields of grain, while a basso narrator intoned, "America! The conscience. The heart. The will." In one irresistibly upbeat sketch, a Texan who kept insisting he didn't believe in "overdoin' things" gradually revealed the gross dimensions of his excess.(!) In another, an immigrant Hungarian obsessed with his people's traditional hostility toward Greeks, reconciled himself to his eldest daughter's marriage to one (while an entire Greek fraternity suddenly surrounded his remaining six daughters). It was an enmity I hadn't heard of before (nor since) but I was quite prepared to believe that it was keeping lots of fine people apart. I'm sure that immigrant family seemed to me rather like my grandparents, with whom I lived, and that I imagined I would grow up rather like the heretical daughter who might just go ahead and marry the Greek, convention be damned, because, after all, we're all Americans. (A fantastic intimation: American problems are the ones that aren't intrinsically *American.*) I wasn't much for Country 'Tis of Thee, nor otherwise impossibly square, but my ancestors had been given some bad times in their Old Countries. I'd heard stories. At night, sometimes, I used to think about how lucky I was to have been born here. My own relation to America was strong and clear. Of course I knew that there were imperfections, vast ones, but I thought almost everybody good (millions of liberals! wearing sandals! listening to The Weavers!) wanted to help change what was bad. I was ready to work, too, and I thought of our problems: "We'll lick 'em." 1952. "Indians" were mentioned once, in a recitation of all the different kinds of real Americans there are. Although it was a "sweeping panorama" no Negro was seen or heard of. Squalor was a homey testing ground for pluck, a purgatory short enough to make heaven seem the cozier. The Korean War did not exist. I remember exactly when I saw *It's a Big Country.* Stevenson had just lost. I was nine years old.

I went to lots of movies as a kid; I could never have guessed that this one, for all its garish mediocrity, influenced me as much, or confirmed as much for me, as any book I ever read. As I watched it again on television, the perfect familiarity of every scene astounded me, for I had no memory of any truth awry, any line or image even slightly extreme. I wish I could have seen it annually, throughout my adolescence, to graph my departure from its lovely vision.

Many people five years older than I (the magic Thirty!) managed to sustain their image of lickable problems into maturity, where it got focused into a hopeful conception of American life, or at least of the forces which stunt that life. Poverty was a toughening up en route to success; Racism, a declining aberration, a Southern psychosis; War, forced upon us from without by foreigners of ruthless, outsized ambition. Even as today, the media takes each Vietnam horror story to be a freakish, notable event, so these elders learned to interpret every tormenting fact of American depravity as a temporary *exception,* learned to cultivate a "full perspective." And as Fitzgerald's great believers wakened to a nation incorrigibly great, so many people five years younger than I wakened to one simply incorrigible, and grew without belief of any kind. We in the middle learned that the enemy was Russia, and later, China, and still later that the enemy was not peculiar to any system, but was the same in all: repression, banality, irrelevance, and all the other uglinesses which conspire to dwarf or extinguish the human personality. We clung desperately to hopes for fixing this, for fixing that, tracing the evil in our national life to misguided policy, until poverty, racism, war and the rest seemed no longer a result of bunglings, no longer accidental, but institutional features of our society. The enormity of the change required seemed, then, to lie altogether beyond our means of change, and numbed us into quietude, or nightmares of apocalypse.

We needed new definitions of livelihood, of maturity and enjoyment, but we could scarcely imagine change so gargantuan it seemed close to reversal, so inaccessible to legislation or "programs" as to demand a radicalism of messianic proportions. America injured us into black experiments, futile bouts; our fists sank into her fat, and disappeared. Some of us were beautiful before going over the edge. The personal histories of friends, and their friends, merged with our own; we shared a common genealogy, and we would share a common fate. One, brimming with compassion, marched and organized. As he ascended ghetto stairwells a kind of targetless hate began to spread inside him, a guilty helplessness, and dread. He was neither poor nor black. He could not pay his dues with nightstick scars, even assuming he could find someone to administer them. His hair and eyes grew wild, but some vestigial love of country froze him in the anarchist's posture. He became an armchair kamikaze; talked of confrontation, interests, guns, resistance, plotted strikes on Lockheed and, at last, provoked a beating from the law in a Westchester shopping center so suburban ladies might see that it could happen there, and to a nice Jewish boy. Succumbing to the romance of guerrilla-hood, he laughed at talk of Asian peasants or disenfranchised blacks, crying that each injustice was but a single head of the Hydra that had to be stilled by a sword through the heart. One day, he was gone, some said to Cuba. Another, with a foot already inside the academy, gave away what he had, wandered barefoot and penniless through Mexico, smoked ganja in Jamaica with

Ras Tafarians and charas in Calcutta with poets; became an animal, howled through the woods of western Pennsylvania, was loved across the boundaries of class and burned for a time with the conviction that it was all *there,* laid out for him, the occult feast, the rites of exploration. "I'm running a whole different flick," he said. Sometimes he talked ideas that unhinged our knees, sometimes his silence was so wise we swore we'd never speak again. And while our leaders reassessed positions, he reassessed for us the meat of consciousness, to make our lives organic, of a piece. Some months ago he turned to vegetable, but until he could no longer wipe himself after toilet, we thought we must also cast off what we still clung to, and follow him. We had sent them out to reconnoiter galaxies, and they, as it happened, plunged too far. We lost radio contact. They lost ground control. We could no longer interpret their fitful vibrations.

Those of us with nerve endings less exposed hung back, holding our acts together, but making little waves. Teen-agers ran a gigantic import industry. (How can you venerate government and law when you commit a felony every day?) Black sophomores propped their black feet up on the prexy's walnut desk. Wheeler-dealer heads took Wall Street for a ride. Ecstatic communitarians grooved to divine potato patches. Children invented music that didn't go Bingo-Bango. They didn't know much; they were suckers for fakery. But we were slow to call any experiment excessive. Within ambient disorder, each seemed somehow appropriate. We felt *ourselves* growing into the people our parents had warned us about. The woods already burning, they spent their strength clucking over our eccentricity. And there were ever reassurances: we would learn; we'd soon be out on the field with the team from VISTA or Dow. Meanwhile, we dug in for the longest "adolescent phase" since adolescence was invented a century ago. Bleak signals flashed across our skies. Legions of our most promising would surely disappear into the prisons. In the Fifties, we never guessed the phonies could become so dangerous. Many wouldn't stick it out. They'd learned why Lao-Tze hopped upon his ox, at last, and rode out beyond the Great Wall. Many others, perhaps stronger and finer, perhaps not yet placing the problems at so terrible a depth, might begin their thousand pinpricks, launch forays into the barren democratic sensibility. By their refusal, their mischief, their infiltration, great numbers could begin to conceive of something more decent than submitting to the culture. There was that vague and fragile chance, and although I had contempt for much my generation spawned, I could not see another chance anywhere I looked.

[October, 1968]

SECTION 3

THE COLOR GAP

Fifth Avenue, Uptown

by James Baldwin

The July 1960 issue celebrated New York. The writers and artists who flocked there were transforming our vision of the world with unprecedented vigor. In sharp contrast to the new energies of the chic downtown set, the editors included this grim and frightening portrait of life uptown in Harlem, where nothing had changed. The seeds of discontent sown there and elsewhere would later erupt into riots in every major city across America. James Baldwin, a prominent black writer, had published a book of essays at the time this article ran, in addition to two powerful novels, Go Tell It on the Mountain *and* Giovanni's Room. Another Country *was published two years later.*

There is a housing project standing now where the house in which we grew up once stood, and one of those stunted city trees is snarling where our doorway used to be. This is on the rehabilitated side of the avenue. The other side of the avenue—for progress takes time—has not been rehabilitated yet and it looks exactly as it looked in the days when we sat with our noses pressed against the windowpane, longing to be allowed to go "across the street." The grocery store which gave us credit is still there, and there can be no doubt that it is still giving credit. The people in the project certainly need it—far more, indeed, than they ever needed the project. The last time I passed by, the Jewish proprietor was still standing among his shelves, looking sadder and heavier but scarcely any older. Further down the block stands the shoe-repair store in which our shoes were repaired until reparation became impossible and in which, then, we bought all our "new" ones. The Negro proprietor is still in the window, head down, working at the leather.

These two, I imagine, could tell a long tale if they would (perhaps they would be glad to if they could), having watched so many, for so long, struggling in the fishhooks, the barbed wire, of this avenue.

The avenue is elsewhere the renowned and elegant Fifth. The area I am describing, which, in today's gang parlance, would be called "the turf," is bounded by Lenox Avenue on the west, the Harlem River on the east, 135th Street on the north, and 130th Street on the south. We never lived beyond these boundaries; this is where we grew up. Walking along 145th Street—for example—familiar as it is, and similar, does not have the same impact because I do not know any of the people on the block. But when I turn east on 131st Street and Lenox Avenue, there is first a soda-pop joint, then a shoeshine "parlor," then a grocery store, then a dry cleaners', then the houses. All along the street there are people who watched me grow up, people who grew up with me, people I watched grow up along with my brothers and sisters; and, sometimes in my arms, sometimes underfoot, sometimes at my shoulder—or on it—their children, a riot, a forest of children, who include my nieces and nephews.

When we reach the end of this long block, we find ourselves on wide, filthy, hostile Fifth Avenue, facing that project which hangs over the avenue like a monument to the folly, and the cowardice, of good intentions. All along the block, for anyone who knows it, are immense human gaps, like craters. These gaps are not created merely by those who have moved away, inevitably into some other ghetto; or by those who have risen, almost always into a greater capacity for self-loathing and self-delusion; or yet by those who, by whatever means—War II, the Korean war, a policeman's gun or billy, a gang war, a brawl, madness, an overdose of heroin, or, simply, unnatural exhaustion—are dead. I am talking about those who are left, and I am talking principally about the young. What are they doing? Well, some, a minority, are fanatical churchgoers, members of the most extreme of the Holy Roller sects. Many, many more are "Moslems," by affiliation or sympathy, that is to say that they are united by nothing more—and nothing less—than a hatred of the white world and all its works. They are present, for example, at every Buy Black street-corner meeting—meetings in which the speaker urges his hearers to cease trading with white men and establish a separate economy. Neither the speaker nor his hearers can possibly do this, of course, since Negroes do not own General Motors or RCA or the A&P, nor, indeed, do they own more than a wholly insufficient fraction of anything else in Harlem (those who *do* own anything are more interested in their profits than in their fellows). But these meetings nevertheless keep alive in the participators a certain pride of bitterness without which, however futile this bitterness may be, they could scarcely remain alive at all. Many have given up. They stay home and watch the TV screen, living on the earnings of their parents, cousins, brothers, or uncles, and only leave the house to go to the movies or to the nearest bar. "How're you making it?" one may ask, running into them along the block, or in the bar. "Oh, I'm TV-ing it"; with the saddest, sweetest, most shamefaced of smiles, and from a great distance. This distance one is compelled to respect; anyone who has traveled so far will not easily be dragged again into the world. There are further retreats, of course, than the TV screen or the bar. There are those who are simply sitting on their stoops, "stoned," animated for a moment only, and hideously, by the approach of someone who may lend them the money for a "fix." Or by the approach of someone from whom they can purchase it, one of the shrewd ones, on the way to prison or just coming out.

And the others, who have avoided all of these deaths, get up in the morning and go downtown to meet "the man." They work in the white man's world all day and come home in the evening to this fetid block. They struggle to instill in their children some private sense of honor or dignity which will help the child to survive. This means, of course, that they must struggle, stolidly, incessantly, to keep this sense alive in themselves, in spite of the insults, the indifference, and the cruelty they are certain to encounter in their working day. They patiently browbeat the landlord into fixing the heat, the plaster, the plumbing; this demands prodigious patience; nor is patience usually enough. In trying to make their hovels habitable, they are perpetually throwing good money after bad. Such frustration, so long endured, is driving many strong, admirable men and women whose only crime is color to the very gates of paranoia.

One remembers them from another time—playing handball in the playground, going to church, wondering if they were going to be promoted at school. One remembers them going off to war—gladly, to escape this block. One remembers their return. Perhaps one remembers their wedding day. And one sees where the girl is now—vainly looking for salvation from some other embittered, trussed, and struggling boy—and sees the all-but-abandoned children in the streets.

Now I am perfectly aware that there are other slums in which white men are fighting for their lives, and mainly losing. I know that blood is also flowing through those streets and that the human damage there is incalculable. People are continually pointing out to me the wretchedness of white people in order to console me for the wretchedness of blacks. But an itemized account of the American failure does not console me and it should not console anyone else. That hundreds of thousands of white people are living, in effect, no better than the "niggers" is not a fact to be regarded with complacency. The social and moral bankruptcy suggested by this fact is of the bitterest, most terrifying kind.

The people, however, who believe that this democratic anguish has some consoling value are always pointing out that So-and-So, white, and So-and-So, black, rose from the slums into the big time. The existence—the public existence—of, say, Frank Sinatra and Sammy Davis, Jr. proves to them that America is still the land of opportunity and that inequalities vanish before the determined will. It proves nothing of the sort. The determined will is rare—at the moment, in this country, it is unspeakably rare—and the inequalities suffered by the many are in no way justified by the rise of a few. A few have always risen—in every country, every era, and in the teeth of regimes which can by no stretch of the imagination be thought of as free. Not all of these people, it is worth remembering, left the world better than they found it. The determined will is rare, but it is not invariably benevolent. Furthermore, the American equation of success with the big time reveals an awful disrespect for human life and human achievement. This equation has placed our cities among the most dangerous in the world and has placed our youth among the most empty and most bewildered. The situation of our youth is not mysterious. Children have never been very good at listening to their elders, but they have never failed to imitate them. They must, they have no other models. That is exactly what our children are doing. They are imitating our immorality, our disrespect for the pain of others.

All other slum dwellers, when the bank account permits it, can move out of the slum and vanish altogether from the eye of persecution. No Negro in this country has ever made that much money and it will be a long time before any Negro does. The Negroes in Harlem, who have no money, spend what they have on such gimcracks as they are sold. These include "wider" TV screens, more "faithful" hi-fi sets, more "powerful" cars, all of which, of course, are obsolete long before they are paid for. Anyone who has ever struggled with poverty knows how extremely expensive it is to be poor; and if one is a member of a captive population, economically speaking, one's feet have simply been placed on the treadmill forever. One is victimized, economically, in a thousand ways—rent, for example, or car insurance. Go shopping one day in Harlem—for anything—and compare Harlem prices and quality with those downtown.

The people who have managed to get off this block have only got as far as a more respectable ghetto. This respectable ghetto does not even have the advantages of the disreputable one, friends, neighbors, a familiar church, and friendly tradesmen; and it is not, moreover, in the nature of any ghetto to remain respectable long. Every Sunday, people who have left the block take the lonely ride back, dragging their increasingly discontented children with them. They spend the day talking, not always with words, about the trouble they've seen and the trouble—one must watch their eyes as they watch their children—they are only too likely to see. For children do not like ghettos. It takes them nearly no time to discover exactly why they are there.

The projects in Harlem are hated. They are hated almost as much as policemen, and this is saying a great deal. And they are hated for the same reason: both reveal, unbearably, the real attitude of the white world, no matter how many liberal speeches are made, no matter how many lofty editorials are written, no matter how many civil-rights commissions are set up.

The projects are hideous, of course, there being a law, apparently respected throughout the world, that popular housing shall be as cheerless as a prison. They are lumped all over Harlem, colorless, bleak, high, and revolting. The wide windows look out on Harlem's invincible and indescribable squalor: the Park Avenue railroad tracks, around which, about forty years ago, the present dark community began; the unrehabilitated houses, bowed down, it would seem, under the great weight of frustration and bitterness they contain; the dark, the ominous schoolhouses from which the child may emerge maimed, blinded, hooked, or enraged for life; and the churches, churches, block upon block of churches, niched in the walls like cannon in the walls of a fortress. Even if the administration of the projects were not so insanely humiliating (for example: one must report raises in salary to the management, which will then eat up the profit by raising one's rent; the management has the right to know who is staying in your apartment; the management can ask you to leave, at their discretion), the projects would still be hated because they are an insult to the meanest intelligence.

Harlem got its first private project, Riverton—which is now, naturally, a slum—about twelve years ago because at that time Negroes were not allowed to live in Stuyvesant Town. Harlem watched Riverton go up, therefore, in the most violent bitterness of spirit, and hated it long before the builders arrived. They began hating it at about the time people began moving out of their condemned houses to make room for this additional proof of how thoroughly the white world despised them. And they had scarcely moved in, naturally, before they began smashing windows, defacing walls, urinating in the elevators, and fornicating in the playgrounds. Liberals, both white and black, were appalled at the spectacle. I was appalled by the liberal innocence—or cynicism, which comes out in practice as much the same thing. Other people were delighted to be able to point to proof positive that nothing could be done to better the lot of the colored people. They were, and are, right in one respect: that nothing can be done as long as they are treated like colored people. The people in Harlem know they are living there because white people do not think they are good enough to live anywhere else. No amount of "improvement" can sweeten this fact. Whatever money is now being earmarked to improve this, or any other ghetto, might as well be burnt. A ghetto can be improved in one way only: out of existence.

Similarly, the only way to police a ghetto is to be oppressive. None of Commissioner Kennedy's policemen, even with the best will in the world, have any way of understanding the lives led by the people they swagger about in two's and three's controlling. Their very presence is an insult, and it would be, even if they spent their entire day feeding gumdrops to children. They represent the force of the white world, and that world's real intentions are, simply, for that world's criminal profit and ease, to keep the black man corraled up here, in his place. The badge, the gun in the holster, and the swinging club make vivid what will happen should his rebellion become overt. Rare, indeed, is the Harlem citizen, from the most circumspect church member to the most shiftless adolescent, who does not have a long tale to tell of police incompetence, injustice, or brutality. I myself have witnessed and endured it more than once. The businessmen and racketeers also have a story. And so do the prostitutes. (And this is not, perhaps, the place to discuss Harlem's very complex attitude towards black policemen, nor the reasons, according to Harlem, that they are nearly all downtown.)

It is hard, on the other hand, to blame the policeman, blank, good-natured, thoughtless, and insuperably innocent, for being such a perfect representative of the people he serves. He, too, believes in good intentions and is astounded and offended when they are not taken for the deed. He has never, himself, done anything for which to be hated—which of us has?—and yet he is facing, daily and nightly, people who would gladly see him dead, and he knows it. There is no way for him not to know it: there are few things under heaven more unnerving than the silent, accumulating contempt and hatred of a people. He moves through Harlem, therefore, like an occupying soldier in a bitterly hostile country; which is precisely what, and where, he is, and is the reason he walks in two's and three's. And he is not the only one who knows why he is always in company: the people who are watching him know why, too. Any street meeting, sacred or secular, which he and his colleagues uneasily cover has as its explicit or implicit burden the cruelty and injustice of the white domination. And these days, of course, in terms increasingly vivid and jubilant, it speaks of the end of that domination. The white policeman, standing on a Harlem street corner, finds himself at the very center of the revolution now occurring in the world. He is not prepared for it—naturally, nobody is—and, what is possibly much more to the point, he is exposed, as few white people are, to the anguish of the black people around him. Even if he is gifted with the merest mustard grain of imagination, something must seep in. He cannot avoid observing that some of the children, in spite of their color, remind him of children he has known and loved, perhaps even of his own children. He knows that he certainly does not want *his* children living this way. He can retreat from his uneasiness in only one direction: into a callousness which very shortly becomes second nature. He becomes more callous, the population becomes more hostile, the situation grows more tense, and the police force is increased. One day, to everyone's astonishment, someone drops a match in the powder keg and everything blows up. Before the dust has settled or the blood congealed, editorials, speeches, and civil-rights commissions are loud in the land, demanding to know what happened. What happened is that Negroes want to be treated like men.

Negroes want to be treated like men: a perfectly straightforward statement, containing only seven words. People who have mastered Kant, Hegel, Shakespeare, Marx, Freud, and the Bible find this statement utterly impenetrable. The idea seems to threaten profound, barely conscious assumptions. A kind of panic paralyzes their features, as though they found themselves trapped on the edge of a steep place. I once tried to describe to a very-well-known American intellectual the conditions among Negroes in the South. My recital disturbed him and made him indignant; and he asked me in perfect innocence, "Why don't all the Negroes in the South move North?" I tried to explain what *has* happened, unfailingly, whenever a significant body of Negroes move North. They do not escape jim-crow: they merely encounter another, not-less-deadly variety. They do not move to Chicago, they move to the South Side; they do not move to New York, they move to Harlem. The pressure within the ghetto causes the ghetto walls to expand, and this expansion is always violent. White people hold the line as long as they can, and in as many ways as they can, from verbal intimidation to physical violence. But inevitably the border which has divided the ghetto from the rest of the world falls into the hands of the ghetto. The white people fall back bitterly before the black horde; the landlords make a tidy profit by raising the rent, chopping up the rooms, and all but dispensing with the upkeep; and what has once been a neighborhood turns into a "turf." This is precisely what happened when the Puerto Ricans arrived in their thousands—and the bitterness thus caused is, as I write, being fought out all up and down those streets.

Northerners indulge in an extremely dangerous luxury. They seem to feel that because they fought on the right side during the Civil War, and won, that they have earned the right merely to deplore what is going on in the South, without taking any responsibility for it; and that they can ignore what is happening in Northern cities because what is happening in Little Rock or Birmingham is worse. Well, in the first place, it is not possible for anyone who has not endured both to know which is "worse." I know Negroes who prefer the South and white Southerners, because "At least there, you haven't got to play any guessing games!" The guessing games referred to have driven more than one Negro into the narcotics ward, the madhouse, or the river. I know another Negro, a man very dear to me, who says, with conviction and with truth, "The spirit of the South is the spirit of America." He was born in the North and did his military training in the South. He did not, as far as I can gather, find the South "worse"; he found it, if anything, all too familiar. In the second place, though, even if Birmingham *is* worse, no doubt Johannesburg, South Africa, beats it by several miles, and Buchenwald was one of the worst things that ever happened in the entire history of the world. The world has never lacked for horrifying examples; but I do not believe that these examples are meant to be used as justification for our own crimes. This perpetual justification empties the heart of all human feeling. The emptier our hearts become, the greater will be our crimes. Thirdly, the South is not merely an embarrassingly backward region, but a part of this country, and what happens there concerns every one of us.

As far as the color problem is concerned, there is but one great difference between the Southern white and the Northerner: the Southerner remembers, historically, and in his own psyche, a kind of Eden in which he loved black people and they loved him. Historically, the flaming sword laid across this Eden is the Civil War. Personally, it is the Southerner's sexual coming of age, when, without any warning, unbreakable taboos are set up between himself and his past. Everything, thereafter, is permitted him except the love he remembers and has never ceased to need. The resulting, indescribable torment affects every Southern mind and is the basis of the Southern hysteria.

None of this is true for the Northerner. Negroes represent nothing to him personally, except, perhaps, the dangers of carnality. He never sees Negroes. Southerners see them all the time. Northerners never think about them whereas Southerners are never really thinking of anything else. Negroes are, therefore, ignored in the North and are under surveillance in the South, and suffer hideously in both places. Neither the Southerner nor the Northerner is able to look on the Negro simply as a man. It seems to be indispensable to the national self-esteem that the Negro be considered either as a kind of ward (in which case we are told how many Negroes, comparatively, bought Cadillacs last year and how few, comparatively, were lynched), or as a victim (in which case we are promised that he will never vote in our assemblies or go to school with our kids). They are two sides of the same coin and the South will not change—*cannot* change—until the North changes. The country will not change until it reexamines itself and discovers what it really means by freedom. In the meantime, generations keep being born, bitterness is increased by incompetence, pride, and folly, and the world shrinks around us.

It is a terrible, an inexorable, law that one cannot deny the humanity of another without diminishing one's own: in the face of one's victim, one sees oneself. Walk through the streets of Harlem and see what we, this nation, have become.

[July, 1960]

The Segs

by Reese Cleghorn

The civil rights efforts of the Sixties had at last opened the doors of all-white schools to black students, but often not without an armed escort of National Guardsmen. Integration was a volatile issue, and many Southerners stood fast in their defense of segregation. In this article published in January 1964, Reese Cleghorn talked with the white supremacist leaders of the Southern Resistance.

The late Senator Theodore G. Bilbo of Mississippi said Negroes should be kept in their place, uneducated as well as segregated, so society would not "spoil a good field hand and make an insolent cook." White supremacy was simpler in those days: Senator Bilbo saw no paramount need to prove Negro inferiority, because to him and most of his constituents it was obvious.

Times have changed, and today the South's leading segregation spokesmen argue their case with what they consider to be clear evidence from genetics, anthropology, anatomy, history, and political science. If their contentions are rejected by the overwhelming majority of geneticists, anthropologists, anatomists, historians and political scientists, they nevertheless can argue that scientists and academicians have been notably wrong before. Even the Supreme Court has reversed itself, and they appear confident that one day it will reverse its recent decisions against segregation.

All this may seem implausible and even preposterous to most Americans. But the hopefulness of what seems a hopeless cause in the South can be understood only in terms of this rationale, developed by what might be

377

called, in the spirit of the times, the Segregation Establishment. When Governor George Wallace proclaims, in the face of heavy evidence to the contrary, "We are winning," he speaks from beliefs that are unknown in most of the country. When university students riot in hope that segregation may yet be preserved, they are acting upon ideas that could be startling on campuses elsewhere.

What are these beliefs and who keeps them alive? The Segregation Establishment can best speak for itself. Outside the South, its spokesmen are virtually unknown. Although fame has come to the bitter-end segregationist governors—Alabama's George Wallace, Mississippi's Ross Barnett, and, less dramatically at present, Arkansas' Orval Faubus—few newspaper readers know much about Leander H. Perez, Sr., Roy Harris, Robert Shelton, Lester Maddox, and William J. Simmons. These five might be called the permanent leaders. They are not all alike in their sentiments or even their goals, but each owes his fame across the South to his professional status as a segregationist. Each works regularly at it. Each has developed a view of life in accordance with that work, a *Weltanschauung* to which he adheres even as his cause seems to be undergoing *Götterdämmerung*.

These five do not typify the Southerner who believes in segregation, any more than James Baldwin or Malcolm X typifies the American Negro who wants to end racial discrimination. Their views are fashioned by the fact that they must appear to be the uncompromising champions of a cause. Whereas a great sea of Southerners hold segregationist views without ever having to fortify their reasons, or even know their reasons, these five men must be masters of the polemics of segregation. They must speak of genetics and perceive the lessons of history. (That Muse, in particular, somehow seems to speak more distinctly to them than to other men.)

So these are not typical white Southerners, or even typical Southern leaders. They are, however, the men who often may be found behind the headlines from the South, or even from Washington, if you look far enough back into the foliage behind the event. When a George Wallace or a Ross Barnett takes office, he is armed with judgments and arguments fashioned by a Bill Simmons or a Roy Harris, and he takes office because of the political climate such men create. When certain Southerners of scrupulous solemnity take the Senate floor to speak, they use arguments from the fact-and-idea mills of the Segregation Establishment.

The products of these factories are tonier now than they used to be, a fact which reflects the growing sophistication of even the no-compromisers. A treatise widely distributed after the Supreme Court's 1954 school-desegregation decision likened Negroes to lizards. Today, although a Leander Perez may explode with wild ferocity, the greater demand among the dedicated segregationists is for material about the fall of

Egyptian civilization, constitutionalism, judicial tyranny, and the consistency of segregation with Christianity.

These segregationists frequently cite what "history tells us" and "anthropology says." But they also sometimes reveal that their thoughts, like Senator Bilbo's, are derived largely from their own way of looking at Negro field hands and Negro cooks. Roy Harris, as a lawyer, has dealt with too many Negro "cuttin's and shootin's." Bill Simmons has seen Negroes shuffling like Africans. Leander Perez has observed that the Negro, after six years, cannot master his hay baler. These would seem to be the real stuffings of the segregationists' beliefs.

But now let the Segregation Establishment speak for itself.

"The Jews are leading the Negroes. They'll resent it and they'll say Perez is anti-Semitic. And when they say that, I say that they are unadulterated damn liars, because I do resent any goddamn Jew trying to destroy our country and our rights and that's what they are doing, and they are using the Negroes for it!" So says Leander H. Perez, Sr., a sturdy dynamite-stick of a man whose fuse burns low after an hour of quieter talk. He had risen now, square and spread-legged behind his desk, with an index finger pointing skyward. Perez is a man who comes to the point. That is one reason he is, at seventy-two, a multimillionaire, a political strongman, and Louisiana's leading segregationist.

"Well, you see, when people are involved in nationwide and worldwide propaganda and conspiracy, there's no question of principle or integrity left. They have an objective. They don't know where their orders come from. It's that unseen web."

Leander H. Perez, Sr. talks often about the conspiracy. "I am not obsessed with the Negro question," he continues in reasonable tones. "I say the turmoil is a flash in the pan, and the Negro question is not that important to the country. It's those who are making common cause with the conspiracy to destroy constitutional government in this country—and that includes the Kennedys, the Warrens, and their ilk. . . . The Negro is just used. No, this is part of the Communists' cold war. It's worldwide. You stir up the racial strife and turmoil and national disunity. It was the Stalin conspiracy to stir up revolution in the Black Belt in this country, among the Negroes and the sharecroppers. It was the Stalin plan then to recognize this Black Belt as an independent state, or nation, and back it up with aggressive military force. Failing in that, naturally, the Communists turned to infiltration. And my God! They have succeeded beyond their fondest dreams. And now the national government, the politicians on a national level, are carrying the ball for the Communists in this cold war."

As the president of the Plaquemines Parish Council, the governing body of an oil-rich Louisiana county, Judge Perez fights this national menace at every opportunity. In fact, he has been imaginatively conducting guerrilla warfare against the federal government, and sometimes the state government, throughout the four decades in which he has run this parish. He has become vastly wealthy, at times held sway over the Louisiana legislature without ever sitting in it, and gained what may be the nearest thing to absolute power in the United States. Perez is Louisiana's most combative segregationist: he has been excommunicated because he fought so bitterly the desegregation of Catholic schools.

He has helped establish private schools for pupils boycotting public and parochial schools, and he works frequently in the interests of the Citizens Councils. To one and all he is "Judge Perez," though he gave up his local judgeship almost forty years ago to become district attorney for Plaquemines and St. Bernard's Parish (his son took over the post three years ago) and from then on to attend to more important matters. His offices today occupy the eighteenth floor of the Commerce Building in New Orleans, where he practices law with his two sons.

To understand his views on racial matters, he says, you have to understand the conspiracy and how far it has progressed. Two men gave John F. Kennedy the Presidency, in his view: David Dubinsky and Walter Reuther. He deems both men to be leaders responsive to "the unseen web," and says they now run the country "through their stooges in high national office."

Is the United States government, then, to be considered under Communist control?

"Control and influence are two different things. You don't need control to influence the events in government. I say there is an unnatural influence, yes, over the course of our government in Washington. If only the Communist-Zionist web could be portrayed to the people of this country it would be the greatest accomplishment that could ever happen."

As an example of Communists in Washington, he cited a former high official who is Jewish.

Had it not been established, he was asked, that this official's name was confused with the name of a man who had once been on a Communist list?

"They can cover it up! Any damn way they want to!" he said.

Was he saying the two persons were the same?

"I don't say it's the same one, but you know damn well it is! I'm only showing you the influence that these organizations have, planting their stooges in key positions in this country."

Was there more than a coincidence that all the people he was naming were Jewish?

"I'll ask *you* about that," he said. "Why did Ben Franklin say that the American people would rue the day that they gave Jews full rights of citizenship in this country? The Jews had been scheming and plotting to destroy Christian government and Christian civilization."

Did Judge Perez think Negroes were inferior?

"Can there be any doubt about Negro inferiority to the white race when over the ages we cannot see results from the Negro's work in lifting himself to any stage of civilization or accomplishment? Yes, I think it's brain capacity. First, because I recall reading in the *Encyclopaedia Britannica,* one of the early editions, a British anthropologist had made a study of the Negro and he had written quite an extensive article on the formation of the Negro's head and cranium and brain capacity. He showed, after extensive study in this country among Negroes, that the Negro brain capacity is so limited that a Negro child at the age of about ten or eleven developed normally, but after that time in life his brain was stunted. Now, that is what I really meant. But I wouldn't pass judgment on that, except I do know from my experience with Negroes—and I've worked with a number of Negroes, employ them on my farm here—I find that in spite of the fact that they may have operated a hay baler for six years, the same hay baler, they make the same mistakes day after day. They have to be told what to do. . . .

"Why, *of course* it's inherent. I have heard over and over again this alibi that it's a product of civilization and the fact that they've been held down. That's all a myth. The Southern Negro has made more advancement than Negroes in their natural state anywhere in the world. Let's compare our Southern Negroes with the Congolese. While there's rape and assault among some of our Negroes over the country, certainly there's nothing to compare with the Negroes in their natural state.

"That business about the Negroes being held down. That's a game, you know, the Franz Boas theory, which has been taken up by the propagandists. They're trying to create an inferiority complex, or rather, a guilt complex, among white folks in this country. Yes, the white people are supposed to be responsible for all the Negro's shortcomings because he's been held down! Which, of course, is not true."

Does the Communist conspiracy have anything to do with the fact that most anthropologists reject assertions of Negro inferiority?

"There's no doubt about it," he said. "Of course. No doubt." He cited Gunnar Myrdal's sociological work with reference to the Supreme Court's 1954 school decision, and noted that "the Carnegie Corp. of Alger Hiss fame" had financed studies by Myrdal. [Hiss, until his trial, was on the Board of the Carnegie Foundation for International Peace.]

Hiss had not participated in Myrdal's famous work, had he?

"No, Hiss was not a part of that report. I said the *Carnegie Corp. of Alger Hiss fame.* I repeat, the *Carnegie Corp. of Alger Hiss fame.*"

Have the Negroes any aspirations of their own?

"The Negroes, of course, are largely emotional," he said quietly, his voice trailing off.

Largely what?

"EEE-MOtional! And UN-THINKing! And they are led and misled, handled through the churches, and the Negro preachers are paid off and bought! The Jews have been using the NAACP to their own purposes. Now this march on Washington, for instance. Do people stop to think what it cost? How many millions—two, three, five million dollars? Who put up that money? The labor bosses, like Walter Reuther! And tax-exempt corporations like the Ford Fund for the Republic and the others.

"I would say the Negroes themselves are satisfied with their lot in this country. They realize they're a whole lot better off than Negroes elsewhere in the world. The stir is caused by the conspiracy. It is not the desire of the Negroes."

Does he accept the theory that Negroes want their civil rights because they're after intermarriage?

"There's no doubt that is the ultimate objective, as W. E. B. DuBois said in a full-page advertisement in a Pittsburgh paper several years ago. He pointed out that that was the ultimate aim. You make a Negro believe he is equal to the white people and the first thing he wants is a white woman. And that's why there are so many criminal assaults and rapes. That's why it isn't safe for white women who are government employees in the Supreme Court building in the nation's capital to leave their offices and go into the streets alone."

Part of the same conspiracy?

"I wouldn't say that there is a drive to encourage Negroes to rape white women. Of course not! But I say it is the natural result of all this upheaval, all of this propaganda, all this project of so-called racial equality, all of this worldwide cold-war conspiracy to stir up racial strife and turmoil."

Does he foresee segregation in the United States a hundred years from now?

"If you mean that we shouldn't have segregation, that we should have all-out integration, that we should have social intercourse, that we should have intermarriage, that ultimately in five or ten generations we should be all one happy mongrelized family, then you are talking about the real Communist plan for America. Because nothing would more certainly destroy America and make it the overripe fruit to fall into the hands of Communist Russia than that. And no matter what Esquire, no matter what *Life* or *Time* or *Look,* or any other magazine, any other propagandists, may want to write on the subject, *that* is the ultimate Communist conspiracy against America. A mongrelized people so helpless that national defense and national security would be a forgotten thing!"

Is segregation, then, the chief safeguard against the Red takeover?

"From the way you ask that question, as if segregation were a dirty word—what do you mean by that? Haaaaaaaah! You know my view damn well. And there's no equivocation about my view. When people are talking hypocritically about civil rights, what are our civil rights? To live our own

life? To choose our own associates? To raise our children in an atmosphere of morality instead of immorality, with Negroes as immoral as they
are? What? Yes, they are inherently immoral! You know the Negroes.
Why, I have a Negro man comes here with a woman and says this is my
wife. But they *ain't married*. It's the way it has been as long as I've known
Negroes, yes. Most of the Negroes, generally, are illegitimates. Most of
them.

"Good-bye! That's all."

But he had an afterthought. "Now when Esquire writes the story, they
can take anything they want to out of context, and personally I just don't
give a damn. Because when we know we are right and when we follow the
rule of reason, we don't mind propaganda. I just don't give a damn, and
you can tell 'em that!"

"If we can keep the segregation fight going for a few years, things are
going to be different," says Roy Harris, of Augusta, Georgia. "When the
Negro invades the suburbs, where the privileged live, it will be all over.
White people are going to run for a while, but then they're going to stand
up and fight." A red headline over the tabloid newspaper on Harris' desk
shouted: "Kennedys Connive With The NAACP To Use U.S. Army To
Force Mixing." Harris, the roly-poly, sixty-eight-year-old lawyer who
edits this tabloid, was once Georgia's political kingmaker. Today his
strange little weekly arms militant segregationists throughout the South
with their hottest ammunition.

Among segregation leaders throughout the South, Roy Harris' *Augusta
Courier* is quoted about as often as Carleton Putnam's peculiar doctrine
on anthropology. Usually the *Courier*'s friends fail to give it credit in
citing its revelations, but when Governor George Wallace of Alabama
testified in Washington on July 15 that Communists control the civil-
rights movement, he displayed a picture and story from The *Augusta
Courier* to prove it. Harris, who started the four-page paper in 1947, "so I
could say what I damn well pleased," says the circulation is seven thousand or so. The masthead once listed the editor as "Old Man Everybody,"
but no editor is listed now, for readers know that Harris, the short, round
man who writes a front-page column, IS The *Augusta Courier*.

Some recent headlines were these: "King's Nonviolent Rioters Are
Trained Outsiders Brought To South"; "Communists Assisted In Organiz-
ing The NAACP In 1909 And Have Been Integrated With It Since That
Time"; "Abraham Lincoln Opposed Integration"; "U.S. Judges Who Play
Martinets Send Their Children To Segregated Schools"; "Ignorant Rich
White People Of North Give Money To Aid Integration"; "Kennedy Boys
Want Votes." As may be seen, the *Courier* views not only the contempo-
rary but also the historical scene, and this is consistent with Harris' idea

that the paper "does not so much influence as arm" segregationists in the South. Harris receives contributions from people all over the country, but carefully screens out the numerous anti-Semitic ones. He regularly clips several daily newspapers for reprints and currently is bearing down upon stories about racial strife in the North, which he takes to be proof that integration cannot work.

"I came up with early practical experience with the Negro people," he said. "I came up working with them on the farm, and usually, you know, back in those days the average white family out there lived among a nest of 'em. You might be the only white family on the farm, see? One white family and half-a-dozen colored neighbors. I came up playing with them. We played and worked together.

"Then, when I got to practicing law, I represented worlds of 'em. I waded through more Negro cuttin's and shootin's and Negro fights, I reckon, than anybody, in the first twenty years I practiced law. And I had an opportunity to know them firsthand. Segregation is the only way two separate, dissimilar races can live together without having riots, and fights, and killin's and cuttin's.

"Then, when you go back and study your history of Egypt, or India, or Portugal, or go down and study Puerto Rico and Cuba, you find that any time you mix the white and the Negro races you have destroyed the white race. Intermarriage will follow—not in mass, but eventually. I think the Negro has some qualities superior to the white man's. He has a certain richness of character in the way of patience, loyalty and the ability to enjoy living which the white man doesn't have. But the Negro never has developed any kind of a civilization of his own, even in Africa.

"When you throw the white and Negro races together, you subject a lot of good white people to a different moral standard that the Negro has. You subject him to being victimized by rapes and beatings, just like it's happened in every integrated community in the North, and at every integrated school they've had to have police. I don't think it's fair to the white people to subject them to this."

Is there an inherent difference between whites and Negroes?

"I think it's basic, and I don't think it'll ever change. I don't want to say that I'm better than any other person, don't care who he is, because I know a lot of people—and a lot of Negroes—that, when it comes down to it, I think are better than I am. But at the same time, that's not true of all of 'em. They've got better hearts in 'em, they do more things for people than I do. But you've got to figure there's a physical difference, and it's just there, and you can't eliminate it."

What is the solution, then?

"Of course old Abe Lincoln, Tom Jefferson and a bunch of them wanted to send them back to Africa. But I don't think you can do that because it could not be a force proposition. And I don't think the Negroes would want to go back."

What will the situation be like a hundred years from now?

"In the next hundred years, I believe, we are going to be resisting just like we are now. And I don't believe it's going to take much more mixing for the pendulum to swing back the other way.

"We're in this shape now because white people didn't stick together. Before long, the white people are going to elect them a candidate. I don't know that this will be the solution, but when it happens we can get together on one."

Would there be national segregation laws?

"If they will make segregation *possible* again, you don't care whether you have any segregation laws or not. In Georgia we've existed practically with no segregation laws. It's a question of who controls the politics."

As for Negro leaders' aspirations, he puts intermarriage high on the list: "The plan of amalgamation of the white and Negro races into a mulatto race, as proposed by the NAACP and CORE, by Martin Luther King's stomp-down, nonviolent type of violence, means the destruction of both races and the creation of a mongrel race of people of the same color."

Harris does not believe in any restrictions on Negro voting, but he thinks registration standards should be higher for all. "I think it ought to be based on education and morals. I don't think you can set up a board to determine a man's morals. I think you've got to take it from your criminal records."

Harris finds it difficult to label his political views in general: "I'm the most liberal person you ever saw to have the reputation of a mossback conservative. I've always led the damn fights for spending money and taxes and for the schools and everything. But by present-day standards, they don't count me a liberal a-tall. By modern-day standards you've got to be soft on Communists, and you've got to embrace the Negro's ambitions, which I can't do. I had always thought that I had been a liberal, but they've changed the meaning of the word."

Over the past thirty years Harris has managed more successful gubernatorial campaigns in Georgia than anyone has at any time, but he has skipped from one side to another in doing it. His biggest switch was from the camp of Eugene Talmadge to that of "liberal" Governor Ellis Arnall, whom he helped as campaign manager and speaker of the Georgia House of Representatives, and back to the Talmadge fold: after Gene Talmadge died in 1946, Harris helped elect his son, Herman, as governor. He has seldom been on the losing side, but it happened in 1962: Carl Sanders defeated Harris' choice, former Governor Marvin Griffin.

His present—and largest—contribution to the segregation fight remains the little paper with the red headlines and sometimes bizarre appraisals of current events. "We've got some good stuff coming up," he says, smiling. "In the next few issues we're going to just devote a little space to some of the troubles they're having up North—in Philadelphia, Chicago and other places. You know, there is little difference between the conditions in New York City today and in the jungles of the Congo."

"The Negro is a diseased animal and can never be our equal. If he was forced into captivity in coming to America, what's so bad about forcing him into captivity and carrying him back to his home?" Impatience shows in the sad eyes of Robert Shelton, the thirty-five-year-old Alabaman who is speaking; impatience, and hurt, almost as if he knows that whatever reasonable words he utters will later be twisted and hurled back in his face, only because he has spoken up for the white man. As Shelton addresses himself to race relations, so does the clattering copying machine outside his personal office, in "Suite 401, United Klans of America, Inc., Knights of the Ku Klux Klan, Imperial Wizard."

"If things are left as they are," Robert Shelton said, "there's no question but that we will have a revolution of the black man against the white man—unless some drastic steps are taken by conservative-thinking people to head off this Communist trend of using Negroes as tools, aggravating them into these dastardly acts. We are all the time reading in the medias that this is a nonviolent demonstration. But there has never been any demonstration carried out by them that has not had violence connected. They have that savage instinct."

Shelton, a tall, lean man with furrows in his forehead, leaned attentively over a desk flanked by big American and Confederate flags. A Bible on the desk was formally centered, opened to Romans ii. Near it was an ashtray made of small, white tile squares with a mosaic of four red "K's." He waited for questions, and when they came he answered seriously. An acquaintance of many years had said that only once had he seen Shelton laugh, and that was over a race joke; he did not smile before, during, or after this interview.

Did he really foresee a Negro revolutionary uprising?

"It's in the planning stage. It's not going to be too long, from activities coming out of Cuba being withheld from the general public. I can see, from conditions that exist today, the upsurging of the Negro element through guidance of the Communist conspiracy. And I don't mean Northerner against Southerner. This is definitely going to lead to a violent revolution between the black man and the white man. There will be no straddling of the fence. And definitely evidence has already shown—actions in Leopoldville, in the Congo—what will happen when you give these Negroes, these crazed savages, the power. So it is something that there will have to be a solution to—a drastic solution, immediately."

What is the drastic solution?

"F.D.R. gave us some of it. We have the fleet in mothballs that could be brought out for transportation back to Africa; and we have the storage of food in Alaska that runs into the billions and billions, which gives them the food; and we also have in Africa over $11,000,000,000 worth of storage homes that belong to the federal government. The only thing that Roosevelt didn't supply was a leader, and I think the Negroes could select their leader, who could send them back as colonies in Africa. Let them have their own government. Let them advance their own strategy, and have their *social equality*."

Is the Negro inferior to the white man?

"Absolutely! I think history has proven that. The white race of people have had a cultured civilization for over two thousand years. The Negro has only been out of the savage actions of the jungles of Africa approximately two hundred years. And the Negro had the same opportunity and resources in Africa to develop himself and his race of people as our forefathers had in America in carving this country from the dense jungles of America. I think we can all realize that the Negro does not have the intitiative, the basic intelligence, to be creative—does not have the ingenuity to devise, invent, create things that the white race does."

Is the inequality permanent?

"Absolutely! Because the climate certainly wouldn't have any bearing facts on what happened in Africa. When the white man went into Africa, they started advancing the Negro even in Africa. I think anatomy has shown that there is a difference in the structure of his jaws. I'm not qualified to speak on anatomy, but from the reports I have read from various groups there seems to be quite a difference."

How far would the Klan go in preventing this imminent overthrow which he foresees?

"We are a law-abiding organization, observing the duly constituted authority of law. And we are not going out provoking or asking trouble or trying to bring about violence. But we are certainly going to maintain self-preservation. The law of nature calls for self-preservation. I'm not going out looking for trouble, or violence, but if it comes to us we're going to protect ourselves."

What about the arrests of Klansmen in various criminal cases, including the one in Alabama in which several of them were sent to prison for castrating a Negro man?

"Once again you're talking about a group of people that are professing to be Klansmen. Now, any group of people can get up five, eight or ten members and profess to be Klansmen and yet not be. They are not Klansmen of this organization. Now, they might call themselves Klansmen and have their own little group. I don't recall that any member of this organization ever has been convicted of any crime they've been charged with. We have always taken steps against violence.

"And you might ask the question: Why, if you wanted to have an organization, why not pick another name besides the Ku Klux Klan? The Ku Klux Klan is the only organization that was organized, formulated and put into effect by Americans, inside American shorelines. So why should you throw away a heritage and a principle? What I'm referring to is a fraternal organization. My grandfather was a member. My father was a member. Because you have people that are associated through their families with the Klan associations, many people are sympathetic with the Klan whether or not they are in it."

Shelton is the leader of only one remnant of the Klan, probably the largest and at the moment the most industrious. But unity has been the most invisible part of the "invisible empire." Besides Shelton's United Klans, there are the Dixie Klans, Federated Klans, Original Klans, Associated Klans and many others. Shelton's office reflects the ambitiousness of his branch, which has shifted the principal Klan leadership from Georgia to Alabama. Shelton himself is the reason.

He makes his living as an air-conditioning salesman, but he goes to the Klan office in the yellow-brick Alston Building in Tuscaloosa, Alabama, almost every day he is in town, riding up in an elevator sometimes operated by a relaxed Negro man in a Klan-red polo shirt. Shelton grew up in Tuscaloosa, graduated from a nearby high school, and has lived in this little city all his life except for some Air Force service. His local fame grew when it was rumored during Governor John Patterson's administration that Shelton, having supported Patterson, had influence with the governor. Shelton denies this. But that brief prominence may have given him an advantage in the struggle for Klan leadership.

Now he is working hard to extend his "empire." His telephone (listed not under the K.K.K., but under the "Alabama Rescue Service") rang a number of times.

"The pendulum is swinging in our favor more and more every day," he said after answering one of the calls. "I think the state of Alabama and the governor is going to be a great part in writing history for this country. People are waking up all over the country."

"Yayss, Sir, if you think about the leaders among the Negro groups at this time you'll seldom ever find one that's not a mulatto," says Lester Maddox. His crinkled eyes have the look of friendly finality as he speaks over a cup of coffee, black, at The Pickrick in Atlanta. Black waiters in white coats tinkle glasses in the kitchen nearby and an old myna bird, black, occasionally greets a customer with a snipped-short "Hello, there!" Maddox's new Pontiac Grand Prix glistens in the sun outside. It, too, is black. But all the customers eating the well-advertised "skillet fried chicken" are and forever shall be white, if Maddox has anything to do with it. His restaurant is the militant-segregationists' banquet hall for convivial fellowship and rededication. And Maddox, forty-eight-year-old some-time candidate for high office, is both their leader and his own court jester.

Lester Maddox is a nondescript man whose coats always seem to flare up at the shoulders and the hips, as if concealing a kite frame. When he is excited, his face flushes, nervous energy exudes, and his tongue is faster. But basically he is not a volatile man. He would look at home behind the counter of a pharmacy (in which he once worked). His speech is somewhat high-pitched, lacking in Southern long-vowel, soft-R mellifluence.

After quitting high school in 1933, a year before finishing ("We didn't have shoes to wear to school, or food to eat at school times"), he went to work in a drugstore at $4 a week. Later he worked at a machine stamping out metal products for Atlantic Steel Company in Atlanta, where his father spent most of his working years as a roll turner. He became a foreman, but wanted his own business. In 1944 he and his wife opened a tiny restaurant-grocery combination, and three years later he bought a site on Hemphill Avenue and built The Pickrick. He will tell you, so rapidly his words flow together, that "pick means to fastidiously eat, and rick means to pile up, to heap, to amass, so we say Pickrick means you pick it out and we'll rick it up."

The restaurant has increased in floor space by seven times. It is a Western-style timber-and-old-brick building in a business area near Georgia Tech, and the food is low-priced. Everyone around Atlanta became aware of The Pickrick when Maddox began to write snappy, column-type advertisements for it in 1949. The ad still begins, as it did in the beginning, with "Pickrick Says," alongside a picture of Maddox. Blocks of lively text follow, divided by short, sharp headlines such as, "I Told You So," "Special to Christians," "Yes, Sir," "Thank God for Gov. Wallace," "Those Do-Gooders," "You Pinks and Punks," "I'm For," and "Sneak of the Year." The ad usually ends with what seems to be an almost irrelevant price list and plug for the restaurant ("Our Sunday Menu"), which may be followed by a social afterthought such as this recent one: "Dine Segregated At No Extra Charge."

Almost from the start, Maddox began to use his ad to get things off his chest. He regularly excoriates the Atlanta daily newspapers, which publish the ad— known to its readers as "Pickrick's Column"—every Saturday. When Maddox decided to run for mayor as a hard-line seg-regationist in 1957, veteran Mayor William B. Hartsfield, who had held the fort for two decades against all comers, beat him 2-1. In 1961 he was beaten again, 2-1, by Ivan Allen, Jr., the present mayor. Maddox has always had higher political prestige among his followers than these results might indicate, however, because he has claimed he received "the majority of the white votes," and "beat everybody but Martin Luther King."

When he was about to be interviewed for Esquire, Maddox remarked that the magazine was no friend of segregation, but he agreed to state some of his views. He was found in a cramped little office off the main restaurant floor. On one wall was a color print of Christ, and on another, fastened with tape and tacks, were letters, cartoons, and membership cards of segregationist organizations. A British .303-caliber rifle stood in a corner near the old-style iron safe ("just in case it's ever needed here," he said).

"I was just making a note from *Advertising Age*," he explained, scribbling over the one bare spot on a scratched wooden desk. "Some of the big companies have been giving in to CORE. We've contacted several hundred major companies on this, and some of our results have been favorable. One company had advertised it was sponsoring an integrated TV show, and they almost apologized for it after they heard from us."

He moved with quick motions, the light flashing now and then on rimless glasses that seem halfway down his face, under a long forehead. "Looka here at the mail," he said, indicating a stack by his hand and a three-foot cardboard box crammed with envelopes. "Did you see this?" He took from an envelope a folded copy of a cartoon, crudely drawn in contemporary bathhouse style, peppered with misspellings. The subject was the marriage of the University of Georgia's first Negro co-ed and a white student. "Look here Nigger," the caption started. "It just came in the mail," Maddox said, indicating little reaction. Then he reached into a pile of papers nearby and handed over another on the same subject, similarly drawn, similarly copied, but not folded. Where had it come from? He shrugged; replied noncommittally.

Walking out now to find a secluded table for talking, he spoke of The Pickrick's institutional role in the segregation fight. "A lot of students come in here to talk to us—from Yale and Harvard and other schools," he said. He pointed to a long bulletin board covered with newspaper clippings, handbills, and pictures. "Kan the Kennedy Klan," said a red-and-black sticker. "Five White Men Shot in Race Riots," a headline said. Nearby was a table filled with segregation literature for customers to take.

"Let's sit down here," Maddox said, indicating a small table in a side room. He explained, as his Negro "help" worked not far away, that he is a segregationist because it is Christian and American, and because he loves his people. "Throughout the Bible we are instructed about the purity of man, the purity of his soul, in all areas. . . ." He rose, found a paper someone had written on the subject, and cited such passages as Deuteronomy 22: 9-10, "Thou shalt not sow thy vineyard with divers seed. . . . Thou shalt not plow with an ox and an ass together"; and instructions given to Isaac not to seek a wife among the Canaanites. "I think it's against the will of God to mix our races, to amalgamate our races."

Maddox's view of the underlying economic aspects of the integration drive are somewhat unorthodox. "I think the major cause behind the move to integrate is not to help the Negro," he said. "It is to help the big financial people— the Carnegies and the Mellons and the Fords and the various big-money people. They're trying to indicate to Africa and other parts of the world that the United States has come to be a leader for doing something for the Negro. They're not really interested in the American Negro as much as they are in pleasing Africa in order to get their products into that area and to get the dollars."

In light of the current integration activity, where does he believe the American Negro will be a hundred years from now?

"With the present no-win policy of our government, and our forcing our people to bow down to dictatorial government, I can't see how we can last a hundred years. I'd be very much surprised if we survive through two more presidential elections as the United States government. I think we'll have a Communist government, unless the people awaken."

What presidential candidate can prevent this debacle?

"None of them at this time would satisfy me," he said. "Goldwater doesn't suit me, but he'd do a much better job. He thinks the American businessman ought to run his business . . . and that the local communities should work out their own racial problems."

Maddox recently formed an organization seeking a solution locally. It is called the People's Association for Selective Shopping (PASS), and the purpose is to boycott businesses that have desegregated or otherwise favored "racial amalgamation." PASS seems to have gotten up no steam. There is much literature in The Pickrick about its prospects. Walking now to the table, Maddox displayed handbills for PASS. Suddenly he was caught up in a group of happy customers on their way in and out. "Here are some friends from Perry and West Point, Georgia," one of them said. Maddox beamed and shook hands; now that the interview was over and philosophical questions were put aside, he looked happy.

"I didn't use the word 'inferiority.' I think you did," said William J. Simmons, uneasily recrossing his long, black-stocking-clad legs. Simmons' appearance and demeanor suggest that he might have been a colonel of the Coldstream Guards if he had not been born in Utica, Mississippi. "The reason I want to be rather precise is that this whole area is loaded with emotional, fuzzy thinking, and the scare words such as 'inferiority' and 'racist' make people's corpuscles rather than their brain cells hop." Then the fastidious forty-seven-year-old administrator of the Citizens Councils of America (home office: Jackson, Mississippi) began to quote directly from his favored scientific authorities. Bill Simmons does not like to sound presumptuous about scientific matters.

"Rather than use a word such as 'inferiority,' " William J. Simmons said, "let me put it in this sense: In terms of the ability to adapt to Western civilization, the colored has shown himself to be less capable than the white. It is a white civilization. In terms of adaptability to the way of life in Africa, the colored is probably superior to the white."

Does he see no difference in the quality of civilization on the two continents?

"I certainly do," he said. But he seemed reluctant to make the judgment his allies frequently make about Negro inferiority. He fenced with the question a bit more, and then said: "I don't see how any white person in the United States could watch newsreel pictures of chanting, clapping colored people shuffling their feet just exactly as they do in Africa and still think that there is not a difference in behavior, a difference in personality, that is *extreme*. I'm unconvinced that the Northern white people are ready to incorporate that sort of thing into their rather antiseptic lives."

Bill Simmons, a banker's son, studied at the Institut de Touraine in France after graduation from Mississippi College. During World War II he served first with the British and then with the U.S. Navy. Afterward, he was assistant treasurer and chief accountant for a natural-gas company before going on to become full-time administrator of the Citizens Councils, which he runs from third-floor offices in the Plaza Building, across the street from the governor's mansion in Jackson, Mississippi. He is not specific about his salary ("very modest"), the Councils' budget (about $200,000 on the state level alone last year and more than that this year, he said) or the Councils' membership (90,000 in Mississippi, he suggested as a guess; others think much less than that). Though he denies having any great influence with Governor Ross Barnett, he is often with the governor on important occasions and has been regarded as a major adviser.

For this interview, he temporarily abandoned a seclusion devoted to writing a book about the integration showdown at the University of Mississippi.

"We in the South now are fighting for survival," he said. "Any talk about white supremacy is like arguing in nineteenth-century terms. What we are concerned about is black supremacy, and we certainly are not in favor of that."

The threat to the South, in Simmons' view, cannot be explained entirely with any simple allusion to a Communist conspiracy or Northern politicians' desire for Negro votes. "I attribute it to a wave of equalitarian philosophy that started in the early part of the twentieth century, primarily with the progressive educationists, such as John Dewey. In time it seemed to permeate the educational field. Dewey and others—Franz Boas among the anthropologists—turned out a number of disciples at Columbia who went into the teaching profession, and this influence grew to a remarkable degree. I think it resulted directly in the Supreme Court school-integration decision. And I think that, although it's predominant now, there's beginning to be a reaction. I think it's going to be reversed."

"Equalitarian" pressures are one thing, however, and segregation pressures are another: "I don't think faculties or administrations are free or ought to be free from community pressures anywhere. I think they ought to be responsive to the views of their community, and there is a very great gap between the views of a certain element of professors at Ole Miss and the views of the majority of Mississippians." He says he thinks these professors should leave.

Simmons believes that the truth of his position may emerge in a case now pending in court. A federal judge in a Brunswick, Georgia, case recently ruled that integration would have a "demoralizing and disorganizing" effect on schools in Brunswick, and the key point in the case was white parents' contention that integration would be damaging psychologically to their children. Allegations were made arguing Negroes' genetic inferiority. "In the Supreme Court 1954 decision," Simmons said, "there was no evidence of a genetic basis. . . . In the new case, interveners did present genetic evidence of racial difference." He says he thinks this case could in effect reverse the 1954 decision. The case, which is being cited by many segregation leaders, including Governor Wallace in his recent defiance of the courts, has not yet made its way through all appellate channels. In the meantime, it is being used to suggest that the doctrine of Negro inferiority has become intellectually respectable.

Simmons says he has read recently that a number of Negro national leaders have identified the American Negro's rights struggle with the aspirations of Africans. "This in effect means that the mass Negro movements have taken their allegiance primarily to Africa—not the United States—to a foreign power or powers. We should remember that the movement for African nationalism has meant that the white man in Africa, in the countries where the blacks have taken over, has been completely deprived of his civil rights, including even the right of life. He's driven into the sea.

"This is the sort of thing to which the leaders of the NAACP, CORE and the other organizations creating this revolution have gravitated. This raises the question that the United States itself is in danger of non-white domination. The non-whites' most potent ally is the liberal-controlled United States government that exists today. The thing that makes this whole thing dangerous is the force and power the government has put behind it. With that, you have the colored masses that exist outside the country. You know the liberals constantly remind us that we must integrate to please the three-fourths of the world which is non-white. This allies the Negroes in the United States with the three-fourths of the non-white world. I'd say the Southern white Protestant is coming rapidly to the position where he can sympathize with the position of the Jews in Nazi Germany."

What is the answer in the light of this startling threat to white people, so largely ignored across the nation?

"Strong organization," he said, with one of the first goals being defeat of "the Kennedys" in 1964. He favors unpledged electors and sometimes is credited with Mississippi's strategy to bring more states behind this plan. The idea is to withhold enough electoral votes from the two major parties to force the election into the House of Representatives, where the South ostensibly would have more bargaining power.

The eventual solution, and "the only real solution," he says, "is a return of Negroes to Africa."

There is no chance now for sending Negroes to Africa, he conceded. "Obviously the weight of opinion is the other way. But these things can change. . . . Generally it has been considered that this ought to be done on a voluntary basis. I think it ought to be voluntary. If this were advanced as a real solution, if real pride of race were instilled in the Negro people, a sense of their own destiny, free of competition and involvement with the white man, I think it's entirely possible that a movement could be started that would begin to sweep them."

Might the Citizens Councils of America undertake this project?

"That I don't know. It hasn't been seriously considered because obviously under present circumstances we think about more immediate problems," he said.

To Simmons, the Citizens Councils are fighting an uphill battle to preserve segregation and constitutional government, defending the views of millions of white Southerners. "I'm a segregationist," he said, "because I believe it's right."

[January, 1964]

The Brilliancy of Black

by Bernard Weinraub

In the late Sixties, new voices began to be heard in the civil rights movement. The inspirational sermonlike speeches of Martin Luther King that asked blacks and whites alike to join forces against racism began to give way to the cries of younger activists intent on building a black-power base. In January 1967, Bernard Weinraub interviewed Stokely Carmichael, leader of the Student Nonviolent Coordinating Committee, who coined the term "Black Power."

Jesus Christ, His arms outstretched and pleading, is painted in lush blues and pinks in the lobby. Inside the church, the aisles are filling with teen-agers, curiously quiet and solemn, who grip programs ("Harlem Youth Unlimited presents . . . 'The Role of Negro Youth in Shaping Their Destinies' "). Stepping through the crowd a slight woman with a lost, desperate smile hands out a "Come Ye Disconsolate" leaflet and cries out that Brothers and Sisters you are all invited to view the Southern Baptist Stars on their twenty-second anniversary at Mount Moriah Baptist Church.

Outside, bare-chested little boys in sneakers watch the white television men set up their cameras. A white cop, a pudgy man with roly-poly fingers and a hard, blue-eyed Irish face, removes a handkerchief from his rear pocket, scrubs off his forehead sweat and gazes up, up, up at the church—a De Mille Corinthian setting that was once a movie threatre, the Alhambra. The Black Muslims are distributing *Muhammad Speaks,* and the television men are nervous and the teen-agers keep surging into the sweltering lobby past the mural of Jesus. It is dusk on Seventh Avenue and 116th Street in Harlem and it is warm and they are waiting for Stokely Carmichael.

Three months earlier, Stokely had taken over the Student Nonviolent Coordinating Committee and had coined those two words "Black Power" that aroused all the white folks and dismayed some of the powerful black folks. He had been on *Meet The Press* television and on the front page of The New York *Times* and had visited Mississippi and Washington, D.C. and Boston and now, finally, he was in Harlem.

The kids waited. They were fifteen, sixteen and seventeen, the boys in pressed olive-drab suits and seersucker jackets, the girls in sandals, dangling earrings, A-line skirts, and kerchiefs, quite chic, on their African cropped hair. They carried paperbacks and chatted quietly. For the past few months they had been in the Haryou-Act anti-poverty program where they worked with the community, and baby-sat for working mothers, and were taught what to wear when they took the A train downtown to apply for a job on Fifth Avenue. And they had read—and discussed—James Baldwin and Chester Himes and explored in heated talks The Role of Negro Youth and The Problems of Negro Youth and What's Ahead for Negro Youth. And now Stokely, who used to play stickball on 137th Street, comes onstage with a half-dozen other speakers and the curious tenseness among the teen-agers bursts. They break into wild applause.

Stokely is surrounded by friends. "Hey, baby, how ya' doin'?" he cries. . . . "Hey Thomas, why the hell aren't you back in Alabama doin' some work. . . . Hey, boy, you lookin' *good*." Stokely looks good too. He wears black Italian boots, a tight blue suit, white shirt, striped tie, a name chain on his wrist. He is six-feet-one and has the build of a basketball guard: a solid chest, slender waist, powerful legs. His smile dazzles—an open, unguarded, innocent smile.

The first speaker is seventeen-year-old Clarissa Williams, a striking girl in a loose green dress. She has a gentle voice: "*Newsweek* and *Life* have conducted their own surveys of black people. Well, baby, no one has to tell us what the black community is like because we know it, we live it. We intend to be the generation which will make black youth to be unlimited. We intend to be the generation that says, Friends, we do not have a dream, we do *not* have a dream, we have a plan. So, TV men, do not be prepared to record our actions indoors, but be prepared to record our actions *on the streets*. . . ." The audience, and Stokely, applaud and cry, "Hit 'em hard, sister."

Clarissa hits them harder and by the time she winds up her tough little speech the audience is electric. And then Stokely rises. His style dazzles. He shakes his head as he begins speaking and his body appears to tremble. His voice, at least in the North, is lilting and Jamaican. His hands move effortlessly. His tone—and the audience loves it—is cool and very hip. No Martin Luther King We Shall Overcome oratory. No preacher harangue. No screaming. He speaks one tone above a whisper, but a very taut, suppressed whisper. His speech—he has made it dozens of times before—varies with the audience, the area, the news that day, his mood. Stokely's words flow musically and build and Stokely pounds into the microphone and stops and the music starts again. The audience is rapt.

"Brothers and Sisters, we have been living with The Man too long. Brothers and Sisters, we have been *in a bag* too long. *We have got to move to a position where we will be proud, be proud of our blackness.* From here on in we've got to stick together, Brothers and Sisters, we've got to join together and move to a new spirit and make of our community a community of love . . . LOVE. There's no time for shuckin' and jivin'. We've got to move fast and we've got to come together and we've got . . . we've got to realize . . . that this country was conceived in racism and dedicated to racism. And understand that we've got to move . . . WE HAVE GOT TO MOVE. . . . We've got to build to a position so that when L.B.J. says, 'Come heah, boy, I'm gonna send you to Veetnam,' we will say, 'Hell, no.' " ("Preach, boy, preach. . . . Tell 'em, Stokely. . . .")

"Brothers and Sisters, a hell of a lot of us are gonna be shot and it ain't just gonna be in South Vietnam. We've got to move to a position *in this country* where we're not afraid to say that any man who has been selling us rotten meat for high prices should have had his store bombed fifteen years ago. We have got to move to a position where we will control our *own* destiny. We have got to move to a position where we will have black people represent *us* to achieve *our* needs. This country don't run on love, Brothers, it's run on power and we ain't got none. Brothers and Sisters, don't let them separate you from other black people. Don't ever in your life apologize for your black brothers. Don't be ashamed of your culture because if you don't have culture, that means you don't exist and, Brothers and Sisters, we do exist. Don't ever, don't ever, don't *ever* be ashamed of being black because you . . . you are black, little girl with your nappy hair and your broad lips, and *you are beautiful*. Brothers and Sisters, I know this theatre we're in—it used to be the Alhambra. Well I used to come here on Saturday afternoon when I was a little boy and we used to see Tarzan here and all of us would yell like crazy when Tarzan beat up our black brothers. Well, you know Tarzan is on television now and from here on in I'm rooting for that black man to beat the hell out of Tarzan. . . ."

The audience roars and is on its feet and Stokely grins and waves. The audience keeps applauding. . . .

Stokely is in the East to build up support, to meet with S.N.C.C. workers in New York, Newark, Boston and Philadelphia. He will make speeches and hold private meetings and endure just a few interviews (he turns down many of them now because of "distortions"). At twenty-five, the most charismatic figure in the Negro movement, Stokely Carmichael rushes from ghetto to ghetto with the drive of a political candidate one week before Election Day. He sleeps just a few hours a night. He eats on the run and drinks milk to keep up his energy. In Mississippi and Alabama, during those five summers of unbearable heat, of prison, of beatings, of death threats, of rifle shots fired at him through car windows, Stokely smoked three packs of cigarettes a day. He doesn't smoke now and doesn't drink.

His base now—and S.N.C.C.'s headquarters—is in Atlanta and his itinerary in other cities is set up by the local S.N.C.C. office, mostly by twenty- and twenty-one-year-old Negroes whom Stokely led in the South. There are, inevitably, the fund-raising parties—S.N.C.C.'s funds have dropped—but mostly just meetings and speeches.

He spends the next day in Newark, a dismal, grey city which has more Negroes than whites. The highlight of the visit is a speech that evening at the anti-poverty board on Springfield Avenue, in the heart of the ghetto, and then a cocktail party at ten-fifteen across town. The anti-poverty board is packed with an older audience than in Harlem. There are mothers with children on their laps and grandmothers with grandchildren on their bosoms; old men in overalls, janitors, civil-service workers, LeRoi Jones, high-school students, tough-looking nineteen-year-olds leaning against the green stucco walls, and several white poverty workers.

Stokely instinctively knows the audience. He stares quickly across the room and then scribbles down notes on the back of an envelope. He rises to warm applause. He smiles.

"Is it okay if ah take off mah jacket?" he says in a too-Southern drawl.

The speech goes well. Stokely begins by warming up the elderly women in the audience and ends with a cry to the students. The themes are the same. "You gotta understand about white power. It's white power that brought us here in chains, it's white power that kept us here in chains and it's white power that wants to keep us here in chains. . . . What they've been able to do is make us ashamed of being black . . . ashamed. I used to come home from school and say, 'Hey, Momma.' And she used to say, 'Sssshh, you know how loud we are.' I wouldn't go outside eating watermelon, no sir. They say we're lazy, so we work from sunup to sundown to prove that we're not lazy. We are tired of working for them, of being the maids of the liberal white folks who consider us part of their families. . . . My mother was a maid for a lady in Long Island and this lady wanted me to go to college and she told my mother, 'Your boy is a bright colored boy and we want to help send him to college.' Well, I hated that woman. She gave my mother $30 a week and all the old clothes her kids didn't want. Well, I didn't want her old clothes. I didn't want her to help send me to college. I wanted my Momma." ("Tell it, Stokely. . . .")

"There is a system in this country that locks black people in, but lets one or two get out every year. And they all say, 'Well, look at that one or two. He's helping his race.' Well, Ralph Bunche hasn't done a damn thing for me. If he's helping his race, then he should come *home*. Brothers and

Sisters, there's nothing wrong about being all white or all black. It's only when you use one to exploit the other—and we have been exploited. You gotta understand what they do. They say, 'Let's integrate.' Well integration means going to a white school because that school is good and the black school is bad. It means moving from a black neighborhood to a white neighborhood because one neighborhood, they tell you, is bad and the other is good. Well, if integration means moving to something white, moving to something good, then integration is just a cover for white supremacy. . . .

"Brothers and Sisters, we have to view ourselves as a community and not a ghetto and that's the only way to make it. The political control of every ghetto is outside the ghetto. We want political control to be *inside* the ghetto. Like the workers in the Thirties, like the Irish in Boston, we demand the right to organize the way we want to organize. Black power is the demand to organize around the question of blackness. We are oppressed for only one reason: because we are black. We must organize. Brothers and Sisters, the only way they'll stop me from organizing is if they kill me or put me in jail. And once they put me in jail I'll organize my brothers in prison. *Organize!*"

The back of Stokely's white shirt is drenched with sweat. As soon as he finishes the speech, the crowd rises and surrounds him and shakes his hand and Stokely seeks out the old ladies who cry, "My, my, *my,* you are somethin' " and gives the younger kids that special handshake reserved only for a black brother or sister—a handshake in which he clasps a hand with his right hand and places his left hand over the linked hands. (When a white man shakes his hand, the smile is guarded, the handclasp unsure, the left hand remains limp.)

Thirty minutes later the cocktail party on Porter Avenue awaits Stokely, who has stopped off in several Negro bars—not to drink, but to meet and talk with some of the customers. The party is given by a short, burly chemist and his wife in the yard in back of their twelve-room stucco house. At least forty people have paid $5 to see Stokely, with about a half-dozen S.N.C.C. workers admitted free. Weak Martinis and Whiskey Sours are ladled out and, curiously, the middle-aged white and Negro couples stand and drink together near the small swimming pool in the center of the yard. The younger white kids stand alone. The young Negroes stand beneath the Rose of Sharon, uncomfortable, hostile, waiting for Stokely.

He arrives late and in a bitter mood. In the car coming to the party Stokely has been told that David Frost, a candidate running in the upcoming Democratic Senatorial primary on an anti-Vietnam ticket, will also speak at the party. Stokely immediately feels that his name is being used to attract people for a political candidate, a *white* political candidate. The money isn't even going to S.N.C.C., as he had been told in New York, but to a local liberal group. Stokely is furious. He walks to the edge of the backyard and has a five-minute talk with Bob Fullilove, the local S.N.C.C. leader. Across the lawn, the young Negroes glower. . . . This is a real put-down, says one girl who is attending Rutgers Law School. Why the hell are they holding this in the backyard? Can't they hold it inside as if it were a regular, *formal* cocktail party? These people are not my kind of people . . . I don't like this scene, man. . . . This is bad news. . . .

Stokely and Fullilove end their talk and Stokely walks beneath the Rose of Sharon with the woman who accompanied him to the party, a six-foot-tall, very cool, very black-skinned woman with piled-high Nefertiti hair. She wears a tight white dress and is, she knows and Stokely knows and the entire party knows, the most stunning woman there. Stokely sips a Coke and the girl glowers at the crowd, which tries very hard to be casual, and not stare at her. A white man walks over, smiling, gripping his Martini.

"I just want to tell you, Mr. Carmichael, I saw you on TV and I really agreed with you on, uh, Vietnam and—"

Stokely cuts him off. "Thank you." Stokely gives him the white man's handshake.

"Attention, attention," cries the hostess, a short chubby woman in a knit dress. "Our guests are all here and our program is beginning."

The young Negroes appear startled. "What program?" Stokely frowns.

"I just want to say a few words," the woman goes on. "We have always been an integrated community. . . ." The Negroes begin shifting uncomfortably. "And we've never cared at all here about money or status, whatever that means."

"Shit," says Stokely in a loud whisper. "She don't know about status? Look at that swimming pool."

As soon as Frost begins speaking, Stokely leaves the backyard and walks toward the front of the house with his date. He leans against an elm, his left hand gentle on the young woman's shoulder. They chat in a whisper. A Negro girl, slightly drunk, and a white man come out of the house and Stokely glares at the girl. She walks over. "I like what you said about being proud of our blackness," she says.

"That means everyone," says Stokely in an angry whisper.

"Let's get out of here," says Stokely's date.

The girl looks at the white man and says, "Be proud of my blackness, my black womanness." She starts laughing and they walk away to a car.

Stokely watches them drive off.

"Let's leave," says Stokely's date.

They return to the backyard and within minutes Stokely—who had been scheduled to speak—and most of the young Negroes are gone; the whites and middle-aged Negroes are left alone.

Stokely is scheduled to take an eight o'clock flight the next morning to

Glens Falls, New York, and then be driven to Benson, Vermont, for a speech at a camp—he's not quite sure what type of camp or who will be there. At two minutes after eight Stokely's cab pulls up to the Mohawk Airlines terminal at LaGuardia Airport and Stokely leaps out and runs toward the ticket desk.

"I'm sorry," the ticket agent behind the desk says with a smile. "The flight just left."

"Oh no, oh no, oh *no*." Stokely pounds his fist on the desk.

"There *is* a flight leaving from Kennedy at eight-forty-five with a stop-off at Albany. And there's another at ten-thirty." The ticket agent smiles again.

Stokely walks away and shakes his head. "I took a cab from the Bronx [his mother's house]. It should have taken twenty minutes to get here. I kept saying, 'Use the bridge, use the bridge, man.' But that son of a bitch kept saying that Bruckner Boulevard was faster. Faster! It took an hour. Oh . . . oh that son of a bitch."

Stokely wears dark glasses, a black shirt with small-flowered print, dungarees and black shoes. He hails a cab for Kennedy Airport and once the cab starts Stokely lifts up the glasses and rubs his eyes—he had gone to bed at five that morning.

"They always do that in Atlanta," he says. "They always give us a hard time with flights down there."

He shakes his head again. The cab glides out of LaGuardia toward the Van Wyck Expressway. The traffic toward Manhattan is heavy; toward Kennedy Airport there are few cars. When Stokely is in New York, he generally spends the night in his mother's South Bronx home (the only Negro family on the block). He had not seen her on this trip, though, since she is working as a maid on a maritime line.

"She's a hard worker and a sharp gal," says Stokely, staring at the cars crawling toward New York. He turns. "She knew, she knows, that if you want to make it you got to hustle, and she hustled from the word go. She took no shit from no one. I got that from my mother. She used to tell me, 'You take nothing from no one, no matter who they are.' She knows the realities of life and she demanded, made sure, that I knew them too."

He smiles. "My old man was just the opposite." Stokely shakes his head and sighs. "He believed genuinely in the great American dream. And because he believed in it he was just squashed. Squashed! He worked himself to death in this country and he died the same way he started: poor and black."

"We came here in '52 from Port-of-Spain. That was a place that was mostly black. It was run by black people and everyone—the cops, the teachers, the civil servants—was black. We came here thinking that this was the promised land. Ha. We went up to the Bronx—I was eleven years old—and I saw this big apartment house we were going to and I said, 'Wow, Daddy, you own that whole thing?' And then eight of us climbed up to a three-room apartment."

"My old man . . ." Stokely takes off his glasses . . . "my old man would Tom. He was such a good old Joe, but he would *Tom*. And he was a very religious cat too— he was head deacon of the church and he was so honest, so very, very honest. He never realized people lied or cheated or were bad. He couldn't conceive of it. He just prayed and worked. Man, did he work. He worked as a cabdriver at night and went to school to study electricity and during the day he worked as a carpenter. He just thought that if you worked hard and prayed hard this country would take care of you. Well, I remember he tried to get into the carpenter's union—and this is a very racist thing. And the only way for him to get into the union was to bribe the business representative. Well, he would have none of that. So one day when my father is out, my mother calls up the business representative and tells him to come to the house and she gives him $50 and a bottle of perfume and my father gets into the union. And when my father comes home and finds out that he's in the union he says, 'You see. You work hard and pray hard and this country takes care.' And my mother and I . . . laughed. Wow. My old man was like the Man with the Hoe. He just felt that there were millions to be made in this country and he died at forty-two—just a poor black man."

The cab pulls up at the Eastern Airlines terminal in Kennedy Airport. Stokely walks in and within seconds a porter walks up and smiles broadly. "I usually hang out with the porters at the airports," he says, walking quickly through the terminal. "A lot of times I don't have money and they just pass the hat. They're good people. In Memphis last week they bought me a steak dinner."

He walks to Gate 2 where a Mohawk flight is taking off at eight-forty-five. He waits ten minutes on standby but the flight is filled. He trudges back to the ticket desk and makes a reservation for the ten-thirty flight and then phones S.N.C.C. to tell them to notify the camp. By now Stokely is hungry and he walks into the cocktail lounge and restaurant in the heart of the terminal. The alcoholics, the hangers-on, the bored travelers, the women catching the nine o'clock flight to Mexico City line the bar, sipping Bloody Marys and beer and Scotch, straight. A waiter hustles over and says, no, the restaurant is not open at this hour, but there's another restaurant at the end of the corridor. A woman at the bar, blonde, tall, tanned, in her late forties, carrying a large white pillbox, turns and stares through dark glasses at Stokely—this hulking, dungareed figure in dark glasses too. Their eyes meet. The woman smiles, just slightly, and Stokely stares at her for a moment and then turns away and walks out.

"Man, this place says something. You can get a drink at nine o'clock, but you can't get food."

At a table in the restaurant Stokely calls the waitress "M'am" and orders orange juice, bacon and eggs, English muffins and two glasses of milk.

"I used to drink," he says with a smile. "I used to like wine. I used to know a hell of a lot of guys who drank wine all day."

The waitress brings his orange juice and he sips it. "In Harlem I used to know a lot of guys like that. I used to know a lot of guys who were addicts and they were some beautiful cats. I'm not kidding. They had this ability, this profound ability to understand life."

While Stokely's father struggled and his mother worked as a maid to help support the family—Stokely has four sisters—he often spent days and weeks with his aunts on Lenox Avenue and 142nd Street in Harlem. "I like Harlem," says Stokely. "It's a very exciting place. It represents life, real life. On one block you have a church and right next door is a bar and they're both packed. On Saturday night people are always in constant motion. You get all of life's contradictions right there in one community: all the wild violence and all the love can be found in Harlem. You get the smells of human sweat and all sorts of bright colors and bright clothes and people in motion. You get preachers on one side of a street and national-ists on the other."

The waitress brings the rest of the order.

Stokely Carmichael grew up in the Bronx and Harlem, a bright, wild, aggressive boy. He attended P.S. 39, P.S. 34, and P.S. 83 and was involved, almost as soon as the family moved to New York, in fistfights and gang intrigues. In the Bronx, he was the only Negro member of the Morris Park Avenue Dukes and was, he admits, a specialist in stealing hubcaps and car radios.

In 1956 quite suddenly Stokely broke with the past. He was admitted to the Bronx High School of Science, a school for some of the brightest children in New York. "My freshman year I wanted to leave," Stokely recalls. "I couldn't intellectually compete with those cats. They were doctors' sons and lawyers' sons and read everything from Einstein to *The Grapes of Wrath*. The only book I knew was *Huckleberry Finn*. It was clear to me I couldn't compete. My mother wouldn't accept it though. She wanted me to go to Science and she would have it no other way. No questions asked. 'Remember one thing,' she would say, 'they're white, they'll make it. You won't unless you're on the top.' "

Stokely began reading—Marx, Darwin, Camus, anything he was given. "I began to read as quickly as I could; anything that anybody mentioned. It was naïve at the time, but it was sincere." For the first time, his friends were upper middle-class whites, wealthy kids who would go on to Harvard, Columbia, Brandeis. He began going out with white girls and making the Greenwich Village scene. He was invited to parties on Park Avenue.

Even as he persisted in friendships with white men and women, however, Stokely realized that the white and black worlds he knew were not linking; in fact they were splitting, irrevocably, apart. "I learned at Science that white people, liberal white people, could be intellectually committed but emotionally racist. They couldn't see *through*. I was everybody's best friend. They would say to me, 'Oh, you're so different.' And they didn't know any other black people. What they meant was I didn't meet their image of black people. And their image, their responses, are governed by the thought that Negroes *are* inferior. I was an exception. I was the accepted Negro. But other Negroes weren't like me. They were bums, lazy, unambitious, inhuman, and that attitude was extended to me. They would say to me, 'Oh, you dance so well,' when I couldn't dance so well. Or they would say to me, 'Oh, you're so sensitive.' Well the only thing I was sensitive to was the fact that they all had maids and they saw no inconsistency between being my friend and exploiting a black maid—paying her $30 a week while they went off and made a damned good living. I went to parties on Park Avenue and they called their maids by their first name and the maids were smiling and serving and I knew full well what was going on in their minds and I knew they didn't want to take all that shit. All these kids—these filthy rich kids—they all had maids and my mother was a maid."

When Stokely was a high-school senior, he began reading about the first sit-ins in the South. His first reaction was negative. "What I said was, 'Niggers always looking to get themselves in the paper, no matter how they did it.' My opinion was that they didn't know what they were doing."

Within months, though, he met several students involved in the sit-ins. As the civil-rights movement spread quickly across the South, Stokely's commitment—and fascination—grew. First, he picketed Woolworth's in New York and then sat-in in Virginia and North Carolina. He turned down scholarships to several white schools and enrolled at Howard University, mostly because he could keep working in the movement while at a Negro school. At Howard, he met other civil-rights activists and immediately engaged in sit-ins and the early freedom rides through Mississippi, Georgia and Alabama. The first ride and the first arrest was in Jackson, Mississippi in 1961. . . .

By now Stokely had finished breakfast at the airport and walked to Gate 2 to board the plane. Almost as soon as he took his seat he began shivering—he is always cold—and he grabbed a blanket off the rack. The plane started and Stokely peered through the window at the rows of A-frame houses below, the cars, the Manhattan skyline. "I went down South when I was nineteen. I was a kid who took nothing from no one.

And, man, I took it." He smiled. "In Mississippi, the beatings are by the cops, not by mobs. The mobs, they throw wild punches and if you're cool you can miss them. But the cops are out to get your ass and you get three cops in a back room who are out to get your ass and. . . ." He shook his head. "In Jackson, before they put me in jail, the cops rode me up and down in an elevator; they kept kicking and using billy clubs and pressing the buttons using their fist. I wanted . . . I just wanted to get my hands on one of them. But like you had to cover your head and . . . and . . . you keep thinking why don't you leave me alone. Why don't you beat your wives instead and just leave me alone?"

Stokely then spent time in jail. "Fifty-three days. Oh, lord, fifty-three days in a six-by-nine cell. Twice a week to shower. No books, nothing to do. They would isolate us. Maximum security. And those guards were out of sight. They did not play, *they did not play*. The sheriff acted like he was scared of black folks and he came up with some beautiful things. One night he opened up all the windows, put on ten big fans and an air conditioner and dropped the temperature to 38 degrees. All we had on was T-shirts and shorts. And it was so cold, so *cold*, all you could do was walk around for two nights and three days, your teeth chattering, going out of your mind, and it getting so cold that when you touch the bedspring you feel your skin is gonna come right off.

"I don't go along with this garbage that you can't hate, you gotta love. I don't go along with that at all. Man you *can*, you *do* hate. You don't forget that Mississippi experience. You don't get arrested twenty-seven times. You don't smile at that and say love thy white brother. You don't forget those beatings and, man, they were rough. Those mothers were out to get revenge. You don't forget. You don't forget those funerals. I knew Medgar Evers, I knew Willie Moore, I knew Mickey Schwerner, I knew Jonathan Daniels, I met Mrs. Liuzzo just before she was killed. You don't forget those funerals."

The worst experience was what Stokely calls a two-day nervous break-down just before the Selma-to-Montgomery march. "I was in the Ben Moore Hotel in Montgomery, getting ready to go downstairs, when they locked the doors. I couldn't get out. And downstairs were the marchers, and the cops began beating and using hoses. I couldn't stand it. I was by my window and I looked down and saw the cops beating and I couldn't get out. I was completely helpless. There was no release. I kept watching and then I began screaming and I didn't stop screaming. Some guys took me to the airport later and I kept screaming and I tried to kick in a couple of windows at the airport. Oh, man."

He shakes his head slowly. "There have been people in the movement who have cracked. Like you can't help it. You always work on the assumption that the worst things will happen, you always work on the assumption that you're going to die. I used to say that the only way they'll stop me is if they kill me. I still think that's true. What bothers me now is if I live through all this I just hope I don't get tired or give up or sell out. That's what bothers me. We all have weaknesses. I don't know what mine are. But if they find out they'll try to destroy me. It's a question of them finding out what my weaknesses are—money, power, publicity, I don't know. And sometimes . . . sometimes . . . you just get so tired too."

Stokely peers out the window at the clean, azure sky and shivers beneath the blanket. Within seconds, he is asleep.

Twenty minutes later the plane is landing at Albany Airport where Stokely will catch a plane for Glens Falls. He steps down the ramp and begins singing: "The empty-handed painter on your street is drawing crazy patterns on your sheet."

He grins and walks into the terminal. "Man, that Dylan is a wild guy."

With thirty minutes free before the next plane leaves, Stokely steps into the airport luncheonette and orders a vanilla ice cream soda. The waitress leaves and Stokely turns toward several persons at the counter reading newspapers. "Look at that, look at *that,*" he says, laughing, pointing to the sports page headline of The New York *Daily News*: "Operate on Whitey's Arm."

"If they flipped that over and put it on the front page they'd sell a million copies," he laughs.

Within the hour Stokely arrives in the small Glens Falls airport—three hours late. As soon as he climbs off the plane, a smiling, crew-cut youth waves and walks over and introduces himself. He is Frank Levy, a Ph. D. candidate in economics at Yale and a member of the camp's staff.

Stokely struggles into Levy's red MG and they drive off to the camp, about fifty miles away. Stokely asks Levy about the camp and is told that it's called the Shawnee Leadership Institute, an annual two-week summer camp for teen-agers who hold discussions on "issues" and listen to invited guest speakers. (The next day, Lord Caradon, the British Ambassador to the United Nations, was coming up.) There are about seventy campers and a staff of thirty, mostly college and graduate students.

Stokely likes Levy and they begin kidding about Vermont: "I wonder if everyone up here smokes pot." The car crosses New York into Vermont on Route 4 and passes Deak's grocery and Frank's Taxidermist. "I've never been to Vermont before," says Stokely.

The elms and pines are just starting to blaze with autumn colors and Stokely settles back and gazes silently at the countryside. He waves at farm boys—who wave back—and laughs as they ride past Crumley's grocery in Fort Ann. "A town like this and you go out of your mind," he exclaims. "I read someplace that suicide rates are very high in Vermont—they must be sick of cutting all that grass."

Just outside of Fort Ann, the car breaks down. Stokely moans and shakes his head and begins laughing. "This is my day," he says. The fan belt is broken and Stokely and Levy struggle with the new belt. After twenty minutes they are off again.

As soon as Stokely arrives at the camp he appears startled, then amused. "Wow," he says, as a half-dozen teen-age interracial couples, their arms around each other, surround the car, "Hey, like I had visions when I heard the name of the camp of old Protestant ladies sitting around campfires talking about love." They shake his hand and escort him to the dining room.

Once inside, Stokely is greeted by an old friend, Julian Houston, who is president of the Student Government at Boston University. Stokely grins and gives Julian the "black" handshake and embraces him. "Man, you should be workin' down in Alabama," cries Stokely.

With Houston and several other camp leaders, Stokely sits down at a wooden table while the campers, awestruck, watch him. Plates of ham and cheese and rolls are brought out and Stokely eats hungrily while a long-haired girl strums a guitar and sings *Ain't Gonna Study War No More*.

After the plates are cleared away, all the campers are called into the wooden dining room. Stokely removes his shoes and begins speaking quietly.

"Black people have not only been told that they are inferior, but the system maintains it. We are faced in this country with whether or not we want to be equal and let white people define equality for us on their terms as they've always done and thus lose our blackness or whether we should maintain our identity and still be equal. This is Black Power. The fight is whether black people should use their slogans without having white people say, 'That's okay.' You have to deal with what white means in this country. When you say black power you mean the opposite of white and it forces this country to deal with its own racism. The 1954 school desegregation decision was handed down for several reasons. It was a political decision—and it was *not* based on humanitarianism, but was based on the fact that this country was going further into nonwhite countries and you could not espouse freedom and have second-class citizens in your own country. The area in which we move now is politics and within a political context. People kept saying that segregation and racism was wrong because it was immoral. But they still didn't come to grips with the two essential things: we are poor and we are black. You can pass 10,000 bills but you still haven't talked about economic security. When someone is poor, it's not because of cultural deprivation, it's not because they need to be uplifted and head-started. When someone is poor, it's because they have no money, that's all. That's all. They say it's our fault, *our fault* that we're poor when in fact it's the system that calculates and perpetuates poverty. They say black people don't know money, that they'll drink it away, they won't work. But we never had money, and it's presumptuous to tell us we won't be thrifty, brave, clean and reverent. You know who the biggest welfare group is in this country? You know who they are? You think it's the black people? Well, it's not. It's the farmers. They are the biggest welfare group in this country. But the difference between them and us is that they run their own programs, they control their own resources and they get something out of it. We must, *we must* take over and control our resources and our programs. And if we don't, the black people will wake up again tomorrow morning, still poor, still black, and still singing *We Shall Overcome*."

The audience responds warmly and as soon as Stokely finishes, the questions begin. Stokely calls on a burly Negro youth who speaks in a thick drawl.

"Stokely, do you believe in God?"

Stokely stares at the youth. "That's a personal question."

The youth smiles. "Oh."

"Where you from?" Stokely asks.

"St. Augustine, Florida, Stokely."

"What you do down there?"

"I worked in the field. Cotton, tobacco, you name it. I worked for $2 a day since I was so high. I worked for $2 a day until I heard Dr. King down there and then I knew I had to join the movement."

"Right." Stokely turns from the boy to the audience. "The reason I joined the movement was not out of love. It was out of hate. I hate white supremacy and I'm out to smash it."

A pause. An older woman rises, a white woman. "Stokely," she asks, a tremor in her voice, "What can we do? What can the whites do?"

"You must seek to tear down racism. You must seek to organize poor whites. You must stop crying "Black supremacy" or "Black nationalist" or "racism in reverse" and face certain facts: that this country is racist from top to bottom and one group is exploiting the other. You must face the fact that racism in this country is a white, not a black problem. And because of this, you, *you* must move into white communities to deal with the problem. We don't need kids from Berkeley to come down to Mississippi. We don't need white kids to come to black communities just because they want to be where the action is.

"Look," says Stokely, leaning forward, speaking in a loud whisper. "Every white man in this country can announce that he is our friend. Every white man can make us his token, symbol, object, what have you. Every white man can say, 'I am your friend.' Well from here on in we're going to decide who is our friend. We don't want to hear any words, we want to see what you're going to do. The price of being the black man's friend has gone up.

"And you must understand," he says, his voice rising, "that as a person oppressed because of my blackness, I have common cause with other blacks who are oppressed because of *their* blackness. It must be to the oppressed that I address myself, not to members—even friends—of the oppressing group."

The audience stirs. Stokely suggests they walk outside so he can get some good country air. Within minutes, the teen-agers sit in a semicircle beneath an evergreen, chatting quietly with Stokely who is lying on his side, his elbow dug into the grass, his chin in his hand. . . .

By dusk, with the apricot-colored sky streaked with violet, the campers implore Stokely to stay the night. He'd love to, he says, he needs the rest and this marvelous clean air, but there are meetings and speeches and appointments the next day.

With Julian Houston, Stokely climbs into a car driven by a Roman Catholic priest from Boston who is on the camp's staff.

"Stokely," says the priest, driving quickly down the darkening road, "what should church people do?"

Stokely pauses. "They should start working on destroying the church and building more Christ-like communities. It's obvious, Reverend, that the church doesn't want Christ-like communities. Christ—he taught some revolutionary stuff, right? And the church is a counterrevolutionary force."

The priest drives a moment in silence. "What should the priest's job be?"

"To administer, through his actions, the teachings of Jesus Christ," says Stokely. "I would also make every church a plain building that could be used for other things, a building that will not be embellished."

"What's next for you, Stokely?" asks the priest.

"Next?" Stokely smiles. "How does the victim move to equality with the executioner? That's what's next. We are the victims and we've got to move to equality with our executioners." He pauses. "Camus never answers that question, does he? We are the victims, they are the executioners. Every real relationship is that—victim and executioner. Every relationship. Love, marriage, school, everything. This is the way this society sees love. You become a slave to somebody you love. You love me, you don't mess around with anyone else. One is the victim, the other the executioner. . . ."

It is dark now and chilly and Stokely begins shivering. He begins gossiping with Houston about old friends who have been lost to the poverty program, the Peace Corps, graduate schools.

At the airport in Burlington, Stokely is told that the plane to New York has been delayed an hour. He shakes his head—"It's my day"—and walks around with Houston. He then has two sandwiches and two glasses of milk and averts the stares of several men at the bar who recognize him.

The plane finally arrives. Stokely shakes hands with the priest and Houston and walks wearily up the ramp. He is cold and tired and sleeps listlessly on the trip to New York.

Shortly before eleven the plane lands at Kennedy Airport. Stokely has a date downtown in Manhattan but decides, instead, just to return to the Bronx and go to sleep. By now he is exhausted. The lack of sleep, the missed and delayed flights, the car trips, the questions, sandwiches on the run, the pressures have taken their toll. He walks through the terminal, breathing heavily, peering blankly through his dark glasses. Once outside, he decides to take a taxi and starts walking to the first cab in line. The driver, who is white, stares at Stokely—dungarees, dark glasses, carrying a paper bag of ham sandwiches, looking vaguely ominous—and drives past him to pick up a laughing white couple who carry cardboard cases of tax-free liquor. Stokely tenses, clenches his fist and takes a deep breath and turns toward the second cabdriver in line. This driver, who is a young Negro, has watched Stokely and is now smiling faintly. Stokely walks over, looks at the cabdriver and begins smiling too. He then opens the door and climbs into the cab and returns home for just a brief rest.

[January, 1967]

An Introduction to Soul

by Al Calloway

While the black community was beginning to take pride in being black, white society as a whole was beginning to take greater notice of Afro-American civilization. Fads in everything from sneakers (Converse tennis shoes as streetwear) to hairstyles (the Afro) that started among black youth were soon copied by whites. In this piece, published in April 1968, Al Calloway, then publisher of an Afro-American magazine called The Probe, *distilled the essence of Soul.*

Soul is sass, man. Soul is arrogance. Soul is walkin' down the street in a way that says, "This is me, muh-fuh!" Soul is that nigger whore comin' along . . . ja . . . ja . . . ja, and walkin' like she's sayin', "Here it is, baby. Come an' git it." Soul is bein' true to yourself, to what is *you*. Now, hold on: soul is . . . that . . . uninhibited . . . no, *extremely* uninhibited self . . . expression that goes into practically every Negro endeavor. That's soul. And there's swagger in it, man. It's exhibitionism, and it's effortless. Effortless. You don't need to put it on; it just comes out.—*Claude Brown*

When I walk on Eighth Avenue, man, I see rhythms I don't see downtown. *Polyrhythms.* You look at one cat, he may be doin' bop, bop-bop bop, bop-bop, and another one goin' *bop*-de-bop, *de*-bop. Beautiful, man. Those are *beautiful* people. Yeah. But when I go downtown to Thirty-fourth Street, everybody's walkin' the same, you dig? They don't put themselves into it. Their walk tells you nothing about who they are. *Polyrhythms.* That's what it is. Like a flower garden in a breeze. The roses swing a little bit from side to side, kind of stiff, not too much. The lilacs swing wide, slow, lazy, not in a hurry. A blade of grass wiggles. It's

411

'cause they're all different and they're bein' themselves. Polyrhythms, like on Eighth Avenue. That's soul.—*Al Calloway*

Soul Is Motion and Sound.

It is stomping and clapping with the gospel music of the First Tabernacle of Deliverance (Spiritual), American Orthodox Catholic Church on Harlem's One Hundred Twenty-fifth Street, and boogalooing the Funky Broadway to the Memphis gospel soul blues of Otis Redding while walking down the street. Soul is "Doin' the Thing" with the church-oriented funky jazz of Horace Silver and just *moving* back down home with John Lee Hooker's gutbucket folk blues. Soul is being natural, telling it like it is. In the plantation fields and later the church, black people were allowed to keep *some* form of their self-expression going. The beautiful simple poetry of spiritual work songs like *Steal Away*—let's sneak back to the "Good Ship Jesus" and sail all the way home—is part of the blues of today, just as the spiritual ecstasy in a Yoruba Temple in West Africa is akin to what is felt in the soul-stirring Sanctified and Baptist churches of America's black ghettos. When Mahalia Jackson sings, the gospel and the blues of Bessie Smith become the *essence* of soul. Ray Charles throws his head back and shouts, "Oh, yeah!" and transmits an inner feeling of goodness. When you've heard it like that, you *know* you have been moved. Then he comes in with, "Don't it make you want to feel all right," and it's like everything has been unraveled and you just lay in there and groove. Ray Charles turns you on. So does Aretha Franklin and "Mister Soul" James Brown. On a warm day in Harlem one can see and feel an infinite variety of rhythms. People stand on tenement stoops and on the sidewalks and sway to jukebox music here, WLIB and WWRL radio there. Some get caught up in front of record shops and just soul dance like they want to. All around you, Watusi, Boston Monkey, Shing-a-ling, Karate, Boogaloo, The Pearl, the Funky Broadway. Storefront-church tambourines ring and two young men in red shirts walk down the street, one playing a sheepskin drum and the other a cowbell or a fife. A saxophone riffs, a trumpet wails, and then there's the shout. The black poet LeRoi Jones calls it "Ka'ba. . . . Our world is full of sound/our world is more lovely than anyone's. . . ."

Soul Heroes.

At Forty-third Street and Langley Avenue, on Chicago's South Side, amid the many storefront churches and dilapidated tenements, stands a soulful monument to African-American folk heroes past and present. Last summer, Billy Abernathy, his wife, and at least a score of other artists and draftsmen within the black community formed the Organization of Black American Culture (O.B.A.C.) and got the building's owner, who happens to be black, to consent to the creation of the revolutionary and historical hand-painted mural. Folk heroes who have made great contributions to the worlds of music, sports and literature adorn the Wall: men like Marcus Garvey, Malcolm X and Stokely Carmichael; men who have steered large masses of black people away from the "assimilation complex" bag that DuBois talked about and guided them to the positive course of *digging* themselves. The Wall is blessed with Dr. DuBois' image too. The great innovators of American music, Charlie Parker, Thelonious Monk, Max Roach, Ornette Coleman and the late John Coltrane, share a large portion of the Wall, along with Sassy Sarah Vaughn and Nina Simone. The mighty men, Muhammad Ali and Wilt Chamberlain, are there because they do their thing with a lot of style, and that's important. The real genius of the Wall is that it generates African-American self-pride. No matter what happens to Chicago, the Wall is sure to stand.

The Nitty-Gritty of Soul.

There's a little piece of real estate in Harlem called Harlem Square, and on and about its four corners the curious, the intellectual and the political meet and exchange ideas. The center of activity there is one of Harlem's landmarks, Michaux's National Memorial African Bookstore. Marcus Garvey, Adam Clayton Powell Jr., Malcolm X and other soul heroes were heard by thousands at many a mass rally that took place in front of Michaux's. Inside the bookshop, every inch of available space is jammed with books by and about black folk. In the back room, where some of the soul heroes sat and wrote their speeches, the walls are crowded with photographs, paintings and drawings of great people of color. Every wall is a wall of respect. It is in Michaux's bookstore ("The House of Common Sense and Home of Proper Propaganda") that you learn about African musicians long ago who mastered the art of circular breathing and the simultaneous playing of instruments made out of elephant tusks and antelope horns. When you *see* the blind soul brother Roland Kirk playing his Manzello (the first saxophone), tenor sax and Stritch at the same time, and frequently blowing long sheets of sound without a breath, you are witnessing soul, baby. —One thing is certain: soul would be nowhere without the great savior, soul food. Black people brought to the Americas a tradition of how to make good food. Being close to the earth was their nature, and it was not difficult for them to find beans and greens that were good and to make good bread out of corn and crackling. It was a good thing that they knew this too, because *the man* would work them in the fields from sunup till dusk and sometimes they had other chores after that. On top of which they had to go all out for self, or the plantocracy would have starved them to death. When it came down to the hog, the planters didn't know anything except ham, bacon, spareribs and chops. The rest of it was no good, or so they thought, and the slaves copped it. They came up with pig tails, pig knuckles, ham hocks, hog maws, pig ears, snout, neck bones, chitlins, tripe and sowbelly. By the time fried or smothered chicken (The Gospel Bird) became a delicacy for special Sundays, black people were making candied yams, sweet-potato pie and fruit cobblers from the vegetables and fruits that they grew in their little patches or gathered from around. Traditionally, black people have congregated at the church for social and spiritual life, because church organization was (is) the only form allowed them. So when the sisters get together with those pots you can bet your life the food's going to be good. If you go into the Victory Restaurant on One Hundred Sixteenth Street in Harlem, you'll dig Bishop Shelton's sisters, with their natural hair and little caps and no makeup and floor-length gowns, serving soul food from eight in the morning till midnight. A plate of knuckles, black eyes and rice, a thick slice of corn bread, a glass of lemonade and a small home-made sweet-potato pie, and you're straight. If you really want to dig deep, get into Adam Powell's bag and cop a mess of chitlins and greens and soak them down with hot sauce. Soul food is why it is still chic to have a soul sister in the kitchen. Everybody digs the way she makes steaks, lobsters, roasts and *mmm* those rolls, pies and cakes.

The Style of Soul.

It is about nurturing creativity, being aesthetic in thought and action as much as possible. It permeates one's entire existence. In Harlem, as in all of America's urban black communities, the style is seen in the way a soul brother selects and wears his vines (suit, coat, tie, shirt, etc.). The hat and shoes are most important. If they are *correct*, it is certain that his whole thing is beautiful. You know that he's a cat who cares about himself. His hat will be a soft beaver, felt or velour, blocked in whatever way he may feel at any given time. He buys the best hat and while he's in his crib playing tunes and laying with his woman he may just let his hands go all over the hat like a potter does his clay. Thus, he creates his thing. A soul brother's shoes are always pointy-toed and so shined that he can almost adjust his hat while looking at them. The Sixties have ushered in a "new" mood among a significant number of soul brothers and sisters, causing a clean break with "anything other than what you really are." As reflected in manner of dress, a little stingy hat without the brim called a *ziki* is worn, or a free-form *fila* which is like a soft bag. The *kufe*, a small round headpiece, is also what's happening. Some soul brothers have gone all the way into a West African thing and are wearing *shokotos* (pants). The style of soul is getting back into the African folk bag. At the House of Ümoja (which means *unity* in Swahili), one of the many African shops in Harlem, soul brothers wear pieces of ivory in their ears and ornament their noses with gold like the Yorubas of West Africa. Wilt Chamberlain wears an African medallion around his neck and so does Jimmy Brown. Lew

Alcindor wears *dasikis* and so does LeRoi Jones. —Soul is what, forever, has made black people hip. And it is what has enticed whites to imitate them without understanding it. Among black people, soul is a congenital understanding and respect for each other. It is the knowledge that one is but a segment of all that is, which is spatial, particled, like the colors in a rainbow; yet like when its colors are all rolled into one it is a deep purple haze . . . like morning . . . like dusk. It makes you humble, peaceful. That is why, above all, soul is wise and weary. It is the self-perception that informs you how and when to groove in your own way while others groove in theirs, and it is the sophistication that knows better than to ask, "Understand me," and settles instead for, "Don't mess with me; I'm in my own thing, baby."

[April, 1968]

Martin Luther King Is
Still on the Case

by Garry Wills

On April 4, 1968, the blast of an assassin's bullet silenced the voice of the mainstream civil rights movement. Martin Luther King had embodied its ideals, created its images: King the leader, moving in the forefront of a march on Washington, surrounded by blacks and whites, young and old; King the preacher, speaking before a hushed crowd about his dream for America. Garry Wills, who began writing for Esquire *in the mid-Sixties, attended Dr. King's funeral. This story was published in August 1968.*

Of course, Mailer had an instinct for missing good speeches—at the Civil Rights March in Washington in 1963 he had gone for a stroll just a little while before Martin Luther King began, "I have a dream," so Mailer —trusting no one else in these matters, certainly not the columnists and the commentators—would never know whether the Reverend King had given a great speech that day, or revealed an inch of his hambone.

—NORMAN MAILER
The Armies of the Night

Nigger territory, eh?" He was a cabdriver, speculative; eyed the pistol incongruous beside him on the seat, this quiet spring night; studied me, my two small bags, my raincoat. The downtown streets were empty, but spectrally alive. Every light in every store was on (the better to silhouette looters). Even the Muzak in an arcade between stores reassured itself, at the top of its voice, with jaunty rhythms played to no audience. Jittery neon arrows, meant to beckon people in, now tried to scare them off. The curfew had swept pedestrians off the street, though some cars with white men in them still cruised unchallenged.

"Well, get in." He snapped down every lock with four quick slaps of his palm; then rolled up his window; we had begun our safari into darkest Memphis. It _was_ intimidating. Nothing stirred in the crumbling blocks; until, almost noiseless—one's windows are always up on safari—an armored personnel carrier went nibbling by on its rubber treads, ten long guns bristling from it (longer because not measured against human forms, the men who bore them were crouched behind the armored walls); only mushroom helmets showed, leaning out from each other as from a single stalk, and, under each, bits of elfin face disembodied.

At last we came to lights again: not the hot insistence of downtown; a lukewarm dinginess of light between two buildings. One was modern and well-lit; a custodian sat behind the locked glass door. This is the headquarters of a new activism in Memphis, the Minimum Salary Building (designed as national headquarters for raising the pay of ministers in the African Methodist Episcopal Church and now encompassing other groups). Its director, Reverend H. Ralph Jackson, was a moderate's moderate until, in a march for the striking sanitation workers, he was Maced by police. Since then his building has been a hive of union officials, Southern Christian Leadership Conference staff, and members of various human-rights organizations.

Next to it is the Clayborn Temple, a church from which marchers have issued almost daily for the past two months. Marchers fell back to this point in their retreat from the scuffle that marred Dr. King's first attempt to help the strikers. Some say tear gas was deliberately fired into the church; others that it drifted in. But the place _was_ wreathed with gas, and a feeling of violated sanctuary remains. Churches have been the Negro's one bit of undisputed terrain in the South, so long as they were socially irrelevant; but this church rang, in recent weeks, with thunderous sermons on the godliness of union dues.

I pay the cabdriver, who resolutely ignores a well-dressed young couple signaling him from the corner, and make my way, with bags and coat, into the shadow of the church porch. In the vestibule, soft bass voices warn me. I stop to let my eyes, initiated into darkness, find the speakers and steer me through their scattered chairs. They are not really conversing; their meditative scraps of speech do not meet each other, but drift off, centipetally, over each one's separate horizon of darkness. This uncommunicative, almost musical, slow rain of words goes on while I navigate my way into the lighted dim interior of the church.

About a hundred people are there, disposed in every combination: family groups; clots of men, or of women; the lean of old people toward each other, the jostle outward of teen-agers from some center (the church piano, a pretty dress on a hanger); or individuals rigid in their pews as if asleep or dead. The whole gathering is muted—some young people try to pick out a hymn on the piano, but halfheartedly. There are boxes of food, and Sunday clothes draped over the backs of pews. The place has the air of a rather lugubrious picnic—broken up by rain, perhaps, with these few survivors waiting their chance to dash out through the showers to their homes. Yet there is a quiet sense of purpose, dimly focused but, finally, undiscourageable. These are garbage collectors, and they are going to King's funeral in Atlanta. It is ten p.m.; in twelve hours the funeral will begin, 398 miles away.

They have been told different things, yesterday and today, by different leaders (some from the union, some from S.C.L.C.). They have served as marshals in the memorial march that very afternoon, and preparations for that overshadowed any planning for this trip. Some have been told to gather at ten o'clock; some at eleven. They believe there will be two buses, or three; that they will leave at eleven, or at twelve; that only the workers can go, or only they and their wives, or they and their immediate families. Yesterday, when they gathered for marshals' school, a brusque young Negro shouted at them to arrive sharply at ten: "We're not going by C.P. Time—Colored People's Time. And if you don't listen now, you won't find out how to get to Atlanta at all, 'cause *we'll* be on the *plane* tomorrow night." The speaker seemed to agree with much of white Memphis that "you have to know how to talk to these people."

And so they wait. Some came before dark, afraid to risk even a short walk or drive after curfew. Some do not realize the wait will be so long; they simply know the time they were asked to arrive. Most will have waited three hours before we start; some, four or five. I try to imagine the mutters and restlessness of a white group stranded so long. These people are the world's least likely revolutionaries. They are, in fact, the precisely *wrong* people—as the Russian fieldworker was the wrong man to accomplish Marx's revolt of the industrial proletariat.

                              People such as these were the first "Memphians" I had met in any number. That was four days ago. And my first impression was the same as that which nagged at me all night in the church: these Tennessee Negroes are not unlikely, they are impossible. They are anachronisms. Their leaders had objected for some time to J.P. Alley's "Hambone" cartoon in the local paper; they say, rightly, that it offers an outdated depiction of the Negro. Nonetheless, these men *are* Hambones. History has passed them by.

I saw them by the hundred, that first morning, streaming past the open casket in a hugger-mugger wake conducted between the completion of the embalmer's task and the body's journey out to the Memphis airport. I had arrived in Memphis several hours after King's death; touched base at the hotel, at the police station, at the site of the murder—dawn was just disturbing the sky; flashbulbs around and under the balcony still blinked repeatedly against the room number—306—like summer lightning. As the light strengthened, I sought out the funeral home police had mentioned—R.S. Lewis and Sons.

Clarence Lewis is one of the sons, he has been up all night answering the phone, but he is still polite; professionally sepulchral, calm under stress. "They brought Dr. King here because we have been connected with the Movement for a long time. We drove him in our limousines when he was here last week [for the ill-fated march]. They brought the body to us from the morgue at ten-thirty last night, and my brother has been working on it ever since. There's so much to do: this side [he pulls spread fingers down over his right cheek and neck] was all shot away, and the jawbone was just dangling. They have to reset it and then build all that up with plaster." I went through the fine old home (abandoned to trade when the white people moved from this area) into a new addition—the chapel, all cheap religious sentiment, an orange cross in fake stained glass. There are two people already there, both journalists, listening to the sounds from the next room (Clarence calls it, with a mortician's customary euphemism, "the Operating Room"), where a radio crackles excerpts from Dr. King's oratory, and men mutter their appreciation of the live voice while they work on the dead body. We comment on the ghoulishness of their task—knowing ours is no less ghoulish. We would be in there, if we could, with lights and cameras; but we must wait—wait through an extra hour of desperate cosmetic work. We do it far less patiently than Memphis garbage men wait in their church. "Hell of a place for Dr. King to end up, isn't it?" the photographer says. "And one hell of a cause—a little garbage strike."

When, at eight o'clock, the body is brought out, bright TV lights appear and pick out a glint of plaster under the cheek's powder. Several hundred people file past; they have sought the body out, in their sorrow, and will not let it leave town without some tribute. But not one white person from the town goes through that line.

Those who do come are a microcosm of the old Southern Negro community. Young boys doff their hats and their nylon hair caps—their "do rags"—as they go by. A Negro principal threatened to expel any child from a local high school who came to class with an "Afro" hairdo. Possessive matrons take up seats in the back, adjust their furs, cluck sympathetically to other women of their station, and keep the neighborhood record straight with bouts of teary gossip. They each make several passes at the coffin; sob uncontrollably, whip out their Polaroid cameras, and try an angle different from that shot on their last pass. One woman kisses the right cheek. Clarence Lewis was afraid of that: "It will spoil the makeup job. We normally put a veil over the coffin opening in cases of this sort; but we knew people would just tear that off with Dr. King. They want to see him. Why, we had one case where the people lifted a body up in the coffin to see where the bullet had gone into a man's back."

Outside, people mill around, making conversation, mixing with stunned friendliness, readjusting constantly their air of sad respect. Again, the scene looked like a disconsolate picnic. Some activists had called him "De Lawd." He always had to be given either his title ("*Doctor* King," even the *Reverend Doctor* King") or his full historic name ("Luther Martin King" one prim lady mourner called him in the funeral home, understandably stumbling over the big mouthful). Even that title "Doctor"—never omitted, punctiliously stressed when whites referred to him, included even in King's third-person references to himself—had become almost comical. He was not only "De Lawd," but "De Lawd High God Almighty," and his Movement was stiff with the preacher-dignities of the South; full of Reverends This and Bishops That and Doctors The-Other. No wonder the militants laughed at it all. And now, damned if he hadn't ended up at a Marc Connelly *fish fry* of a wake—right out of *The Green Pastures*.

Connelly learned to read by poring over the pages of the Memphis *Commercial Appeal* and he learned his lesson well: he was able to create a hambone God: "Dey's gonter to be a deluge, Noah, an' dey's goin' to be a flood. De Levees is gonter bust an' everything dat's fastened down is comin' loose." These are unlikely people, I thought at that sad fish fry, to ride out the deluge whose signs had already thundered from several directions on the night King died. But then, so was Noah an unlikely candidate. Or Isaac, who asked: "Does you want de brainiest or the holiest, Lawd?" "I want the holiest. I'll make him brainy." And there was one note, at King's makeshift wake, not heard anywhere in Connelly's play. As one of the mammy types waddled out the front door, she said with matter-of-fact bitterness to everyone standing nearby: "I wish it was Henry Loeb lying there"—handsone lovable Henry Loeb, the city's Mayor, who would later tell me, in his office, how well he liked his Negroes; unaware, even now, that they are not his. Connelly's "darkies" do not hate white people: "the white folk" simply do not exist in his play, which was meant to fortify the Southern conviction that "they have their lives and we have ours," an arrangement convenient to the white and (so whites tell themselves) pleasant for all. The whites get servants, and the blacks get fish fries. That whole elaborate fiction was shattered by the simple words, "I wish it was Henry Loeb." Massah's not in the cold, cold ground. She wishes he were. These people may be Hambones, but not J.P. Alley's kind. They are a paradox, a portent white Memphis still must come to grips with—hambone militants, "good darkies" on the march. When even the stones rise up and cry out, the end has come for Henry Loeb's South.

The signs of it are everywhere—at the Lorraine Motel, where King died; it is an extension of the old Lorraine Hotel, once a white whore-house. Then, when the neighborhood began to go black, it was thrown to a Negro buyer as, in the South, old clothes are given to "the help." A man named William Bailey bought it, and laboriously restored it to respectability. King stayed there often on his visits to Memphis. It is now a headquarters for the S.C.L.C.'s Project Memphis, a program designed—as its assistant director says—"to make Memphis pay for the death of Dr. King." Yet the Lorraine is run by a man who could pose for "Uncle Ben" rice ads—an ex-Pullman porter who is still the captain of porters at a Holiday Inn. He works for the white man, and does it happily, while he owns and runs a black motel where activists plot their campaigns. "I'm very proud to be part of the Holiday Inn family," he told me. "Why, the owners of the whole chain call me Bill Bailey." That's the Negro Henry Loeb has always known. It is the other side of him—the owner of the Lorraine, the friend of Dr. King—that is the mystery.

King made the mistake of staying, on his penultimate visit to Memphis, at one of the posher new Holiday Inns—in the kind of place where Bill Bailey works, not in the motel he owns. The Memphis paper gleefully pointed out that King *could* stay in the Inn because it had been integrated—"without demonstrations." But the Lorraine is not integrated (except in theory). Neither was the white flophouse in which the sniper lurked. It is good that King came back to the real world, the de-facto segregated world, to die. He was in the right place, after all. Memphis indeed, had taught him to "stay in his place"—a thing it will come to regret. For "his place" is now a command post, a point where marches are planned, and boycotts, and Negro-history classes.

These garbage men are that new thing, Hambones in rebellion—and they have strange new fish to fry. The people who filed past King's body had said no to the whole city of Memphis; said it courteously, almost deferentially (which only made it more resounding); they had marched every day under their employers' eyes; boycotted the downtown; took on, just for good measure, firms like Coca-Cola and Wonder Bread and Sealtest Milk; and were ready, when the time came, to join with King in taking on Washington. Patience radiates from them like a reproach. Perhaps that is why the white community does not like to see them in a mass—only in the single dimension, the structured encounter that brings them singly into the home or the store for eight hours of work. These Negroes seem almost too patient—wrong people for rebels. Yet their like has already made a rebellion. A tired woman in Birmingham was the wrong sort to begin all the modern civil-rights activism; but Rosa Parks did it. King was drawn into that first set of marches and boycotts almost by accident—as he was involved, finally, in the garbage men's strike: "Dat's always de trouble wid miracles. When you pass one you always gotta r'ar back an' pass another."

The buses were late. They were supposed to arrive at eleven-thirty for loading baggage (each man had been told to bring toothbrush, change of underwear, change of outer clothes if he wanted it, and most wanted it.) Besides, there had been talk of a bus for teen-agers, who were now giggling and flirting in the dark vestibule (surrendered to them by their elders). Jerry Fanion, an officer of the Southern Regional Conference, scurried around town looking for an extra bus; like all Negroes, he was stopped everywhere he went. Police recognized him, and they had been alerted about the men who would be leaving their homes for the funeral; but they made him get out of the car anyway, and laboriously explain himself. He never did get the bus. Later in the week, the teen-agers made a pilgrimage to King's grave.

Meanwhile, the wives in the Clayborn Temple still did not know whether they could go with their husbands. About eleven-thirty, T.O. Jones showed up, with P.J. Ciampa. Jones is the spheroid president of the sanitation local—a man too large in some ways and too small in others for any standard size of shirt, coat, pants. He is content with floppy big pants and a windbreaker that manages to get around him, but only by being too long in the sleeves and too wide in the shoulders. He is a quiet man in his early forties, determined but vague, who began the strike by going to the office of the Director of Public Works and—when the Director told him there was an injunction against any strike by city employees—changing into his "prison clothes" on the spot.

Ciampa is the fiery Italian organizer who came into town for the union and amused people with televised arguments against Mayor Loeb (who insisted that all negotiations be carried on in public). Jones and Ciampa have lost the list of men signed up for the buses; they don't know how many buses are coming, how many can ride on each. They try to take two counts—of workers alone, and workers with their wives; but it's difficult to keep track of those who wander in and out of shadows, doors, anterooms.

After an hour of disorder, it becomes clear that everyone can fit into the three buses if folding chairs are put down the aisles. T.O. had told me to save a seat for him, but the chairs in the aisle barricade us from each other. I sit, instead, with a sleepy young man who describes the route we *have* to take, and then finds confirmation of his theory, with a kind of surprised triumph, all along the way. The route one travels through Mississippi and Alabama is a thing carefully studied by Southern Negroes. After giving T.O. a check for the bus drivers, Ciampa went back to the hotel, T.O. swung onto the lead bus, and we pulled out.

In the seat behind me, a woman is worried over the teen-agers still standing by the church, hoping they will get a bus. "How they gonna get home?" she asks. "Walk, woman," her husband growls. "But what of the curfew?" "What of it?" "I don't trust those police. If I hadn't got on the

bus with you, I'd have stayed all night in the church." As the bus rolls
through downtown Memphis, on its way South, the woman sees cars
moving. "What are they doing out during the curfew? Why aren't *they*
stopped?" She knows, of course. Her husband does not bother to answer
her.

In our bus, all the animation comes from one voice in the back. A tall
laughing man I had watched, in the church, as he moved from one cluster
to another, mixing easily, asked to sit beside me while I was still saving a
seat for T.O. I was sorry later I had not said yes. As the riders shouldered
sleepily into their chair backs, he joked more softly, but showed no signs
of fatigue himself—though he had been a marshal all the long afternoon
of marching. And as fewer and fewer responded to him, he moved
naturally from banter and affectionate insults to serious things: "That Dr.
King was for us." The response is a sigh of yesses. "He didn't have to
come here." A chorusing of noes. As he mused on, the crowd breathed
with him in easy agreement, as if he were thinking for them. This
"audience participation" is what makes the Southern preacher's sermon
such an art form. I had been given a dazzling sample of it three days
before in the garbage men's meeting at the United Rubber Workers Union
Hall. That was the day after King's death, and a formidable lineup of
preachers was there to lament it. They all shared a common language,
soaked in Biblical symbol: Pharoah was Mayor Loeb, and Moses was Dr.
King, and Jesus was the Vindicator who would get them their dues
checkoff. But styles were different, and response had to be earned. The
whole hall was made up of accompanists for the improvising soloist up
front. When he had a theme that moved them, they cheered him on: "Stay
there!" "Fix it." "Fix it up." "Call the roll." "*Talk* to me!" "Talk *and a
half.*" The better the preacher, the surer his sense of the right time to tarry,
the exact moment to move on; when to let the crowd determine his pace,
when to push against them; the lingering, as at the very edge of orgasm,
prolonging, prolonging; then the final emotional breakthrough when the
whole audience "comes" together.

Memphis is not really the birthplace of the blues, any more than Handy
was the father of them; but these are the same people who created the
form—the triple repeated sighing lines, with a deep breathing space
between each, space filled in with the accompanists' "break" or "jazz."
That is the basic pattern for the climactic repetitions, subtle variations,
and refrains of the preacher's art. That kind of sermon is essentially a
musical form; and the garbage men are connoisseurs. When a white pastor
from Boston got up, he gave them slogans and emotion; but without a
response from the audience—he didn't know the melody.

Nor did all the black preachers succeed, or win equal acceptance. The
surprise of the afternoon, at least for me, came when an S.C.L.C. delegation reached the hall, and the Reverend James Bevel got up to preach. He

and his associates looked almost out of place there amid the "do rags" and scarred ebony skulls; they were immaculately dressed, with educated diction, wearing just the proper kind of "natural" and a beard.

Bevel was the fourteenth, and last, speaker of the afternoon. It seemed that earlier emotional talks would have drained these men of all response left them after the shock of the preceding night. But Jim Bevel slowly built them up, from quiet beginnings, to an understanding of what it means to be "on the case." (This is a phrase he invented a year ago to describe musicians who are perfectly interacting; it is now an S.C.L.C. phrase of wide applicability.) "Dr. King died on the case. Anyone who does not help forward the sanitation workers' strike is not on the case. You getting me?" (They're getting him.) "There's a false rumor around that our leader is dead. *Our* leader is not dead." ("No!" They know King's *spirit* lives on—half the speeches have said that already.) "That's a *false* rumor!" ("Yes!" "False." "Sho' nuff." "*Tell* it!") "Martin Luther King is not—" (yes, they know, not dead; this is a form in which expectations are usually satisfied, the crowd arrives at each point *with* the speaker; he outruns them at peril of losing the intimate ties that slacken and go taut between each person in the room; but the real artist takes chances, creates suspense, breaks the rhythm deliberately; a snag that makes the resumed onward flow more satisfying)—"Martin Luther King is not our *leader!*" ("No!" The form makes them say it, but with hesitancy. They will trust him some distance; but what does he mean? The "Sho' nuff" is not declamatory now; not fully interrogatory, either; circumflexed.) "*Our* leader—("Yes?")—is the *man*—("*What* man?" "Who?" "Who?" Reverend Abernathy? Is he already trying to supplant King? The trust is almost fading)—who led *Moses* out of *Israel*." ("*Thass* the man!" Resolution; all doubt dispelled; the bridge has been negotiated, left them stunned with Bevel's virtuosity.) "*Our* leader is the man who went with Daniel into the lions' den." ("Same man!" "Talk some.") "Our leader is the man who walked out of the grave on Easter morning." ("Thass the leader!" They have not heard, here in hamboneland, that God is dead.) "Our leader never sleeps nor slumbers. He cannot be put in jail. He has never lost a war yet. *Our* leader is *still on the case*." ("*That's it!*" "*On* the case!") "Our leader is not dead. One of his prophets died. We will not stop because of that. Our staff is not a funeral staff. We have friends who are undertakers. We *do business*. We *stay on the case*, where our leader is."

It is the most eloquent speech I have ever heard. I was looking forward, a day later, to hearing Bevel again, before a huge audience in the Mason Temple. He was good—and gave an entirely different speech. But the magic of his talk to the sanitation workers was gone. It was not merely the size of the crowd (though that is important—the difference between an intimate combo and some big jazz band only partially rehearsed). The makeup of the crowd was also different. Those in the Union Hall were predominantly male. Men accompany; women compete—they talk over the preacher's rhythms. Their own form is not the jazz combo, but the small group of gospel singers, where each sister fights for possession of the song by claiming a larger share of the Spirit. In a large place like the Mason Temple, women set up nuclei around the hall and sang their own variations on the sermon coming out of the loudspeakers.

But that night in the bus, there was no fighting the jolly voice that mused on "Dr. King's death." Responses came, mingled but regular, like sleepy respirations, as if the bus's sides were breathing regularly in and out. This is the subsoil of King's great oratory, of the subtly varied refrains: "I have a *dream* . . . *I* have a dream today." He must have been a great preacher in his own church; he could use the style out in the open, before immense crowds. He made the transition more skillfully than Bevel had—and far better than Abernathy does. That very day, the Monday before King's funeral, Abernathy had paused long on the wrong phrases: "I do not *know* . . . I do not *know*." He had let the crowd fool him by their sympathy; he took indulgence for a *demand* to linger. He did not have King's sure sense of when to move.

I suppose I heard thirty or forty preachers on that long weekend of religious eloquence; but not one of them reached King's own level of skill in handling a crowd. That was the mystery of King. He was the Nobel Prize winner and a Southern Baptist preacher; and, at places like the Washington Mall in 1963, the two did not conflict but worked together. As the man in the bus kept saying, "He was for *us*." (Unh-*hmmn*!") "He was *one* with us." ("That he was." "That he was.")

But King's rapport with his people was not the natural thing it seems now. He had to learn it, or relearn it. The man's voice rose behind us in the bus: "You know what Dr. King said?" ("What?") "He said not to mention his Nobel Prize when he died." ("Thass what he *said*.") "He said, 'That don't mean nothing'." ("Sho' nuff.") "What matters is that *he* helped *us*." ("Thass the truth." "That *is* the truth." "*That* is.")

In several ways. King was very bright, a quick study. He skipped two grades to finish high school at the age of fifteen. He was ordained at eighteen; graduated from college at nineteen. It was a fast start, for a career that is one long quick record of youthful accomplishment. He got his theology degree at the age of twenty-two. While a pastor (from the age of twenty-five), he got his Ph.D. from Boston University at twenty-six. And he went direct from graduate school to a position of national leadership. His major achievements were already behind him when he became the youngest man (thirty-five) to receive the Nobel Prize. He was dead before he reached the age of forty; and there are constant little surprises in remembering how young he was—as when Harry Belafonte, speaking in Memphis, referred to King as his junior by a year. Was "De Lawd" really younger than that baby-faced singer? And why did we never think of him as young?

He had the strained gravity of the boy who has moved up fast among his elders. That unnatural dignity is in his writing, too, which labors so for gravity that it stretches grammar: "President Kennedy was a strongly contrasted personality . . . trying to sense the direction his leadership could travel." His acceptance speech will not rank with the great Nobel speeches: "transform this *pending* cosmic elegy into a creative psalm . . . unfolding events which surround . . . spiral down a militaristic stairway . . . blood-flowing streets. . . ."

The young King wanted to study medicine. He majored in sociology at Morehouse College. He thought preachers not quite intellectually respectable, though his father and grandfather and great-grandfather had all been preachers. Even when he accepted ordination, he thought he should become a theologian-minister, perhaps a professor, rather than a mere preacher. He took his first parish—in Montgomery—to get "pastoring background" before accepting a teaching post. To the end of his life he talked of turning to an academic career.

But he was never convincing as a scholar. An account of his own intellectual development reads as if it were lifted from a college catalog: "My intellectual journey carried me through new and sometimes complex doctrinal lands, but the pilgrimage was always stimulating, gave me a new appreciation for objective appraisal and critical analysis, and knocked me out of my dogmatic slumber." He was not even a very perceptive commentator on the men who created his doctrine of civil disobedience—Thoreau and Gandhi. When he began the Montgomery boycott, he liked to refer vaguely to Hegel as the prophet of "creative tensions." It was not till someone suggested more likely patrons of nonviolent rebellion that he began referring to Gandhi and Gandhi's American forerunner—*referring* to them—as saints. He never really discusses their philosophy. And his most ambitious defense of civil disobedience—the Letter from a Birmingham Jail, written eight years after the Montgomery boycott—does not even *refer* to Gandhi or Thoreau. Instead, King uses tags from Augustine and Aquinas (hardly anti-authoritarians). Nor does the Letter deserve high marks for logic. It offers as the model of civil disobedience, not Gandhi, but Socrates, the stock Platonic figure suborned for all noble causes, but something of an embarrassment in this context, since Plato makes him preach history's most rigorous sermon against civil disobedience in the *Crito*. The Letter gives three qualifications for a valid act of civil disobedience: 1) that it be open, 2) that it be loving (nonviolent), and 3) that those engaged in it accept their punishment willingly. Then he gives as a historical example of this the Boston Tea Party, whose perpetrators: 1) were clandestine (they disguised themselves as Indians), 2) were armed for violence (they forced wharf guards away and were ready to repel any interruption), and 3) evaded all punishment (Sam Adams and his Committee of Correspondence *dared* England to attempt punishment). Indeed, none of the historical examples of civil disobedience given in King's Letter meets the three requirements he had just set up.

Like Moses, he was not "de brainiest." He only knew one book well—the Bible. It was enough. All the other tags and quotes are meant to give respectability to those citations that count—the phrases sludged up in his head from earliest days like a rich alluvial soil. He could not use these with the kind of dignity he aspired to unless he were more than "just a preacher." Yet the effect of that *more* was to give him authority *as* a preacher. By trying to run away from his destiny, he equipped himself for it. He became a preacher better educated than any white sheriff; more traveled, experienced, poised. He was a Hambone who could say "no" and make it sound like a cannon shot.

It is interesting to contrast him with another preacher's son—James Baldwin. Baldwin became a boy preacher himself as a way of getting out into the secular world. King became a student as a way of getting into a larger world of *religion,* where the term "preacher" would not be a reproach. He needed a weightiness in his work which only that "Doctor" could give him. He needed it for personal reasons—yes, he had all along aspired to be "De Lawd"—and in order to make Southern religion relevant. That is why King was at the center of it all: he was after *dignity*, which is the whole point of the Negro rebellion. His talent, his abilities as a "quick study," his versatility, his years studying philosophy and theology (for which he had no real natural bent) were means of achieving power. His books and degrees were all tools, all weapons. He had to put that "Doctor" before his name in order to win a "Mister" for every Southern Negro. They understood that. They rejoiced in his dignities as theirs. The Nobel Prize *didn't* matter except as it helped them. As T.O. Jones put it, "There can never be another leader we'll have the feeling for that we had for him."

Our three buses had a long ride ahead of them—ten hours, an all-night run, through parts of Mississippi, Alabama, and Georgia. They were not luxury buses, with plenty of room; the Greyhound company had run out of vehicles and leased these from a local firm. One could not even stretch one's legs in the aisle; the folding chairs prevented that. Ten hours there. Ten hours back.

Minutes after our departure, the man behind me said, "We're in Mississippi now." "Oh no!" his wife groaned. It is well to be reminded that our citizens are afraid to enter certain states. The man most frightened was T.O. Jones. He knows what risks an "uppity" Negro takes in the South. He does not give out his address or phone number. The phone is changed automatically every six months to avoid harassment. He has lived in a hotel room ever since the beginning of his union's strike, so his wife and two girls will not be endangered by his presence in the house. "This is risky country," he told me. "And it gets more dangerous as you go down the road. That Mississippi!" We were going down the road.

The lead bus had no toilet, and the chairs in the aisle effectively barricaded it from anyone's use in the other buses. The technique for "rest stops" was for all three buses to pull off into a darkened parking lot; the chairs were folded; then people lined up at the two toilets (one bus for men, one for women). At our first stop, some men began to wander off into the trees, but T.O., sweating in the cool night, churning all around the buses to keep his flock together, warned them back. "Better not leave the bus." I asked him if he expected trouble. "Well, we're in Mississippi, and folk tend to get flusterated at—" He let it hang. He meant at the sight of a hundred and forty Negroes pouring out of buses in the middle of the night. "You didn't see that man over there, did you—in the house by the gas station? There was a man at the door." Some had tried to go near the dark station, to get Cokes from an outdoor vending machine. T.O. pulled them back to the buses. He carries his responsibility very self-consciously.

Back in the bus, there was a spasm of talk and wakefulness after our stop. The deep rumbling voice from the rear got chuckles and approval as he mused on the chances of a strike settlement. "We got Henry Loeb on the run now." ("Yeah!" "Sure do!") "He don't know what hit him." Fear is not surprising in the South. This new confidence is the surprising thing. I had talked to a watery little man, back in the church, who seemed to swim in his loose secondhand clothes—a part-time preacher who had been collecting Memphis' garbage for many years. What did he think of the Mayor? "Mr. Loeb doesn't seem to do much thinking. He just doesn't *understand*. Maybe he can't. The poor man is just, y'know—kinda—*sick*." It is King's word for our society, a word one hears everywhere among the garbage men; a word of great power in the Negro community—perhaps the key word of our decade. It is no longer a question of courage or fear, men tell each other; of facing superior white power or brains or resources. It is just a matter of understanding, of pity. One must be patient with the sick.

Henry Loeb does not look sick. He is vigorous, athletic, bushy-browed, handsome in the scowling-cowboy mold of William S. Hart and Randolph Scott. And he has a cowboy way of framing everything as part of his personal code: "*I* don't make deals. . . . *I* don't believe in reprisals. . . . . *I* like to conduct business in the open." There is an implicit contrast, in that repeatedly emphasized pronoun, with all the other shifty characters in this here saloon. He even has a cowboy's fondness for his "mount"—the P.T. boat he rode during the war, a loving if unskilled portrait of which hangs behind his desk. (His office biography makes the inevitable reference to John F. Kennedy.)

Loeb is an odd mixture of the local and the cosmopolitan. He comes from a family of Memphis millionaires; he married the Cotton Carnival Queen. Yet as a Jew he could not belong to the Memphis Country Club (he has become an Episcopalian since his election as Mayor); and he went East for his education. A newsman who knows him made a bet with me: "When he hears you are from a national magazine he will not let five minutes go by without a reference to Andover or Brown." When I went into his office, he asked for my credentials before talking to me (he would later boast that he talks to anyone who wants to come see him). Then he asked where I live. Baltimore. "Oh, do you know so-and-so?" No. Why? "He was in my class at Andover, and came from Baltimore." That newsman could clean up if he made his bets for money.

Loeb did not mention Brown. But he did not need to. As I waited for him in his office, his secretary took the Dictaphone plug out of her ear and began flipping through her dictionary, and confided to me, as she did so, "The Mayor was an English major at Brown University, and he uses words so big I can't even find them." Later, his executive assistant found occasion to let me know that his boss was "an English major at Brown University."

But the Mayor also plays the role of local boy protecting his citizens from carpetbaggers out of the North. He has the disconcerting habit of leaving his telephone amplifier on, so that visitors can hear both ends of a conversation; and when a newspaperman with a pronounced Eastern accent called him for some information, he amused local journalists, who happened to be in his office, by mimicking the foreigner in his responses. When a group of white suburban wives went to his office to protest his treatment of the garbage strikers, he listened to them, then slyly asked the five who had done most of the talking where they were from; and his ear had not betrayed him—not one was a native "Memphian." He has a good ear for classes, accent, background. He wanted to know where I had gone to college. The South is very big on "society."

But Loeb has no ear at all for one accent—the thick, slow drawl of men like T.O. Jones. He knows they haven't been to college. I asked him whether he thought he could restore good relations with the Negro community after the sanitation workers settlement. "There is good understanding now. I have Negroes come to me to firm up communications—I won't say to reestablish them, because they had not lapsed." I told him I attended a mass rally at Mason Temple, where more than five thousand Negroes cheered as preacher after preacher attacked him. "Well, you just heard from a segment of the community whose personal interests were involved. Why, I have open house every Thursday, and just yesterday I had many Negroes come in to see me about different things." Imagine! And Massah even talked to them! And they came right in the front door, too! It is the conviction of all Henry Loebs that the great secret of the South, carefully hidden but bound to surface in the long run, is the

Negro's profound devotion to Henry Loeb. After all, look at everything he has done for them. "*I* took the responsibility of spending fifteen thousand dollars of city money—multiplied many times over by federal food stamps—to feed the strikers." *Noblesse oblige.*

The odd thing is that white Memphis really *does* think that—as citizen after citizen tells you—"race relations are good." Its spokesman cannot stop saying, "How much we have done for the Negro" (the Southern bigot is nothing but the Northern liberal caricatured—we have *all* done so much for the Negro). A journalist on the *Press-Scimitar,* the supposedly "liberal" paper in town, says, "We have been giving Negroes the courtesy title" (that is, calling Mr. and Mrs. Jones *Mr.* and *Mrs.* Jones) "ever since the Korean War." (It embarrassed even the South to call the parents of a boy killed in action *John* and *Jane* Jones.) But the executive secretary of the local N.A.A.C.P. was considered a troublemaker when, arrested in a demonstration supporting the strikers, she held up the booking process time after time by refusing to answer the officer's call for "Maxine" instead of Mrs. Smith. ("Why, *isn't* your name Maxine?" one honestly befuddled cop asked her.)

Mrs. Smith is one of the many Negroes who protested the morning paper's use of the "Hambone" cartoon. But she ran up against the typical, infuriating response: "Hambone" was actually the white man's way of saying how much he *loves* the Negro. It was begun in 1916 by J.P. Alley, who—this is meant to settle the question once for all—won a Pulitzer Prize for attacking the Klan. It was kept up by the Alley family (one of whom is married to the morning paper's editor), and Memphis felt it would lose a precious "tradition" if their favorite darkie disappeared from their favorite newspaper—as, at last, a month after King's death, he did; with this final salute from the paper: "Hambone's nobility conferred a nobility upon all who knew him."

Nowhere is the South's sad talk of "tradition" more pitiful than in Memphis. The city was founded as part of a land deal that brought Andrew Jackson a fortune for getting Indians to give up their claims to the site. The city's great Civil War hero—to whom Forrest Park is dedicated—could not belong to the antebellum equivalent of the Memphis Country Club because he was not a "gentleman"—that is, he was not a slave *owner* but a slave *trader.* After the war, however, he took command of the Ku Klux Klan, which made him "society." The Memphis Klan no doubt boasted of all the things it did for the Negro, since it *was* more selective and restrained than the Irish police force, which slaughtered forty-six Negroes in as many hours during 1866. Later in the century, yellow fever drove the cotton traders out of town; and Irish riffraff took over; the municipality went broke, surrendered its charter, and ceased to exist as a city for a dozen years. Then, just as Memphis regained its right of self-government, a small-town boy from Mississippi, Ed Crump, came up the pike and founded the longest-lasting city "machine" of this century. The main social event for the town's "aristocracy"—the Cotton Carnival—goes back only as far as 1931, when it was begun as a gesture of defiance to the Depression: the city is built on a bluff, and run on the same principle.

When Dr. King's planned second march took place, four days after his death, men built the speaker's platform inconveniently high up, so Mrs. King would be standing before the city emblem, above the doors of City Hall, when she spoke. It was meant, of course, as a rebuke to the city. But her standing there, with that background, is henceforth the only tradition Memphis has worth saving.

Yet the city keeps telling itself that "relations are good." If that is so, why was Henry Loeb guarded by special detectives during and after the strike? (One sat in during my session with him; they stash their shotguns under his desk.) Why did some white ministers who supported the strike lose their jobs? Why are black preachers called Communists in anonymous circulars? But the daily papers will continue to blink innocently and boast on the editorial page: "Negro football and basketball players figure prominently in all-star high-school teams selected by our Sports Department." What *more* do they want?

When dawn came, our buses had reached Georgia, the red clay, the sparse vegetation. By the time we entered Atlanta, it was hot; the funeral service had already begun at Ebenezer Church. The bus emptied its cramped, sleepy load of passengers onto a sidewalk opposite the courthouse (Lester Maddox is hiding in there behind *his* bodyguard, conducting the affairs of office on a desk propped up, symbolically, with shotguns). The garbage men who brought their good clothes have no opportunity to change. The women are especially disappointed; the trip has left everyone rumpled. Men begin to wander off. T.O. does not know what to do. He ends up staying where the bus stopped, to keep track of his flock. Some men get the union's wreath over to the church. Others walk to Morehouse College. But for most, the long ride simply puts them in the crowd that watches, at the Capitol, while celebrities march by.

It was a long ride for this; and the ride back will seem longer. The buses leave Atlanta at eight-thirty on the night of King's burial, and do not reach Memphis until six the next morning. But no one regretted the arduous trip. T.O. told me he *had* to go: "We were very concerned about Dr. King's coming to help us. I talked with the men, and we knew he would be in danger in Memphis. It was such a saddening thing. He was in Memphis for only one reason—the Public Works Department's work stoppage. This is something I lay down with, something I wake up with. I know it will never wear away."

A week after the funeral, Mayor Loeb finally caved in to massive pressures from the White House. The strike was settled, victoriously. At the announcement, T.O. blubbered without shame before the cameras. It was the culmination of long years—almost ten of them—he had poured into an apparently hopeless task, beginning back in 1959 when he was fired by the city for trying to organize the Public Works Department. After the victory I went with him to an N.A.A.C.P. meeting where he was introduced, to wild applause, by Jesse Turner, head of the local chapter: "Our city fathers tell us the union has been foisted on us by moneygrubbing outsiders. Well, here's the outsider who did it all, Carpet-bagger Jones." The applause almost brought him to tears again: "I was born in Memphis, and went to school here. I haven't been out of the state more than three days in the last ten years. Is that what they mean by an outsider?" A man got up in the audience and said, "When my wife saw you on television, she said 'I feel sorry for that fat little man crying in public.' But I told her, 'Don't feel sorry for him. I've seen him for years trying to get something going here, and getting nowhere. *He* just *won*.' "

When the strike was still on, Henry Loeb, if asked anything about it, liked to whip out his wallet and produce the first telegram he got from the union's national office, listing nine demands. He would tick off what he could and couldn't do under each heading, giving them all equal weight, trying to bury in technicalities the two real issues—union recognition and dues checkoff. When I went to see him after the settlement, he brought out the tired old telegram, now spider-webbed with his arguments and distinctions. Then he searched the grievance-process agreement for one clause that says the final court of appeal is the Mayor (still built on a bluff). He assured me that, no matter how things look, *he* does not make deals. They really settled on *his* terms. But isn't there a dues checkoff? No. The *city* does not subtract union dues before pay reaches the men; their credit union does (a device the union had suggested from the outset). What about recognition of the union; wasn't that guaranteed? No, it was not. There is no contract, only a memorandum signed by the City Council. Well, is that not a binding agreement—i.e., a contract? "No, it is a *memorandum*" (see how useful it is to be an English major?)—"but we have a way of honoring our commitments." The code. Well, then, didn't the union get a larger raise than the Mayor said it would? Not from the *city*. Until July 1, when all city employees were scheduled for a raise, the extra demands of the union will be met by a contribution of local businessmen. *Noblesse oblige*—see what we have done for our Negroes. Will the Mayor handle promised union agitation by the hospital and school employees in a new way, after the experience of the garbage strike? "No. Nothing has changed."

Wrong again, Henry. Everything has changed. The union is here to stay, it will spread: Jesse Epps and P.J. Ciampa and T.O. Jones will see to that. The S.C.L.C. is here to stay: Jim Bevel is in charge of Project Memphis. The city is his case now, and he is on it. A coalition of local preachers that backed the strikers has made itself a permanent organization, Community on the Move for Equality; preachers like James Lawson, better educated than some Brown graduates, are convinced that the God of Justice is not dead, not even in Memphis. Most important, Memphis is now the place where Dr. King delivered one of his great speeches—those speeches that will outlive his labored essays.

The excerpt most often published from that last speech told how King had been to the mountaintop. But those who were there at the Mason Temple to hear him, the night before he died, remember another line most vividly.

He almost did not come to that meeting. He was tired; the weather was bad, he hoped not many would show up (his first march had been delayed by late spring *snows* in Tennessee); he sent Ralph Abernathy in his stead. But the same remarkable people who rode twenty hours in a bus to stand on the curb at his funeral came through storm to hear him speak on April 4. Abernathy called the Lorraine and told King he could not disappoint such a crowd. King agreed. He was on his way.

Abernathy filled in the time till he arrived with a long introduction on King's life and career. He spoke for half an hour—and set the mood for King's own reflection on the dangers he had faced. It was a long speech—almost an hour—and his followers had never heard him dwell so long on the previous assassination attempt, when a woman stabbed him near the heart. The papers quoted a doctor as saying that King would have died if he had sneezed. "If I had sneezed," he said, he would not have been in Birmingham for the marches. "If I had sneezed—" ("Tell it!" He was calling the roll now, talking "and a half," tolling the old cadences.) He could never, had he sneezed, have gone to Selma; to Washington for the great March of 1963; to Oslo. Or to Memphis.

For the trip to Memphis was an important one. He did not so much climb to the mountaintop there as go back down into the valley of his birth. Some instinct made him return to the South, breathing in strength for his assault on Washington, which he called the very last hope for nonviolence. He was learning, relearning, what had made him great—learning what motels to stay at; what style to use; what were his roots. He was learning, from that first disastrous march, that he could not come in and touch a place with one day's fervor; that he had to *work with* a community to make it respond nonviolently as Montgomery had, and Birmingham, and Selma.

It is ironic that the trouble on that first march broke out on Beale Street, where another man learned what his roots were. W.C. Handy did not come from Memphis, like Bessie Smith; he did not grow up singing the blues. He learned to play the trumpet in Alabama from a traveling bandmaster, a real Professor Harold Hill. Then he went North, to tootle transcribed Beethoven on "classical cornet" afternoons in Chicago. It was only when he came back South, and saw that the native songs *worked* better with audiences, that he began to write down some of those songs and get them published.

King, after largely ineffectual days in Chicago, returned to Memphis, the deracinated Negro coming home. Home to die. His very oratory regained majesty as he moved South. He had to find out all over what his own movement was about—as Marc Connelly's "Lawd" learns from his own creation: "Dey cain't lick you, kin dey Hezdrel?" Bevel said the leader was not Martin King. That was true, too, in several ways. In one sense, Rosa Parks was the true leader. And T.O. Jones. All the unlickable Hezdrels. King did not sing the civil-rights blues from his youth. Like Handy, he got them published. He knew what *worked*—and despite all the charges of the militants, no other leader had his record of success. He was a leader who, when he looked around, had armies behind him.

This does not mean he was not authentic as a leader. On the contrary. His genius lay in his ability to articulate what Rosa Parks and T.O. feel. Mailer asks whether he was great or was hamboning; but King's unique note was precisely his *ham* greatness. That is why men ask, now, whether *his* kind of greatness is obsolete. Even in his short life, King seemed to have outlived his era. He went North again—not to school this time, but to carry his movement out of Baptist-preacher territory—and he failed. The civil-rights movement, when it left the South, turned to militancy and urban riots. Men don't sing the old songs in a new land.

Yet it may be too soon to say that the South's contribution has been made. After all, the first two riots in 1968 were in South Carolina and Tennessee. The garbage strike opens a whole new possibility of labor-racial coalition in those jobs consigned exclusively to Negroes throughout the South. And, more important, the Northern Negro, who has always had a love-hate memory for the South, begins to yearn for his old identity. The name for it is "soul."

The militant activists insist on tradition (Africa) and religion (Muslim-ism, black Messianism, etc.) and community (the brothers). Like the young King, many Negroes feel the old Baptist preachers were not dig-nified. Better exotic headdress and long gowns from Africa than the frock coat of "De Lawd." But the gowns and headgear *are* exotic—foreign things that men wear stiffly, a public facade. There are more familiar Negro traditions and religion and community. Black graduate students have earned the right to go back to hominy and chitlins and mock anyone who laughs. The growth of "soul" is a spiritual return to the South—but a return with new weapons of dignity and resistance. Religion, the family, the past can be reclaimed now without their demeaning overtones. In this respect, the modern Negro is simply repeating, two decades later, King's brilliant maneuver of escape and reentry. He got the best of both worlds—the dignity that could only be won "outside," and the more familiar things which that dignity can transform. King was there before them all.

He remained, always, the one convincing preacher. Other civil-rights pioneers were mostly lawyers, teachers, authors. They learned the white man's language almost too well. King learned it, too; but it was always stiff. He belonged in the pulpit, not at the lectern. Bayard Rustin, with his high dry professional voice and trilled r's, cannot wear the S.C.L.C.'s marching coveralls with any credibility. The same is true, in varying measure, of most first-generation "respectable" leaders. Some of them would clearly get indigestion from the thinnest possible slice of watermelon, Adam Powell, of course, can ham it with the best; but his is a raffish rogue-charm, distinguished by its whiff of mischief. King, by contrast, was an Uncle Ben with a degree, a Bill Bailey who came home—and turned the home upside down. That is why he infuriated Southerners more than all the Stokelys and Raps put together. In him, they saw *their* niggers turning a calm new face of power on them.

King had the self-contained dignity of the South without its passivity. His day is not past. It is just coming. He was on his way, when he died, to a feast of "soul food"—a current fad in Negro circles. But King was there before them. He had always loved what his biographer calls, rather nervously, "ethnic delicacies." He never lost his "soul." He was never ashamed. His career said many things. That the South cannot be counted out of the struggle yet. That the Negro does not have to go elsewhere to find an identity—he can make his stand on American soil. That even the Baptist preacher's God need not yield, yet, to Allah. God is not dead—though "De Lawd" has died. One of His prophets died.

[August, 1968]

PART V

LIVING UP
TO OUR
COMMITMENT
IN VIETNAM

Hell Sucks

by Michael Herr

During the years of the Vietnam War, a new kind of cynicism was born. Official Army statements, body counts, congressional investigations, presidential speeches—all these were expressions merely of whatever truth seemed to fit the purpose. In an effort to get at the reality of the war, Esquire *sent a young writer named Michael Herr to Southeast Asia. The reports he sent back remain among the war's most vivid and believable, and were later collected in a book called* Dispatches. *This piece was published in August 1968 after the Tet offensive had begun.*

There is a map of Vietnam on the wall of my apartment in Saigon, and some nights, coming back late to the city, I'll lie out on my bed and look at it, too tired to do anything more than just get my boots off. The map is a marvel, especially absorbing because it is not real. For one thing, it is very old. It was left here years ago by a previous tenant, probably a Frenchman since the map was made in Paris. The paper has buckled, and much of the color has gone out of it, laying a kind of veil over the countries it depicts. Vietnam is divided into its older territories of Tonkin, Annam and Cochin China, and to the west, past Laos and Cambodge, sits Siam, a kingdom. That's old, I told the General. That's a really old map.

The General is drawn to it too, and whenever he stops by for a drink he'll regard it silently, undoubtedly noting inaccuracies which the maps available to him have corrected. The waters that wash around my Indochine are a placid, Disney blue, unlike the intense, metallic blues of the General's maps. But all of that aside, we both agree to the obsolescence of my map, to the final unreality of it. We know that for years now, there has been no country here but the war. The landscape has been converted to terrain, the geography broken down into its more useful components;

439

corps and zones, tactical areas of responsibility, vicinities of operation, outposts, positions, objectives, fields of fire. The weather of Vietnam has been translated into conditions, and it's gone very much the same way with the people, the population, many of whom can't realize that there is an alternative to war because war is all they have ever known. Bad luck for them, the General says. As well as he knows them (and he knows them well), he seldom talks about them except to praise "their complexity, their sophistication, their survivability." Endearing traits.

Everyone is terribly sorry about what the war is doing to Vietnam and the Vietnamese, especially since the cities have been brought into it, although somehow most of the official expressions of grief have about them that taint of Presidential sorrow, turning a little grinny around the edges. The Tet Offensive changed everything here, made this an entirely different war, made it Something Else. ("Nonsense," a colonel told me. "We're just doing the same things in the cities that we've done in the boonies, why . . . for *years*!" He was not the same man who said, "We had to destroy Bentre in order to save it," but he might have been. He'd be hip to that.) Before Tet, there was some clean touch to jungle encounters, some virtue to their brevity, always the promise of quick release from whatever horror there was. The war went on in bursts, meeting engagements; and covering it—particularly in the Highlands and the Delta, II Corps and IV Corps—you were always a tourist, a tripper who could summon up helicopters like taxis. You would taxi in, the war would break over you suddenly and then go away, and you would taxi out. Enough chances were taken to leave you exhilarated, and, except for the hangovers that any cheap thrill will give you, it was pleasant enough. Now, it is awful, just plain awful, awful without relief. (A friend on The New York *Times* told me that he didn't mind his nightmares so much as his waking impulse to file on them.) It has finally become that kind of conventional war that the Command so longed for, and it is not going well. And for every month that it continues not going well, the scope of its destruction is enlarged. We are not really a particularly brutal people, certainly no more brutal now than we've been in other wars, acquiring it as the war goes on. But our machine is devastating. And versatile. It can do almost everything but stop.

And after all these years, we were caught in midwinter with the blunt truth that our achievement in Vietnam had been less than epic, a fact that touched everyone but the men who run the war. It became finally clear that General Westmoreland did not understand this war ("This is a different war than Americans have ever been asked to fight," he told the Examining Angels. "How is it different?" they asked. "Well, you know, it's just . . . different"), and he was asked to leave it. The immediate official response was manic; after years and years of posing along the rim, the Mission joined hands and leapt through the Looking Glass. It was as though Swift's vault had been plundered to meet the public doubt. They trotted out their kill ratios, their curious estimates of enemy morale (there wasn't any), their poor, salvaged shards of Pacification (that good American idea; it would have worked wonderfully in New Mexico), strange redemption profiles of the countryside's lost security. The same incantations, the heavies, moderates and lights of this statistic-obsessed war, were sung again, and optimism was spent at the same excessive rate which we had previously maintained in the expending of ordnance. This antic Thumbs-Upmanship was best pegged by a British correspondent who compared it all to the captain of the *Titanic* accouncing, "There's nothing to be alarmed about, ladies and gentlemen. We're only stopping briefly to take on some ice." And I remembered an Indian lady I once knew who shipped a trunk to her family in Calcutta. She had lost the key but found another, the key to one of her closets, and she mailed that on after the trunk. She knew it wouldn't open the trunk, but she so wanted it to work that she sent it anyway. Strange story, but I expect it might touch our Ambassador, and possibly even our former Commanding General.

When the battle for Hué was all over, they entered it into the records, gauged its terrible cost and battlegrammed it, so that it took on the dry, tactical stamp of the West Point Atlas of American Wars. When future observers come to it, it will seem that some order had been apparent during the twenty-seven days that it took to get the North Vietnamese and Vietcong forces out of the Imperial City, and that will not be exactly the truth. Hué was not the bloodiest battle of the Vietnam war (unless you enter in the more than four thousand civilian dead and the tens of thousands who were wounded, not likely in any forthcoming revised edition of the W.P.A.O.A.W.), but it was the hardest and the bitterest, and for those of us who were a part of it, even the coldest chronicles will be enough to recall the texture of its dread. If the war was changing, Hué was that turn of the screw which locked the new terms into place for good, taking you beyond that cutoff point where one war becomes just like all other wars. You would get twinges of this feeling any time that you were on the line, with the troops; but still, before Hué, you thought of yourself as a dove or a hawk, felt that our involvement was criminal or proper, obscene or clean. After Hué, all of your lines of reasoning turned into clumsy coils, and all of the talk got on your nerves. Hué finally gave you what you had expected, half yearned for, in the days of the war that ended with the Offensive. It got up memories, vicarious enough, stored from old copies of *Life* magazine, old movie newsreels, Pathé sound tracks whose dirge-disaster music still echoed: the Italian Campaign, the fight for the Reservoir, gruesome camp, evocations of '44 and '50.

Going in, there were sixty of us packed in a deuce-and-a-half, one of eight trucks moving in convoy from Phubai, bringing in over three hundred replacements for the casualties taken in the earliest fighting south of the Perfume River. There had been a harsh, dark storm going on for days, and it turned the convoy route into a mud bed. It was terribly cold in the trucks, and the road was covered with leaves that had either been blown off the trees by the storm or torn away by our heavy artillery. The artillery had done a job here, touched everything. Many of the houses had been completely collapsed, and not one had been left without at least heavy pitting from shell fragments. Hundreds of refugees held to the side of the road as we passed. Many of them had been wounded during the shelling. The kids would laugh and shout the standard, "You you you! Okay?" The old would look on with that quiet tolerance for misery that makes so many Americans uneasy, which is usually misread as indifference. But the younger men and women would often give us looks of unmistakable contempt, pulling their cheering children back from the trucks.

So we sat there, grinning at the bad weather and the discomfort, sharing the first fear, glad that we were not riding point or closing the rear because, man, the middle is good. They had been hitting our convoys regularly, and a lot of the trucks had been turned back. The houses that we were passing so slowly made the best kind of cover for snipers, and one B-40 rocket could have made casualties out of a whole truckload of us. All the Grunts were whistling and no two were whistling the same tune, and it sounded like a locker room just before a big game. A friend of mine, Sergeant Dale Dye, a Marine correspondent, sat with a tall yellow flower sticking out of his helmet cover, a really outstanding target, the kind of idiosyncracy the Marines will indulge in. His eyes rollicked, and below his big moustache his wicked, shy smile said, "Oh yes, Charlie's got his shit together here, this will be oh-so-bad, indubitably." It was the same smile I saw later when a sniper's bullet tore up the wall two inches above his head inside the Citadel. Odd cause for merriment in anyone but a Grunt.

There's something you see in the faces of Marines that you'll never see in the Army, some extra character etched in by the training and by more hard times than you'd believe, by constant intimidation, by the widespread conviction that you will get yours if you hang in there long enough. They're each of them like the hardest man on the block (You ain't been cut, you ain't my man) and they all have that wild, haunted, going-West look that says it is perfectly correct to be here where the fighting is worst, where you won't have half of what you'll need, where it is colder than the Nam ever gets. To pass the time, I started reading the stuff they'd written on their helmet covers and flak jackets. There were the names of campaigns and the names of their girls, nicknames (The Entertainer, The Avenger, Short Time Safety Moe), the slogans that touch on their lonely, severe fantasies (Born to Lose, Born to Raise Hell), and general graffiti (Hell Sucks, Time is On My Side, Yossarian Lives, Just You and Me God—Right?). There was nothing on the truck as good as the scrawl on the wall in Khesanh that said, "I Think I'm Falling In Love With Jake," but it passed the time.

And they are all giving you that mock-astonished look. "You mean you don't *have* to be here? And you're *here*?" But they are glad you're here, really very grateful. "Hey, Esquire! Hey, you want a story, man? Write this: I'm up there on 881, this was May, I'm up there walkin' the ridgeline an' this Zip jumps up smack into me, lays this AK-47 fuckin' right *into* me, only he's so surprised I got my whole clip off 'fore he knew how to thank me for it. Grease one." After twenty kilometers of this, in spite of the roiling dark sky ahead, we could see the smoke coming up from the far side of the river, from the Citadel of Hué.

The bridge was down that spanned the canal dividing the village of An Cu and the southern sector of Hué, blown the night before by the Vietcong, and the forward area beyond the opposite bank was not thought to be secure, so we bivouacked in the village for the night. It had been completely deserted, and we set ourselves up in empty hootches, laying our poncho liners out over the litter of shattered glass and brick. At dusk, while we were all stretched out along the canal bank eating dinner, two Marine gunships came down on us, strafing us, sending burning tracers up along the canal, and we ran for cover, more astonished than scared. "Way to go, mother-lover, way to pinpoint the motherin' enemy," one of the Grunts screamed, and he set up his M-60 machine gun in case they came back. "I don't guess we gotta take *that* shit." Patrols were sent out, guards posted, and we went to the hootches to sleep. For some reason, we were not even mortared that night.

The next morning we knew that the area must have been secured beyond a reasonable doubt, because the A.R.V.N. were there. Good little fighters, the A.R.V.N.; ask any U.S. adviser in the field. Most of them here were not even armed. They needed both hands free for their work that morning, which consisted of thoroughly combing every house and store in the village, turning out drawers, tipping over chests and urns, raiding chicken coops and liquor cabinets, kicking in all the glass cases they could find, and forcibly relieving refugees on the road of radios, wine, ducks, clothing, anything. What they couldn't carry, they wore. One soldier moved up the road in an old felt hat that fell down over his eyes and a blue gabardine overcoat at least eight sizes too large, so that it trailed around him in the mud as he walked. I thought he was going to ask me the way to Floogle Street, but he only smiled proudly at his good luck and ducked into one of the shops.

It was the same after we'd crossed the canal on a two-by-four and started walking in. We tried to flag down a lift, but the jeeps all seemed to be driven by A.R.V.N. officers out on organized looting parties. We walked along in the open toward the river, talking in an offhanded way about how superb the N.V.A. snipers were supposed to be, until we came across the very first of the hundreds of civilian dead that we were to see in the next weeks: a little girl who had been hit while riding her bicycle and an old man who lay arched over his straw hat. They'd been lying out like that for over a week, and for the first time I was grateful for the cold.

Along the Perfume River's south bank there is a long, graceful park that separates Hué's most pleasant avenue, Le Loi, from the riverfront. People will talk about how they'd sit out there in the sun and watch the sampans moving down the river, or watch the girls bicycling up Le Loi, past the villas of officials and the French-architected university buildings. Many of those villas had been destroyed and much of the university permanently damaged. In the middle of the street a couple of ambulances from the German Mission had been blown up, and the Cercle Sportif was covered with bullet holes and shrapnel. In the park itself, four fat green dead lay sprawled around a tall, ornate cage, inside of which sat a small, shivering monkey. One of the correspondents along stepped over the corpses to feed it some fruit. (Days later, I came back to the spot. The corpses were gone, but so was the monkey. There had been so many refugees and so little food then, and someone must have eaten him.) The Marines of 2/5 had secured almost all of the central south bank and were now fanning out to the west, fighting and clearing one of the major canals. We were waiting for some decision on whether or not U.S. Marines would be going into the Citadel itself, but no one had any doubts about what that decision would be. Didn't it always come to that with the Grunts? Didn't it, every goddam time? We sat there taking in the dread by watching the columns of smoke across the river, receiving occasional sniper rounds, infrequent bursts of .50 caliber, watching the Navy L.C.U.'s on the river getting shelled from the wall. One Marine next to me was saying that it was just a damned shame, all them poor people, all them nice-looking houses. He was looking at the black napalm blasts and the wreckage along the wall. "Looks like the Imperial City's had the schnitz," he said.

It stayed cold for the next ten days, cold and dark, and that damp gloom was the background for the footage that we all took out of the Citadel. The little sunlight there was caught the heavy motes of dust that blew up from the wreckage of the East Wall, held it until everything you saw was filtered through it. And most of what you saw was taken in from unaccustomed angles, prone positions or quick looks from a crouch; lying flat out, hearing the hard dry rattle of shrapnel scudding against the debris around you, listening to the Marine next to you who didn't moan, "Oh my God, Oh Sweet Jesus, Oh Holy Mother save me," but who sobbed, instead, "Are you *ready* for this? I mean, are you *ready* for this?" Once, when the noise from a six-round mortar attack stopped, I heard some singing in back of me. There were three Grunts huddled together holding onto their helmets, looking more mischievous than scared. "We gotta get out of this place," they sang, "if it's the las' thing we ever do-woo." With all of that dust blowing around, the acrid smell of gunpowder would hang in the air for a long while after fire fights, and there was also some CS gas that we'd fired at the N.V.A. blowing back in over our positions. It was impossible to get off a clean breath with all of that going on, and of course there was that other smell too, that most special of all smells that came up from shallow graves and from shattered heaps of stone wherever an air strike had passed. It held to the lining of your nostrils and worked itself into the weave of your fatigues, and weeks later, miles away, you would wake up from a dream in the middle of the night and it would be there in the room with you. The N.V.A. had dug themselves so deeply into the wall that air strikes had to destroy it meter by meter, dropping napalm as close as three hundred meters from our positions. Up on the highest point of the wall, on what had once been a tower, I looked across the Citadel's moat and saw the N.V.A. moving quickly among the rubble of the opposing wall. We were close enough to be able to see their faces. A rifle went off a few feet to my right, and one of the figures across the moat started forward and then dropped. A Marine sniper leaned back from his cover and grinned at me.

By the end of that week, the wall had cost the Marines roughly one casualty for every meter taken, a quarter of them K.I.A. 1/5, which came to be known as the Citadel Battalion, had been through every tough battle the Marines had had in the past six months, and now some of its companies were down to below platoon strength. They all knew how bad it was, the novelty of fighting in the streets had become a nasty, spooky joke, and not many of them really believed they'd ever get out alive. Everyone wanted to get wounded.

There was a tough, quiet Negro who called himself Philly Dog. He'd been a gang lord in the streets of North Philadelphia, and in Hué he was the best man to be with, the only one who really understood how it was when you had no cover and no rear. He was better here than the hottest jungle fighter, better than those lean, mean Nam veterans with their proficiency badges for coaxing water out of palm roots, filleting snakes and reading moss. Philly Dog was the only scout you could feel right about in Hué.

"Just hold onto it, man," he'd say. "You doan go out there. That's Charlie." He pointed up the road.

We were in among the makings of a former villa, with only the rear wall still standing. I couldn't see anything up the road past one of our tanks, only a few houses, scattered trees and wires and a gigantic portion of collapsed wall.

"How do you know?" I asked.

" 'Cause if I was Charlie, that'd be my spot." And he was right, almost every time.

At night, in the battalion C.P., the Major in command would sit reading his maps, staring vacantly at the trapezoid of the Citadel. It could have been a scene in a Norman farmhouse twenty-five years ago, with candles burning on the tables, bottles of red wine arranged along damaged shelves, the cold in the room, the high ceilings, the heavy ornate cross on the wall. The Major had not slept for five nights, and for the fifth night in a row he assured us that tomorrow would get it for sure, the final stretch of the wall would be taken, and he had all the Marines he needed to do it. And one of his aides, a tough mustang of a first lieutenant, would pitch a hard, ironic smile above the Major's stare, a smile that rejected good news and opted for doom, and it was like hearing him say, "The Major here is full of shit, and we both know it."

We found a villa near the C.P. and set ourselves up in it for the night. We never stayed in the same area two nights in a row, since it never took the N.V.A. very long to get us zeroed in. In the living room of the villa there were photographs of a Vietnamese family that had been taken in the States; the father in a dark business suit standing somewhere in New York; Mom, Dad and the kids at Disneyland. The Grunts could never get over the fact that there were wealthy Vietnamese, and these pictures filled them with awe. Dale Dye was there (after the sniper had barely missed him, he had gotten rid of that flower), and some of the guys had found a bottle of Veuve Cliquot. Usually they'd scarfe up the 7 Crown or the Calvert's and leave four-star cognacs sitting on the shelves, but the champagne intrigued them. Most of them had never tasted it. One tall kid was saying that where he came from, it only got poured at weddings. Dye popped the cork, and one of them went chasing after it, giggling at how gala this was getting to be. Dye passed the bottle to the tall boy, who put it to his lips as if it might go off before drinking it. "It tickles m'nose," he said, and Dye broke up, shaking his head. "It's a good champagne," he said. "Not a great champagne, but a good champagne."

We slept so soundly that night that a sixty-round mortar barrage a little before dawn failed to wake us.

After the Catholic chaplain was killed, the Protestant had to give communion. His name was Takesian, an Armenian from Boston, one of those hip, blunt clerics who loved to talk, as though talking itself contained ritual powers of redemption. He wasn't one of your grizzled battle chaplians, but he was very brave, and very much affected by the particular ugliness of the Hué fighting. It was not physical fear that put him off, but the mood of bitterness that no one seemed to be able to shake, and he would sit for long stretches by himself, staring at the wounded through his thick steel-rimmed glasses. He was using sliced C-ration white bread and canteen water to deliver the sacramants, and some of the Grunts were skeptical about receiving them from a Protestant. "Listen, you silly bastards," Takesian said. "You could all get your ass shot off any time now out there. Do you think God gives a damn *how* you've been blessed?"

Sometimes one of the companies would find itself completely cut off, and it would take hours for the Marines to get their casualties out. I remember one Marine with a head wound who finally made it up to the Battalion C.P., only to find himself stuck in a stalled jeep. He finally jumped out of the jeep and started to push it, knowing it was the only way out of there. Most of the tanks and trucks which carried casualties had to move up a long, straight road with no cover, and they began calling it Rocket Alley. Every tank the Marines had had been hit at least once there. An epiphany of Hué turned up in John Olson's great photograph in *Life,* the wounded from Delta Company piled hurriedly on the tank. Sometimes, on the way out to the Battalion Aid Station, the more seriously wounded would take on that bad color, the grey-blue fishbelly promise of death that would spread upwards from the chest and cover the face. There was one Marine who had been shot through the neck, and all the way out the corpsmen massaged his chest. By the time they reached the station, though, he was so bad that the doctor triaged him, passed him over to treat the ones that he knew could be saved, and when they put him into the green canvas body bag there was some chance that he was still clinically alive. The doctor had never been in a position before where he had had to choose like that—there were so many wounded—and he never got used to it. During the lulls, he'd step outside for some air, but it was no better out there. The bodies were stacked together, and there was always a crowd of A.R.V.N. standing around staring, death-enthralled like all Vietnamese. Since they did not know what else to do, and not knowing how it would look to the Marines, they would smile vacantly at the bodies there, and a couple of ugly incidents occurred. The Marines who had volunteered for the body details were overworked and became snappish, ripping packs off of corpses angrily, cutting gear away with bayonets, heaving bodies into the green bags. One of the dead Marines had become stiff and they had trouble getting him to fit. "Damn," one of them said, "didn't this mother have big feet on him?" And he finally forced the legs into the canvas. In the station, there was the youngest-looking Marine I'd ever seen, so young that his parents must have had to sign for him at enlistment. He'd been caught in the knee by a large piece of shrapnel, and he had no idea at all of what they would do with him now that he'd been wounded. He lay out on the stretcher while the doctor explained how he would be choppered back to the Phubai hospital and then put on a plane for Danang, and then flown back to the States for what would probably be the rest of his hitch. At first the boy was sure that the doctor was kidding him, then he started to believe a little of it, and when he knew that it was true, that he was actually getting out, he couldn't stop smiling, and enormous tears of happiness ran down into his ears.

It was at this point that I began to recognize almost every casualty, remember conversations we'd had days and even hours earlier, and that's when I got out, riding a Medevac chopper with a lieutenant who was covered with blood-soaked bandages. He'd been hit in both legs, both arms, the chest and head, his ears were filled with caked blood, and he asked a photographer named Art Greenspon who was in the chopper if he'd get a picture of him like this so he could mail it to his wife.

But at this point, the battle for Hué was almost over. The Cav was working the northwest corner of the Citadel, and elements of the 101st had come in through what had formerly been an N.V.A. resupply route. Vietnamese Marines and some of the 1st A.R.V.N. Division, who had fought well from the beginning, had been moving the remaining N.V.A. down toward the wall. The N.V.A. flag that had flown for so long over the South Wall had been brought down, and in its place an American flag had been put up, a sight which must have thrilled those most xenophobic of all Vietnamese, the people of Hué. Two days later the Hoc Bao, Vietnamese Rangers for whom this privilege had been reserved, stormed through the walls of the Imperial Palace, but there were no enemy troops left inside. Except for a few corpses that bobbed sluggishly in the moat, most of the dead had been buried. Nearly seventy percent of Vietnam's one lovely city was destroyed, and if the landscape seemed desolate, imagine how the figures in that landscape looked.

There were two official ceremonies marking the expulsion of the N.V.A., both flag raisings. On the south bank of the Perfume River, two hundred refugees from one of the camps were recruited to stand in the rain and watch the G.V.N. flag being run up. But the rope snapped, and the crowd, thinking the V.C. had shot it down, broke up in panic. (There was no rain in the stories that the Saigon papers ran, there was no trouble with the rope, and the cheering crowd numbered thousands.) As for the other ceremony, the Citadel was still thought by most people to be insecure, and when the flag finally went up there was no one there to watch it except a handful of Vietnamese troops.

In the first weeks after the Tet Offensive began, the curfew began early in the afternoon, and was strictly enforced. By two-thirty each day Saigon had the look of the final reel of *On the Beach,* a desolate city whose long avenues held nothing but refuse, windblown papers, small, distinct piles of human excrement and the dead flowers and spent firecracker casings of the Lunar New Year. Alive, Saigon had been depressing enough, but once the Offensive began it became so stark that, in an odd way, it was invigorating. The trees along the main streets all looked like they'd been struck by lightning, and it became unusually, uncomfortably cold; one more piece of bad luck in a place where nothing was in its season. With so much filth growing in so many streets and alleys, an epidemic of plague was feared, and if there was ever a place that suggested plague, demanded it, it was Saigon in the Emergency. Large numbers of American civilians, the construction workers and engineers who were making it here like they'd never made it at home, began openly carrying weapons, 45's and grease guns and AK's, and no mob of Mississippi sheriff's boys ever promised more bad news. You'd see them at ten in the morning on the terrace of the Continental Hotel, waiting for the bar to open, unable to light their own cigarettes until it did. The crowds on Tu Do Street looked like Ensor processions, and there was a corruption in the air that had nothing to do with government officials on the take. After seven in the evening, when the curfew became total, nothing but police vehicles and M.P. jeeps moved in the streets, except for a few very young children who raced up and down over the rubbish, running newspaper kites up into the chilling wind. Shortly after dark, I could expect to see the headlights of the General's jeep coming up the street toward my apartment.

The General is a great favorite of the press here. He is commonly thought to be candid, articulate and accessible, which is absolutely the highest compliment the press corps can pay to any member of the American Mission. He is less accessible now that the war has begun to go badly, but he still finds time most nights to drop around for a quick drink, before returning to his headquarters and, I imagine, a late night's work. I have never really understood our growing friendship, since there is not a single point touching the war that we agree on. It is thought by outsiders that the General and I spend our evenings playing chess, but in fact I never learned the game, and its abstractions make the General nervous. My colleagues think that he drinks with me instead of them because I am accredited to a monthly, but of course there's more to it than that. For one thing, the General never condescends to me, while I take a lot of trouble trying not to understand him too quickly. I suppose that we are both, in our own way, aesthetes. The General is an aesthete of insurgency and counterinsurgency, a choreographer of guerrilla activity, and he has been at it a long, long time. Some of the older hands here remember seeing him in Vietnam at the time of the Indochina War. He was a captain then, and he would turn up in odd, remote corners of the country dressed in black pajamas. He is supposed to have spoken fluent Vietnamese then, although he now flatly denies any familiarity with that language, which he will actually mimic quite cruelly, breaking into protracted fits of laughter. It's said that he took a break in service during the early Sixties, two years in which he all but completely disappeared. He has no command designation as such, but is connected vaguely with something called Special Operations, about which he refuses to speak.

One is immediately struck by the clean-lined ruggedness of his features, although the longer you observe him the more you notice something delicate there, some softness behind the eyes that is almost feminine. The eyes are ice-blue but not cold, and they suggest his most interesting trait, an originality of mind that one never associates with the Military, and which constantly catches you off balance. It's impossible to guess his age to a certainty (I'd never think of asking him), but he is probably around fifty.

"How's the war going, General?" I'll ask him.

"You're a correspondent, you tell me."

"Seriously."

"Oh, how does it ever go, Mike? Slowly. Damned slowly."

He accepts his drink, lights a Bastos and sinks into a chair.

"We're hurting him," he says. "We know we're hurting him. What we don't know is how much more of it he can take. We're killing him." He raises his glass. "To absent friends."

We talk about many things: Blake, Mexico, the Beethoven Quartets, Oriental women, the Saints, wines, the Elizabethans, classic automobiles and, obviously, Vietnam, which I don't really understand that well. Before the Offensive, we would argue about whether the American position here was morally defensible. I believed it was not, the General believed it was beside the point. In fact (we never said this, but somehow mutually acknowledged it) the subject bored us both. Now, since Tet, I've been more concerned with whether or not our position is even militarily defensible, and the General is optimistic there. Sometimes, he worries about me, about my safety and, even more, about my sanity. I have what he refers to as "this thing about death," an unhealthy fascination with so much of what I've had to see here. He respects it intellectually (one of our other constant topics is suicide) but finally he finds it morbid and unprofitable. Worst of all, he finds that I have a tendency, when discussing the dead, to not only dwell on them, but to personalize them as well. "That way lies you-know-what," he says, tapping his temple; but he lets me get it out, lets me talk about the victims, about the dead and the disposition of the dead.

The first dead I saw in Vietnam was a Cambodian Mercenary serving with the Special Forces in the Seven Mountains Region of the Delta. He had accidentally shot himself in the head while cleaning his .30-caliber rifle. Mercenaries live in a compound with their families, and this one had his parents, his grandparents and his wife with him at the time. The medics bandaged his entire head so that he looked like something you'd see in relief on an old temple wall, some dead prince, very dignified in repose. The women squatted over his body, and their moaning built up into a terrible wail, falling off and beginning again, hour after hour. Some blood and brine from the wound had seeped through the bandages and filled a small dent in the canvas, so that when they carried him from the stretcher some of it spilled over my boots. "Sorry," one of the medics said. "Got some on you." The next dead that I saw were in a mass of over one hundred, Vietcong who had tried to overrun the perimeter of an outpost of the 25th Infantry Division near Tayninh. They had been stopped by 105's firing fléchette canisters, thousands of steel shafts that cut them up in the most incredible way, leaving them almost unrecognizable as human beings, although you could see that some of them were very young and some were women. In Cantho, on the morning after the Offensive began, there were around forty V.C. piled up at the end of the airstrip, and one of them was a medic who had died huddled over his aid case. One of the Americans worked him loose with his feet, jammed a cigar into the clenched teeth and photographed it. Another American was screaming at a very young dead, almost sobbing, "There, you silly bastard, there! You got it now? You got it?" Americans often admonish the dead like that, particularly the young ones. The bodies were all loaded into the back of a truck, where they lay all day, growing stiff in the positions which they had taken in death. When the truck finally started, one of them fell off the back. He was so rigid that he landed exactly on both knees and one elbow (a perfect three-pointer, one of the guys called it) with no other part of him touching the ground, and he had to be lifted up into the truck like a heavy wrought-iron figure.

Later that day, in the provincial hospital at Cantho, the friendly dead began accumulating in the corridors. The Vietcong shelled the hospital for over seven hours from Cantho University, which they had captured and held until it was finally bombed flat, and even if we had wanted to leave we couldn't have. They needed help desperately that day. Over four hundred civilian wounded were brought in, most of them children ("Who shot you, V.C. or U.S.?" the Psywar types kept asking), and we had to cleanse the wounds, cut away dead tissue, or just lean on them, hold them still while the surgeons worked. Outside of the operating rooms there were all of those who were beyond saving, already going grey before death. They just waited there, and you could see they knew. There was an odd piece of graffiti up on the wall of one of the hospital rooms, and I passed it a hundred times that day, always meaning to find out who had written it, and why. It said, "How do you feel about decay, Senator?" In spite of the mortars, a number of Vietnamese came into the hospital carrying wounded children, strangers whom they'd found lying out in the streets, and a number of others came in simply to help. At this point in the fighting the IV Corps Commander, General Manh, was absorbed in constructing a solid five-block perimeter around his house, a strange sort of defense plan considering that the most precious region of the country was at stake, and we were not permitted to drive our jeeps through this perimeter because they drew fire. We had to drive instead through sniper-infested sections of the city, frequently through ambushes along the road, and there were certainly a lot of dead to be seen there.

Of course it is much closer to you when the dead are Americans, and closer still when you've known them. I'm always being told about our comparatively heightened regard for human life, and a lot of us here think that it's exclusively American. I knew a G.I. in Bu Dop who could look at blown-up Vietnamese all day, V.C. or friendly, men, women and children, it didn't much matter. "Hell, they ain't people," he said. "Them're Slopes." But the sight of one quite cleanly killed American made him vomit. The war was a very simple one for him, and you can bet that he had a solution for ending it. But we did agree that it was a bad thing that Americans were getting killed. I'd spent enough hours flying out of combat LZ's in choppers shared with the dead. Often enough, they had no faces left at all, and some died with that wincing sucking-in of breath that shows the full pain of it, some with the dreamy smiles of the drowned, and one that I particularly remember with full staring eyes and a look of mighty outrage, like some Old Testament picture of wrath at the injustice of it. Some just get Blown Away, and sometimes, if they can't reassemble a more or less total corpse from the found parts, they will enter it as Missing. "Shitty way to buy the farm," one kid told me.

For me, though, the very worst dead was a Vietnamese who had been killed near a canal in southern Hué, on the road leading to the Hotel Company C.P. The very top of his head had been shaved off by a piece of debris, so that only the back of his scalp remained connected to the skull. It was like a lidded container whose contents had poured out into the road to be washed away by the rains. Perhaps something had driven over it, or perhaps it had just collapsed during the ten days or more that it had lain there, but I couldn't get the image of it out of my mind. I spent that afternoon with the commander of Hotel, checking their defense perimeter. He was a great, decent Marine named Captain Christmas. This was not a wealthy section of Hué. The homes were modest, sometimes nothing more than elaborate hootches, but walking around Hotel's positions you could see that the entire section had been planned and landscaped, its arranged pathways decorated with statues, its gardens formally designed. Christmas was very moved by this, and his men had strict orders to respect the homes, the grounds and the people. But when it came to spending the night there, my nerves gave out. The Grunts probably assumed that I was afraid of a mortar attack, which was ridiculous since one could be and usually was mortared almost anywhere in Hué, at any time. It was that dead out there with his hinged scalp. I knew that if I stayed here he would drift in over me that night, grinning and dripping, all rot and green-black bloat. After I'd decided to go, I knew that I'd have to pass him again on the way out, and when the time came I forgot my promise and looked back at him one more time. . . .

The General holds up his hand. He's been leaning forward, listening like a crack therapist, and his eyes have gone narrow. He's been tuned into it, all right.

"Yes. Of course," he says. "It's terrible. I didn't really expect it to happen this way. If they'd listened to me then."

"Who? When?"

He shakes his head and a guarded smile comes over his face. Outside, there is a gecko chittering and screaming, and a cluster of magnesium flares are settling down over the perimeter beyond Tan Son Nhut. The General's driver, a giant Khmer called Lurch, is sleeping behind the wheel of the jeep down by the curb.

"Sometimes," the General says, "I think I'm the only man in the world who understands this thing."

"It must be very lonely for you."

"Mike, it comes with the job. But you. If you hate this all so much, why do you stay?"

He has me there. I wait a moment before answering. "Because, General, it's the only war we've got."

And he really smiles now. After all that talk, we're speaking the same language again.

[August, 1968]

An American Atrocity

by Normand Poirier

For the American soldier, Vietnam was a war of ambiguities, with no clear battle lines or battle zones, where the enemy could be anyone—an old man, a woman. There were stories of children throwing live grenades into Army helicopters. Some soldiers came to scorn not only the Vietcong, but all Vietnamese. A few nursed this scorn into an abiding hatred that led them to commit brutal acts of violence against innocent people. Published in August 1969, this powerful piece by Normand Poirier reports the horrifying facts of one such incident.

First Squad drew the night's ambush. While Second and Third Squads of Second Platoon had slogged all day over wooded hills and barren dunes, First Squad had stood security back at Platoon C.P. So First Squad drew the night's ambush and at dusk, as Second and Third Squads filed into the C.P. perimeter—grousing at still another day of no contact with Vietcong—the nine men of First Squad set out in a light wind-whipped rain for their ambush site. Their orders: proceed three hundred yards to the junction of a certain stream and forest trail, deploy in ambush, remain in ambush until 11 p.m., abandon the ambush and check several huts for V.C. suspects and weapons, return to the C.P. by 12:30 a.m. For the Marines in Second Platoon, a routine patrol. Soldiering in their sector of Trà Bông Township had tamed off sharply since the arrival of the Marines in battalion strength four months earlier. The Vietcong had pulled out to mountains in the west and overt enemy activity had dwindled to stray rounds of sniper fire. Second Platoon had neither taken nor inflicted a casualty in weeks. Battalion officially considered the sector pacified. By all odds, First Squad's night ambush should have been uneventful.

But something unusual occurred. After crossing three hundred yards of alternately swampy and sandy terrain, the men of First Squad—a sergeant, a lance corporal, six privates first class and a hospitalman—reached the junction of stream and trail. Three men checked security around the site, standard operational procedure, and then the squad gathered together in a tight huddle of hushed talk deliberately inaudible above the babbling of the nearby stream. At this point, standard operational procedure called for the sergeant to assign ambush positions. The parley that took place did not follow S.O.P.: the sergeant did none of the talking; the talk lasted too long to be concerned only with a routine ambush. Five minutes. Ten minutes. Fifteen minutes. Dusk turned to dark around them. The rain stopped. After twenty minutes, the men stood up. They removed from their collars the small metal insignia denoting grade. They rolled their sleeves down to cover wristwatches and I.D. bracelets. They removed rings from their fingers. The sergeant radioed back to the C.P. that the squad had been positioned off and that the ambush was set. Then the men set out in single file on the trail they were supposed to have ambushed toward the hamlet of Xuan Ngoc a half-mile away. As they walked, the clouds parted and the moon broke through. It would be a clear night.

There were no lights in the hut as the men of First Squad observed it in silence from thirty yards away. At a signal from one, the last three men in the column moved stealthily toward it. They were numbers seven, eight and nine. No names would be used in this operation as a precaution against later identification. Each man had a number. Numbers seven, eight and nine were rear security. At the signal, they fanned out around the house, one to the rear and two to the sides. Numbers one, two and three would break in through the front door. Four and five would stand security out front.

Nguyen Luu had lived in the little hamlet of Xuan Ngoc all of his sixty-one years. He was a rice farmer and a carpenter and had helped build many of the two-dozen thatched-roof bamboo huts that housed his relatives and neighbors in the hamlet. He spent his days in the rice paddies or in his hut making benches and tables or repairing other farmers' wooden plows. Marine patrols passed by his paddies and his hut every few days, stopping now and then to check his I.D. cards and ask about V.C., but for the most part Nguyen Luu was left alone with his wife, who was almost seventy, his two younger sisters, and two nieces, not yet in their teens, who lived in the hut with him. He knew of six men from the hamlet who were Vietcong. He had once seen them with weapons. But everyone in the hamlet knew them and the hamlet chief had long since given their names to the U. S. troops and they had either been arrested or had fled into the mountains. And Nguyen Luu was satisfied. Since the

Marines arrived, the V.C. had stayed away and a measure of peace had settled over Xuan Ngoc.

So Nguyen Luu, asleep in his one-room hut with his wife, two sisters and two nieces, bolted upright in terror when the front door crashed open and dark figures swarmed in, shouting and knocking over furniture and filling the room with screams from the women and children. A light flashed in his face and a hand grabbed his hair and jerked his head back and an angry voice yelled, "Veecee! Veecee! Veecee!" He tried to shake his head no, but the hand that gripped his hair dragged him out of his bunk face down onto the floor and a heavy boot kicked him in the ribs. "No Veecee! Vietnamese!" he cried out and looked up to see his old wife's toothless face in the spot of light and a hand holding her head back by the hair. Her eyes were white with panic and her mouth moved soundlessly. The hand shoved her back on the bunk and Luu felt the boot again in his back. He was lifted to his feet and pushed through the front door to the patio, where two men stood with rifles. One of them punched him in the stomach and the other knocked him down with a blow to the face. He started to say that he was not a V.C., but he was kicked in the stomach and he could not catch his breath. He felt a gun barrel jab into his neck and he was terrified that he would be shot before he could get his breath back to explain that he had an I.D. card. Again he was raised to his feet and, while four Marines shouted at him and threatened him with their rifles, he saw his wife and two sisters and the two children being led away from the hut by two other Marines. He saw one Marine kick his sister Tran Thi Dat when she held out her I.D. card. The women and children were crying. Luu pleaded no one knew about V.C. but the Marines understood only his headshaking and one of them punched him in the face and another slashed his face with the barrel of his rifle. Luu fell down again. Two Marines went into the hut and ripped it apart, smashing furniture, tearing shelves from walls, slashing the matting of the walls. Luu rose to his knees, sobbing, and held out his I.D. card. A Marine grabbed it, looked at it, and tore it up. Luu could hear the women and children crying from the paddy next to the hut and he begged the Marines not to shoot them, realizing as he did that they did not understand him. The two Marines stomped out of the house angrily and kicked him again. Then they led him off to the paddy and made him squat with the women and children. For ten minutes the Marines terrorized the family, shouting about V.C., aiming at them with their rifles as though they would shoot them, kicking them, menacing them with bayonets. And then, with a final kick into Luu's back, the Marines filed off into the darkness in the direction of the hut of Nguyen Truc.

Nguyen Truc, a thirty-eight-year-old rice farmer, was asleep with his wife. Their five children, ranging in age from two to nine, were sleeping on a second bunk in the hut's one room. The front door burst open with a loud crack and a beam of light searched the room. The mother bounded out of bed toward her children but a Marine caught her by the arm and swung her to the door, where another Marine grabbed her. Truc jumped toward her but he was rammed back against the wall and held there by two men who flashed the light in his face. "You Veecee! You Veecee!" the men screamed at him and he shouted back that he was not. But they began punching him around the room. He was knocked sprawling against furniture, against the walls, once into his children, who were crying and screaming on their bunk. He heard his wife screaming outside and fought ferociously to reach the front door, but the Marines beat him until he was too weak to stand. They dragged him to the patio, where there were more Marines, and there two men grabbed him by the legs and held him upside down—his head off the ground—and a third delivered a kick to the face that knocked him out. He came to with the sound of his wife's hysterical sobbing in his ears and he saw that Marines were carrying pieces of firewood into the house and he asked his wife where the children were and she screamed that they were inside and that the troops were going to burn them. Truc went berserk and strained to his feet, screaming that they could not kill his children, blood streaming from the gash in his forehead. He was punched to the ground. The Marines surrounded him and his wife and shouted about V.C. and the couple wailed that they knew nothing and begged for their children. They were grabbed by the arms and led inside their house and were shown by flashlight their five children on the bunk covered by pieces of firewood. The couple screamed and sobbed and struggled to get to their children and the Marines barked at them furiously about V.C. Then the Marines shoved them across the room to their children and left.

Nguyen Thi Mai was not in her hut when the Marines broke into it. She was in a low-ceilinged dirt-walled bunker made of bamboo and sand at the rear of the hut. The bunker had been constructed by a neighbor for protection against mortar shellings. Nguyen Thi Mai had not used it for months because the shelling had stopped with the arrival of the U. S. troops. But this night she and her mother and her mother's sister had heard screams carried on the night breeze from the direction of Nguyen Truc's house, and screams in the night were not a good omen. So, as they had done during the period of the mortar shellings, Nguyen Thi Mai and the two older women packed their valuables— clothing and dishes—into an old suitcase and went to the bunker for the night. They were talking softly by the light of an oil lamp when they heard the racket and the sound of men's voices at the house. It sounded as though the men were tearing the house apart. The three women sat frozen in fear, Nguyen Thi Mai in a unique fear because she knew she was pretty, well-formed and only sixteen years old. None of the three thought to extinguish the lamp.

Nguyen Thi Mai stared at the narrow waist-high door to the bunker. A face appeared. A black man's face. The man stared at the women, called out to the other men, then waved the women out. The two older women went out but Nguyen Thi Mai couldn't move. She cringed on the bunk. The man reached in and pulled her out by the leg. Outside, her mother and aunt chattered nervously that they had their I.D. cards and that the troops should be careful of the suitcase because it contained their most precious items and that Nguyen Thi Mai didn't need an I.D. card because she was not yet eighteen. But the Marines merely shouted at the two women and tore up their I.D. cards and stuffed them back into the bunker and placed a board over the low doorway to block their view. Then one trooper grabbed Nguyen Thi Mai around the neck and slapped a hand on her mouth. Two others grabbed her legs and she was thrown to the ground on her back. A hand felt for the top of her pajama pants and ripped it off. She tried to scream, but the sounds died in her throat. She tried to kick and twist her body, but hands like vises gripped both her arms and both her legs and she couldn't move. The men talked excitedly and laughed and then her legs were forced open. She wanted to scream for her mother but the rough hand over her mouth and nose killed off all sound but the futile grunt in her throat. She could hear her mother wailing inside the bunker: God save my baby! God save my baby! She saw one of the troopers kneel between her legs with a flashlight and she cried at the shame of it. She knew they were going to do to her what no man had done to her and she cried for her mother. Then the vises on her arms and legs let go and the hand that had covered her mouth slapped her hard across the face and she was free. She screamed and ran in horror to the cover of the woods behind the bunker to hide her nakedness. She stayed there a long time after the Marines had left and then she crept back to the bunker and asked her mother to hand out a pajama pants from the suitcase. She put it on and went inside and joined her mother and aunt on the bunk, but no one spoke of what had happened because they were all too ashamed.

The men of First Squad raided six more huts. They ransacked but found neither weapons nor contraband; they beat and terrorized the villagers but elicited no information about Vietcong. When they reached the tenth hut—the home of Bui Thi Huong—they were frustrated and enraged. Bui Thi Huong was eighteen and the mother of a three-year-old boy, Dao Thien. Her husband, Dao Quang Thinh, was twenty, a farmer too ill with a chronic skin disease to be in the army. They lived in the hut with his mother, Nguyen Thi Lanh, fifty, his sister, Pham Thi Tan, twenty-nine, and his sister's daughter, Dao Thi Tao, aged five. They were sleeping when the men of First Squad battered their way into the hut. They yanked Thinh out of his bunk and accused him of being a V.C. He shook his head that he wasn't and repeated over and over, "No Veecee!" but they punched him in the head and stomach. Other Marines were dragging the three screaming women from the hut to the open concrete patio in front of the hut. Thinh managed to break free and dashed through the door to the patio but two Marines tackled him and began pounding him with fists and boots. One Marine came out of the hut holding a hand grenade and as he shouted to the other troopers he pointed to the grenade and to Thinh, indicating it as proof that Thinh was a V.C. Thinh shook his head and denied in wide-eyed terror that it was his grenade but the troopers formed a ring around him and punched him until he was nearly unconscious. They propped him up against the front of the hut and ordered his sister and mother and the two young children to sit beside him. While two Marines stood guard over them, five of the men assembled at the side of the house where Thinh's young wife had been dragged. She had heard her husband's protests of innocence and his cries as he was beaten and the cries of her mother-in-law and sister-in-law and the wailing of the children. But she could not even cry out because a man had a hand over her mouth and two others held her arms and legs and they had her on her back on the ground. When there were five men around her they forced open her legs and ripped her pajama pants away and tore open the top of her pajamas. She felt rough hands on her breasts and strained to break free but the grips on her arms and legs were like steel clamps. The hand on her face squeezed until she thought her nose would break. She felt the point of a knife jab into her forehead. A man knelt between her legs with a light and the others talked and laughed. She strained at the clamps and bit the hand over her mouth and when the hand flew off she let out a scream that pierced the night. The hand cracked her face back and forth and she felt blood trickle down her chin. Then the hand came down on her face again, this time holding a cloth cap, and she could neither scream nor see. She felt the first man go inside her and she prayed for her husband and baby. Then a second man raped her. She could hear her mother-in-law and sister-in-law wailing on the patio. They didn't understand, they were saying. They were not V.C. and the Americans just that day had checked their I.D. cards. O God, what were they doing to Bui Thi Huong, little mother. God save our little mother. God save our little father. Our little father was not V.C. Why did they beat our little father? Bui Thi Huong prayed while the second man raped her and she became so exhausted and pained that she fell off into unconsciousness. She felt water splashing on her face and she came to to see a man standing over her pouring water from a canteen. Another man was tapping her cheeks and she was relieved that no one was on her and inside her. The canteen was handed to two men standing beside her and they washed their genitals. All the men were talking and laughing and then a third man raped her. Tears streamed from her eyes but her sobs caught in her throat because of the hand over her mouth. She was so tired that she wished for unconsciousness again, but it did not come. She heard her husband's voice again, but she could tell from it that he was in great pain. He was asking what they had done with his wife. After the third man was finished, a fourth man raped her. And then a fifth man. Her husband's voice was loud now. He was screaming for his wife, hysterically, and the screams would carry all over the hamlet. The Marines shouted at him back on the patio but he kept screaming. The men around her raised their voices in anger and yelled back at the men on the patio but her husband yelled still louder. The man who was raping her finished and the troopers walked off to the patio. She heard them shout at her husband and she heard him scream as they hit him. He was hysterical with hatred because, he said, he knew what they had done to her. He knew. He knew! They could not understand him and they shouted things that she could not understand. But then she heard the first burst of gunfire. An angry, deafening blast of gunfire. And then she didn't hear her husband's voice any more. Only the wailing of her mother-in-law and sister-in-law and the crying of the children. Then she heard another burst of gunfire. And her mother-in-law's voice was gone. And then another burst, two or three bursts together, and there were no voices. My baby, she thought. My baby! She got to her knees and heard bamboo snap and saw a blinding flash of light and felt a searing pain in her right arm and breast and felt herself lifted and spun around and plopped down on the ground. She knew she was dead. Then the ground beneath her shook from a violent explosion and she felt a rain of debris and dirt pelt down on her. She lost consciousness.

First Squad reported by radio to the lieutenant at Platoon C.P. that the ambush had sprung and that three V.C. had been killed—two women and a man. The two women had been dragged off by the V.C., the lieutenant was told. This radio message was heard also by the captain of "B" Company, the lieutenant's commanding officer, at his C.P. He radioed the lieutenant for an immediate report on details of the skirmish. The lieutenant ordered his squad to return to the Platoon C.P. There, the men of First Squad told the lieutenant that the shootings had not taken place at the assigned ambush site. They had taken place a mile away. The men had panicked while checking out hooches and had accidentally killed civilians.

The lieutenant hiked back to the scene with his men. He froze when he saw on the patio the bodies of a man, a woman and two young children. The body of the older woman, the grandmother, had been blasted back inside the hut. Bui Thi Huong's body was around to the side of the hut.

"My God! What have you done!" the lieutenant said.

He turned to his men for an answer but before anyone could speak a sharp cry came from one of the two blood-splattered children. The lieutenant spun around and all ten men stared, without moving, at the bodies. The lieutenant spoke quietly to two men then ordered the dead man's body to be carried back to the original ambush site. At the site, he detailed five men to remain there with the body and track up the area to simulate an ambush action. The lieutenant then radioed to the captain that the ambush had triggered contact, that his squad had taken eight rounds and returned forty, that two females and one male V.C. had been killed, that the two females had been dragged away by V.C., and that pursuit had been broken off. The lieutenant then led the remaining four members of the squad back to Platoon C.P.

The five men he left behind proceeded to doctor up the ambush site. They dragged the man's body in the sand to make the trails for the two vanished female V.C. They removed their shoes and left the footprints of the ambushed V.C. They scattered empty cartridge shells. But then, instead of returning to the C.P., they went back to the hut. They set about policing the area. They lifted the body of the grandmother onto one bunk. They carried the body of the younger woman to the second bunk and placed the body of the little boy next to her. When they started to lift the body of the five-year-old girl, the child cried out. So they left her on the patio. They spread hay over the pools of blood on the patio and then gathered around the child. They looked down at the naked, blood-streaked form and debated. Four of them walked off a few yards but the fifth man stood over the child and with his M14 rifle bashed its brains in. The body was thrown into the hut, the splintered door was shut, and the five men headed back to Platoon C.P. First Squad's patrol was over.

At the C.P., the lieutenant warned the men of First Squad that they had better get together on one version of what had happened because he was going to report that version to his company commander in the morning. The men huddled for an hour, then reported this story to the lieutenant: they were set in at the ambush site; they saw several figures running through the woods; they followed the figures to a group of hooches; they heard screams and saw someone running from the hooches; somebody panicked and opened fire and they all opened up. The civilians were accidentally killed.

Bui Thi Huong didn't move when she came to. She listened for sounds from the hut but she heard only the wind through the banana trees. Her stomach ached and her right arm and chest throbbed and burned and her body was slick with blood. She didn't know how long she'd been unconscious and she didn't know whether the soldiers had left. It was still night. The moon was bright. When she did look up she could see in the moonlight that her little house had partly caved in from the explosion. The back wall and part of one side wall had been blown out. She was afraid her whole family was dead. My baby! My husband! She crawled, using her good arm, to the patio and through the sticky blood on the patio into the hut. In the gloom, she made out the bodies on the bunks. She crawled to the nearest bunk where her sister-in-law was sprawled and she held her hand to her sister-in-law's nostrils to feel if she was breathing. She felt nothing.

"O my sweet sister!" she whispered and began to weep. She crawled to the other bunk and held her hand to her mother-in-law's nostrils and knew that she was dead.

"O my sweet mother!" she said. And then she saw her own baby and picked him up with her good arm and knew immediately that he was not alive. She held him against her and rocked him and then she lay on the floor with him. She knew her husband was outside, dead, but she was too weak to look for him. She remained awake with her baby on the floor until dawn.

Then she was suddenly aware that it was light out and that someone was staring at her. At the front door she saw her neighbor, Mrs. Tho, peering in at her.

"Everybody is dead," Bui Thi Huong said, "American soldiers. . . ."

Mrs. Tho entered the hut. She observed the bodies and saw that Bui Thi Huong was without pajama pants. She went back to her own hut and returned with a pair. She helped the young woman into them and told her that they would have to go to a Vietnamese medic in the marketplace for her wounds. Bui Thi Huong nodded in agreement. She kissed her baby and placed him on the bunk next to her mother-in-law and, leaning on Mrs. Tho, started off for the marketplace at Ky Chanh village. Neither woman talked during the long walk and though they passed a score of curious villagers—her pajama was bloodied and her face and hair were caked with dirt—they were spoken to by no one. At the marketplace, the Vietnamese, who had had some medical training, cleaned and bandaged her wounds. He put her on a military van that served the area as a bus and told the driver to let her off at the Marine base. There was a hospital there. There were two long benches against either side of the van but she was afraid she might create a disturbance by fainting and falling off so she sat on the floor between the two rows of passengers and rode that way the five bumpy miles to the base. She stood outside the main gate until a Vietnamese interpreter noticed her and took her to a medical aid station. Through the interpreter, she told Lieutenant Anthony Fathman, a Navy doctor, that she had been raped and shot and that her whole family had been murdered by Marines. The doctor examined her and concluded that she had, indeed, been raped. He had her taken to the base hospital and drove off to report her rape and murder charges to the commanding officer of the battalion.

While Bui Thi Huong was making her way from her hut to the Marine base, the lieutenant and the men of his First Squad were marching to the base with the body of her husband. The lieutenant was Stephen J. Talty, a rugged twenty-three-year-old Marine. The report he made to his C.O., Captain J. P. T. Sullivan, was the most distasteful task he'd been called on to make in his ten months in the Corps. He had lied in his radio report the night before, he told the captain. His men had not killed three V.C. during an ambush; they had killed four innocent civilians accidentally in a moment of panic while searching out hooches for V.C. He had lied in his radio report, the lieutenant said, because he had not wanted to go on the air with talk of civilian killings.

Captain Sullivan was irritated by the report. Only three days before, General Westmoreland had issued a directive warning against mistreatment of Vietnamese, "physical and otherwise," because of the resultant bad publicity in the Saigon press. The publicity, the directive pointed out, was "damaging to the image of the Marine Corps." Henceforth, the directive went on, all such incidents of mistreatment would be reported up through channels to his office. The captain did not relish being brought to General Westmoreland's attention in this capacity.

He set off in a jeep for the office of the commanding officer of the battalion. The colonel was just then listening to a Navy doctor who was relaying a Vietnamese woman's claims of rape and murder.

The nine men of First Squad were sitting in the shade beside the green frame chapel—two M.P.'s standing guard over them—when Major James T. Elkins drove up. His sergeant-chauffeur ordered them inside the chapel and Major Elkins read off their names, to which they answered.

Sgt. Ronald L. Vogel
L/Cpl. Robert W. Monroe
Pfc. Clifton G. Hobson
Pfc. Jerry D. Sullivan
Pfc. Danny L. McGhen
Pfc. John D. Potter Jr.
Pfc. James W. Henderson
Pfc. James H. Boyd Jr.
Hn. Jon R. Bretag

Henderson, a slender six-foot-four, and Hobson, nearly a foot shorter but muscular, were Negro. The seven others were white. Major Elkins called Sergeant Vogel forward and led him to the chaplain's office where he interrogated him about the previous night's mission. Elkins began by advising him that under Article 31 of the Uniform Code of Military Justice he had the right to remain silent, that anything he said could be used against him in court, and that he had the right to counsel. Vogel said that he understood his rights and that he had no objection to being questioned about the patrol.

For a half hour, Sergeant Vogel related in a slow drawl the story that he and his men had fabricated for the lieutenant—the ambush, the running figures, the pursuit to the huts, the panic, the gunfire, the dead civilians. Under questioning, however, Vogel was vague, imprecise, confused. He labored to answer the simplest questions and Major Elkins decided that Vogel was either lying or a dullard. He settled for the latter. He tried Vogel to what he considered the limit and asked him if he had any objections to writing down on paper what he had related. Vogel said he had no objections. The major provided him with pencil and pad and told him he would return in fifteen minutes. As the major opened the door to leave the room, Vogel said:

"I can't."

"You can't what?" Elkins asked.

"I can't write it because it's all a lie. I'm sick of it!"

"What's a lie?"

"The whole bullshit story I just told you," he said, shaking his head. "We made it all up."

Then Sergeant Vogel told Major Elkins what had really happened.

The Inquiry

Master Sergeant Charles W. Ellis sat in his cubicle in the Division Legal quonset hut at Chu Lai and mulled over the story Major Elkins had just related to him. It was 9:30 p.m. on September 24, 1966, the night after the raid on the hamlet of Xuan Ngoc, and Ellis was about to interrogate the nine men who had been trucked over from the Battalion C.P. on Hill 54 ten miles west. Ellis had been a criminal investigator for seventeen of his twenty-three years in the Marine Corps and his credentials were impeccable. Besides his training at military police schools, he had graduated from the F.B.I. National Academy, the Federal Bureau of Narcotics training school, and the school for U. S. Treasury agents. He was considered one of the ablest investigators in the Corps with experience in every area of criminal activity. But this case had elements that baffled him. Sergeant Vogel had told Major Elkins at the chapel that when his squad reached the ambush site one of his men—Pfc. Potter—took command of the squad with the claim that he had been given secret orders by Lieutenant Talty. Potter, according to Vogel, then briefed the squad to this effect: that the lieutenant was fed up with patrols and ambushes that did not produce; that the lieutenant was convinced the local Vietnamese were withholding information about V.C.; that the only way to obtain information was through fear; that the ambush was a cover to satisfy the Company Commander, Captain Sullivan, who had to approve all night missions; that under this cover, the lieutenant wanted the squad to stage a raid of terror; that the lieutenant had said that anything goes—beating up on people, wrecking hooches, raping, killing; that the only restriction was on burning, fires that might be observed from the Company C.P.

Ellis found it difficult to believe that a lieutenant would issue such an order. He would be exposing himself to the severest repercussions. And why would he bypass his sergeant, the leader of the squad, and give the order to a Pfc.? And why would a sergeant let a Pfc. usurp his authority? And why would eight men acquiesce to a plan of beating, raping and deliberate murder? Why would eight men, a corporal and sergeant included, take orders they knew to be criminal from a Pfc.? Vogel would have to be lying. And yet such a raid had taken place. There were five dead bodies. There was one wounded and raped woman. There were statements piling up from the farmers who had been terrorized. Vogel's story was a bizarre one and yet there it all was, the debris.

"Why do you suppose," Ellis asked Major Elkins, "they went back and killed the little girl? Afraid she might testify?"

"Vogel was very vague about that child. He remembered less about that part of it than anything else," Elkins said.

"Well, let's see if we can't help him remember," Ellis said.

The interrogations were conducted under irksome conditions: Ellis' cubicle was cramped; a huge generator growled outside the window; jets roared in deafening takeoffs right over the building; and everyone had been through a long stifling day. Especially Sergeant Vogel. Nervous, scared, he had not slept or eaten in thirty hours. The other men in the squad had been fed C-rations that afternoon but Vogel, after making his statement to Major Elkins, had been isolated in an M.P. shack and no one had thought to feed him. When he walked into Ellis' cubicle he was tired and hungry and utterly dejected. At twenty-three, he'd been a Marine for four years, straight out of high school. He had been in Vietnam over a year and had seen action in Operations Wyoming, Apache, Colorado and Napa. His four-year hitch had ended in July but he volunteered for another six months in Vietnam even though he wanted desperately to be back home with his wife and their little girl, Robin Lee. Only a few days before the raid on Xuan Ngoc, Vogel had received word from his wife that the final adoption papers on Robin Lee had come through.

The interrogation of Sergeant Vogel, as did all subsequent interviews, began with Ellis warning him that he was suspected of murder and rape and advising of his right to remain silent and of his right to counsel. Vogel waived his rights.

"All right now. I think it will be a lot easier for both you and me if you told your story first. Start right at the very beginning. Go through it slow. If need be I'll ask you questions from time to time. . . ."

Ellis has a deceptively gentle manner. He is soft-spoken and calm. He has a greying crew cut and pronounced cheekbones. There is no menace in his style.

With the spools of a tape recorder turning slowly on the desk in front of him, Vogel told his story in a sluggish Southern drawl. At about 7:30 p.m. at the Platoon C.P., Lieutenant Talty told him that his squad had the night's ambush. Vogel picked up his gear and joined his squad where Pfc. Potter greeted him with, "Are you going?" He said he certainly was and Potter told him, "You don't have to go." Vogel told him that the lieutenant had told him to go and that it was his squad and that he was going. Potter shrugged and the squad set out for the ambush site.

"Who was in control of the squad?" Ellis interrupted.

"Pfc. Potter and Lance Corporal Monroe, sir."

"Why?"

"Well, I didn't know anything about it, sir. The lieutenant didn't brief me. I couldn't tell them what to do. I didn't know anything about the ambush or anything."

Ellis studied Vogel's face. "But you're a sergeant, the appointed squad leader, the senior man present, and yet you let a lance corporal or a Pfc. take your command away from you without taking action to find out what the hell was going on?"

"I didn't know about the ambush," Vogel said.

"And you made no effort to call back to the lieutenant and find out what the hell the scoop was?"

"No sir. No excuse. I should have but I didn't. I. . . ."

"We'll talk about it later. Go ahead."

At the ambush site, Vogel said, Potter told the men that he had orders from the lieutenant to pull a raid on hooches and destroy, rape and terrorize.

"Were those the words he used?"

"I don't know the exact words. Go out and terrorize and find out where the V.C. were. Harass, destroy, beat up on people. Rape if there were some young girls around. And shoot anybody that got in the way and wreck their houses. Then he gave us numbers. I was number six. . . ."

He told of the raids on the huts, the beatings, the assault on the sixteen-year-old Nguyen Thi Mai. "Some of the men were going to rape her but the Doc examined her with a flashlight and thought she had clap so they left her." Vogel became increasingly nervous and vague, stammering, as he tried to reconstruct the scene at the hut of Bui Thi Huong where the rape and murders occurred. He denied having participated in either. He said that while Bui Thi Huong was being raped he was on the patio guarding the man and the woman and children. Once he walked over to the side of the house when one of the men yelled for water. He had a canteen. The woman had fainted and Pfc. Sullivan was tapping her cheeks so Vogel poured water on her face to revive her. He saw Potter climb on the woman and then he went back to the patio. Later, the man on the patio, Bui Thi Huong's husband, started screaming and nothing would shut him up. Vogel thought of stuffing his mouth with straw but Doc Bretag pulled a bandage from his bag and tried to gag him with it. The man fought the gag and continued screaming until the Marines at the side of the house returned to the patio, angry, and one of them said that "We're going to have to shoot them." Somebody else said, "We better get outta here!" Vogel said that at this point he walked away from the house to a trail twenty-five yards away where he waited for his squad. Henderson and Bretag were on the trail with him. A few minutes later, he heard shooting from the house.

"But you said one of the men said that these people would have to be shot," Ellis broke in.

"Yes."

"So when you heard those rifle shots go off you knew that they were killing those people back there."

"Yeah," Vogel said.

"But you were a squad leader! Why didn't you go back and see what was happening? Why didn't you leave your position on that trail and walk back down there and find out what was happening? You already *knew* what was happening!"

"Yes sir."

"Why didn't you go down and try and stop it?" Ellis persisted. "You had a weapon, did you not?"

"Yes, but I did not have no rounds. We left in a hurry . . . I. . . ."

"I'm not interested in whether you had rounds or not!" Ellis snapped angrily. "You had a weapon, didn't you?"

Vogel remained silent. He looked away from Ellis to Major Elkins and then to the ceiling; his gaze had nowhere to go.

"Vogel, were you afraid of Potter?"

The sergeant remained silent.

"Were you physically afraid of these men?"

"Probably," Vogel finally answered, "when they had their rifles and they were firing."

Major Elkins pulled out a pack of cigarettes and offered one to Vogel, who reached for it with a trembling hand. Ellis watched Vogel fumble with the matches. What had he lied about? Had he lied about not raping the woman? Or his part in the murders? Or was he shaking because he knew his lie was still ahead of him? Elkins had said Vogel had been vaguest about the wounded little girl and Ellis asked Vogel to relate what had happened when the squad returned to the hut with Lieutenant Talty.

"We went there and were looking around and the lieutenant said, 'Oh my God, what have you done!' Or some words like that. He started talking to Potter and Monroe and all of a sudden a baby screamed, cried out, and the lieutenant jumped."

"Did the lieutenant or anybody go over and check this baby?"

"No. They looked at it but didn't do anything about it."

"You could see two babies, right?"

"Yes sir. The lieutenant was saying, 'What have you done!' and 'What are we going to tell the captain!' and 'We're going to have to do something.' "

"He included himself in this statement?"

"Yes sir. Then it was all quiet for a while. And then he said let's take the man's body back to the ambush site. The whole squad went and we took the man's body."

Vogel described how at the ambush site, a thousand yards from the hut, the lieutenant left five men behind with instructions to 'Make it look like an ambush took place if it takes you all night.' The five were Potter, Monroe, Hobson, McGhen and Vogel. The lieutenant and the rest of the squad returned to the Platoon C.P. Vogel and the others dragged the body through the sand and across the stream, leaving trails of the two nonexistent female V.C.'s who had been dragged away. They took off their boots and left the tracks of the nonexistent V.C. who had tripped the ambush. They dropped empty cartridges that had been fired at the hut. And then the five returned to the hut.

"We put the bodies inside the hut . . ." Vogel said, hurriedly.

"Whoa!" Ellis barked.

". . . except for the baby," Vogel corrected himself. "I started to pick it up and it screamed. . . . Potter said the baby was going to die anyway. . . ."

"But it was screaming. It was living."

"Yeah, the baby was still living, but the way it looked. It was just bloody."

"You don't know how much damage was done to that baby, do you?"

"No."

"You don't know if the baby was going to die, do you?"

"It . . . it looked like it was hit by a frag," Vogel offered.

"Did you look at it to see what the nature of its injuries were? Did you look at it close?"

"No," Vogel said and sighed. "No, I did not."

"Vogel, who decided the baby would have to be killed?"

The sergeant said he didn't know for sure.

"But Potter said it isn't going to live anyway. . . ."

Vogel nodded and blurted, ". . . and he said who's going to do it and everybody turned around. Couldn't do it . . . everybody looked out. . . ."

"What do you mean 'looked out'?"

"Just looked out. . . ."

"Looked out where? You just looked out at rockets going off?"

"Just looking in the distance . . . nobody could do it . . . then Potter did it . . ." he said, his voice trailing off.

"Speak up, Vogel! How do you know he did it?"

"I don't know."

Ellis' questions came rapidly, one on the other, so that Vogel had no time to think. He was swept along on a racing current of questions.

"You were looking out?"

"No. Everybody turned around . . . Potter was standing. . . ."

"But they turned around and looked at Potter!"

"Potter was standing over. . . ."

"You looked at him!"

"Yes! Yes! I did! We all looked at him!"

"And you all knew what Potter was going to do!"

"Yeah. . . ."

"What did Potter do when you were looking at him while he was standing over the baby?"

"He had his rifle in his hands . . ." Vogel said.

"What did he do. . . ."

"He said, 'Somebody count for me!' "

"Somebody count what?" Ellis asked.

"Count! Just count!"

"Count cadence?"

"No, just count for him. So I started counting. I turned around and started counting. . . ."

"You *looked* at him and then you started counting! You can't make it any easier."

"I said one . . . two . . . three. . . . And he was hitting the baby with the butt!"

"How was he doing it?"

"Dropping it down."

"Picking it up and smashing it down or just letting it fall down?"

"Picking it up and hitting it down," Vogel said, softly.

"Like a baseball bat or like he was chopping wood or straight up and down like a butt stroke? Did you ever see anyone churn butter?"

"It was straight up and down."

"Like someone churning butter," Ellis said in conclusion.

"Yeah," Vogel said. And after a long pause he said: "Then it was quiet and someone said to Potter, 'You sure got some balls to do that.' "

Vogel's interrogation lasted from 9:45 to 10:30 p.m. and the eyes of the other eight men in the squad followed him as he was led by an M.P. past them.

They could not have been encouraged. His face was ashen. His shirt was soaked through with sweat. More significantly, he returned none of their stares. The men had suspected, since Vogel had been whisked away from the chapel by Major Elkins, that he had talked. The sight of him as he emerged from Ellis' office did nothing to dispel that feeling.

Nevertheless, Hospitalman Jon R. Bretag, a twenty-year-old Navy medic from Albuquerque, New Mexico, decided to try the concocted version of the previous night's incident on Ellis. Ellis let him relate it—the ambush, the chase to the hooches, the shadowy figure, the panicked gunfire, the accidental killings. A high-school graduate, Bretag had been a good student. His father, a Chief Warrant Officer in the U.S. Army Reserves, worked for the Bureau of Indian Affairs, and his mother was a Registered Nurse. He had enlisted in the Navy a year before and had volunteered for duty in Vietnam in July. On September 21, two days before the raid on Xuan Ngoc, he was assigned to Lieutenant Talty's platoon. Ellis let him tell his version of the killings and then abruptly stopped him.

"What about the woman you raped, Doc?"

"Rape?"

"The rape at the house where you killed those people. You remember that? You examined a girl for clap, like you examined one earlier, and you raped her."

"Well . . . I . . . we . . ." he stammered. "I examined her but I didn't see the men do anything. They were just standing around her chatting."

"What were they chatting about, Doc?"

"I don't remember."

"Doc, little bits of amnesia isn't going to help you a bit. Let's face it, you are as much in trouble as every one of these men who are involved."

"I know, sir."

Ellis got up, took two or three steps to the window, leaned his elbow on the sill, and stared out at Chu Lai's plane-lined strip.

"It probably started out as a big gag, a big joke," he said, his voice lined with sarcasm. "A big joke. And then it got a little horrible toward the end. But let's stick to the joke part, where we are still in the fun-and-games business, all right? You made an examination on the woman. Now you didn't do it to pass the time out there. What did they have in mind?"

"They had rape on their minds, sir."

"Now how do you know that?"

"Well, they wanted to know who was going to be first and all this. . . ."

"Did they flip a coin or how did they arrive at who was going to go first?"

"I . . . I don't remember. . . ."

Ellis fixed Bretag with a stare and said:

"There's been a hell of an injustice here, Doc! A hell of a crime! You got it on your conscience to live with the rest of your life. Those were human beings out there! There was no provocation. If you can let that kind of thing go on you're in a pretty bad way!"

"I didn't know what I was getting into," Bretag pleaded. "I volunteered for this patrol because I was new and I wanted to have the experience. This was my first patrol. I didn't know what I was getting into!"

Then the young seaman told Ellis what he wanted to know. "When we got to our ambush site Potter said the lieutenant told him the purpose of this patrol was, as much as I could gather . . . it didn't seem right to me . . . was that we were supposed to, you can say, raid these huts, raising hate and discontent. Potter said we were to beat up people, tear up the hooches, rape and kill. Spoke up and asked him why we were doing this. And he looked hard at me and said the people wouldn't turn the V.C. in but if we created enough fear they would. I went along as just a medical personnel. We went through some huts, the men were beating up on people. . . ."

He told how he had examined the sixteen-year-old girl with a pocket flashlight while Marines held her pinned to the ground and told them that she looked diseased. They became angry but they didn't do anything to the girl.

"How about the second girl, Doc?"

"Well, I was guarding this man and woman and two kids on the patio of this hut and they called me over to the side of the house. They had a woman stretched out and they told me to check her for clap. I did and I said I didn't know if she did or not. Well, Potter said, 'Who's going to go first?' Two of them said they couldn't get a hard on. A third got on her. I went back to the patio for about ten minutes. When I came back . . . well . . . he had got off her . . . I guess I got on and had intercourse. . . ."

He looked up at Ellis and waited for Ellis to say something but Ellis just returned his look and he continued.

"Then two others got on her after me. Then the woman appeared to have passed out. Potter asked if she was dead. Vogel poured water on her and Sullivan tapped her cheeks. Potter was standing there with his penis out trying to get an erection. That's when I went back to the patio. . . ."

There the young father, Bui Thi Huong's husband, was propped up against a wall of the hut. His sister sat near him with the two children and the grandmother was squatting just inside the hut.

"There was a wailing chant," Bretag said. "That's the only way I can describe it. Then the man started crying loudly and all the Marines wanted to keep him quiet so they began wrestling with him and hitting him. I tried to tie a bandage around his mouth but each time I went to tighten it it would slip down around his neck and I'd be strangling him. Then the men from the side of the house had come around to the front now. They didn't leave anybody over there for security so I went to the side. I heard yelling, screaming, you shut up, shut up, and then a couple of bursts of automatic fire, then some semiautomatic fire. I don't know how many bursts, how many rounds.

"I walked back to the house and looked at the people. The man was laying up against the house. The woman was laying next to him. I didn't see any of the children . . . except for one by the old lady. Someone said, 'We'll have to make it look good. I'm going to throw in a hand grenade. Everybody get behind the sand.' I got behind the sand pile and the grenade was thrown. After that, I didn't walk back. I didn't want to see what was—what happened. I'd seen enough and I was getting sick. It was my first patrol and the first time I'd seen 'em, people shot, laying there. . . ."

Pfc. Danny L. McGhen of the McKeesport, Pennsylvania, area, did about-faces in his statement to Ellis as smartly as he had ever done them for a drill instructor. Like Bretag, McGhen launched into the spurious version of the murders. He had advanced through three simple declarative sentences when Ellis slammed a fist on his desk.

"Let's stop right there, McGhen! We've been through all the bullshit! It's all over with. We know exactly what happened. Do I make myself clear? There is 720 feet of tape there and none of it is a lie. Now nothing about any noises in front of the ambush site or any of that jazz."

"Right, sir!"

Ellis took McGhen straight to the rape of Bui Thi Huong and the murders.

"You saw what was being done to that girl?"

"It was dark but I still had an idea what was going on, sir."

"You know damn well what was going on, McGhen."

"The men were trying to rape her, sir."

"Trying?"

"Were raping her, sir."

"Fine, McGhen. Now how did the shooting start?"

"Well, sir, the man was making a lot of noise. Everybody got scared. I know I was. I guess in my mind I finally started realizing what was happening. I went around to the front of the house because I couldn't . . . I guess I went crazy because I couldn't stand that noise anymore. I kept thinking in my mind, somebody is going to tell and we're all going to get in real trouble over it . . . if we weren't in already! So I went out front and I kept trying to get the man to be quiet and I *think* . . ." He looked up at Ellis and corrected himself. ". . . I *know* I did . . . hit him a couple of times. To get him quiet. And he wouldn't get quiet and by this time everybody was getting around. I don't know who it was, somebody said, 'We'll have to shoot them!' and as soon as they did somebody opened up."

"Who?"

McGhen gave the names of those he was "pretty sure" opened up.

"I think I shot at the man and the old lady both, sir," he said. "But I think I might have hit the old lady."

"Who fired at the young girl with the baby?"

"I think Boyd was standing there, sir. Boyd, I'm pretty sure it was."

"What happened after the shooting?"

"We picked up the man's body and we were going to take him back to the ambush site and say that he was caught in the ambush and let it go at that. So we did this and we were even crazy enough, stupid enough, to make trails like bodies were drug away and leave cartridges around."

Ellis asked him who killed the second child at the house.

"Potter did, sir. He stood there and went mashing up and down with his rifle. It was his own idea, sir. Nobody else could do it."

"Then what?"

"Then, sir? Nothing, sir. Nobody said nothin'. I just said as we looked down at the baby that I was glad this wasn't in the United States."

Ellis stared at McGhen for a full minute. When he spoke his voice crackled with anger. "What the hell difference does it make where it's at! You murdered five people!" He picked up a book and slammed it on the desk. "What difference does it make where you did it at? You raped one woman and tried to murder her. Does it really make any difference where it happened?"

"No sir. I guess it don't," McGhen replied, sheepishly.

"Do you have a religion, McGhen?"

"Evangelical United Brethren, sir."

"Are they in favor of killing?"

"No sir."

"What do they teach about it? Murder, I'm talking about, not just war-time killing."

"It's not done, sir."

"It's against the law of God?"

"Yes sir."

"So what difference does it really make when you murder somebody exactly where it takes place?" Ellis asked. "You've deprived two children of sixty years of life!"

Ellis sighed, shook his head, and sat down. He knew he should not have gotten into the religious thing for the tape. The statements would be introduced at the formal pretrial investigation and defense counsel would harangue him for his unprofessionalism. He continued:

"How long have you been overseas, McGhen?"

"About thirty days, sir."

"You just come out of boot camp?"

"Yes sir."

"How old are you?"

"Nineteen, sir."

Pfc. James H. Boyd Jr. was eighteen, the youngest man on the patrol. He was probably also poorest equipped to be in Vietnam. He was slightly built, almost scrawny. And his score of 24 on the Armed Forces Qualification Test gave him a Class IV rating, the lowest class the Marine Corps will accept. Cutoff score is 21. He was raised in Coon Rapids, Minnesota, and his parents were divorced when he was eleven. He repeated fourth and tenth grades and after finishing tenth grade he enlisted because his father was out of a job. He had been in Vietnam five months before the incident at Xuan Ngoc and had fought in Operation Colorado and Operation Napa and had written numerous letters home filled with his fear and his anger and his bewilderment at the death of his buddies.

It was after two a.m. when he was called into Ellis' office and both Ellis and Boyd were so bone-tired that neither bothered to fence with the pre-arranged story.

"Who'd you shoot, Boyd?" Ellis asked.

"I didn't shoot anybody."

"You fired your rifle," Ellis stated.

"I didn't . . . I don't know if I hit anyone. . . . But I didn't shoot. . . ."

"Who did you shoot at, Boyd?"

"I don't know. One of the women, sir."

"Did you hit her?"

"I don't know, sir."

"You fired directly at her? From a very short distance?"

"Yes sir."

"Very small chance of you missing her, Boyd?"

"Very."

He said Potter and others blasted the old lady and the man with automatic bursts. He said one child was in her grandmother's arms and was killed with her by these bursts. The baby was in his father's arms and was hit but not killed.

"Now how do you know he wasn't?"

"Because he was bawling when we left."

Sergeant Ellis did not interrogate Lieutenant Talty until four days later. Talty was in the field and Ellis was busy with routine detective work. He inspected the scene of the murders and collected physical evidence—spent slugs embedded in beams in the hooch and in trees, cartridge casings, the spoon from the grenade tossed into the hooch. He had pictures taken of the hut, patio and grounds around the hut. He had the squad's weapons collected and sent off to a military ballistics expert in Japan along with the recovered slugs and casings. Through interpreters he took statements from Bui Thi Huong, Nguyen Thi Mai, and a score of Vietnamese who had been visited by the raiders. The bodies of the five murder victims had been buried by relatives and neighbors the day after the incident and he tried to have the bodies exhumed for autopsy but S-5, the Marine Civil Affairs Branch, advised him that the Vietnamese refused to allow their dead to be dug up. It would be disrespectful. Ellis conceded that there had been enough disrespect. He learned from S-2, intelligence, that none of the murdered—needless to say, not the children—had been V.C. suspects or V.C. sympathizers. In fact, S-2 said, none of the people harassed by the squad were known to have any V.C. connections. The hamlet of Xuan Ngoc was considered a pacified area.

Ellis, with Major Elkins present, interviewed Lieutenant Talty on September 28 in the same cubicle in the quonset hut at Chu Lai where the lieutenant's men had been questioned. Talty was twenty-three, a birthday he had celebrated two weeks after his arrival in Vietnam on July 9, and in his ten weeks as a platoon leader in Bravo Company had shown himself to be a dependable and commendable officer, though he had come fresh from training schools. He had enlisted in the Corps in December, 1965. He was a native of Buffalo, New York, where his father was a public-school supervisor and his mother a nurse. He had served as an altar boy for seven years while a pupil at St. Thomas Aquinas Grammar School, graduated from Bishop Timon High School, and earned above-average grades at St. Bonaventure U. in Buffalo where he got his B.A. in English in 1965. For three summers during college he was a lifeguard at a Buffalo Recreation Department swimming pool. He mixed weight lifting with folk singing as an undergraduate and was good enough at the latter to get paying jobs for his group around the Buffalo area. He failed, as a sophomore, in his first try to pass the test for Marine Officers' school and was sorely disappointed. When he made it in 1965 he was elated. When he reached Vietnam he was a proud Marine. He was proud of the Corps, proud of his part in it. He was especially close to and careful for his men. He surveyed their gear closely and made sure they had what they needed in clothes and weapons. He sat down with them and made sure their pay and allotments were properly taken care of. Not all officers were so diligent. Under fire he was cool and resourceful. In less than ten weeks he had taken part in Operations Colorado, Napa, and Monterey, and numerous smaller operations against insurgent V.C. forces. His immediate superior officers said he was a good leader of men. His men thought of him as a good officer. Master Sergeant Ellis, as he tried to understand what had gone wrong with First Squad at Xuan Ngoc hamlet, was not so sure.

Ellis advised Talty that an Article 31 investigation into murders, rape and assaults was underway and that the lieutenant was a possible suspect and that he did not have to say anything and that he had the right to counsel. Talty said that he would answer all questions without counsel. He proceeded to detail the events of the night of September 23:

At 7 p.m., he gathered a squad around him at Platoon C.P. and briefed them on their patrol. They would proceed to a stream junction 300 meters from the perimeter, set up an ambush, and remain at the site until 11 p.m. The squad would then check out several hooches in the area for V.C. and return to the C.P. by 12:30 a.m. At 7:30 p.m., he received a radio message from the squad reporting the men were in position. At 9 p.m. he received another message that three V.C. had been killed, two males and one female. But the message was garbled due to faulty transmission. A later message reported two females and one male had been killed. The squad had received eight rounds of V.C. fire. Soon after, the squad returned to the C.P. and told the lieutenant that civilians had been killed in an accident. The lieutenant went to the site with them and saw the bodies. He said, "My God, what the hell have you done here!" They told him it had been an accident. The company commander, Captain J.P.T. Sullivan, radioed for information on the incident and the lieutenant told him that he had one male body but that the two female bodies had been dragged away.

"We moved the body back to the ambush site and I left five men there," Talty said. "Potter, Monroe, McGhen, Vogel and Hobson. I told them to make it look like an ambush. Then I went to the C.P., sat down, gathered my wits, questioned the other three I brought in, separately, Henderson, Boyd and Sullivan. Doc was with us, too. They said they were all rear security and didn't know anything. I sent a team out with the platoon sergeant to bring the others back. I wanted to find out what happened. So I said to leave the body until the morning and we will get our story straight on this. So we all sat down and they told me what happened. I hit the sack at 1:30 a.m. in the morning, I told them to get the body and they did and took it to Hill 54. I told the C.O. what happened. I didn't tell him I moved the body. I just told him I made it look like an ambush. The reason I had done this—it was a mistake on my part—it was just to give me time to think and to find out just exactly what happened."

"Now, lieutenant," Ellis began, "Among those dead bodies at the hut there was a live baby, wasn't there?"

Talty said there was.

"Did you take any action to check the condition of that baby?"

He said he had not, and Ellis asked him why he had not.

"I thought probably she would be alive in the morning when they looked over the area," he said.

"Isn't that a pretty big chance to be taking, sir?"

"Yes it is."

"That she could have survived an ordeal, a thing like that?" There was a guarded reprimand in the question. "That she *might* just be alive in the morning if somebody *happened* to wander out and look at the area?"

"Yes, Sergeant Ellis, it is."

"Is there any question you should have taken some steps?"

"I'm positive I should have, now," Talty said, coolly.

"Now some of your men, lieutenant, claim that you ordered them to return to the hut and dispose of those bodies, to police up the area?"

"I gave no such orders."

"They did, in fact, though, return to that house and moved the bodies from the patio to the interior of the house," Ellis said. "And in the course of doing this—the reason we bring this up—is that the young child that made the sounds while you were at the house was murdered by Potter. He bashed its brains out with a rifle butt in the presence of four men, lieutenant."

"I did not give them any orders at all to return to that house."

"Then somebody countermanded or disobeyed your orders?"

"I told them to stay at the ambush site."

Ellis looked through some notes and set off on a new tack. He asked Talty to repeat what he had reported to Captain Sullivan the morning after the murders. Talty said he had told the C.O. that his men had accidentally killed four civilians and that. . . .

"I'm sorry, lieutenant, would you repeat this?" Ellis interrupted.

"I told the C.O. that my men had accidentally killed four civilians."

"Now while you were relating this story to the captain, did you tell him that there was one live baby out there?"

"No, I didn't. I just told him . . . I just ran through it quickly and I told him there were some civilians killed and. . . ."

"You said there was *four* civilians, lieutenant."

"I wasn't trying to keep it from him."

"Lieutenant, you said that you told the captain there were *four* civilians killed!"

"Right!"

"Which would have been a man, a woman, and two children because that's what you saw on the patio that night. And yet we both know that the child was alive when you were out there. So there were only *three* civilians killed and one wounded. A baby."

"Well," Talty paused, "from what they told me there was two women, a man and one child."

"But you *saw* two children!" Ellis argued.

"Right!"

"So isn't that a little confusing, sir?"

"Right. It is."

"You reported what they told you instead of what you saw? And you didn't tell anyone that the baby was alive? Why?"

"I don't know."

"Lieutenant, did you know that morning that the baby was, in fact, not alive?"

"Definitely not!" Talty said, angrily. "How would I know that?"

Talty looked at both Ellis and Elkins but got no answer.

Ellis switched to another line of questioning. He asked Talty for his professional opinion of Sergeant Vogel.

"I don't think he is very competent. Potter runs the squad and he is a damn good man. I hate to see this happen. He is a damn good man, one of the best point observers and a good trooper. Monroe we kind of put on mess duty there for a while until after Operation Colorado. He was kind of shaky because one of his best buddies got shot up, but he is a real good man, too. We got a good squad."

Ellis asked in what ways Sergeant Vogel was incompetent.

"He was always yelling at his men, screaming at them, trying to show them he was the boss and still he actually didn't know his job. He went about it all in the wrong way, I think."

Major Elkins asked if his leadership could have been undermined by Potter and Monroe.

"I don't think so, I don't think that was true. I don't think that was true at all."

"You say Monroe and Potter were running the squad. What do you mean they were running it? Wasn't Sergeant Vogel there?"

"They were the ones doing all the work in the field actually. They were the ones who knew what was going on. They were just handling themselves better and quicker."

"Well, lieutenant, you see the dilemma that we are faced with. For some reason your men disobeyed your orders to remain in a combat ambush for a specified time. They jumped the time and left several hours early and went on a reign of terror for about two-and-a-half hours. It all boils down to this point, lieutenant, that Potter and Monroe allegedly had a private briefing and they passed on the briefing to the patrol not in your presence. After they left the ambush they briefed the patrol themselves and they said that these were your instructions—to rape, rob, terrorize!"

"I gave them no such orders!" Talty shot back angrily.

"Why would they move out of the ambush early?"

"I asked Vogel at the hut and he said he didn't know. Nobody knew."

"No one knew why they had moved?" Ellis asked. "No one came up with a good concrete answer? Do you suppose it was everybody's idea to move at one time?"

"They said they had seen something."

"What had they seen?"

"A man running."

"But this house is a considerable distance from the ambush site, right?

Doesn't that seem a little odd to you that they would chase a man a mile or almost a mile and a half across the sand?"

"They weren't chasing. . . ."

"Everything they had been taught was dead against it!"

"I said to them why the hell did you go so far."

"And what was the answer?"

"None."

"Well, lieutenant, this is where we are at now, trying to determine just what was told to these people that would give them the idea or reason to believe that they might have the semblance of backing from somebody to jump out of the ambush site for no reason and go on this terror strike."

Ellis stared across the desk into Talty's eyes but Talty did not answer.

"Quite frankly," Ellis said, smiling wanly, "it has me puzzled! I haven't run across a situation similar to it—where a squad has just deliberately disobeyed an order . . . just deserted an ambush and literally terrorized the countryside. . . ."

Again he stared at Talty and again there was no answer.

"Let me ask you a question, lieutenant, that might be a little involved. You're the leader of these people. You knew they were screwed up when you walked up to that house, even before you got to that house. You walked into that scene and the first thing you see is the bodies of two small children.

"Now lieutenant, there is nothing—*nothing*—I can think of, using all my experience, I can't think of *anything* that would lead you to believe that two small children could be gunned down at that time of night by accident!"

"I disagree there!" Talty said, pointing a finger at Ellis.

"How can you say that!"

"I disagree because of knowing the reaction of any squad, any normal squad when they are in combat! They see something or something startled them and one opens up and then they automatically all of them do and that's what I thought happened. That they had killed the two individuals by doing that. Something startled them and they just opened up. That's the first thing that came to my mind. Things like that, I mean I don't know how you figure it, but things like that can happen by accident. It doesn't have to be mischievous or anything else and that's what I thought it was."

Ellis stared wide-eyed at him. "Are you still entertaining the idea that this was *nothing more than an accident*? A very regrettable accident?"

Talty hesitated then said: "I don't know. I don't know what it was."

"But you have heard the story! We have told you that there were two or three hours of *terror*! People were raped! People were beaten up! People were . . . you've been told this before . . . people were hung up by the *heels* and kicked in the head and five people were murdered! Now, do you still think it was an accident?"

"No, I don't," Talty conceded.

"What do you think it was now, lieutenant?"

"It was . . ." he paused for the right word . . . "brutal."

"Brutal! We have two men who were running that squad who were supposed to be outstanding men, Potter and Monroe. They were the ones who had the leadership. Are they still outstanding troops, lieutenant?"

"Well!" Talty hesitated. He crossed his legs. "If you're asking me if I would take them into combat with me, yes."

"You still trust them?"

"I think so."

"Knowing what they did!"

"I wouldn't turn my back on them, if that's what you mean." The lieutenant could not get comfortable in his chair.

"Do you think you could trust them!"

"It's a hard question to answer."

"All right, lieutenant!" Ellis said sternly. "This thing is being put in such a way that it leaves the question in mind as to whether—by implication or straight orders—you engineered the whole thing. This is what it boils down to."

"I know it does!" Talty said.

"Someone is giving us stories and facts that come together in such a way that there was a secret briefing held by you with Monroe and Potter and that they in turn relayed the briefing to the squad. It looks as though you engineered this thing. By implication if nothing else. Or by saying, 'Go to your ambush site and at a specific time go out and rape, rob, beat and terrorize these goddamned people and get these zipper heads or gooks, shoot them, and don't bring any prisoners.' This is the word that was passed on to the squad. So it looks as though this word came from you originally. This is the position that you are being put in."

Talty's face grew redder as Ellis spoke.

"I see what they are trying to do! They are trying to blame the whole thing on me! But that day. . . ."

"We're just relaying to you what was related to us and showing you what this involves," Ellis said, quietly.

"Well, I'll tell you something!" Talty exploded. "I gave them no orders to kill anyone or rape or pillage or anything else! And earlier that day or I think it was the day before we had been sitting down, the platoon sergeant and myself and a bunch of guys, and it was first indicated that we move at night and raid a few places and find out if there were V.C. coming in. And then there was the usual kidding around about hanging them by the neck and beating them up and . . . well, I'm not an advocate of this! Why, it pisses me off to see them go out in the field and grab a chicken and kill a chicken and have some chicken! But I'm not telling these guys . . . these guys have heads of their own . . . if they want to go out and kill somebody . . . I would never in my life . . . to me . . . I mean these people are human beings and I'm not going to tell them . . . it's like trying to kill my own family . . . I'm not going to give them orders to go out and rape and burn. . . ."

Talty was breathing hard and beads of sweat rolled down his forehead. He wiped his brow with his sleeve, then looked at the stain.

"You say this bullshit session went on? This kidding around?"

"Yes, *kidding* around!"

"Were you involved in the kidding around, too?"

"Oh yes I was involved in it," he replied quickly. "But they are not going to take that and call it an order! That's what they're trying to do, though!"

Ellis paused. When he spoke it was in his weary, grey voice.

"Could it be that they might have thought this was the way the lieutenant felt about it?"

The lieutenant mopped his face with his handkerchief. "Well, that's bad, I guess."

"You see, lieutenant, somewhere something went wrong," Ellis suggested. "Some *word* was misconstrued, misunderstood, some *act* was misunderstood. And this was the end result."

"I gave them no orders!"

"You have to backtrack and find out where this bad seed came into it, if in fact the bad seed ever existed."

"When I gave them the briefing I gave it in front of everybody and they were grouped around me and if they took anything . . . I mean there were a lot of other people that day . . . and there had been a lot of other joking around in the Marine Corps, as far as that goes . . . when you're out in the field you joke around sometimes . . . and if these guys are going to take it like that . . . take it like it was an order from me . . . I wasn't the only one goofing around or anything like that . . . if they took that as an order from me . . . then . . . then . . . they are sick!"

"What exactly was said during this kidding around?"

"I said that we are going to try moving in on these hooches at night and try to find some V.C. with their weapons. Try to catch them making time with their wives. And then somebody would say, 'We ought to go in there and rape and burn,' or things like that . . . but *I* didn't say anything like that!"

"How about the destruction of other people's property?"

"Things like that, when they go to a place, about beating up on civilians and tearing things apart? I let it be known that I didn't go for that. I told them never let me catch them doing that stuff."

"Would you concur with this, lieutenant? A squad is sent out on what is supposed to be a combat mission. They are sitting in an ambush with specific instructions on the time to move out and for some reason they jump the gun and leave their position quite early and do in fact go to houses and commit acts of atrocity, they rape, they hang a man by his heels and kicked him in the head, and tore up another man's house almost apart and beat him and his wife and threw their children out in the patio and covered them up like they were going to burn them. And then they get to this house and they massacre the whole family. Doesn't it seem odd that these people would do this without feeling that they had implied backing? They just can't arbitrarily get up and move out without feeling some sense of security that someone is behind them. Someone has to have, by some form or other, communicated, implied. . . ."

"I gave them nothing like that."

"Do you concur that they *might* have been thinking this?"

"No I don't!" Talty said, emphatically. "It's impossible that they could have."

"Why, lieutenant! They done it!" Ellis exclaimed. "They done just what I said they done and it took them several hours to do it. Now, they must have felt somewhere along the line by some form of communication or another that someone had implied that this sort of action is just what was supposed to be taken."

"They couldn't have," Talty maintained, shaking his head. "I gave them specific. . . ."

"They left their ambush early!"

"To search out a couple of hooches. . . ."

"But what about all the atrocities?"

"Search for V.C. . . . search for V.C. . . . that's what I gave them the flashlight for . . . search for V.C. . . ."

"Then we have them hanging people by their heels and actually going on a terror spree!"

Talty shook his head as though he didn't want to listen to Ellis.

"I gave them no such orders . . . I. . . ."

"They took it in their heads to do it all by themselves?" Ellis asked, incredulously. "Is it *possible* it might have been something you said? Or some implication?"

"No! I don't think so at all!"

"Then it would have to be one individual who gave the orders. Either that or the whole squad decided together to do it."

"It would have to be," Talty agreed.

"Well," Ellis stated angrily, "that would mean that every man in the squad is an animal!"

"Not necessarily! I'm not saying that!"

"Either one man leads, lieutenant, or the whole pack is an animal and they operate on the same level! They all get the same idea at the same time! Either that or it would have to be one man leading."

"Not necessarily one," Talty suggested, weakly.

"Well, let's say two then," Ellis said and his voice softened. "I'll give it the benefit of the doubt. Would you say that Boyd was capable of coming up with the idea?"

"No."

"That Vogel was capable of coming up with this?"

"No."

"Or Henderson? Even with his size?"

"No."

"The Doc?"

"No."

"What about Potter and Monroe?"

"I don't think they would actually *plan* something like this," Talty said. "I don't know. It's hard to say. I didn't think they were the type to do anything like that, that's all. It's still hard for me to believe that they have done it. . . ." Talty frowned at the thought of his guilty men. ". . . I mean they are my own men, you know, and I have worked with them and I have *never* seen any of this maltreatment . . . and I let it be known that I was against it . . . and I never seen it done . . . I just can't believe that all of a sudden they would do that. . . ."

The Verdict

Sergeant Ellis' inquiries into the facts surrounding the raid on Xuan Ngoc lasted from September 24, the day after the crimes were committed, to October 9. The formal pretrial investigation was conducted in the quonset hut at Chu Lai from October 24 to November 2. Under Article 31 of the Uniform Code of Military Justice, a pretrial investigation officer hears all witnesses and evidence against suspects and recommends to higher authority whether they should be charged and tried. The process is the approximate equivalent of the grand jury system in civilian courts; to indict or not indict. The pretrial investigation officer in this case was a Lieutenant Colonel John L. Zorack, a wiry, sharp-featured career Marine in his early forties. The ten suspects, including Lieutenant Talty, were present, with a variety of captains and majors to represent them as counsel.

The hearing dragged on through six days of sweltering heat. Wide latitude is allowed in cross-examinations in these preliminary hearings and the battery of six defense lawyers (four acted for two suspects) took full advantage of it. The hearing bogged down further because most of the witnesses were Vietnamese who had to be questioned through an interpreter. The interpreter, to complicate matters still more, was weak in English (he had taken a six-month course in an American school) and not overly familiar with the Vietnamese dialect spoken in the Xuan Ngoc area.

Lieutenant Colonel Zorack, after hearing the six days of testimony, recommended that the following be charged and tried by general courts-martial:

Sergeant Ronald Vogel: Murder and rape.

Lance Corporal Robert W. Monroe: Murder, rape, assault, assault to commit murder, assault to commit rape.

Pfc. John D. Potter Jr.: Murder, rape, assault, assault t/c rape.

Pfc. Danny L. McGhen: Murder, rape, assault, assault t/c murder, assault t/c rape.

Pfc. James H. Boyd Jr.: Murder, assault t/c murder.

Pfc. Clifton G. Hobson: Rape, assault t/c rape, assault.

Pfc. Jerry D. Sullivan: Rape, assault t/c rape.

Pfc. James W. Henderson: Rape, assault t/c rape, assault.

Hn. Jon R. Bretag: Rape, assault t/c rape.

Lieutenant Stephen J. Talty: Making a false report to a superior officer.

In a footnote to his recommendations, Lieutenant Colonel Zorack suggested that the charge against Lieutenant Talty be dropped. It was Zorack's understanding, he said, that the lieutenant had submitted his resignation. The lieutenant had exercised extremely poor judgment, Zorack conceded, but in view of the relative insignificance of the charge of making a false report, the investigating officer recommended that the resignation be accepted.

The Commanding General of the First Marine Division, the authority to which Zorack addressed his recommendations, disagreed. He ordered that the lieutenant be court-martialed not only for making a false report but also for violation of Article 78 of the Uniform Code of Military Justice: accessory after the fact of murder.

Lieutenant Talty and his nine men were tried by courts-martial separately at Chu Lai during January of 1967.

Pfc. Potter, the real leader of the squad, the man charged with rape, the murder of five people including that of the five-year-old Dao Thi Tao, did not take the stand in his defense. He was revealed to be, nevertheless, an excellent Marine. "Potter was the kind of man that I wanted in my platoon," testified Gunnery Sergeant Jerald L. Hass, a veteran Marine, and platoon sergeant in Bravo Company. "Potter was forceful, excellent, above average." Blond, of medium build, Potter had been in the Marines two years, the last ten months in Vietnam. He had seen a lot of action— Operations Jackson, Osage, Montgomery, Colorado, and numerous smaller sweeps against V.C. On June 22 he had been wounded in the groin by shrapnel and had been awarded the Purple Heart. He had come from Satartia, Mississippi, a hamlet near Yazoo City. His father, a deacon in the Methodist Church, ran a grocery store. An above-average student in high school, Potter transferred to the Chamberlain-Hunt military academy in

Port Gibson, Mississippi, where he easily made second lieutenant and became a cadet leader. After one year at Mississippi State College, he enlisted in the Marines.

A psychiatrist's report read at his court-martial brought out that Potter, after ten months in Vietnam, "gave a history of frustration, anger and nervous tension. In this war the enemy is always hidden and Marines know that he is hidden by the citizenry. Potter was angry and he looked forward to raiding the village. This mental strain, however, didn't prevent him from being fully mentally responsible."

Potter was found guilty. He was sentenced to a dishonorable discharge "and hard labor for the rest of your natural life." He was twenty. Over the two years since his trial, as a prisoner at the Portsmouth, New Hampshire, naval prison, he has exhausted all routes to appeal. Preparations were being made at this writing to transfer him to the Federal penitentiary at Leavenworth where he will serve his sentence.

As Potter was revealed at his court-martial to have been a forceful Marine, Sergeant Vogel was drawn as a weak leader.

Sergeant Pedro Laredo of Bravo Company testified: "Potter and Monroe took care of the squad. Both Captain Sullivan and Lieutenant Talty were aware of Vogel's shortcomings. Vogel wasn't getting the work done. He wasn't showing leadership at all. That ambush was going to be his last patrol. They were going to transfer him next morning due to incompetence."

And Gunnery Sergeant Hass: "Sergeant Vogel was to be administratively busted. If I had my way he wouldn't of had that squad. There was nothing Mr. Talty could do. This man's background and his capabilities at leading men was well known within this Company. He had no business having the squad. We were going to solve the problem within a week. If he didn't snap out of his shit, we were going to take the squad away from him and administratively bust him."

Vogel was charged as a principal in the murder of the five-year-old girl in that he aided and abetted Potter by counting one, two, three. He was charged as a principal in the rape of Bui Thi Huong, though he did not physically rape her, because he aided and abetted by pouring water on her to revive her. He was found guilty on both charges.

In a final plea to the court before sentencing, Vogel, the Marine with the adopted daughter waiting for him back home, said: "I don't know how to say this or what to do. I'll take the blame for all of it. It was my fault I was not carrying out my duties as a sergeant and because I was the senior man present. If I could do anything to bring those people back I would do so. I would even give up my own life. But I can't do so. I'm going to have to leave it up to you men and whatever you decide."

The men decided to sentence him to fifty years in prison. Last May, Vogel's sentence was cut by the Naval Board of Review to ten years. The

Board reversed the rape conviction in the belief that Vogel, when he poured water on Bui Thi Huong, might have been performing a humane act. He is serving his time at the Portsmouth naval prison.

Even the prosecution saw the pathos in the case of Pfc. Boyd, the low achiever from Coon Rapids who pleaded guilty to murder in that he fired a single shot at one of the women as she was falling from Potter's burst.

"This is a sad and pathetic case, a classic example of where a man is a victim of circumstances," the trial counsel said, adding to the weight of defense counsel's plea for leniency in sentencing.

The pathos was not lessened when defense counsel read the court a letter from the defendant's mother:

". . . we belonged to the Methodist Church until our eleven-year-old daughter led us to a bible-believing church which is the Coon Rapids Baptist Church. Here is where we accepted Jesus as our personal savior and by the grace of God we were saved. Jim accepted Jesus as his personal savior before he went to Vietnam and by the grace of God he was also saved. . . ."

Strangely, the Marine Corps was able to determine *after* the incident at Xuan Ngoc, that the eighteen-year-old Boyd had "a long-standing character and behavior disorder manifested by lack of normal interpersonal relationships, immaturity, poor judgment and almost complete disregard for the accepted social, moral and legal codes of society. Boyd usually acts in an impulsive and immature manner without taking time to consider his actions beforehand."

And the court sentenced him to four years at hard labor. Boyd, with time off for good behavior, has been released from Portsmouth and is now at liberty.

Bretag, the Navy medic who had the misfortune to make his first volunteer patrol in Vietnam a raid on a sleeping village, also pleaded guilty to the rape of Bui Thi Huong.

"I've always tried to perform my duties as a Corpsman to the best of my ability," he told the court before sentencing. "But on the night of the twenty-third I let myself down and I let my family and my fellow Corpsmen down. As being so weak as to follow the group and stand by and not try to stop what was happening. If there was some way that I could rectify what happened that night I'd very much do so."

Bretag was sentenced to six months at hard labor.

Clifton G. Hobson and James W. Henderson, the two Negro Pfc.'s in the squad, both pleaded not guilty to the charges of raping Bui Thi Huong and assaulting Nguyen Thi Mai with intent to commit rape. Henderson, twenty-one, well over six feet and slender, had enlisted in the Marines in 1963 after finishing junior high school in Philadelphia. His mother was a widow. Hobson was short and stocky. He played football and basketball in junior high school in his native Monroe, Louisiana, and his one fear as a boy was that he wouldn't fill out enough to play football in high school and college. He did but his father, the game's injuries in mind, asked him not to go out for the sport and Clifton complied. Both his mother and father were teachers, his mother principal of an elementary school in Monroe. An uncle was a high-school principal, an aunt a supervisor of instructors, and another uncle a doctor. He had a sister in college. After graduating from Carroll High School in Monroe, Hobson spent a year at Grambling College. He had been in Vietnam three months before Xuan Ngoc and, like Henderson, had made a good record.

Both men were found guilty. Henderson was sentenced to two years at hard labor and Hobson to three years. Both men's convictions on the charges of raping Bui Thi Huong were later reversed on appeal. In Henderson's case, the court found that the mere testimony that the defendant was seen on top of the alleged victim was not proof of guilt, that forcible entry had to be proved. Hobson's conviction was set aside because the Board of Review was unconvinced by the evidence against the accused. The convictions on the charges of assaulting the sixteen-year-old girl with intent to commit rape were affirmed in both instances, however, and the sentences were reduced to six months. Both men are now free.

Lance Corporal Monroe, Pfc. Jerry Sullivan, and Pfc. Danny McGhen were found not guilty on all charges in their courts-martial. McGhen and Sullivan are out of the Marines but Monroe is now a sergeant at Camp LeJeune, North Carolina.

Lieutenant Talty was court-martialed at Chu Lai on March 13 and 14 of 1967. He pleaded not guilty to charges of being an accessory after the fact of murder in that he assisted his squad in order to prevent the detection and apprehension for murders of Vietnamese civilians and of making a false official statement to a superior officer.

The question of the lieutenant's mood on September 23, the day of the raid on Xuan Ngoc, was not brought up at his court-martial but it had been at Potter's court-martial. Defense counsel had asked a Corporal Dedmon, one of the lieutenant's men, about Talty's state of mind that day.

"Well, our platoon had been sort of fouling up in garrison, seemed like everything we did, and we wanted to get some V.C. so we could more or less prove that we were as good as anyone else because we had a lot of pride in our platoon and we wanted real bad to get some V.C. that day."

The trouble was that V.C. were scarce, if not absent, in the Xuan Ngoc area. Captain Sullivan, who had been company commander at the time of the raid, testified by deposition at Talty's trial:

"When we first came into the [area] in May, V.C. activity was, shall we say, moderate. The more we stayed inside the area, it became decreasing, that is it became decreased. Smaller and smaller. In September . . . we had no incident in the Xuan Ngoc area that I can recall."

The lieutenant testified that his instructions to the squad were to set up an ambush, remain at the ambush site until 11:30 p.m., search out any hooches in the immediate area, and return by 12:30 a.m. He admitted that after the squad showed him the bodies at Bui Thi Huong's house he radioed the company commander, Captain Sullivan, with the false report that a male and two female V.C. had been killed in the ambush and that the two females had been dragged away. He admitted that he then instructed the squad to carry the man's body a thousand yards back to the ambush site and "make it look like an ambush if it took all night. Drag the body around, walk around in bare feet, I didn't care what they did. I didn't want to tell the company commander what happened. I was very shocked."

"Did you give them any instructions about returning to the house?"

"No sir, I did not. One man suggested that we go back and get rid of the bodies, put them in the shack and burn it, but I said, 'No, you should never go back to the house.' "

The lieutenant was asked by his counsel why he had instructed the men to simulate an ambush action.

"They were obviously wrong in what they had done. They left the ambush site. I wasn't altogether protecting them. I was protecting myself in a way. I knew there would be repercussions because of what happened. They left the ambush site, they killed these civilians who, I assume, were innocent. But I had no idea. Murder didn't enter my mind at all. I thought it was a brutal, tragic accident. And I was willing to help them. I'd helped them before."

Gunnery Sergeant Hass, who had to be told by the referee Law Officer to keep his language slightly less salty, testified that when Lieutenant Talty returned to the C.P. after viewing the bodies, the lieutenant said, "Well, they really fucked up this time!"

The prosecutor asked Talty why he had made such a remark.

Talty said that Potter and Monroe more or less ran the squad "and when they got together anything could happen."

"What do you mean?"

"They've often been told before about maltreatment of the people."

"You knew they had antagonism for the people?"

"Yes sir."

"You knew that in the past they were guilty of antagonism and brutality toward the Vietnamese people?"

"I wouldn't say brutality."

"Pushing around?"

"Yes."

"Hitting on occasion?"

"I have never seen it but I had heard it."

"You knew the victims of their acts, roughhousing, were innocent people?"

"That's correct."

"And yet you let them run the squad?"

"They were both good troopers. Very good."

"Did you take measures to correct these propensities?"

"Yes sir. And I thought they had taken effect."

The prosecutor then probed Talty's motives for making his false report to the captain and ordering his men to fake the ambush.

"You said you thought the killings were an accident. Didn't you go to an awful lot of trouble to cover up an accident?"

"Yes sir, but I knew there would be repercussions. I just wanted to get away from that house. I wanted to get the hell away from there."

"But why go to such great lengths? Why not tell the C.O. it was an accident?"

"There would be an investigation. There would be repercussions. I would be relieved, the squad leaders would be relieved, everybody would be relieved. The captain would be relieved. But I wasn't going to cover up the incident. I was going to tell about it."

"You were going to tell them you covered it up and made it look like an ambush? Then why were you doing it?"

"I don't know," Talty said. "I just wanted to get away from there."

Lieutenant Talty was found not guilty of the more serious charge, accessory after the fact of murder. He was found guilty of making a false report and sentenced to dismissal from the Corps, forfeiture of $100 per month pay for five months, and loss of 300 numbers in rank. The Board of Review affirmed the conviction but set aside the sentence of dismissal. The lieutenant petitioned the Court of Military Appeals for a review of his case but the court turned him down. It then forwarded the case, in accordance with established practice, to the Secretary of the Navy for possible clemency. Attached were two enclosures: the Judge Advocate of the Navy recommended no clemency. Lieutenant General L. W. Walt, now Assistant Commandant of the Marine Corps, recommended:

"This officer submitted a false and misleading statement to his superiors in an attempt to prevent the discovery of murders committed by his men and to protect himself. An officer who is guilty of such conduct could never be trusted. An officer who cannot be trusted is of no value."

Talty and six of his men are back in civilian life. One is a sergeant in the Corps, two are still in prison.

All cases in the Xuan Ngoc incident are in the Judge Advocate General's "finished" file.   [August, 1969]

The facts of this report are available for public inspection in the office of the Judge Advocate General of the Navy in Washington, D.C.

PART VI
CREATIVE AGONIES

Some Children of the Goddess

by Norman Mailer

Experimentation was the norm in the Sixties, and every talented writer was groping for a new form or a new style that would change the direction of American fiction. The competition was stiff, and Norman Mailer in no way hid the fact that he was playing to win. In this piece, originally published in July 1963 under the title "Norman Mailer Versus Nine Writers," Mailer, who had commented before on his competition, reviewed their latest books and came up with what he called some "further evaluations of the talent in the room."

I doubt if there is any book I read in the last few years which I approached with more unnatural passion than *Set This House on Fire*. Styron's first novel, *Lie Down in Darkness*, was published when he was twenty-six, and it was so good (one need today only compare it to *Rabbit, Run* to see how very good it was) that one felt a kind of awe about Styron. He gave promise of becoming a great writer, great not like Hemingway nor even like Faulkner whom he resembled a bit, but great perhaps like Hawthorne. And there were minor echoes of Fitzgerald and Malcolm Lowry. Since his first novel had failed to make him a household word in America, he had a justifiable bitterness about the obscurity in which good young writers were kept. But it poisoned his reaction to everything. One of the traps for a writer of exceptional talent, recognized insufficiently, is the sort of excessive rage which washes out distinction. Styron was intensely competitive—all good young novelists are—but over the years envy began to eat into his character. Months before James Jones's *Some Came Running* was published (and it had the greatest advance publicity of any novel I remember—for publicity seemed to begin two years before publication), Styron obtained a copy of the galleys. There were long nights in

493

Connecticut on "Styron's Acres" when he would entertain a group of us by reading absurd passages from Jones's worst prose. I would laugh along with the rest, but I was a touch sick with myself. I had love for Jones, as well as an oversized fear for the breadth of his talent, and I had enough envy in me to enjoy how very bad were the worst parts of *Some Came Running*. But there were long powerful chapters as well; some of the best writing Jones has ever done is found in that book. So I would laugh in paroxysms along with the others, but I was also realizing that a part of me had wanted *Some Came Running* to be a major book. I was in the doldrums, I needed a charge of dynamite. If *Some Came Running* had turned out to be the best novel any of us had written since the war, I would have had to get to work. It would have meant the Bitch was in love with someone else, and I would have had to try to win her back. But the failure of *Some Came Running* left me holding onto a buttock of the lady—if she had many lovers, I was still one of them. And so everything in me which was slack and conservative could enjoy Styron's burlesque readings. Yet I also knew I had lost an opportunity.

A few months later, I ceased seeing Styron—it would take a chapter in a novel to tell you why. I liked the boy in Styron, disliked the man, and had vast admiration for his talent. I was hardly the one to read *Set This House on Fire* with a cool mind. Nine years had gone by since *Lie Down in Darkness* was published, and the anticipation of the second novel had taken on grandiloquent proportions among his friends and his closest enemies. One knew it would be close to unbearable if his book were extraordinary; yet a part of me felt again what I had known with *Some Came Running*—that it would be good for me and for my work if Styron's novel were better than anything any of us had done. So I read it with a hot sense of woe, delighted elation, and a fever of moral speculations. Because it was finally a bad novel. A bad maggoty novel. Four or five half-great short stories were buried like pullulating organs in a corpse of fecal matter: overblown unconceived philosophy, Technicolor melodramatics, and a staggering ignorance about the passions of murder, suicide and rape. It was the magnum opus of a fat spoiled rich boy who could write like an angel about landscape and like an adolescent about people. The minor characters were gargoyles, and badly drawn. Here and there quick portraits emerged, there was one excellent still-life of an Italian police official who was Fascist, the set pieces were laid out nicely, but the vice of the talent insisted on dominating. Whenever Styron didn't know what to do with his men and women (which was often, for they repeated themselves as endlessly as a Southern belle), Styron went back to his landscape; more of the portentous Italian scenery blew up its midnight storm. But Styron was trying to write a book about good and evil, and his good was as vacuous as the spirit of an empty water bag:

I can only tell you this, that as for being and nothingness, the one thing I did know was that to choose between them was simply to choose being, not for the sake of being, or even the love of being, much less the desire to be forever—but in the hope of being what I could be for a time.

Which is a great help to all of us.

His evil character took on the fatal sin of an evil character: he was not dangerous but pathetic. A fink. Styron was crawling with all ten thumbs toward that ogre of mystery who guards the secrets of why we choose to kill others and quiver in dread at the urge to kill ourselves. But like a bad general who surrounds himself with a staff which daren't say no, Styron spent his time digging trenches for miles to the left and miles to the right, and never launched an attack on the hill before him. It was the book of a man whose soul had gotten fat.

And yet, much as I could be superior to myself for having taken him thus seriously, for having written predictions in *Advertisements for Myself* that he would write a very good book which the mass media would call great, much as I would grin each day after reading a hundred pages of hothouse beauty and butter bilge, much as I would think, "You don't catch the Bitch that way, buster, you got to bring more than a trombone to her boudoir," much so much as I was pleased at the moral justice which forbids a novelist who envied too much the life of others to capture much life in his own pages, I was still not altogether happy, because I knew his failure was making me complacent again, and so delaying once more the day when I would have to pay my respects to the lady.

And indeed I lost something by the failure of *Some Came Running* and *Set This House on Fire*. I never did get going far on my novel. I wrote a four-hour play and essays and articles, two hundred thousand words accumulated over the years since *Advertisements for Myself*, and I showed a talent for getting into stunts, and worse, much worse. Years went by. Now once again, in this season, ready to start my novel about the mysteries of murder and suicide, I found by taking stock of psychic credit and debit that I had lost some of my competitive iron. I knew a bit of sadness about work. I did not feel sure I could do what I had now settled for doing, and to my surprise I was curious what others were up to. If I couldn't bring off the work myself, it might be just as well if someone else could give a sign of being ready to make the attempt. In this sad dull mellow mood, feeling a little like a middle-aged mountaineer, I read at one stretch over three weeks the novels I want to write about here.

There was a time, I suspect, when James Jones wanted to be the greatest writer who ever lived. Now, if *The Thin Red Line* is evidence of his future, he has apparently decided to settle for being a very good writer among other good writers. The faults and barbarities of his style are gone. He is no longer the worst writer of prose ever to give intimations of greatness. The language has been filed down and the phrases no longer collide like trailer trucks at a hot intersection. Yet I found myself nostalgic for the old bad prose. I never used to think it was as bad as others did, it was eloquent and communicated Jones's force to the reader. It is not that *The Thin Red Line* is dishonest or narrow; on the contrary it is so broad and true a portrait of combat that it could be used as a textbook at the Infantry School if the Army is any less chicken than it used to be. But, sign of the times, there is now something almost too workmanlike about Jones. He gets almost everything in, horror, fear, fatigue, the sport of combat, the hang-ups, details, tactics, he takes an infantry company through its early days in combat on Guadalcanal and quits it a few weeks later as a veteran outfit, blooded, tough, up on morale despite the loss of half the original men, gone, dead, wounded, sick or transferred. So he performs the virtuoso feat of letting us know a little about a hundred men. One can even (while reading) remember their names. Jones's aim, after all, is not to create character but the feel of combat, the psychology of men. He is close to a master at this. Jones has a strong sense of a man's psychology and it carries quietly through his pages.

The Thin Red Line was of course compared to *The Naked and the Dead*, but apart from the fact that I am the next-to-last man to judge the respective merits of the two books, I didn't see them as similar. *The Naked and the Dead* is concerned more with characters than military action. By comparison it's a leisurely performance. *The Thin Red Line* is as crammed as a movie treatment. No, I think the real comparison is to *The Red Badge of Courage*, and I suspect *The Red Badge of Courage* will outlive *The Thin Red Line*. Yet I don't quite know why. *The Thin Red Line* is a more detailed book; it tells much more of combat, studies the variations in courage and fear of not one man but twenty men and gets something good about each one of them. Its knowledge of life is superior to *The Red Badge of Courage, The Thin Red Line* is less sentimental, its humor is dry to the finest taste, and yet . . . it is too technical. One needs ten topographical maps to trace the action. With all its variety, scrupulosity, respect for craft, one doesn't remember *The Thin Red Line* with that same nostalgia, that same sense of a fire on the horizon which comes back always from *The Red Badge of Courage*.

No, Jones's book is better remembered as satisfying, as if one had studied geology for a semester and now knew more. I suppose what was felt lacking is the curious sensuousness of combat, the soft lift of awe and pleasure that one was moving out onto the rim of the dead. If one was not too tired, there were times when a blade of grass coming out of the ground before one's nose was as significant as the finger of Jehovah in the Sistine Chapel. And this was not because a blade of grass was necessarily in itself so beautiful, or because hitting the dirt was so sweet, but because the blade seemed to be a living part of the crack of small-arms fire and the palpable flotation of all the other souls in the platoon full of turd and glory. Now, it's not that Jones is altogether ignorant of this state. The description he uses is "sexy," and one of the nicest things about Jim as a writer is his ease in moving from mystical to practical reactions with his characters. Few novelists can do this, it's the hint of greatness, but I think he steered *The Thin Red Line* away from its chance of becoming an American classic of the first rank when he kept the mystical side of his talents on bread and water, and gave his usual thoroughgoing company-man's exhibition of how much he knows technically about his product. I think that is the mistake. War is as full of handbooks as engineering, but it is more of a mystery, and the mystery is what separates the great war novels from the good ones. It is an American activity to cover the ground quickly, but I guess this is one time Jones should have written two thousand pages, not four hundred ninety-five. But then the underlying passion in this book is not to go for broke, but to promise the vested idiots of the book reviews that he can write as good as anyone who writes a book review.

When you discuss eight or ten books, there is a dilemma. The choice is to write eight separate book reviews, or work to find a thesis which ties the books together. There is something lick-spittle about the second method: "Ten Authors in Search of a Viable Theme," or "The Sense of Alienation in Eight American Novelists." A bed of Procrustes is brought in from the wings to stretch and shorten the separate qualities of the books. I would rather pick up each book by itself and make any connections on the fly. The thesis of the Bitch is thesis enough for me. Its application to Jones would say that *The Thin Red Line* is a holding action, a long-distance call to the Goddess to declare that one still has one's hand in, expect red roses for sure, but for the time, you know, like there're contacts to make on the road, and a few Johns to impress.

Another Country, by James Baldwin, is as different from *The Thin Red Line* as two books by talented novelists published in the same year can turn out to be. It does not deal with a hundred characters, but eight, and they are very much related. In fact there is a chain of fornication which is all but complete. A Negro musician named Rufus Scott has an affair with a white Southern girl which ends in beatings, breakdown, and near-insanity. She goes to a mental hospital, he commits suicide. The connection is taken up by his sister who has an affair with a white writer, a friend of Rufus' named Vivaldo Moore, who in turn gets into bed with a friend named Eric who is homosexual but having an affair with a married woman named Cass Silenski, which affair wrecks her marriage with her husband Richard, another writer, and leaves Eric waiting at the boat for his French lover Yves. A summary of this sort can do a book no good, but I make it to trace the links. With the exception of

Rufus Scott who does not go to bed with his sister, everybody else in the book is connected by their skin to another character who is connected to still another. So the principal in the book, the protagonist, is not an individual character, not society, but a milieu, not a social organism like an infantry company, but indeed is sex, sex very much in the act. And almost the only good writing in the book is about the act. And some of that is very good indeed. But *Another Country* is a shocker. For the most part it is an abominably written book. It is sluggish in its prose, lifeless for its first hundred pages, stilted to despair in its dialogue. There are roles in plays called actor-proof. They are so conceived that even the worst actor will do fairly well. So *Another Country* is writer-proof. Its peculiar virtue is that Baldwin commits every *gaffe* in the art of novel writing and yet has a powerful book. It gets better of course; after the first hundred pages it gets a lot better. Once Eric, the homosexual, enters, the work picks up considerably. But what saves the scene is that Baldwin has gotten his hands into the meat and won't let go. All the sex in the book is displaced, whites with blacks, men with men, women with homosexuals, the sex is funky to suffocation, rich but claustrophobic, sensual but airless. Baldwin understands the existential abyss of love. In a world of Negroes and whites, nuclear fallout, marijuana, bennies, inversion, insomnia, and tapering off with beer at four in the morning, one no longer just falls in love—one has to take a brave leap over the wall of one's impacted rage and cowardice. And nobody makes it, not quite. Each of the characters rides his sexual chariot, whip out, on a gallop over a solitary track, and each is smashed, more or less by his own hand. They cannot find the juice to break out of their hatred into the other country of love. Except for the homosexuals who can't break into heterosexual love. Of all the novels talked about here, *Another Country* is the one which is closest to the mood of New York in our time, a way of saying it is close to the air of the Western world, it is at least a novel about matters which are important, but one can't let up on Baldwin for the way he wrote it. Years ago I termed him "minor" as a writer, I thought he was too smooth and too small. Now on his essays alone, on the long continuing line of poetic fire in his essays, one knows he has become one of the few writers of our time. But as a Negro novelist he could take lessons from a good journeyman like John Killens. Because *Another Country* is almost a major novel and yet it is far and away the weakest and worst near-major novel one has finished. It goes like the first draft of a first novelist who has such obvious stuff that one is ready, if an editor, to spend years guiding him into how to write, even as one winces at the sloppy company which must be kept. Nobody has more elegance than Baldwin as an essayist, not one of us hasn't learned something about the art of the essay from him, and yet he can't even find a good prose for his novel. Maybe the form is not for him. He knows what he wants to say, and that is not the best condition for writing a novel. Novels go happiest when you discover something you did not know you knew.

Baldwin's experience has shaped his tongue toward directness, for ur-
gency—the honorable defense may be that he has not time nor patience to
create characters, milieu, and mood for the revelation of important com-
plexities he has already classified in his mind.

Baldwin's characters maim
themselves trying to smash through the wall of their imprisonment. William Burroughs gives what may be the finest record in our century of the
complete psychic convict. *Naked Lunch* is a book of pieces and fragments,
notes and nightmarish anecdotes, which he wrote—according to his preface—in various states of delirium, going in and out of a heroin addiction.
It is not a novel in any conventional sense, but then there's a question
whether it's a novel by any set of standards other than the dictum that
prose about imaginary people put between book covers is a novel. At any
rate, the distinction is not important except for the fact that *Naked Lunch*
is next to impossible to read in consecutive fashion. I saw excerpts of it
years ago, and thought enough of them to go on record that Burroughs
"may conceivably be possessed by genius." I still believe that, but it is one
thing to be possessed by genius, it is another to be a genius, and *Naked
Lunch* read from cover to cover is not as exciting as in its separate pieces.
Quantity changes quality, as Karl Marx once put it, and fifty or sixty
three-page bits about homosexual orgies, castration, surgeon-assassins,
and junkie fuzz dissolving into a creeping green ooze leaves one feeling
pretty tough. "Let's put some blue-purple blood in the next rape," says
your jaded taste.

This is, however, quibbling. Some of the best prose in America is
graffiti found on men's room walls. It is prose written in bone, etched by
acid, it is the prose of harsh truth, the virulence of the criminal who never
found his stone walls and so settles down on the walls of the john, it is the
language of hatred unencumbered by guilt, hesitation, scruple, or complexity. Burroughs must be the greatest writer of graffiti who ever lived.
His style has the snap of a whip, and it never relents. Every paragraph is
quotable. Here's a jewel among a thousand jewels:

Dr. Benway . . . looks around and picks up one of those rubber vacuum
cups at the end of a stick they use to unstop toilets . . . "Make an incision,
Doctor Limpf. . . . I'm going to massage the heart." . . . Dr. Benway washes
the suction cup by swishing it around in the toilet-bowl. . . .

Dr. Limpf: "The incision is ready, doctor."

Dr. Benway forces the cup into the incision and works it up and down.
Blood spurts all over the doctors, the nurse and the wall. . . .

Nurse: "I think she's gone, doctor."

Dr. Benway: "Well, it's all in the day's work."

Punch-and-Judy. Mr. Interlocutor and Mr. Bones. One, two, three,
bam! two, four, eight, bam! The drug addict lives with a charged wire so
murderous he must hang his nervous system on a void. Burroughs'

achievement, his great achievement, is that he has brought back snow-flakes from this murderous void.

Once, years ago in Chicago, I was coming down with a bad cold. By accident, a friend took me to hear a jazz musician named Sun Ra who played "space music." The music was a little like the sound of Ornette Coleman, but further out, outer space music, close to the EEEE of an electric drill at the center of a harsh trumpet. My cold cleared up in five minutes. I swear it. The anger of the sound penetrated into some sprung-up rage which was burning fuel for the cold. Burroughs' pages have the same medicine. If a hundred patients on terminal cancer read *Naked Lunch*, one or two might find remission. Bet money on that. For Burroughs is the surgeon of the novel.

Yet he is something more. It is his last ability which entitles him to a purchase on genius. Through the fantasies runs a vision of a future world, a half-demented welfare state, an abattoir of science fiction with surgeons, bureaucrats, perverts, diplomats, a world not describable short of getting into the book. The ideas have pushed into the frontier of an all-electronic universe. One holds onto a computer in some man-eating machine of the future which has learned to use language. The words come out in squeaks, spiced with static, sex coiled up with technology like a scream on the radar. Bombarded by his language, the sensation is like being in a room where three radios, two television sets, stereo hi-fi, a pornographic movie, and two automatic dishwashers are working at once while a mad scientist conducts the dials to squeeze out the maximum disturbance. If this is a true picture of the world to come, and it may be, then Burroughs is a great writer. Yet there is sadness in reading him, for one gets intimations of a mind which might have come within distance of Joyce, except that a catastrophe has been visited on it, a blow by a sledgehammer, a junkie's needle which left the crystalline brilliance crashed into bits.

Now beyond a doubt, of all the books discussed here, the one which most cheats evaluation is Joseph Heller's *Catch-22*. It was the book which took me longest to finish, and I almost gave it up. Yet I think that a year from now I may remember it more vividly than *The Thin Red Line*. Because it is an original. There's no book like it anyone has read. Yet it's maddening. It reminds one of a Jackson Pollock painting, eight feet high, twenty feet long. Like yard goods, one could cut it anywhere. One could take out a hundred pages anywhere from the middle of *Catch-22*, and not even the author could be certain they were gone. Yet the length and similarity of one page to another gives a curious meat-and-potatoes to the madness; building upon itself the book becomes substantial until the last fifty pages grow suddenly and surprisingly powerful, only to be marred by an ending over the last five pages which is hysterical, sentimental and walleyed for Hollywood.

This is the skin of the reaction. If I were a major critic, it would be a virtuoso performance to write a definitive piece on *Catch-22*. It would take ten thousand words or more. Because Heller is carrying his reader on a more consistent voyage through Hell than any American writer before him (except Burroughs who has already made the trip and now sells choice seats in the auditorium), and so the analysis of Joseph H.'s Hell would require a discussion of other varieties of inferno and whether they do more than this author's tour.

Catch-22 is a nightmare about an American bomber squadron on a made-up island off Italy. Its hero is a bombardier named Yossarian who has flown fifty missions and wants out. On this premise is tattooed the events of the novel, fifty characters, two thousand frustrations (an average of four or five to the page) and one simple motif: more frustration. Yossarian's colonel wants to impress his general and so raises the number of missions to fifty-five. When the pilots have fifty-four, the figure is lifted to sixty. They are going for eighty by the time the book has been done. On the way every character goes through a routine *on every page* which is as formal as a little peasant figure in a folk dance. Back in school, we had a joke we used to repeat. It went:

"Whom are you talking about?"

"Herbert Hoover."

"Never heard of him."

"Never heard of whom?"

"Herbert Hoover."

"Who's he?"

"He's the man you mentioned."

"Never heard of Herbert Hoover."

So it went. So goes *Catch-22*. It's the rock and roll of novels. One finds its ancestor in Basic Training. We were ordered to have clean sheets for Saturday inspection. But one week we were given no clean sheets from the Post laundry so we slept on our mattress covers, which got dirty. After inspection, the platoon was restricted to quarters. "You didn't have clean sheets," our sergeant said.

"How could we have clean sheets if the clean sheets didn't come?"

"How do I know?" said the sergeant. "The regulations say you gotta have clean sheets."

"But we can't have clean sheets if there are no clean sheets."

"That," said the sergeant, "is tough shit."

Which is what *Catch-22* should have been called. The Army is a village of colliding bureaucracies whose colliding orders cook up impossibilities. Heller takes this one good joke and exploits it into two thousand variations of the same good joke, but in the act he somehow creates a rational vision of the modern world. Yet the crisis of reason is that it can no longer comprehend the modern world. Heller demonstrates that a rational man devoted to reason must arrive at the conclusion that either the world is mad and he is the only sane man in it, or (and this is the weakness of *Catch-22*—it never explores this possibility) the sane man is not really sane because his rational propositions are without existential reason.

On page 178, there is a discussion about God.

". . . how much reverence can you have for a Supreme Being who finds it necessary to include such phenomena as phlegm and tooth decay in His divine system of creation. . . . Why in the world did He ever create pain?"

"Pain?" Lieutenant Scheisskopf's wife pounced upon the word victoriously. "Pain is a useful symptom. Pain is a warning to us of bodily dangers."

. . . "Why couldn't He have used a doorbell instead to notify us, or one of His celestial choirs?"

Right there is planted the farthest advance of the flag of reason in his cosmology. Heller does not look for any answer, but there is an answer which might go that God gave us pain for the same reason the discovery of tranquilizers was undertaken by the Devil: if we have an immortal soul some of us come close to it only through pain. A season of sickness can be preferable to a flight from disease for it discourages the onrush of a death which begins in the center of oneself.

Give talent its due. *Catch-22* is the debut of a writer with merry gifts. Heller may yet become Gogol. But what makes one hesitate to call his first novel great or even major is that he has only grasped the inferior aspect of Hell. What is most unendurable is not the military world of total frustration so much as the midnight frustration of the half world, Baldwin's other country, where a man may have time to hear his soul, and time to go deaf, even be forced to contemplate himself as he becomes deadened before his death. (Much as Hemingway may have been.) That is when one becomes aware of the anguish, the existential *angst*, which wars enable one to forget. It is that other death—without war—where one dies by a failure of nerve, which opens the bloodiest vents of Hell. And that is a novel none of us has yet come back alive to write.

With the exception of *Another Country*, the novels talked about up to now have been books written for men. *Catch-22* was liked, I believe, by almost every man who read it. Women were puzzled. The world of a man is a world of surface slick and rock knowledge. A man must live by daily acts where he goes to work and works on the world some incremental bit, using the tools, instruments, and the techniques of the world. Thus a man cannot afford to go too deeply into the underlying meaning of a single subject. He prefers to become interested in quick proportions and contradictions, in the practical surface of things. A book like *Catch-22* is written on the face of solemn events and their cockeyed contradictions. So it has a vast appeal: it relieves the frustration men feel at the idiocy of their work. *Naked Lunch* fries the surface in a witch's skillet; the joy in reading is equal to the kick of watching a television announcer go insane before your eyes and start to croon obscenely about the President, First Lady, Barry Goldwater, Cardinal Spellman, J. Edgar. Somewhere in America somebody would take out his pistol and shoot the set. Burroughs shatters the surface and blasts its shards into the madness beneath. He rips the reader free of suffocation. Jones wrote a book which a dedicated corporation executive or an ambitious foreman would read with professional avidity because they would learn a bit about the men who work for them. *The Thin Red Line* brings detail to the surprises on the toughest part of the skin. So these three books are, as I say, books for men. Whereas *Another Country*, obsessed with that transcendental divide keeping sex from love, is a book more for women, or for men and women. So too is *Set This House on Fire*. And much the same can be said of *Rabbit, Run* and *Letting Go*.

On record are the opinions of a partisan. So it is necessary to admit the John Updike's novel was approached with animus. His reputation has traveled in convoy up the Avenue of the Establishment, The New York Times *Book Review* blowing sirens like a motorcycle caravan, the professional muse of *The New Yorker* sitting in the Cadillac, membership cards to the right Fellowships in his pocket. The sort of critics who are rarely right about a book— Arthur Mizener and Granville Hicks, for example—ride on his flanks, literary bodyguards. *Life* magazine blew its kiss of death into the confetti. To my surprise, *Rabbit, Run* was therefore a better book than I thought it would be. The Literary Establishment was improving its taste. Updike was not simply a junior edition of James Gould Cozzens. But of course the Establishment cannot nominate a candidate coherently. Updike's merits and vices were turned inside out. The good girlish gentlemen of letters were shocked by the explicitness of the sex in *Rabbit, Run*, and slapped him gently for that with their fan, but his style they applauded. It is Updike's misfortune that he is invariably honored for his style (which is atrocious—and smells like stale garlic) and is insufficiently recognized for his gifts. He could become the best of our literary novelists if he could forget about style and go deeper into the literature of sex. *Rabbit, Run* moves in well-modulated spurts at precisely those places where the style subsides to a ladylike murmur and the characters take over. The trouble is that young John, like many a good young writer before him, does not know exactly what to do when action lapses, and so he cultivates his private vice, he *writes*. And there are long over-fingered descriptions in exacerbated syntax, airless crypts of four or five pages, huge inner exertion reminiscent of weight lifters, a stale sweet sweat clings to his phrases.

EXAMPLE: *Redbook, Cosmopolitan, McCall's.*
Boys are playing basketball around a telephone pole with a backboard bolted

to it. Legs, shouts. The scrape and snap of Keds on loose alley pebbles seems to catapult their voices high into the moist March air blue above the wires. Rabbit Angstrom, coming up the alley in a business suit, stops and watches, though he's twenty-six and six-three. So tall, he seems an unlikely rabbit, but the breadth of white face, the pallor of his blue irises, and a nervous flutter under his brief nose as he stabs a cigarette into his mouth partially explain the nickname.

EXAMPLE: *True Confessions.*
Outside in the air his fears condense. Globes of ether, pure nervousness, slide down his legs. The sense of outside space scoops at his chest.

EXAMPLE: *Elements of Grammar.*
His hands lift of their own and he feels the wind on his ears even before, his heels hitting heavily on the pavement at first but with an effortless gathering out of a kind of sweet panic growing lighter and quicker and quieter, he runs. Ah: runs. Runs.

It's the rare writer who cannot have sentences lifted from his work, but the first quotation is taken from the first five sentences of the book, the second is on the next-to-last page, and the third is nothing less than the last three sentences of the novel. The beginning and end of a novel are usually worked over. They are the index to taste in the writer. Besides, trust your local gangster. In the run of Updike's pages are one thousand other imprecise, flatulent, wrynecked, precious, overpreened, self-indulgent, tortured sentences. It is the sort of prose which would be admired in a writing course overseen by a fussy old nance. And in Updike's new book, *The Centaur*, which was only sampled, the style has gotten worse. Pietisms are congregating, affirmations à la Archibald MacLeish.

The pity is that Updike has instincts for finding the heart of the conventional novel, that still-open no-man's-land between the surface and the deep, the soft machinery of the world and the subterranean rigors of the dream. His hero, Rabbit Angstrom, is sawed in two by the clear anguish of watching his private vision go at a gallop away from the dread real weight of his responsibility. A routine story of a man divided between a dull wife he cannot bear to live with, and a blowsy tough tender whore he cannot make it with, the merit of the book is not in the simplicity of its problem, but in the dread Updike manages to convey, despite the literary commercials in the style, of a young man who is beginning to lose nothing less than his good American soul, and yet it is not quite his fault. The power of the novel comes from a sense, not absolutely unworthy of Thomas Hardy, that the universe hangs over our fates like a great sullen hopeless sky. There is real pain in the book, and a touch of awe. It is a novel which could have been important, it could have had a chance to stay alive despite its mud pies in prose, but at the very end the book drowns in slime. Updike does not know how to finish. Faced with the critical choice of picking one woman or another (and by the end, both women are in fearful need), his character bolts over a literal hill and runs away. Maybe he'll be back tomorrow, maybe he'll never be back, but a decision was necessary. The book ends as minor, a pop-out. One is left with the expectation that Updike will never be great, there is something too fatally calculated about his inspiration. But very good he can be, a good writer of the first rank with occasional echoes from the profound. First he must make an enemy or two of the commissioners on the Literary Mafia. Of course a man spends his life trying to get up his guts for such a caper.

Letting Go, by Philip Roth, has precisely the opposite merits and faults. As a novel, its strategy is silly, tiresome, and weak. But its style, while not noteworthy, is decent and sometimes, in dialogue, halfway nice. It is good time spent to read any ten pages in the book. The details are observed, the mood is calm, the point is always made. It is like having an affair with a pleasant attentive woman, the hours go by neatly. It is only at the end of a year that one may realize the preoccupations of the mistress are hollow, and the seasons have been wasted.

Letting Go is a scrupulous account in upper Jewish New Yorker genre of a few years in the lives of two English Department college instructors, one married to that most coveted of creatures, a fragile dreary hangup of a heroine, the other a bachelor and lover of worried proportions. Very little happens. The wife goes on being herself, the husband remains naturally frozen and stingy, and the instructor-lover has a small literary breakdown. One can say, well isn't this life? didn't Chekhov and de Maupassant write about such things? And the answer is yes they did, in five pages they did, and caught that mood which reminds us that there is sadness in attrition and grinding sorrows for decency. But Roth is not writing a book with a vision of life; on the contrary, one could bet a grand he is working out an obsession. His concentration is appropriated by something in his life which has been using him up in the past. Virtually every writer, come soon or late, has a cramped-up love affair which is all but hopeless. *Of Human Bondage* could be the case study of half the writers who ever lived. But the obsession is opposed to art in the same way a compulsive talker is opposed to good conversation. The choice is either to break the obsession or enter it. The compulsive talker must go through the herculean transformation of learning to quit or must become a great monologuist. Roth tried to get into the obsession—he gave six hundred pages to wandering around in a ten-page story— but he did it without courage. He was too careful not to get hurt on his trip and so he does not reveal himself: he does not *dig*. The novel skitters like a water fly from pollen spread to pollen spread, a series of good short stories accumulate en route, but no novel. The iron law of the conventional novel, the garden novel, is that the meaning of the action must grow on every page or else the book will wither. It is Updike's respectable achievement in *Rabbit, Run* that he writes just such a book, or

tries to until the last three pages when he vanishes like a sneak thief. Roth
never gets into the game. One senses a determined fight to maintain
Letting Go as a collection of intricately intercollected short stories.

But the short story has a tendency to look for climates of permanence—an event occurs, a man is hurt by it in some small way forever.
The novel moves as naturally toward flux. An event occurs, a man is
injured, and a month later is working on something else. The short story
likes to be classic. It is most acceptable when one fatal point is made.
Whereas the novel is dialectical. It is most alive when one can trace the
disasters which follow victory or the subtle turns that sometimes come
from a defeat. A novel can be created out of short stories only if the point
in each story is consecutively more interesting and incisive than the point
before it, when the author in effect is drilling for oil. But Roth's short
stories in *Letting Go* just dig little holes in many suburban lawns until
finally the work of reading it becomes almost as depressing as must have
been the work of writing it. Roth has to make a forced march in his next
book, or at the least, like Updike, get around to putting his foot in the
whorehouse door. If he doesn't, a special Hell awaits his ambition—he
will be called the Rich Man's Paddy Chayefsky, and Paddy without his
grasp of poverty is nothing much at all.

It is necessary to say that the four
stories about the Glass family by J. D. Salinger, published in two books
called *Franny and Zooey* and *Raise High the Roof Beam, Carpenters,*
seem to have been written for high-school girls. The second piece in the
second book, called *Seymour an Introduction*, must be the most slovenly
portion of prose ever put out by an important American writer. It is not
even professional Salinger. Salinger at his customary worst, as here in the
other three stories of the two books, is never bad—he is just disappointing. He stays too long on the light ice of his gift, writes exquisite dialogue
and creates minor moods with sweetness and humor, and never gives the
fish its hook. He disappoints because he is always practicing. But when he
dips into Seymour, the Glass brother who committed suicide, when the
cult comes to silence before the appearance of the star—the principal, to
everyone's horror, has nausea on the stage. Salinger for the first time is
engaged in run-off writing, free suffragette prose, his inhibitions (which
once helped by their restraint to create his style) are now stripped. He is
giving you himself as he is. No concealment. It feels like taking a bath in a
grease trap.

Now, all of us have written as badly. There are nights when one comes
home after a cancerously dull party, full of liquor but not drunk, leaden
with boredom, somewhere out in Fitzgerald's long dark night. Writing at
such a time is like making love at such a time. It is hopeless, it desecrates

one's future, but one does it anyway because at least it is an act. Such writing is almost always unsprung. It is reminiscent of the wallflower who says, "To hell with inhibitions, I'm going to dance." The premise is that what comes out is valid because it is the record of a mood. So one records the mood. What a mood. Full of vomit, self-pity, panic, paranoia, megalomania, *merde*, whimpers, excuses, turns of the neck, flips of the wrist, transports. It is the bends of Hell. If you purge it, if you get sleep and tear it up in the morning, it can do no more harm than any other bad debauch. But Salinger went ahead and reread his stew, then sent it to *The New Yorker*, And they accepted it. Now, several years later, he reprints it in book covers.

There is social process at work here. Salinger was the most gifted minor writer in America. *The New Yorker*'s ability is to produce such writers. The paradox comes from the social fact that *The New Yorker* is a major influence on American life. Hundreds of thousands, perhaps millions of people in the most established parts of the middle class kill their quickest impulses before they dare to act in such a way as to look ridiculous to the private eye of their taste whose style has been keyed by the eye of *The New Yorker*. Salinger was the finest writer *The New Yorker* ever produced, but profoundly minor. The major writer like James Jones, indeed James Jones, leads the kind of inner life which enables him to study victories as well as defeats; Salinger was catapulted by a study of excruciating small defeats into a position of major importance. The phenomenon in the nation was the same those years. Men of minor abilities engaged America in major brinkmanships.

But it is always dangerous when the Literary Mafia (*The New Yorker*, the *Saturday Review*, The New York Times *Book Review*, *Time* magazine's book reviews, and the genteel elements in publishing) promote a minor writer into a major writer. A vested interest attaches itself to keeping the corpse of the violated standards buried. Readers who might be average keen in their sense of literary value find their taste mucked up. The greatest damage in this case, however, seems to have been to Salinger himself. Because a writer, with aristocratic delicacy of intent and nerves so subtle that only isolation makes life bearable for him, has been allowed to let his talent fester in that corrupt isolation. Salinger has been the most important writer in America for a generation of adolescents and college students. He was their leader in exile. The least he owed them for his silence was a major performance.

But it's a rare man who can live like a hermit and produce a major performance unless he has critics who are near to him and hard on him. No friend who worried about Salinger's future should have let him publish *Seymour an Introduction* in *The New Yorker* without daring to lose his friendship first by telling him how awful it was. Yet there was too much depending on Salinger's interregnum—he was so *inoffensive,* finally. So a suspension of the critical faculty must have gone on in the institutional wheels of *The New Yorker* which was close to psychotic in its evasions.

As for the other three stories in the two books, they are not as good as the stories in *Nine Stories.* Affectations which were part once of Salinger's charm are now faults. An excessive desire to please runs through his pages. There is too much sweetness. He is too pleased with himself, too nice, he lingers too much over the happy facility of his details in a way Fitzgerald never would. He is no longer a writer so much as he is an entertainer, a slim much-beloved version of Al Jolson or Sophie Tucker, the music hall is in the root of his impulse as much as the dungeons and mansions of literature. Does one desire the real irony? There is nothing in *Franny and Zooey* which would hinder it from becoming first-rate television. It is genre with all the limitations of genre: catalogs of items in the medicine chest, long intimate family conversations with life, snap with mother, crackle and pop. If I were a television producer I'd put on *Franny and Zooey* tomorrow. And indeed in ten years they will. America will have moved from One Man's Family to the Glass Family. Which is progress. I'd rather have the Glass Family on the air. But don't confuse the issue. The Glass stories are not literature but television. And Salinger's work since *The Catcher in the Rye* is part of his long retreat from what is substantial, agonizing, uproarious, or close to awe and terror. *The Catcher in the Rye* was able to change people's lives. The new books are not even likely to improve the conversation in college dormitories. It is time Salinger came back to the city and got his hands dirty with a rough corruption or two, because the very items which composed the honor of his reputation, his resolute avoidance of the mass media and society, have now begun to back up on him. There is a taste of something self-absorptive, narcissistic, even putrefactive in his long contemplation of a lintless navel.

The value of past predictions by this critic may be judged by the following about Saul Bellow. It is taken from page 467 in *Advertisements for Myself.*

When and if I come to read *Henderson the Rain King*, let me hope I do not feel the critic's vested interest to keep a banished writer in limbo, for I sense uneasily that without reading it, I have already the beginnings of a negative evaluation for it since I doubt that I would believe in Henderson as a hero.

Well, one might as well eat the crow right here. Henderson is an exceptional character, almost worthy of Gulliver or Huckleberry Finn, and it is possible that of all the books mentioned in this piece, *Henderson the Rain King* comes the closest to being a great novel. Taken even by its smallest dimension, and its final failure, it will still become a classic, a fine curiosity of a book quite out of the mainstream of American letters but a classic in the way *The Innocents Abroad,* or *The Ox-Bow Incident, The Informer,* or *High Wind in Jamaica* is classic.

Bellow's main character, Henderson, is a legendary giant American, an eccentric millionaire, six-four in height, with a huge battered face, an enormous chest, a prodigious potbelly, a wild crank's gusto for life, and a childlike impulse to say what he thinks. He is a magical hybrid of Jim Thorpe and Dwight Macdonald. And he is tormented by an inner voice which gives him no rest and poisons his marriages and pushes him to go forth. So he choose to go to Africa (after first contemplating a visit to the Eskimos) and finds a native guide to take him deep into the interior.

The style gallops like Henderson, full of excess, full of light, loaded with irritating effusions, but it is a style which moves along. *The Adventures of Augie March* was written in a way which could only be called *all writing.* That was one of the troubles with the book. Everything was mothered by the style. But Henderson talks in a free-swinging easy bang-away monologue which puts your eye in the center of the action. I don't know if Bellow ever visited Africa, I would guess he didn't, but his imaginative faculty—which has always been his loot—pulls off a few prodigies. I don't know if any other American writer has done Africa so well. As for instance:

> I was in tremendous shape those first long days, hot as they were. At night, after Romilayu had prayed, and we lay on the ground, the face of the air breathed back on us, breath for breath. And then there were the calm stars, turning around and singing, and the birds of the night with heavy bodies, fanning by. I couldn't have asked for anything better. When I laid my ear to the ground, I thought I could hear hoofs. It was like lying on the skin of a drum.

After a series of tragicomic adventures, Henderson reaches a royal almost Oriental tribe with a culture built upon magic and death. He is brought to the King, Dahfu, who lives in a wooden palace attended by a harem of beautiful Amazons. (One could be visiting the royalest pad in Harlem.) Dahfu is a philosopher-king, large in size, noble, possessed of grace, complex, dignified, elegant, educated, living suspended between life and death. The King, delighted with his new friend, takes him into the secrets of his mind and his palace, and one begins to read the book with a vast absorption because Bellow is now inching more close to the Beast of mystery than any American novelist before him. Dahfu is an exceptional creation, a profoundly sophisticated man with a deep acceptance of magic, an intellectual who believes that civilization can be saved only by a voyage back into the primitive, an expedition which he is of course uniquely suited to lead.

As the action explores its way down into an underworld of plot and magical omens, one ceases to know any longer whether Dahfu is potentially an emperor who can save the world, or a noble man lost in a

Faustian endeavor. The book is on the threshold of a stupendous climax—for the first time in years I had the feeling I was going to learn something large from a novel—and then like a slow leak, the air goes out of the book in the last fifty pages. Dahfu is killed in a meaningless action, Henderson goes home to his wife, and the mystery that Bellow has begun to penetrate closes over his book, still intact.

He is a curious writer. He has the warmest imagination, I think, of any writer in my generation, and this gift leads him to marvelous places—it is possible that Bellow succeeds in telling us more about the depths of the black man's psyche than either Baldwin or Ellison. He has a widely cultivated mind which nourishes his gift. He has a facility for happy surprises, and in Henderson, unlike Augie March, he has developed a nose for where the treasure is buried. Yet I still wonder if he is not too timid to become a great writer. A novelist like Jones could never have conceived *Henderson the Rain King* (no more could I), but I know that Jones or myself would have been ready to urinate blood before we would have been ready to cash our profit and give up as Bellow did on the possibilities of a demonically vast ending. The clue to this capitulation may be detected in Bellow's one major weakness, which is that he creates individuals and not relations between them, at least not yet. Augie March travels alone, the hero of *Seize the Day* is alone, Henderson forms passionate friendships but they tend to get fixed and the most annoying aspect of the novel is the constant repetition of the same sentiments, as if Bellow is knocking on a door of meaning which will not open for him. It is possible that the faculty of imagination is opposed to the gift of grasping relationships—in the act of coming to know somebody else well, the point of the imagination may be dulled by the roughness of the other's concrete desires and the attrition of living not only in one's own boredom but someone else's. Bellow has a lonely gift, but it is a gift. I would guess he is more likely to write classics than major novels, which is a way of saying that he will give intense pleasure to particular readers over the years, but is not too likely to seize the temper of our time and turn it.

For those who like the results of a horse race, it should be clear that the novels I liked the most in this round of reading were *Henderson*, *Naked Lunch*, and *Catch-22*. *The Thin Red Line* if not inspired was still impressive. *Another Country* suffered from too little style but compensated by its force. *Rabbit, Run* was better than expected but cloyed by too much writing. *Set This House on Fire* was rich in separate parts, and obese for the whole. *Letting Go* gave a demonstration of brilliant tactics and no novelistic strategy at all. *Franny and Zooey* and *Raise High the Roof Beam, Carpenters* was a literary scandal which came in last.

It has been said more than once that Tolstoy and Dostoevsky divided the central terrain of the modern novel between them. Tolstoy's concern—even in the final pessimism of *The Kreutzer Sonata*—was with men-in-the-world, and indeed the panorama of his books carries to us an image of a huge landscape peopled with figures who changed that landscape, whereas the bulk of Dostoevsky's work could take place in ten closed rooms: it is not society but a series of individuals we remember, each illuminated by the terror of exploring the bad jungle of themselves. This distinction is not a final scheme for classifying the novel. If one can point to *Moby Dick* as a perfect example of a novel in the second category—a book whose action depends upon the voyage of Ahab into his obsession—and to *An American Tragedy* as a virile example of the first kind of novel, one must still come up short before the work of someone like Henry James, who straddles the categories, for he explores into society as if the world were a creature in a closed room and he could discover its heart. Yet the distinction is probably the most useful single guide we have to the novel and can even be given a modern application to Proust as a novelist of the developed, introspective, still-exploitive world, and Joyce as a royal, demented, most honorable traveler through the psyche. The serious novel begins from a fixed philosophical point—the desire to discover reality—and it goes to search for that reality in society, or else must embark on a trip up the upper Amazon of the inner eye.

It is this necessity to travel into one direction or the other up to the end which makes the writing of novels fatal for one's talent and finally for one's health, as the horns of a bull are final doom for the suit of lights. If one explores the world, one's talent must be blunted by punishment, one's artistic integrity by corruption: nobody can live in the world without shaking the hand of people he despises; so an ultimate purity must be surrendered. Yet it is as dangerous to travel unguided into the mysteries of the Self, for insanity prepares an ambush. No man explores into his own nature without submitting to a curse from the root of biology since existence would cease if it were natural to turn upon oneself.

This difficulty has always existed for the novelist, but today it may demand more antithesis and more agony than before. The writer who would explore the world must encounter a society which is now conscious of itself, and so resistant (most secretly) to an objective eye. Detours exist everywhere. There was a time when a writer had to see just a little bit of a few different faces in the world and could know that the world was still essentially so simple and so phrased that he might use his imagination to fill in unknown colors in the landscape. Balzac could do that, and so could Zola. But the arts of the world suffered a curious inversion as man was turned by the twentieth century into mass-man rather than democratic man. The heart-land which was potential in everyone turned upon itself; people used their personal arts to conceal from themselves the nature of

their work. They chose to become experts rather than artists. The working
world was no longer a congerie of factories and banks so much as it was
reminiscent of hospitals and plastic recreation centers. Society tended to
collect in small stagnant pools. Now, any young man trying to explore that
world is held up by pleasures which are not sufficiently intense to teach
him and is dulled by injustices too elusive to fire his rage. The Tolstoyan
novel begins to be impossible. Who can create a vast canvas when the
imagination must submit itself to a plethora of detail in each joint of
society? Who can travel to many places when the complexity of each pool
sucks up one's attention like a carnivorous cess-fed flower? Of all the
writers mentioned here, only Jones, Heller and Burroughs even try to give
a picture of the world, and the last two have departed from conventional
reality before financing the attempt. It may be that James Jones is indeed
the single major American writer capable of returning with a realistic
vision of the complex American reality. But by his method, because of the
progressively increasing confusion and contradiction of each separate
corner in American society, he will have to write twenty or thirty books
before he will have sketched even a small design.

Yet a turn in the other direction, into the world of the Self, is not less
difficult. An intellectual structure which is cancerous and debilitating to
the instinct of the novelist inhabits the crossroads of the inner mind.
Psychoanalysis. An artist must not explore into himself with language
given by another. A vocabulary of experts is a vocabulary greased out and
sweated in committee and so is inimical to a private eye. One loses what is
new by confusing it with what may be common to others. The essential
ideas of psychoanalysis are reductive and put a dead weight on the
confidence of the venture. If guilt, for example, is neurotic, a clumsy part
of the functioning in a graceful machine, then one does not feel like a hero
studying his manacles, nor a tragic victim regarding his just sentence, but
instead is a skilled mechanic trying to fix his tool. Brutally, simply, mass
man cannot initiate an inner voyage unless it is conducted by an expert
graduated by an institution.

*Set This House on Fire, Another Country, Rabbit, Run, Letting Go,
Henderson,* and the Glass stories were all amateur expeditions into the
privacy of the Self, but they are also a measure of the difficulty, because
one could sense the exhaustion of talent in the fires on the way, as if a
company of young untried men were charging a hill which was mined and
laid across with fire lanes for automatic weapons.

Yet the difficulty goes beyond the country of psychoanalysis. There are
hills beyond that hill. The highest faces an abyss. Man in the Middle Ages
or the Renaissance, man even in the nineteenth century, explored deep
into himself that he might come closer to a vision of a God or some dictate
from eternity, but that exploration is suspect in itself today, and in the

crucial climactic transcendental moments of one's life, there is revealed still another dilemma. God, is it God one finds, or madness?

The religious temper of these books is significant. Of them all, *The Thin Red Line, Naked Lunch, Another Country,* and *Letting Go* have no overt religious preoccupation. Yet altogether one could make a kind of case that *Naked Lunch* and *Another Country* are not divorced from religious obsessions. The suggestion of still another frontier for the American novel is here. A war has been fought by some of us over the last fifteen years to open the sexual badlands to our writing, and that war is in the act of being won. Can one now begin to think of an atttack on the stockade—those dead forts where the spirit of twentieth-century irreligious man, frozen in flop and panic before the montage of his annihilation, has collected, like castrated cattle behind the fence? Can the feet of those infantrymen of the arts, the novelists, take us through the mansions and the churches into the palace of The Bitch where the real secrets are stored? We are the last of the entrepreneurs, and one of us homeless guns had better make it, or the future will smell like the dead air of the men who captured our time during that huge collective cowardice which was the aftermath of the Second War.

[July, 1963]

Back on the Open Road for Boys

by Alice Glaser

The Fifties had seen the birth of the Beat generation. In his classic, On the Road, *Jack Kerouac celebrated the Beats' code of existential freedom and brought their philosophy to a wider audience. For the July 1963 issue,* Esquire *editor Alice Glaser tracked down one of the best-known Beat poets, Allen Ginsberg, in India.*

On the bank of the Ganges between Delhi and Calcutta is the dusty city of Benares—a city tingling with ricksha bells, teeming with sages and scavengers, smelling of yak and marijuana. Eighteen months ago it was discovered by two wandering poets, Allen Ginsberg and Peter Orlovsky, probably the only two Beats still on the road. Even Kerouac, their god, had settled down on Long Island with his mother, and the whole Beat movement seemed threatened unless the will could be revived and a new hopland could be found. Benares seemed the perfect place. Sandals were only four cents a pair, and pads were going for $2 a month. The streets were lined with beggars carrying monkeys, with naked holy men, and with big buffaloes that the children pulled down to the Ganges and washed all over, intimately, soaping and scrubbing them and finally polishing them with banana oil and waiting for the defecation so they could scoop it up, roll it in dust and straw, and later convert it to fuel.

Such sights and smells charmed the Beats and, though Ginsberg and Orlovsky dined mostly on borsch and scrambled eggs, they otherwise quickly adapted to this Indian scene. They wore long, billowy gowns and beards not unlike the Sikhs, who wear bangles on their left wrists and their masculine organ on the right side.

514

Their poets' pad, on the third floor of a hot Hindu tenement, over-looked two temple tops and a blind woman rocking in the shade, back and forth, saying nothing. On their first week in Benares, the poets, their hair and beards untrimmed, gleefully sprinted down to the Ganges in blue swimming trunks. A buffalo began to lick Orlovsky.

"What does it feel like?" Ginsberg asked.

"Like the tongue you buy in stores," said Orlovsky.

Ginsberg seemed disappointed.

For the rest of the year they remained in Benares, undiscovered by the Trends Editors of *Vogue*, unmissed by Orville Prescott. But early this spring, wondering if they might not have a message for the hipsters back home, I flew to Benares and, after a bumpy ricksha ride across town toward the Ganges, I soon found myself knocking on the heavy wooden door of the poets' pad.

"How old are you?" asked Ginsberg, lying on the floor, inhaling deeply and blowing the sweet, cool smoke into the hot room.

"In my mid-thirties," I said.

"I'm thirty-six," he said.

"How about some tea?" asked Orlovsky, a delicate, thin blond of twenty-nine, standing in a gown over a small alcohol stove.

The bowls on the shelves were buzzing with flies and sticky with old hairs, and, declining politely, I took a seat on the floor.

"Do you mind if I comb out my hair?" Ginsberg asked, raising his head. "I'm not used to having hair so long." He removed from under a carpet a long, dirty comb and teased his brunet locks slightly upward.

"Are you here on a grant?" I asked.

"Guggenheim turned me down twice," Ginsberg said. "They think I'm a creep."

"Well, where does your money come from?"

"I get from $800 to $1,200 a year from the publisher, Lawrence Ferlinghetti; about $50 or $60 more from the Eighth Street Bookshop in Greenwich Village, and not much from the magazines because I sell to the crappy, experimental ones that don't pay much. Although I did get an advance from *Playboy* to do a piece on India. Any excess money, I plow back into the literary scene, such as that little magazine in New York we shall euphemistically call *Mother*. It's a magazine of culture written in a really frantic, freakish camp. *Mother, A Magazine of the Arts*."

"How do you spend your days?"

"Burning bodies," Ginsberg said. "Next door, at the Manikarnika Ghat, they usually have at least four or five bodies going up there. When you die here, you know, your body gets burned up. There is never any fear of death, either. Death is no worse than a hamburger stand."

"You mean you just stand around and watch?"

"We help out, too. Burning bodies is a holy rite. After they're burned, it's a sweet smell—they empty everything into the Ganges, which is very sterile, you know, because of the mineral content of the water. A dead cow can go floating down it and you can go swimming in the same spot two minutes later without getting infected by anything."

"How has your writing been going?"

He inhaled, blew out more smoke, and cheerfully presented a section from his journal, which I read as follows: ". . . so we ate cold chicken squatting on a mattress, twenty-five rupees, five dollars' worth, while the old lady beggar I have been watching on the clothshop corner steps downstairs rocked back and forth on her heels under a grey mattress for the fourth successive day. No sleep last night, and all morn feeding bannanas [sic] to monkeys on the roof, sunrise and then to the police to give papers registration address—the policeman a jolly type baffled by our presence. 'Why do you want to stay here in India so long?' "

"Well," I said, putting the journal aside, "why *do* you stay in India so long?"

Peter Orlovsky, leaning against a wall across the room, said, "I like living here. There's so much going on all the time. Wherever it happened, and whenever it's going, it's here right now."

Ginsberg nodded. Then he pulled out some photographs of himself, William Burroughs, Orlovsky and other Beats taken earlier in the year on another journey. One photograph showed Orlovsky naked with his hands modestly clasped over his genitalia; another showed Orlovsky, naked, facing the camera, no hands.

"I got mad in Greece," Orlovsky explained. "I wanted to pose naked in front of the Parthenon but the guide was afraid he'd get into trouble. . . ."

"You're like Dali," said Ginsberg, turning. "Dali sat naked to newsmen for an interview once. Dali's a European Spaniard from an earlier scene. That's especially why he's a Catholic and Monarchist, also a Dadaist."

Then I asked Ginsberg about some writers he has known, and he said, "Kerouac uses his friends in his books: Peter is usually 'George.' I've known Kerouac and Burroughs since 1943; Jack had a sort of sympathy about his family, a sort of despairing tenderness. One critic, Podhoretz, called Jack a juvenile delinquent, and then got fond of Mailer, and when Mailer stabbed his wife all those Columbia people got upset. Mailer was influenced by Burroughs, you know. He read *Naked Lunch* and got very influenced. Mailer got up and praised Burroughs at the Edinburgh Conference. Burroughs has always been a kind of loner. About the stories of Burroughs cutting pages down the middle, this is in the Gertrude Stein direction; this is how *Soft Machine* is. It's a transition from tonal to atonal—it takes a while to accustom the ear to it but it does become familiar after a while."

"What are your plans, if any?"

"Well," he said, inhaling again, and again lying on the floor, "we're going to stay here for a while and then maybe go to Japan. But not just yet. One of these days I'll go to Canada to speak at the University of Toronto, then to New Jersey to see my father, and back here to pick up Peter for Japan."

"Then what?"

"To be real, that's what," he said. "And to reserve all my charms and determination for private life rather than be hypocritical and nasty in public. See, the old tradition was to be pompous in public and if you preferred a private perversion or two, never say so, making the public somehow different from what the private thoughts were, dig?"

"Dig," I said, but before I could ask another question I realized both were sleeping, and so I kissed them and left.

[July, 1963]

The Night Senator and Mrs. Javits, Robert Rauschenberg, Niki de Sainte-Phalle, Jean Tinguely, Merce Cunningham, the Stewed Prunes, *Life*, *Newsweek*, *Harper's Bazaar* and *Show* magazines, the Canadian Broadcasting Corporation and the Cream of New York's Upper Bohemia all saw, at last, what was Happening

by John Wulp

Happenings were all the rage in the Sixties. No longer did an artist have to sit, tortured, alone in a room with a canvas to create art. Now he could make art out of anything, and if he did it in front of an audience, then it was a Happening. The participants were the original performance artists. The author John Wulp has variously earned a living as photographer, writer, painter, theatrical producer, designer, and cook.

In the Spring of 1962 I was in control of the Maidman Playhouse, a rather plush off-Broadway theatre on West Forty-second Street. I had taken a year's lease on the theatre which had begun in midwinter, but since that time I had produced two shows, a musical and an evening of one-act plays, both of which had been disastrous failures.

After that I tried renting the theatre, but with no better luck. One show had already opened to good reviews, but it had failed to attract an audience and quickly closed. Another show was scheduled to open the end of May, but the script was so bad I knew it had little chance of running—as things turned out it never even opened.

If I wanted to hang onto the theatre I had to think up something to do that would enable me to pay the rent through the summer months—and fast.

I was sitting in the office of the theatre brooding about these problems one day toward the end of April when the telephone rang. It was Kenneth Koch, a poet and playwright with some reputation among the *avant-garde* in New York. He was the author of a ten-minute epic called *Bertha*, which had been included among the plays in the *Theatre of The Absurd* produced off-Broadway the year before, and also of a slightly longer epic called *George Washington Crossing The Delaware*, one of the three one-act plays I had recently produced.

"Hello, John," said Kenneth. "How are things?"

"I don't know," I said. "How are things with you?"

"Just great," said Kenneth. "Say, John, I was wondering what's going on at your theatre now?"

"Nothing much," I said. "I've got the Stewed Prunes on Monday nights, but that's about all." The Stewed Prunes were a pair of comedians consisting of MacIntyre Dixon, fair and short and phlegmatic, and Richard Libertini, dark and tall and volatile, who had persuaded me to allow them to use the theatre on Monday nights to try out new material. They generally played to an audience of ten or twelve people.

"What sort of business are they doing?" said Kenneth.

"Pretty good," I said. "Why?"

"Well, a group of us were sitting around talking last night and we thought it might be fun to do something," said Kenneth.

"Who's we?" I said.

"Oh, you know," said Kenneth. "Bob Rauschenberg, Niki de Saint-Phalle, Jean Tinguely. You know them, don't you?"

"The only one I know is Bob Rauschenberg," I said. Bob Rauschenberg is a painter of "Neo-Dadaist" tendencies. He got a start toward international fame several years before when he had smeared his bed with paint and then exhibited the bed (quilt, sheets, and stuffed pillow case) as a work of art. This provoked a minor scandal among the art-world followers, and Bob Rauschenberg's reputation was made.

I had met him several years before, when I went to his studio to see if he might be interested in designing the scenery for a play that I had written which was about to be produced in New York. I had never seen his work before. In one corner stood a stuffed goat whose face had been daubed with paint and whose body was encased by an automobile tire. In another corner stood an orange crate that had been pasted with photographs and smeared with paint and on which stood a stuffed white chicken.

"Is this your work?" I inquired, somewhat timorously.

"Yes, but it isn't plugged in yet," Bob Rauschenberg replied, whereupon he put a plug into a wall socket and a naked light bulb in the orange crate began to blink on and off.

The matter of his designing the scenery for my show never worked out, but I had seen Bob Rauschenberg several times since then and we had a nodding acquaintance with each other.

"Well, certainly you've heard of Jean Tinguely," said Kenneth.

"What has he done?" I said.

"Oh, you know," said Kenneth. "He's the guy that does the self-destroying machines. They had a show of his a few years ago in the courtyard of the Museum of Modern Art. You must have read about it in the newspapers. It was on all the front pages."

"I remember now," I said. "That was the night the self-destroying machine failed to destroy itself. Didn't the fire department have to come and put it out?"

"We won't go into that," said Kenneth.

"What do you mean?" I said.

"Oh, the fire department didn't really have to put it out," said Kenneth. "They were just showing off. They probably wanted some free publicity."

"He's French, isn't he?" I said.

"Who?" said Kenneth.

"Jean Tinguely," I said with some exasperation. "Who do you think we're talking about?"

"He's Swiss, but that's all right," said Kenneth.

"Who's Niki de Saint-Phalle?" I said.

"She's the girl who fires rifles at paint-filled bags concealed on various objects," said Kenneth. "You've heard about her, haven't you?"

"I don't think so," I said.

"Oh, sure you have," said Kenneth. "You must have read about her someplace or seen her on television."

"Well, anyhow, what are you planning to do?" I said.

"I don't know," said Kenneth. "As I say, we were only talking about it last night."

"You must have some idea," I said.

"Well, I thought maybe I'd write something about Boston," said Kenneth. "You know, I went to Harvard and Bob Rauschenberg's been there one or two times. Niki's never been there, but she says she loves the sound of the place."

"I still have no idea what you're planning to do," I said.

"I don't know," said Kenneth. "I have no idea what Bob Rauschenberg is planning to do. Who can tell with him? Jean says he's going to do something with balloons. I don't know. He blows them up, I suppose. Niki will probably paint by firing a rifle. I don't know. I don't know."

"Who's going to direct this thing?" I said.

"We're trying to get Merce Cunningham," said Kenneth.

"Do you really think he'll do it?" I said. Merce Cunningham is a famous *avant-garde* dancer and choreographer in New York, and I was surprised that he would be willing to be associated with a project that seemed so nebulous.

"Sure, why not?" said Kenneth. "Bob Rauschenberg is a good friend of his."

"Do you suppose anybody will come?" I said.

"Who can tell?" said Kenneth. "I should imagine so. They're all very big names in the art world right now."

"Well, I don't know—" I said. "Do you have any money?"

"Are you kidding?" he said.

"I'll tell you what," I said. "I've got a show coming in the end of May, but I think we can work out some sort of schedule so that you can do your show if you can get it on within the next couple of weeks."

"That's all right," said Kenneth. "Jean is leaving for Europe in a couple of weeks so we'd have to get it on before then anyhow. How much do you want for rent?"

I swallowed hard and said the biggest figure I thought I had a chance of getting. "A hundred and fifty dollars."

"Don't you think that's a little steep?" said Kenneth.

"You can take it or leave it," I said.

"Let me talk it over with the others and call you back," said Kenneth.

A few days later he called back to say that he had discussed my terms with the other people involved, and they had all decided to go through with the venture.

The performance was scheduled to be held at ten in the evening of Friday, May 4. It was then around the end of April, so that left just a week and a half for preparations.

It was agreed that Kenneth Koch would write a short epic poem to be called *The Construction of Boston*, and Bob Rauschenberg, Niki de Saint-Phalle and Jean Tinguely would appear in this work. Merce Cunningham had by this time definitely consented to direct it. It was still necessary to get two actors to read the poem, but I said I would take it upon myself to persuade the Stewed Prunes to do this without being paid. Kenneth Koch and his friends thought they could assemble the rest of the performers.

There were to be two paid ads in The New York *Times*. The first was to appear on the Wednesday before the performance, the second on the day of the performance itself. Both ads would be paid for by Leo Castelli, a New York gallery owner and a friend of the artists.

No tickets would go on sale until ten o'clock in the morning on the day of performance. All tickets would be three dollars. There would be no complimentary tickets—not to friends of the artists and the performers, not even to critics.

Once this had been settled wheels began to turn.

I got in touch with the Stewed Prunes. They said they were reluctant to perform for nothing, although it was no secret between us that they had never earned a cent on one of their Monday nights. Nevertheless, I managed to persuade them that the prestige of appearing on the same stage with such well-known artists as Bob Rauschenberg, Niki de Saint-Phalle, and Jean Tinguely might be beneficial to their careers, and they finally said yes.

It was not long after this that Kenneth Koch called me again to set up an appointment for me to meet with Merce Cunningham and the others for the purpose of showing them the stage.

We met at the theatre around four o'clock on a Sunday afternoon.

"This really is a lovely little theatre," said Merce.

"Is all this yours?" Bob Rauschenberg said to me. He was enviously eyeing the debris that had accumulated backstage.

"Please feel free to use anything you find lying about," I said.

"You wouldn't have a costume for Jean?" said Niki de Saint-Phalle. Jean Tinguely spoke very little English: whenever he had anything to say, he said it in French and Niki de Saint-Phalle translated it for him.

"I'll show you what we have in the costume room," I said. I led them down a winding metal stairway to the costume room.

"You don't have to worry about us damaging anything we use," said Bob Rauschenberg. "We're real artists."

When I opened the costume room Niki de Saint-Phalle and Jean Tinguely immediately began going through the racks trying to find a costume for Jean. All the while they were searching, Jean kept putting on a series of funny hats to the accompaniment of giggles and squeals from Niki. Finally, she uttered a cry of delight.

"Look, Jean! Look what I've found!" she said. "It's *you!*"

Niki de Saint-Phalle and Jean Tinguely came hurrying out of the costume room and went into one of the dressing rooms so that Jean could get a better look at himself in the mirror when he tried on his costume. He stripped himself to the waist, revealing a hairy black chest. Then he tried wriggling into an elegant evening dress that turned out to be sizes too small for him.

"Oops, careful!" said Niki de Saint-Phalle, who was helping him. "You'll split the seams."

A look of horror must have come over my face because the evening dress had once been a very expensive costume.

"Don't worry," said Bob Rauschenberg to reassure me. "We're real artists."

Jean Tinguely was unable to get into the dress. He stood with it bunched around his hips, holding the top part over his hairy chest as he sadly surveyed himself in the mirror.

"What a shame!" said Niki de Saint-Phalle. "That one would have been perfect for you."

When I saw what they were after I brought them one dress after another from the costume room, but all of them were shabbier and less expensive than the dress Jean had first tried on and they found some reason to reject each one.

"No, that won't do," said Niki de Saint-Phalle. "No! No! Jean must look elegant."

"We're real artists," said Bob Rauschenberg.

They decided there was nothing to do but rent a costume for Jean Tinguely.

During the following days the preparations for the performance grew more and more frantic. Bob Rauschenberg and a group of friends he had recruited to help him were busy as ants carrying various objects into the theatre. They brought bathtubs and toilets. They brought beds and dressers and chairs. They brought rubber tubing and tangles of electrical wiring. On their last trip they wheeled into the theatre an enormous replica of the Venus de Milo that Niki de Saint-Phalle had made out of plaster of Paris.

"Jean has a reputation for destroying things," said Niki de Saint-Phalle to me one afternoon as we were talking in the lobby. "So for this performance he has decided he would like to build something for a change."

"That will be nice," I said.

Shortly thereafter a load of cinder blocks was delivered to the theatre and neatly stacked in the lobby.

"What are the cinder blocks for?" I said when I next encountered Niki de Saint-Phalle.

"Jean has decided to build a wall," she replied.

"A wall?" I said.

"Yes," said Niki de Saint-Phalle. "It's going to fill the entire proscenium opening."

"Won't that make it difficult for the audience to see?" I said.

"That's the idea," said Niki de Saint-Phalle.

The dress rehearsal was scheduled to begin at eleven o'clock on the night before the actual performance. When I arrived at the theatre I discovered an assorted group of people sprawled out on seats in various parts of the auditorium drinking cups of black coffee. In addition to the Stewed Prunes, I recognized two dancers, Henry Geldzahler, an associate curator of American painting and sculpture at the Metropolitan Museum, and Maxine Groffsky, a girl who was working as a reader in a large publishing house. All the others were unknown to me.

"Hello, dear," said Maxine, as soon as she spotted me. She was sitting in the front row with her feet propped up on the stage.

"Maxine!" I said. "What are you doing here?"

"I wish I knew," said Maxine. "I'm sleepy."

It was difficult to tell very much about what the show would be like from the dress rehearsal. None of the costumes had arrived and the artists could do little more than walk through their paces and describe the actions they would eventually perform.

"This is where I make rain," said Bob Rauschenberg.

"This is where I fire the cannon," said Niki de Saint-Phalle.

After the dress rehearsal, everyone met to compare notes.

"I know it looks rough," said Merce, "but we'll get it tidied up by tomorrow night."

"How long did it run?" said Kenneth.

"A little under fifteen minutes by my watch," said Bob Rauschenberg.

"What will we do?" said Kenneth. "Do you think the audience will be furious at paying three bucks a ticket for a show that runs less than fifteen minutes?"

"It will run longer in actual performance," said Niki de Saint-Phalle.

"Maybe nobody will come anyhow," said Kenneth.

"I think the whole thing is crap," said Henry Geldzahler.

I sensed that something was wrong with the Stewed Prunes. I had noticed MacIntyre Dixon stretched out on a couch in the lobby with his eyes tightly closed while Richard Libertini bent over him solicitously, but I thought it best not to say anything at the time. However, as soon as I was able to get Merce Cunningham alone, I asked him what had happened.

"Oh, one of the parts from Jean's weather machine came loose and hit the little Stewed Prune (what's his name? I can never tell the two of them apart) on the forehead," said Merce.

"Is it anything serious?" I said.

"I don't think so," said Merce. "But he's threatening to walk out on the show."

"What will you do?" I said.

"Kenneth's talking to him now," said Merce.

"If there's any way I can be of help, let me know," I said.

"The Stewed Prunes don't understand my artistic principles," said Merce. "I understand their artistic principles, but I'm not interested in them."

When I arrived at the theatre to open the box office around nine-thirty on the morning of the performance, I found a line of people waiting to buy tickets and all three box-office telephones ringing frantically. It quickly became obvious to me that I was not going to be able to handle the box office by myself, so I put in a hurried call to Bob Foley, an unemployed actor who had appeared in one of my shows.

"Get over here as fast as you can!" I said. "This place is a madhouse!"

"But I'm not up yet!" said Bob Foley. "I haven't had my coffee!"

"Don't ask any questions!" I said.

Bob Foley arrived at eleven o'clock, rubbing the sleep out of his eyes, but by that time, between the telephone reservations and the window sales, the two hundred tickets for that evening's performance were completely sold out. From that point on it became a question of dealing as diplomatically as possible with the mobs of people who showed up at the theatre or called in by telephone.

"No, I'm sorry, we're completely sold out," I said over and over again.

"Yes, that's right. The tickets only went on sale at ten o'clock, but we were completely sold out by ten-thirty. I can put your name on a list and if there are any cancellations. . . ."

"No, I'm sorry, we're completely sold out," said Bob Foley on another telephone. "If you want me to put your name on a list. . . ."

"Hello, I'm————. I'm calling for Leo Castelli—I'm Mr. Castelli's secretary."

"Yes?" I said.

"Mr. Castelli would like to reserve forty-eight tickets for tonight's performance."

"I'm sorry, we're completely sold out," I said.

"Oh, dear, I thought the tickets were only supposed to go on sale at ten o'clock."

"That's right, but we're completely sold out already," I said.

"Oh, dear, you're completely sold out? Mr. Castelli has invited a party of forty-eight people."

"I'm sorry," I said.

"Some of the people Mr. Castelli has invited are very important in the art world."

"I'm sorry," I said.

"You know Mr. Castelli paid for the newspaper ads?"

"If there are any cancellations I'll let you know," I said.

"Hello, this is————, at *Harper's Bazaar*. I'd like to reserve twelve tickets for tonight's performance."

"I'm sorry, there are no tickets left," I said.

"You must have a few tickets put aside for the press. We were planning to send our entire art staff."

"We're completely sold out," I said.

"In that case, do you suppose it might be possible to squeeze one of our photographers into your theatre somehow? Our readers couldn't afford to miss this."

By one o'clock, what with special requests of one sort or another, I had considerably oversold the house and there was a waiting list of several hundred people. When Bob Rauschenberg, Niki de Saint-Phalle, and Jean Tinguely heard this there was some debate as to whether or not they should schedule a second performance, but they finally decided against it.

"It's better if we don't make it too easy to get in," said Niki.

The phone never stopped ringing.

"Hello, this is Nan Rosenthal at *Show* magazine. I was wondering if you could tell me a little bit about tonight's performance."

"I'm sorry, there are no tickets left," I said.

"You don't seem to understand. This is Nan Rosenthal at *Show* magazine."

"There are no tickets left," I said.

"I'm the art editor at *Show* magazine. You must have made some arrangements to accommodate the press."

"There's a small cubicle at the back of the theatre," I said. "Maybe I could fit you in there."

"Will I be able to see?"

"You'll have a partially obstructed view of the stage," I said.

"No, no, you don't seem to understand. This is Nan Rosenthal at *Show* magazine."

"It's the best I can do," I said.

"Well, all right. Put two tickets aside for me. The name is Nan Rosenthal at *Show* magazine."

"There are no complimentary tickets," I said.

"I'm Nan Rosenthal, at *Show* magazine."

"We're not giving complimentary tickets to anyone," I said.

"But if I'm interested I might do a piece on tonight's event for *Show* magazine."

"What good is that going to do me?" I said.

"Don't you want free publicity? Think how much a plug in *Show* magazine might boost your business."

"There's only going to be one performance and we're sold out already," I said.

"I've never heard of such a thing," said Nan Rosenthal, and hung up, indignant.

During the afternoon several New York newspapers called. *Life* called. *Newsweek* called. A man from The Newark *News* called. They all wanted to send either reporters or photographers. I said I would try to accommodate them somehow, but they would have to pay for their tickets.

"Hello, I was wondering if you would be so kind as to give me some information about tonight's event."

"I'm sorry, we're completely sold out." I said.

"Oh dear, I've come all the way down from Boston. You see, I'm on the program committee for the Boston Museum of Fine Arts. We saw your advertisement in the newspapers and were *so* intrigued by the title. Do you think your show might be suitable for the Boston Museum of Fine Arts?"

"You'd have to decide that for yourself," I said.

"Couldn't you just give me some hint as to the nature of the program?"

"It's sort of difficult to describe," I said. "If you're at all familiar with the work of Bob Rauschenberg or Jean Tinguely, you'll know what I mean."

"It sounds absolutely fascinating. Are you sure there's no way I could get in?"

"Well, I was thinking of opening up a small cubicle at the back of the theatre," I said.

"Will I be able to see all right?"

"You'll be able to see enough to tell what's going on," I said.

"Oh, if you could get me in I would be ever so grateful. You see, I'm on the program committee for the Boston Museum of Fine Arts. . . ."

"Hello, I was wondering what my chances are for getting into tonight's performance."

"There are no tickets left," I said.

"Well, actually I wasn't interested in getting a ticket so much as I was interested in getting into the theatre with my equipment."

"Your equipment?" I said.

"Yes, this is————, from the Canadian Broadcasting Corporation. We thought we'd like to do a broadcast of the show you're having at your theatre tonight."

"How big is your equipment?" I said.

"It doesn't take up much room at all."

"Perhaps we could wedge you in next to one of the columns at the side of the auditorium," I said.

"Anything will be fine."

Around six o'clock the artists began to arrive to make final preparations for the performance, but still the telephone continued to ring, and still more and more people continued to arrive at the box office.

Around nine o'clock, just before the audience began to file into the theatre, I met Merce Cunningham in the lobby. Merce was on his way out to get a sandwich and a glass of milk before the performance. He looked worn and tired.

"Is everything all set?" I said.

"Who knows?" said Merce. "I have no idea what's going to happen tonight."

"What about MacIntyre Dixon?" I said.

"He's agreed to go through with it," said Merce. "We've worked it out so he can read his lines from in front of the proscenium where he won't be in any danger."

The audience was an impressive one.

Marcel Duchamp was there, making a rare public appearance.

Virgil Thomson was there, in a party that included a young rock-and-roll composer and his attractive actress wife.

The art director of *Harper's Bazaar* was there along with several members of his staff.

Leo Castelli had finally gotten in, although he was forced to stand.

Every available seat in the house was filled. People were standing about twenty deep in each of the doorways, and the little cubicle at the back of the auditorium that I thought might hold twelve people was crammed with twice that number. I told Bob Foley to lock the doors. There was a mob of fifty to a hundred people in the outer lobby still hoping to get in.

Just then the telephone in the box office rang.

"Hello," said the voice on the other end of the line. "Are you having some sort of show at your theatre tonight?"

"I'm sorry, there are no tickets left," I said wearily.

"Now, wait a minute," said the voice at the other end of the line. "Are you having some show called—what the hell is it? *The Construction of Boston*—at your theatre tonight?"

"There are no tickets left," I said.

"I'm sure you can always find room for a few more," said the voice at the other end of the line.

"There are no tickets left," I said. I was beginning to get angry.

"I'm calling for Senator and Mrs. Javits," said the voice at the other end of the line.

That calmed me down very quickly. "I'm sorry, I'd like to help you," I said, "but there's a line of about a hundred people ahead of you."

"What time does the show start?" said the voice at the other end of the line.

"It's just about to begin," I said.

"We'll be right over."

Kenneth Koch was supposed to have programs printed, but in his excitement he had forgotten to do so. Therefore, it had been decided that I should read the list of credits to the audience. Just as I was about to step in front of the red curtain, however, Merce Cunningham stopped me.

"I don't want my name mentioned," said Merce.

"Why not?" I said.

"I just don't want my name mentioned," said Merce.

I stepped in front of the curtain.

"Good evening, ladies and gentlemen," I said. "I have been asked to read the program for tonight's event. The show you are about to see is called *The Construction of Boston*. It was written by. . . ."

And I began the list of credits.

Bob Rauschenberg, Niki de Saint-Phalle, and Jean Tinguely were each playing themselves. They each also had alter egos bearing the same names but played by other people. I felt this was too complicated to explain so I simply recited the information that Kenneth Koch had written down.

"The part of Jean Tinguely will be played by Jean Tinguely," I read. And, after that, "The part of Jean Tinguely will be played by Henry Geldzahler."

Much to my astonishment, the audience broke into guffaws which increased each time I read the similar listings for the other artists.

After I had finished reading the program, I stepped in back of the red curtain once again and walked to the side of the stage. I was just about to look for a spot from which I might watch the show when Bob Foley came rushing up to me.

"John, you've got to do something about that mob in the lobby," said Bob Foley. "There's some guy out there who's pounding on the doors trying to get in."

As I walked to the back of the lobby, I could hear the pounding.

I angrily pulled open the door only to be confronted by Senator Javits. A woman I presumed to be Mrs. Javits was standing beside him.

"Good evening, Senator Javits," I said.

Senator Javits simply smiled.

"This is Senator and Mrs. Javits," said a man in a sharkskin suit who was behind the Senator.

"Yes, I know," I said. And then I pointlessly repeated, "Good evening, Senator Javits."

Senator Javits smiled again.

"Senator and Mrs. Javits would like to see this little show you're going to have here tonight," said the man in the sharkskin suit.

"What am I going to do?" I said. "As I told you over the phone I don't have any more room and there are all these people ahead of you."

"You don't seem to understand," said the man in the sharkskin suit. "This is Senator and Mrs. Javits."

"If I let the Senator in, I have to let everyone else in," I said.

"Surely you can find some place for the Senator and his wife," said the man in the sharkskin suit.

"Well, if they don't mind standing—" I said.

Senator Javits finally spoke.

"How much do I owe you?" he said. He reached into his pocket and took out a roll of bills.

"How many people are in your party?" I said. "Six? That means you owe me eighteen dollars."

"I'm sorry," said Mrs. Javits, smiling to the angry mob of people in the outer lobby.

But Mrs. Javits' smile did not appease them. After the Senator and his party had stepped into the theatre, there were angry grumbles of resentment.

"What are you going to do about that?" said Bob Foley.

"Let them in! Let them all in!" I said. "To hell with the fire laws. I'm sure nobody is going to lock me up as long as I've got a Senator on the premises."

By the time I had freed myself from the Senator and his party, the performance had already begun. I was unable to see over the heads of the people in the doorways, so I went backstage and climbed into the scenery loft. About thirty people had gotten there before me. Those who had arrived first were the only ones who had an unobstructed view of the stage. They were sitting on the edge of the platform, their legs dangling in midair. The others had to crane their necks to see. They were perched on the railing or leaning out from the uprights. In one corner of the platform a lady reporter from the Canadian Broadcasting Corporation was speaking into her microphone.

I looked down on a scene of wild confusion.

The two Stewed Prunes were reading from their scripts on opposite sides of the proscenium so that it was difficult to see or hear them. But there were enough other things going on to occupy my interest whenever I was able to get a glimpse of the stage.

Jean Tinguely made his entrance wearing a white ball gown with a large flounce at the bottom. The black hair on his chest was showing over the top of the gown. On his head he wore a wide-brimmed Lillian Russell picture hat covered with multicolored ostrich plumes which was tied beneath his chin with a large satin bow. He was pushing a wheelbarrow loaded with cinder blocks which he dumped in the center of the stage. Then he turned and went into the wings to reload the wheelbarrow.

The audience cheered.

Henry Geldzahler, who was impersonating Jean Tinguely's alter ego followed Jean onstage. Henry was also wearing a ball gown. He held his script in one hand and a cigar in the other.

"I am *ze* spirit of Jean Tinguely," said Henry Geldzahler, affecting a French accent. But the rest of his words were lost because Jean Tinguely had returned with the second load of cinder blocks which he again dumped in the center of the stage.

The audience cheered.

In one corner of the stage a facsimile of a small apartment had been set up consisting of a bed, a dresser, one or two chairs, a cast-iron bathtub, an ice box, a hot plate, a Maxfield Parrish drawing, and other assorted objects. Here the male dancer and the female dancer silently went about the acts of daily living, completely unmindful of everything else that was happening onstage. An alarm clock went off. The male dancer, wearing pajamas, got out of bed to silence it. He yawned. He brushed his teeth. He did a few setting-up exercises. In the meantime, the female dancer, wearing a nightgown, had gotten out of bed. She yawned. She dressed herself in a soiled cotton wrapper. She lit the hot plate and put on a pot of coffee.

By this time Bob Rauschenberg had come onstage followed by his alter ego. They were both dressed in Army-surplus rain capes with illuminated photo reflectors where their heads should have been. Bob Rauschenberg's alter ego didn't have any lines to read. Whenever the script called upon Bob Rauschenberg to say something, his alter ego projected his speeches in writing upon the back wall of the stage.

The Stewed Prunes commanded Bob Rauschenberg to make weather for Boston and he obliged by setting in motion a mechanical contraption he had erected at the side of the stage. A feather duster began to spin around scattering a whole bunch of plastic balls that were delicately balanced above it into the audience and about the stage. As soon as MacIntyre Dixon heard the whirring sound of the machine from which the metal part had come loose in rehearsal, he covered his head with both hands.

Next, the Stewed Prunes commanded Bob Rauschenberg to supply the elements for Boston. He filled a bucket with water from the cast-iron bathtub and poured this into a toilet seat imbedded in an old automobile tire.

After this the Stewed Prunes commanded Bob Rauschenberg to beautify the Boston landscape. He hauled what looked to me like part of an air-conditioning duct onstage and attempted to plant a rose bush in it. His efforts were continually hampered by the fact that he kept getting tangled in the wires that supplied the current for the light in his photo reflector.

Finally, the Stewed Prunes commanded Bob Rauschenberg to produce rain for Boston. He pulled a rope which was connected to a network of black rubber hose he had strung around the ceiling and a stream of water was released, drenching everyone onstage.

The audience cheered.

By now the two dancers had changed into street clothes.

The male dancer was cooking bacon and eggs in a frying pan.

The female dancer was arranging flowers in a vase. When she had finished she put the vase of flowers in the icebox.

Jean Tinguely had at last transported all the cinder blocks onstage and had begun to construct a wall across the proscenium opening. He labored first on one side of the stage and then on the other, leaving the center free for entrances and exits and also so that the audience could see what was going on. As he worked the flounce of his ball gown kept getting caught in the cinder blocks and Jean continually had to wrench himself free. Finally he removed the ball gown altogether and angrily threw it into the wings. From this point on Jean worked in his trousers, bare from waist up.

The performance was coming to a climax.

The Stewed Prunes called upon Niki de Saint-Phalle to appear and supply culture for Boston. Thereupon, Niki made her entrance down the center aisle of the auditorium, dressed in the uniform of a Napoleonic cannoneer. Two assistants, similarly attired, followed her.

The audience cheered.

Niki de Saint-Phalle's alter ego came onstage dressed in a costume identical to Niki's and sang a little ditty about culture. But the song was completely lost in the noise of Jean Tinguely's hurling the cinder blocks into place.

Maxine Groffsky wheeled the veiled plaster-of-Paris replica of the Venus de Milo onstage.

The statue was now unveiled.

One of Niki de Saint-Phalle's assistants handed her a loaded rifle. She took careful aim at the statue and fired. Luminous paint began to ooze from the statue.

The audience cheered.

She took aim and fired a second time. More luminous paint.

The audience cheered.

During these events I could hear the lady from the Canadian Broadcasting Corporation speaking into her microphone in hushed but breathless tones: "The applause you hear is for Niki de Saint-Phalle who has just made her entrance through the audience, followed by two assistants. Miss de Saint-Phalle has just come onstage. She is dressed—I believe—as George Sand, while her two assistants seem to be wearing some sort of military uniforms. An enormous plaster-of-Paris statue has just been wheeled onstage. They've just uncovered it. If I'm not mistaken I would say the statue is supposed to be a very rough replica of the Venus de Milo. One of Miss de Saint-Phalle's assistants has just handed her a rifle. She is taking aim. She fires! I believe that's green paint I see, yes, luminous green paint is oozing from the left nipple of the statue. . . ."

I couldn't help but wonder what the radio audience in Canada must be thinking.

Niki de Saint-Phalle kept aiming and firing at the statue. As soon as one rifle was empty, an assistant would hand her another loaded one. By the time Niki had fired all her ammunition the statue was riddled with holes and discolored with blotches and drippings of luminous paints. Then Niki's two assistants went into the wings and returned pulling a small cannon behind them.

The male dancer was listening to a news commentator on the radio.

The female dancer was washing the breakfast dishes in the bathtub.

Niki de Saint-Phalle's two assistants stuffed the cannon with newspapers, then they poured in gunpowder, and finally inserted a pellet of white paint. Niki lit the fuse.

The cannon went off with a loud explosion. It reared back and went hurtling across the stage, almost falling into the laps of the spectators in the front row. Niki de Saint-Phalle had intended that the paint in the cannon would make the statue entirely white again, but because the statue simply turned a muddy shade of grey, everyone assumed that Niki had missed her aim.

The audience booed.

Now Jean Tinguely set about in earnest to complete the center portion of the wall. Everyone onstage pitched in to help him so the work proceeded rapidly. As the cinder blocks rose higher and higher it became more and more difficult for the actors to deliver their lines. Henry Geldzahler managed to speak through a small aperture in the wall, but

Niki de Saint-Phalle's alter ego was forced to climb a ladder in order to make herself seen and heard above the din. The spectators in the front rows began to head for the exits, all the while glancing apprehensively over their shoulders.

No one was quite sure when *The Construction of Boston* had been completed. As soon as Jean Tinguely ran out of cinder blocks and it was no longer possible to see or hear any of the performers, the houselights were turned on. There was a moment of stunned silence. A few people clapped, some booed. The Stewed Prunes, suddenly realizing they were stranded in front of the wall, tried frantically to find some way of getting backstage without going through the auditorium, but were forced to nudge and jostle their way through the former members of the audience who were now crowding the aisles and the lobby.

The entire performance had taken about fifteen minutes.

After the performance the stage was littered with paint and plaster of Paris and broken fragments of cinder block, but this did not deter the mobs of people who descended on the artists and performers.

In addition to friends and well-wishers, there were reporters and photographers from *Life, Newsweek,* and *Harper's Bazaar.*

Out of the corner of my eye I noticed the lady from the Canadian Broadcasting Corporation threading her way through the crowd, shoving her portable microphone into people's faces and asking them if they had any opinions for the Canadian listening audience.

Senator Javits and his wife posed for photographs with Bob Rauschenberg. Senator Javits said that he found the performance "interesting," an opinion which his wife must have shared because four days later she devoted a large part of her short-lived newspaper column to her interpretation of the event.

I willingly posed for group photographs with the others, a circumstance which nettled Kenneth Koch.

"John, you're standing right in front of me," he said.

I turned and smiled. At first I thought Kenneth must be kidding.

"Damn it, John," said Kenneth. "I think I should be in the center of the photograph. After all, this whole thing was my idea."

When all the spectators had left the stage and only the people who had participated in *The Construction of Boston* were left, there was some debate as to whether to clean up the stage that night.

"Let's do it now," said Bob Rauschenberg. "I know everyone is tired, but it's better to do it now while we're all still here."

Everyone agreed with him and the whole group set to work at once.

I left the others to their cleaning chores and went out to the box office to count up the receipts with Bob Foley. The total income for the evening came to nearly eight hundred dollars. Even after I deducted the rent, the money for taxes, and various incidental expenses, I was still able to turn over more than six hundred dollars to Kenneth Koch when he came by the box office to get a final accounting.

As soon as he saw the amount of money, Kenneth's eyes lit up. He was all set to do a whole series of similar evenings.

"It's such a great idea," he said, "and it's all so simple. I don't see how I ever thought it up. I mean, there's London and Paris and Rome. We can go on forever until we've exhausted all the cities of the world."

The idea stuck in my mind, and the more I thought about it the more it seemed as though Kenneth Koch might have the solution to my financial problems. It was obvious that there was a large audience for the sort of show he and his friends had presented. Nearly as much money had been taken in at the box office for *The Construction of Boston* as had been taken in during the short runs of each of the shows that had been presented at the theatre during the winter, and each of those shows had cost over ten thousand dollars to produce.

The following Sunday afternoon I took a walk in Greenwich Village and was still pondering this state of affairs, when, quite by accident, I bumped into Niki de Saint-Phalle and Jean Tinguely. They were having dinner at the Albert French Restaurant and invited me along.

Naturally, we began to discuss the events of the previous Friday.

"It just goes to prove what I've always suspected," said Niki de Saint-Phalle. "People are tired of the theatre and movies. They want *real* entertainment."

Jean Tinguely spoke in French.

"Jean says that artists have become the new movie stars," translated Niki. "Jean says he may become the new Humphrey Bogart."

We all laughed.

I told them about the difficulties I was having in holding onto the theatre, and I said I was wondering if it might not be a good idea not to do any more plays but instead to present a series of events similar to the one on Friday night. They both agreed that this was a splendid idea, but Jean raised the objection that it would not be wise to present such an event too often. He felt that a great deal of the success of *The Construction of Boston* was due to its novelty. I replied that then I would still be without any way of meeting my monthly rent.

"Maybe we could charge ten or fifteen dollars a ticket," said Niki.

"Twenty-five," I said.

Jean spoke. "Jean says fifty," translated Niki.

We all felt confident that we would have no trouble getting fifty dollars a ticket, and that this money could be raised by subscription so the theatre rent would be covered in advance.

As soon as this obstacle had been passed, none of us could speak fast enough to get out all the wild and fanciful ideas that came crowding into our heads. We could get real poets to write the scripts and real actors to recite the lines.

Jean spoke, and Niki de Saint-Phalle translated: "Jean says maybe we could get Richard Burton." Then, turning to me, she inquired seriously, Can he speak well?"

[November, 1963]

On Experiencing Gore Vidal

by William F. Buckley Jr.

On August 28, 1968, two of the nation's most eloquent debaters exchanged insults in front of ten million people in a broadcast that "rocked television." William F. Buckley Jr. and Gore Vidal had been asked by ABC to deliver commentaries on the 1968 political conventions from the conservative and liberal viewpoints, respectively. Each writer's explanation of the incident proved no less heated or controversial than the original outburst. Buckley's account was published in August 1969. Vidal was granted equal time in the September 1969 issue.

I have here a recent issue of *The East Village Other* featuring a piece entitled "Faggot Logic" which is about me, or more precisely about a column I wrote on Senator McGovern which highly displeased this demi-mondaine journal. "Following faggot logic," my critic writes, "is disturbing at any time of year, and Buckley's spiteful spewlings today have just pissed me off, even more than usual." That is certainly an icebreaker, even in *The East Village Other,* and I read on, my interest aroused to learn something about the nature of faggot logic. "On the Right," the author went on, referring to the logo of my thrice-weekly column, "is nearly invariably an exercise in faggot dialectic. And since I think this peculiar mode of intellect is worthless at best and generally inimical to the public weal, then I'd like, just once—Christmas season notwithstanding—to engage in a point-by-point vivisection of one of his scabrous evacuations."

Alas, many many words later, the reader is left knowing nothing he didn't know before about the nature of faggot logic, which in my case was nothing at all, and moreover glumly aware that he would not likely come to apprehend the meaning of anything in any way elusive under the guidance of the writer in question, whose thought proved to be as barren as his wit: so that after jogging alongside him over an endless stretch of indignation, one arrives at the cheerless conclusion (hardly reassuring to poor Senator McGovern), that the author likes the senator, dislikes me, and thinks we should get out of Vietnam instantly.

Even so the piece sticks in the mind because here is a licentious rhetorical effort at homicide—in which the author arms himself with all the bad words; and yet he selects as the killer-word: "faggot." That was the warhead. Very interesting. And particularly revealing in the context of the general attitude of that journal towards faggotry, the unmetaphorical practice of which it explicitly panders to, or so it would seem. On page 17 of the same issue there are advertisements as plainspoken as Macy's for garden furniture. "NUDE MALE FILM CLUB. . . . There will be continuous screenings nightly . . ."—is just one display ad. Another, discreetly sequestered in the classified section, positions wanted, "WHEEL AND DEAL": "Bi-Sexual, nude model, handsome, tall, trim, blond, hung, well-built, 30, will pose for sketches or you name it. $20 per session. . . ." And for those choosy readers who desire a synoptic view of the area and its possibilities there is the "1969 Gay Guide for gay guys, 'N.Y., N.J. baths, bars, glory holes, restaurants, movies, etc.' "

Why is faggotry okay, but the imputation of it discreditable? Is there a platonic coinage, which is bad—even as the real thing becomes okay? Is that a culture lag, of sorts? Rather like saying about somebody that he is impious (which is unfriendly) even though, as everybody knows, explicit impiety is perfectly okay.

At this point my mind moved to Gore Vidal, and the dismal events of the Summer of 1968, when he and I confronted each other a dozen times on network television, leading to an emotional explosion which, it is said, rocked television. Certainly it rocked me, and I am impelled to write about it; to discover its general implications, if any; to meditate on some of its personal implications, which are undeniable and profound; to probe the question whether what was said—under the circumstances in which it was said—has any meaning at all beyond that which is most generally ascribed to it, namely: Excessive bitchery can get out of hand. But first the narrative.

   In the late Fall of 1967 I had a telephone call from Mr. James Haggerty, vice-president of the American Broadcasting Company and former White House press chief for President Eisenhower. Would I, he asked, consent to confer with Mr. Elmer Lower and Mr. William Sheehan concerning ABC's coverage of the 1968 political conventions? Yes I said—obviously. We met then, the heads of ABC News and Special Events and of ABC Television News and they disclosed their plans for 1968. Instead of covering the political conventions "gavel to gavel," ABC would condense the day's events into ninety minutes of nightly television, divided into five segments. The fourth segment was conceived as broad-ranging commentary on the convention, and the forthcoming election, and on politics in general.

They had in mind that two people would share that time, one of them a conservative, the other a liberal. Would I?

I asked a few mechanical questions, and indicated it would probably work out, and then asked them who would be my adversary. They replied that he had not been selected, did I have any suggestions? I thought a while and gave them eight or ten names, among whom were some of the obvious people (Schlesinger, Galbraith, Mailer), and some a little less obvious (for instance Al Lowenstein, Carey McWilliams Jr.). Was there anyone at all I would refuse to appear alongside? I wouldn't refuse to appear alongside any non-Communist, I said—as a matter of principle; but I didn't want to appear opposite Gore Vidal (I said), because I had had unpleasant experiences with him in the past and did not trust him. A few months later the announcement was made that Gore Vidal had been selected as my opposite number. "We knew we wanted Buckley," Elmer Lower told a reporter in Miami at the outset of the Republican Convention, "because we were well familiar with him. . . . It was a question of who would best play off against him. We considered a number of people and did some 'auditions,' sort of surreptitiously that is, watching people on the air without them knowing we were watching them. It looked as though Buckley would play better with Vidal than with any of four or five other people." In one sense he was right. Even before Chicago—a good week or ten days after Miami—there were those who took pains to record their misgivings. For instance—not exactly typical, but singularly interesting—Stephanie Harrington, who wrote in *The Village Voice,* looking back on our first series of encounters at Miami:

"What political analysis ABC did try for turned out to be the most embarrassing ingredient in its grand innovation. This was its attempt to elevate the affair to the level of intelligent discussion by bringing together nightly Gore Vidal and William Buckley for their comments—which [discussions] had far more to do with their contempts for each other than [with] their impressions of the convention. It was clearly a sequel to that painful moment some years back when Buckley, during a televised debate with Vidal, descended to his unique level of argument and in a typically Buckleyesque display of dirty debater's tricks, destroyed his opponent not by logic but by using his personal life against him. [I interrupt Miss Harrington to bring you a special announcement: remember that phrase, 'personal life.'] Indeed, he tried again this time, dismissing Vidal's political opinions on the grounds that he is the kind of man who would write a book like *Myra Breckinridge.* It was obvious that Buckley's heroics about the show going on despite the broken collarbone he suffered in a fall on his boat [—heroics? I simply went. Heroism, maybe; heroics, no—] had less to do with interest in the convention than with eagerness to get his claws into Vidal again."

Now under the stress of my conversations with ABC, we see that the anchor of Miss Harrington's argument is uprooted, and her analysis drifts away into fantasy. *Still*, she did say a few things concerning which there has been considerable speculation which *is* relevant: so that (fulldisclosurewise) I now divulge the history, abbreviated but not censored, of my dealings with Mr. Vidal, acknowledging Miss Harrington's and others' suspicions that those dealings figured, yes indeed, in the meetings at Miami and Chicago.

In January of 1962, appearing on the Jack Paar program to promote his play *Romulus*, Vidal went out of his way to observe that I had "attacked" Pope John XXIII for being "too left wing": which sorrowful recording of my impiety drew from the audience horrified tremors.

Paar was evidently pressured to invite me to reply, which he had and I did, on an evening Paar once reminisced about as having been among the most memorable of his career, such was the ensuing uproar. Said uproar, for once, directed not against me, but against Paar's assault on me after I had left the studio, which assault stimulated, by the count of one NBC spokesman, seven thousand (anti-Paar) telegrams of protest and one (pro-Paar) phone call from the White House. That is by the way—what I liked most in terms of the theatre of the episode was that instants after I left the studio, Paar ingenously announced to the studio audience, "*I just got a call here. Gore Vidal's coming back tomorrow night!*" Now Paar's shows were taped three hours before they were telecast. So that he couldn't have received a telephone call from Gore Vidal reacting to my appearance—because the show would not go out over the air-waves for another three hours. (And they used to talk about Tricky Dick.)

Anyway, Vidal showed up, and after cooing about him ("Notice the difference in manner and approach and reasoning") for a few minutes Paar asked what *had* I actually said about the Pope and the encyclical?

Vidal: Yes, well what he actually said—and I went back and looked it up . . . in the month of August, Buckley attacked the Pope in a piece in his magazine, and the piece was called "A Venture in Triviality."

(a, I did not "attack the Pope." b, There was no "piece," merely a one-paragraph, unsigned editorial. c, The paragraph was not called "A Venture in Triviality"; it bore no title; one phrase in it said "[the encyclical] must strike many as a venture in triviality coming at this particular time in history.")

V.: It was a vicious piece, and *America*, which is the Jesuit weekly in the United States, attacked Buckley in an editorial declaring that he owes his readers an apology, unquote.

(The demand by *America* for an apology was unrelated to the editorial in question.)

V.: And Buckley's answer to the Jesuits was: "You are impudent."

(My answer to the Jesuits was in 2500 words, one sentence of which stated that it was impudent for *America* to ask a non-Catholic journal of opinion to apologize for a transgression—even assuming that that is what it was—against exclusively Catholic protocol; and of course I was right.)

V.: I mean, who is he? Here's a guy who has never worked for a living . . . has never had a job.

(I had held down one part-time job, as a member of the faculty of Yale, 1947-1951; and three full-time jobs before going to work for *National Review*, in 1955, which is at least a full-time job.)

V.: He's got two sisters.

(Six.)

V.: One said while she was at Smith . . .

(It was ten years after she graduated.)

V.: . . . that the faculty was filled with Communists.

(She said four faculty members had Communist-front connections, which was true.)

V.: The other was at Vassar and started the same thing at Vassar.

(She said that at Vassar the bias in the social-science departments was predominantly liberal, and of course she was right, ask Mary McCarthy.)

V.: Meanwhile their brother was at Yale and wrote *God and Man at Yale* and said that was full of Communists.

(My book did not charge or intimate that there was a single Communist at Yale.)

V.: He feels free to correct, through his little magazine of his, the actions of all our Presidents and the Pope, and philosophers . . . on the subject of philosophy I thought *this* might interest you, Jack—of Albert Schweitzer—who is one of the great men of our time, and whose philosophy is reverence for life—he wrote of Albert Schweitzer, quote: He is more destructive than the H Bomb, unquote.

(The quotation is not from me, but from a book review in *National Review*—by a Ph.D. in philosophy. I do not censor the book reviewers.)

V.: On the subject of integration, Mr. Buckley wrote, quote: Segregation is not intrinsically immoral, unquote. Well, that's a double negative which means I don't quite dare to come out and say I'm in favor of segregation, so I'll put it in a double negative.

(a, It isn't a double negative. b, It is a litotes, and should be recognized as such by a professional writer. The litotes has been around as a necessary rhetorical refinement for years; was used, for instance, by that old evader, Homer. c, I didn't in fact write that phrase, I spoke it in the presence of a Catholic liberal, John Cogley, who d, agreed with me.)

V.: . . . but that's exactly what it means, which goes against not only Catholic doctrine but I would think any humane—you put your finger on it, you know, when you said there's no humanity there.

But Mr. Vidal was not through.

V.: I was just going to say one more thing struck me, listening to Mr. Buckley. He said (and I was quite fascinated because it's amazing the things perhaps you can *just* get away with, this side of libel). . . . He said that Harry Truman had called Eisenhower an anti-Semite and anti-Catholic.

Paar: Yes, he did say that. But what—

Vidal: There's no evidence that Harry Truman ever said this. Now I would like to say right now, on the air, that I will give $100 to the *National Review*, which is Buckley's magazine, if he can prove that Harry Truman ever said any such thing: and if he cannot prove it, why I think he should then be regarded as what he is, which is an irresponsible liar. . . . As someone once said . . . [the Buckleys] are sort of the sick Kennedys.

I flew early the following morning to Switzerland, leaving a telegram to be dispatched by my office to Jack Paar. It read: "PLEASE INFORM GORE VIDAL THAT NEITHER I NOR MY FAMILY IS DISPOSED TO RECEIVE LESSONS IN MORALITY FROM A PINK QUEER. IF HE WISHES TO CHALLENGE THAT DESIGNATION, INFORM HIM THAT I SHALL FIGHT BY THE LAWS OF THE MARQUIS OF QUEENSBERRY. HE WILL KNOW WHAT I MEAN. WILLIAM F. BUCKLEY JR." The telephone was ringing when I reached my destination in Switzerland, as I half expected it would be. Come on now, calm down, whaddaya say, forget it, write a piece about the whole thing instead. So I finally withdrew the telegram, and contented myself instead to send a letter to Jack Paar:

Dear Mr. Paar:

[I have been informed of what Mr. Gore Vidal said on your show on February 1.]

1. The documentation, taken in each case from The New York *Times*, is as follows: On October 9, 1952, President Harry Truman accused the Republicans generally of supporting "the discredited and un-American theory of racial superiority." On October 17, Assistant Secretary of State Howland Sargeant read a message from Mr. Truman to the Jewish Welfare Board in Washington. Eisenhower, Truman said, "cannot escape responsibility" for his endorsement of Senator Revercomb, "the champion of the anti-Catholic, anti-Jewish provisions of the original D.P. bill." Truman charged that Eisenhower "has had an attack of moral blindness, for to-

day he is willing to accept the very practices that identify the so-called 'master race' although he took a leading part in liberating Europe from their domination."

2. The following day, Rabbi Abba Hillel Silver, ex-President of the Zionist Organization of America, expressed "shock that an irresponsible statement of that character could be made. The attempt by implication to identify a man like General Eisenhower with anti-Semitism and anti-Catholicism, is just not permissible even in the heat of a campaign."

3. Please instruct Mr. Vidal to make out a check for $100 to the National Conference of Christians and Jews.

Paar, directed to do so by NBC's lawyers, read, or rather caused to be read, the letter aloud over his program, during a station break, following which he made no reference to it whatever. Vidal made no acknowledgment, tendered no apology, did not reply in any way to a couple of letters asking him to make out the check.

It is not my habit to review the material that appears in the back of the book section of *National Review*, so that I saw for the first time in the published magazine, weeks later in Switzerland, a review by Noel E. Parmentel Jr. of Vidal's play, *Romulus*. The review was unfavorable to the play, but generous—one should say accurate—in its appreciation of Vidal's talents as a playwright. One aspect of *Romulus* the reviewer found offensive, and was not alone in the critical community in doing so. "All in all," he wrote, "*Romulus* adds up to (with the possible exception of *Sail Away*) the most offensive instance of 'inside' theatre, which such diverse types as the late Ernie Kovacs and New York *Times* drama critic Howard Taubman have chosen to call 'effeminate' and which the boys in Lindy's are calling '*la nouvelle fague.*' "

Parmentel went on. "Although the critics have generally ridiculed the Vidal literary product, he is far from being a jejune hack. He has certainly traveled an odd road. During his early career as a 'serious' novelist, he evinced an interest in homosexuality equalled only by that of the editors of *One*. Many of his novels and stories are clinical, apparently informed commentaries on the problem. [Notice what Vidal would consider the planted axiom:—the *problem*.] In spite of all this high purpose, critic William Peden was once moved to note that the Vidal output constituted 'a rather dreary landmark in the literature of homosexuality.' "

And there followed a crack I confess I have repeated here and there mostly because I thought it funny, still do. "Always the seeker after truth, Vidal lived for a time in the ruins of a sixteenth-century monastery in Guatemala, where he gathered material for an anti-United Fruit Company novel—positively, as a local wag observed, the *only* anti-fruit novel Vidal ever wrote."

And then, more seriously, "At another point he made a pilgrimage to the bedside of André Gide. It is reported that the great French writer liked Vidal and gave him an inscribed first edition of his controversial *Corydon*. Vidal carried his almost obsession with homosexuality into the movies. Although he is quite a proficient scriptwriter, he once wrote a scenario about Billy the Kid, acted by a bewildered Paul Newman, in which the legendary outlaw appeared as a misunderstood homosexual. It was only natural that Sam Spiegel should call on Vidal's specialist skills for Tennessee Williams' *Suddenly Last Summer*."

The operative word is "obsession." And it wasn't only *National Review*, as Parmentel made clear, that thought it a—problem. Our sister publication on the Left, *The New Republic*, carried a review of *Romulus* by Robert Brustein who is now the dean of the Yale Drama School. He wrote that Vidal had "transform [ed] Dürrenmatt's tough parable into an effeminate charade. . . . To make the Romans into homosexuals," he concluded, "is simply in bad taste." *Why* bad taste?

The months passed, and David Susskind asked me if I would appear *mano a mano* with Vidal on his *Open End*—just the two of us. And discuss what? I asked. *Everything*, said Susskind. All right, I said.

Now no discussion of "everything" nowadays can be counted upon not to touch on sex. Accordingly I was prepared, should the subject arise, to attempt to state the case, biological, cultural, and religious, for heterosexuality (that sounds funny, doesn't it?)—prepared to go so far as to defend its "normalcy"; to defend, even, the idea that normalcy in this instance at least is related to what is normative: to defend, one might say, the conservative position.

It seemed to me utterly natural—one is tempted to say utterly normal—that in defending heterosexuality I should furtively consult my own preferences in that direction, and accordingly that in defending bisexuality, the question of Vidal's preferences would reasonably arise. I had read, in preparation for our meeting, his book of essays, *Rocking the Boat*, in which his own intellectual sympathies, at least, were quite candidly stated. "Now it is an underlying assumption of twentieth-century America," he wrote—and the student of rhetoric knows already, the "now" being a dead giveaway, that the writer is about to introduce an assumption with which he disagrees—"that human beings are either heterosexual or, through some arresting of normal psychic growth, homosexual, with very little traffic back and forth. To us, the norm is heterosexual; the family is central; all else is deviation, pleasing or not, depending on one's own tastes and moral preoccupations. Suetonius"—Vidal was reviewing a translation of *The Twelve Caesars* by Robert Frost—"reveals a very different world. His underlying assumption is that man is bisexual and that given complete freedom to love—or, perhaps more to the point in the case of the Caesars, to violate—others, he will do so, going blithely from male to female as fancy dictates. Nor is Suetonius alone in this assumption of man's variousness. From Plato to the rise of Pauline Christianity, which tried to put the lid on sex, it is explicit in classical writing. [Nonsense, as it happens. E.g. Aristophanes, who mocked Plato's homosexuality; Juvenal, who stigmatized the Greek-aristocratic homosexuality; Catullus, who found Caesar's bisexuality, in the words of Gilbert Highet, 'ridiculous and disgusting.'] Yet to this day Christian, Freudian and Marxian commentators have all decreed or ignored this fact of nature in the interest each of a patented approach to the Kingdom of Heaven. . . ."

Now in fact the subject did not come up, though the question was raised, I think (I do not exactly remember and I do not have the transcript) as to whether practicing homosexuals working in sensitive government agencies were security risks, like, say, drunkards. I have never been convinced, by the way, that they are, but I did recite the reasons given by security officials (susceptibility to blackmail, primarily), and I do not know whether I loosed an inflection that burrowed into the memory of Miss Harrington. I cannot conceive that if I had made a major, or even a minor statement, about Gore Vidal's "personal life," that it would have escaped the attention of every single one of the television critics who watched and reported on the program, and there were apparently many of them, none of whom made the slightest reference to the cause of Miss Harrington's trauma. Could she have had in mind a personal reference to Vidal's relations to the Kennedys? But the only thing I knew about his private life in that connection (Vidal had not yet fallen out with the Kennedys) was that his sometime stepfather is Jacqueline Kennedy's incumbent, a nexus that connects an awful lot of people with an awful lot of people and is neither newsworthy nor scandalous.

On the other hand, I gather that I spoke sharply to Vidal (I should hope so!). One reviewer who was also covering the opening of the Lincoln Center that night, wrote that every so often he "would switch over to an independent channel where a fair-haired barracuda named William Buckley Jr. was nibbling at the flesh of a young sea robin named Gore Vidal. . . . In the only complete sentences spoken on this piscatorial orgy, we heard Mr. Vidal saying he couldn't imagine Mr. Buckley in the role of an abolitionist and Mr. Buckley saying that he was an abolitionist for the slaves of Eastern Europe, which Mr. Vidal wasn't." There was no masking, I gather, the mutual dislike, which in Mr. Vidal's case was spontaneously generated, in mine evolved as a reaction to his hit-and-run network disparagement of my family and myself earlier in the year. "The debate," another reviewer wrote, "got entrenched in so much personal opprobrium nothing really was decided other than Buckley's clear debating superiority. . . . When it came to historical and political facts and interpretation, Vidal, frustrated in realistic fencing, resorted to personal disdain, never an attractive effect. . . . Both indulged the sort of ad hominem needling that dazzles and spins off sparks and delights viewers who adore such exercise of forensic fisticuffs, but it does keep issues muddled while delighting the more sadistic semantic fight fans." Vidal said a while later on the Les Crane program that I had beaten him badly, and gave as the reason that he, Vidal, had permitted himself to become "emotionally involved," whatever that means.

It was during the Republican Convention at San Francisco in 1964 that I resolved I would not again debate with Gore Vidal. It was the memory of that encounter, added to everything else, that made me suggest to ABC that I'd prefer not to debate with him, and now I gather that his exclusion graveled him. Indeed over the intervening years I had never asked him to appear on *Firing Line*, which was launched early in 1966. "The one forum on which they have not met is Buckley's syndicated series, *Firing Line*," a reporter wrote, after interviewing Vidal. "Buckley invited the novelist to the program, but 'I refused to give him that much help,' Vidal smiled thinly." (I'd have smiled thinly too if I told a reporter I refused Ed Sullivan's invitation to tap dance on his show because I didn't want to give Sullivan that much help.) At San Francisco it wasn't just the usual things that aroused me, but an insight I got into what I now concluded was more than a merely episodic insensibility to the truth. Specifically, Vidal announced on a television program, once again "moderated" by Susskind (Susskind's advocacy of Vidal's positions competed with the positions themselves in burdening Vidal), that I had that very afternoon importuned Barry Goldwater to accept a draft of an acceptance speech I had written for him, and that Goldwater had brusquely turned me down, all of this in the presence of John Jones, a Goldwater aide. I told him, a) that I had not laid eyes on Goldwater that afternoon, b) that I had not written nor suggested to anyone that I write a draft of Goldwater's acceptance speech, and that c) although I knew very well who John Jones was, in fact I had never laid eyes on him in my entire life. Vidal not only refused to modify let alone to withdraw his allegation, he reasserted it several times. The next day, Susskind (over Vidal's protests, Susskind subsequently told me) read over the air a letter from Jones confirming my denials. (Goldwater, it happened, had tuned in on the program, and was as nonplussed as Jones.)

There were one or two other instances of the same kind of thing, and I remember that it occurred to me then, as it did a couple of times in Miami and Chicago, that perhaps Vidal makes his own reality, which is, all things considered, sufficient reason to understand his philosophical melancholy, even as the order of reality would be melancholy if it had conceived Vidal. At any rate, one wants to stay away from such people, at least publicly. Yet once again the debate had been lively. One reviewer, who took pains to disavow any sympathy with my politics, said that, in the service of "the radical right, [Buckley] was far more successful than Susskind and Vidal on the medium left . . . Susskind and Vidal rocked back and forth like two old harpies and spat at him with no visible effect on their target nor, I suspect, on viewers." The other reviewer "got the impression . . . that Susskind was a zookeeper trying to prevent two hissing adders from killing each other. But the hissing was always wreathed in benign smiles." August 7, 1968, The Rockford *Star*, " 'I haven't seen Buckley since 1964 at the Cow Palace,' Vidal recalled. 'His last words to me were that he never wanted to see me again.' " Needless to say, I did not say those words. But they represented, accurately, my thoughts.

I find only two unpleasant references to Vidal written by me between 1964 and 1968. Commenting on an article by Vidal in Esquire on the Kennedy family, I wrote, "It is of course ironic that Mr. Vidal, the super-liberal super-thinker who in pursuit of the good life has tried everything, but everything in the world, including icon-smashing with a vengeance, now engages an icon he had a hand in molding." The other reference was exhumed by the drama editor of The Miami *Herald* who wrote at the beginning of the Republican Convention that "Vidal is worried the broadcasts may be a bit dull, feeling the allotted twenty minutes or so won't really give them time to get into things. That seems like an obscure worry as only a couple of years ago, in his newspaper column, Buckley referred to Vidal as 'the playwright and quipster who lost a congressional race a few years ago but continues to seek out opportunities to advertise his ignorance of contemporary affairs.' "

Bent on promoting their forthcoming programs, the people at ABC set up a lunch for me to meet the area's television critics, and subsequently did as much, I assume, for Vidal. Such meetings, as every writer knows, are something of a strain: because you are generally made to feel that you can only please by being viperish. What will I want to say about the conventions when face to face with Vidal? I didn't know. My line on Vidal was that I thought his dissatisfaction with America and with American politics was such as to make him almost necessarily sour on anything that was likely to happen at either convention.

Vidal was evidently much more detailed. One critic wrote that according to Vidal he had "accepted ABC's offer, even though he was to be teamed with Buckley, a man with whom he has had video encounters before and for whom he has utter contempt." Another quoted Vidal as saying, "Bill, of course, will try to personalize our shows. He thrives on insults. But I'll try to stick to politics. He never sticks to a subject because he's on such weak ground." Another wrote that Vidal "was not the least bit reluctant to discuss his adversary. Vidal welcomed the chance to be quoted. Apparently he relishes the vaudeville-team approach to interpretative journalism employed by ABC television for the national conventions and is anxious to allow the churlish nature of their on-screen rapport to carry over into off-screen conversation. . . . 'though I don't like being brought down to his level. That's the reason I've refused to appear with him over the last four—or is it six?—years. . . . Buckley is frivolous, superficial and often very entertaining.' "

And he told Mr. Hal Humphrey, whose column is widely syndicated, that he would "stipulate at least one ground rule. . . . 'When I'm talking I want the camera on me and not on Bill's face doing all those wild expressions of his while I'm just a voice off-stage.' " Later he told a correspondent that he had complained to the director of getting insufficient camera time, and the director had promptly complied with his requests. On these and related matters he proved most fastidious. "Buckley," a Miami reporter wrote, ". . . is as conservative about being pictured in the make-up chair as he is in his political philosophy. He submitted to a brief [make-up], a quick swish of a comb by his wife Patricia who had accompanied him. On the other hand, his fellow program jouster Gore Vidal was thoroughly liberal about being touched up. No hurry-up job, this. Miss May leisurely cleansed the skin with an antiseptic lotion, added a cream-type foundation and powder and commented on his hairline: 'He has a good hairline.' 'I don't have a wig,' he quipped. 'Tell your photographer not to make me look as though I have. Past pictures have. See how vain I am. I'm letting you take my bad side,' gesturing to his right."*

In general, the press anticipated the forthcoming debates with unmitigated glee. In Toledo the headline was, "Politicians Are Forewarned/Bill, Gore May Steal Show." The Washington *Post* announced that "The best show during the Republican and Democratic Conventions next month will not be on the convention floors or in hotel corridors but in an ABC studio. . . . In Buckley and Vidal, ABC has a dream television match. They are graceful, shrewd, cool antagonists; paragons of caustic wit and established observers of the American political scene." "It's anybody's ball game," wrote the New York *Daily News* about the G.O.P. Convention, "as they've been telling us the past couple of days, but right now the inside dope at the convention is that Bill Buckley and Gore Vidal have it practically sewed up. As a team, Buckley is in the No. 1 slot, naturally, since he's thoroughly committed, with Vidal, an expert sniper, as his running mate. And the beauty part of it is that, disliking one another intensely and both gifted in invective (they are far and away the best infighters in Miami Beach), they're a cinch to provide challenging leader-

---

* *"We have found, especially in persons whose libidinal development has suffered some disturbance, as in perverts and homosexuals, that in the choice of their love-object they have taken as their model not the mother but their own selves."*—Freud, On Narcissism, II.

ship." "A rare stroke of good television programing . . ." said the Philadelphia *Daily News.* "As an ABC spokesman puts it, 'We fully expect the
fur to fly when those two come together,' and there wasn't a dissenting
comment from his listeners."

So there we were, Saturday, August 3, on
duty for our first broadcast, suddenly re-scheduled in a makeshift studio at
the Fontainebleau Hotel because the ceiling had caved in two days before
over the studio at the convention site. We were instructed that we must
prerecord an initial statement of a sentence or two, and I knew, when I
heard Vidal's, that the session was going to be grim. "To me," he said,
"the principal question is, can a political party based almost entirely upon
human greed nominate anyone for President for whom the majority of the
American people would vote?" Now there was an interval of eight or ten
minutes before we swung into the live portion of the program. Diagonally
across from us, William Lawrence was well into his political forecast,
which had followed a pastiche of the day's events screened by ABC
producers. Across from us was Howard K. Smith, suave, intelligent,
mildly apprehensive, rehearsing with his lips the lines he would presently
deliver, directly in touch with the controls, where twenty officials and
technicians called the signals, to Smith, to Lawrence, to the thirty-
forty-fifty technicians, reporters, directors, who filled the enormous room,
at one corner of which, earphones attached, Vidal and I awaited the sound
of the bell. We had exchanged minimal amenities, and I scribbled on my
clipboard to avoid having to banter with him, and he did the same, and I
felt my blood rising in temperature as I reflected on the malevolent inanity
of his introductory observation, and then the resolution evolved that I
would hit him back hard with a *tu quoque* involving *Myra Breckinridge*
—which I had not then read. . . . But Howard K. Smith derailed me by asking me not, as I had expected, to initiate the exchange by commenting on
Vidal's description of the Republican Party, but rather to answer a specific
question—who, in my judgment, was the Best Man at Miami? We were off.

I answered: Reagan and Nixon, and said why, more or less. Vidal came
back with Rockefeller—"I cannot possibly imagine Richard Nixon President of the U. S." He backed this failure of his imagination by reciting an
arresting catalog of Nixon's sins, so livid up against the exigencies of the
day:

"And here you have a man who when he was in Congress voted against
public housing, against slum clearance, against rent control, against farm
housing, against extending the minimum wage. . . . He said, 'I am
opposed to pensions in any form as it makes loafing more attractive than
working.' And now today he offers us a program for the ghettos which he's
made much of, and what is it? Well, he is going to give tax cuts to private
businesses that go into the ghetto and help the Negroes. Now in actual fact
private business is set up to make private profits. . . . So I would say
that so far as Mr. Nixon goes he is an impossible choice domestically."

Now up against an extended barrage like that, a debater has problems. Point-by-point refutation is clearly impossible. As a rule one doesn't have handy the relevant material for coping with such arcana. And anyway, in network situations, an elementary sense of theatre (which if you don't have it, you won't ever face the problem of what to do in network situations) disciplines you in the knowledge that you simply don't have the time it takes for detailed confutation. Nixon hadn't been in Congress for *sixteen* years. Just to begin with, whatever Nixon did in Congress between 1947 and 1952 was largely irrelevant. Apart from that, what on earth does it mean, Nixon "voted against," say, "rent control"? Rent control survives in only a few places, primarily New York City. How can *any* attitude he took toward "farm housing" eighteen years ago bear on his present qualifications for the Presidency? And what sort of a "farm housing" bill did he vote against? How can we know?—maybe it was the same farm housing bill that the Americans for Democratic Action also opposed? And anyway, wasn't Nixon selected in 1952 by Eisenhower because he had a reputation as a domestic liberal (one of Christian Herter's boys) and as a tough anti-Communist—a good combination in 1952? Hadn't Nixon's preference for Eisenhower over Taft situated him in the liberal wing of the G.O.P.?

And then there was the problem of the directly quoted sentence. Vidal quoted Nixon as saying, "*I am opposed to pensions in any form as it makes loafing more attractive than working.*" The debater knows by the application of rudimentary discriminatory intelligence that no politician in the history of the world ever said that, and most probably no non-politician: and certainly not anyone who ever contemplated running for the Presidency. The mind needs to work quickly in such situations, canvassing rapidly the possibilities that a direct challenge might lead him into a carefully planned ambush. . . . So one comes in on the subject from the other direction: If Nixon had ever uttered a sentence so preposterous—condemning pensions paid even to ninety-year-old widows, on the grounds that they are conducive to sloth—wouldn't a fatuity so lapidary have instantly become a part of the political folklore, like, for instance, Mr. Agnew's "If you've seen one slum you've seen them all"? The answer is of course yes; so that in debate, under these circumstances, you can feel safe in saying, "Nixon never said that"—even though such a denial is itself a) unprovable, and b) silly; since no one on earth is familiar with every statement Nixon ever made; and no one therefore can know as a certitude that he never made *any* particular statement. What to do?

I decided to do nothing. To go back and challenge the over-arching axiom planted by Vidal at the outset—more damaging, more readily exposable, than what he said about Nixon. . . .

B.: It seems to me that the earlier focus of Mr. Vidal here on human greed—you remember that he said he found himself wondering whether the party that was devoted to the concept of human greed could ever hope to get a majority of the American people to vote for it. Now the author of *Myra Breckinridge* is well acquainted with the imperatives of human greed—

Vidal broke up—reacted quite extraordinarily. . . .

V.: Ha, ha, ha. If I may say so, Bill, before you go any further, that if there were a contest for Mr. Myra Breckinridge, you would unquestionably win it. I based the entire style polemically upon you—passionate and irrelevant.

B.: That's too involuted to follow. Perhaps one of these days you can explain it—

V.: You follow it.

I didn't and don't. In any case, we were off.

B.: For Mr. Vidal to give us the pleasure of his infrequent company by coming back from Europe where he lives in order to disdain the American democratic process and to condemn a particular party as one that has engaged in the pursuit of human greed, requires us to understand his rather eccentric definitions. . . .

I went on to point out that Senator Robert Kennedy, not Nixon, had first suggested the tax rebates, and that the Republican Party's support of the costly Vietnam war was hardly an exercise in greed. Vidal answered that the Republicans were big businessmen who made profits from the war, I pitched for the free enterprise system; he said the Republicans denigrate the poor and the minority groups, and that if by some terrible accident Nixon became President, "I shall make my occasional trips to Europe longer."

B.: Yes, I think a lot of people hope you will. As a matter of fact, Mr. Arthur Schlesinger Jr., who is a member of *your* party, not mine, [has] remind[ed] you of your promise to renounce your American citizenship unless you get a satisfactory party in November.

V.: Now, now, Bill, that isn't quite what I said. I said it would be *morally* the correct thing to do but I can behave as immorally as the Republicans.

B.: I can believe that, too.

What Vidal had written, in the book Authors Take Sides on Vietnam, *published only a few months before Miami, was* "For myself, should the war in Vietnam continue after the 1968 election, a change in nationality will be the only moral response." *So already, pre-Gethsemane, the statement turned out to be nothing more than moral bravura.*

Vidal returned to the theme of Republicans-as-believers-that-welfare-is-immoral. He managed to intrude a feline reference to Ronald Reagan, which so help me God if I had said such a thing about Adlai Stevenson, I hope I'd have gone off and joined the Trappists. He warmed up by attributing to Reagan, as he had done to Nixon, a statement Reagan never made—

V.: Meanwhile, with several denunciations [by Reagan] like I quoted to you, on free-loaders on welfare and how it encourages immorality and divorce—I assume he was on unemployment insurance when he divorced Jane Wyman—

And on he went. Another evening (August 6) he would motivate Reagan's liberal-to-conservative switch in the early Fifties on Reagan's falling in love with the daughter of "a very prominent brain surgeon." I asked how come, under the circumstances, Reagan had achieved the extraordinary plurality of 1966? Well, the people make mistakes.

Vidal suddenly switched the topic, electing to allude to my "intimacy" with Reagan and Nixon. In order to do so, he assigned to the word "neurosis" a meaning I have never heard it given, not even by conventional neurotics.

V.: . . . Since you're in favor of the invasion of Cuba, in favor of bombing the nuclear potentiality of China, since you're in favor of nuclear bombing of North Vietnam, I'd be very worried about your kind of odd neurosis: neurosis being a friend of anybody who might be a President. If I were one of the candidates I'd say Bill Buckley don't stay home. [I know, I know, I don't get it either.]

B.: I'd be very worried too, if you had such a hobgoblinized view—but I've never advocated the nuclear bombing of North Vietnam.

V.: I'll give you the time and place if it amuses you.

B.: Well, you won't.

V.: I will.

B.: I advocated the liberation of Cuba at the same time that Mr. Kennedy *ordered* the liberation of Cuba.

V.: No, no, Bill, keep to the record. You said we should enforce the Monroe Doctrine and invade Cuba the sooner the better in your little magazine whose name will not pass my lips in April, 1965. You favored bombing Red China's nuclear production facilities the 17th of September, 1965, in *Life* magazine . . .

I had said to *Life: "I have advocated bombing Red China's nuclear production facilities. But it becomes more and more difficult to do . . . as Red China takes pains to diffuse and protect its facilities. But technically, it is still possible. How do we justify the bombing in terms of world opinion? On the grounds the good guys of this earth have got to keep the bad guys from getting nuclear bombs."*

V.: . . . and you suggested the atom bombing of North Vietnam in your little magazine which I do not read but I'm told about, the 23rd of February, 1968. So you're very hawkish, and if both Nixon and Reagan are listening to you, I'm very worried for the country.

I told him he was misquoting me.

V.: No, Bill Buckley, let me make it clear to you that the quotation is exact. . . . Are you saying that you didn't say that?

B.: I'm saying that I didn't say it, that your misquotations—

V.: Tune in this time tomorrow night and we will have further evidence of Bill Buckley's cold war turned hot. . . .

I responded limply, and Howard Smith relieved us, and I would suppose the national audience, from the misery, by telling us how "enjoyable" it had been to hear us "articulate" our "points of view."

That was August 3. Today (as I write) is February 19, 1969, and I have just now reached for the bound volume of *National Review* 1968, and leaf through to find the issue of February 23, 1968. It does not exist. I look back, to the issue of February 13—surely that was what he meant? Nothing there about nuking North Vietnam. Perhaps the following issue—February 27? Ha! P. 206: "Vietnam and Partisan Politics" by W.R.B., second column third paragraph. "If Lyndon Johnson's reasoning is correct that bombing the North is justified, then it is also correct to bomb the harbor of Haiphong and prevent the delivery there of the hundreds of thousands of tons of material being used against us so effectively." That is the most bellicose paragraph in the issue. Could Vidal have had in mind a column, written about that time, though never published in *National Review,* advocating the use of tactical nuclear weapons in Vietnam? Who knows. Yes, I have advocated (and most ardently continue to do so) their use, only after pointing out that they are conceived as more efficient than conventional artillery, under certain circumstances, and that their firepower is more discriminatory, and therefore less damaging to extra-military targets than, for instance, the mass bombings by the B-52's used in the defense of Khesanh.

I wondered what, say, a court would have done under parallel circumstances? "You know," the prosecution declaims, "on February 23, 1968, the Supreme Court, in Minelli *v.* Illinois, declared that anyone who. . . ." And, later, an inquisitive legal researcher discovers that the Supreme Court didn't declare *anything* on February 23, 1968, and that Minelli and the State of Illinois, far from fighting with each other, were always on the very best of terms. What happens? Contempt of court? Reversal? Disbarment? I'll tell you what happens when the audience is not the judge, the jury, and Minelli's kinfolk, but ten million people. What happens is nothing.

Reflections on the first meeting?

From Vidal: "I don't mind his condemning my books," he told one reporter. "The President of Bantam Books, which is bringing out the paperback edition in September, phoned me last night and asked me to encourage the attacks on *Myra* because the book wholesalers have been calling all day with orders. . . . Bill refuses to deal with the issues because he doesn't know what they are, so he uses the personal attack. I spend my time reading statements of Nixon, Reagan and Rockefeller, and I'm able to deal with their positions. Buckley doesn't do much reading. He just arranges his prejudices." Vidal was very pleased by his performance. The television people, he explained, learned greatly from it. "Did you notice," he asked another critic, "that after our first meeting the other commentators began to change their style—to try for wit and candor? Even Cronkite tried to be funny. It's possible that ABC is exploiting our names and reputations. But I couldn't turn down the audience. Just think of how many millions of people who never heard of either of us now know who we are," he crowed. "He went over each encounter," the critic reported, "claiming that he 'absolutely destroyed' Buckley in their first preview meeting. . . . 'The camera did focus on Buckley too much during Tuesday's session, but I put a stop to that,' Vidal said. 'The next night there were not so many full-face reaction shots of him.' "

The press wasn't, or at least not all of it, quite so appreciative. Dean Gysel, who had talked about the dream team, referred to the shows' "waspish bitchery." "Vidal was especially guilty of making personal attacks," said another reviewer. "There was something positively obscene," wrote Terrence O'Flaherty, who had written four years earlier about the San Francisco encounter, sounding a note of warning . . . "about . . . [the] face-splitting exchange [which] was irresistible as well as embarrassing. . . . It was not the dialogue itself that made the conversation obscene; it was the expression of almost sensual relish which flashed across their faces as they thrust and stabbed—for obviously they enjoyed these duels as much as the audience. [Point: what is obvious may not be true, and in this case, speaking authoritatively about my own state of mind, I not only didn't enjoy the evening, I detested it.] [But] suddenly the conversation gets the teeth on edge." And Jack Gould, of The New York *Times:* "[Their] petty confrontations should qualify them as the week's major bores in Miami Beach. . . ." Sure, there was also the world of the satisfied. "Both stress style over content," one critic wrote, "but it is high style. Both may be irrelevant, but they are passionately irrelevant. The polemics are such that the rubber band often breaks, but then they define their positions." And the ratings were very high.

My own feeling was that the encounter had confirmed my misgivings. On Sunday morning I telephoned to Wally Pfister, the producer, and suggested the possibility of alternative formats: perhaps two or three minutes of Vidal, followed by two or three minutes of Buckley, but no cross-talk. He reported back the conclusion of the brass that that would make for uninteresting fare. To a television critic he spoke without making reference to my expressed dissatisfactions. . . . "Pfister revealed that the day after the first debate, Vidal called him and said: 'I sure took care of him [Buckley] last night, didn't I?' Later, Buckley called him and said: 'I certainly made him [Vidal] look silly, didn't I?' The mighty are human, too," the critic concluded. The mighty are unmighty too, he'd have better concluded.

Vidal's political philosophy is, I discovered fairly early in our association, elusive. His attitudes, if you look them up in the yellow pages, are neatly left-liberal in purely conventional terms. However there are anomalies. There is a strain of populism. But populism, after all, should be popular. I have heard John Kenneth Galbraith call himself a populist, always on the understanding that he does not thereby deprive himself of his right to intellectually aristocratic habits, e.g. in the case of Galbraith cultural elitism, and in the case of Vidal, that much at least; and, touching on the point already raised, sexual singularity as well. But on the whole, populists should be not only expert but enthusiastic at reasoning through to the justification of the people's demands. Vidal isn't good at this at all: or rather, one comes across an impenetrable barrier to the understanding. Towards "the people," he has ambiguous relations, though he appears not to be able to do without them, at least not for as long as twenty network minutes. Even though "they" are, strangely, always out to get him. "Vidal expresses the hope," wrote Hal Humphrey in a syndicated story, "that security provisions at the conventions are especially good because, he says, for the first time in his life (he's forty-two) he has a fear of physical danger to himself. 'I get more threatening mail each day, and from reading it I wonder that there isn't more violence in our country than there is. You know, of course, that one of every five people in the U.S. is mentally disturbed?' " (The inference is that he gets threatening mail from those who are disturbed, rather than from those who are undisturbed.)

Now anyone plugged in to reality will recognize this as sheer fantasy. If Vidal got five threatening letters in 1967, I'll deliver him J. Edgar Hoover as a bodyguard. But it was a cherished theme: "While in Miami Beach," reported Tom Mackin, "he was the subject of considerable hostility. 'I hear hissing in the lobby of the Fontainebleau and people shrink from me,' he said."

Possibly his difficulty in understanding "the people" accounts for his rather extraordinary record as political forecaster. In 1963 he wrote that Goldwater could not be nominated in 1964, in 1968 he predicted that Reagan would be nominated, at Miami he said that Nixon could not be elected, a few days later he predicted that he would be elected—but having predicted something which actually came to be, he left the impression that he made this prediction not so much because his observation of political events led him to the conclusion, as because he needed to massage his *Weltschmerz* which he proceeded to do in *The New York*

Review of Books, after the nomination of Nixon, with masturbatory diligence. Gloom is his chic, and when he remembers to blame "them," it is "the people" who are responsible for the melancholy state of public affairs. On the occasions when he forgets to blame the human condition on "the people," it is the people's leaders who are responsible, the people's leaders being the Vested Interests. "I think," Vidal told a writer for the *Saturday Review,* who asked him what his thoughts turned to on contemplating the city of Rome—"I think," said Vidal, "not only of Marc Antony, Caesar and Cicero, but of our own representatives who take their name from this"—he pointed to history—"the Roman senate. I contemplate their follies and mistakes. I see Washington in ruins as something perfectly portended. . . . Americans have no sense of the past, and indeed hate it." (Even though they are reactionaries.) ". . . We're in the third world war already," he sighed to an interviewer in The Washington *Post* last winter, "and it is going straight to the terminus." It isn't exactly clear why we have not yet reached the terminus. Away back in 1961 Vidal was writing that "we have become a passive, ill-informed, fearful society," whose right wing "has not yet had the courage to propose that some people be allowed to vote and some not to vote according, say, to the size of their income but that is what they [who?] are after. For they mistrust and dislike the majority."

Now wait a minute. The right wing mistrusts and dislikes the majority. As much as Vidal mistrusts and dislikes the majority? Indeed, shouldn't we *all* distrust and dislike the majority—if, among other things, the majority's memory "is about four weeks at best," as Vidal announced it to be in Miami? *"One must never underestimate the collective ignorance of that informed electorate for whom Thomas Jefferson had such high hopes,"* he told us in the Spring of 1963. And now, a few years later, the majority was in even worse odor. Because *"it could be said that with almost the best will in the world, we have created a hell and called it The American Way of Life."*—On the other hand, in other moods, and to suit other purposes, it is "the people" who are the foilees, rather than the foilers. At Miami, Vidal wrote, "the public liked Lindsay but the delegates did not. They regarded him with the same distaste that they regard the city of which he is mayor, that hellhole of niggers and kikes and commies, of dope and vice and smut. . . . [One is left to infer, by Vidalian logic, that "the people" should, and one supposes, really *do,* approve of dope and vice and smut.] So they talk among themselves until an outsider approaches; then they shift gears swiftly and speak gravely of law and order and how this is a republic not democracy." "The people" were pronounced good by Vidal in an opening statement at Chicago. "At Miami Beach," he reminisced about the people, "the people wanted Rockefeller but the politicians wanted Nixon. Here, in Chicago, the people want McCarthy but the politicans seem to want Humphrey. On

Wednesday night, we shall discover just how democratic the two political parties are." Two days later he was saying in despair that the Presidents we tend to get saddled with, in the instant case Lyndon B. Johnson, "reflect the mood of the country." Which would certainly appear to be "the people's" fault, it being "the people" who make up the mood of the country, right? At a moment when the Gallup poll was showing that Nixon was decisively and exactly equally ahead of both Humphrey and McCarthy, Vidal simply ignored the McCarthy showing, his endeavor being, at that moment, to prove that the people were against Humphrey. ". . . there is a poll about to be released," he said, ". . . which is going to show that Humphrey has got something like twenty-seven percent of the vote against Richard Nixon who's got something like sixty in that trial heat. . . ." But of course the trouble with putting Humphrey down, vis-à-vis Nixon, was that to do so required that Nixon be put up; and of course this interfered hugely with the anti-democratic melodrama of Miami Beach, where Vidal had announced that if Nixon were nominated, in the teeth of the demands of the people who wanted Rockefeller, the people would not forgive the Republican Party. . . .

By election night, of course, Vidal was utterly confounded, because "the people," in going towards Nixon, obviously weren't behaving themselves. "I have always felt," he explained, "that we must never underestimate the essential bigotry of the white majority in the United States." If the white majority is bigoted, why did it want McCarthy at Chicago and Rockefeller at Miami? Or, all along, did he really mean the *minority*? Let's see—the minority who wanted Rockefeller-McCarthy; or the minority who is bigoted? And then at Chicago (August 25) Vidal had said, "Well, it is the greater wisdom, finally to trust the people. In any case, we *are* trusting the people, since the major politicians are *entirely* dominated by what the polls say, as we witnessed at Miami Beach. . . ." So: the people—who are good—even though their memory is only four weeks old—but they are wise—and wanted Rockefeller and McCarthy—in spite of their essential bigotry—but the politicians paid no attention to the people—even though the politicians are entirely dominated by the people:—and so on, into the mists of unintelligibility.

Whatever difficulty Mr. Vidal had with "the people," he had none at all with the poor people, with whom he identifies altogether. He does have difficulty in deciding how many poor people there are all told, though he is quite certain on the point that they will not be cared for by a Republican administration.

"The United States," he announced on August 5, "has thirty million poor people in the ghettos, people that I am afraid voted against you so heavily when you ran for Mayor, Bill, when you kept reminding the Negroes in Harlem in one of your first efforts, to throw the garbage out the window for that." [I don't know, you figure it out.]

I challenged the figure but was sharply rebuked.

"I would say that Mr. Buckley as always has misstated the case on poverty as he has on so much else. There are over thirty million people living at the poverty line and the Republican Party, according to the platform, which I read very carefully, is going to benefit the insurance agencies, the private interests, in great detail and nothing at all for the people."

Vidal's little-Marxist assumption that material interests always govern occasionally got him into trouble, as when he was challenged to recite the practical Presidential qualifications of Eugene McCarthy, which he promptly gave as McCarthy's unfortunate support of Humphrey's anti-Communist bill of 1954, and

V.: . . . also, on two occasions, [McCarthy] supported the . . . oil lobby on the depletion of oil resources allowance of which I must say liberals take a very dim view, but I suspect you, with your oil interests and liking for that sort of lobby, would find quite commendable. So he can indeed make those "practical elisions" that you so much admire. I think he is a practical man.

B.: Do you think that Minnesota is such a heavy oil state?—

V.: If Minnesota—what has that got to do with anything?

B.: What was the advantage in [McCarthy's] yielding to the oil interests?

V.: I dread to think but I—

B.: I know you dread to think. That's obvious. . . .

Two days after giving the figure of thirty million, Vidal suddenly rescued millions of Americans from poverty.

"As far as the mutiny in the land which Mr. Buckley refers to, of course, there is mutiny in the land. When you have sixteen million people in poverty and six million in abject poverty—these are actual statistics—and when something like ten to eleven billion dollars is needed to end it all according to Health, Education, and Welfare, I suspect that you are going to need some sort of a program."

So now there are not "over thirty million" but twenty-two million poor (whose poverty will end, we note in passing, with a one-time subsidy of five hundred dollars each). That was Wednesday. That weekend, Vidal wrote an article for *The New York Review of Books,* bewailing the events of Miami Beach, and speaking gloomily about the prospects, under a Republican Administration—"for the forty million poor."

In the interval between Miami and Chicago, I read *Myra Breckinridge.* I have thought and thought about it, and resolved finally to describe and evaluate it and its purposes mostly by quoting from reviewers of the novel who cannot be suspected of sexual or cultural homeguardism.

"Really," said Gore Vidal during the spring after his novel's appearance, to an interviewer from *The National Observer,* "the state of reviewing in this country is *so* low. There is so much dealing in personalities, even in respectable publications. You know, I had originally intended to let *Myra* go under a pen name—not because I was ashamed of her, but because I wanted her to stand on her own. I wish now I'd done that. . . . [But] I wanted to make *Myra* the kind [of book] I'd read myself. I did. I'm delighted."

From *Myra,* a sample—a bowdlerized sample—: "I touched the end of [his] spine, a rather protuberant bony tip set between the high curve of buttocks now revealed to me in all their splendor . . . and splendor is the only word to describe them! Smooth, white, hairless except just beneath the spinal tip where a number of dark coppery hairs began, only to disappear from view. Casually I ran my hand over the smooth slightly damp cheeks. To the touch they were like highly polished marble warmed by the sun of some perfect Mediterranean day. I even allowed my forefinger the indiscretion of fingering the coppery wires not only at the tip of the spine but also the thicker growth at the back of his thighs. Like so many young males, he has a relatively hairless torso with heavily furred legs. . . ."

In England, the authorities did not permit the distribution of the American original. However, the *New Statesman* observed, "Despite the famed mutilations, the British *Myra* hasn't been severely ravaged: the operation leaves no fiery scars. The cuts are mainly in the rape scene: pink sphincters, rosy scrotum, 'the penis . . . was not a success.' The cruelty of this particular charade is so triumphant that it survives censorship. Also, it's far more gruesome than erotic—for those who don't love pain. In fact, *Myra* is more cerebral than bawdy."

Indeed.

"Oh," said Vidal on the Merv Griffin show (November 18, 1968), "*Myra*'s not pornographic. It's extremely graphic, I suppose. It's a—describe certain sexual activities in great detail, but I don't think—pornography is written to stimulate people in order to make money for the writer. And I was not—I didn't—I don't write books to make money."

Griffin: "You don't?"

"Vidal: "People, though I'm not—I think now, I must say, in a way I would be more interested in exciting people perhaps than in writing for money."

Indeed. Vidal, the reviewers seem to agree, was engaged in other pursuits than moneymaking, even if he did not resent the pennies from heaven; it is gratifying, in fact, to make money from intellectual pursuits. "In an 'Afterword' to his revised early novel, *The City and the Pillar,*" the *New Stateman* observes, "Mr. Vidal announced that everyone is bisexual, while 'the idea that there is no such thing as "normality" is at last penetrating the tribal consciousness. . . .' "

In order to establish the abnormality of normality, the vehicle is homosexuality. "Not only are these nasty consequences in Vidal's little morality tale," wrote Marvin Barrett in *The Reporter,* "he takes his lofty homosexual theme of twenty years back (then all high-toned sentiment), grinds it to sludge, and flushes it away with a lewd satiric chuckle.

"Only half kidding," Barrett continues—and there is the operative phrase—"he has Myra/Myron say: 'In the Forties, American boys created a world empire because they chose to be James Stewart, Clark Gable and William Eythe. By imitating godlike autonomous men, our boys were able to defeat Hitler, Mussolini and Tojo. Could we do it again? Are the private eyes and denatured cowboys potent enough to serve as imperial exemplars? No. At best, there is James Bond . . . and he invariably ends up tied to a slab of marble with a blowtorch aimed at his crotch. Glory has fled and only the television commercials exist to remind us of the republic's early greatness and virile youth.' "

"Glory" has fled—along with—necessarily with?—the convention in favor of heterosexuality as the "normal" sexual relationship. We move in a different direction, as we are emancipated from surely the only prejudice commonly shared by St. Paul, Marx, and Freud. . . . "Some novels," writes Michael O'Malley in *The Critic,* "smell of beer, others of marijuana or perfume. . . . This one is soaked in estrogen. A tone entirely estrous: everyone in continual heat, an itchy, yowling, manic, pussycat heat that is right out of *The Pearl* and as ludicrous, as depressing. . . . The whole thing seems to have been written from a point of observation to the rear of the characters and about eighteen inches off the pavement. This may be a privileged angle to some but for me it produces almost at once a severe pain in the neck. The story itself is Odds and Ends. Rear ends. There are more bottoms here than in *Twenty Thousand Leagues Under the Sea.* The heart of the book—and the part where you throw up your hands *and* your lunch and realize that you're dealing with yet another pale echo of Genet's masturbatory daydreams—is this rape. It just goes on and on with an interminable homosexual nittyness. . . . Other Odds against you include a masochist with a touch of nymphomania, the rapee who turns sadist homosexual, a Negro queen called Irving Amadeus, the profoundly lesbian Miss Cluff, a rock group that practices bestiality, the bisexual Gloria Gordon, a bit of a satyr, the obligatory Hollywood orgy scene, and some business lifted from Catullus to add tone. Catullus did it better."

But then Catullus had other things on his mind, whereas *Myra* is plainly intended as allegory, in the continuing crusade of Gore Vidal not only to license homosexuality but to desacralize heterosexuality: in the interest of a *true* understanding of human nature, such as has not been nobly or ignobly understood by any dominant philosophical or imperial figure since Plato and the Twelve Caesars; and (bonus!) is in any case desirable if only as the humane solution to pressing social problems. "In other words," *Time* magazine commented, "the remedy for overpopulation might be homosexuality."

But the allegory fails, straining vainly against paradigms artistic as well as moral. "Is this *Paradise Lost*," asks *The Times Literary Supplement*, in a review entitled "Pathetic Phallusy," "or merely a *Golden Ass* penetrated? Milton, Blake said, was 'of the Devil's party without knowing it'; Vidal, it seems, is of the Devil's party—and knows it. For he connives with his temptress, his tutelary female, the eternal aggressive whore, or *porné* incarnate, deflating, deflowering the tumescent males. Myra Breckinridge herself sees all life as a naming of parts, an equating of groins, a pleasing and/or painful forcing of orifices. Which is the essence, after all, of pornography. All is referred to the phallic point, the reductio ad absurdum of the genitalia. Nor is the response spiked, but silkily sensuous to male buttocks, nipples, pubic hair, and the whole repertory of male adornment from jockey briefs to T-shirt and jeans. . . . Pornography, then, is exhibited as the final metamorphosis of Existentialism: 'The only thing we can ever know for certain is skin.'

"Today," the *T.L.S.* concludes—even as the *New Statesman* sighed that "the sexual cook-outs will disturb many, as they are meant to; but the trans-sexuality can't be rejected as fantasy; since a fantasy that's so popular has surely acquired universal flesh"—"Today," *T.L.S.* succumbs, Kinsey-like, "sex is metamorphosed as freely as fancy dress. And in his role of *arbiter elegantiae,* Gore Vidal can write, without recourse to preposterous tableaux,

" '*It is the wisdom of the male swinger to know what he is, a man who is socially and economically weak, as much put upon by women as by society. Accepting his situation, he is able to assert himself through a polymorphic sexual abandon in which the lines between the sexes dissolve, to the delight of all. I suspect that this may be the only workable pattern for the future, and it is a most healthy one.'* " Vidal has thought seriously about the future. One year after writing *Myra,* he proposed (Esquire, October 1968) the dissolution of the family. Breeding complications? None he cannot handle: "The endlessly delicate problem of who should be allowed to have children might be entirely eliminated by the anonymous matching in laboratories of sperm and ova."

There is nothing left to be said about *Myra.* It attempts heuristic allegory but fails, giving gratification only to sadist-homosexuals, and challenge only to taxonomists of perversion: for the rest, for the millions, only the same excitement that depravity gives, that de Sade has given to six generations of people altogether healthy. But the homiletic failure of the allegory does not rob it of the seriousness of the effort. *Myra* is indeed more intellectual than bawdy, even as de Sade was. Vidal is fond of recalling that Alfred Whitehead once said that one gets at the essence of a culture not by studying those things which were said at the time, but by studying those things which were not said. It will surely be said about *Myra Breckinridge,* not that the shrewdest readers of it failed to get the message. But that the responsible community betrayed itself, finally, as indifferent: to so acute, so crazed an assault on—traditional, humane sexual morality: on the family as the matrix of society: on the survival of heroism, on the very idea of heroism. It may be that the cognoscenti consider that Vidal is a trivial literary figure, and hardly a philosophical menace; that their toleration of his effronteries, indeed their ignoring of them, is merely an application of the Jeffersonian principle that one's tolerance of those who would tear down the republic is a monument to our democratic self-assurance. But Jefferson said that such toleration was appropriate on the assumption that "reason is left free to combat" the nihilists. Reason is free all right. But who is using it? ABC-TV? The half dozen young black racist anti-Semites in the New York Public School system are not about to usher in Buchenwald. Even so, reason and passion were quickly and decisively mobilized against them. The editor of a prominent newsweekly, renowned for its liberal opinions, told me that *Myra* was the only book he had taken pains to hide from his adolescent daughter—who probably read it before her father did, assuming she can get the $1.25 to buy the paperback edition and has a normal curiosity. Censorship is probably not the answer. But with the repudiation of censorship, something very strange happened. The corollary was unthinkingly accepted that no one is censurable. "And on my left, Mr. Gore Vidal, the liberal author, and playwright, and novelist, whose most recent book is *Myra Breckinridge.* Mr. Vidal, could we have your views on the moral qualifications of the Republican nominee, Mr. Richard Nixon, to serve as President?"

And so we met again, at Chicago. No need to describe the surrounding tumult. The unhappy delegates could not give satisfaction. Lyndon Johnson was still powerful, but not so much so as to risk a personal appearance, not even to celebrate his birthday. Eugene McCarthy—it was somehow intuited—simply wouldn't do; indeed the Kennedy forces had, in inexplicit recognition of McCarthy's Presidential shortcomings, extruded Senator George McGovern, who, in his few personal appearances, had captivated the beholders; but he was a staying operation, clearly so—his practical role being secondarily the tacit repudiation of McCarthy and primarily a foot in the door for a blitzkreig by Senator Kennedy.

For a while the official attitude towards Mayor Daley was tolerant—his was an adamantine history of pro-Kennedyism, and he foreswore on Sunday the expected endorsement of Hubert Humphrey. So that the pressure on Daley mounted, and his ensuing ineptitudes might have been stagemanaged by Lowenstein and Unruh. In the turmoil, the delegates—and the public—reached hagiologically for the single nominee they knew they could not conscript, because Bobby Kennedy was dead. But his name, especially now that he was dead, was holy; even as Goldwater's would have been, if he had been assassinated minutes after triumphing over Rockefeller in the California primary (I can see John Lindsay at the Communion rail).

I trafficked on Robert Kennedy's prestige, though not, I like to think, in a way he'd have disapproved of. . . . It was on Tuesday and the Vietnam plank was on the agenda. After a while Vidal made a pass at realpolitik. He yearned for the diplomacy of the nineteenth century, shorn of morality and pietism, and wondered whether, in fact, it wouldn't be clever of the United States to back Ho Chi Minh, on the grounds that he and Mao Tse-tung were natural enemies. (Virginia Kirkus was to comment on Vidal's *Reflections Upon a Sinking Ship*, "Vidal seems fatally addicted to the worldly skeptical tone with a Boy Scout aria tagged on at the end, rather like Vidal imitating Talleyrand imitating Walter Lippmann.")

At the mention of Ho Chi Minh and the Vietcong, I saw an opening I had been waiting for. . . .

B.: Mr. Vidal's suggestion that perhaps it would be in our interest to support Ho Chi Minh suggests [to me] that as a matter of testamentary integrity, I should reveal a concrete proposal contained in a letter sent to me by Senator [Robert] Kennedy about six months ago,* the P.S. of which was:

"I have changed my platform for 1968 from 'Let's give blood to the Vietcong' to 'Let's give Gore Vidal to the Vietcong.' "

V.: May I see that?

B.: I think, however, that [giving Vidal to the Vietcong] would be immoderate.

Vidal was reeling.

V.: I must say . . . I must say, I am looking at this. What a very curious handwriting. It also slants up, sign of a manic depressive. I did see that. Whether you forged it or not, I don't know. I would have to have my handwriting experts, the graphologists would have to look at it. I put nothing beyond you, not even in the Dreyfus case when we had such evidence brought into court. [Poor Vidal had been reduced to blithering unintelligibility] . . . But it is very, very amusing and has nothing to do with the case. In fact, his writing [you] makes me terribly suspicious of him as a Presidential candidate. I will say that. . . . Yes, I realize that. I recognize the handwriting. Makes me very suspicious of what he might have been like as President.

Vidal had been oh-so-careful to stay clear of the history of his feelings towards the Kennedys, for reasons both self-serving and charitable. He had begun as an ardent admirer of J.F.K. Then there was the affair at the White House, after which he turned anti-

* *I should have said "about a year ago." The letter was sent in early April, 1967.*

Kennedy. It was rather hard for him to become convincingly anti-J.F.K., in the teeth of his own fulsome praise of him; but he took it out against the Kennedy family and Bobby in particular (Vidal worked conspicuously for Senator Keating against Bobby in 1964) in two interesting and discerning articles published in Esquire. But now Robert Kennedy, freshly assassinated, had emerged as the stricken savior of young idealism, so that not once had Vidal, in all the previous sessions, spoken about Kennedy. Indeed shortly after the assassination Vidal had treated it as a personal affront, final proof of everything he had been saying for years and years and years about America. Interviewed by *Stern*, he gave a most remarkable explanation for the murder of Robert Kennedy, namely the intensity of the hatred of Kennedy in the town of Pasadena which, he explained to his German readers, had housed and reared the killer.

"Sirhan grew up in Pasadena, a center of the John Birch Society, a center of radical right reactionaries, a despicable blot on this earth. The people of Pasadena are well-off. They hate the Jews, they hate the Negroes, the poor, the foreign. I find these to be really terrible people. Sirhan grew up in this atmosphere and I do not doubt that he heard many anti-Kennedy speeches. He simply accepted the way people in Pasadena think. He decided that Bobby Kennedy was evil and he killed him. . . ."

One wonders what exactly the people of Pasadena read, that so inflamed the assassin's heart?

"There is no doubt that when Bobby goes before the convention in '68 he will seem beautifully qualified. . . . But there are flaws in his *persona* hard to disguise. For one thing, it will take a public-relations genius to make him appear lovable. He is not. His obvious characteristics are energy, vindictiveness, and a simplemindedness about human motives which may yet bring him down."

Was that *the passage that caught the eye of Sirhan?*

"To Bobby the world is black or white. Them and Us. He has none of his brother's human ease; or charity. . . . He would be a dangerously authoritarian-minded President."

Can't permit such a man as that *to become President, can we, sons of Pasadena?*

"In their unimaginative, fierce way, the Kennedys continue to play successfully the game as they found it. They create illusions and call them facts, and between what they are said to be and what they are falls the shadow of all the useful words not spoken. The cold-blooded jauntiness of the Kennedys in politics has a remarkable appeal for those who also want to rise and find annoying—to the extent they are aware of it at all—the moral sense . . . to entrust him [Bobby] with the first magistracy of what may be the last empire on earth is to endanger us all."

The words of course are all Vidal's—did Sirhan read them? Vidal did not speculate on the question. The reporter from *Stern* did not question him on the subject. Vidal had little to fear from a reporter who accepted unquestioningly Vidal's learned intelligence that Sirhan Sirhan came by his anti-Semitism from the public school children of Pasadena, California.

By nomination-time, Vidal had cataloged a considerable indictment of the opposition, and of me. The Republican platform was "war-minded"; Ronald Reagan was merely an "aging Hollywood juvenile actor"; I was what he had in mind in writing *Myra Breckinridge*; Nixon had "no discernible interest except his own" for running. He had denounced Nixon as a hypocrite who accepted racist support. He had deplored my "almost Stalinist desire to revise history," and pronounced me "the leading warmonger in the United States."

Chicago was seething with tension, objectified in the demonstrators' encounters with the Chicago police. ABC devoted itself, in the filmed segment preceding our own commentary, to an impassioned excoriation of the Chicago police superintended by ABC commentator John Burns. Vidal was thereupon asked by Howard Smith for the usual preliminary statement.

V.: One of the more vivid pleasures [what a strange word to use] of Chicago has been the spectacle of a Soviet-style police state in action. The police here are brutal. The citizens are paralyzed, and the right of peaceful assembly has been denied by Mayor Daley, who believes in order without law.

B.: [Trying to focus on the political vectors—after all, Humphrey had just been nominated.] The selection of Mr. Humphrey is what in a Republican context would be hilariously applauded as the choice of a moderate over against an extremist. But the American Left are very poor losers and therefore it means trouble for the Democratic Party.

The attempt to bring the discussion around to the nomination of Humphrey as Presidential candidate was ignored.

V.: I think there's very little that we can say after those pictures that would be in any way adequate. It's like living under a Soviet Regime. . . . [He proceeded heatedly along the same lines until finally,]

Howard Smith: I wonder if we can let Mr. Buckley comment now for a short while?

B.: The distinctions to be made, Mr. Smith [I had found that, under stress, I was better off addressing the moderator than Vidal], are these: Number One, Do we have enough evidence to indict a large number of individual Chicago policemen? It would seem from what Mr. Burns showed us, that we do. However, the effort here—not only on your program tonight, but during the past two or three days in Chicago—has been to institutionalize this complaint so as to march forward and say that, in effect, we have got a police state going here, we have got a sort of fascist situation.

One young man approached me, last night, and said, "Are you aware that Mayor Daley is a fascist?"—to which my reply was, "No. And if that *is* the case, why didn't John Kennedy and Bobby Kennedy, whose favorite mayor he [Daley] was, indict him as such, and teach us that we should all despise him as a fascist?"

The point is that [some] policemen violate their obligations just the way [some] politicians do. If we could all work up an equal sweat and if you all would be obliging enough to have your cameras handy every time a politician commits demagogy or a businessman passes along graft or bribes, or every time a businessman cheats on his taxes, or every time a labor union [man] beats up people who refuse to join his union—then maybe we could work up some kind of impartiality in resentment. As of this moment, I say: go after those cops who were guilty of unnecessary brutality, [and] develop your doctrine of security sufficiently so that [you can know] when you *don't* have as many cops as you should have had—for instance, in Dallas, in November of 1963. You don't [then] go and criticize the F.B.I. for not having been there, for not having taken sufficient security measures. But don't do what's happening in Chicago tonight, which is to infer from individual and despicable acts of violence, a case for implicit totalitarianism in the American system.

Vidal responded emphatically that nothing less than a constitutional issue was at stake, that the demonstration had sought nothing more than constitutionally-guaranteed opportunities to voice their dissent.

V.: These people came here with no desire other than anybody's ever been able to prove, than to hold peaceful demonstrations.

B.: I can prove it.

V.: How can you prove it?

B.: Very easily. By citing the recorded words of Mr. Hayden of the S.D.S., of Mr. Rennie Davis of the Coordinating Committee—whose object has been to "break down the false and deceptive institutions of bourgeois democracy sufficient to usher in a revolutionary order." Anybody who believes that these characters are interested in the democratic process is deluding himself. I was fourteen windows above that gang last night, [above] these sweet little girls with their sun-baked dresses that we heard described a moment ago, and the chant between eleven o'clock and five o'clock this morning, some four or five thousand voices, was sheer, utter obscenities directed at the President of the United States, at the Mayor of this city, plus also the intermittent refrain, "Ho Ho Ho/Ho Chi Minh/The N.L.F./Is sure to win!"

This is the way [they have chosen] of accosting American society concerning their brothers, their sisters, their uncles, their fathers, who are being shot at by an enemy which wrongly or rightly nevertheless we are fighting. I say it is remarkable that there was as much restraint shown as was shown for instance last night by cops who were out there for seventeen hours without inflicting a single wound on a single person even though that kind of disgusting stuff was being thrown at them and at all American society.

Smith: Our reporter, Jim Burns, said there ought to be a different way to handle situations like that.

B.: I wish he would invent it. Why don't you ask him next time—Maybe tomorrow?—to tell us *how* to handle it. Because I'm sure the Republican Party and the Democratic Party would [gladly] form a joint platform which would suggest how to do it. . . .

V.: The right of assembly is in the Constitution, in the Bill of Rights.

B.: Nothing on earth is absolute.

V.: That's right. We live in a relativist world. However, it is the law, it is the Constitution and . . . [Vidal, agitated,—as I was—groped frantically for his ideological querencia] and let us have no more sly comments in your capacity as the enemy of the people.

The discussion turned blisteringly to the question of what does the Constitution guarantee, what doesn't it, with Vidal insisting on the blamelessness of the demonstrators. . . .

V.: When they were in the parks on Monday night, when I observed them, watched the police come in like this from all directions, standing. They were sitting there, singing folk songs. There were none of the obscenities which your ear alone seems to have picked up. [What I and my wife had heard, fourteen stories high was: F--- L.B.J.! . . . F--- Mayor Daley! . . . —how do you begin producing witnesses when there are, say 50,000 of them available?] They were absolutely well-behaved. Then, suddenly, the police began. You'd see one little stirring up in one corner. Then, you'd suddenly see a bunch of them come in with their night clubs and I might say, without their badges, which is illegal,—

Smith: Mr. Vidal, wasn't it a provocative act to try to raise the Vietcong flag in the park, in the film we just saw? Wouldn't that invite—raising a Nazi flag in World War II, would have had similar consequences?

Vidal explained that there are different points of view about the Vietnam war, and that "I assume that the point of American democracy is you can express any point of view you want—"

B.: (garbled).

V.: Shut up a minute.

B.: No, I won't. The answer is: they were well-treated by people who ostracized them and I am *for* ostracizing people who egg on other people to shoot American marines and American soldiers.

And then it came—

V.: *As far as I am concerned, the only crypto Nazi I can think of is yourself, failing that, I would only say that we can't have.* . . .

Smith.: *Now let's not call names.*

B.: *Now listen, you queer. Stop calling me a crypto Nazi or I'll sock you in your goddamn face and you'll stay plastered—*

Smith: *Gentlemen! Gentlemen! let's not call names.* . . .

B.: *Let Myra Breckinridge go back to his pornography and stop making allusions of Nazism.* . . . *I was in the infantry in the last war.*

V.: *You were not in the infantry, as a matter of fact you didn't fight in the war.*

B.: *I was in the infantry.*

V.: *You were not. You're distorting your own military record.*

Through it all one hears the pleading voice of Howard Smith: *Gentlemen, please, gentlemen, I beg of you;* and then, taking the conversation by the horns,

Smith: Wasn't it a provocative act to pull down an American flag and put up a Vietcong flag even if you didn't agree with what the United States is doing?

V.: It is not a provocative act. You have every right, in this country, to take any position you want to take because we are guaranteed freedom of speech. We've just listened to a certainly grotesque example of it.

I muttered something about lawful acts which are nevertheless provocative, citing the projected hate-Jew rally that George Lincoln Rockwell had planned to stage in New York City a few years before, which Mayor Wagner aborted by denying him a license. Vidal maintained that such freedoms are absolute, and Smith, reacting to instructions from the control board at which the mesmerized executives finally rallied, no doubt to tell him to get the two madmen off the air, interrupted:

S.: I think we have run out of time, and I thank you very much for the discussion. There was a little more heat and a little less light than usual, but it was still very worth hearing.

But it wasn't over. Situated as we were, in one corner of the immense studio, at other parts of which ABC continued ineluctably with its live broadcast for another twenty minutes, we had, as was customary, very quietly to unharness ourselves from our ear sets and then tread noiselessly out of the studio. My pulse was racing, and my fingers trembled as wave after wave of indignation swept over me—and then suddenly, about to deposit the earphones on the table stand, I stopped, frozen. Vidal, arranging his own set, was whispering to me. "Well!" he said, smiling. "I guess we gave them their money's worth tonight!"

I reached my trailer after taking great strides through the maze of technicians operators executives reporters guests, all of whom looked at me as I stomped by and then, quickly, looked away; afraid, perhaps, that I would greet anyone guilty of a lingering glance with a sock on his goddamn face. I reached my trailer and there was chaos there among my half dozen friends, and my wife, who had watched on the closed-circuit television. Everyone spoke at once, and then the door swung open—it was Paul Newman, longtime friend of Vidal. I want you to know, he said, working his jaw like Hud, I think that was the foulest blow I ever saw. I approached him feverishly: "Have you ever been called a Nazi?" I spat the words out at him. His voice mellowed. "That," he explained, opening his hands wide as one does in expressing the obvious, "was purely *political*. What *you* called *him* was personal!" I despaired; and motioned to the door, a gesture which the clamorous company, silent since Newman's arrival, by the strain of their necks and the inflection of their eyes, seconded by acclamation. And he left, slamming the door behind him.

The reaction was voluble. There were those who did not conceal a sense of bawdyhouse excitement. *Time* magazine wrote that "Commentators William F. Buckley Jr. and Gore Vidal made Mayor Daley and his cohorts look like amateurs in invective." ABC, which was in uproar, withheld the entire exchange from the western United States, where it would normally have run two hours after being seen live in the rest of the country. That would account for some papers' (e.g., the Oakland *Tribune*) otherwise unaccountable failure to remark the provocation—"The boys were discussing the police violence, Vidal attacking the police and Buckley defending them," wrote Bob MacKenzie. "The insults became more and more heated. Finally Buckley blew his famous cool entirely. . . ." The New York *Daily News*'s Kay Gardella delivered a prim rebuke for our "disgraceful" language, and reported that a spokesman of ABC-TV had said that after the telecast Vidal "apologized to Buckley in his trailer office at the convention site. . . . [However] an apology was adamantly denied by Vidal when reached in his Ambassador Hotel suite in Chicago. 'What would I have apologized for?' he asked. 'It's Mr. Buckley who begins the personal attack. I simply respond in kind.' " "ABC official Elmer Lower," the same story reported, "referred to the verbal volley yesterday as 'intemperate language.' He said that 'ABC was upset about what happened, but what can you do except talk to the individuals and ask that it not happen again?' " Well you can of course do that much, which in fact ABC did not do.

I wondered as the clippings came pouring in at the all but universal conclusion that my outburst had identified me as the equal of Vidal in intemperance. And worse. *Commentary* magazine, shrewd and deliberate, wrote that "It was really rather irresponsible to choose this pair as the chief editorialists on the ABC team. Though their political opinions certainly added up to a rather perilous balance, the shameful pleasure of watching them match wits had less to do with a search for political enlightenment than with such archaic or illegal entertainments as cockfighting, duels to the death, and fliting. The effect was the opposite of edifying. Certainly, Dr. Frederick Wertham must have been worried by Buckley's scarcely controlled ferocity as he shook his fist and drawled. . . . After drama like that, who could be content to turn back to the maunderings of Carl Albert?" I wondered that the editors of *Commentary,* of all people, should apparently think it irrelevant to specify what it was that catalyzed the scarcely controlled ferocity. One wonders how the editor of *Commentary* would have reacted if he had been called a crypto Nazi in the presence of a dozen million people. Would he take the position that that was merely a *political* charge, in a response to which one has no reason to lose one's cool? If, in non-academic circumstances, you call a man a Nazi, are you evoking ethnocentric nationalism—or Buchenwald? A single editorialist—in *The Arizona Republic*—caught the point.

"This was a smear of the worst kind. The New York *Times,* which was so mad it couldn't see straight when Spiro Agnew said Hubert Humphrey was soft on communism, ignored it completely. . . . In order to put the incident in better perspective, just suppose that Buckley had called Vidal a pro or crypto Communist. . . ."

For days and weeks, indeed for months, I tormented myself with the question, What should I have said? Obviously my response was the wrong one if it is always wrong to lose one's temper, as I was disposed ("the wrath of man worketh not the righteousness of God") to believe that it is. Was my mistake that of going on TV at all, in the light of the abundant warnings, with Vidal (who says A, must say B)? Assume that. But even so the question is not then answered: What *might* have been done within the narrow context? Could it be that my emotional reaction was defensible and even healthy, but that my words were ill-chosen? "The higher the stakes," C. S. Lewis wrote, "the greater the temptation to lose your temper. . . . We must not over-value the relative harmlessness of the little, sensual, frivolous people. They are not above, but below, some temptations. . . . If they had perceived, and felt as a man should feel, the diabolical wickedness which they"—let us say the Nazis—"[were] committing and then forgiven them, they would have been saints. But not to perceive it at all—not even to be tempted to resentment—to accept it as the most ordinary thing in the world—argues a terrifying insensibility. . . . Thus the absence of anger, especially that sort of anger which we call *indignation,* can, in my opinion, be a most alarming symptom. And the presence of indignation may be a good one. Even when that indignation passes into bitter personal vindictiveness, it may still be a good symptom, though bad in itself. It is a sin; but at least shows that those who commit it have not sunk below the level at which the temptation to that sin exists—just as the sins (often quite appalling) of the great patriot or great reformer point to something in him above mere self. If the Jews cursed more bitterly than the Pagans, this was, I think, at least in part because they took right and wrong more seriously."

Can it be that the rhetorical totalism of the present day has etiolated *every* epithet? It was a commonplace at Chicago to call the police and the mayor Fascists and Nazis, and the country yawned, indeed much of it expected that so should the police and mayor have yawned. Everybody gets away with everything. Paul Krassner of *The Realist,* addressing the kids at the Coliseum at L.B.J.'s "unbirthday party," attaches the very highest importance to impunity. "I have it on good authority," he yelled into the loudspeaker, "that when someone privately asked L.B.J. why he kept up the war, he answered, 'The Commies are saying F--- you L.B.J.; and nobody gets away with that.' Well, tonight, as a birthday present, we are all going to say 'F--- you L.B.J.—*and get away with it.*' " To that Coliseum William Burroughs dispatched a congratulatory message calling the cops dogs, and Jean Genet topped him and called them mad dogs, and Terry Southern said they weren't dogs but swine. Can such men understand the causes of anger in others? Understand the special reverence we need to feel for that which is hateful? I do not believe that anyone thought me a Nazi because Vidal called me one, but I do believe that everyone who heard him call me one without a sense of shock, without experiencing anger, thinks more tolerantly about Nazism than once he did, than even now he should.

And then finally, the word I did use, which was "personal" in the understanding of Paul Newman—and a few others. Perhaps if I had merely threatened to hit him, that would have been all right. But to call him a queer—"I've been aware of you," one man wrote me, months after the affair, and apropos of nothing, "since the old days when you were on the debating team at Yale and I sat and watched and listened. I admired you then, and since—until you called Vidal a 'homosexual' on TV. This reminded me—somehow and so much—of *Of Human Bondage* when Mildred called the doctor a 'cripple.' I mean, he *did* have a clubfoot, a limp, true, but it was wildly cruel of her to mention it. Dramatic, yes, but really hitting below the belt. I can't recall your doing this sort of thing in New Haven. Have you changed that much—and if so, why?" I don't know. I hope not (though unquestionably Yale hopes so). But don't you see, Vidal does not consider that he is clubfooted, rather that the conventional morality is. He is no more reluctant to suggest his tastes than Swinburne was—and everyone from Carlyle to Edmund Wilson has spoken and written about them—intending to be wildly cruel? "In some ways," Vidal has written, "I was lucky to be brought up with no sense of sexual guilt. I was never told that . . . it was particularly wicked to go to bed with boys or girls. I also went into the army a month after my seventeenth birthday, and there was very little [there] one didn't do. That established a promiscuous pattern which I'm sure has had its limiting side. But there have been compensations." Vidal as usual writes loosely. One must suppose that very little of what we know is "wicked" we know because somebody took us aside and told us so. I don't remember, e.g., being "told" that it was particularly wicked to kill someone, but I have nevertheless always supposed it to be so. And anyway, what does Vidal mean by the "limiting side"? And has that limiting side any obligation to try to survive? Evangelists for bisexuality must endure evangelists for heterosexuality. And the man who in his essays proclaims the normalcy of his affliction, and in his art the desirability of it, is not to be confused with the man who bears his sorrow quietly. The addict is to be pitied and even respected, not the pusher.

Such then have been my thoughts, acknowledgedly self-serving, but not empty, I think, of objective interest. It remains a fact that, as I began by acknowledging, faggotry is countenanced, but the imputation of it—even to faggots—is not. There may be occasions when the clinical imputation is justified, such occasions as were mentioned earlier—Robert Brustein's reviewing a play. But the imputation of it in anger is not justified, which is why I herewith apologize to Gore Vidal.

[August, 1969]

A Distasteful Encounter
with William F. Buckley Jr.

by Gore Vidal

During the evening of May 13, 1944, Christ Episcopal Church at
Sharon, Connecticut was vandalized. According to *The Lakeville Journal*:
"The damage was discovered by worshipers who entered the church for
early communion the following day. The vandalism took on the appearance of similar occurrences in New York, according to witnesses. Honey
mixed with feathers was smeared on seats, obscene pictures were placed in
prayer books, among other desecrations." According to the local police
lieutenant "the crime [was] one of the most abominable ones ever committed in the area."

Twenty-four years later, on Wednesday, August 28, at nine-thirty
o'clock, in full view of ten million people, the little door in William F.
Buckley Jr.'s forehead suddenly opened and out sprang that wild cuckoo
which I had always known was there but had wanted so much for others,
preferably millions of others, to get a good look at. I think those few
seconds of madness, to use his word, were well worth a great deal of
patient effort on my part.

Last month, in a lengthy apologia, Buckley reprinted this exchange
which, he proudly tells us, "rocked television." For purpose of reference, I

must briefly reprise what happened. On the night of August 28, the Chicago Police riot was at its peak. Predictably, Buckley took the side of the police. This was particularly hard to do since, just before we went on the air, ABC had shown a series of exchanges between police and demonstrators which made it quite clear that the boys in azure blue were on a great lark, beating up everyone in sight. Buckley attacked me for defending the victims. That did it. I was now ready for the *coup de grace*. I began: "The only pro crypto Nazi I can think of is yourself. . . ."* As Buckley knew, there was more to come. He created a diversion: "Now listen, you queer. Stop calling me a pro crypto Nazi or I'll sock you in the goddamn face and you'll stay plastered. . . ." It was a splendid moment. Eyes rolling, mouth twitching, long weak arms waving, he skittered from slander to glorious absurdity. "I was," he honked, "in the Infantry in the last war." Starting as always with the last improvisation first, I said, "You were not in the Infantry, as a matter of fact you didn't fight in the war." I was ready to go into that but by then he was entirely out of control and, as our program faded away on much noise, a few yards from us Hubert Humphrey was being nominated for President. All in all, I was pleased with what had happened: I had enticed the cuckoo to sing its song, and the melody lingers on.

For eleven nights we had "debated" one another on television, first at the Republican Convention in Miami Beach and then at the Democratic Convention in Chicago. The American Broadcasting Company had asked us to discuss politics, and so I had spent a number of weeks doing research on the major candidates as well as on my sparring partner. From past experience, I knew that as a debater Buckley would have done no research, that what facts he had at his command would be jumbled by the strangest syntax since General Eisenhower faded from the scene, that he would lie ("McCarthy never won a majority in any state he ever ran in . . .") with an exuberance which was almost but not quite contagious; and that within three minutes of our first debate, if the going got tough for

* *There is some confusion about what was actually said on the telecast. The word "Nazi" was first introduced into the discussion by Howard K. Smith who felt that to raise a Vietcong flag in Grant Park was the equivalent to raising a Nazi flag during the Second War. I said it was not the same thing: officially there is no war between us and Hanoi. More to the point, a sizeable minority in the U.S. disapprove of their government's policy and if flaunting a North Vietnamese flag gives them comfort they have every constitutional right to do so (as it later developed, the "flag" raised was underwear). Buckley once again attacked the dissenters; I defended their right to dissent. Unfortunately, two lines of his preceding my "pro crypto Nazi" remark are not clear on the tape. It is my recollection they had to do with communism and the dissenters' relation to the Great Conspiracy. Whatever they were, my own outburst was not a declarative sentence but the beginning of a response to Buckley which was—so notoriously—cut short. Incidentally, I had not intended to use the phrase "pro crypto Nazi." "Fascist-minded" was more my intended meaning, but the passions of the moment and Smith's use of the word "Nazi" put me off course.*

him on political grounds, he would mention my "pornographic" novel *Myra Breckinridge* and imply its author was a *"degenerate."* This is of course what happened. This is what always happens when Buckley performs. As columnist or debater, he has made sniggering sexual innuendos about a range of public figures, and there is some evidence that what may have begun as a schoolboy debater's trick to save a losing argument has now become morbid obsession.

Study the technique. Discussing the "left opposition" to President Johnson on the Vietnam war, Buckley writes (June 17, 1966, Los Angeles *Times*): "At the eye of the hurricane, taking advantage of the centrifugal quiet of his station, is Bobby, whose way is swept clean by the ravaging winds of his associates. He must of course occasionally lisp into the act. . . ." Now the late Senator's voice was known to us all and he did not lisp. Why say that he did? Because the word "lisp" suggests softness, weakness, and, above all, effeminacy. The mad cuckoo behind the little door could not resist casting a shadow upon the virility of his enemy, just as the cuckoo astonishingly characterized those who demonstrated against the war in New York, October 1965, as "epicene" and "mincing" slobs, thus slyly assigning to Sodom's banner such unlikely recruits as I. F. Stone, Ossie Davis, and Father Philip Berrigan. Charity forbids me mentioning what he has written or said of many others; it is all, however, in the record, as his great idol Joe McCarthy used to say.

In any event, having indicated that he lost the debates to me by "losing his cool," Buckley now hopes to regain by writing what he lost through performing. From where I sit, it looks as if our old friend Hugh Bris is back in town. Apparently Buckley has spent the better part of a year brooding over his disaster. "I tormented myself," he declares in a tone which, for sheer plangency, has not sounded since Whittaker Chambers sang among the pumpkins. And so, to relieve his torment, at extraordinary length, he has given us the passion of William Buckley "on experiencing Gore Vidal," a document which deserves at least appendix-status in any study of paranoia American Style. It is obvious that Buckley spent a great deal of effort on this work and though it is about as accurate as those newspaper columns he writes in twenty minutes, it is still a most revealing work—though not, as I hope to demonstrate, in quite the way he thinks.

Buckley begins his tirade with, I should have thought, a most dangerous quotation from *The East Village Other* to the effect that Buckley has been found guilty of exercising "faggot dialectic." The implication is plain. The writer thinks that Buckley is a faggot. He is not alone. Norman Mailer even shouted the word "fag" at Buckley during a Les Crane taping: it was cut from the show . . . how innocent television was before Chicago last summer! Now Buckley's private life should be a matter of no concern to *The East Village Other* or even to that vivacious compendium *The Homosexual Handbook* whose listing of well-known degenerates includes, on page 261, "*William F. Buckley:* Writer, professional candidate, Mr. Buckley hosts a television program and conducts it with a flourish and a zest, with such brilliant gestures and hand movement, that Gore Vidal is reported to have called him 'the Marie Antoinette of American politics.' " Now to include Buckley in a list of homosexuals is doubtless slanderous. In any case, every public figure is vulnerable to this sort of rumor, which is why it seems to me odd that someone like Buckley, himself suspect, should be so quick to smear others as "queers." It is a most unbecoming trait in him, and more than a little mad.

Buckley's reaction to being called a "faggot logician" in *The East Village Other* was very peculiar. Quoting with obvious excitement from a series of personal ads in the paper soliciting homosexual partners, he asks, "why is faggotry okay, but the imputation of it discreditable?" This is sophistical, to say the least. When Buckley imputes faggotry to others, he means no compliment; nor were the liberal editors of the paper paying him a compliment by calling him a "faggot logician." Though Buckley is hardly a logician, he is—at his level—a kind of syllogist, and this is what I think he is trying to say: If liberals think faggotry okay and I call one of them a faggot, why is that wrong in their eyes since there is nothing wrong in being one? Yet when they call *me* one, they imply there is something very wrong about being a faggot.

I believe I can straighten this out for him. People often use terms which are blunt but not necessarily unkind. Agnew's "fat Jap," let us say, or Aristophanes needling Socrates for being a pederast which Buckley reminded us of in his garble of classical history ("I really loved your novel *Julian*," Bill whispered softly to me in Miami as we waited to go on the air) when Aristophanes was himself an apologist for pederasty (read Plato's *Symposium* for the inside story and don't forget you saw it here first!). People have a tendency to be ambiguous about sex and sexual words. Succumbing to his constant vice of name-dropping, Buckley described how at Chicago Paul Newman ticked him off for having shouted "you queer" at me. Buckley described the conversation accurately except for Newman's last statement, "You," said Newman with that preciseness that made him such a formidable campaigner in the 1968 primaries, "are a male c-asterisk-asterisk-t." Now this did not mean that the heterosexual movie star and father of six in any way deplored the c-asterisk-asterisk-t, ("The last fantasy which is of course the first reality." *Myra Breckinridge*, p. 245), it just meant that the word in that context was nicely evocative, even traditional, since the word "hysterical" derives from the Greek noun for womb, and by his own admission Buckley was a "madman" that night. In other words, it is possible to designate someone as a faggot in one context while, in another, regard the whole subject with a permissive eye. By Newman's standard, Buckley behaved like a male womb, by mine he was hysterical, and since that anomaly—the male womb—ought to be excised, I hope that this present exercise will prove to be a successful hysterectomy.

Just as I had predicted, no sooner had I begun to discuss the various political positions of Nixon and Reagan, Buckley launched an attack on *Myra Breckinridge*, as a pornographic potboiler, even though he now admits in his *mea culpa* that he had not read the book at the time he attacked it. Would that he were always so candid! But his motive was plain. *Myra Breckinridge* is about a homosexual who becomes a woman, falls in love with a girl and then becomes, more or less, a man again. To connect me with the book would mean, to certain simple souls, that the author was a homosexual who had become a woman who had then become a man, etc.—because books are true, aren't they? This is pretty simple-minded reasoning but Buckley himself has a simple mind; it is only his neurosis that is rich and strange. Needless to say, identifying authors with their works is a feckless game. Simply to go by their books, Agatha Christie is a mass murderess, while William Buckley is a practicing Christian. But we are dealing now with tribal emotions. There was nothing that Buckley was not prepared to invoke in order to keep me from establishing him as anti-black, anti-Semitic, and pro-war. After I had pointed out, pleasantly I hope, how much he resembled Myra Breckinridge, particularly in his use of logic, I was able to get the subject back to politics. I confronted him with a series of statements he had made. He then did something I have never seen anyone do on television before or since. He simply denied having written what I had said he had written. It was the obverse of Joe McCarthy's, "I have a paper here in my hand." This time I had the paper with each statement neatly checked and dated, and he denied it all. As Goebbels used to say, in somewhat similar circumstances, the big lie is always more powerful than the small plausible one. Still upset over those quotations, he now tells us that he carefully checked his records and the dates I had given him and so on were wrong.

He makes a great to-do over my statement that he favored the atom-bombing of North Vietnam, on the ground that my quote was from the *National Review*, 23 February 1968. Apparently there is no such issue. The quote, as prepared for me by a researcher, and which, incidentally, appeared in Buckley's *On the Right* column of 22 February 1968, reads, "The use of limited atomic bombs for purely military operations is many times easier to defend on the morality scale than one slit throat of a civilian for terrorism's sake." I thought this most illustrative of the Buckley morality scale. But then, denying he had made the statement, he writes, "Could Vidal have had in mind a column, written about that time, though never published in *National Review*, advocating the use of tactical nuclear weapons in Vietnam? Who knows? Yes, I have advocated (and most ardently continue to do so) their use. . . ." He then appeals to the reader: what is he to do with someone who invents facts on television?

There is a solemn lunacy about all this. Incidentally, in the text of his article that I was sent by Esquire, *he crossed out the following exchange from our first performance*:

Vidal: According to you, it's [the people] made nothing but errors since 1932 with an eight-year interregnum of a man you didn't much admire. In fact you criticized Richard Nixon for his unctuous love and attention of the great general. Unctuous is a rather good word.

Buckley: I can account for these errors other than by using the neurotic terms that you're so fetched by. . . .

Buckley crossed out this exchange. Reading it, I wondered why. Admittedly, his response makes no sense—just which of the terms I had used was "neurotic"? A few lines later I understood the reason for the cut.

"Vidal suddenly switched the topic, electing to allude to my 'intimacy' with Reagan and Nixon."

Buckley does indeed like to give the impression that he is "the tablet keeper of history" for the movers and shakers, and his journalism is filled with little anecdotes as to how Reagan introduced him as a speaker one night in California, or "I have had exclusive interviews with Mr. Rockefeller and Mr. Nixon in recent weeks." (*National Review*, 9 April 1968.) I knew, as shall be later demonstrated, that in the words of *The Wall Street Journal*, his ". . . ideological stance seem [s] to have closed off for him, at least for the present, any close public contact with political figures in the major parties." (31 January 1967.)

"In order to do so, [Vidal] assigned to the word 'neurosis' a meaning I have never heard it given, not even by conventional neurotics."

Aware that I had simply played back the word "neurotic," Buckley thought it wise to suppress that part of the dialogue which showed him as provocateur. He then gave the following exchange:

Vidal: Since you're in favor of the invasion of Cuba, in favor of bombing the nuclear potentiality of China, since you're in favor of nuclear bombing of North Vietnam, I'd be very worried about your kind of odd neurosis [I meant "neurotic"] being a friend of anybody who might be a President. . . .

Denying everything, Buckley did admit, righteously, that: "I advocated the liberation of Cuba at the same time that Mr. Kennedy ordered the liberation of Cuba."

Vidal: No, no, Bill, keep to the record. You said we should enforce the Monroe Doctrine and invade Cuba the sooner the better in your little magazine whose name will not pass my lips.

I then gave the date when he favored an invasion—20 April 1965, four years after Kennedy's attempt at "liberation." ("What Republican leader has done anything to dramatize the need for the restoration of the Monroe Doctrine and *all that it signifies* in terms of *our axiomatic obligation* to our own hemisphere?" [Italics mine] *N.R.* 20 April 1965.) He continues with my testimony, beginning:

Vidal: You favored bombing Red China's nuclear production facilities the 17th of September 1965 in *Life* magazine, and you suggested the atom bombing of North Vietnam in your little magazine which I do not read but I'm told about, the 23rd of February 1968. So you're very hawkish, and if both Nixon and Reagan are listening to you, I'm very worried for the country.

Buckley abandons the transcript to observe, "I told him he was misquoting me." Was I? Here is what I quoted from *Life* magazine September 17, 1965: "I have advocated bombing Red China's nuclear production facilities. . . . How do we justify the bombing in terms of world opinion? On the grounds that the good guys of this earth have got to keep the bad guys from getting nuclear bombs."

On television I called Buckley a warmonger because the preemptive strike which he favors against China would lead to a war with China, because the use of nuclear weapons against the North Vietnamese would undoubtedly bring the Chinese into that already disastrous operation, and because his call for an invasion of Cuba is plainly a call for war. I quoted him accurately. And his response? I had invented everything. I suspect that the thought of a Republican administration in 1969 made him not want to be reminded of more zealous days. Always ambitious to be accepted by the nation's establishment, he wanted desperately to appear to be in the placid mainstream of our political life—yet there I was revealing him as an eccentric war-lover of the right. He was not happy. As we left the studio, after the first debate, he whispered to me, "You'll be sorry."

During the next twelve debates, I did my best to discuss the issues. I came to each session armed with quotations from Nixon, et al. Buckley came with a set of prejudices, uncompromised by fact. He was at a constant disadvantage and he knew it. The best he could do was simply say that whatever source I quoted was false. He makes particularly heavy weather in his epilogue of my quotation from Nixon: "I am opposed to pensions in any form as it [sic] makes loafing more attractive than working." According to Buckley, "no politician in the history of the world ever said that, and most probably no non-politician." The second part of this hyperbole is quite mad: most right-wingers say this sort of thing all the time. As for the first part, Nixon did make the statement, and it can be found in *Labor*, 18 October 1952.

When the evidence was too clearly against Buckley, he would again revert to sexual innuendo, attacks on *Myra*, and, finally, Bobby Kennedy. With unexpected naïveté, Buckley thought I would be embarrassed to have the audience reminded that I had written unkind things about Bobby. The opposite is true. And so, contrary to expectation, I enjoyed Buckley's reading of Bobby's letter to him, suggesting that not blood but Gore be sent to the Vietcong. I also noted that at the end of the letter Bobby had scribbled, "And please, when you put it in—please don't twist it." He knew Buckley. Needless to say, this part was not read aloud on the air.

Apropos of the second Kennedy murder, Buckley quotes from an interview I gave to the German magazine *Stern* in which I said that I thought it significant that Sirhan was brought up in Pasadena, a city rich in anti-Jews, anti-blacks, anti-poor. In fact, Los Angeles County, California, is one of the strongholds of the virulent Right Wing. Now obviously Pasadena is not solely responsible for making Sirhan do what he did, but it was certainly a contributing factor. You cannot live unaffected in a community where so many tote guns and talk loudly about how this Commie and that Jew and that nigger ought to be shot. Needless to say, Buckley defends Pasadena. He then quotes various unflattering things I had written about Bobby, asking rhetorically, "Was that the passage that caught the eye of Sirhan?" This is pure Goebbels. But where Buckley is more than usually bird-brained is that I can quote him at equal length in dispraise of Bobby, and I, too, can cry, "Is this the phrase that caught the madman's eye and drove him to kill?"

Yet there is a demagogic strategy in all this. If one is lying, accuse others of lying. On television this sort of thing is enormously effective in demoralizing the innocent and well-mannered who, acting in good faith, do not lie or make personal insults. Buckley has made many honorable men look dishonest fools by his demagoguery, and by the time they recover from his first assault and are ready to retaliate, the program is over. Fortunately, I had Buckley night after night and was so able to remind him and the audience of those facts he found inconvenient. My favorite exchange occurred when we were discussing Eugene McCarthy. At the end of one debate, in which I had claimed that McCarthy was the popular choice of the party, if not of its leaders, Buckley suddenly exclaimed, "McCarthy never won a clear majority in any state he ever ran in. Name one state. Name *one!*" Honking and hissing, flapping his arms, he made it impossible for me to answer that McCarthy had won the Wisconsin primary by fifty-seven percent, a clear majority. The next night, however, I brought up the subject again. Buckley began to writhe. He tried to deny the figures. Then tried to deny saying what he had said. Finally: "But Wisconsin was an uncontested primary and I meant a *contested* primary." I pointed out that since there were other names on the ballot, that meant a contest and, in any case, that is not what he had said, et cetera. Childish. Typical. Appealing? To whom, I wonder.

As the debates continued their turbulent way, Buckley began to show the strain. His hands shook, eyes grew wild, he sweated constantly. As I doggedly and, probably rather boringly, discussed the positions of the candidates, he would go off on wild tangents of his own. I lived in Europe

(I also live in America). I was a pornographer. I was making up my newspaper quotations. Whenever he did this, I would reply in kind. Although careful to avoid discussing his personal life, I set out to establish him not only as a war-lover but as a totalitarian, in the general sense of someone with an authoritarian disposition who wishes to use the state for such ends as placing the "chronic welfare cases" of New York City in "rehabilitation centers" outside the city (a proposal made in the mayoralty campaign of 1965). No matter what I said, he denied it. Yet here are some of the quotations:

"I am convinced that Martin Luther King belongs behind bars along with everyone else who conspires to break the law."

After King's death, he wrote:

"The martyrdom [King] seemed sometimes almost to be seeking may commend him to history and to God, but not likely to Scarsdale, New York, which has never credited the charge that the white community of America conspires to ensure the wretchedness of the brothers of Martin Luther King. . . ."

After Adam Clayton Powell was suspended from Congress, the *National Review* printed a lip-smacking comment wittily subtitled, "The Jig Is Up, Baby."

"If the entire Negro population in the South were suddenly given the vote and were to use it as a block and pursuant to directives handed down by some more demagogic Negro leaders, chaos would ensue."

This statement is a paradigm of the Buckley technique, and should be analyzed. If the Negroes are given the vote, and if they all decided to vote as a block, and the leader of the block was Rap Brown, say, then there would be chaos. Conclusion: don't give them the vote. Yet (a) there is no evidence that they would necessarily vote in any more of a self-serving block than those New York Irish cops who voted for Buckley; (b) it is well known that extremist black leaders like Rap Brown have almost no influence among the Southern blacks; (c) how could there be "chaos" when the only choice offered the blacks in a general election like that of 1968 would be Nixon or Humphrey? Perhaps their block support of Humphrey is Buckley's idea of chaos. In any case, the thought of the blacks exercising their constitutional right to vote is displeasing to one who regards the blacks not only of America but of Africa with distaste, even going so far as to characterize Patrice Lumumba and Joseph Mobutu as "semi-savages in the Congo." (The New York *Times,* 23 August 1961.)

In his epilogue, Buckley had some good fun with my statistics on poverty. I am supposed to have said, sometimes there were forty million poor and at other times twenty million, and so on.

The point to throwing doubt on my statistics (supplied by the Department of Health, Education and Welfare) was to give the impression that poverty is really not much of a problem. But then Buckley's attitude toward the poor is singularly cruel. "It is estimated that in New York one half of the chronically poor are disorganized poor, who cannot be persuaded even to flush their own toilets." (*N.R.*, 4 June 1968.) He also affects not to understand my reference to garbage thrown out of the windows of Harlem. I was not able to complete the sentence on television. But here it is. During a television exchange with Buckley, James Baldwin blamed the white owners of the black slums for their condition. Buckley's response: And I suppose the white landlords go pitty-pat uptown and throw the garbage out the windows.

I first became aware of the Buckleys as a family when I was running for Congress as a Democrat in upstate New York, close to Sharon, Connecticut, where the Buckleys live. Campaigning in America (a town I carried) I heard a good deal about the family, none of it flattering. Until then, I had been vaguely aware of someone called William F. Buckley Jr. who had written an attack on the faculty of Yale's "intellectual drive toward agnosticism and collectivism," a defense of Joe McCarthy and McCarthyism as "a movement around which men of goodwill and stern morality can close ranks," and who edited an unsuccessful magazine called *National Review* (according to *The Wall Street Journal,* January 31, 1967, between 1955 and 1964, the operating deficit was $2,181,000; it is now more). I had dismissed him as a sort of Right Wing Liberace.

Then, on a January night in 1962, on *The Jack Paar Show,* there was a discussion of the Right Wing. I mentioned Buckley in a half sentence, something to do with his dismissal of Pope John's encyclical *Mater et Magistra* as "a venture in triviality." Buckley was not mentioned again. Then, unfortunately, this was the opportunity he had been waiting for, according to Buckley, "Paar was evidently pressured to invite me to reply." Needless to say, Paar was not seriously "pressured" by anyone except Buckley who rang him up and asked for "equal time." Buckley had now managed to get himself on national television. It was a heady moment. The fact that Paar cut him up badly made no difference. Buckley had finally hit the big time as a TV entertainer, and that was all that mattered. It is a source of some pain to me that, unwittingly, I helped Buckley lose his richly deserved anonymity.

We met for the first time on David Susskind's program of September 23, 1962. For two hours, we debated. I had been reluctant to appear with Buckley on the ground that simply to sit next to him would make me look the same sort of nut of the Left Wing that he was of the Right. But Susskind persuaded me. It is my recollection that the program was dull.

We next met in San Francisco, 1964, during the Goldwater convention. We appeared for an hour on a program moderated by Susskind. Here is Buckley's version of what happened: ". . . Vidal announced . . . that I

had that very afternoon importuned Barry Goldwater to accept a draft of
an acceptance speech I had written for him, and that Goldwater had
brusquely turned me down, all of this in the presence of 'John Jones,' a
Goldwater aide. I told him that I had not laid eyes on Goldwater that
afternoon. . . ." I never said Buckley went to Goldwater . . . in fact,
just the opposite. It was, all in all, a fine comic interlude, beginning earlier
the day of the telecast, when Douglas Kiker, then of the New York *Herald
Tribune,* took Norman Mailer and me to see Goldwater's press secretary
"John Jones." What "Jones" said about Goldwater was to be off the
record. I could not resist, however, asking what Buckley's role would be in
the campaign if Goldwater were the nominee. "Jones" sighed. "That guy!
The telephone's been ringing all day, him wanting to talk to the Senator.
Then he sent over some stuff for the acceptance speech and I took it into
the Senator, and he said, 'What's all that crap?' " I confess to having
prepared a trap for Buckley. Once we were on air, I inquired innocently as
to what his role would be in a Goldwater campaign. Buckley looked
positively roguish, his *éminence* becoming more *grise* by the moment. I
egged him on. He grew more and more expansive about his relations with
Goldwater. Hinted at closeness. Then, to my shame, I allowed the trap to
shut. I repeated—somewhat paraphrased—what "Jones" had told Mailer,
Kiker and me. Buckley raved: it was all lies! The next day "Jones," quite
predictably, wrote Buckley a letter denying what he had said and Buckley
sent a copy to me with a covering letter to the effect that he never wanted
to see me again. I found this sentiment agreeable. In any case, aside from
my two witnesses, Mailer and Kiker, events proved me right: Buckley
played no part in the campaign of '64, and the G.O.P. national chairman
Dean Burch ascribed this to "a matter of personality."

After San Francisco, Buckley tells us he decided not to debate me again
and declares that "over the intervening years I had never asked him to
appear on *Firing Line* [Buckley's television program]"; according to
Buckley, this "exclusion gravelled him." Here we have two misstatements.
First, I was hardly "gravelled" at the thought of not appearing on *Firing
Line.* Second, I was one of the first people approached to appear on *Firing
Line.* As Buckley's luck would have it, the producer of the program rang
me while I was giving an interview to Gerald Walker. I turned the
producer down flat, hung up, then explained to Walker that one of the
regrets of my life was allowing Buckley to use me to get himself attention.
Walker recorded all this in his interview, which appeared in *Writer's
Yearbook, 1965.*

Now before we return to Chicago and the crack-up, I
think I should answer certain charges Buckley has made about my work. I
am, apparently, such a dedicated proselytizer for homosexuality that
I have, in the words of *National Review*'s daintiest hack, produced in

Romulus (a play taken from Dürrenmatt about the last Roman emperor) ". . . the most offensive instance of 'inside theatre' . . . effeminate. . . ." In actual fact, there is nothing "effeminate" about the play. No character is a homosexual, and the subject is never mentioned. Buckley also quotes New Haven's mevin for all drama seasons Robert Brustein as objecting to the play as an "effeminate charade." What can they mean? They mean, simply, that the leading actor, Cyril Ritchard (now a widower, but for years a happily married man) is known as a camp actor —and doesn't camp mean effeminate mean homosexual? Since no one listens in the theatre (or to television), the actual drama went unnoticed. Fortunately, the text can be found with Dürrenmatt's original in a Grove Press edition, and the curious will discover that this "effeminate charade" is a thoughtful meditation on power and responsibility, and makes no mention of sex of any kind. The *N.R.* writer also tells us that "[Vidal] once wrote a scenario about Billy the Kid . . . as a misunderstood homosexual." A) Leslie Stevens wrote the Screenplay for *The Left Handed Gun*, based upon a television play by me; B) in neither version was Billy the Kid shown to be homosexual.

Now for *Myra Breckinridge*. As literary critic, Buckley is—how to put it?—lightly equipped. But that does not deter him. He will take on any subject with insolent pluck, confident that his readers are bound to be even more ignorant than he. He is probably right. To support his case against *Myra,* he quotes most selectively, from some of the more troubled American reviews. Now I am not about to explain or defend my work, but since he has quoted at length from such obscure periodicals as *The Critic* (a house organ for the Knights of Columbus?), I shall quote from two well-known English critics.

First, Michael Ratcliffe in *The Times* (London): "Most British reviews have taken Mr. Vidal with total seriousness, up to a point, but to conclude, as some have, that *Myra Breckinridge* is a novel about sex as the source of all ultimate power is greatly to underrate its subtlety. Gore Vidal remains, after all, a proclaimed classicist, a writing professional and a patrician who suffers fools and shamateurs less gladly than ever . . . and it is impossible when reading *Myra Breckinridge* not to sense his impatience that the headlong flight into apparent sexual libertarianism has produced a nightmare of idiotic thinking and cant and even that, as an anthropological phenomenon, sex has become wildly overrated. . . . Mr. Vidal has drawn the line between absurdity and obscenity, between satire and daft thinking with such a delicate exactness that future sociologists will be hard put to distinguish the fantasy from the real thing."

Second, Brigid Brophy in *The Listener*: "The high baroque comedy of bad taste is a rare genre. *Myra Breckinridge* belongs to it and is a masterpiece: the funniest event since *Some Like It Hot* (and some can't recommend more highly than that). . . . The trans-sex fantasy explodes,

I suspect, at a level even deeper than the one from which it liberates the homosexual imprisoned in every heterosexual and also, of course, the heterosexual in every homosexual (for what, after all, was a respectable, presumed-exclusive queer like Myron doing taking such an erotically detailed interest in lady film stars?). . . . Because the baroque is so analytically formal, the baroque mode and his baroque subject matter are a perfect metaphor for Mr. Vidal's satiric purpose.

"He finds intellectual sloppiness destructive. He destroys it by an explosive, centrifugal force far more inherently destructive than its enemy, but which he controls and creatively deploys into an artistic form."

In England literary critics tend to write about books for the newspapers; in the United States journalists like Buckley do most of the reviewing, with the result that one gets a good deal of intellectual sloppiness and much moralizing at the Billy Graham level. Muddling *Myra*'s views with my own, Buckley indicates that I prefer homosexuality to heterosexuality. Now I want to make one thing absolutely clear, as Richard Nixon would say: I do not prefer homosexuality to heterosexuality—or, for that matter, heterosexuality to homosexuality. Unhappily, somewhere along the way, those who write for newspapers decided that since I thought homosexuality as *natural* as heterosexuality, I must then hate heterosexuality and love homosexuality. One of the sad characteristics of popular journalism is that what *ought* to be true is true. Contrary evidence is not admitted, including the two million words which I have published in the last twenty-five years, nowhere stating that homosexuality ought to be the preferred form of sexuality. It is true that at one point *Myra* makes a case for homosexuality on the ground that it might help contain the population explosion. That was a joke. Incidentally, though Buckley quotes at length from the scene in which Rusty is raped, he makes no mention of the many pages devoted to Myra's attempted seduction of Mary-Ann and the long and I think quite beautiful apostrophe to the uterine mystery.

"But tonight she was subtly changed. I don't know whether it was the snaps at Scandia or the cold bright charm of the powerful Letitia or the knowledge that Rusty would never be hers again but whatever it was, she allowed my hand to rest a long moment on the entrance to the last fantasy which is of course the first reality. Ecstatically, I fingered the lovely shape whose secret I must know or die, whose maze I must thread as best I can or go mad for if I am to prevail I must soon come face to face with the Minotaur of dreams and confound him in his charneled lair, and in our heroic coupling know the last mystery: total power achieved not over man, not over woman but over the heraldic beast, the devouring monster, the maw of creation itself that spews us forth and sucks us back into the black oblivion where stars are made and energy waits to be born in order to begin once more the cycle of destruction and creation at whose apex now I stand, once man, now woman, and soon to be privy to what lies beyond the uterine door, the mystery of creation that I mean to shatter with the fierce thrust of a will that alone separates me from the nothing of eternity; and as I have conquered the male, absorbed and been absorbed by the female, I am at last outside the human scale, and so may render impotent even familiar banal ubiquitous death whose mouth I see smiling at me with moist coral lips between the legs of my beloved girl who is the unwitting instrument of victory, and the beautiful fact of my life's vision made all too perfect flesh."

While we are on Buckley's favorite subject, sex, I will try to unmuddle his distortion of what I have said about bisexuality. We are all bisexual to begin with. That is a fact of our condition. And we are all responsive to sexual stimuli from our own as well as from the opposite sex. Certain societies at certain times, usually in the interest of maintaining the baby supply, have discouraged homosexuality. Other societies, particularly militaristic ones, have exalted it. But regardless of tribal taboos, homosexuality is a constant fact of the human condition and it is not a sickness, not a sin, not a crime . . . despite the best efforts of our puritan tribe to make it all three. Homosexuality is as natural as heterosexuality. Notice I use the word "natural," not normal. Buckley likes the word normal. It conjures up vigorous Minute Men with rifles shooting Commies, while their wives and little ones stay home stitching hoods. But what is the sexual norm? By definition it is what most people do most frequently. Therefore, the norm is neither homosexual nor heterosexual. The most frequent (if not most preferred!) sexual outlet of most people of the time is masturbation, making onanism the statistical norm from which all else is deviation. Yet I don't think even Mrs. Portnoy's son would want to make a case for that particular normality.

As for being an "evangelist of bisexuality," I am not an evangelist of anything in sexual matters except a decent withdrawal of the state from the bedroom. There will, of course, always be morbid twisted men like Buckley sniggering and giggling and speculating on the sexual lives of others, and nothing's to be done about them. But the sex laws must be changed. It was Dr. Kinsey who pointed out that if all the laws were enforced, ninety percent of the men in the United States would be in jail. One final point: Buckley quotes an American reviewer who was horrified at my explicit description of a male body (as usual, no mention of the equally explicit description of a female body). To me this reviewer's objection perfectly reflects the sickness of the society we live in. On the one hand, such critics hold that we are made in the very image of God, a bit of proud, primitive lunacy still obtaining in certain Christian sects, and yet, without any awareness of paradox, they also hold nudity to be obscene, the body disgusting, and certain parts of it horrifying. Yet if we are made in God's image, the body must be divine. Conversely, if the body is vile, then its maker must be vile. Unfortunately, our primitives are beyond mere logic. They have their tribal prejudices and find both comfort and glory in their confusion.

"The only pro crypto Nazi I know is you," I said to Buckley on the night of August 28. He tells us that this so maddened him, he went to pieces with righteous anger. Looking and sounding not unlike Hitler, but without the charm, he began to shriek insults in order to head me off, and succeeded, for by then my mission was accomplished: Buckley had revealed himself. There was no need to discuss his anti-Semitic background. He had demonstrated most vividly what I could only have stated. But now that he has seen fit to relive his failure at Chicago, I am now obliged to write what I chose not to say on the air.

William F. Buckley Sr. was a Texan and an oil speculator who made a small fortune and had ten children. Politically, he was a perfect example of what Professor Richard Hofstader has called the "paranoid style" in American political life. A nouveau riche of limited intelligence but powerful prejudices, Buckley Sr. felt that he should have more influence in the country than indeed he had. In this he follows what Professor Hofstader has shown to be a classic pattern. Whenever a member of one of the immigrant groups to the United States moves from poverty to affluence, his first response is a sense of letdown that he is still no closer to the levers of power than he was before. If he is of a paranoid disposition, he will suspect conspiracy; he will blame *them*. The John Birch Society is a particular haven for this kind of malcontent. It seems likely that Buckley Senior felt insufficiently acknowledged. Despite the legend of his great fortune, he was never listed in *Who's Who in America, Current Biography, Poor's Register of Corporations, Directors, and Executives,* or even the *Social Register.* Like a cut-rate Joe Kennedy, he then decided to compensate through his children. They were taught total conservatism. They were privately tutored. All were sent to England to acquire patrician accents. William Jr.'s did not quite take. The result was a vigorous, highly articulate brood who, in the words of one (John), "are all good conservatives and, thank heavens, we all married conservatives." The family is as devoted to one another as the Kennedys, and on the important issues, they think alike. When Buckley Junior was attacking the faculty at Yale for "collectivist" tendencies, two sisters opened up separate fronts at Smith and Vassar.

Though Buckley Jr. is usually candid about his love of war and distaste for the blacks, he is extremely wary of appearing anti-Semitic. In this he resembles Robert Welch, though not the late irrepressible George Lincoln Rockwell. Very seldom does he betray his actual feelings as he did on Tex McCrary's radio program 25 September 1964. ". . . they [the Jews] tend to construct an engaging political myth, centered around the Hitlerian experience which more or less suggests that Hitler was the embodiment of the ultra-Right, and that the true enemies of Hitler, many of them—that the true enemies were, in fact, many of them Communists during the early Thirties. And under the circumstances they, I think, emotionally feel a kind of toleration for Communist excesses in this country. . . ." Arnold Forster of the Anti-Defamation League of B'nai B'rith answered Buckley four days later·on the same program. To Buckley's charge that Jews feel a kind of toleration for Communist excesses in this country, Forster replied: "That of course, Tex, is nothing more than insidious slander. . . . And notice how easy he finds it to generalize, Tex, about Jews. Millions of human beings in one group." The question of course is why does Buckley find it so easy insidiously to slander, in Forster's phrases, millions of human beings? I know the answer and Buckley, knowing that I knew it at Chicago, terrified that I would discuss it on the air, saw fit to interrupt me with calculated hysterics.

On March 4, 1944, Mr. and Mrs. Sully Berman bought a house on the green at Sharon. The Bermans were Jews. Now in Sharon, there was a gentleman's agreement to keep out Jews. Needless to say, the arrival of the Bermans was considered by the village gentry to be a betrayal of that agreement, and the town's wrath was directed not so much at the Bermans as at the real-estate agent who had done such an un-Christian thing as to admit Jews to Sharon. The agent was Mrs. Francis James Meadows Cotter. Her husband was the Episcopal minister at Sharon, and Rector of Christ Church. The Cotters were a well-liked family, and their two daughters were contemporaries and friends of the young Buckleys. Buckley Sr., however, was a most unforgiving man. He complained loudly and bitterly about what Mrs. Cotter had done and, like Henry II, vowed revenge. Shortly thereafter, on Saturday, May 13, Christ Episcopal Church was vandalized. Honey and feathers were poured over the velvet cushions of the pews. Prayer books were defaced. Obscene photographs were inserted in the Bible.

There was considerable uproar the next morning when the Reverend Cotter and his flock assembled. Who had done it? The high-spirited Buckleys were immediately suspected. Acting on a tip, detectives went to the Buckley house and there found the magazines from which had been torn the nudes, the oatmeal and syrup containers still set out on the kitchen table. Minimal sleuthing revealed which of the young Buckleys had been in town that night. The detectives then confronted the three vandals and got them to sign confessions. The case came to court June 10, and the three (one was in college and two in prep school) were found guilty by a Justice of the Peace and each fined $100 for damaging the church. Buckley Sr. did his best to take further revenge on the Cotters, even going so far as to request the Episcopal Bishop of Connecticut to remove Cotter from Christ Church, but by then village sentiment was entirely on the side of the Cotters and Buckley Sr. dropped the matter. But he had made his point as far as his family was concerned and therein lies the key to his son's character. Buckley Jr. has never accepted any view of the world other than his father's. He is forever the little boy trying to impress Daddy by hating what Daddy hates. To be fair, Buckley Sr.'s prejudices were not much different from those of, let us say, Joe Kennedy or Senator Gore, my grandfather, but Joe Kennedy's sons and Senator Gore's grandson changed as they made their way in the world, learned charity or at least good sense, but not Bill—he is still the schoolboy debater echoing what he heard in his father's house, and for this post-poned maturity he must suffer the fate of having been irrelevant to his own time, a mere entertainer with a gift for mischief.

"A man like Titus Oates occurs like a slip of the tongue, disclosing the unconscious forces, the nightside of an age. . . ." So wrote Graham Greene and so one might write of Buckley. In examining Eichmann's career Hannah Arendt came to the conclusion that evil could be banal. Buckley's career suggests that evil can be fatuous. But banal or fatuous, the result is the same if to the fool or his friends falls the power of the state. Buckley is not of course a "pro crypto Nazi" in the sense that he is a secret member of the Nazi party (and I respond to Buckley's charming apology to me with mine to him if anyone thought I was trying to link him to Hitler's foreign and domestic ventures). But in a larger sense his views are very much those of the founders of the Third Reich who regarded blacks as inferiors, undeclared war as legitimate foreign policy, and the Jews as sympathetic to international communism.

Since I began this operation with a story from *The Lakeville Journal*, a sense of symmetry impels me to end with another newspaper quotation. During Buckley's campaign for Mayor of New York, The New York *Times* took exception to his "slurs on Negroes," and accused him of pandering to "brutish instincts." Buckley wanted to know to what brutish instincts he was appealing, and The *Times* made answer, "Those instincts are fear, ignorance, racial superiority, religious antagonism, contempt for the weak and afflicted, and hatred for those different from oneself."

[September, 1969]

Acknowledgments

Grateful acknowledgment is given for permission to reprint the following articles, all of which first appeared in *Esquire:*

"The American Establishment" by Richard Rovere, first appeared in the May 1962 issue. Used by permission of Eleanor B. Rovere on behalf of the author.

"Kennedy Without Tears" by Tom Wicker, first appeared in the June 1964 issue. Used by permission of the author.

"On Experiencing Gore Vidal" by William F. Buckley Jr., first appeared in the August 1969 issue. Used by permission.

"Come Alive, America" by Charles Remsberg and Bonnie Remsberg, first appeared in the February 1965 issue. Used by permission of the authors.

"Frank Sinatra Has a Cold" and "The Loser" by Gay Talese, first appeared in the April 1966 and March 1964 issues, respectively. Used by permission of the author.

"A Distasteful Encounter with William F. Buckley Jr." by Gore Vidal, first appeared in the September 1969 issue. Used by permission.

"Superman Comes to the Supermarket" and "Some Children of the Goddess" by Norman Mailer, first appeared in the November 1960 and July 1963 issues, respectively. Used by permission.

"Life and Death of a Hippie" by Anthony Lukas, first appeared in the May 1968 issue. Used by permission of the author.

"Fifth Avenue, Uptown" by James Baldwin, first appeared in the July 1960 issue. Used by permission of the author.

"The Coming of the Purple Better One" by William Burroughs, first appeared in the November 1968 issue. Used by permission.

"Twirling at Ole Miss" and "How I Signed Up . . . with the C.I.A." by Terry

Southern, first appeared in the February 1963 and June 1963 issues, respectively. Used by permission of the author.

"The Members of the Assembly" by Jean Genet, first appeared in the November 1968 issue. Used by permission.

"The Naked Luncheon" by Gina Berriault, first appeared in the March 1966 issue. Used by permission.

"Literary Notes on Khrushchev" by Saul Bellow, first appeared in the March 1961 issue. Used by permission.

"The Brilliancy of Black" by Bernard Weinraub, first appeared in the January 1967 issue. Used by permission.

"My Generation" by Frank Conroy, first appeared in the November 1961 issue. Used by permission.

"Hell Sucks" by Michael Herr, first appeared in the August 1968 issue. Used by permission.

"Bogie in Excelsis" by Peter Bogdanovich, first appeared in the September 1964 issue. Used by permission of the author.

"Martin Luther King Is *Still on the Case*" by Garry Wills, first appeared in the August 1968 issue. Used by permission of the author.

"The Segs" by Reese Cleghorn, first appeared in the January 1964 issue. Used by permission of the author.

"The Dark Side of L.B.J." by James Deakin, first appeared in the August 1967 issue. Used by permission of the author.

"Las Vegas (What?) Las Vegas (Can't Hear You! Too Noisy) Las Vegas!!!" and "That Kandy-Kolored Tangerine-Flake Streamline Baby" from *The Kandy-Kolored Tangerine-Flake Streamline Baby* by Tom Wolfe. Copyright © 1963, 1964 by Tom Wolfe. Reprinted by permission of Farrar, Straus and Giroux Inc.

"The Last Kennedy" by Burton Hersh, first appeared in the September 1968 issue. Used by permission of the author.

The Introduction to the First Edition by Harold Hayes. Used by permission of the author.

Grateful acknowledgment is also extended to three whose assistance in the preparation of this collection proved to be invaluable: Catherine H. McBride, Rebecca Bartlett, Constance Wood.